The
Problem of Slavery
in the Age of
Emancipation

The
Problem of Slavery
in the Age of
Emancipation

DAVID BRION DAVIS

ALFRED A. KNOPF
New York
2014

THIS IS A BORZOI BOOK
PUBLISHED BY ALFRED A. KNOPF

Copyright © 2014 by David Brion Davis

www.aaknopf.com

Knopf, Borzoi Books, and the colophon are
registered trademarks of Random House LLC.

Portions of chapter two were originally published in "The Impact of
the Haitian and French Revolutions" from *Inhuman Bondage: The Rise and
Fall of Slavery in the New World* (New York: Oxford University Press, 2006).
Reprinted by permission of Oxford University Press, U.S.A.

Portions of chapters three and four are taken from a Tanner Lecture on
Human Values by the author delivered at Stanford University in 2006.
Reprinted by permission of the Tanner Lectures on Human Values,
a Corporation, University of Utah, Salt Lake City, Utah.

Library of Congress Cataloging-in-Publication Data
Davis, David Brion.
The problem of slavery in the age of emancipation / by David Brion Davis.—
First edition.
pages cm
ISBN 978-0-307-26909-6 (hardback) ISBN 978-0-385-35165-2 (eBook)
1. Slavery—United States—History—19th century.
2. Slaves—Emancipation—United States. 3. Free African Americans—
History—19th century. 4. Antislavery movements—United
States—History—19th century. 5. Antislavery movements—Great
Britain—History—19th century. 6. African Americans—Colonization—
Africa. 7. American Colonization Society. I. Title.
E449.D24 2014
306.3'62097309034—dc23   2013032893

Jacket images © Dimitar Todorov/Alamy
Jacket design by Chip Kidd

Manufactured in the United States of America
First Edition

To my beloved sons, Adam and Noah,
And their wonderful families

Contents

Preface   xi

INTRODUCTION   3

Discovering Animalization   3

Some Evidence of Animalization   9

1   **SOME MEANINGS OF SLAVERY AND EMANCIPATION:
    DEHUMANIZATION, ANIMALIZATION,
    AND FREE SOIL**   15

The Meaning of Animalization, Part I   15

The Meaning of Animalization, Part II   22

The Search for the Animalized Slave   26

Domestication and Internalization   35

2   **THE FIRST EMANCIPATIONS: FREEDOM
    AND DISHONOR**   45

Self-Emancipation: Haiti as a Turning Point   45

Freedmen and Slaves   52

Freedmen's Rights   61

Loss of Mastery   65

The "Horrors of Haiti"   74

3   COLONIZING BLACKS, PART I: MIGRATION AND
    DEPORTATION   83

    The Exodus Paradigm   83
    Precedents: Exiles   90
    Precedents: The Displaced   97

4   COLONIZING BLACKS, PART II: THE AMERICAN
    COLONIZATION SOCIETY AND AMERICO-LIBERIANS   105

    Liberating Liberia   105

5   COLONIZING BLACKS, PART III:
    FROM MARTIN DELANY TO HENRY HIGHLAND
    GARNET AND MARCUS GARVEY   126

    Nationalism   126

6   COLONIZATIONIST IDEOLOGY: LEONARD BACON
    AND "IRREMEDIABLE DEGRADATION"   144

    Bacon's "Report" of 1823   144
    The Paradox of Sin and "Irremediable Degradation"   155
    Some Black Response   162

7   FROM OPPOSING COLONIZATION TO IMMEDIATE
    ABOLITION   167

    Paul Cuffe and Early Proposals for Emigration   167
    James Forten and Black Reactions to the American
    Colonization Society   171
    The Search for Black Identity and Emigration to Haiti   176
    Russwurm, Cornish, and Walker   179
    Blacks and Garrison   185

8   FREE BLACKS AS THE KEY TO SLAVE EMANCIPATION   193

    Recognition of the Issue   193
    Abolitionist Addresses to Free African Americans   197
    David Walker and Overcoming Slave Dehumanization   209
    James McCune Smith and Jefferson's "What further is
    to be done with these people?"   216

9   FUGITIVE SLAVES, FREE SOIL, AND THE QUESTION
    OF VIOLENCE   226

    Frederick Douglass as a Fugitive   226
    The Underground Railroad and Runaway Slaves   232
    Harriet Jacobs as a Female Fugitive   238
    Fugitive Slaves and the Law   244

10 THE GREAT EXPERIMENT: JUBILEE, RESPONSES,
    AND FAILURE   256

    An Eschatological Event and America's Barriers   256
    The Enactment of British Emancipation   261
    Some American Responses to British Emancipation   271
    From Joseph John Gurney to the Issue of Failure   277

11 THE BRITISH MYSTIQUE: BLACK ABOLITIONISTS IN
    BRITAIN—THE LEADER OF THE INDUSTRIAL
    REVOLUTION AND CENTER OF "WAGE SLAVERY"   291

    Frederick Douglass Confronts the World   291
    African Americans Embrace the Mother Country   294
    The Problems of Race, Dehumanization, and Wage
    Slavery   304
    Joseph Sturge, Frederick Douglass, and the Chartists—
    the Decline and Expansion of Antislavery in the 1850s   315

    EPILOGUE   320

    Acknowledgments   339
    Notes   345
    Index   405

Preface

During the decades it took to write this trilogy on "The Problem of Slavery"—this volume was preceded by *The Problem of Slavery in Western Culture* (1966) and *The Problem of Slavery in the Age of Revolution* (1975)—people repeatedly asked me, "What led to your great interest in race and slavery?" It therefore seems appropriate to begin this final volume with a fairly brief reply.

Given the national racial segregation of my childhood and youth, it is not surprising that while I and my parents made eight interstate moves across the country, and I attended five high schools in four years, I never shared a classroom with an African American. After turning eighteen, in early 1945, I became exposed to the appalling racism of the Jim Crow South, where I received months of combat training for the invasion of Japan. After the war unexpectedly ended, I found myself on a large troopship bound for Europe. Though seasick, I was ordered to take a club, go down into the hold, and keep the "jiggaboos" from gambling. In this highly segregated army, I had never dreamed there were any blacks on the ship. But after descending a long winding staircase, I came upon what I imagined a slave ship would have looked like. Hundreds and hundreds of near-naked blacks jammed together, many of them shooting craps. After answering the question "What you doin' down here, white boy?," I hid in the shadows for four hours until relieved of "duty."

Months later, as a member of the army's Security Police in Germany, I witnessed armed and bloody conflicts between white and black American troops, mainly evoked by white fury over the sight of black soldiers dating and dancing with German girls. I also heard incredibly racist speeches from American officers, including General Ernest N. Harmon, who came from New England but denounced the government for ever sending black soldiers to Europe.

These experiences had a strong and lasting effect on my mind when I went on to attend Dartmouth College and graduate school at Harvard. Because of what I saw in the army, I read and was especially impressed by the Nobel Laureate Gunnar Myrdal's *An American Dilemma: The Negro Problem and Modern Democracy,* which influenced the landmark 1954 decision *Brown v. Board of Education,* and by President Truman's Committee on Civil Rights' 1947 report, *To Secure These Rights.* While I failed to become actively involved in the civil rights movement, I became deeply shocked by the discovery that slavery and racism had been largely ignored in my undergraduate and graduate courses. I owed this discovery to Kenneth M. Stampp, who came to Harvard from Berkeley as a visiting professor the year before the publication in 1956 of his landmark book *The Peculiar Institution: Slavery in the Ante-Bellum South.* Since, happily, he lived close to me, we became friends and had enlightening discussions on the subject of his book.

When I was lucky enough to become an assistant professor of history at Cornell the next year, I was determined to emphasize the importance of slavery in my teaching and to write a book that would provide an *antislavery* counterpart to the work of Stampp. But after studying some of the writings of abolitionist William Lloyd Garrison, I turned to the intellectual and international "background" of responses to slavery in Western culture. This expanded vision was partly the result of my undergraduate concentration on the history of political thought and philosophic views of human nature (I majored in philosophy). My decision to write *The Problem of Slavery in Western Culture* also owed much to a Guggenheim Fellowship that allowed me to do a significant amount of my initial research in Great Britain.

The three volumes of this trilogy differ from one another in very important ways, so it is essential at the start to describe the goals and scope of this book. Since I began writing *The Problem of Slavery in the Age of Emancipation* by 1980, my publication of other books, particularly *Slavery and Human Progress* in 1984 and *Inhuman Bondage: The Rise and Fall of Slavery in the New World* in 2006, radically changed the book's plan and freed me from doing a broad "survey" of slavery and emancipation from the Haitian Revolution to the outlawing of slavery in Brazil in 1888. I have instead focused on writing a highly selective study of significant and often neglected aspects of this broad subject, centered especially on Britain and the United States. Yet the basic subject of the book is the incredible moral achievement of the "Age of Emancipation"—the fact that from the 1780s to the 1880s, thanks largely to abolitionist movements, slavery was outlawed from Canada and New England to Chile and Brazil.

I highlight Britain because of its unprecedented and powerful abolition movement, public mobilization, and peaceful but controversial act of freeing 800,000 colonial slaves. Britain not only provided a model of emancipation in the 1830s but had earlier become a global leader in promoting the abolition of oceanic slave trading.

I concentrate on America because the nation possessed by far the largest, most productive, and expanding slave population in the New World; because the example of freeing the slaves in all the Northern states raised the central issue of whether and how large numbers of freed blacks could coexist in a white world (quite unlike the West Indies); and because the unexpected Civil War led to the sudden freeing of some 4 million slaves, a critical turning point in the Age of Emancipation that redefined the meaning of British emancipation and exerted a profound influence on Cuba and Brazil.

As for subject matter, this book begins with an extensive discussion of the issue of dehumanization and its implications—the treatment of slaves as if they were domesticated animals and the continuing need of African Americans to confront and counteract the kind of white psychological exploitation that deprived them of the respect and dignity needed for acceptance as equals in a white society. I have long interpreted the problem of slavery as centering on the impossibility of converting humans into the totally compliant, submissive, accepting chattels symbolized by Aristotle's ideal of the "natural slave." Throughout the book, I devote much attention to the views of free blacks and former slaves who refute the belief that blacks are in some way subhuman but who also deplore the fact that extremely brutal treatment sometimes leads slaves to act like compliant "brutes." This perceived "animalization," implied by the language of such figures as David Walker and Frederick Douglass, took a different form when whites expressed fear of vicious, noncompliant, animal-like blacks intent on rebellion and revenge, as exemplified by the Haitian Revolution. Or when prominent Northern clergymen attacked slavery but insisted that the "Irremediable Degradation" of slaves required the "colonization" of free blacks outside the United States. These issues of black inferiority reached one kind of climax in Britain, as we see in the last chapter, when the lecturing of African American abolitionists helped to destroy British support for the American Colonization Society and when the lecturers expressed amazement over the lack of racism and basked in the public recognition of their full humanity. As Walker had predicted, despite his frequent despair, "Treat us like men, and there is no danger but we will all live in peace and happiness together."

Free blacks, I argue, provided the key to slave emancipation. Frederick Douglass, a former slave and the most prominent African American of the nineteenth century, replied to a question posed by Harriet Beecher Stowe by stressing that slaveholders benefited most from the low condition of the American free colored population and that "The most telling, the most killing refutation of slavery, is the presentation of an industrious, enterprising, thrifty, and intelligent free black population." One crucial chapter of the book describes how black leaders, aided by white men and women abolitionists, struggled to achieve this goal, and how a few blacks, like Dr. James McCune Smith, attained the highest standards of education and success. Another chapter counters widespread misinterpretations and shows how free blacks played the main role in sustaining antislavery agitation in the 1820s, overcoming the colonizationists and launching the radical "immediatist" movement of the 1830s.

As we see in the chapter on Haiti, free blacks like Toussaint Louverture played a central part in the Haitian Revolution, which showed that blacks could defeat the seasoned armies of Napoleon as well as the British. The Haitian Revolution continued to inspire and be celebrated by free African Americans. But the international response to Haiti helped to create a picture of national ineptitude and incompetence as well as a genuinely impoverished nation that replaced what had been the richest and most productive colony in the New World. The chapter on the impact of Haiti is followed by a set of chapters on the colonization movements in America, which were strongly influenced by the fear of a Haitian-like revolution in America (and in the 1820s, thousands of American free blacks accepted the Haitian government's invitation to migrate to Haiti, much to the regret of most everyone).

The issues of colonization and migration are extremely complex and have generally been misunderstood. From the time of Jefferson until and including that of Lincoln, most American leaders, to say nothing of a large majority of whites, believed that any total ending of American slavery would require an extensive system of colonizing freed slaves in Africa, the Caribbean, or Central America. Given the increase and persistence of racism and the deplorable conditions that African Americans faced, a succession of black leaders from Paul Cuffe in the early nineteenth century to Marcus Garvey in the 1920s promoted their own plans for emigration to a promised land. For this reason I devote some attention to the influential biblical Exodus narrative of Israelite slaves escaping from Egypt, to historical examples of migration and expulsion, to the history of Liberia, and even to Garvey's leadership of a true mass movement as "the final act" in a long play.

But, as I have already mentioned, it was free African Americans who took the leadership in counteracting and checking the colonization movement and in convincing white abolitionists that it was a racist cause. As black writers and journalists contributed to an evolving black culture, it contained a genuine pride in the way African American workers had helped create the United States and how African American ancestors had fought in the American Revolution and the War of 1812. This patriotism underlay the crucial goals of elevating and improving the free black population and freeing its members from subservience, dishonor, and persecution simply because of their color.

While many chapters focus on race as the major barrier to slave emancipation, the book rests on the premise that the Age of Emancipation depended on the Anglo-American abolition movements. I wholly endorse the economists and historians who have emphasized the economic strength and vitality of the slave system and who reject any theory that it was on the road to natural extinction. As the historian Seymour Drescher has argued, the Nazis and Soviets restored a huge and highly profitable slave regime in the 1940s.

As I have tried to demonstrate in my trilogy, the abolition of slavery depended on a fundamental change in the Western moral perception of the institution, followed by the rise of antislavery movements in Britain, America, France, and eventually Brazil. Accordingly, this book devotes much thought to abolitionism, especially in Britain, where it achieved the most dramatic results. Yet by the 1850s there was a broad consensus that Britain's emancipation act had been an economic failure, even if the freed slaves were better off. This issue directed more attention to the outcome of antislavery in the United States, where I turn to such questions as fugitive slaves, free soil, and the acceptance of violence.

The discussion of abolitionism in Britain also leads to the vital question of whether this particular reform, challenging a form of private property and an institution that had been globally accepted from biblical times onward, could become a model for other kinds of protest and radical change. Most American abolitionists were proud of America's political democracy and strongly supported democratic movements abroad. Ironically, abolitionism reached its first great success, especially in mobilizing a large part of the total population, in a monarchic and aristocratic nation that also led the way in the Industrial Revolution, with its exploitation of countless men, women, and children in factories and mines. I therefore give some attention to the growing ties between British abolitionists and the radical Chartist movement against "wage slavery," an issue that visiting American abolitionists such as William Lloyd Garrison and Frederick Douglass had to confront. In the Epilogue I also continue to consider the Age of Emancipation, as a model for other reforms and as probably the greatest landmark of willed moral progress in human history.

But the epilogue also stresses the extraordinary fortuity and contingency of this outcome, which owed much to the highly unpredictable nature of the American Civil War. Surprisingly, despite Britain's global leadership in antislavery, the British government, press, and upper classes took a very hostile view of the Northern cause early in the war. This was partly the result of complex historical relations between the two countries, reinforced by widespread misunderstanding of the constitutional limitations on Lincoln's government, to say nothing of British dependence on Southern cotton and aristocratic fear of democratic reforms. The British government, prodded by France, came close to recognizing the Confederacy's independence and to intervening to stop the war. Many leading newspapers even denounced Lincoln's Emancipation Proclamation, though the public increasingly celebrated this turning point and finally responded with enthusiasm to the Thirteenth Amendment's liberation of all slaves.

But I also argue, in the epilogue, that if the Southerners had achieved independence by winning or avoiding the war, or by British and French intervention, it is clear that slavery would have continued well into the twentieth century. By 1860, two-thirds of the wealthiest Americans lived in the South, where the value of slaves continued to soar along with a major export economy. Moreover, many slaveholders dreamed of annexing an expanding tropical proslavery empire ranging from Cuba to Central America, and it is conceivable that an independent Confederacy might have moved in that direction. In 1857 a prominent Southerner even briefly became president of Nicaragua and restored both slavery and the African slave trade. The Southern goal of presenting a wholly "modernized" version of racial slavery would have been reinforced by the shocking rise and spread of "scientific racism," in Britain and Europe as well as America.

But there were many contingent events that seemed almost "providential," such as Union general William T. Sherman's great victory at the Battle for Atlanta, which ensured Lincoln's defeat of the almost proslavery Democratic candidate, George B. McClellan, in the presidential election of 1864 (Lincoln had earlier doubted whether he could win). This opened the road to the possible enactment of the Thirteenth Amendment, something inconceivable at the beginning of the war. While much can be said about the later failure of Reconstruction, the following century of Jim Crow discrimination and segregation, and the persistence of various forms of penal servitude and human trafficking, I conclude by viewing the Thirteenth, Fourteenth, and Fifteenth Amendments as the culmination of the Age of Emancipation—the award not only of liberation but of citizenship and the right to vote to the most oppressed class of Americans for well over two hundred years.

The
Problem of Slavery
in the Age of
Emancipation

Introduction

Long ago, when I began looking for salient features of "the Age of Emancipation"—the century of struggle, debate, rebellion, and warfare that led to the eradication of slavery in the New World—I was struck by the significance of two subjects that have received surprisingly little emphasis from historians: the Haitian Revolution and the American colonization movement.

The former, which was intertwined in complex ways with the French Revolution and European wars for empire, destroyed from 1791 to 1804 the richest and most productive colony in the New World—French Saint-Domingue. White refugees, their slaves, and black seamen carried news of this first large-scale emancipation of slaves in modern history to the rest of the Caribbean and South America as well as to New Orleans, Charleston, Virginia, Philadelphia, and New York. Even the vaguest awareness that blacks had somehow cast off their chains and founded the new republic of Haiti brought a glimmer of hope to thousands of slaves and free blacks who were the common victims of a remarkably unified Atlantic slave system. The crucial role of free blacks in the revolution, including the great leader Toussaint Louverture, highlighted a group that would continue to have central importance in the Age of Emancipation, especially in their efforts to counteract white beliefs in the slaves' incapacity for freedom.[1]

But the very words "Santo Domingo," which English-speakers used to refer to the doomed French colony of Saint-Domingue, evoked at least a moment of alarm and terror in the minds of slaveholders throughout the Americas, despite poetic and other tributes to Toussaint Louverture, whose capture and death in a French prison dissociated him from the grimmer consequences of the revolution. Sometimes this example of self-liberation was dismissed as the freakish result of French legislative and military blunders exacerbated by the subversive ideology of British and French abolitionism and the tropical diseases that decimated the British and French armies. Sometimes abolitionists vacillated between a policy of ignoring the explosive subject and warning that insurrections and racial war would be inevitable unless the slaves were peacefully emancipated and converted into grateful free peasants. But whether the Haitian Revolution hastened or delayed the numerous emancipations of the following century, imagery of the great upheaval hovered over the antislavery debates like a bloodstained ghost. No Internet was needed to distribute Bryan Edwards's unforgettable descriptions of a white infant impaled on a stake, of white women being repeatedly raped on the corpses of their husbands and fathers, and of the fate of Madame Séjourné:

> This unfortunate woman (my hand trembles while I write) was far advanced in her pregnancy. The monsters, whose prisoner she was, having first murdered her husband in her presence, ripped her up alive, and threw the infant to the hogs.—They then (how shall I relate it) sewed up the head of her murdered husband in ———!!! ———Such are thy triumphs, Philanthropy![2]

The idea of deporting or colonizing emancipated blacks outside the North American states or colonies long preceded the Haitian Revolution. But in the United States the specter of Haiti, reinforced by the Virginia slave conspiracies of 1800 and 1802 and the massive Barbadian insurrection of 1816, all of which were influenced by the Haitian Revolution, gave an enormous impetus to the colonization movement. Some advocates understood colonization as a way of making slavery more secure by removing the dangerous (as Haiti had shown) free black and colored population. But colonization was more commonly seen as the first and indispensable step toward the gradual abolition of slavery. In effect, it would reverse and undo the nearly two-century flow of the Atlantic slave ships and by transporting the freed slaves back to Africa would gradually and peacefully redeem

America from what James Madison called "the dreadful fruitfulness of the original sin of the African trade."[3] The very thought of shipping from 1.5 to over 4 million black Americans to an inhospitable Africa has seemed so preposterous and even criminal that many historians have tended to dismiss the subject of colonization out of hand (despite the success of white Americans in "removing" Indians to the West and ultimately to "reservations"). This means, however, that historians have never really explained why the coupling of emancipation and colonization appealed to leading American statesmen from Jefferson to Lincoln, why this formula won the endorsement by 1832 of nine state legislatures, and why William Lloyd Garrison, Theodore Weld, the Tappan brothers, Gerrit Smith, James G. Birney, and virtually all the other prominent and radical abolitionists of their generation accepted colonization before finally embracing the doctrine of "immediate emancipation." The American fusion of antislavery and colonization—what historian William W. Freehling has termed the "conditional termination" of slavery—gave a distinctive stamp to America's Age of Emancipation and to the abolitionism that suddenly erupted in the 1830s from an almost religious disavowal and repudiation of the colonizationist faith.[4]

Later chapters will explore the Haitian and especially the colonizationist models of slave emancipation. However, it was only after I had worked on these subjects for several years that I began to realize that both of them focused attention on the dehumanization of black slaves, a subject that lies at the center of debates over emancipation.

As seen in the Bryan Edwards quotation, descriptions of the Haitian rebels, especially those transmitted by refugees, accentuated their "vicious" and "animal-like" behavior as they inflicted revenge upon whites and ultimately massacred or expelled most whites from Haiti.

Leading colonizationists such as Connecticut's Reverend Leonard Bacon later argued, in assessing slaves' alleged incapacity for freedom, that whites could only faintly imagine how generations of oppression had degraded the black slave,

> whose mind has scarcely been enlightened by one ray of knowledge, whose soul has never been expanded by one adequate conception of his moral dignity and moral relations, and in whose heart hardly one of those affections that soften our character, or those hopes that animate and bless our being, has been allowed to germinate.

According to Bacon, who saw slavery as an intolerable national evil, the African American could never be raised "from the abyss of his degradation." Not in the United States, that is, where the force of racial prejudice was understandably magnified by the fear of a black biblical Samson "thirsting for vengeance" and bursting his chains asunder. With Haiti obviously in mind, Bacon warned that "the moment you raise this degraded community to an intellectual existence, their chains will burst asunder like the fetters of Sampson [sic], and they will stand forth in the might and dignity of manhood, and in all the terrors of a long injured people, thirsting for vengeance."[5] In this example, having raised blacks from their "abyss" of degradation to the "dignity of manhood," Bacon clearly rejected any thought of inherent inferiority. Nevertheless, his major argument tied degradation with an incapacity for peaceful coexistence. And the dismal history of black Haiti, whose freedpeople had no way of migrating to Canaanite "free soil," seemed to underscore their incapacity for economic success and genuine freedom.

As I concluded in *The Problem of Slavery in the Age of Revolution*, the debate over slavery in the period of the American Revolution had "helped to isolate the Negro's supposed incapacity for freedom— whether inherent or the result of long oppression—as the major obstacle to emancipation." Largely because of the widespread enthusiasm for liberty and equal rights, both opponents and defenders of slavery minimized the economic value and importance of the institution and helped make race, a concept which personified "incapacity," the central excuse for human bondage.[6] Slavery might very well be a genuine evil, as the Jeffersons and Madisons acknowledged, but what would be the consequences of suddenly discharging and losing control over hundreds of thousands of "dehumanized" human beings—people whose animal-like bondage had supposedly deprived them of all self-discipline as well as the skills, knowledge, frugality, and moral values needed for responsible participation in society? How would the existing free white population respond to and interact with such "liberated" people? This fear was magnified by the bleak early history of Haiti, a nation shunned by the rest of the world and soon almost bankrupted by reparation payments to France for even the willingness to trade and taking the step of seeking recognition as an independent nation. Hardly less discouraging was the fate of thousands of freed slaves in the Northern United States, who, being barred from schools and respectable employments, quickly sank into an underclass—the first of many generations of African Americans who privately struggled, in a world dominated by whites, with the central psychological issue of self-esteem.

In short, it was the new possibility of eradicating slavery—which became meaningful only in the late eighteenth century, with the beginning of gradual emancipation in the Northern United States, followed by the Haitian Revolution and France's revolutionary emancipation act of 1794—that greatly magnified the importance of race.[7] And a belief in a people's dehumanization had become the key to race. The later growth of "scientific racism" reinforced the much earlier speculation of some white travelers and writers that black Africans were inherently inferior and even closer to African apes than to fully human Caucasians. But such views were wholly repugnant to many white Christians, even Southern slave owners, who fervently defended the biblical belief in a common human creation "in the image of God." Leonard Bacon was far from alone in rejecting any view of inherent black incapacity and in stressing the corrupting and dehumanizing effects of slavery itself.[8]

But it is crucial to begin by examining the ways in which "being treated like animals" could lead to "being perceived as animalized humans"—and vice versa. This was the central accusation in most antislavery writing from John Woolman and Anthony Benezet to Theodore Dwight Weld and even Charles Darwin. Weld's classic *American Slavery as It Is: Testimony of a Thousand Witnesses,* published by the American Anti-Slavery Society in 1839 and based on voluminous research in Southern sources, illuminates the theme of animalization and deserves to be quoted at some length:

> [The slaveholder] does not contemplate slaves as human beings, consequently does not *treat* them as such; and with indifference sees them suffer privations and writhe under blows, which, if inflicted upon whites, would fill him with horror and indignation. . . . [S]laveholders regard their slaves not as human beings, but as mere working animals, as merchandise. The whole vocabulary of slaveholders, their laws, their usages, and their entire treatment of their slaves fully establish this. The same terms are applied

to slaves that are given to cattle. They are called "stock." . . . [T]he female slaves that are mothers, are called "breeders" till past child bearing. . . . Those who compel the labor of slaves and cattle have the same appellation, "drivers"; the names which they call them are the same and similar to those given to their horses and oxen. The laws of slave states make them property, equally with goats and swine; they are levied upon for debt in the same way; they are included in the same advertisements of public sales with cattle, swine, and asses; when moved from one part of the country to another, they are herded in droves like cattle, and like them are urged on by drivers. . . . [W]hen exposed for sale, their good qualities are described as jockeys show off the good points of their horses; their strength, activity, skill, power of endurance &c. are lauded,—and those who bid upon them examine their persons, just as purchasers inspect horses and oxen; they open their mouths to see if their teeth are sound; strip their backs to see if they are badly scarred, and handle their limbs and muscles to see if they are firmly knit. Like horses, they are warranted to be "sound," or to be returned to the owner if "unsound."[9]

Since I will be focusing on the dehumanization of North American slavery, it is important to recognize that black slaves were treated like animals throughout the hemisphere, as Charles Darwin discovered while living in Brazil and Argentina during the first stage of the long *Beagle* voyage. Because he had grown to maturity in an ardently antislavery British family, Darwin's experience solidified his commitment to the belief in a common humanity with a common origin:

Near Rio de Janeiro I lived opposite to an old lady, who kept screws to crush the fingers of her female slaves. I have lived in a house where a young household mulatto, daily and hourly, was reviled, beaten, and persecuted enough to break the spirit of the lowest animal. I have seen a little boy, six or seven years old, struck thrice with a horse whip (before I could interfere) on his naked head, for having handed me a glass of water not quite clean. . . . I will not even allude to the many heart-sickening atrocities which I authentically heard of;—nor would I have mentioned the above revolting details, had I not met with several people so blinded by the constitutional gaiety of the negro, as to speak of slavery as a tolerable evil.[10]

As we shall see, the antislavery indictment, exemplified by the accusation that the animal-like coercive "breeding" of slaves explained the unique rapid population growth of American slaves, was confirmed by the abundant testimony of former slaves; dehumanization was absolutely central to the slave experience. Moreover, this aspect of oppression, as suggested by the classic Exodus narrative in the Bible, which was familiar to many American slaves, led white colonizationists and even many blacks at times to conclude that true freedom was impossible in the land of bondage and required a change of place—an eventual movement from cage-like enclosure to "free soil" or even to a promised land.

Though historians have long recognized dehumanization as an aspect of slavery, they have not—despite the significant clue Aristotle provided when he called the ox "the poor man's slave"—really explored its bestializing aspects. This neglected point seems to me fundamental, especially for an understanding of slavery and racism in the United States. Former slave Henry Highland Garnet conveyed this message when he addressed Congress in 1865. Garnet praised the Thirteenth Amendment, a consummation of the Age of Emancipation, and bitterly denounced those American leaders who had continued to tolerate an institution that embodied the "concentrated essence of all conceivable wickedness," "snatching man from the high place to which he was lifted by the hand of God, and dragging him down to the level of brute creation, where he is made to be the companion of the horse and the fellow of the ox."[11]

SOME EVIDENCE OF ANIMALIZATION

While everyone is familiar with the casual as well as hostile comparison of human beings to certain animals, I came to see that the more systematic animalizing of African Americans, as a way of denying their capacity for freedom and preventing their "amalgamating" with white society, carried far-reaching and complicated meanings that deserve more careful examination. It was really this form of extreme dehumanization—a process mostly confined to the treatment of slaves and to the perceptions of whites—that severed ties of human identity and empathy and made slavery possible.

Some historians have argued that white masters and overseers necessarily recognized the full humanity of blacks when they had sex with slave women, an intimate act that would have been condemned and punished as bestiality or "buggery" if the blacks had been seen as "beasts."[12] But military gang raping in the twentieth century should have taught us that sexual intercourse can exemplify the most dehumanizing, degrading, and exploitative act of conquest or warfare, including the infliction of the conqueror's genes on an enemy group.[13]

In contrast to Latin America, Southern planter society officially condemned interracial sexual unions and tended to blame lower-class white males for fathering mulatto children. Yet there is abundant evidence that many slave owners, sons of slave owners, and overseers took black mistresses or in effect raped the wives and daughters of slave families. This abuse of power may not have been quite as universal as Northern abolitionists claimed. But the ubiquity of such sexual exploitation was sufficient to deeply scar and humiliate black women, to instill rage in black men, and to arouse both shame and bitterness in white women.[14]

Historian Mia Bay, by thoroughly exploring the vast WPA narratives of elderly former slaves, has dramatically proved that Garnet's animal metaphors were not limited to the highly literate former slave elite. As Bay concludes, after summarizing thousands of pages of testimony: "Identifying not with their masters' dependent children but with their masters' four-legged chattel, ex-slaves remembered being fed like pigs, bred like hogs, sold like horses, driven like cattle, worked like dogs, and beaten like mules."[15] Memories of animalization, in other words, largely undercut the slave owners' pretentions of "paternalism."

It is important to note that most of the WPA interviewers were white and, in the 1930s, often recently descended from slaveholders. The blacks, surrounded by flagrant racism and Great Depression poverty, were cautious and seldom criticized slavery as an institution. Nevertheless, the ex-slaves in numerous Southern states repeatedly remembered that like animals they did not know their age or birthdays and as children often even ate like and with animals: "Dey was a trough out in de yard [where] dey poured de mush an milk in[,] an us chillum an de dogs would all crowd 'roun it an eat together . . . we sho' had to be in a hurry 'bout it cause de dogs would get it all if we didn't." "The white folks et the white flour and the niggers et the shorts," one woman reported, and "the hogs was also fed the shorts." Even the few ex-slaves who praised their masters' generosity mentioned animals.

According to a freedman in South Carolina, "Master Levi kept his niggers fat, just like he keep his hogs and hosses fat, he did."[16]

As Professor Bay points out, the slaves not only were surrounded night and day by mules, horses, donkeys, and other work animals but, like those domesticated species, their only reason for existence was to perform labor for their white owners in exchange for care and feeding. Yet "what the slaves resented most were slaveowners who treated them like animals rather than workers." Josephine Howard recalled that in Texas "Dey wan't nothin' de whites don't do to 'em—work 'em like day was mules an' treat 'em jes' like day don't have no feelin'." In Oklahoma a white preacher exhorted Robert Burns and his fellow slaves, "Only white people had souls and went to heaven. He told dem dat niggers had no more soul than dogs, and dey couldn't go to heaven any more than could a dog."[17]

Confined like captured or domesticated animals to cage-like spaces, slaves knew that if they tried to escape, they would be pursued by armed patrollers who canvassed the country "just like dogs hunting rabbits." And once seized for any offence, as Joe Ray recalled his childhood on an Arkansas plantation, "Dere was two overseers on the place and dey carried a bull whip all the time. . . . I saw a slave man whipped until his shirt was cut to pieces! Dey were whipped like horses." If the master "didn't want dem beat to death . . . Dat's too much money to kill," "they would take your clothes off and whip you like you was no more than mules."[18]

From antiquity, chattel slavery was modeled on the property rights traditionally claimed for domestic animals, which meant that human beings could be bought, sold, traded, leased, inherited, included in a dowry, gambled, or lost as debt—abrupt changes in identity that negated or deeply compromised marriage, parenthood, or family relations in what historian-sociologist Orlando Patterson has termed a state of "social death." As the American freedwoman Mollie Barber recalled, every time her owners "need[ed] some money, off dey sell a slave, jest like now dey sell cows and hogs at de auction places." And Professor Bay quite convincingly sees the auction, to which slaves were driven on foot by mounted white men, as the epitome of bestialization:

One ex-slave explained: "Speclators uster buy up niggers jest lak dey was animals, and dey would travel around over de country and sell an' sell 'em. I've seen 'em come through there in droves lak cattle." Once at auction, the slaves were scrutinized by prospective buyers. "A large crowd of masters gathered 'round,' " one slave witness recalled, "and dey would put de slaves on the block and roll de sleeves and pantlegs up and say, 'Dis is good stock; got good muscles, and he's a good hardworking nigger.' Whey dey sold 'em just like you see 'em sell stock now. If de woman was a good breeder she would sell for big money, 'cause she could raise children. They felt all over the woman folks."[19]

In recent decades historians have shown that from 1790 to 1860 the southwestern expansion of slavery in the United States depended on such animalizing auctions and on a vast internal movement of over a million slaves, conducted by coastal slave ships as well as by overland coffles of chained men, followed by slave women and children, often trudging seven or eight weeks on foot as they moved toward Louisiana or Texas.[20]

I should emphasize that Bay's evidence on "being treated like animals" is repeatedly confirmed by numerous earlier slave narratives addressed to Northern audiences; but the WPA testimony is especially convincing, since animal parallels were clearly far removed from the white Southern proslavery mythology of that time. The elderly freedpeople's language signified an enduring black experience. By the same token, Bay shows that freed blacks long continued to use animal comparisons in Southern Jim Crow society. If they were no longer regularly whipped or sold at auctions, many felt they had been turned loose like aged horses and cows without their own fields in which to graze. For the black day laborer, prison farm worker, or sharecropper, still stigmatized by race, emancipation failed to lead to some kind of humanizing "free soil." And, as we shall see, the theory of inherent black bestiality acquired a kind of tsunami force in the 1880s and 1890s, given the obsession of radical Southerners with lynching as an antidote to the supposedly near-universal desire of black men to rape white women.

Bay's thesis stresses the continuing determination of African Americans, both slave and free, to reject and counteract all attempts at animalization. Even the few blacks who accepted the argument that Noah's biblical "curse of Ham" had justified their enslavement, joined in the continuing defense and assertion of their humanity. Yet, as we will see, a very few radical blacks who called for a slave revolt also condemned black slaves for a docility and subservience that seemed to be the result of unprecedented oppression.

But dehumanization has clearly been a central aspect of slavery from ancient times, and what I have referred to as "the problem of slavery" involves the impossibility, seen throughout history, of converting humans into totally compliant, submissive chattel property. Nevertheless, from ancient Greece to the development of New World colonies and on to the prosperous American South in the mid-nineteenth century, slave labor has proved to be remarkably productive, effective, and economically successful. And racial slavery generated new forms of racism, which encouraged efforts at animalization in extreme and systematic forms. In the next chapter we will explore how the whites' projection on blacks of unwanted "animal" traits and attributes highlighted the slaves' supposed incapacity for freedom—a crucial issue for the "Age of Emancipation." Animalization also raised the issues of psychological internalization and black self-esteem—questions that by no means disappeared with emancipation. Accordingly, before turning to the Haitian Revolution, black colonization, and other highly selective aspects of the "Age of Emancipation," I want to explore in some detail some subjects that lie at the heart of slavery's "problem."

1

Some Meanings of Slavery and Emancipation: Dehumanization, Animalization, and Free Soil

God's first blunder: Man didn't find the animals amusing,—
he dominated them, and didn't even want to be an "animal."
—NIETZSCHE, *Der Antichrist*

THE MEANING OF ANIMALIZATION, PART I

Traveling through the South in 1856, the famous journalist and land-scape designer Frederick Law Olmsted remarked to a white overseer that it must be disagreeable to punish slaves the way he did. The overseer replied, "Why, sir, I wouldn't mind killing a nigger more than I would a dog."[1]

Does this mean that blacks who were treated like animals were literally seen as "only animals," or as an entirely different species from humans? The answer is clearly no, except perhaps in some extreme cases and for very brief periods of time—as for example in the post-emancipation lynching era, when many black men accused of raping white women were hanged or tortured, dismembered, and burned alive, occasionally before immense cheering crowds of Southern white men, women, and children.[2]

Degradation and insult are reinforced every day when people call other people curs, pigs, swine, apes, bitches, and sons of bitches, terms which momentarily dehumanize one party while enhancing the "non-animal" superiority of the other. But animalization can cover a spectrum from superficial insult to the justification of slavery and on to lynching and genocide.

Thus the use of such animal metaphors as lice, vermin, microbes, and cockroaches, as in the Nazi Holocaust, lowers the process to a different level, justifying the complete extermination of an impure enemy group that supposedly threatens the basic health of society and therefore has no right to exist. I am mainly concerned here with the psychological and linguistic process, as a way of dealing with the question of whether humans who were treated like animals were ever literally seen as "only animals," since a discussion of diverse motives would lead us far astray. The world had never seen such an extreme and systematic engine of dehumanization as the Nazi propaganda machine, epitomized by Joseph Goebbels's assertion in an early speech (March 7, 1942) that "It is a life-or-death struggle between the Aryan race and the Jewish microbe. No other government and no other regime would have been able to muster the strength to find a general solution to this issue." Nearly a year later, SS Reichsführer Heinrich Himmler would expand the point in a speech to SS officers:

> Antisemitism is exactly the same as delousing. Getting rid of lice is not a question of ideology. It is a matter of cleanliness. In just the same way, antisemitism, for us, has not been a question of ideology, but a matter of cleanliness, which now will soon have been dealt with. We shall soon be deloused. We have only 20,000 lice left, and then the matter is finished within the whole of Germany.[3]

Given the Nazi example, it is worth noting that the antipode of this animalizing can be seen in a universal tendency to project our potentiality for self-transcendence, freedom, and striving for perfection onto images of kings, dictators, demagogues, and cultural heroes of various kinds. This form of idolatry, which ancient Judaism fortunately singled out as the most dangerous sin facing humanity, can also appear in various kinds of narcissism and egocentrism, as when an individual imagines that he is godlike and free from all taint of finitude and corruption.

There is actually a long history to the links between animalization and genocide or ethnic cleansing, and the formula by no means ended with the Nazis. In 1994, when the Hutu slaughtered some 800,000

Tutsi neighbors in Rwanda, the victims were repeatedly likened to *inyenizi*, or cockroaches.[4]

But were Jews and Tutsis truly seen as nonhumans, as the actual equivalent of microbes, lice, or cockroaches? Given the appalling realities of mass murder, we are intuitively inclined to think yes. Why else would Himmler try to persuade SS officers that their actions would be exactly the same as delousing? Fortunately, philosopher Kwame Anthony Appiah has insightfully clarified this issue as his discussion of ethics moves from social hierarchy to insiders/outsiders and on to genocidal massacres. In accounting for genocide, "the familiar answer" presumes that members of some outgroup are not considered "human at all." Yet that "doesn't explain the immense cruelty—the abominable cruelty," which is not evident even in the extermination of pests. As Appiah then reasons:

> The persecutors may liken the objects of their enmity to cockroaches or germs, but they acknowledge their victim's humanity in the very act of humiliating, stigmatizing, reviling, and torturing them. Such treatment—and the voluble justifications the persecutors invariably offer for such treatment—is reserved for creatures we recognize to have intentions and desires and projects.

Appiah adds in an endnote that the victimizers always "tell you why their victims—Jews or Aztecs or Tutsi—deserve what's being done to them."[5] That was emphatically true of the Nazis, who pictured the Jews not only as an active global threat to civilization throughout history, but in World War II as the hidden conspiratorial force behind both their Soviet and Western enemies. Clearly this retention of a human element fails to make animalization more humane. Quite the contrary.

At this point it should be clear that "dehumanization" means the eradication not of human *identity* but of those elements of humanity that evoke respect and empathy and convey a sense of dignity. Dehumanization means the debasement of a human, often the reduction to the status of an "animalized human," a person who exemplifies the so-called animal traits and who lacks the moral and rational capacities that humans esteem. As Appiah implies, this extreme dehumanization deprives the victims even of the kind of sympathy and connectedness often given to Alzheimer patients or those in a coma.

I would only add that since the victims of this process are per-ceived as "animalized humans," this double consciousness would probably involve a contradictory shifting back and forth in the rec-ognition of humanity. When Henry Smith, an African American accused of rape, was tortured and killed in 1893 before a Texas mob of some ten thousand whites, many in the crowd no doubt saw him momentarily as "nothing but an animal" as they watched hot irons being pressed on his bare feet and tongue and then into his eyes, and heard him emit "a cry that echoed over the prairie like the wail of a wild animal."[6] Conversely, we have reports of German soldiers who momentarily recognized the true humanity of individual Jews as they were herded toward the gas chambers.

In any event, the creation of "animalized humans" can produce a mental state in the victimizers and spectators that disconnects the neural sources of human identification, empathy, and compassion, the very basis for the Golden Rule and all human ethics. In extreme cases, this means the ability to engage in torture or extermination without a qualm. But the focus on extreme cases can obscure the fact, emphasized by David Livingstone Smith, that "we are all potential dehumanizers, just as we are potential objects of dehumanization."[7] No doubt many situations arise, especially in war, where people kill or inflict pain without misgivings and without any explicit animaliza-tion.[8] But the victims must still be *dehumanized* in similar ways. And animalization, which also appears in such group differentiations as class, caste, and ethnicity, as well as race, clearly makes the process easier for large collective groups.[9]

One explanation, as already suggested, involves the projection on victims or on groups such as slaves of an exaggerated version of the so-called animal traits that all humans share and often fear and repress.[10] This psychological process deprives the dehumanized of those redeeming rational and spiritual qualities that give humans a sense of pride, of dignity, of being made in the image of God. At the same time, the projection enables the victimizers to become almost psychological parasites, whose self-image is immeasurably enhanced by the dramatic contrast with the degraded and dehuman-ized "Other." But why have we humans been so concerned with our "animality," and what is the ultimate source of this desire to animal-ize other humans—apart from the quite diverse motives of slavehold-ers, white supremacists, and Nazis? Here I would turn to Reinhold

Niebuhr's view of the core of human "distinctiveness," as opposed to other animals, in the fear, self-doubt, anxiety, and even pride and confidence generated by the dilemma of finitude and freedom. The dilemma that prompts us to ask, "Who am I?" "Why am I here?" "What is it all about?" As Niebuhr remarks, while surveying the ways we distinguish the self from the totality of the world, "The vantage point from which man judges his insignificance is a rather significant vantage point."[11] If one samples some typical quotations on the human condition, we see a single answer in the tension between our sense of our existential animal finitude (evoked by our discovery in childhood that we are certain to die) and our capacity for self-reflection, for making ourselves our own object. Countless poets and philosophers have agreed with Charles Caleb Colton (1780–1830): "Man is an embodied paradox, a bundle of contradictions."

As expressed by the great French Renaissance essayist Montaigne, "Man sees himself lodged here in the mud and filth of the world, nailed and fastened to the most lifeless and stagnant part of the universe, in the lowest story of the house, at the furthest distance from the vault of Heaven, with the vilest animals; and yet, in his imagination, he places himself above the circle of the moon, and brings Heaven under his feet." Or according to Edward Tyson, a founder of comparative anatomy whose dissection of a chimpanzee in 1698 led him to the view that "*Man* is part a *Brute*, part an *Angel*; and is that *Link* in the Creation, that joyns them both together." Or Edward Young, an eighteenth-century religious poet much favored by the later British abolitionists: "*Helpless* Immortal! Insect *infinite*! / A worm! a God! I tremble at myself, / And in myself am lost! At home a stranger." And Lord Byron, first in Sardanapalus: "I am the very slave of circumstance / And impulse—borne away with every breath! / Misplaced upon the throne—misplaced in life. / I know not what I could have been, / but feel I am not what I should be—let it end."

But then, in Byron's Sonnet to Chillon: "Eternal spirit of the chainless mind! / Brightest in dungeons, Liberty! thou art, / For there thy habitation is the heart, / The heart which love of thee alone can bind."[12]

When I think of myself wholly in terms of my eating, sleeping, urinating, defecating, cutting toenails (claws), scratching an itch, aging and dying, there can be no question that I am a finite mammal. This exercise, which runs against the grain of a lifetime of "civilizing" and self-idealizing, requires some concentrated effort. But as we define ourselves as rational animals, *Homo sapiens,* we continue to marvel over our amazing capacity for self-reflection and rational analysis—for viewing ourselves from a vantage point outside the self, for analyzing our own introspection, and for imagining what it would be like to be someone else, including their own imaginings, even a slave or animal. The 100 billion neurons in our brains enable us even to study and understand *their* own actions.

Much human behavior is driven not by simple desires for food, money, sex, and security, but by our need to respond to this paradoxical nature. According to Niebuhr's classic analysis, the anxiety generated by this paradoxical condition can lead to a denial of our capacity for rationality and self-transcendence, in the sin of sensuality; or, far worse, to a denial of our animality itself, the sin of pride.[13] Animalizing other people is clearly an expression of the sin of pride and was long encouraged, as we will see, by the constant ubiquity and interaction with domesticated animals, as well as by the sharp conceptual division between humans and animals imposed by Western culture.

The psychological mechanism of animalization has been so deeply implanted in white culture, with respect to African Americans, that most white Americans have been unaware of their usually unconscious complicity as well as the significant benefits they have reaped from their "transcendent whiteness." Especially during the period of racial slavery, the process of animalizing blacks enhanced the whites' sense of being a rational, self-disciplined, and ambitious people, closely attuned to their long-term best interests. Racism became the systematic way of institutionalizing and justifying the individual white's projection of an "animal Id" upon blacks. It took the form of an intellectual theory or ideology, cloaked in science, as well as actions and behavior legitimated by laws, customs, and social structure.

As I wrote in a review of Winthrop D. Jordan's landmark book *White Over Black,* "The counter-image of the Negro became the living embodiment of what transplanted Europeans must never allow themselves to become."[14] This parasitic relationship gave special force to the whites' sense of historical mission, the "American Dream" of overcoming the limits and boundaries of past history. But as I briefly explore later, a long succession of African American writers, beginning in the eighteenth century and including even Barack Obama, have conveyed the deeply felt effects of this process on individual and collective black self-esteem.

Yet the animalization of black slaves obviously differed markedly from that of groups in danger of genocide. For one thing, slaves were valuable as chattel property and as investments, and in nineteenth-century America their value soared as they became increasingly important to the economy. Far from being in danger of extermination, the lives of slaves were at least legally protected by state laws and interpretations of common law that ruled that the murder of a slave was a crime punishable by death.[15]

But if state laws and courts repeatedly recognized the humanity of slaves, Thomas Jefferson was far from being alone in fearing an eventual war between the races, a war that many whites predicted would end in the extermination of all "Negroes."[16] And the related subject of black colonization, which had immense theoretical support among the American antebellum white population, promised an eventual removal of the black population by "peaceful means"—an option that even Hermann Göring and some other Nazi leaders favored for the Jews before World War II and "the final solution."

Finally, as we have seen, the populist lynching of blacks began to reach epic levels in the 1880s and '90s. The widespread acceptance of scientific racism, a central prop for Jim Crow segregation and white supremacy, reinforced the traditional fear of sexual contamination, through rape or intermarriage—the invasion of the black Id, a reprisal of all the animalistic traits that had been projected on blacks to achieve white purity. In 1897, Rebecca Latimer Felton, a prominent Georgia feminist, journalist, and eventually the first woman to become a U.S. senator, aroused national attention with a near hysterical speech on the peril of black rapists: "[I]f it takes lynching to protect woman's dearest possession from drunken, ravening human beasts," she cried, "then I say lynch a thousand [blacks] a week if it becomes necessary." Later, emphasizing the "moral retrogression" of blacks since the days of slavery, Felton accused the "promoters of Negro equality" of preparing the way for an imminent "revolutionary uprising" that "will either exterminate the blacks or force the white citizens to leave the country." Fortunately, such extremists never came close to shaping federal policies, but it is significant that at the turn of the twentieth century the Chief Statistician of the U.S. Census,

Professor Walter Francis Willcox, and other prominent statisticians, happily predicted the gradual extinction of the Negro race.[17]

THE MEANING OF ANIMALIZATION, PART II

It is almost impossible for us today to imagine the ubiquity and variety of animals that would closely surround us if we had lived at any time from the Bronze Age to the early twentieth century. When I hear the word "animal" today, I do not automatically picture horses, oxen, donkeys, mules, cows, goats, pigs, sheep, chicken, ducks, rabbits, and geese. Yet, as we saw in the testimony of former slaves regarding the animalization of blacks, that was the context everyone had in mind. Everyone depended on beasts of burden for every kind of pulling and hauling as well as for transport. The food they ate required the aid of animals in plowing fields as well as the hunting of all sorts of game. Every day most people interacted with animals, especially horses, as much as we do with cars and computers.

Even in towns and cities residents kept a variety of animals in addition to pets. Our "liberation" from this proximity and total dependence must be taken into account if we are to understand the past. The linguistic legacy of labeling some people brutish and beastly arose in the context of human "dominion" over an immense range of species from bees to bulls. Ironically, despite this daily intimacy and proximity with animals, Western culture long posited an almost unbridgeable gap between humans and animals that has now been greatly eroded, thanks to a major cultural transformation regarding cruelty (originally focused on slaves and animals), as well as scientific discoveries from Darwin to DNA.[18]

The animalization of people first required the "animalization" of animals, beings that can of course be described and understood in an infinite number of ways.[19] *The Oxford Thesaurus* of 1992 equates "animal" with "physical, fleshly, sensual, gross, coarse, unrefined, uncultured, uncultivated, rude, carnal, crude, bestial, beastlike, subhuman." An older Webster's *Dictionary of Synonyms* typically states that "When applied figuratively to human beings, animal either throws the emphasis on purely physical qualities or implies the ascendancy of the physical nature over the rational and spiritual nature. . . ." The *Free Online Thesaurus* tells us that "animalization" is "an act that makes people cruel or lacking in normal human qualities."[20] As historian

Keith Thomas has written, Renaissance Europeans repeated the proverb "as drunk as a dog," though they had of course never seen a drunken dog:

> Men attributed to animals the natural impulses they most feared in themselves—ferocity, gluttony, sexuality—even though it was men, not beasts, who made war on their own species, ate more than was good for them and were sexually active all the year round. It was as a comment on human nature that the concept of "animality" was devised. As S. T. Coleridge would observe, to call human vices "bestial" was to libel the animals.[21]

Such examples of the animalization of animals are part of the wider and deeper phenomenon of "anthropodenial," a term popularized by philosopher Martha Nussbaum and primatologist Frans de Waal—meaning the opposite of the anthropomorphism we often apply especially to pets: "a blindness to the humanlike characteristics of other animals, or the animal-like characteristics of ourselves." According to Nussbaum, this insistence on a brick wall separating humans from the rest of the animal kingdom, despite the fact that our DNA is roughly 98 percent like that of chimpanzees, leads not only to appalling cruelties in treating animals but to certain failures of compassion for human suffering.[22] While the forms of anthropodenial have changed over the centuries, having been strongly influenced by the ancient Greeks (though Plato famously referred to "the wild beast within us"), this dualism separating man from beast lives at the heart of the Judeo-Christian worldview, beginning with the Bible.

But before turning to the Bible, we should remember that domestication did require the creation of close bonds between humans and animals. And for millennia men and women have loved all kinds of pets, have treated animals as companions, and have even worshipped animals as deities. Though slaves were denied such godhood, they could sometimes be loved or become trusted companions. And the view that slaves were essentially children was often a variant on the animal metaphor. The permanent child would be equivalent in some ways to a dehumanized adult, a human who lacks the capacities of reason and self-introspection and analysis. And, like children, animals are petted, cuddled, and nurtured, or made to perform tricks as well as labor. Indeed, in many cultures small children were referred to and treated as if they were animals: "little deer," "little bear or wolf," "little lion"; and in antiquity, partly to avoid starvation, untold thousands of babies and children were sold into slavery or abandoned so that others would bring them up as slaves. However loved or cherished a slave might be, animalization implied the excision or removal of some inner human qualities that helped to protect an adult man or woman from being treated as a mere object—as opposed to a moral "center of consciousness."

Now to the Bible. On the authority of Genesis, God first creates all the moving, living creatures, the "creeping things," fowls, whales, cattle, beasts of the earth. He blesses them, tells them to be fruitful and multiply, and sees that "it was good." Then God says,

> *Let us make man in our image, after our likeness: and let them have dominion over the fish of the sea, and over the fowl of the air, and over the cattle, and over all the earth, and over every creeping thing that creepeth upon the earth.*
>
> *So God created man in his own image, in the image of God created he him; male and female created he them.*
>
> *And God blessed them, and God said unto them, Be fruitful, and multiply, and replenish the earth, and subdue it: and have dominion over the fish of the sea, and over the fowl of the air, and over every living thing that moveth upon the earth.*[23]

After God has given humans dominion over all animal species, he "brought them unto Adam to see what he would call them." Adam then symbolically exercises human power by giving "names to all cattle, and to the fowl of the air, and to every beast of the field." Human dominion then increases substantially after the Fall from the Garden of Eden and after Noah rescues all the surviving animal species from the disastrous flood. Upon leaving the ark, Noah builds an altar to the Lord and sacrifices a member of every "clean" beast and fowl as burnt offerings. God is so pleased by the "sweet savour" of the fumes that he promises "I will not again curse the ground any more for man's sake . . . neither will I again smite any more every thing living, as I have done." The biblical language suggests that the ritual of sacrificing animals (like animalizing other people) became a way of purging humans of "animality" and thus of a major source of sin.

In addition to being needed for regular sacrifice, animals will now be wholly subordinate, a source of food for humans:

And the fear of you and the dread of you shall be upon every beast of the earth, and upon every fowl of the air, upon all that moveth upon the earth, and upon all the fishes of the sea; into your hand are they delivered. Every moving thing that liveth shall be meat for you; even as the green herb have I given you all things.[24]

It is important to stress that over the ages these words of Genesis have shaped fundamental assumptions and values in Western culture—even for early church fathers who were more concerned with counteracting pagan views of human-animal interchangeability, and for the countless people who did not literally accept all the details of the story of creation. Moreover, Keith Thomas, in his invaluable account *Man and the Natural World*, shows that from 1500 to 1800, the biblical sense of human uniqueness and privilege gained considerable new strength in Western Europe. As Europeans entered a wholly new stage of exploration, conquest, and colonization, including the transportation of millions of African slaves to all parts of the New World, there was a skyrocketing confidence in man's right and ability to exploit the surrounding world of nature.

Renaissance men could draw on Plato, Aristotle, and other ancient Greek writers to reinforce the biblical view that everything in the natural world existed solely to serve man's interests—that everything had a human purpose. Since beasts supposedly had no souls and no conception of a future, domesticated animals were said to be much better off than their wild brethren, who had to fend for themselves and were vulnerable to predators and the sufferings of old age.[25] Besides, whether wild or tame, most animals were designed to provide food for humans, and Western Europeans were especially carnivorous. Even in the Middle Ages, the more affluent people ate an astonishing variety of meat, increasingly mixed with large quantities of spices from the East. One notable cook in medieval Savoy "instructed his purveyors to set out with forty horses six weeks or even two months before a two-day banquet to acquire deer, hares, partridges, pheasants, small birds . . . doves, cranes, and herons."[26]

Keith Thomas points out that Western Europeans were shocked and expressed "baffled contempt" when they learned of the Buddhists' and Hindus' respect for animals, even insects.[27] By the 1630s, any such respect was further weakened philosophically by the emerging work of the so-called Father of Modern Philosophy, René Descartes. As a great mathematician, it was perhaps natural for Descartes to conclude that "thinking" was his essence, the only thing about himself that could not be doubted ("I think, therefore I am"). Hence his body was like a machine, a matter of extension and motion that followed the laws of physics and was controlled by his wholly separate mind and soul. Since he became certain that animals lacked both a cognitive mind and soul, they were really automata, like clocks, capable of complex behavior but totally incapable of speech, reasoning, or perhaps even sensation (a conclusion endorsed by some of his disciples). While Thomas writes that Descartes had limited direct influence in Britain, he had "only pushed the European emphasis on the gulf between man and beast to its logical conclusion," "thus clearing the way for the uninhibited exercise of human rule." Even in England "the doctrine of human uniqueness was propounded from every pulpit."[28]

The widening gulf between man and beast had important implications for what we might term social control and the spread of Christian civilization. Christians had regularly portrayed the devil as a mixture of man and animal, and the Antichrist as a beast. There had always been a tendency to animalize the serfs and peasants, especially those who worked daily with animals and were darkened by manure and soil as well as the sun.[29] Thomas points out that bestiality, the ultimate sexual crime, became a capital offense from 1534 to 1861. The chains, bridles, and cages linked with domestication were used at times for beggars and the insane as well as for criminal offenders. Edmund Burke expressed a typical dehumanizing view of social class when contemplating the French Revolution: "Learning will be cast into the mire, and trodden down under the hoofs of the swinish multitude."[30]

Like domestic animals, African slaves transported to the New World were supposed to benefit by being saved from human sacrifice, cannibalism, and other cruel practices of savages in the uncivilized world; given a "purpose" in life, they would work for the good of society while being guaranteed food and shelter; some, if they had souls, might even be Christianized.

THE SEARCH FOR THE ANIMALIZED SLAVE

It was Western Europe's unprecedented expansion that extended the animalizing process, usually epitomized by enslavement, to increasing numbers of outsiders, beginning with Slavs, Moors, Canary Islanders, Irish, Native Americans, and numerous peoples of West and East

Africa. And the widening of the gap between man and beast, symbolized by Descartes, coincided with much more intense interaction with diverse outsiders, especially sub-Saharan Africans, whose alleged "beastly living" and proximity to apes greatly enhanced the Western Europeans' rising self-image as the exemplars of global civilization.

In this section we will briefly describe how the search for the ideal animalized slave—a human who, as Aristotle put it, was clearly "born to be a slave"—led to the racist stereotyping of black Africans by the late eighteenth century. In the section on "Domestication and Internalization," below, I will specifically show how Aristotle's ideal slave pointed to the model of animal domestication and raised the issue of slaves "internalizing" their masters' attempts at dehumanization—an issue related to the theme of the blacks' alleged incapacity for genuine freedom in a democracy, which lies at the heart of the long historical legacy of slavery, especially in America.

From very early times, slaveholders had much preferred outsiders—"barbarians" (*barbaroi*) in the case of the ancient Greeks. While the Greeks did enslave one another in their wars, they favored foreigners who spoke barbaric languages and were thus "ignorant of the political institutions and cultural characteristics of the city."[31] Even more striking was the way ancient Israelites sought to mitigate the servitude of their own people (mostly debt slaves, with seven years of service) and limit perpetual chattel slavery, which involved more dehumanization, to outsiders and foes, especially Canaanites. As later Christians searched the Old Testament for proslavery sanctions, they found this crucial justification in Leviticus:

> *Such male and female slaves as you may have—it is from the nations round about you that you may acquire male and female slaves. You may also buy them from among the children of aliens resident with you, or from their families that are among you, whom they begot in your land. These shall become your property: you may keep them as a possession for your children after you, for them to inherit as property for all time. Such you may treat as slaves. But as for your Israelite brothers, no one shall rule ruthlessly over the other.[32]*

This portentous if very human distinction between people like us and the foreign outsiders not only validated perpetual slavery but even seemed to imply that non-Hebrew slaves could be ruled ruthlessly or, as phrased elsewhere, "with rigor." Yet Leviticus and Exodus also proclaim versions of the Golden Rule: "You shall not oppress a stranger, for you know the feelings of the stranger, having yourselves been strangers, in the land of Egypt." Both Jews and Christians have long struggled to reconcile these oppressive and compassionate passages and precepts. (Some later captains of slave ships claimed that their treatment of Africans conformed to the Golden Rule.)[33]

Even when the forces of demand and supply often led to the enslavement of local debtors and abandoned babies, it was surely easier to dehumanize the foreigners captured in wars and often traded by merchants who specialized in such commerce.[34] It is highly significant that beginning in the tenth century, Western Europeans began attaching a foreign ethnic connotation to their words for "slave" as they purchased increasing numbers of bondspeople from the Dalmatian coast. The Latin words *servus* and *mancipium* were gradually replaced by *sclavus*, meaning a "Slav" or person of Slavic descent, which became the root for the English word *slave* and its counterparts— *schiavo* in Italian, *esclave* in French, *esclavo* in Spanish, *sklave* in German. And from the early thirteenth to the late fifteenth century, Italian merchants participated in a booming long-distance seaborne trade that transported tens of thousands of "white" Armenian, Bulgarian, Circassian, Mingrelian, and Georgian slaves from regions around the Black Sea and the Sea of Azov to Mediterranean markets extending from Muslim Egypt and Syria to Christian Crete, Cyprus, Sicily, and eastern Spain. Such slave labor was increasingly used for the production of sugar.[35] As a remnant of this white slave trade, which was cut off after the Ottoman Turks captured Constantinople in 1453, there were a few Greek and Slavic slaves in Spanish Havana as late as 1600.[36] But by the late 1500s, the Portuguese settlers in Brazil, having earlier relied on Indian captives, were turning almost exclusively to black African slaves, and a century later, after the "Africanization" of the Caribbean, the English colonists in Virginia and Maryland were following the same path.

Historians long engaged in a debate over whether antiblack racism preceded the widespread enslavement of Africans or emerged as a result of that enslavement. There is some truth on both sides, but in general the second alternative is supported by more evidence. It is easy enough to dwell on the negative symbolism of the "noncolor" black or even to point to a preference for dark-skinned slaves on the part of the Aryan invaders in India or the T'ang Dynasty Chinese. Beginning in the sixteenth century, the first English voyagers and traders described sub-Saharan Africans as "a people of beastly living, without a God, lawe, religion, or common wealth." Such writers drew on earlier non-English precedents, among them the Moroccan Christian convert Leo Africanus, who in the 1520s described the blacks' "beastly kind of life, being utterly destitute of the use of reason, of dexteritie of wit, and of all arts." Numerous commentators noted the blacks' near nakedness and their supposed unrestrained lust, symbolized by the male's large penis.[37] With respect to human-animal relations, it was a "tragic happenstance of nature," as Winthrop Jordan put it, that Europeans discovered the chimpanzee, then called "orang-outang," in the same West African regions where they purchased slaves. As a result, while it was not claimed that black Africans were themselves a species of apes, there was much comparison of their low and flat nostrils, thick lips, and other features with those of the tailless apes. There was also much continuing lore about male "orang-outangs" having sex with black women.[38]

But in the sixteenth century, the English were well aware that the Portuguese had long been purchasing and transporting thousands of African slaves to Iberia and the Atlantic Islands, a fact that already made them seem like a people "made to be slaves." Moreover, the Portuguese had shown respect for African rulers and traders and had dealt with them as equals. To complicate matters further, a study of the image of black Africans in Western art suggests that medieval European culture, prior to New World slavery, can hardly be described as "racist," at least with respect to black Africans (as opposed to Jews).[39]

Countless whites derived their first impressions of Africans from depictions of Mansā Mūsā, the very wealthy black king of Mali, laden with gold on his pilgrimage to Mecca; or from numerous pictures of a black African magus, or wise man, in scenes of the Nativity; or from illustrations of the black Queen of Sheba or even a black Virgin Mary. While churches also portrayed black-faced executioners in the Passion of Christ, the distinctive African facial features were far more evident in the many paintings and statues of the heroic Saint Maurice, a black African clothed in armor who appeared in churches and cathedrals in Germany and Switzerland. Amazingly, Saint Maurice was supposedly a leader of the Teutonic Knights in the Holy Roman Empire's crusade against the pagan Slavs to the east! Despite the negative depictions of West Africans in later English traveler accounts, a relative absence of antiblack racism extended on into the Renaissance and beyond, as evidenced in Western European literature and the humanistic portraits of blacks by Memling, Rubens, Hals, Rembrandt, and others.

The much earlier Muslim experience underscores the way that the increasing enslavement of blacks could lead to antiblack racism in both ideology and behavior. By 869 CE, when thousands of black slaves rose in revolt in the marshlands of the Tigris-Euphrates delta, in modern Iraq, Arabs and Persians had imported, especially by sea, countless numbers of black slaves from East Africa. And it would appear that the connection between dehumanizing labor, on the one hand, and people with a highly distinctive physical appearance, on the other, led Muslim writers in increasing numbers to describe blacks in terms that fit Aristotle's image of natural slaves (whether they had heard of Aristotle or not). In fact, the Arabic word for slave, 'abd, came in time to mean only a black slave and, in some regions, referred to any black whether slave or free—surely an indication that black slaves were thought to have an incapacity for genuine freedom. Many Arab writers echoed the racial contempt typified by the famous fourteenth-century Tunisian historian Ibn Khaldūn, when he wrote that black people were "characterized by levity, excitability, and great emotionalism," and were "as a whole submissive to slavery, because Negroes have little that is essentially human and have attributes that are quite similar to those of dumb animals."[40] The historian Gernot Rotter shows that Arab and Persian writers frequently associated blacks with apes; a thirteenth-century Persian concluded that the Zanj [Bantu-speaking peoples from East Africa] differed from animals only because "their two hands are lifted above the ground," and that "many have observed that the ape is more teachable and more intelligent than the Zanji."[41]

It should also be noted that while medieval and early-modern Arab and Persian writers usually attributed the blacks' physical traits to climatic and environmental forces, they increasingly invoked Noah's biblical curse of Canaan, the son of Ham, to explain why the "sons of Ham" had been blackened and degraded to the status of natural slaves as punishment for their ancestor's sin.[42] Still, there were voices like that of Muslim jurist Ahmad Baba of Timbuktu, who exclaimed that "even assuming that Ham was the ancestor of the blacks, God is too merciful to punish millions of people for the sin of a single individual.[43]

There can be no doubt that the increasing purchase or capture of sub-Saharan African slaves, usually for the most degrading kinds of labor, generated an early form of racism as well as an Islamic literature defending the humanity and equality of blacks by explaining the supposed environmental origins of their physical difference.

For many medieval Arabs, as for later Europeans, the blackness of Africans suggested sin, damnation, and the devil. Despite the protests of free black writers themselves, some medieval Muslims continued to describe the Zanj as being ugly, stupid, dishonest, frivolous, light-hearted, and foul-smelling, but gifted with a sense of musical rhythm and dominated by unbridled sexual lust (again, symbolized by the large penis). Point by point, these stereotypes of medieval Muslim writers resemble those of the later Spaniards, Portuguese, English, and Americans. I should stress that many Muslim jurists and theologians continued to reject the popular idea that black Africans were designed by nature to be slaves, and insisted that human beings were divided only by faith: all infidels or pagans, regardless of skin color or ethnic origin, could lawfully be enslaved in a jihad.[44]

Though much further research is needed, it seems highly probable that many racial stereotypes were transmitted, along with black slavery itself (to say nothing of algebra and a knowledge of the ancient Greek classics) from Muslims to Christians as the two groups traded and fought over many centuries from the eastern Mediterranean and Holy Land on to that melting pot of religions and cultures, the Iberian Peninsula. As historian James H. Sweet has emphasized, "by the fifteenth century, many Iberian Christians had internalized the racist attitudes of the Muslims and were applying them to the increasing flow of African slaves to their part of the world." Sweet even concludes that "Iberian racism was a necessary precondition for the system of human bondage that would develop in the Americas during the sixteenth century and beyond."[45]

Of course, preconditions do not determine the actual flow of events, and the settlement of African slaves in the New World from the early 1500s to the early 1700s was haphazard, unsystematic, and dependent on diverse local circumstances and conditions. Even in the early sixteenth century, the demand for black slaves in the Spanish colonies was tempered by what would become a universal fear that an excessive number of Africans would endanger security—a fear confirmed sporadically by slave revolts. In some regions, like the

Chesapeake colonies, the status of black servants was ambiguous for a time and blacks interacted with white indentured servants until large importations of African slaves in the later 1600s generated racist laws and attitudes that reinforced a sense of a superior white identity and, eventually, white "equality."[46]

Nevertheless, the rising hemispheric demand for cheap labor, coupled with the seemingly limitless supply of slaves from Africa (well over 12 million were exported) led to the dispersal of black slaves from Chile to Canada. While the great majority were concentrated in Brazil and the Caribbean, black slaves comprised for a time more than half the populations of Lima and Mexico City, and beginning in 1688, the governor and other Canadian officials of New France begged the French kings to authorize direct shipments of African slaves to Canada, arguing that slave labor was responsible for the economic success of both New York and New England.[47]

As a result of this nearly universal New World demand for cheap and productive labor, the eighteenth century became the great century of the African slave trade, and the rapid growth of the New World slave population was further accelerated by the unique *natural* growth of the slave population in North America. Not surprisingly, given the Muslim example, these demographic events were accompanied in Western Europe as well as in the Americas by the slow and erratic evolution of an antiblack racism that went beyond any earlier precedents. The century also witnessed the evolution of a wholly new *antislavery* moral ideology and activism which gave an added stimulus to scientific racism, especially in the nineteenth century, as the most effective weapon to block slave emancipation.

While slavery had always involved some animalization, as a form of dehumanization, and had relied on xenophobia and ethnocentrism with respect to outsiders, it long existed without explicit racism. The ancient stereotypes of slaves, including Plato and Aristotle's depictions of a kind of inferiority rooted in nature, had anticipated the stereotypes of blacks in much racist writing. But the scientific racism that developed in the late eighteenth and nineteenth centuries became a systematic way of institutionalizing and justifying the individual white's projection of an "animal Id" upon blacks. It took the form of an intellectual theory or ideology, cloaked in science, as well as actions and behavior legitimated by laws, customs, and social structure. As historian George M. Fredrickson has emphasized, racism "either directly sustains or proposes to establish *a racial order,* a permanent group hierarchy that is believed to reflect the laws of nature or the degrees of God."[48]

The offhand racist remarks of such preeminent philosophers of the Enlightenment as David Hume, Voltaire, and Immanuel Kant, writing in the mid-eighteenth century, indicate how deeply the anti-African stereotypes from New World slavery had penetrated some of the highest levels of secular culture—the same Enlightenment culture that would make important contributions to antislavery movements. On the other hand, the Enlightenment focused attention on environmental causality and any argument for the African's innate, genetic inferiority challenged the most fundamental and cherished Christian belief in the common origin and unity of all mankind.

Voltaire spoke of the "prodigious differences" between whites and blacks, dramatized not only by the latter's "round eyes, their flat noses, their lips, which are always thick, their differently shaped ears, the wool on their head," but by "the measure even of their intelligence." Kant agreed that the "substantial" difference between the two races "appears to be as great in respect to the faculties of the mind as in color," and that therefore "the Negroes of Africa have received from nature no intelligence that rises above the foolish." Hume suspected that blacks were "naturally inferior to the whites" since they had produced "no ingenious manufactures . . . no arts, no sciences." And Kant noted that Hume "invites anyone to quote a single example of a Negro who has exhibited talents." In short, given the Enlightenment's broader context of promoting freedom and equality to replace traditional feudal hierarchies, some intellectual leaders discovered a race that, because supposedly lacking a rational mind and dominated by animal passions, exhibited an incapacity for genuine freedom and thus presented a serious problem when living in a white society. Yet it should be stressed that Hume, Voltaire, and Kant were by no means defenders of slavery.[49]

This seeming paradox is mirrored in the phenomenon of the Enlightenment's encouragement of science and secular thinking, which led to an increasing recognition of the close ties between humans and other animals and to the classification of human groups in the manner of classifying plants and animals. Ultimately this methodology contributed to various forms of scientific racism and to the view that black Africans were closer to apes than whites, or were even a separate species with a separate origin.

The great Swedish botanist Carl Linnaeus and German zoologist Johann Friedrich Blumenbach led the way in devising extremely influential classifications of the human species within the primate genus.[50] Thus Blumenbach affirmed the essential unity of the human species while differentiating Caucasians, Mongolians, Ethiopians, American Indians, and Malays. The last four groups had supposedly diverged or degenerated from the original form set by the Caucasians, who were named for the supposed beauty of the people living in the mountainous region between the Black and Caspian seas (a curious point considering the long enslavement of such so-called Slavs). While Linnaeus and Blumenbach did not rank human races, and Blumenbach tried to refute the common claim that Africans were "nearer the apes than other men," the great French naturalist Georges-Louis de Buffon found an environmental explanation for the Africans' intellectual inferiority as well as skin color.[51]

By 1799, Charles White, a British surgeon and member of the Royal Society, drew on comparative anatomy in his account of nature's Great Chain of Being—the belief in a continuous gradation from plants and animals to human beings, an idea long debated in the eighteenth century. While disavowing any support for "the pernicious practice of enslaving mankind," White assembled an unprecedented array of physiological details to prove that "ascending the line of gradation" between separate human species, the white European was the "most removed from brute creation" and "the most beautiful of the human race." Refuting the Judeo-Christian doctrine of a common human origin, he affirmed that Negro sensuality and intellectual inferiority rested on the evidence that the African more closely resembled the ape and "seems to approach nearer to the brute creation than any other of the human species." While contrary to White's stated intentions, this attempted scientific animalization of the black African contributed to proslavery theories of "inherent inferiority," one of two ways of finding Aristotle's natural slave.[52]

But, given the strength of Christian opposition, it would not be until the 1840s, partly in response to the flourishing abolitionist movements in Britain and the United States, that the racist behavior long embodied in all examples of New World slavery would be intellectually structured in a widely accepted science, later greatly aided by neo-Darwinism, that would flourish well after emancipation and persist with little effective criticism until after the First World War. Yet Aristotle himself had pointed to an alternative source of natural slavery when he compared the natural slave with domesticated animals, who in the course of being "trained" had *internalized* human needs and desires.

DOMESTICATION AND INTERNALIZATION

As Aristotle contemplated the social stratifications of his time, he concluded that "from the hour of their birth, some men are marked out for subjection, others for rule." Notably, his analysis of human inequalities begins by stressing the parallel between slaves and domesticated beasts:

> Tame animals are naturally better than wild animals, yet for all tame animals there is an advantage in being under human control, as this secures their survival. And as regards the relationship between male and female, the former is naturally superior, the latter inferior, the male rules and the female is subject. By analogy, the same must necessarily apply to mankind as a whole. Therefore all men who differ from one another by as much as the soul differs from the body or a man from a wild beast (and that is the state of those who work by using their bodies, and for whom that is the best they can do)—these people are slaves by nature, and it is better for them to be subject to this kind of control, as it is better for the other creatures I have mentioned.

Aristotle then goes on to claim that nature "must have intended" to give slaves stronger bodies and feebler minds than free people:

> For a man who is able to belong to another person is by nature a slave (for that is why he belongs to someone else), as is a man who participates in reason only so far as to realize that it exists, but not so far as to have it himself—other animals do not recognize reason, but follow their passions. The way we use slaves isn't very different; assistance regarding the necessities of life is provided by both groups, by slaves and by domestic animals. Nature must therefore

have intended to make the bodies of free men and of slaves different also; slaves' bodies strong for the services they have to do, those
of free men upright and not much use for that kind of work, but
instead useful for community life.[53]

Aristotle did acknowledge that on occasion "slaves can have the
bodies of free men" and that free men could have "only the souls and
not the bodies of free men." Even more troubling, he observed, was
the fact that people "of the most respected family" sometimes become
slaves "simply because they happened to be captured and sold." But
such instances of injustice could not weaken his conviction, which
would help shape virtually all subsequent proslavery thought, that "it
is clear that there are certain people who are free and certain people
who are slaves by nature, and it is both to their advantage, and just,
for them to be slaves."

I am sure most readers have noticed that Aristotle linked the
natural slave with an affirmation of female inferiority, as a supposedly obvious example of natural inequality. It has been convincingly
argued that the earliest and archetypal human slaves were women.[54]
In patriarchal societies, women were treated like domesticated or pet-
like animals in order to ensure their dependence and submission. In
the Hebrew Bible, as in Homer and other early sources, male captives
were typically killed on the spot; otherwise they might have escaped
or risen in revolt. Before the rise of societies capable of absorbing large
numbers of male slaves, women captives seem to have been customar-
ily enslaved as workers or concubines. Aristotle's association of female
inferiority with a discussion of the natural slave also calls to mind a
kind of ideological animalization, partly concealed by paternalistic
idealization—that is, an almost universal focus on the female body
in terms of sex, menarche, childbearing, and nursing—all accentu-
ating women's resemblance to the females of other species, with an
implied exclusion of the "higher" rational capacities of mind and
self-awareness.

As an example of Aristotle's continuing influence, it is significant that his theory of the natural slave formed the framework for
the momentous debate in Spain, in 1550–51, between Juan Ginés
Sepúlveda and Bartolomé de Las Casas, on whether American Indians had been created to be natural slaves (with Las Casas attacking
that conclusion, but not Aristotle's basic premises). In 1495, Columbus

had transported some five hundred Native American slaves to Spain and dreamed of a profitable slave trade of American Indians to Iberia, Italy, and Sicily. But, for various reasons, after Las Casas had called for the protection of Indians and the importation in America of African slaves, both the Church and the Spanish government attempted to prohibit the genuine enslavement of Native Americans.[55]

While scientific racism eventually offered one way of arguing that a given group conformed to the ideal of the natural slave, Aristotle's making an analogy with domesticated animals pointed to the possibility that animalistic treatment might result in a psychological and even genetic transformation based on the internalization of slaveholders' desires.

After drawing on comparisons of slaves with domestic animals that have been made throughout history, historian Karl Jacoby has argued convincingly that the domestication of sheep, goats, pigs, cattle, horses, and other animals during the Neolithic revolution might well have served as a model for enslaving humans.[56] Whether used for food, clothing, transport, or heavy labor, these social animals underwent a Darwinian evolutionary process of neoteny, or progressive "juvenilization." That is, they became more submissive than their wild counterparts, less fearful of strangers, and less aggressive (which in physical terms was reflected in a shortening of the jawbone and a decrease in the size of the teeth). Far from being chance occurrences, these changes in anatomy and behavior were closely geared to human needs, especially in farming, though of course the human domesticators learned by trial and error and had no knowledge of the mechanisms of genetic engineering. Many mammals, such as zebras, successfully resisted domestication.[57]

To control domesticated beasts, human beings devised collars, chains, prods, whips, and branding irons. They also castrated some dangerous males and subjected animals to selective breeding. More positive incentives arose from a kind of paternalism in which human beings replaced the dominant male animal that had exercised some control over the social group. Unlike later, inanimate resources such as coal and oil, animals were self-reproducing but had to be kept healthy and protected as much as possible from disease.

As Jacoby astutely observes, once economic development led to an increasing need for male labor for agriculture and public works, similar means of control were applied to human captives (including even castration), whose foreign languages may have made them seem more like animals than men. After the harvests and livestock accumulated by agricultural societies had revolutionized the objectives of warfare, a well-planned raid to steal the wealth that a foreign community had saved from a year of labor might also involve the kidnapping of groups of workers, who could then be identified by different clothing, hair cutting, branding, collars, and other symbols. Xenophon, like many other early writers on the management of slaves, "compared the teaching of slaves, unlike that of free workers, with the training of wild animals."[58]

Yet, despite the countless attempts to equate human captives with domestic animals (the first African slaves shipped to Lisbon in the mid-1400s were stripped naked and marketed and priced exactly like livestock), slaves were fortunately never held long enough in distinct, isolated groups to undergo significant genetic change (as we can tell from DNA). Even so, juvenilization, the development of childlike characteristics in slaves, was clearly the goal of numerous slaveholders, despite their lack of any scientific understanding of how domestication had changed the nature and behavior of animals. Even Aristotle's description of the natural slave's mind and body pictured at least superficially what a human being would be like if "tamed" by neoteny.[59]

Black abolitionists, such as fugitive slave Henry Highland Garnet, fully grasped this point. In a famous speech to free blacks, urging slaves to resist, Garnet spelled out the goal of animalization:

> In every man's mind the good seeds of liberty are planted, and he who brings his fellow down so low, as to make him contented with a condition of slavery, commits the highest crime against God and man. Brethren, your oppressors aim to do this. They endeavor to make you as much like brutes as possible. When they have blinded the eyes of your mind—when they have embittered the sweet waters of the light which shines from the word of God—then, and not till then has American slavery done its perfect work.[60]

As Garnet suggests, the slaveholder's dehumanizing methods could lead to some internalization, some acceptance or contentment, "with a condition of slavery," even if no genetic domestication took place. Orlando Patterson, the great historian of comparative slavery, has argued that the "Sambo" stereotype, with its "total absence of any hint of 'manhood,' " has been "an ideological imperative of all systems of slavery." Patterson quotes the famous description by historian Stanley Elkins:

> Sambo, the typical plantation slave, was docile but irresponsible, loyal but lazy, humble but chronically given to lying and stealing; his behavior was full of infantile silliness and his talk inflated with childish exaggeration. His relationship with his master was one of utter dependence and childlike attachment: it was indeed this childlike quality that was the very key to his being.[61]

Writing in the late 1950s, Elkins wished to emphasize the unprecedented harshness of American (as opposed to Latin American) slavery, but his portrait of the infantilized "Sambo" infuriated liberals and radicals of the 1960s and 1970s who wished to celebrate slave autonomy and slave resistance. Patterson, who could not have been more aware of defiant and rebellious slaves throughout history, emphasized that the "Sambo" image "is no more realistic a description of how slaves actually thought and behaved than was the inflated conception of honor and sense of freedom an accurate description of their masters." But without suggesting that slaves significantly internalized "the conception of degradation held by their masters," he recognized that slaves could hardly escape some feelings of being dishonored and degraded. This could mean an ability to play the role of "Sambo" as a way of deceiving whites. Countless black writers have referred to the "masks" blacks feel a need to wear when dealing with whites. But Patterson also quotes slaves expressing self-hatred and "psychological violence against [themselves]": "De Massa and Missus was good to me but sometime I was so bad they had to whip me. . . . I needed de whippin'."[62]

Of all the slaves or former slaves who left testimony, Frederick Douglass would seem to be the last one we could imagine to have internalized even the slightest sense of white degradation. Very likely the son of his white owner, Douglass led a highly privileged boyhood, learned to read and write and school himself, and succeeded at age twenty in escaping to the North, where he became one of the few American "giants" of the nineteenth century. He became "one of the most meritorious men, if not the most meritorious man, in the United States," as President Abraham Lincoln put it—a leading abolitionist, best-selling author, editor, spellbinding lecturer, adviser to President Lincoln, and U.S. ambassador.[63] Yet at age sixteen Douglass discovered the harsh realities of slavery, when his relatively new owner, Thomas Auld, chose to work him in the fields and have him disciplined by a so-called slave-breaker, Edward Covey. After he had been "tamed" by interminable work and countless whippings, Douglass recalled: "Mr. Covey succeeded in breaking me. I was broken in body, soul, and spirit. My natural elasticity was crushed, my intellect languished, the disposition to read departed . . . the dark night of slavery closed in upon me; and behold a man transformed into a brute!"

While Douglass eventually achieved a true sense of psychological freedom by fighting Covey and vanquishing him, at other times he had deeply felt that learning to read "had been a curse rather than a blessing . . . I envied my fellow-slaves for their stupidity. I have often wished myself a beast." After noting that on Sundays he spent his leisure time "in a sort of beast-like stupor, between sleep and wake, under some large tree," Douglass admitted that "I was sometimes prompted to take my life." And even in 1846, when Douglass had won repeated acclaim in Britain as an abolitionist speaker, a British reformer wrote to a prominent American abolitionist that Douglass was "a sort of reclaimed wild beast—and . . . it don't do to judge him by our civilized rules."[64] As that quotation suggests, Douglass, despite his fame and even as the son of a white father, could not escape the biological heritage of Africa and the cultural heritage of white responses to dark pigmentation of skin.

Given the slavery-based culture of white dehumanization, a theme of self-hatred and ambiguous self-esteem runs through African American writing, from the eighteenth century's Phillis Wheatley ("Some view our sable race with scornful eye,/Their color is a diabolic die./Remember, Christians, Negroes, black as Cain,/May be refined, and join th'angelic train") to James Baldwin and Toni Morrison. In 1971, Baldwin, who had much earlier asserted that he had been conditioned to "despise" black people, related that racial self-hatred to both animalization and the heritage of slavery:

The American triumph, in which the American tragedy has always been implicit, was to make Black people despise themselves. When I was little I despised myself, I did not know any better. And this meant, albeit unconsciously, or against my will, or in great pain, that I also despised my father. And my mother. And my brothers. And my sisters. Black people were killing each other every Saturday night out on Lenox Avenue, when I was growing up; and no one explained to them, or to me, that it was *intended* that they should; that they were penned where they were, like animals, in order that they should consider themselves no better than animals. Everything supported this sense of reality, nothing denied it: and so one was ready, when it came time to go to work, to be treated as a slave.[65]

Toni Morrison has also emphasized that her fictional account of a black girl's longing for blue eyes was based on "racial self-loathing." This assertion of racial beauty was definitely not

a reaction to the self-mocking, humorous critique of cultural/racial foibles common in all groups, but against the damaging internalization of assumptions of immutable inferiority originating in an outside gaze. I focused, therefore, on how something as grotesque as the demonization of an entire race could take root inside the most delicate member of society: a child, the most vulnerable member: a female.[66]

Following two and a half centuries of American slavery and a century of Jim Crow legal discrimination, conditions did of course improve in significant ways. But even in the mid-1980s, when Barack Obama began working as a community organizer in South Side Chicago, he discovered that black self-hate was far from being a marginal or exceptional problem—a matter he felt free to describe in his 1995 book, *Dreams from My Father*. Perhaps because Obama had had so little involvement with black communities, a friend impatiently asked, " 'What are you surprised about? . . . That black people still hate themselves?' " After analyzing the blacks' self-destructive symptoms of "color consciousness," including concern over "good hair, bad hair, thick lips or thin," and the hostile use of "nigger," the future president of the United States expressed an understanding of the allure of black nationalism and the grim reality of "all the black people who, it turned out, shared with me a voice that whispered inside them—'You don't really belong here.' "

Yet, as Obama further reflected, "to admit our doubt and confusion to whites, to open up our psyches to general examination by those who had caused so much of the damage in the first place, seemed ludicrous, itself an expression of self-hatred." While he overcame this fear, he also felt "there seemed no reason to expect that whites would look at our private struggles as a mirror into their own souls, rather than yet more evidence of black pathology."[67]

In dealing with slavery and its subsequent antiblack racism, there has always been a danger of exaggerating a kind of passive victimhood that elicits white pity as well as contempt for a "damaged black psyche." The image of blacks as psychologically damaged victims can reinforce the belief in white superiority and has in fact been used to oppose racial integration and civil rights.[68] As Obama implies and as this chapter was meant to establish, the central pathology is a *white* pathology intent on animalization as a form of projection for the benefit of whites of all social classes. If this psychological exploitation resulted in some black internalization and even pathology, it also evoked black resistance, from the time of slavery to the thousands of ex-slaves in the South who were routinely arrested for "crimes" like vagabondage and were then leased out by states to work in mines, plantations, and factories, to say nothing of the later blacks who refused to sit in the back of a bus or to step off a sidewalk to make way for white superiority.

It was often said in the antebellum South that the existence of a debased and slavish race made even poor whites feel equal to the privileged elite. But this was only part of a larger paradigm. A dialectical and historical connection developed between American slavery and American freedom, between the belief in an inferior, servile race and the vision of classless opportunity. Blacks represented and sometimes absorbed the finitude, imperfections, sensuality, self-mockery, and depravity of human nature, thereby amplifying the opposite qualities in the white race. And this parasitic relationship came to be driven by the special nature of the American "mission" and dream of overcoming the limits and boundaries of past history. However conceived, "the Negro problem" meant that blacks were associated metaphysically with everything that compromised or stood in the way of the American Dream—with finitude, failure, poverty, fate, the sins of our fathers, nemesis. In short, with dark reality.

As we will see, the antebellum decades were filled with dreams and fantasies of removing or colonizing this black Id, a vision based on the proposition that the Id would become Ego—that the Negro, if removed from the prejudicial environment of America and returned to Africa, would become a civilized *Black American* who would help *Americanize* Africa. But along with the grimmer models of deporting British criminals to Australia and expelling groups like Jews and Moriscos from late-medieval Spain, the biblical Exodus had been the archetype for countless groups, including the English Puritans, to escape oppression and search for a Promised Land. If slaves were caged like domestic animals and deprived of any true freedom of movement, would they not need to travel to "free soil" upon emancipation, in order to gain genuine liberation? In the 1820s thousands of American free blacks sailed off to Haiti with such expectations. And while the overwhelming majority of free blacks rejected the appeals of the white American Colonization Society, there were continuing black "back to Africa" movements, culminating in the first African American mass movement, led in the early 1920s by Marcus Garvey. Barack Obama's reference to the occasional black feeling that "you don't really belong here" is also confirmed by the many black intellectuals, such as W. E. B. Du Bois, who became expatriates.

Nevertheless, despite the persistence of slavery's legacy—the continuation of much black deprivation, inequality, and white racism even into the twenty-first century—African Americans have remained steadfast in their loyalty and commitment to a special American identity. The arrival and reelection of a black family in the White House has signified a momentous change and a generational transformation with respect to race. It would not be relevant for a book on slavery and emancipation even to summarize the slow and incomplete erosion of racism in the twentieth century. Yet given my emphasis on dehumanization and psychological parasitism, I want to mention the long-term interactions between white and black cultures, from nineteenth-century white black-face minstrels to the role of blacks in professional and college sports and white responses to black hip-hop. If most whites profited from psychological projection, increasing numbers also succumbed to the appeal of "the Negro Id." This nineteenth-century opening eventually enabled African American culture to transform popular music and many other aspects of American culture itself.

Race, as we have seen, came to personify blacks' supposed incapacity for freedom in the sense of voluntary work, self-discipline, moral responsibility, and civilized behavior. It became the major justification for slavery, often obscuring the actual and indispensable economic value of slave labor. Yet the Haitian Revolution, to which we now turn, shook the entire New World and conveyed two contradictory messages with regard to racial capacity and freedom. As we briefly saw in the introduction, there were images of docile slaves suddenly engaged in beastly slaughter, rape, and unimaginable atrocities. On the other hand, supposedly incapable blacks organized military forces that continued to fight for more than twelve years, creating a new independent nation after defeating not only their white masters but the best armies of France, Britain, and Spain.

2

The First Emancipations:
Freedom and Dishonor

SELF-EMANCIPATION: HAITI AS A TURNING POINT

On January 2, 1893, Frederick Douglass rose to deliver a speech dedi-
cating the Haitian Pavilion at the Chicago World's Fair. Douglass was
intimately involved in planning the pavilion. As the recent United
States minister and consul general to Haiti and exposition commissioner of the Haitian government, the now elder statesman was
pleased with the result. Douglass called the pavilion "a city set upon
a hill," invoking the words of the New Testament, and their use by
John Winthrop to Puritan settlers in 1630 on the deck of the *Arbella*.
Douglass took the opportunity of his speech to negate the common
stereotype that Haitians were lazy barbarians who devoted their leisure time to "Voodoo" and child sacrifice. But what's more significant
is that Douglass used the speech to reflect back on the past century of
slave emancipation. Douglass, after all, was born a slave. And he had
won international fame through his writing and oratory in the service
of black emancipation. As the most prominent black spokesman and
statesman of the New World, Douglass had no difficulty in identifying
one of the central events in the history of emancipation:

> We should not forget that the freedom you and I enjoy to-day; that
> the freedom that eight hundred thousand colored people enjoy
> in the British West Indies; the freedom that has come to the col-

ored race the world over, is largely due to the brave stand taken by the black sons of Haiti ninety years ago. When they struck for freedom . . . they struck for the freedom of every black man in the world.[1]

Douglass made sure to note that blacks owed much to the American and British abolitionists, including antislavery societies in countries around the world. But blacks, he noted, "owe incomparably more to Haiti than to them all." It was Haiti that struck first for emancipation; it was "the original pioneer emancipator of the nineteenth century." Haiti had instructed the world about the dangers of slavery, and had demonstrated that the latent powers and capabilities of the black race had only to be awakened. Once awakened, the former slaves of Saint-Domingue demonstrated their strength in defeating fifty thousand of Napoleon's veteran troops. Not only that, but these insurgents turned to establish an independent nation of their own making. The white world could and would never be the same. Until Haiti spoke, Douglass pointed out, "no Christian nation had abolished Negro slavery. . . . Until she spoke, the slave trade was sanctioned by all the Christian nations of the world, and our land of liberty and light included. . . . Until Haiti spoke, the church was silent, and the pulpit dumb."[2]

The history, of course, was more complex than Douglass's depiction. He knew that. For whites, Haiti was "a very hell of horrors." The "very name was pronounced with a shudder," as he noted at the beginning of his speech. And indeed the revolution had inevitably had contradictory effects. As an abolitionist from 1841 to 1865, Douglass avoided mention of the Haitian Revolution in his public speeches, debates, and interviews.[3] In the ears of his white audiences, the abolitionist Douglass knew the perceptions of the event all too well. For some, the revolution had been an object lesson in the inevitable social and economic ruin that would attend any form of emancipation. For others, it signaled blood—a veritable white massacre, a racial nightmare made real. Yet this did not change Douglass's conviction that the Haitian Revolution was a watershed event.

Douglass's address of 1893 contained an inescapable truth: the Haitian Revolution was a turning point in history. Like 9/11 for modern day Americans, the Haitian Revolution could not be escaped, however much its meaning was rationalized, suppressed, or avoided.

The event demonstrated the possible path of any slaveholding society. Therefore, the Haitian Revolution impinged in one way or another on the entire emancipation debate from the British parliamentary move in 1792 to outlaw the African slave trade to Brazil's final abolition of slavery ninety-six years later. It is helpful, then, to briefly discuss the significance of Haiti's birth in order to review some of the ways in which New World slavery was being transformed in the Age of Revolution.

It is important to understand that in the 1780s, the French colony of Saint-Domingue was no backwater of the New World slave system. It was the centerpiece. The colony produced more than half the world's coffee. In 1787, it exported almost as much sugar as Jamaica, Cuba, and Brazil combined. But the "pearl of the Antilles" was destroyed from 1791 to 1804 by revolution and civil war. The slaves and free descendants of slaves shook off not only their masters but the most formidable armies of Spain, Britain, and France. Douglass made the situation clear. Unlike the American Revolution, which had been led by "the ruling race of the world" who "had the knowledge and character naturally inherited from long years of personal and political freedom," the Haitian rebels represented a race that "stood before the world as the most abject, helpless, and degraded of mankind."[4] Haiti's freedom "was not given as a boon" by the standing powers "but conquered as a right!" "Her people fought for it. They suffered for it, and thousands of them endured the most horrible tortures, and perished for it."

This heroic achievement evoked little applause from whites, even those who rejoiced over other movements of national liberation. For reasons that we shall explore later on, the Haitian Revolution reinforced the conviction that emancipation in any form would lead to economic ruin and to the indiscriminate massacre of white populations. The waves of fear traveled even faster than the Dominguan refugees who streamed westward to Cuba and Jamaica and northward to Spanish Louisiana and the port cities and towns of the United States. Throughout the Americas, planters and government officials learned to live in a state of alert.

But fear seldom overcomes greed. Planters in Cuba, Brazil, Jamaica, and Trinidad clamored for more African slaves who could help make up the deficit in world sugar and coffee production left by the devastation of Saint-Domingue. In one of the ironies of history, the destruction of slavery in Saint-Domingue gave an immense stimulus to plantation slavery from neighboring Cuba to far-off Brazil. In December 1803, just after the disease-ridden French army had finally capitulated to Jean-Jacques Dessalines's ex-slaves, South Carolina reopened the slave trade and in the next four years imported some forty thousand Africans. As Charleston's merchants well knew, the defeat of Napoleon's New World ambitions had opened the way for the Louisiana Purchase, which ensured that American slavery could expand westward without foreign interference into the Lower Mississippi Valley.

On the other hand, even Cuba, South Carolina, and other slave-importing regions sought to exclude bondsmen from colonies in which blacks had been exposed to revolutionary ideas. Although slave insurrections had usually been associated with a labor force containing a high proportion of recently imported Africans, white leaders were now far more fearful of blacks who had been contaminated by French or abolitionist conceptions of liberty. Haiti thus represented the fullest effects of the contagion of liberty among slaves. Measures had to be put into place to stop the spread of people inordinately exposed to the germ of freedom. It could spread.

In Britain and the United States abolitionists argued that slavery itself was the obvious cause of slave revolts. Early in 1792, Thomas Clarkson insisted that while the French Revolution had presented the slaves with an opportunity to vindicate their humanity, the insurrection in Saint-Domingue could be attributed only to the slave trade and the oppressive system it produced. Far from being an argument against Britain's antislave-trade petitions, the events in Saint-Domingue showed that it was sheer madness for the British to continue transporting Africans who, having "the passions of men," would sooner or later avenge their wrongs.[5] Such reasoning was clearly influential in the United States, where planters could rely on a rapid natural increase in the slave population and where opposition to further slave importation had won sanction from the War of Independence. The nation as a whole was outraged and alarmed by South Carolina's reopening of the slave trade in 1803; the Haitian Revolution strengthened the political argument for outlawing the American slave trade in 1808, the earliest date allowed by the Constitution.[6] The Haitian example, supplemented by a major slave conspiracy in Virginia, also led to laws restricting manumission and nourished interest in deporting free blacks to some distant colony.

Haiti's effects on British policy were more ambiguous. Like their French neighbors, British planters lived as small white minorities surrounded by vast slave majorities. But they were accustomed to risk and were convinced that their fortunes depended on a labor force that would soon die off unless replenished by continuous imports from Africa. The catastrophe in Saint-Domingue, they claimed, showed the dangers of abolitionist agitation, not of a labor supply on which the Caribbean colonies had always depended. Even in 1795–96, when the British colonies were most seriously threatened by racial warfare and by French armies that included large numbers of emancipated slaves, Parliament deferred to the West India planters and merchants and failed to renew a 1792 resolution calling for an end to the slave trade in four years. Indeed, the British successfully defended their slave colonies only by enlisting black troops directly from the slave ships. It would be difficult to show that fear of another Haitian Revolution motivated Parliament's crucial votes in 1806 abolishing the slave trade to rival foreign markets, and in 1807 abolishing the British slave trade altogether.[7]

Yet it cannot be denied that both the government and the British public had learned a lesson from William Pitt's disastrous attempt to conquer Saint-Domingue, restore slavery, and subdue Toussaint Louverture. In 1796, nearly three years after the first British forces landed in Saint-Domingue, the Pitt administration sent off to the West Indies one of the greatest expeditionary forces in British history. Before the end of the year Edmund Burke heard that ten thousand men had died in less than two months. It was reported in the House of Commons that almost every Briton had a personal acquaintance who had perished in the Caribbean campaigns. Burke wrote caustically of "recruits to the West Indian grave" and of fighting to conquer a cemetery. Although the mortality figures were somewhat exaggerated and British casualties were much heavier in the Windward Islands than in Saint-Domingue, there were good grounds for public outrage and for opposition party attacks on the conduct of the war. The loss in the Caribbean of nearly fifty thousand British soldiers and seamen, to say nothing of the expenditure of more than £16,000,000, underscored the cost of defending colonies that might at any moment become replicas of Saint-Domingue.[8] The West Indian "image," already tarnished by years of antislavery literature and iconography, never recovered from Britain's defeat in Saint-Domingue.

In this broad sense the Haitian Revolution surely contributed to the British government's decisions, beginning in 1797, to limit the expansion of plantation agriculture in Trinidad, an undeveloped frontier that Britain had just seized from Spain. There were many competing political and economic interests involved in the government's disposition of the rich crown lands in Trinidad, and after 1803 in the conquered Dutch Guianan colonies. But shrewd politicians and reformers were able to dramatize the extreme danger of any policy that would encourage the unlimited importation of slaves. The failure of British and French armies to subjugate Saint-Domingue fostered discussion of alternative forms of labor and made it easier for government leaders to restrict the flow of slaves to Trinidad and Guiana, despite pressure from planters and investors who were eager to profit from the rising world demand for cotton, sugar, coffee, and other plantation staples.[9]

In the short run, however, the Haitian Revolution seriously damaged the antislavery movement. As abolitionists were increasingly portrayed as inciters of violence, there was a marked decline in antislavery activity and publication in both Britain and America. In France the movement virtually disappeared. Even after 1815 abolitionists found it difficult to escape the stigma of Saint-Domingue and the need to defend the record of Haiti, as if the rights of every black in the hemisphere depended on the virtue and magnanimity of Haiti's rulers. As a result of the trauma that swept much of the white world, especially after Dessalines ordered the extermination of the whites remaining in Haiti, abolitionists were long obsessed with disavowing violence or any form of slave resistance. Until the mid-nineteenth century we find few white abolitionists like "Philmore," who had argued in 1760 that since blacks were held in slavery by unjust force, they may "lawfully repel that force with force, and to recover their liberty, destroy their oppressors"; or Jean de Pechméja, who had written in 1774 that "whoever justifies so odious a system deserves scornful silence from the philosopher and a stab with a poniard from the Negro."[10]

But there was another side to this legacy. Abolitionist literature had tended to portray slaves as passive victims or as sentimental objects of benevolence, typified by Josiah Wedgwood's famous cameo of the kneeling, chained slave, supplicating the viewer with the inscription *Am I Not a Man and a Brother?* The emphasis on the slave's meekness and humility contrasted with a literary tradition descending from Aphra Behn's Oroonoko, the heroic African slave rebel, to the Abbé Raynal's "Black Spartacus," who would lead the slaves "to vengeance and slaughter" and redeem the honor of the human species. The Haitian Revolution not only brought Oroonoko and Spartacus to life but showed that the slave masses could fight indefatigably for their own liberty. While antislavery writing would continue to invent and reinvent Uncle Toms, the significance of such figures could never be separated from the knowledge that hundreds of thousands of black slaves had won their freedom by force of arms. In their very eagerness to prove the safety of emancipation and the capability of blacks for freedom, abolitionists covertly challenged the claim that black slaves were either so content or docile that they could never seriously threaten a plantation regime.

Most important was the effect of the Haitian Revolution on blacks themselves, both slave and free.[11] In 1893 Frederick Douglass simply reaffirmed an argument that runs through African American culture from the time of Toussaint Louverture's initial victories. Later on we shall examine some specific black responses to this central liberating event. For now it is sufficient to consider Douglass's key point. Learned Southerners like Thomas Jefferson had been fond of comparing the achievements of white slaves in antiquity with the dismal record of modern Negroes. But where in Greek or Roman history, Douglass asked, could one find an example of nobler daring?

> It will ever be a matter of wonder and astonishment to thoughtful men, that a people in abject slavery, subject to the lash, and kept in ignorance of letters, as these slaves were, should have known enough, or have had left in them enough manhood, to combine, to organize, and to select for themselves trusted leaders with loyal hearts to follow them into the jaws of death to obtain liberty.[12]

Black slaves had revolted, of course, from the time of the first New World settlements. But it was only in Saint-Domingue that slaves began to fight against the institution of slavery itself; and there, for the first time, they proved that white power was not invincible.[13] It was the example of Haiti, in Douglass's view, that first "startled the Christian world into a sense of the Negro's manhood."

Geographically, Haiti lay near the center of a galaxy of slave systems that depended on the fiction that slaves were incapable of acquiring or exercising power. Slaveholders needed to interpret their slaves' powerlessness as a natural condition, as the result of inherent limitations. Throughout the ages, the behavior of slaves of all races had normally lent support to this interpretation. By definition a "slavish" person was a cringing Sambo, degraded and dependent, totally lacking in manly or womanly honor. Even the children of Israel, in their paradigmatic exodus from bondage, cried out to Moses that they would have preferred to serve the Egyptians than to be slain by Pharaoh's pursuing army.[14] On rare occasions, circumstances encouraged seemingly docile slaves to cut their masters' throats. But throughout the New World, the same whites who armed themselves to suppress possible insurrections spoke with contempt of the blacks' cowardice and contentment. As Douglass intimated, when the Dominguan slaves vindicated the honor and true character of the black man, the message was as important for self-doubting blacks as for arrogant and self-deluding whites.

FREEDMEN AND SLAVES

Since the Haitian Revolution was precipitated by a demand for freedmen's rights, the cataclysm drew attention to the anomalous condition of the free black and colored populations of the New World.[15] Did the presence of such people breed unrest among slaves and pose a danger to the slave system? Would planters be more secure if they widened or narrowed the distinctions between freedman and slave status? What did the behavior of freedmen suggest with respect to the slaves' capability for eventual freedom and "civilization"? If racial slavery was dangerous to the long-term safety and virtue of any social order, as many political leaders agreed, did the condition of freedmen provide a preview of post-emancipation society or suggest that slavery could not be abolished without producing even worse social problems?

The Age of Revolution, roughly defined as the half-century between the onset of the American Revolution and the conclusion of the Napoleonic wars and Latin American struggles for independence, marked a dramatic growth in the free black and colored populations of the New World. In colonial Brazil and Spanish America, this was part of a long-term trend encouraged by sexual intermixture and relatively frequent manumission, especially of women and small children. By the late eighteenth century, free African Americans outnumbered slaves in most of Spanish America; even in Cuba over 45 percent of the African American population was free.[16]

In regions where manumission had always been extremely rare, such as the British mainland and Caribbean colonies, the number of free nonwhites now multiplied at an unprecedented rate. Some of this growth was attributable to natural reproduction at a time when most slave populations were not self-sustaining. Various slaveholding societies, including Saint-Domingue, sought to restrict manumissions, which were increasingly seen as a threat to white supremacy. But military needs reinforced religious zeal, paternal goodwill, and revolutionary ideology, inducing many masters to free their slaves during the American and French revolutions and then in the Hispanic wars of independence. Thousands of North American slaves won their freedom by joining forces with the British army or British loyalists. The British, during their protracted struggle with France for control of the Caribbean, found it necessary to enlist thousands of African slaves in special West Indian regiments and by a single legislative act to free some ten thousand of these veterans.[17] The disruptions of war and revolution enabled untold numbers of slaves to escape and find precarious niches where they could at least pass as freedmen. The fluidity and uncertainties of the Age of Revolution provided blacks with opportunities to take new initiatives and to express their own values and aspirations, though often in contradictory and self-divisive ways.

We are not concerned here with the impact of revolution on the economics of slavery. Our point of departure is the relevance of the rapidly expanding free black and colored populations to subsequent debates over the feasibility and probable consequences of general emancipation. As we shall see, the volcanic upheavals in the French colonies were widely attributed to the free coloreds' struggles for equal rights. In the United States, the large-scale emancipations that resulted from the American Revolution evoked a backlash of racial discrimination that increased support for plans to colonize free blacks in West Africa or other refuges. And it was the militant reaction against colonization, initiated by blacks themselves, that gave a distinctive stamp to American abolitionism. In the United States, far more than in any other New World society, the condition of free blacks as the beneficiaries of "the first emancipation" set the framework for later debates over the abolition of slavery.

At the outset it is important to clarify the relationship between manumission and slavery. Throughout history slaveholders have used manumission as a reward for faithful and diligent labor, for heroic acts or military service, for favored concubines and children. In some societies slaveholders enhanced their profits by allowing enterprising slaves to purchase their freedom in installments and by using the proceeds to buy new and younger laborers. From comparative studies of slave societies, we know that the frequency of manumission proves nothing about the relative harshness of slave treatment or the strength of a slave regime. In regions where masters could rely on a continuing supply of fresh slaves, as in ancient Rome and colonial Brazil, frequent manumissions probably strengthened slavery as a social and economic system. Whether freedmen and their descendants were assimilated within a few generations or were consigned to a stigmatized caste, their status had little effect on the fate of the mass of slaves. This is not to say that manumission and the status of freedmen were unrelated to the total pattern of variables that defined a given slave system. But the history of slavery gave no support to the assumption, widely held after the American Revolution, that an increasing incidence of manumission would lead automatically to universal emancipation.[18]

It is true that the Age of Revolution heightened fears that freedmen would ally themselves with slaves and encourage slave discontent, resistance, and revolt. But here one is easily misled by the later example of black abolitionists and fugitive slaves in the Northern United States and Brazil. The relations between freedmen and slaves were always complex and varied according to demographic and racial patterns, economic opportunities for freedmen, white acceptance of racial intermixture, and other factors.[19] Making allowance for the immense variations in slave societies, it is clear that freedmen were characteristically torn between a sense of loyalty to slave friends and kin and a more powerful drive to distance themselves from all reminders of their former degradation. Manumission was generally an individual and divisive act, a transfiguring gift of life or rebirth that transformed a person's status while preserving the status quo. Unlike an act of general emancipation, manumission implied no prior or universal right to liberty. It was a reward, granted at the discretion of a master, judge, or government to a slave who had been selected for some reason from the corporate mass. The process of selection favored slaves who were most likely to identify their interests with the master class that freed them. Yet this very dependence, especially when aggravated by a continuing stigma of inferiority and dishonor, generated resentments that could lead backward to an identification with slaves.

In the Southern United States as well as the British West Indies, slaveholders listened attentively to the warnings of white refugees from the French colonies. The French planters insisted that their slaves had been docile and content until the free coloreds began agitating loudly for equality and natural rights. When freedmen succeeded in winning a hearing and in elevating themselves to the level of whites, the slaves inevitably followed suit and vowed to break their chains.[20] In an era of egalitarian rhetoric, it appeared that the racial subordination of all African Americans was an essential bulwark of slavery. On the other hand, in Saint-Domingue, the free colored population had owned slaves and generally supported the slave system. They had first taken up arms against rebellious white colonists who sought to deprive them of property and elemental rights. The *gens de couleur libres*, who included blacks as well as mulattoes, fought to suppress the slave insurrection in the North Province and limited their own demands to the guarantee of full legal equality with whites. What plunged Saint-Domingue into anarchy and civil war was the growing racism of whites, especially poor whites, who were determined to maintain their superiority over all descendants of slaves and to prevent the revolutionary government of France from responding to the grievances of colored citizens.[21]

This lesson was not wholly ignored in other slaveholding societies. In 1803, for example, when the Barbadian Assembly and Council debated a bill to limit the property rights of freedmen, a prominent member of the council pointed out that the free coloreds' property holding, including slaveholding, helped to preserve public security by uniting the interests of freedmen and whites. "But if we reduce the free coloured people to a level with the slaves," he predicted, they must unite with them, and will take every occasion of promoting and encouraging a revolt." Similarly, a few delegates to the Tennessee and North Carolina constitutional conventions in the mid-1830s opposed disfranchising free blacks on the ground that deprivation of the free coloreds' traditional liberties had sparked the revolution in Saint-Domingue.[22] In the United States, however, this argument carried little weight.

Southern slaveholders were particularly prone to see subversive freedmen behind every suspected slave conspiracy. Freedmen often had the opportunity to assimilate revolutionary ideology and they sometimes assumed leading roles in slave conspiracies or insurrections: one thinks of Toussaint Louverture in Saint-Domingue, Alexandre Pétion in Curaçao, José Chirino in Venezuela, José Antonio Aponte in Cuba, Denmark Vesey in South Carolina, and Joseph Pitt Washington Franklin in Barbados.[23] On the other hand, freedmen also won praise from whites by exposing a conspiracy, as in the case of Vesey's plot in 1822, or by helping to suppress an insurrection, as in Louisiana in 1811 and Barbados in 1816. In eighteenth-century Jamaica, even the maroons, the fiercely independent black fugitives and descendants of fugitives who struggled to preserve their own de facto freedom, cooperated with white authorities by catching runaway slaves and helping to put down slave revolts. And in 1795 the Accompong Maroons, aided by slave rangers and free colored militiamen, played a central part in defeating the rebellious Trelawny Town Maroons, who, when finally transported to Sierra Leone, dutifully put down an insurrection there.[24] Rebels do not necessarily ally with other rebels.

Slaveholders everywhere would have preferred restricting arms to white troops and militia, although black soldiers had established an impressive record of loyalty and courage from the time of the first New World settlements. Given the large white population of the northern mainland colonies at the time of the Revolution, it was at least conceivable that a war against Britain could be fought without enlisting black troops. This was the policy agreed upon late in 1775 by Washington's officers and a delegation from Congress. But when the Northern states found it difficult to meet enlistment quotas, they soon began accepting blacks who volunteered or were offered as substitutes for their white owners. By 1779, when the military situation was becoming desperate in the Deep South, even South Carolinians— including Governor John Rutledge and the Laurens family—were calling on Congress to mobilize an army of black slaves. Unfortunately, though Congress offered to compensate slave owners in Georgia and South Carolina in order to raise a force of 3,000 black troops, it had no way of overriding the resistance of the Georgia and South Carolina legislatures.[25]

In 1795 the Jamaican legislature mounted similar resistance to Britain's proposal to enlist thousands of slaves and free coloreds in permanent West Indian regiments. Demographic realities had long reconciled West Indian whites to the use of blacks for military labor and even combat, though for limited periods and under strict local control. The Caribbean colonies simply could not attract enough whites for self-defense; the white troops sent from Europe died in appalling numbers from yellow fever and other tropical diseases. By 1795, after two years of warfare with France, it was clear that Britain could not send out sufficient reinforcements to conquer Saint-Domingue, reconquer Guadeloupe, suppress rebellions in Grenada, Saint Vincent, and Jamaica, and defend all the colonies against French agents who were trying to use France's emancipation decrees as a means of inciting slave insurrections against the British. Jamaican whites thought it madness, in such an inflammatory environment, to raise regiments of armed slaves. Planters, like those in the American South, also resisted even the compensated loss of their most valuable property, since any appreciable drain of manpower could destroy the value of their estates. The British government therefore resorted to the policy of buying thousands of Africans from the slave ships, outfitting them with red coats and arms, and mustering them in special regiments. And surprisingly, the planters' fears proved to be ill-founded. For the rest of the long war, Britain relied on a largely Africanized military force to defend and garrison the West Indian colonies. Although white colonists were shocked by the sight of black troops fraternizing with slaves and of black noncommissioned officers commanding white soldiers, the West Indian regiments helped to preserve the slave system even in the conquered French islands. It was the French, with their emancipation decrees, who lost an empire.[26]

West Indian whites had wanted to avoid a dependence on black military power that inevitably eroded the racial boundaries of caste. In every New World society, African ancestry was a visible badge of slave origin and thus dishonor. Free blacks and coloreds everywhere occupied a marginal and ambiguous status, neither slave nor genuinely free; disdained by whites and often by privileged slaves, they were circumscribed by legal disabilities and barred from the more prestigious occupations and professions. But in regions where slaves outnumbered freedmen and free blacks were almost as numerous as whites, it was impossible to maintain a rigid color line that equated all the privileges of freedom with white skin. In describing Latin American and Caribbean slave societies, historians have referred to a three-tiered or three-caste system in which a free colored population, composed largely of mulattoes and lighter-skinned African Americans but including dark blacks, served as a protective buffer between a small white minority and a black slave majority. Freedmen and their descendants, however marked off as a separate caste, were often related to white families by ties of kinship, concubinage, and clientage. Such connections were far more manifest in the Caribbean and Latin America than in the United States, where racial intermixture was generally concealed and saturated in guilt. While no single determinant can begin to explain the complex variations in the way freedmen were defined and treated, it is clear that demography—and the socioeconomic forces that shaped demography—were of central importance.[27]

For example, in 1810, Jamaica contained well over 300,000 slaves, who accounted for some 86 percent of the colony's total population. This was a fairly characteristic proportion in the British and French Caribbean. While the Upper South held over twice as many slaves as Jamaica, they constituted in 1810 only 31 percent of the population; the comparable figure for the Lower South was 45 percent, though the density of slaves in some local regions was similar to that in the Caribbean. In the South as a whole, about 63 percent of the population was white; in the British West Indies the proportion of whites ranged in 1810 from a high of 17 percent in Barbados to 5 percent in Nevis, 2.6 percent in Grenada, and 1.7 percent in Berbice. Obviously the small white minorities in the British and French Caribbean faced a very different world from that found in the slave states of North America. By coincidence, the proportion of black and colored freedmen was very similar in the total populations of Jamaica, Barbados, and the Upper South. The more significant figure, however, was the free black and colored percentage of the total free population. In 1810 this ranged from some 56 percent in Demerara-Essequibo to 14 percent in Barbados, 6 percent in the Upper South, and 3 percent in the Lower South. In Jamaica the proportion of free blacks and coloreds continued to increase until the 1820s, when nonwhites clearly formed a majority of the free population.[28]

As one might expect, freedmen were most sharply distinguished from slaves in colonies like Jamaica, which also gave informal recognition to a hierarchy of color ranging upward from free blacks and sambos (the offspring of a black and a mulatto), to mulattoes, quadroons, mustees, and persons deemed white because of being four generations or more removed from a black ancestor.[29] While the freedmen were divided among themselves by color, wealth, occupation, and town or rural residence, they shared a common quest for equality with whites and an orientation to white values. They were "eager for honor," to use the words of a Spanish priest referring to the free colored in Puerto Rico, and they were quick to take affront if anyone implied that they were darker in color than their own self-image. Since Jamaican society openly sanctioned informal conjugal unions between white men and black women, some of the most respectable and refined colored women thought it more honorable to be the mistress of a white man, and to bear children who might be considered white or near-white, than to marry a colored husband.[30] This general pattern prevailed through much of the Caribbean and Latin America, where white males greatly outnumbered white females and where generations of intermixture had produced a large class of free coloreds.[31]

Similar racial distinctions could be found in parts of the Lower South, especially in Charleston, which absorbed many free colored refugees from the French West Indies, and in Louisiana, which also became a haven for refugees and which had acquired under French and Spanish rule a tradition of open racial intermixture. The Lower South was relatively flexible in its treatment of freedmen, at least until the later antebellum period. Despite restrictions on manumission, South Carolina and the Gulf states made room for a small number of privileged free mulattoes, some of whom became slaveholding planters.[32]

William Ellison, for example, was born a slave in 1790 in upcountry South Carolina. As a young apprentice he learned the new and highly prized craft of making and repairing cotton gins. After apparently purchasing his own freedom in 1816, Ellison bought freedom for his wife and daughter and shrewdly won the respect of his white clients and neighbors. He bought slaves to work in his gin shop and eventually became a cotton planter and owner of sixty-three slaves. By 1860, Ellison's property holdings placed him among the richest 10 percent in South Carolina's wealthy Sumter District. He owned more slaves than 97 percent of the state's slaveholders. Since the combined personal estate of all the other 328 free blacks in the district amounted to only $7,580, Ellison's personal property was seven times greater than their combined total and more than five hundred times greater than the free colored mean. In Louisiana there were a few black planters who were even richer than Ellison.[33]

But if parts of the Lower South approached the West Indian model, Barbados shared certain characteristics with the Southern slave states. As Britain's oldest West Indian colony apart from St. Kitt's, Barbados had a relatively large population of native-born whites whose racism and fear of freedmen paralleled that of their North American brethren. And in Barbados, as in the Upper South, a large proportion of the freedman population was black. Yet the Barbadian freedmen generally supported the slave regime and pressed for legal reforms that would remove their invidious disabilities and protect them from being insulted or assaulted by slaves and lower-class whites.[34]

In the Upper South, freedmen and slaves were more united by common interests, since the large white majority tended to treat them as a single inferior group. In no other New World society were freedmen regarded with such hostility or subjected to such a humiliating and slavelike status. Like the free states to the North, the Upper South had pretensions of being a white man's country, a land in which the presence of black slaves was an unfortunate and perhaps temporary accident. Obsessed with the fear of racial amalgamation, Upper South whites could not tolerate a middle ground between black and white or between bondage and freedom. In actuality, free blacks provided nonslaveholders with an indispensable pool of cheap labor for temporary hire. But however useful to the Upper South's increasingly diversified economy, free blacks could be accepted only if their status differed little from that of slaves. Accordingly, as African Americans developed their own churches, fraternal societies, and other institutions, freedmen and slaves frequently intermingled.[35]

To be sure, even in the West Indies the relations between freedmen and slaves were extremely complex. Some slaves were light-skinned; some were better off in material terms than most freedmen. Freedmen intermarried with slaves and engaged in less-formal sexual contacts; throughout the New World they accumulated the funds, often after many years of labor, to purchase the freedom of slave parents, wives, children, and other relatives. Some of the "slaves" nominally owned by free blacks, especially in the United States, were family members whose manumission was prevented by various legal restrictions. Freedmen and slaves also traded and fraternized with one another, and in the Upper South, especially, freedmen sometimes aided and gave shelter to fugitives.

But such instances of racial solidarity were the result of common racial oppression. Even in the Upper South, most free blacks were far too prudent and realistic to challenge the slave system. Elsewhere, a free colored elite accepted slavery as an unalterable fact of life and joined white planters in resisting emancipation. From their first organized protests in Saint-Domingue, freedmen demanded an equal right to participate in the system, so that wealth rather than race would be the criterion of status. For whites, however, the somatological traits of African ancestry symbolized the dishonor and degradation that were inseparable from chattel slavery. If manumission were itself sufficient to wipe away what the Jamaican Assembly termed the "corruption of blood," slavery would lose its ideological basis. As the example of Saint-Domingue suggested, the freedmen's drive for equal rights carried implications that extended far beyond any intended objectives.

FREEDMEN'S RIGHTS

Discussions of the later debates over slave emancipation seldom mention the spectacular growth of freedman populations in the late eighteenth and early nineteenth centuries. The world marveled over the fact that after 1790 the total United States population continued to double in less than twenty-five years, representing a rate of increase of about 35 percent each decade. From 1790 to 1830 the American slave population grew at a decadal rate of about 30 percent. But the free black population shot ahead by 82 percent in the decade 1790–1800 and by 72 percent in the decade 1800–1810.[36]

Although the Northern states were gradually abolishing slavery in this period, the free black population increased at a faster rate in the South—in the Lower South by 99 percent between 1790–1800, and by 223 percent between 1800 and 1810. The latter figure was inflated by the acquisition of Louisiana and by the influx of West Indian free coloreds. But in Virginia, where the numbers involved were considerably larger than in the states farther south, the free black population grew from an estimated 2,000 in 1782 to 20,000 in 1800 and to more than

30,500 in 1810. During the twenty years from 1790 to 1810, the number of free blacks in Maryland more than quadrupled; the slave population increased by a mere 8 percent. Until the 1830s, when restrictions against manumission began taking effect, free blacks were the fastest growing segment of the Southern population.[37]

The available statistics, which probably underestimate the actual growth of the free black population, are far less satisfactory for the West Indies. It is clear, however, that in Saint-Domingue the freedman population grew at a faster rate than in the British colonies and had equaled or even surpassed the white population by the first years of the French Revolution. The number of free coloreds in Saint-Domingue doubled from 1770 to 1780 and more than doubled from 1780 to 1789. In Jamaica the free black and colored population increased by 170 percent between 1768 and 1789 and by more than 280 percent in the thirty-six years between 1789 and 1825. In Barbados the comparable figures are 163 percent for the period 1786–1801 and 133 percent for the period 1801–1829.[38]

What were the implications of this soaring freedman population? The lessons from Latin America, which had always been more tolerant of manumission, were ambiguous. In countries that never became dependent on a plantation economy and that could draw on a large supply of indigenous peon labor, manumissions and mortality gradually eroded the slave population; ultimately, slave owners could offer little resistance to general emancipation laws. But in Cuba and Brazil the emergence of a large free colored population did not inhibit the continuing growth of plantation economies based on the African slave trade. Presumably, slave labor would have been no less viable in Cuba and Brazil if planters had been able to rely, as in the United States, on a slave population that grew rapidly from natural reproduction.

Moreover, in marked contrast to Latin American societies, the proportion of freedmen in the total black population of most Southern states never rose above 5 percent. After the 1820s the percentage stabilized or declined. Only in Delaware and northern Maryland did the number of freedmen surpass the number of slaves—in Delaware as early as 1800, a trend that continued to 1860, when free blacks outnumbered slaves by more than nine to one.[39] Even without considering the rising demand for slaves, the growing number of slave owners, and the great migration of slaves and their masters to the Old Southwest, it is clear that manumissions were not sapping the vitality of the peculiar institution except in parts of the upper Chesapeake, where tobacco and slaves had given way to wheat, free labor, and economic diversification. On the other hand, any thoughtful observer living in the late eighteenth and early nineteenth centuries had good grounds for wondering how long slavery could survive if free blacks continued to multiply at a much faster rate than either whites or slaves.

The very existence of a growing freedman population posed a political problem for societies committed to eighteenth-century ideals of citizenship and representative government. The Age of Revolution was an age of petitioning for legal and political rights. From the 1770s to the 1820s, freedmen in various parts of the New World became keenly attuned to the political rhetoric of the time and developed a highly coherent sense of their rights. On rare occasions even slaves drafted petitions, perhaps with the aid of freedmen, asking to be released from unmerited and unjustifiable bondage.

Beginning in 1773, for example, groups of Massachusetts slaves sent petitions to the General Court describing their hardships and appealing to the principles of colonists "who have made such a noble stand against the designs of their fellow-men to enslave them." In 1777, a petition from New Hampshire slaves spoke of freedom as "an inherent right of the human species" and condemned public tyranny and slavery as "alike detestable to minds conscious of the equal dignity of human nature." Sometimes free blacks signed the petitions of slaves who demanded the restoration of their natural rights, as in the case of Prince Hall, a Barbadian immigrant who organized a black Masonic lodge in Boston and who struggled there to improve the condition of free blacks. Some of the New England petitions looked beyond the formal act of emancipation and asked for a grant of land that could be settled by blacks or for assistance in emigrating to Africa, "where we shall live among our equals and be more comfortable and happy, then [*sic*] we can be in our present situation." In 1780, seven free blacks petitioned the Massachusetts Council and House of Representatives to relieve them from the burden of paying taxes as long as they were denied the vote and "influence in the election with those that tax us." This appeal was signed by Paul Cuffe, a young mariner and future sea captain who would later play an important role in the African emigration movement.[40]

A few individual slaves had won freedom suits in the courts before the 1770s, especially in Massachusetts; in Jamaica a few free blacks and coloreds had won special legislated privileges, including the right to a jury trial and even equal civil rights. But it took the American and French revolutions to inaugurate a new era of group consciousness and political action. Unfortunately, there were few legislative bodies like those in New England that would receive petitions from freedmen, let alone slaves.

In 1791, when some free blacks in Charleston petitioned the state senate to repeal a law barring them from testifying in court against whites, they deferentially claimed that they did not "presume to hope" that they would be put on an equal footing with white citizens "in general." The following year Jamaican legislators expressed alarm over a petition, written in "the language of fanaticism," in which free coloreds complained that they paid taxes but were denied the right to give evidence in court and were subject to discriminatory punishments and restrictions on bequeathing property. In 1799, Absalom Jones and other free blacks in Philadelphia sent a respectful and cautiously worded petition to Congress complaining that many freedmen were being kidnapped on the shores of Maryland and Delaware and sold as slaves in Georgia. The petitioners called for a revision of the fugitive slave law, an end to the slave trade, and measures that would ameliorate the hardships of slaves and prepare the way for eventual emancipation. For two days Congress engaged in heated debate over the threat the petition posed to national security. George Thatcher, a Federalist from the Maine district of Massachusetts, described slavery as "a cancer of immense magnitude" that would destroy the nation unless Congress began to take remedial action; he admitted that he actually admired the French for emancipating their slaves. John Rutledge Jr., a Federalist from South Carolina, declared that the petition was an "entering wedge" that placed the country in "imminent danger"; he then reviewed the recent history of Saint-Domingue, which confirmed all the earlier unheeded warnings of the French West Indian planters.[41]

During the previous decade, New World slaveholders had learned that freedmen's rights could become a fatally explosive issue even when taken up by an extremely cautious but revolutionary French assembly. Only six brief years separated the achievement of American independence, won with the aid of French land and naval forces that included an impressive number of West Indian freedmen, from the onset of the French Revolution. The 1780s seethed with agitation for various kinds of reform, in the slave states and colonies as well as in Britain and France. Despite bitter resistance, Virginia led the way among Southern states in removing restrictions on private manumission; five Northern states either abolished slavery by judicial decision or enacted statutes for gradual emancipation (a sixth state, Vermont, had already adopted a constitution that outlawed human bondage). British and then French reformers began pressing for international suppression of the African slave trade. The *gens de couleur* in the French West Indies asserted their right to legal equality with whites, nominally guaranteed by the seventeenth-century *Code noir*, and sent delegates to plead their cause to the French ministry. Since some of the wealthiest *gens de couleur* lived in France, the summoning of the Estates General in 1789 presented an opportunity to win a national hearing and to nullify the humiliating colonial laws that defined them as an inferior caste.

For the Western world, as we have already begun to see, Saint-Domingue was a crucial test of reform—of the possibility of elevating freedmen to the status of citizens without jeopardizing the richest plantation regime the world had yet seen (in 1789 the colony accounted for roughly 40 percent of the total value of France's foreign trade and by some estimates was responsible for the livelihood of more than one-sixth of the French population).[42] Since the Haitian Revolution involved the issue of freedmen's rights and also became the most terrifying paradigm of slave emancipation in human history, it is essential to review the sequence of events that were later interpreted in such contradictory ways.

LOSS OF MASTERY

Of all the freedman groups in the New World, the *gens de couleur* were in the best position to redress their grievances in a revolutionary crisis. No legal restrictions had curbed their acquisition or inheritance of property, and in Saint-Domingue a small minority had prospered at the cultivation of coffee, cotton, and indigo, which unlike sugar required relatively little capital investment. Julien Raimond and other colored representatives in France claimed that the freedmen owned more than one-quarter of Saint-Domingue's slaves and between one-quarter and one-half of the productive land. They outnumbered whites in the South and West provinces and even in the North were indispensable as the managers of sugar estates. In the militia and especially the rural police they provided the security forces that captured runaway slaves, kept the maroons at bay, and preserved the colony's peace.

But from the mid-eighteenth century to the Revolution, white colonists expressed increasing alarm over the growth and power of these "dangerous people." The French mulattoes were accused of fraternizing with slaves and sheltering fugitives while also aping the manners and customs of whites, forgetting their dishonorable origins, and aspiring to intermarry with the best white families. As the racist reaction progressed, the *gens de couleur* were prohibited from holding meetings or assemblies, from sitting with whites at meals or in church or the theater, from wearing European dress or playing European games, from taking the title of Monsieur or Madame, from traveling to France without special authorization, and from entering the professions and more prestigious trades. Although many of these laws and customs were not strictly enforced—for example, the colored elite continued to seek education and a less hostile environment in France—no other freedman population had achieved such economic power while being proscribed as a contemptible caste.[43]

At the beginning of the French Revolution, the white West Indian proprietors and investors who lived in France organized an influential lobby, the Club Massiac, to defend West Indian interests. The proprietors hoped to prevent a reckless French Assembly from interfering with colonial affairs. They particularly feared that the Constituent Assembly, intoxicated by the Declaration of the Rights of Man, would decree equal rights to all colored citizens if the question ever reached the floor. The Club Massiac knew that the *gens de couleur* then living in Paris had formed their own *Société des colons américains* ("American" being reserved to describe colonists of mixed blood, as distinct from "Europeans" and "Africans"), and that Julien Raimond was haunting the corridors of the Assembly as well as the antechambers of the royal ministry. Some of the proprietors and West India merchants thought that direct concessions to the *gens de couleur* would be a way to bypass the Constituent Assembly and to unite property owners of both races against the radical demands of colonial *petits blancs*. But the ensuing discussions between the *gens de couleur* and the Club Massiac came to naught. At best, the absentee proprietors could offer no more than support for future concessions from colonial assemblies.

And most proprietors knew that the white colonists, already in rebellion against royal officials and absentee control, would never tolerate outside infringements on white supremacy. While the white colonial interests were divided by various commercial and political disputes, they were able to join in a campaign to prevent the *gens de couleur* from winning an official hearing that could easily lead the colonies to secession and civil war.[44]

Although the *gens de couleur* resented the high-handed treatment they received from the Club Massiac, they shared the whites' uncertainties over the wisdom of consigning colonial questions to an unpredictable National Assembly. For a time some of the coloreds continued to hope that the ministry or absentee white planters would support full citizenship for the lightest-skinned *gens de couleur* who, being farthest removed from a slave ancestor, had superior claims to honor and respectability, to the status of "new whites." But by October 22, 1789, when a delegation of *gens de couleur* appeared before the bar of the National Assembly to petition to be seated as colonial deputies, they demanded equal citizenship for all free persons, blacks as well as coloreds. Mirabeau had earlier challenged the credentials of white deputies elected in the West Indies. He had not only questioned the logic of counting slaves in apportioning representation but had also asked how the deputies could claim to represent a large population of free coloreds who owned property and paid taxes but were not allowed to vote. Members of the Assembly were generally sympathetic to the freedmen's grievances, and their petition and credentials were accepted for future consideration. But the Assembly faced the urgent need to draft a constitution for France and feared taking any precipitous actions that might risk losing the colonies.[45]

The *gens de couleur* soon found unexpected allies among the *Amis des noirs,* a humanitarian and Anglophile association that had followed the lead of British reformers in attacking the slave trade and preparing the way for the gradual abolition of slavery. The Amis, like the British abolitionists, had earlier shown no interest in freedmen's rights, which they considered a subsidiary issue that might distract attention from the horrors of the African slave trade. Moreover, the *gens de couleur* repeatedly professed their support for colonial slavery and agreed only reluctantly to oppose the African slave trade. But both groups shared an interest in circumventing the obstructionist tactics of the colonial deputies and in bringing colonial issues to the floor of the Constituent Assembly. The Abbé Grégoire, who sat on the Assembly's credentials committee and who championed the rights of freedmen as well as the rights of Jews, became a spokesman for both the *gens de couleur* and the abolitionists.[46]

This fortuitous alliance carried momentous implications for free blacks and coloreds throughout the New World. Grégoire and the *gens de couleur* continued to insist that freedmen could be enfranchised without endangering the slave system. Yet Grégoire, in an impassioned tract defending the rights of the *gens de couleur*, condemned the slave trade, praised pioneer abolitionists, and envisioned a millennial emancipation as "a general insurrection in the universe, extinguishing tyranny and resurrecting liberty."[47] Colonial propagandists had already charged that the Amis des noirs, instigated by the visiting English abolitionist Thomas Clarkson, were plotting to incite slave insurrections and to destroy the French colonies. Clarkson's close ties with Grégoire and with colored leaders seemed to confirm the suspicion that abolitionist conspirators had chosen freedmen's rights as a battleground that could lead to victory on all fronts. In an early version of the domino theory, the proprietors and colonial deputies made a defense of the color line a defense of slavery and thus of France's most vital colonial interests.

In the fall of 1790 an abortive rebellion in Saint-Domingue reinforced the view that the *gens de couleur* had become the agents of an abolitionist conspiracy orchestrated by perfidious Albion. Vincent Ogé, a colored merchant and goldsmith who owned part of a Saint-Domingue plantation, had been a leading spokesman for freedmen's rights before becoming involved with Grégoire and especially Clarkson. The Club Massiac, which warned officials in Saint-Domingue that Ogé had embarked on a revolutionary mission, claimed that Clarkson had raised funds in England that enabled Ogé to purchase arms and munitions in the United States. The intentions of Ogé's backers remain obscure but there is no evidence that they envisioned a racial war or slave insurrection.[48]

In March the Constituent Assembly had granted colonists the right to draft their own constitutions, subject to metropolitan approval, and had stipulated that the initial colonial assemblies should be elected by "all persons" over twenty-five who owned landed property or paid taxes. The ambiguous phrasing provoked sharp debate but was generally interpreted to mean that the existing colonial assemblies could define "all persons" as they saw fit without requiring the National Assembly to sanction racial exclusion. Ogé, however, was determined to force the white authorities of Saint-Domingue to accept a literal reading of the disputed article. Presenting himself as a spokesman for French law, he tried to negotiate with the authorities at Le Cap and pledged his support for the slave system. Although some free coloreds had already taken up arms to resist the growing racial tyranny, Ogé failed to consolidate this potentially rebellious mass. After his small force was defeated and dispersed, Ogé fled to Spanish Santo Domingo. He was then extradited, tried, broken on the wheel, and executed. For the freedmen and French abolitionists, Ogé had become a martyr to liberty. For white colonists, Ogé symbolized the danger of free colored subversion. When the Constituent Assembly ordered the dissolution of colonial legislatures, in response to continuing white rebellion and the collapse of French authority, it also promised, as a conciliatory gesture, that France would never intervene with respect to the status of persons unless requested to do so by the colonies.[49]

In May 1791, when the Assembly debated a proposed constitution for the colonies, the West Indian deputies demanded a confirmation of this self-denying pledge.[50] By then, however, it was impossible to separate the colonial question from the theatrical politics of the French Revolution. In a flaming oration, Robespierre exposed the national disgrace of officially sanctioning slavery and ominously linked the enemies of freedmen's rights with the enemies of the constitution. The Assembly now listened to the testimony of free colored colonists, who described the humiliations suffered by respectable planters, merchants, and professionals who were descended, however distantly, from a black slave. Julien Raimond, the freedmen's leading spokesman and pamphleteer, assured the Assembly that only the free coloreds could keep the slaves subdued.

On May 15, the Assembly finally adopted a compromise amendment pledging that France would enact no law on the status of "persons not free, other than those born of free mothers and fathers." The decree sent to the colonies reaffirmed the colonists' autonomy in defining the status of slaves and the vast majority of freedmen, but insisted that the children of two free parents, regardless of color, should enjoy the full rights of citizenship. The compromise betrayed the prevalent fear that the immediate descendants of slaves might in a crisis identify with slaves. For the colonial deputies, however, the May 15 decree was a fatal breach in the color wall that opened the way to slave emancipation and racial war. The Assembly had set a precedent for direct intervention to enforce inalienable rights. The same reasoning could be used to defend the rights of all freedmen and slaves, and French opinion was turning strongly in favor of equal rights for all free coloreds. Indeed, the debates over freedmen's rights had already elicited proposals for gradual slave emancipation. The West Indian deputies encouraged colonial resistance by denouncing the decree and walking out of the Assembly. White colonists saw the proceedings as a betrayal of the Assembly's earlier promise that it would pass no laws on the status of persons. They refused to accept the new measure, arguing that France could not enfranchise the descendants of slaves without destroying slavery itself. There was open talk of political independence or an alliance with England.[51]

There is no need here to describe the conflicts that divided the colonial whites, that forced the free coloreds to fight for their rights, and that led in August 1791 to a massive slave insurrection in Saint-Domingue's North Province. The origins of this great revolt are still obscure and hot with controversy, but it is clear that the thousands of slaves who suddenly began to kill whites and set fire to the estates and cane fields were a truly revolutionary force, capable of devastating guerrilla warfare even after the black generals had capitulated. No doubt the objectives of the slaves were at first ambiguous; it took years for them to unite in a struggle for freedom and independence. But contemporary commentators, like many later historians, only obscured the central message when they pointed to outside abolitionist agitators, to the "tragic" division between whites and mulattoes, and to the yellow fever, which, as David Geggus has observed, became unbearable only when most of the blacks refused to tolerate slavery.[52] The inescapable fact, which jolted the administrations of George Washington and William Pitt as well as the French National Assembly, was that the blacks themselves had seized the initiative and were destroying the plantation regime that oppressed them.

This message was conveyed in the most negative way by widely publicized descriptions of a white infant impaled on a stake and of white women being raped on the dead bodies of their husbands. As American newspapers printed the most recent tales of black atrocities recounted by refugees and the captains of ships returning from Saint-Domingue, the white public recoiled in horror and anxiously scrutinized the faces of the blacks in their midst. A few brave radicals like Abraham Bishop, a Yale classmate in the 1770s of Joel Barlow and Noah Webster, pointed out that the Dominguan blacks were fighting for the same principles Americans had consecrated in their own revolution. After mocking the hypocrisy of most Americans, including abolitionists, Bishop sadly concluded that "from us the blacks had a right to expect effectual assistance. They are pursuing the principles which had taught them, and are now sealing with their blood, the rights of men: yet Americans are sending assistance to their enemies."[53] The Washington administration was so convinced that the black revolution threatened vital American interests that it advanced the white colonists $726,000 for the purchase of arms, munitions, and supplies. The legislatures of Pennsylvania and South Carolina also voted to extend aid, and a few American volunteers fought on the planters' side. The desirability of suppressing the black insurgents was one objective on which Thomas Jefferson and Alexander Hamilton were in complete accord.[54]

The Boston *Columbian Sentinel*, like the London *Times*, traced the cause of the "calamity" to the French Assembly's decision to grant the rights of citizenship to the free coloreds.[55] While this explanation oversimplified an extraordinarily complex revolution, the conflict over freedmen's civil rights clearly aggravated the struggles involving royalists, Jacobins, secessionists, and French officials. Alarmed by the danger of continuing slave revolts, white colonial leaders finally negotiated a series of concordats with the *gens de couleur*, or *affranchis*, confirming or extending the rights guaranteed by the May 15 decree. But then the Constituent Assembly tried to backtrack again and renounced jurisdiction over the "status of persons" in the colonies. This regression encouraged local racism, infuriated the coloreds, and provoked savage racial warfare that persisted into the early summer of 1792, when Saint-Domingue learned that on April 4 the new French Legislative Assembly had decreed equal rights and citizenship for all free persons, regardless of color, and had resolved to send civil commissioners and six thousand troops to enforce the law and restore peace.

In 1792 the French free blacks and coloreds finally won the civil rights for which other New World freedmen would long struggle. The law of April 4 appeared for a while to strengthen the slave regime. For the most part, whites and *affranchis* joined in a common effort to suppress slave rebellions and restore plantation discipline. But the vacillating policies of the National Assembly had alienated the white leaders of Saint-Domingue, who increasingly called for Spanish or English intervention as the only means of preserving colonial slavery. The whites feared that the French commissioners, backed by a Jacobin army, would emancipate the slaves. This nightmare became, in effect, a self-fulfilling prophecy.

When, after much delay, the commissioners finally arrived in Saint-Domingue, they faced hostile white leaders, some of them royalists, who were actively promoting secession. While trying to purge what they saw as counterrevolutionary treason, the commissioners turned to the "citizens of April 4" for support. By no means did all free coloreds rally to the Republican side, but those who did were often rewarded with unprecedented positions of authority. Military needs continued to erode racial barriers. After France declared war on England and Spain, early in 1793, all the Caribbean combatants recruited slaves as military manpower. Léger-Félicité Sonthonax, the leading French commissioner, promised freedom to any rebel slaves in the North who would join the Republican cause. On August 29, 1793, two months after the black insurgents had stormed the port city Le Cap, forcing thousands of terrified whites to evacuate by sea, Sonthonax finally issued a general emancipation decree as a last desperate measure to win black support. Sonthonax had neither the legal authority nor the effective power to enforce such a measure, but the alliance of blacks with Spanish invaders made his situation so perilous that any means seemed justified to keep Saint-Domingue French. As the planters had originally feared, France's attempt to enforce the racial equality of all free persons had led to an emancipation proclamation—although the planters themselves bore a heavy responsibility for this outcome. The *affranchis*, enhanced in power by the exodus of thousands of whites, would now play a critical role in the preservation or destruction of black bondage.[56]

But the *affranchis* were no less divided than the whites. A few of them, along with an even fewer number of *petits blancs*, joined groups of rebellious slaves. Some of the wealthier free coloreds sided with the white planters, some fought against slaves who had been armed by white planters, and others incited slaves to revolt. Alliances kept shifting and differed dramatically from one locality to another. Colored soldiers, some of them veterans of the American War of Independence, led the forces of the French Republic. Others welcomed the invading armies of Spain and Britain. (It is well to remember that Toussaint Louverture, the black general and former slave, fought originally on the side of the Spanish.) Whatever their immediate objectives, the *gens de couleur* were eager to preserve their civil rights and superiority over the mass of black slaves. These goals might have been achieved by an alliance with the British, who landed in Saint-Domingue in September 1793 and who soon occupied one-third of the colony. Sir Adam Williamson, the British governor, was convinced that with the coloreds' support he could easily conquer the West and South provinces and pacify the slaves. But such support, he informed London, would depend on his authority to abolish legal distinctions of color.[57]

In Britain, however, racial dogma took precedence over military strategy. Refugee French royalists and proprietors, reinforced by British West Indian planters, convinced the government that the color line was an indispensable foundation of the slave system. If equality of color were granted in Saint-Domingue, how could it be withheld in neighboring Jamaica? Curiously, this was an issue to which British abolitionists paid little if any attention. The official propositions worked out to govern British occupation of foreign West Indian territories specified that the free coloreds would have the same status as the free coloreds in the British colonies. In Saint-Domingue the *affranchis* refused to accept this provision in the capitulation agreements, and British commanders promised for a time to maintain equal rights. But by the summer of 1794 British policy had encouraged white racism and growing discrimination in the occupied zones. Some whites talked openly of exterminating the free coloreds or of deporting them to Botany Bay. Dismayed by this turn of events, the *affranchis* plotted rebellions and wavered uneasily between the British and French sides. Toussaint, who had also wavered and who had finally committed himself to the Republicans when the French Convention decreed the emancipation of slaves, deeply mistrusted the *gens de couleur*. But he succeeded in skillfully undermining their alliance with the British.[58]

Free coloreds throughout the West Indies had tried to keep their aspirations distinct from those of slaves. But events in Saint-Domingue suggested that agitation for racial equality could provide slaves and freedmen with a common enemy and destroy the most successful slave regime in the Americas. It made little difference for planters in other countries that the slaves had revolted well before the *affranchis* were granted equal rights, or that the British might well have subdued Saint-Domingue if they had reaffirmed this policy and had mobilized the free colored forces. Most slaveholders believed that black slavery would be untenable if free blacks and coloreds were accorded equal status with whites. In the eyes of British leaders, Jacobin and abolitionist principles threatened by 1795 to subvert the entire West Indian world. In Saint-Domingue, Toussaint's ex-slaves had won brilliant victories and were closing in on Britain's disease-ridden troops; armies of ex-slaves and free coloreds had expelled the British from Guadeloupe and Saint Lucia; racial warfare raged in Grenada and Saint Vincent; French free colored agents were blamed for inciting the Maroon War in Jamaica. As we have seen, the British responded by recruiting their own slave troops with promises of eventual freedom. In Saint-Domingue thousands of blacks fought for the British and thus for the maintenance of the slave regime until 1798, when many joined the evacuation to Jamaica. It is significant that Sir Adam Williamson defended the recruiting and freeing of male slaves on the ground that they would mostly die or reenlist and would not add to the long-term growth of the *affranchi* population. David Geggus, in the most exhaustive study of the British occupation, concludes that British intervention weakened the *gens de couleur,* contributed to the growing power of the blacks, and helped to destroy the slave regime the British were trying to preserve.[59]

THE "HORRORS OF HAITI"

The defeat of the Spanish, British, and French armies of occupation is especially remarkable in view of the persistent division between blacks and mulattoes, which continued to dominate the history of independent Haiti. The distinction of color partially overlapped the distinction between the *anciens libres,* those who owed their freedom to prerevolutionary acts of manumission, and the *nouveaux libres,* the recently emancipated slaves. Color and the timing of freedom both symbolized the degree by which a person was removed from the degradation and humiliation of bondage. The *anciens libres* included large landholders who had themselves owned slaves. Their interests and outlook were often at odds with those of the black military elite associated with Toussaint Louverture. Toussaint did not win mastery of Saint-Domingue until he had crushed mulatto resistance and defeated the mulatto general, André Rigaud.

On the other hand, Toussaint himself was an *ancien libre* who had owned land and slaves and had become reasonably affluent.[60] His ex-slave lieutenants, Henri Christophe and Jean-Jacques Dessalines, made fortunes from Toussaint's reinstitution of the plantation system.[61] Black and mulatto leaders shared a common interest in encouraging exports that could pay for the arms and supplies, mostly imported from the United States, needed for the island's defense. Their experiences with white oppression also gave them the sense of sharing a common African heritage. Although Toussaint was willing to acknowledge nominal French sovereignty and even tried to induce refugee white planters to return to Saint-Domingue, he and his black and mulatto followers were determined to prevent the restoration of either slavery or the color line. Toussaint's constitution of 1801 abolished slavery forever, prohibited distinctions according to color, and affirmed equal protection of the law—measures that were appended to the United States Constitution in compromised form only after the Civil War.[62]

General Charles Leclerc, whom Napoleon dispatched with some ten thousand troops to subjugate Saint-Domingue as soon as Europe was at peace, knew he would have to pledge support for these high principles. Yet Napoleon had secretly resolved to restore colonial slavery, the African slave trade, and white supremacy. Leclerc hoped to deceive and divide the blacks and mulattoes while wooing their leaders, pacifying the countryside, and reestablishing French sovereignty. Leclerc was wholly unprepared for the skillful and heroic resistance he encountered. But, after incredibly bloody warfare, the French succeeded in enlisting the services of Christophe and Dessalines, and in seizing Toussaint by a ruse after first negotiating a surrender. But Leclerc's army, though reinforced by more than thirty thousand men, could not subdue the black guerrillas in the hills.[63]

In the summer of 1802, when Napoleon's veterans were being decimated by yellow fever and malaria, news arrived that slavery had been restored in Guadeloupe. Leclerc complained in frantic letters to Napoleon and the minister of marine that "the moral force I had obtained here is destroyed. I can do nothing by persuasion." Just when a political settlement seemed in sight, Leclerc wrote, his work was undermined by the revelation of French intentions and by the return from exile of planters and merchants who talked only of slavery and the slave trade. As blacks took up arms to defend their freedom, Leclerc reported to Napoleon that "these men die with an incredible fanaticism; they laugh at death; it is the same with the women. . . ." Thousands of mulattoes joined the rebel forces when they learned that the French had reestablished the color line in Guadeloupe. The defectors included Alexandre Pétion, a mulatto officer who had fought Toussaint and had then joined Leclerc's expedition in France. In the fall of 1802, when Leclerc died of yellow fever while pleading to Napoleon for more troops, Christophe and Dessalines deserted the French. Leclerc's successor, General Rochambeau, then resorted to a policy of virtual genocide. The French concluded that Saint-Domingue could be pacified only by exterminating most of the existing black and mulatto population, which could later be replaced by African slaves.[64]

The race war of 1802–3 carried profound implications for every black and mulatto in the New World. Napoleon's reversal of French policy showed that a white nation could reinstitute slavery, strip the free descendants of slaves of their rights, and kill even children of the stigmatized race if they had been contaminated with ideas of liberty. The rebels' response showed that blacks and mulattoes could unite and defeat a professional European army. White commentators insisted that the army had really been defeated by disease and by the naval blockade the British imposed when war resumed in 1803. It was difficult to deny, however, that the blacks won battles and knew how to make the most of the yellow fever and British blockade. The blacks turned the entire white cosmos upside down when they forced the French to evacuate Saint-Domingue and when Dessalines and other former slaves then proclaimed the independence of Haiti. Every New World society was familiar with slave rebellions; some maroon communities, established by escaped slaves, had resisted conquest for many decades and had even negotiated treaties, as in Jamaica, with colonial authorities. But no slaves in history had ever expelled their former masters and established their own nation-state.

The very existence of Haiti challenged every slaveholding regime in the New World (and for that matter in the Cape Colony and Indian Ocean colonies). As the London *Times* put it, "a Black State in the Western Archipelago is utterly incompatible with the system of all European colonisation."[65] Hoping to allay white fears and ease the way for diplomatic recognition, Dessalines and his successors disavowed any interest in interfering with the domestic institutions of neighboring countries. Except for invading and annexing Spanish Santo Domingo, the eastern part of the island from which various enemies could threaten Haitian independence, Haiti posed no military danger to slaveholders.[66] Despite temporary panic over reports of Haitian agents inciting slaves in the Caribbean colonies and southern United States, slave revolts were never again so frequent as in the 1790s. There is fragmentary evidence, however, that slaves in various localities were well aware of the Haitian Revolution and of the possibility of actually destroying the system to which they were violently subjected. Even in 1791, Jamaican slaves sang songs about the Saint-Domingue insurrection within a month after the uprising began.[67]

After the great Barbadian insurrection of 1816, which resulted in the execution of more than two hundred blacks, some of the slave testimony pointed to Haiti as a model. Nanny Grigg, a literate house servant who apparently concluded from news of the parliamentary debates over slave registration that Britain intended to emancipate colonial slaves on New Year's Day 1816, urged her brethren to fight for the freedom their owners had withheld and to set fires, "as that was the way they did in Saint Domingo." Earlier, whites had blamed the Dominguan example for slave revolts in such far-flung spots as Maracaibo, in Venezuela, and Pointe Coupée, in Spanish Louisiana. In view of Louisiana's heavy influx of white, free colored, and slave refugees from Saint-Domingue, it seems almost certain that knowledge of the revolution had spread among the hundreds of slaves who in 1811 rose in rebellion and marched to within eighteen miles of New Orleans before being defeated by an American militia. In this instance Governor William Claiborne shrewdly enlisted as militiamen free colored refugees who had recently fled from revolutionary destruction in the French colonies.[68]

Planters and government officials expected Haitian-inspired subversion and were eager to attribute domestic unrest to outside influence. But they also sought to suppress information that might undermine the official doctrine that black slaves were helpless, degraded beings whose servitude was as natural as the force of gravity. It is therefore extremely difficult to assess the actual influence of the Haitian Revolution on the behavior of slaves and free blacks. For example, the arrival in Virginia of a motley assortment of French colonists and their slaves seems to have been related to increasing white complaints about black "insolence" and unrecoverable runaway slaves. But little can be said about the sources of the great Gabriel Prosser slave conspiracy of 1800, except that court testimony indicated that the insurgents planned to spare the lives of Frenchmen and that the *Virginia Argus* opined that the insurrection had been organized "on the true French plan."[69]

The Haitian inspiration was much clearer in Cuba, where in 1812 José Antonio Aponte and his rebel followers flew the Haitian colors and wore Haitian hats before being defeated, tortured, and put to death.[70] Like Cuba, Jamaica simmered with rumors of conspiracy as refugees streamed in from Saint-Domingue and as Jamaican slaves escaped to Haiti. In 1815 an assembly committee reported that young blacks had vowed to kill off the white population if they were not granted their freedom. Although the Jamaican free coloreds generally supported the slave system, by 1823 they began to address their appeals for civil rights to influential Englishmen who were already calling for the gradual abolition of slavery. This reprise of Dominguan events of the 1780s alarmed Jamaican officials. Significantly, they arrested two colored merchants, Louis Lecesne and Edward Escoffery, whose white fathers had much earlier fled to Jamaica from Saint-Domingue. Lecesne and Escoffery were charged with arming and training slaves for a general insurrection, and both men were deported without a trial to Haiti. For white Jamaicans this move proved to be counterproductive since the blatant racial hysteria played into the hands of British reformers. In 1830, Lecesne and Escoffery were repatriated and financially compensated for their losses, a reversal that was part of Britain's general extension of civil liberties to the colonial free coloreds.[71]

Denmark Vesey, the free black leader of the supposedly momentous 1822 slave conspiracy in Charleston, South Carolina, had worked as a slave in Saint-Domingue in the early 1780s. After winning his freedom in a Charleston lottery in 1800, Vesey took a lively interest in the Haitian Revolution. In the trials following the exposure of the alleged plot, one rebel testified that Vesey "was in the habit of reading to me all the passages in the newspapers that related to St. Domingo, and apparently every pamphlet he could lay his hands on that had any connection with slavery." Other slave testimony referred to letters to Haiti requesting aid and to one of Vesey's followers promising "that St. Domingo and Africa would come over and cut up the white people if we only made the motion here first." The evidence suggested that Vesey may have hoped to gain assistance from Haiti and the North and to sail to Haiti after exterminating the whites and destroying Charleston. Henry William Desaussure, South Carolina's leading jurist, spoke of the rebels appealing to the Haitians "as their natural allies." He predictably used the history of Haiti as an example of the destructive civil wars that would inevitably follow any move toward slave emancipation.[72]

While the Haitian example inspired a few violent conspiracies, it had a deeper and more enduring impact on the self-image and nascent national identity of free blacks, especially in the Northern United States. From the outset the Haitian Revolution stirred the free black community of Philadelphia, a port city long involved in West Indian commerce. What impressed a black leader like James Forten, a prosperous sailmaker and entrepreneur, was not the violence that could be attributed to war and to slavery itself. It was rather the providential message that the black people "would become a great nation" and "could not always be detained in their present bondage." By the 1820s, when blacks in various Northern cities began celebrating the anniversary of Haitian independence, the revolution became a symbolic negation of everything slavery represented. As one speaker in Baltimore put it, Haiti had become "an irrefutable argument to prove . . . that the descendants of Africa never were designed by their Creator to sustain an inferiority, or even a mediocrity, in the chain of being; but they are as capable of intellectual improvement as Europeans, or any other nation upon the face of the earth." David Walker, in his revolutionary *Appeal to the Coloured Citizens of the World,* urged his brethren to read the history of Haiti, which he termed "the glory of the blacks and terror of tyrants." A decade earlier Robert Wedderburn, a Jamaican mulatto who had emigrated to London, merged the cause of blacks with the cause of Britain's working class. A member of Thomas Spence's circle of ultraradicals, Wedderburn appealed to the precedent of Haiti when he called on West Indian blacks to "slay man, woman and child" and exhorted English wage-slaves to revolt against their oppressors.[73]

Yet, as a model of liberation, the Haitian Revolution suffered from inherent liabilities. One clue to this no-win dilemma can be seen in the white response to the ex-slaves' military performance. In popular imagery the blacks were either cowards or fiends, excited barbarians who panicked when hard pressed or demons capable of unthinkable atrocities. Toussaint's sudden capitulation in 1802 evoked scorn for the blacks and confident reassurances that white discipline could always overcome, as young Henry Brougham put it, "the vast numbers and ferocious strength of a savage people."[74] Racial stereotypes of "savagery" reinforced the fear and contempt that slaves had always aroused among nonslaves. When the French were finally defeated, even abolitionists found it difficult to acknowledge that the degraded blacks of Saint-Domingue had vindicated their honor in a way comparable to the American patriots of 1776 (or the patriots of the later Latin American or Greek struggles for independence).[75]

It is true that in the late 1790s, American Federalists became so fearful of the infidel French that they praised Toussaint and provided his army with indispensable supplies and even naval support. After Britain resumed war against Napoleon in 1803, various writers tried to portray the Haitians as heroic allies in a common struggle for freedom. Toussaint, once he had perished in Napoleon's prison in the Jura mountains, became a legitimate martyr and even a man of honor, largely because he could serve as a foil to the treacherous "Enslaver of Nations." But since Britain had a compelling self-interest to protect Haitian independence, what is really striking is the relative absence of popular sympathy for the Haitians when compared, let us say, to Napoleon's Continental subjects or to the Greeks in their later War of Independence. The enduring memory of the Haitian Revolution was not of Toussaint the tragic hero but of Dessalines the butcher of whites. For an age obsessed with the problem of freedom and order, the Haitian Revolution suggested the unleashing of pure Id.[76]

Haiti faced a similar double check in the field of political economy. When black leaders beginning with Toussaint sought to revive the export economy by resorting to forced labor on the plantations, they were accused of reinstituting slavery. When they accommodated the peasants' desires for small plots of land and acquiesced in a sharp decline in exports and the dominance of subsistence farming and local markets, the world perceived Haiti as regressing to savagery. The seeming alternatives of regimented labor or tropical indolence were hailed by proslavery writers as proof of two irrepressible truths: that blacks would not work unless coerced, and that in tropical climates slavery was indispensable for progress. Few commentators questioned the desirability of the plantation system itself.

British abolitionists were eager to celebrate Haiti's material and moral progress as proof of the blacks' capability for freedom and civilization. The very fact that the new nation could be burdened with such momentous expectations meant that the issue of capability was in doubt, that the Haitians' friends had put them before the bench of world opinion as the defendants of their race. It would have been alien to the age, however, to propose economic aid for a region devastated by thirteen years of civil war. Indeed, beginning with Jefferson's presidency, the United States quarantined Haiti as a potential source of racial subversion, and England postponed even partial recognition of Haitian independence until 1825—after France finally gave up hope of reconquering the rebellious colony. Even after Napoleon's fall, Haiti's leaders faced a genuine danger of French invasion or less direct forms of conquest. In 1825 Haiti's president, Jean-Pierre Boyer, finally won French recognition only by agreeing to a staggering indemnity of 150 million francs and to reduced customs charges for French ships, concessions that made the republic fatally dependent on foreign credit and foreign economic control.[77]

During the first third of the nineteenth century, Haiti stood as the single decisive example of mass emancipation. Britain had established a small colony of freed blacks at Sierra Leone, which helped to inspire the later American settlement of Liberia. But it was difficult to extrapolate any general principles from these faltering experiments. The northeastern states from New Jersey to Vermont might have presented more suitable laboratories if the freedmen had not confronted immense white majorities and an enveloping racism that deprived them of the most elemental rights and opportunities. Abolitionists in both England and America made remarkably few references to the Northern states' emancipation acts and their consequences. For a time, however, they did pin their hopes on Haiti.[78]

In most respects the very existence of Haiti was a godsend for the abolitionists' opponents. Sanguine accounts of the moral and educational advance of the people, of economic enterprise that would soon lead to thriving towns and to Haitian ships entering the harbors of the world, increasingly gave way to reports of political upheaval and hopeless poverty. The tacit comparison with the fruits of North American independence locked the abolitionists into a defensive posture. It became necessary to explain why Henri Christophe's Anglophile kingdom collapsed, why President Boyer imposed a draconian labor code, why exports plummeted, why the economy stagnated, why the mulattoes and blacks contested for power, why the Haitians should be compared to the British barbarians of Roman times rather than to peoples who had benefited from centuries of progress.[79] While it is impossible to measure public opinion on such matters, the negative images of Haiti probably reinforced the conviction, especially among American whites, that free blacks were incapable of civilized life.

As we have already seen, however, the Haitian Revolution conveyed a different message to free blacks and to a few white abolitionists. For them it was not simply a matter of black power and capability, though the ex-slaves' creation and governance of an independent nation, however poor and unstable, clearly contradicted the stereotypes of black inferiority. The birth of Haiti was also viewed as an unprecedented and unforeseen historical event, a revelation of God's will and a harbinger of universal emancipation. Pompée Valentin Vastey, Christophe's publicist and adviser, wrote of a global liberation in which "five hundred million men, black, yellow, and brown" would reclaim their natural rights and privileges.[80] The constitution of Alexandre Pétion's southern republic invited the black and colored populations of other New World countries to a kind of aliyah that would in effect convert Haiti into a black Israel. In the 1820s, President Boyer's appeal for African American immigrants stirred the free black communities of the northern American states. Although thousands who emigrated to Haiti became quickly disillusioned and many returned to the United States, Haiti remained a symbol of hope, a historical reassurance, as Frederick Douglass later affirmed, that bondage was not an inevitable or eternal fate.

3

Colonizing Blacks, Part I: Migration and Deportation

THE EXODUS PARADIGM

The Haitian Revolution coincided in time with the founding of Sierra Leone and with the growth of Anglo-American interest in African colonization. While it should be stressed that African colonization had earlier and independent origins, there can be no doubt that the eminent Virginians who helped found the American Colonization Society in 1816 were deeply influenced by the specter of Haiti and the continuing conspiracies it seemed to inspire among slaves and free blacks from Virginia to Barbados. If Haiti symbolized one of the possible outcomes of slave emancipation, the emigration or removal of free blacks represented a quite different "solution" to the problem of slavery, at least in the United States. About the voluntary character of this proposed migration there was considerable ambiguity and debate. But between the American Revolution and the Civil War, the hope that a dangerous population could be gradually drained away and that black missionaries could be enlisted to carry Christian civilization to Africa profoundly influenced the public controversy over emancipation.

From Jefferson to Lincoln, most of America's major leaders insisted that the blight of slavery could not be overcome unless a distant refuge were found for the black beneficiaries of freedom. This premise was angrily rejected by Northern free blacks, who took the lead in challenging the motives of white colonizationists. After 1831, white abolitionists increasingly made the disavowal of colonization the core of their confession of faith; they attacked the American Colonization Society and its colony Liberia as vehemently as they attacked slavery itself. But, despite denunciations by abolitionists and Southern defenders of slavery, the idea of black resettlement kept rebounding after apparent defeats. Various black leaders, such as Paul Cuffe, Henry Highland Garnet, Martin R. Delany, Alexander Crummell, and James Theodore Holly, promoted their own increasingly nationalistic projects for an African or Caribbean homeland. Delany, according to Edward Wilmot Blyden, a black advocate of Liberian colonization, had the qualifications to become "the Moses to lead in the exodus of his people from the house of bondage to a land flowing with milk and honey."[1] The essential distinction between choosing to emigrate and being colonized by others has usually obscured the fact that the early speeches and reports of the white American Colonization Society anticipated the central themes and expectations of black emigrationists from Garnet and Delany, in the slavery era, to Marcus Garvey, in the 1920s.

Modern historians have understandably been hostile to the ACS and its diverse supporters. The colonization movement often embodied and encouraged the most insidious forms of white racism. Historians have frequently quoted the expressions of racial contempt, fear, condescension, and hypocrisy that contributed to the colonizationists' appeal to American whites. There is evidence that this prejudice alienated blacks who might otherwise have found in the colonization ideology a ground for racial pride and solidarity. For now it is sufficient to emphasize that colonization, as a movement seeking white consensus, embraced a variety of contradictory motives, interests, hopes, and visions. The simple dichotomy between the ACS Antichrist and the abolitionist Redeemers, which abolitionists perpetuated as a way of explaining their own journey from spiritual blindness to a new Reformation, can only obscure our understanding of both movements.

Although colonizationists have conventionally been dismissed as hopelessly impractical visionaries, for example, they were clearly more realistic than the abolitionists when they argued that white racial prejudice would remain intractable for generations to come, that the achievements of a few individual blacks would not benefit the masses, that progress would depend on black solidarity and collective effort, and that the formal act of emancipating slaves could not be divorced from the need for an economic and social environment in which freedmen could exercise their full capacities for human development. This is not to say that the program of the ACS was the right solution. But if the colonization movement actually represented a dangerous obstacle to African American self-fulfillment, we will never understand or even recognize similar obstacles if we rely on negative caricature and fail to grasp the complexity of the movement's appeal. Instead of recapitulating the well-known history of the ACS, it seems more promising to approach the issues of deportation and colonization from several comparative perspectives that may point to unsuspected relationships and configurations of meaning.[2]

At first glance the distinction between emigration and expulsion seems clear-cut. In the archetypal story of Exodus, God enabled the Israelites to flee from Egyptian bondage and undergo the trials and self-purgation that prepared them for a life of freedom in the Promised Land. Some five centuries later, when the children of Israel in the Northern Kingdom sinned against "the LORD their God, who had freed them from the land of Egypt," by worshipping idols and practicing pagan rites and enchantments, they were punished, according to the Hebrew prophets, by an Assyrian conquest that led to mass deportations from Samaria to Upper Mesopotamia and Media, where ten tribes of Israelites lost their historic identity.[3] In Christian theology, it might be said, the saved emigrate to heaven; sinners are deported to hell or perhaps to purgatory, where they gain a second chance.

On closer inspection, however, voluntary migrations have seldom been free from pain, nostalgia, and regret; involuntary exiles have sometimes found a promised land. Images of colonization and expulsion, particularly since the Protestant Reformation, have been enriched by biblical narratives that were known to some degree by the lowest classes of society and that reach back to the earliest human memories of migration, conquest, deportation, and longing for a lost homeland. Psychologically, such experiences have also echoed the stages of individual life from weaning and the departure from a natal family to aging, death, and the succession of generations. Historically, the appeal of a new beginning has usually been mixed with fears of disinheritance, of exile from the graves of ancestors, of becoming, like Cain, "a ceaseless wanderer on earth," dispossessed of place and society.

If we wish to move beyond a parochial view of the debate over colonization, it will be helpful to examine precedents that illustrate a wide range of motives and meanings associated with deportation and escape. Because the Exodus narrative became so vitally important for the Puritan settlers in North America, for interpreters of America's struggle for independence from England, and for blacks advocating a return to Africa as well as for black slaves longing for emancipation, we should begin by reviewing several points that might not be familiar to modern "secular humanists" who seldom read the Bible.

Most surprising, perhaps, is the continuing allure of the land of bondage. As Michael Walzer reminds us, "the great paradox of the Exodus, and of all subsequent liberation struggles, is the people's simultaneous willingness and unwillingness to put Egypt behind them." The biblical commentaries "are full of stories of Israelite assimilation in Egypt . . . Many Israelites admired the very people who oppressed them, copied Egyptian ways, curried Egyptian favor. And other Israelites feared and repressed the impulse to act similarly in themselves."[4] If the Hebrews resented the disabilities that had deprived them of Egyptian luxuries, memories of relative well-being erupted at times of rebellion, as when Dathan and Abiram asked Moses, "is it not enough that you brought us from a land flowing with milk and honey [Egypt] to have us die in the wilderness, that you would also lord it over us?"[5] Such dissent could be mitigated, at least, by reminding the Hebrews of the oppression they had suffered as slaves and "strangers" in Egypt. This biblical theme, coupled with a liturgical reexperiencing of bondage and deliverance, became absolutely central to Judaism and to its expressions of love and gratitude to a monotheistic God. As early as 1808 the Reverend Absalom Jones, a former slave who had purchased his own freedom and had helped found the African Church of Philadelphia, told his congregation that just as Passover linked every Jew to their historic deliverance from slavery, so American blacks should commemorate events like Haitian independence in order to "remember the history of the sufferings of our brethren, and of their deliverance," and to ensure that this experience would descend "to our children, to the remotest generations."[6]

Although the book of Exodus gives relatively little detail on the rigors of bondage in Egypt, the injustice of the oppression is signified by God's wrath, the succession of ten plagues, and the annihilation of the Pharaoh's army at the Sea of Reeds. Future slaveholders could draw little comfort from this model of emancipation, or from the example of the Hebrews plundering their masters, by way of restitution, of gold, silver, clothing, and flocks and herds.

On the other hand, it would appear that for God even the creation was an easier task than liberating slaves. When American abolitionists like the Reverend George Barrell Cheever invoked the Mosaic precedent, they condensed biblical history and overlooked the extraordinary difficulties of emancipation and "reconstruction," a process not quite finished at the end of the Pentateuch.[7] While the Hebrews' deliverance depended at every stage on God's decisive acts, God in turn required a human leader who was not a lowly slave but the Hebrew foster son of the Pharaoh's daughter, a man of double identities who had killed a bullying Egyptian taskmaster and was yet "much esteemed" among the Pharaoh's courtiers and the Egyptian people. First it was necessary for God to persuade a reluctant Moses to become a truly voluntary leader and deliverer. Then Moses, working through his brother Aaron, needed to perform miraculous signs to convince the Israelite elders that God would liberate His people. Although Moses had access to the Pharaoh for repeated negotiations that sometimes gave ground for hope, God taught a lesson in the realities of human power by hardening the Pharaoh's heart and showing that only the worst afflictions could force the king to give in. In effect, the Pharaoh finally combined emancipation with immediate deportation, ordering Moses and the Israelites to leave Egypt in the middle of the night. After overcoming these prodigious obstacles, Moses soon discovered that the Egyptians had changed their minds and that his own people, catching sight of the pursuing army, cried out: "Is this not the very thing we told you in Egypt, saying, 'Let us be, and we will serve the Egyptians, for it is better for us to serve the Egyptians than to die in the wilderness?' "[8]

The act of physical liberation, we soon learn, is not sufficient; long trials and discipline are needed to prepare a people for the obligations of authentic freedom under covenant with God. This message took on poignant meaning for African American emigrationists. In 1820, when the first expedition sent out by the American Colonization Society and United States government settled at a swampy, unhealthful spot on Sherbro Island, off the coast of Sierra Leone, the colonists were soon decimated by disease. Before dying, the society's white agent granted his commission as leader to Daniel Coker, a mulatto minister and teacher who on shipboard may have prevented a black rebellion against white authority. At times of crisis Coker had repeatedly prayed that "He that was with Moses in the wilderness be with us," and that "He that divided the waters for Israel will open our way, I know not how." By May 1821, Coker confided in his journal that "Moses was I think permitted to see the promised land but not to enter in. I think it likely that I shall not be permitted to see our expected earthly Canaan. But this will be of but small moment so that some thousand of Africa's children are safely landed." A century later, Marcus Garvey employed the same precedent in a speech restating the goals of the Universal Negro Improvement Association (UNIA): "It was because of lack of faith in the children of Israel that they were held up for so long in the wilderness and why so many of them died without seeing the Promised Land. That same lack of faith will be the downfall of many of us."[9]

The Exodus narrative has been central to the Judeo-Christian idea of God shaping the course of human history through a succession of warnings, promises, punishments, and rewards. Taken as the literal transcription of God's revelation to Moses, the story has been recapitulated and transmogrified not only in the Old and New Testaments but through much of Western history. It has conveyed the astounding message that in the past God actually heard the cries of the oppressed and was willing to free slaves from their masters. Indeed, God passed over the brilliant and powerful peoples of the ancient Near East and chose a group of degraded slaves to bear the awesome responsibility of receiving and transmitting His law. Exodus has therefore furnished a model for every kind of deliverance, whether by escape, revolution, or spiritual rebirth. It has helped people understand the suffering, rebellious "murmuring," and moral testing that mark the road toward the Promised Land.

Although Christian theologians generally interpreted the Mosaic Exodus as a prefiguration of Christ's redemption of humankind, numerous Christian groups have identified their own sins, afflictions, rewards, and mission with those of ancient Israel. Such views of similitude have ranged from momentary and casual analogies to a sustained sense of reenacting sacred history. There is no need here to consider the convolutions of Protestant covenant theology, the different meanings assigned to "Israel," or the chasm that increasingly separated a small group of religious skeptics from the multitudes who felt empowered by their direct access to the Word of God. It is sufficient to note that by the late sixteenth century, English preachers thought it self-evident that God had chosen England for special blessings and responsibilities because, as numerous sermons put it, "we are like unto the children of Israel." As Michael McGiffert has shown, the parallels perceived between ancient Israel and Protestant England made a base upon which the clergy "built the towering scaffold of moral nationalism." The Israelite paradigm, by affirming the continuity of sacred history and the consistency of God's judgment of nations, enabled preachers to draw upon the matchless eloquence of the Hebrew prophets as they condemned the sins of the land.[10] The evolving Jeremiad, with its enumeration of collective crimes and its alternative visions of national holocaust and a New Jerusalem, created a framework for interpreting both the Puritan Exodus to America and the English civil wars. The Israelite paradigm became so embedded in Anglo-American Protestant culture that such diverse groups as the English and American Puritans, clerical supporters of the American Revolution, the Mormons, and black emigrants and "Exodusters" pictured themselves being delivered from Egypt.[11]

While the experiences of such groups were in some ways incommensurable, Michael Walzer suggests that the endless repetition of the Exodus story established a cultural pattern that has shaped Western perceptions and understandings of liberation. He also provides valuable insight into the continuing tension between "Exodus politics" and a messianism that emerges from the Exodus experience but looks forward to "a new heaven and a new earth," which finally appears (though not mentioned by Walzer) in the book of Revelation after "the first heaven and the first earth were passed away."[12]

The Land of Canaan, Walzer points out, was simply the antipode of Egypt—a specific geographic place to which Israelites could return, work as free farmers, and enjoy their milk and honey. Exodus politics were attuned to the realities of life, power, and human fallibility. Permanent liberation from Egyptian bondage required social discipline and education. It was not sufficient to survive the march across the desert, to train a new generation that had not been debased by slavery, to conquer Canaan and build a new nation. Far more difficult was the task of remaining true to the covenant, of preventing the reemergence of Egyptian corruptions from within. The fall of Jerusalem and the destruction of the First Temple in 586 BCE signified the failed hopes of the first Exodus. To escape the Babylonian conquest, many Jews even fled to Egypt.[13]

Jewish messianism arose in the period of the Babylonian exile when the prophets began to envision a new Exodus, a new covenant, and a restored Israel as the new Promised Land. As the prophet Jeremiah made clear, God's new covenant would be qualitatively different from the Sinai covenant, "when I took them by the hand to lead them out of the land of Egypt, a covenant which they broke, so that I rejected them." For God would soon forgive past iniquities and inscribe His law upon the hearts of His people, "in their inmost being," so "all of them, from the least of them to the greatest, shall heed Me."[14] These visions of forgiveness and redemption nourished traditions of Jewish and then Christian messianism that confidently awaited a total transformation of human nature, the restoration of Adamic innocence and Edenic peace. Instead of opposing Egyptian bondage with a free but worldly Canaan, the messianic writers opposed all the evils of the existing world with a millenarian paradise that would appear, often after a series of apocalyptic terrors, at "the end of days."[15] The spiritualizing tendencies of messianism were countered in postbiblical Jewish thought by a sense of historical continuity with the patriarchal age and the specific worldly event of the Exodus from Egypt, leading to the revelation of God's law. Yet the Jews' continuing experience of persecution and exile also generated heightened dreams of a second Moses, a final Exodus, and a "definitive redemption."[16] As we shall later see, a similar tension pervaded the American colonization and abolitionist movements. If the abolitionists' demand for "immediate emancipation" represented in one sense a moral Exodus from the Egypt of colonization, it also relied on a spiritual regeneration sufficient to overcome not only racial prejudice but every vestige of the Kingdom of Darkness.

PRECEDENTS: EXILES

American colonizationists were hardly eager to identify the United States with Pharaonic Egypt or to associate their cause with the notorious expulsions of European history.[17] When Thomas Jefferson wrote that "we should in vain look for an example in the Spanish deportation or deletion of the Moors," he seems to have meant that, compared to Spain, Virginia would reap far richer benefits and escape far worse calamities by beginning, while "it is still in our power to direct the process of emancipation and deportation, peaceably, and in such slow degree, as that the evil will wear off insensibly." In 1832, a fellow Virginian and ardent colonizationist, Jesse Burton Harrison, stressed that "the very last cases to which we would compare such gradual withdrawal . . . would be the expulsion of the eight hundred thousand Jews from Spain under Ferdinand and Isabella, or that of nearly a million of Moors under Philip III, or that of the Huguenots from France." The difference had little to do with consent, since Harrison spoke frankly of the "deportation" of freed slaves, contrary to the usual rhetoric of the Colonization Society. The difference lay in the avoidance of sudden, disruptive change and in the alleged worthlessness to Virginia of the black population. In contrast to America's blacks, Harrison affirmed, the Jews, Moors, and Huguenots "carried with them greater personal wealth in proportion to their number, finer skill, and more thriving habits than were left behind them."[18]

The movement to colonize America's blacks can be put in clearer perspective if we examine some of the precedents or antiprecedents that were at least vaguely familiar to late-eighteenth- and nineteenth-century Americans. These historical examples should help us understand the ways in which the colonization movement combined some of the features of deportation with an idealized picture of seventeenth-century English migrations to North America.

Any expulsion or exodus is bound to be seen in a wholly different light by the world's Pharaohs and Israelites. Like the biblical Pharaoh and America's post-Revolutionary whites, the persecutors have typically voiced alarm over the supposedly *sudden* growth of a population of dangerous "strangers" or heretics. Yet the desire to expel or exterminate these unwanted subversives has been restrained, at least temporarily, by a realistic knowledge of their services. In medieval Europe, for example, the Church's obsession with religious uniformity was often counterbalanced by a secular recognition that Jews could be extremely useful to the state because of their knowledge of commerce, credit and banking, medicine, and the languages and customs of distant Christian and Muslim lands. In thirteenth-century England, the Crown derived a significant share of its revenue from a few extraordinarily wealthy Jewish magnates. It was not until Henry III's ruinous taxes had impoverished the Anglo-Jewish community that the way was open for the famous expulsion edict of 1290. Two centuries later, when Spain deported a far larger Jewish population, officials tried to keep the irreplaceable Jewish physicians from leaving the country. At the turn of the seventeenth century, proposals to exterminate or expel Spain's Moriscos were resisted by landlords and creditors who relied on their labor.[19]

Such self-interested resistance could be overcome by a belief in two kinds of danger: the fear that the subject population would rise in armed revolt or aid neighboring enemies; and the fear that an unassimilated group would corrupt the purity of a religious or national mission. Often the two fears overlapped, as in the prophecies of Jefferson and other white leaders that the continuing presence of America's blacks would either undermine the experiment in republican government or provoke what Jefferson described as the "exterminating thunder" of "a god of justice," who in an armed struggle would favor the oppressed.[20]

Internal security served as a pretext, at least, for the expulsion of some 275,000 Moriscos from early modern Spain. Centuries of Christian reconquest had led to the subjugation of large Muslim populations that were often indispensable to the economy but that also rebelled and collaborated with Muslim armies. In the thirteenth and fourteenth centuries, Spanish Christians enslaved and massacred the Moors but also intermarried with them; Christian kings prohibited Moors from emigrating to Muslim lands and also expelled them as security risks.[21] The dilemma persisted long after the conquest of Granada purged Spain of Muslim rulers. The Spanish Moriscos, while nominally Christian, rebelled in the late 1560s, when the Crown tried to eradicate their Moorish customs and culture. Envied for their industry and fecundity, the Moriscos were perceived as internal enemies who might support Turkish attacks on Spain. Philip III's decree of 1609, ordering the Moriscos to leave Spain, won enthusiastic popular support at the very moment when Spaniards felt humiliated by concessions to the victorious Dutch; the decree was also hailed as an act of mercy to a population that deserved extermination.[22]

Unlike the Moors and Moriscos, the Spanish Jews had no potential military allies or traditions of armed rebellion. Although Christians repeated and embellished all the libels fabricated during centuries of anti-Semitic persecution, the Edict of Expulsion of 1492 focused on the problem of assimilation, a problem experienced in different form by nineteenth-century free blacks who sought acceptance in the United States. Following the anti-Jewish riots and massacres of 1391, many Spanish Jews converted to Christianity. To prove the authenticity of their own faith, a few of these Marranos, or "New Christians," accused others of secret Judaizing practices. Using torture, the Inquisition extracted a sufficient number of confessions to cast doubt on anyone with a trace of Jewish ancestry. The Spanish preoccupation with purity of blood, or *limpieza de sangre*, merged racism with religious prejudice. In theory, Marranos were not denied the possibility of Christian redemption. In actuality, they could always be accused of Judaizing practices and be banished or burned alive. By 1492, when the Reconquista finally subjected Granada to Christian rule, Ferdinand and Isabella concluded that the Marranos and their descendants would never be free from corruption as long as Jews were allowed to live in Spain, where they could secretly instruct the New Christians and persuade them "to follow the Law of Moses." One is reminded of the fear expressed by Southern slaveholders that slaves would never unquestioningly accept their status as long as free blacks could poison their minds and represent the possibility of a different way of life. Because Ferdinand and Isabella were determined to prevent "our holy Catholic faith" from being "debased and humbled," they ordered all Jews to leave Spain within three months.[23]

Even such classic examples of expulsion usually implied a degree of individual choice and self-definition. Thousands of Spanish Jews, including prominent rabbis, accepted last-minute conversion to Christianity as a lesser of evils. Two centuries later, thousands of French Huguenots preferred Catholicism to exile or death. The French Acadians, whom the British deported in 1755–56 from Nova Scotia and adjacent territories, could probably have remained in their homeland had they accepted an unconditional oath of allegiance to the British Crown that would have denied, in effect, the political authority of the pope. Some seventy thousand American Loyalists, the first refugees from a modern, secular revolution, also rejected the alternative of a loyalty oath and political conversion. To win acceptance none of these exiles, with the arguable exception of several thousand black American Loyalists, faced the impossible requirement of changing the color of his skin.[24]

Yet, for many Spanish Jews, Huguenots, and other religious and political refugees, the choice of conversion was equivalent to a choice of enslavement. The alternatives were roughly comparable to those offered to a small number of Southern bondsmen who were given the choice of emigrating to Liberia or remaining in America as slaves. The meaning of consent is also transformed by violent persecution, which can sometimes bring the oppressors and the oppressed to agree that further coexistence is impossible, especially when the oppressed are perceived and begin to perceive themselves as a separate "nation." This point is crucially important for an understanding of the occasional cooperation between black emigrationists and white racists after free blacks had been subjected to mob attacks in Northern cities and had finally been defined by the Supreme Court as "beings of an inferior order" with "no rights which any white man was bound to respect." A few references to twentieth-century events will help us appreciate how even coercive colonization can be interpreted as a providential escape.

To take the most extreme example, in 1938 the Nazis' persecution of Jews entered a new phase with the Kristallnacht beatings, murders, and attacks on Jewish homes, shops, and synagogues. A few days after Kristallnacht, Hermann Göring explained privately that the goal of such violence was to force Jews to leave Germany and settle in a distant colony like Madagascar. State Secretary Ernst von Weizsäcker and other officials subsequently devoted considerable time to the Nazis' "Madagascar Project." The idea of colonizing Jews in Madagascar had actually appeared in anti-Semitic literature in the 1920s and had led the Polish government, which was eager to get rid of Poland's "superfluous" Jews, to sound out the governor-general of the French colony. After finally receiving French consent, Poland dispatched a commission to Madagascar in 1937 to investigate the possibility of founding a Jewish settlement there (the two Jewish members of the commission found the island inhospitable and objected to the commission's report). The fact that Poland and even France were interested in reducing their Jewish populations suggests why neighboring governments refused to take Nazi anti-Semitism seriously or to open their gates to more than a trickle of Jewish refugees. Although some German officials were still considering the goal of colonizing all European Jews in distant territories as late as the summer of 1940, "resettlement" soon became a Nazi euphemism for unprecedented mass extermination.[25]

This experience has dramatized both the urgency and the difficulty of finding asylum for peoples subjected to increasingly violent persecution. Few refugee groups in history have been as fortunate as the French Huguenots, who for all their suffering were often aided by foreign neighbors and were able to escape by the tens of thousands to Protestant regions in Switzerland, Holland, the Rhineland, and England. When we evaluate the nineteenth-century African colonization movement, we should keep in mind the range of emotions aroused in modern times by the plight of Soviet Jews, by the conflict between the British and Irish, by the demand of right-wing Israeli groups that all Arabs be expelled from Israel, and by Israel's "Operation Moses," which rescued thousands of black Falashas from Ethiopia before being disclosed to the world in 1984. Aiding the persecuted does not usually imply even tacit moral approval of the persecutors; it may, however, serve as a humanitarian cloak for prejudice or imply a pragmatic acceptance of the persecution as an irremediable fact of life.

Despite their humiliation and suffering, exiles and refugees have often found it difficult to view their rejection as permanent. Groups of Spanish Jews, Huguenots, Acadians, and other expatriates addressed kings with petitions or monetary offers in the hope of securing a right to return. Moriscos who retained Christian practice and who found themselves despised in Barbary slipped back into Spain at the risk of being discovered and condemned as galley slaves. Hundreds of the Acadians who had been dispersed among Francophobic and anti-Catholic colonists to the American South welcomed the open boats and supplies provided by the governments of Georgia and South Carolina, and sailed up the Atlantic coast in desperate attempts to reach the Bay of Fundy.[26] For at least two generations after the revocation of the Edict of Nantes, many Huguenots awaited the providential event that would enable them to return to France and convert their countrymen to Protestantism. Although some groups of refugees, such as the Huguenots, soon lost their distinctive identity, victims of persecution were no less bound than other emigrants to the culture of their former homelands. In northern Africa, Italy, Flanders, and Turkey, Sephardic Jews continued to take pride in their

Spanish language, manners, and culture, which gave them an air of cosmopolitan superiority. When America's black refugees returned to the United States from Haiti, Canada, and Liberia, or preserved American customs and institutions abroad, they were not thereby betraying their distinctive African American subculture or diluting their resentment toward racist oppression.[27]

Historical comparisons also provide perspective on the mixture of exuberance and despair felt by many exiles as they sought to explain their loss of homes, property, and community as well as the frightening uncertainty of the future. For faithful Muslims, Jews, and Christians alike, such cataclysms could be comprehended only as the will of God. The Moriscos, according to Henry Charles Lea, arrived at the Spanish port of Alicante "with music and song, as though going to a festival, and thanking Allah for the happiness of returning to the land of their fathers." Although many Moriscos mistrusted Philip III's offer of free transport and chartered their own ships, others interpreted Spain's sudden reversal of policy as a providential opportunity, as one leader put it, " 'to go to the land of our ancestors, under our king the Turk, who will let us live as Moors and not as slaves, as we have been treated by our masters.' "[28]

In 1492, many Jews expressed a similar sense of exaltation and ecstasy as they compared their suffering and banishment to the Mosaic Exodus or saw it as a "third exile," confirming their unique relationship with God. According to Leon Poliakov, it was said that this Exodus would be followed "by a promised land of glory and honor. Others added that it would not be long before Spain recalled her children, so certain exiles, after selling their property, buried their money in the soil of the mother country." After receiving a warm welcome in Turkey, one Jewish poet proclaimed that God had at last provided a safe asylum in which Jews could cast off corruptions and recover ancient truths:

> Great Turkey, a wide and spreading sea, which our Lord opened with the wand of His mercy (as at the exodus from Egypt), that the tide of thy present disaster, Jacob, as happened with the multitude of the Egyptians, should therein lose and exhaust itself. . . . In this realm thou art highly favored by the Lord, since therein He granteth thee boundless liberty to commence thy late repentance.[29]

Some Huguenot leaders compared their persecution to that of the Spanish and Portuguese Jews; they also complained that their followers, "like the Israelites, noe sooner past the sea but they forget their deliverance and goe a Stray." For Huguenot exiles, however, the central meaning of the Israelites' Exodus was that God would not abandon the faithful who remained within His covenant. The punishment He had inflicted upon such persecutors as Pharaoh and Herod, in the Old and New Testaments, showed that Catholic tyrants would inevitably pay for their crimes; the agonies suffered by Protestants within France would soon cease. While Huguenot leaders, such as Pierre Jurieu, recommended emigration to America as a way of escaping conversion to Catholicism, they associated deliverance with the return to a purified France, not with a new promised land. Still, it is noteworthy that when Mademoiselle de Sers wrote to her mother and father, a Huguenot pastor, while sailing to America in 1688, she compared the way God had delivered the Israelites from the hands of Pharaoh to the way He had enabled her faithful compatriots to escape their persecutors and joyfully cross the sea. Mademoiselle de Sers was bound for Saint-Domingue. She could not foresee the chain of events that would arouse hopes similar to hers, 136 years later, among shiploads of American free blacks bound for the same island.[30]

PRECEDENTS: THE DISPLACED

When exiles and refugees recalled the biblical Exodus, they seldom referred to its darkest side. When the founders and supporters of the American Colonization Society asserted that "this scheme is from God!" and that "to labour in this work is to co-work with God," they envisioned the salvation of Africa, not the slaughter or displacement of its natives. When Edward Wilmot Blyden wrote to his fellow African Americans from Liberia, telling them that God had mandated their return to an African homeland, he quoted from Deuteronomy: "Behold, the Lord thy God hath set the land before thee: go up and possess it, as the Lord God of thy fathers had said unto thee; fear not, neither be discouraged." But Blyden did not point out that this passage precedes God's angry complaint that the Israelites had been fearful of trying to conquer "a people stronger and taller than we, large cities with walls sky-high."[31]

In Deuteronomy, at the end of the forty years' preparation in the wilderness, the Lord informs the Israelites that they are about to invade and occupy "seven nations much larger than you." He promises He "will dislodge those peoples before you little by little; you will not be able to put an end to them at once, else the wild beasts would multiply to your hurt." After guaranteeing victory over the idolatrous nations that occupy the Promised Land, God issues an unequivocal command: "You shall not let a soul remain alive." And when Joshua's troops eventually capture Jericho, the Bible reports, "they exterminated everything in the city with the sword: man and woman, young and old, ox and sheep and ass."[32]

In actuality, archeological evidence indicates that the Israelites slowly infiltrated the Land of Canaan and did not exterminate their enemies; God's war sermon probably reflects a post-settlement lament that the Israelites' adoption of idolatrous customs and intermarriage with Canaanites could have been prevented by killing off the native inhabitants.[33] Talmudic and medieval rabbinic commentators insisted that God's ruthless commandment could never serve as a precedent for other times and peoples. Even the New England Puritans, who sometimes referred to Indians as Canaanites and Amalekites, were extremely reluctant to invoke God's commandments to annihilate specific pagan tribes. Nevertheless, the conquest of Canaan provided an example of divinely sanctioned colonization and violent displacement that was not lost on the English colonizers of Ireland and North America.[34]

Before examining the subject of displacement, it is important to clarify a source of possible confusion when one compares the relations between colonists and natives in North America and West Africa. During the half century following the War of Independence, white Americans subjected Indians and free blacks to increasing persecution. Demands for the removal of both groups presupposed their replacement by white citizens. There were enormous differences, however, between Indian nations who inhabited land desired by whites and communities of free blacks who tended to seek what refuge and employment they could find in crowded cities. Historically, whites had often expressed an abstract admiration for Indians that was definitely not extended to blacks. The contrast widened as writers, painters, and poets romanticized the noble savage as the primordial American.[35] Yet the blacks, unlike the Indians, were also portrayed by the American Colonization Society as latter-day Pilgrims who would carry to Africa the seeds of Christianity and American civilization. Frequently likened to the founders of Plymouth and Jamestown colonies, the Liberian settlers occupied their own "Canaan" and confronted their own natives, whose population had not been depleted in advance by alien diseases such as those that wiped out whole communities of eastern Indians before Plymouth was settled.[36]

The visionary goals of the American Colonization Society cannot be understood without some discussion of the ideology of colonization that helped create the United States. We can catch a glimpse of this point in Benjamin Franklin's extremely influential "Observations Concerning the Increase of Mankind," first published in 1755, which contains some of the fundamental premises and prejudices of the later colonization movement, although Franklin's essay never advocates the removal of emancipated blacks.

Like many colonizationists, Franklin maintained that the perpetuation of black slavery was contrary to the national interest: slave labor could never be as cheap in America as free labor had proved to be in a densely populated country like England; the presence of slaves impeded the growth of white population and corrupted whites by encouraging pride and idleness. Second, Franklin expressed a desire to make America a white man's country: "Why increase the Sons of Africa, by Planting them in America, where we have so fair an Opportunity, by excluding all Blacks and Tawneys, of increasing the lovely White and Red?" Thirdly, Franklin showed that "natural Generation" could quickly replace any loss in population such as those created by the expulsion of Protestants from France, the emigration of English settlers to America, or the sale of African slaves to the New World. Finally, when illustrating the connections between public policy and human progress, Franklin hailed as "Fathers of their Nation" the rulers and legislators who encouraged trade, economic improvements, and the growth of population. Pride of place went to "the Prince that acquires new Territory, if he finds it vacant, or removes the Natives to give his own People Room."[37] As Franklin's friend Joseph Banks discovered in 1770, when he and Captain James Cook landed at a place in Australia that Cook named Botany Bay, "new" territories were very seldom vacant.

Colonization began to acquire new meanings in the sixteenth and seventeenth centuries, when modern nation states supported the

founding of overseas plantations that went far beyond trading settlements and military outposts.[38] In Ireland, which became the training
ground for England's appropriation of territories in the New World,
the English evicted Gaelic natives in order to extend plantations
beyond the traditional pale of English settlement. Proposals to exterminate or expel the "wild Irishmen," whom the English regarded as
no more civilized than American Indians, were rejected, according to
T. W. Moody, because "the deputy and council believed in 1540 that it
would be impossible to furnish Ireland as a whole with 'new inhabitants,' since no prince could spare so many people from his own country." By the early seventeenth century, however, population growth
encouraged the English to promote Scottish emigration to Ulster.
Irish rebellions, leading ultimately to Oliver Cromwell's invasion and
subjugation of the Irish in 1649, gave a pretext for confiscating millions of acres of land and driving the "wild Irishmen" who were not
slaughtered into the bogs and wastelands of Ulster. Like Franklin's
ideal "Prince," British rulers from Henry VIII to Cromwell established a precedent for removing the natives to give room to their own
people.[39]

In 1516, when Europeans were just beginning to reflect on the
significance of a New World, Sir Thomas More sketched out some
basic ideas regarding ideal settlement in his fantasy of a "Utopia."
He found a justification for settling colonies and removing natives
that contained the basic ideas Anglo-Americans would embody in
Indian policy from the time of Sir Humphrey Gilbert, a veteran of
sixteenth-century Irish conquests who received one of the first charters to found a settlement in North America, to the time of Andrew
Jackson. More's Utopians felt free to establish a colony "wherever the
natives have much unoccupied and uncultivated land." The Utopians
gladly assimilated those natives who were willing to live "according
to their laws" and to learn agricultural techniques that made "the
land sufficient for both [peoples], which previously seemed poor and
barren to the natives." Recalcitrant natives were simply driven from
the territory. The Utopians considered it "a most just cause for war
when a people which does not use its soil but keeps it idle and waste
nevertheless forbids the use and possession of it to others who by the
rule of nature ought to be maintained by it."[40]

Three centuries later, President James Monroe elaborated the same theme as he celebrated the imminent settlement of the southern Mississippi Valley:

> In this progress, which the rights of nature demand and nothing can prevent . . . it is our duty to make new efforts for the preservation, improvement, and civilization of the native inhabitants. The hunter state can exist only in the vast uncultivated desert. It yields to the more dense and compact form and greater force of civilized population; and of right it ought to yield, for the earth was given to mankind to support the greatest number of which it is capable, and no tribe or people have a right to withhold from the wants of others more than is necessary for their own support and comfort.[41]

Seventeenth-century Puritans put this utilitarian argument within a wider framework of God's governance and appointment. Leaders of the Puritan Exodus to America repeatedly compared themselves with the ancient Hebrews: "Let Israel be the evidence of the Doctrine, and our glass to view our Faces in." As a chosen people, sifted from the chaff of English Protestantism, by the very act of migrating to a wilderness the emigrants took on the obligations of a new covenant with God. If they kept the covenant, John Winthrop affirmed, "wee shall finde that the God of Israell is among vs." But when Winthrop's expedition was about to embark from Southampton in 1630 to settle the colony of Massachusetts Bay, John Cotton's farewell sermon, "God's Promise to His Plantations," found a theological charter not in Exodus or Deuteronomy but in a proleptic text from the second book of Samuel. Cotton chose the verse in which the Lord, speaking through the prophet Nathan, promises King David that "I will appoint a place for my people Israell, and I will plant them, that they may dwell in a place of their owne, and move no more."[42]

This passage precedes God's prediction that one of David's seed ("I will be his father, and he shall be my son") will establish an everlasting kingdom. Since Christians believe that David was an ancestor of Jesus, Cotton could reinterpret Canaan as both a material and a spiritual inheritance promised to those who, through rigorous self-examination, discerned that they were "in Christ" and were settling in a place appointed to them by the hand of God. Otherwise, Cotton told the Puritans, "we are but intruders upon God." Despite the appealing imagery of a New Jerusalem and a New Canaan, Cotton and other clerical leaders warned that heathen natives could not be killed or driven away, without provocation, unless God had given a nation a special commission, "such as the Israelites had." The promoters of the earlier Jamestown venture, who also spoke of crossing the Red Sea, wandering in the wilderness, and finding the Land of Canaan, made the same point. As William Crashaw put it, "The Israelites had a commandment from God to dwell in Canaan, we have leave to dwell in Virginea: they were commanded to kill the heathen, we are forbidden to kill them, but are commanded to convert them."[43]

Cotton made room for the utilitarian argument by emphasizing the universal "charter" given to Adam and Noah, who were told to "Multiply, and replenish the earth, and subdue it." The Old Testament furnished numerous precedents for claiming "vacant" land in sparsely populated territories and establishing a right to the soil by bestowing "culture and husbandry upon it." When Abraham found that his well at Beersheba had been seized by the natives, Cotton pointed out, he did not tell King Abimelech that his right derived from a divine calling, "for that would have seemed frivolous amongst the Heathen." Rather, according to Cotton's interpretation, Abraham based his successful plea on "his owne industry and culture in digging the well." To illustrate the point that Canaan contained enough vacant space for the heathen and elect alike, Cotton also referred to Jacob, who pitched his tents at Shechem and purchased a parcel of land from the children of Hamor: "There was roome enough as Hamor said, Let them sit down amongst us."[44]

But, as many of Cotton's American-bound listeners surely knew (and this immensely influential sermon was reprinted and quoted in New England for more than a century), Hamor made these conciliatory remarks at a time of crisis. Hamor's son had just raped one of Jacob's daughters, Dinah, whom he was determined to marry; Jacob's sons had then deceitfully agreed to intermarriage between the two groups if the males of Shechem submitted to circumcision. While the obliging Canaanites were disabled by the pain of this operation, two of Jacob's sons slaughtered them and the others plundered the town and carried away the women and children as captives. Since Cotton explicitly recognized the right of "lawfull war" against natives who failed to recompense wrongs committed against uninvited settlers, this biblical precedent boded ill for the Indians—even those who accepted baptism, the Christian equivalent of circumcision. Cotton concluded with a plea to "offend not the poore Natives, but as you partake in their land, so make them partakers of your precious faith." Seven years earlier, John Robinson, the nonemigrating minister of the Pilgrims who founded Plymouth, had already received news in Holland of a bloody retaliation against Indians by the colonists. "Oh, how happy a thing had it been," he wrote Governor William Bradford, "if you had converted some before you had killed any!"[45]

The Virginia Company also expressed benevolent concern for the Native Americans. English settlers would introduce them to the Bible, "cover their naked miserie, with civill use of foode, and cloathing," teach them how to make productive use of their time and land, and welcome them with "equall priviledges" into the English community. As the historian Edmund S. Morgan puts it, the promoters of colonization hoped for more than profits: "Theirs was a patriotic enterprise that would bring civility and Christianity to the savages of North America and redemption from idleness and crime to the unemployed masses of England."[46] The failure of all these expectations did not kill the initial dream or deter Virginians and other Americans from applying a very similar formula, more than two centuries later, to the colonization of Africa.

The English settlers' assurance of divine guidance seldom bred humility. Even Thomas Morton, the anti-Puritan trader and adventurer who reveled with the Indians at "Marry-mount," accepted the common belief that "the hand of God" was responsible for the epidemic that killed so many Indians and made Massachusetts "more fitt, for the English Nation to inhabit in, and erect in it Temples to the Glory of God." Although the first English colonists were saved from starving by Indian generosity and Indian agricultural technology, they credited their survival to God and tended to picture the land as empty and "devoid of all civil inhabitants." When Indians resisted English paternalism and responded to continuous encroachments on their land with surprise hit-and-run attacks, they were not seen as sovereign peoples repelling an invasion. Infuriated by the Pequots' unconventional ways of war, the Puritans had no compunctions about exterminating members of the tribe, regardless of age or sex. Preachers might interpret the Indians' destruction of New England villages as a divine punishment for the sins and unfaithfulness of "our Judah"; but they also asserted that heathen tribes who thwarted God's larger plan for "the English Israel" could be dispossessed and put to the sword.[47]

Belief in a divinely guided mission made it easier to combine benevolent paternalism with the kind of brutal slaughter God had sanctioned in the Old Testament. English professions of altruism and goodwill toward the Indians survived Opechancanough's devastating attack on Virginia's settlements and King Philip's attempt to wipe out New England. Benevolent goals seemed perfectly compatible with burning Indian villages, with killing the inhabitants or selling them as slaves in the West Indies, and with signing treaties whose duplicitous intent rivaled that of Jacob's sons. Moral scruples could not be allowed to protect barbarians who violently resisted the progress of Christian civilization.

4

Colonizing Blacks, Part II: The American Colonization Society and Americo-Liberians

LIBERATING LIBERIA

In 1924, when W. E. B. Du Bois proclaimed from Liberia that "Africa is the Spiritual Frontier of human kind—oh the wild and beautiful adventures of its taming!," he described Monrovia as "a city set upon a hill." This was the figure, taken from the Sermon on the Mount, that John Winthrop had made synonymous with New England's and America's mission to the world (and that Frederick Douglass had extended, as we have seen, to Haiti). In 1924, Du Bois's model of tropical paradise was the antipode to Winthrop's ideal of a disciplined, enterprising Christian commonwealth, an ideal accepted in large measure by the nineteenth-century black and white founders of Liberia. A native New Englander and the first black to earn a Ph.D. from Harvard, Du Bois had long been fascinated by the African roots of American black culture. Late in 1923 he had been sent to Liberia as President Coolidge's envoy and minister plenipotentiary for the inauguration of President C. D. B. King. After walking for hours in the bush and visiting a Kru village, Du Bois made the romantic discovery that "efficiency and happiness do not go together in modern culture," that "laziness; divine, eternal, languor is right and good and true." Even as he resisted the compulsions of his own internalized work ethic, Du Bois's allusion to the "mud town Plymouth Rock" and to the "city set upon a hill" reinforced the central hope of Liberia's history: that African Americans, having been cruelly excluded from the promise of American life, which they had helped create, could find fulfillment and dignity in a regenerated "America" on the shores of Africa.[1]

Du Bois's rhapsodic response to African culture illustrates the complexity of modeling African colonization on the myth of America as the Promised Land. Unlike Du Bois, Liberia's nineteenth-century settlers had not studied anthropology and failed to share his poetic delight in "the ancient witchery" of Africa's medicine and his appreciation of the villagers' "breeding" and "leisure of true aristocracy, leisure for thought and courtesy, leisure for sleep and laughter." With a few exceptions, the Americo-Liberians were no less ethnocentric than the white settlers of North America. They too sought to escape an Egypt or Babylon and build a city on a hill that would reap the full material and spiritual rewards of Christian civilization. They too experienced uncertainty and homesickness as they struggled to find a new identity that would help to liberate their brethren from the oppressions of history.

Like the Puritans, the Liberian settlers and their patrons were alert to the dangers of "counter-conversion"—of colonists assimilating the ways of Canaan. Ralph Randolph Gurley, the Connecticut-born and Yale-educated secretary and vice president of the ACS, warned that without the "means of Christian improvement," the Americo-Liberians would quickly become indistinguishable from the African natives "except by the sturdiness and variety of their vices."[2] The location and very meaning of a promised land were complicated by the need to conquer Canaan while looking backward across the sea for standards of justification and moral assessment. Would New England or Liberia redeem their flawed progenitors, or become dissolute clearings in a distant wilderness?

Among the world's emigrants and colonists, the Puritans and Quakers were exceptional in their relative affluence, education, and political experience, a point frequently noted by free black critics of the American Colonization Society who objected to the apparent absurdity of expecting similar feats of nation-building from illiterate former slaves.[3] Although English Puritans were despised and persecuted by their High Church countrymen, their errand into the wilderness was not governed and interpreted by a Puritan Colonization Society that regarded them as a "vile excrescence" and a "foul stain" upon the nation.[4] Such epithets, pervasive among white supporters of black colonization, had been applied to Jews, Moriscos, convicts, and other victims of deportation. But the voluntary emigrants to Liberia found themselves in a bizarre and unprecedented position: they were assigned the mission of "saving" America by vindicating their race and civilizing Africa—as President John Tyler put it, "Monrovia will be to Africa what Jamestown and Plymouth have been to America"— yet they themselves were the "corruption" whose purgation would supposedly purify the United States.[5]

A further point should be made about analogies between the colonizers of Liberia and New England. The Puritans' errand into the wilderness was oriented to England and Europe. As the New England leaders redefined their mission in the 1640s, in response to the apocalyptic English conflict from which they appeared to have fled, they endeavored to build a model Christian commonwealth that would help purify England of religious corruption and "save" the Protestant Reformation.[6] In similar fashion, the more articulate supporters of African colonization, especially the religious activists, viewed their own errand as a providential opportunity to cleanse the United States of slavery and racial conflict, the twin diseases that imperiled America's Christian and republican mission. The official journal of the ACS even claimed that colonizationist activity was rapidly dispelling white racial prejudice, since "it is impossible, in the nature of things, that unkind feelings or prejudice towards a people can long survive benevolent efforts for their improvement."[7] Benevolent actions, in other words, would purify the more negative motives and emotions that might have brought support to those very actions. Spokesmen for the ACS, including some Southern slaveholders, confidently predicted that American blacks would prove their capability for civilization and vindicate their race as soon as they were freed from the degrading and demoralizing effects of racial prejudice. Modern historians, influenced by the misleading accusations of abolitionists, have seldom taken note of George Fredrickson's discovery that "one can go through much of the literature of the [colonization] movement from 1817 to the late 1830s without finding a single clear and unambiguous assertion of the Negro's inherent and unalterable inferiority to whites."[8] Although antebellum America was afflicted with a deep and profound racism, there was also a widespread belief in what one might term radical environmentalism—the belief that human character changes rapidly and radically as the result of changed environment. As we will see in chapter 8, this was the theme of an important essay by the great black antebellum physician James McCune Smith.

According to Robert Goodloe Harper, the aristocratic Maryland lawyer and politician who gave Liberia its name, the blacks who were hopelessly debased in the United States by the stigma of racial slavery would be wholly transformed within an environment of dignity and equality: "They would become proprietors of land, master mechanics, shipowners, navigators, and merchants, and by degrees schoolmasters, justices of the peace, militia officers, ministers of religion, judges, and legislators." Once they were removed from the social and psychological oppression of whites, Harper affirmed, America's blacks would "soon become equal to the people of Europe, or of European origin, so long their masters and oppressors." George Washington Parke Custis, grandson of the first president, contrasted the bloodshed of the Spanish conquest of America with the redemptive role America would soon play in Africa: future generations of Africans "will not think of Cortes or Pizarro—the name of America will be hailed with enthusiasm by millions on that vast continent that are now unborn."[9]

The bombastic style of many colonizationist orations served only to reinforce the ritualistic and self-justificatory power of the myth of America. Evils alleged to be of European origin, such as slavery and the racial dilemma, were to be overcome by movement to an uncorrupted space where victims of oppression could prove by their own exertions that they were worthy of the Promised Land. The ultimate fate of millions of American slaves—and, by implication, of America's republican institutions—would depend on the black colonists' success in civilizing Africa, eradicating the slave trade, and building a free and prosperous society that would be as attractive to American blacks as the United States had proved to be for European immigrants. Liberia's mission was so abstract and grandiose that it almost precluded serious discussion of capital investment, technological assistance, labor skills, and markets.

The American Colonization Society was aware that parallels with New World colonization could be double-edged. By 1820 American history had shown that a few small and dubious settlements, ravaged by disease and harassed by "savages," could grow into a great and prosperous nation. But more than two centuries of continuing Indian warfare had also given pause to free blacks who considered themselves good Americans, entitled to the security and amenities of civilized life, who were now asked to found new Jamestowns and Plymouths. Two lines of argument were addressed to such misgivings. First, unlike the Europeans who colonized America, blacks were not aliens in Africa. They were being offered the opportunity to return to their ancestral homeland, a point underscored by John Kizzel, a former slave from South Carolina who had finally settled in Sierra Leone after being freed by the British and evacuated to Nova Scotia during the Revolution. In 1818, Kizzel and ten other black refugees from America addressed the following appeal to their American brothers and sisters:

> Brethren, you know the land of Canaan was given to Abraham and to his seed; so Africa was given to our forefathers and to their children. . . . Joseph was sold into a strange land wrongfully by his brethren; and, dear friends, you know many of you were sold wrongfully into a strange land:—and you have increased in the land where you are. Word was sent by God unto the children of Israel for them to return into the land of Canaan, and you have the same word sent unto you to return into your own land. The hand of God is in this business. The children of Israel brought the ark of God into their land, and you will bring the gospel into your land. . . . It is God who has put it into the hearts of these good men to assist you back to your country.[10]

The Colonization Society happily endorsed this analogy and added a second crucial argument: missionaries had found that the "native tribes" in the Sierra Leone region were eager to welcome an American colony. The Africans were "more mild, amiable, and docile; less warlike than the aborigines of America." Reports from Sierra Leone proved that "instead of the war-whoop of the savages, armed with the implements of death and torture, they go to meet their friends and brothers, a generous, humane, hospitable race, who already welcome their approach, as the harbinger of civilization and social happiness." If the American settlers would take as their model the "gentleness, forbearance, and moderation" of the Quaker founders of Pennsylvania, they could be assured the same rewards of uninterrupted peace and friendly intercourse with the aborigines.[11]

In 1834, Philadelphia and New York colonizationists actually founded a settlement in Liberia based on Quaker principles of pacifism and antislavery. The next year King Joe Harris's Kru warriors wiped out this Bassa Cove community in a midnight attack, killing twenty of the colonists while the survivors fled in panic through the forests to Monrovia. The response from the settlers' *Liberia Herald* was predictable: "Such is the dastardly, unprincipled disposition of these half cannibals, that nothing but a knowledge of superiority, in point of physical force, on the part of foreigners, will keep them to the terms of any compact made with them." Before long Americo-Liberian clergymen were reported to be saying, "the best way to civilize these Natives is with powder and ball."[12]

Despite the optimistic rhetoric of the Colonization Society, conflicts between settlers and African ethnic groups had erupted with disturbing frequency since 1787, when Britain established a precarious colony at Sierra Leone as a refuge for London's indigent blacks. In 1789, for example, a Temne king destroyed Sierra Leone's main settlement, Granville Town, in retaliation for the burning of a Temne village by British marines. Aided by fugitive settlers and tribal allies, the Temnes' King Tom led full-scale attacks on Fort Thornton in 1801 and 1802. Ironically, the rebellious Trelawny Maroons who had been deported from Jamaica and then sent to Sierra Leone from Nova Scotia helped to save the colony. Counteroffensives were required to pacify the natives and force them to accept British interpretations of treaties and land cessions.[13]

Neither the British nor the Americans had learned much from the disastrous mistakes of New World colonization. Apart from choosing unhealthful sites that guaranteed devastating mortality from disease, they failed to comprehend that non-Europeans would not willingly accept Western ideas of land use, private property, and political authority. Christian humanitarians, eager to replace the slave trade with legitimate commerce, never anticipated that increasing exports of camwood, rice, ivory, palm oil, and hides would simply increase the demand for slave labor in domestic African economies. The power of West African political regimes and alliances hinged on the control of trade routes as well as on access to Western firearms, textiles, rum, tobacco, and iron tools and utensils. For centuries the diverse ethnic groups of Upper Guinea and the Grain Coast had preserved their sovereignty while conducting business with European traders. Merchants of mixed African and European ancestry, who greatly outnumbered the Europeans residing temporarily at posts along the coast, often served as intermediaries between two economic and cultural worlds. But the survival and expansion of British Sierra Leone, which became a training center for African missionaries, introduced new sources of conflict. Africans learned that self-professed benefactors not only endangered the slave trade and internal commercial networks but claimed exclusive and perpetual jurisdiction over land that could be sold but should always be governed, in native eyes, by traditional custom. The Anglo-American humanitarians could not see that they were building an entrance ramp on the road to imperialism.[14]

When the Reverend Samuel J. Mills and Ebenezer Burgess explored the Sierra Leone coast in 1818, searching for a site that would satisfy the needs of the American Colonization Society, they found "great tracks" of uninhabited land on Sherbro Island. After dispensing rum and other gifts to numerous African officials and chieftains, they discovered that these "children of nature" were incapable of understanding the benevolent objectives of the Colonization Society and were unwilling to sell even vacant land. Three years later, Eli Ayers and Captain Robert Field Stockton, a United States naval officer, encountered still greater resistance at Cape Mesurado, east of Sierra Leone on the Grain Coast. Only after aiming cocked pistols at King Peter's head were Stockton and Ayers able to extort a treaty ceding the Cape, for less than $300 in trade goods, to the Colonization Society. In 1822, Ayers, Jehudi Ashmun, and the first black settlers quickly learned that their security required more than a treaty and professions of peace and goodwill. Though weakened by fever, Ashmun exploited African tribal divisions while mounting a brass cannon and building a stockade and martello tower. By November he was prepared for the mass assault of hundreds of native warriors who nearly overwhelmed the thirty-odd defenders before the cannon's repeated charges of grapeshot tore bloody holes in their ranks. In a second confrontation, twenty days later, Matilda Newport supposedly turned the tide when she ignited a field piece at point-blank range with the coals from her pipe, decapitating an African priest and inciting panic among the native troops. For Americo-Liberians, these legendary exploits signified the triumph of civilization over barbarism, much as similar victories over Indians became part of a mythology justifying the white Americans' possession of North America.[15]

Like the seventeenth-century English colonists and the chartered companies that subsidized them, the Americo-Liberians and white ACS officials insisted that their purchases of land would not deprive "the Natives of the Country" of a single "real advantage." On the contrary, according to the prevailing ideology, memorably expressed in a deed for land along the St. Paul River, the settlements would "improve [the natives] and advance their happiness, by carrying Christianity and civilization to the doors of their Cabins."[16]

This progressive objective was closely tied to the United States government's belated commitment to enforce its laws prohibiting Americans from participating in the African slave trade. Although President Monroe had been persuaded by his cabinet that the Constitution barred the government from purchasing land or directly supporting a colony for America's free blacks, the Slave Trade Act of 1819 provided a pretext for indirect aid. Monroe concluded that government funds could be used to prepare and support a site for resettling Africans rescued from the illicit slave trade by a special United States naval squadron. The privately governed colony of Liberia thus became an official refuge for Africans saved by the United States government from becoming slaves in Cuba or other parts of the New World. Federal funds appropriated to benefit African recaptives helped initially to subsidize Liberian housing, education, defense, and the purchase of agricultural equipment.[17] Natives who resisted the extension of Americo-Liberian settlements along the coast were accordingly portrayed as enemies not only of Christian civilization but of selfless efforts to suppress the primal crime that had crippled and corrupted Africa. While the ACS continued to stress the "friendly character" of the colony's relations with native tribes, it also underscored the colonists' need and desire for naval protection: "The influence of the United States squadron on the African coast has been of vast advantage to Liberia. It has given the native tribes a better idea of the American character and resources, and has tended to quell their turbulent feelings and cause them to seek . . . a closer connection with the commonwealth of Liberia."[18]

The free blacks and mulattoes who first emigrated to Liberia were dependent on the coastal peoples for food, trade, and knowledge of the environment. The Dei and other coastal groups viewed the black and mulatto settlers as "Americans" or even "white men." Though cautiously willing to profit from the methods of the non-African world, they often looked with contempt upon former slaves or the descendants of slaves. If the darker-skinned Americo-Liberians seemed African in appearance, they still deferred to whites, not to the authority of local kings.

For their part, the settlers felt infinitely superior to seminaked heathen who had no understanding of individual land ownership, who believed in trial by an ordeal of poison, and who enslaved and sold their neighbors. Like numerous other groups of exiles and refugees, the Americo-Liberians attempted to replicate the culture they and their forebears had syncretized in their recent homeland. The more privileged settlers relished imported American foodstuffs and disdained such local staples as cassava, plantain, and palm oil. In the sultry heat they wore black toppers, long frock coats, and heavy silk gowns. Amid the "riotous" vegetation, under the "pitiless" African sun that later enraptured W. E. B. Du Bois, they tried to reconstruct the churches, lyceums, benevolent societies, schools, poorhouses, and fraternal orders of Jacksonian America. Ironically, in cities like Philadelphia, it was precisely such institution-building that had most enraged American whites who wanted to keep blacks in their servile "place." In view of the Liberian context, there is a further irony: in the United States blacks had honored such voluntary institutions with the proud adjective "African."[19]

The settler society, to be sure, was anything but homogeneous. While sharing a common heritage of persecution, the Americo-Liberians were divided by distinctions of complexion, class, wealth, skills, and education. By 1841, when Joseph Jenkins Roberts replaced the last white governor, a small merchant and mostly light-skinned oligarchy had won control of the colony's productive resources and political power. Roberts, a wealthy octoroon merchant and philanthropist, belonged to a network of elite families, many of them from Virginia, who had been born free and had immigrated during the first years of settlement. If this oligarchy curtailed opportunities for later immigrants, the majority of whom were former slaves, their achievements also challenged theories of racial incapability. A widening *inequality* between individuals has often been the proof required for an acceptance of equality between groups or nations.[20]

One should not generalize about Americo-Liberian culture from the behavior of the elite families or even from the hundreds of surviving letters of former slaves who became artisans and farmers in Liberia. These literate blacks, though often suffering from privation and poverty, were a privileged group by virtue of their literacy.[21] Furthermore, their letters were crafted for the eyes of former owners, benefactors, and ACS officials. Yet the very existence of such a correspondence is highly significant. Few exiles and expatriates have cared to address their former oppressors and describe their achievements and hardships, their hopes and grievances. Few oppressors have shown continuing solicitude for members of a despised and outcast group. The former slaves who appealed for aid, approval, and family news also rejoiced over finding a land they described as free of racial prejudice, a land where even whites addressed them as "Mister" instead of "boy" (they failed to mention that Americo-Liberians used "boy" when addressing grown native men). While the letters from Liberia may have minimized the Africanisms of Americo-Liberian culture, they gave expression to a governing ideology that extolled enterprise and self-respect and that decried the life of "savages" who rejected the clothing, tools, and Bible of civilized life.[22]

In 1840 Peyton Skipwith almost mimicked the rhetoric of an American frontiersman when he described his adventures in a punitive expedition against Getumbe, a Gola chieftain who led a federation of native rebels some fifty miles inland from Monrovia. Skipwith, a skilled mason and devout Christian, had been emancipated in 1833 by John Hartwell Cocke, a Virginia planter, reformer, and active leader of the ACS. Cocke had sent Skipwith, together with his wife and six children, to Liberia. It was in a letter to Cocke that Skipwith recounted his march, "Rifle in hand," through "the wild bush" with some three hundred militiamen led by Joseph Jenkins Roberts, who eight years later would become the first president of the independent republic. Skipwith reported that "a savage host" of about four hundred men had attacked a missionary village defended by "three Americans" who "whipt the whole enemy. They killd on the feeld above 20 dead, and god he only knows how many was wounded and carread away. . . . The Battle lasted about one Hour fifteen minutes. How this was done they had and over quanty [i.e., a surplus] of musket loded and had nothing to do but take them up and poor the Bullets in thire flesh and they would fall takeeng fingers and tearing the flesh assunder."[23]

Sion Harris, one of the defenders of the mission houses, described the same surprise attack "by about 3 or 4 hundred warriors" in a long letter to Samuel Wilkeson, president of the ACS board of directors. After firing repeated volleys into the enemy's ranks, Harris found himself facing "the head man": "Goterah returned back to the kitchen which he seized and shook with one hand and brandished a dreadful knife with the other, about six inches broad. And about a hundred and 50 men came up to the fence to whom he said, let us go in. I took deliberate aim at him (he was half bent, shaking) and brought him to the ground, cut off his knee, shot him in the lungs and cut of[f] his privets." Harris later delivered Goterah's head, which had been cut off by an African recaptive, to the governor of the colony.[24]

Skipwith saw little kinship between his own family, who were intent on improving themselves in grammar school and at the Baptist Church Sunday School, and the "crooman" (Kru) who was about to be executed for brutally killing "an american boy." Skipwith reflected that "it is something strange to think that these people of Africa are calld our ancestors. In my present thinking if we have any ancestors they could not have been like these hostile tribes in this part of Africa for you may try and distill that principle and belief in them and do all you can for them and they still will be your enemy."[25]

There were, of course, profound cultural differences between the eastern woodland Indians of North America and the sixteen African ethnic groups that eventually fell under the political hegemony of Liberia. The Mandinka, to cite only one example, were skilled in metallurgy and political organization and were successful in converting many Vai and members of other ethnic groups to Islam. Nevertheless, colonization threatened West Africans and Native Americans in somewhat similar ways. Like the white colonists in North America, the Liberian settlers were initially unprepared for agricultural life in a foreign environment. As merchants and middlemen who had access to American credit and exports, they increasingly monopolized the natives' supply of imported commodities while insulating themselves in self-contained communities. As their numbers increased and their settlements expanded, they also destroyed forests and game; exploited tribal rivalries; endangered traditional commercial networks, including the lucrative slave trade; and demanded obedience to their own laws in exchange for schools, markets, and police protection. Above all, they spoke of civilizing the natives and of enlarging their territory, as Edward Wilmot Blyden put it at the time of the American Civil War, "by fair purchase and honourable treaty stipulations, preparatory to the influx of our worn-out and down trodden brethren from abroad."[26]

While some West Africans welcomed the settlements and even sent their children to Monrovia to be "made Americans," King Bowyah appealed in 1851 for British aid against Liberian infringements on Afro-British trade. Writing to the British consul in Monrovia shortly before an African attack on a Bassa Cove settlement, Bowyah complained that the "Americans" were trying to seize his country: "I write this to let you know that this Country is not belong to Americans, and I will not sell it. I have this Country from my Fore Father, and when I die, I wish to left to my sons. I want all English to come here and make trade with my people." Such appeals, even from native slave traders, became a pretext for British and French territorial encroachments and gunboat diplomacy.[27]

As high-handed imperialists, however, the Americo-Liberians were difficult to outmatch. By 1853, when prominent American blacks were reevaluating the alternative of African emigration, a report issued by the Colored National Convention held at Rochester strongly condemned the oppression of Liberia's native population. This attack on all forms of colonialism was written by James W. C. Pennington, a fugitive slave and former blacksmith who had received an honorary degree from the University of Heidelberg and had become an active abolitionist and the pastor of America's largest black Presbyterian church. Determined to dissociate the benefits of Christian missions from the "rapine" and "plunder" of colonization, Pennington compared the Dutch and English exploitation of southern Africa with the expansion of Liberia: "The Liberians themselves, with their government backing them, are pursuing precisely, the same policy, that other colonizers have for the last hundred years in Africa: They boast that they have made their arms so often felt, that 'no combination of the natives can be induced to fight them.' " According to Pennington, it was a "singular coincidence" that Britain chose an African colony (at the Cape of Good Hope) "to relieve herself from what she believed to be [her] over-grown population; America, to relieve herself from what she calls obnoxious population." In both cases, the colonizers "paid no regard to the African's love of home or veneration for his father's grave."[28]

Pennington might have added that the Americo-Liberians, deeply influenced by the American systems of slavery and racial caste, tended to regard physical labor as a degrading fate ideally suited for the unenlightened, such as African natives and the so-called Congos who had been liberated from slave ships by the United States Navy. From the outset, Liberia was in theory a beachhead of free soil, a deadly threat to the slave markets of Africa. In practice, the settlers adapted African customs of pawning—borrowing for an indefinite period of time the services of a son, daughter, wife, or other person—to American notions of servitude. Even poor settler families could adopt a Congo as a "ward" and receive $150 dispensed for annual maintenance and rehabilitation by the United States government.

As one would expect, there are conflicting reports of wards and pawns being treated like chattel slaves and also being acculturated into families, freed, and endowed with property. It is clear that under U.S. supervision the Americo-Liberians succeeded in assimilating large numbers of African recaptives or Congos, who learned English, wore Western dress, and welcomed the opportunity to become citizens. These exiles had already been violently uprooted from family and kin; the fear of reenslavement, reinforced by memories of kidnapping or trumped-up judicial proceedings, may have contributed to their adaptability. Because the recaptives were familiar with African crops and agricultural techniques, they were more successful than the Americo-Liberians as farmers and pioneers. They also found it easier to interact with the indigenous populations. The mediating role assumed by these emancipated slaves showed the wisdom of the Liberian government in according them citizenship and rejecting petitions to deny them land and reduce them to perpetual dependency.[29]

For the most part, however, the government lacked any effective political or judicial institutions that could have protected native African laborers even if there had been a will to do so. Supplied with cheap servants, succeeding generations of Americo-Liberians sought careers in trade or politics. Because they disdained industry and technological skills, they found it increasingly necessary to raise revenue by taxing the natives or exporting native labor to such productive regions as the Transvaal, Libreville, and Fernando Po (now Bioko). Charles Spurgeon Johnson, a member of the League of Nations International Commission of Inquiry into the Existence of Slavery and Forced Labor in the Republic of Liberia, quotes the Liberian secretary of state complaining in 1930 that "our only truly exploitable commodity is labor." Before being exploited, however, the natives had to be subdued.[30]

As late as 1887, Americo-Liberian captives released by Dwallah Zeppie, a Gola leader, reported that their captor intended to drive the settlers back to the sea. Fearing that the Gola and Mandinka threatened the crucial supply of rice from interior farms, President Hiliary R. W. Johnson dispatched an expeditionary force that in 1890 finally captured Dwallah Zeppie and pacified the St. Paul River region. At this time the Liberian troops refrained from the kind of wholesale slaughter that in 1890 brought the American Indian wars to a shameful end at Wounded Knee. Yet, in the early twentieth century, when with U.S. assistance the government organized a Liberian Frontier Force to impose order in the hinterland, the troops plundered villages, raped native women, hanged local chieftains, and seized livestock and slaves.

This ruthless oppression represented something more than the greed of undisciplined soldiers. The highest government officials continued to profit from a system that subjected Liberia's indigenous majority to corrupt and inequitable tax levies and allowed the forcible recruitment of slavelike laborers. As late as 1929, Frontier Force commanders threatened to destroy villages that failed to furnish a specified number of "boys." After raiding and looting native towns, Liberian troops regularly seized and bound thousands of laborers. Some were sent to build badly planned roads or to work on the Firestone rubber plantations. The least fortunate, who often failed to return, were shipped to the Spanish island of Fernando Po. There, on the unhealthful cocoa plantations, they often worked for the black planter descendants of slaves once liberated by British cruisers.[31]

We should not lose sight of the obvious and monumental differences between African and North American colonization. The settlers of Sierra Leone and Liberia did not advance across the continent, seizing all the land and herding the native inhabitants into a few barren reservations. Africans were far less vulnerable than the Native Americans to alien diseases and cultural disintegration. In Liberia, despite a low incidence of intermarriage, racial affinity doubtless encouraged a more reciprocal acculturation and a closer sense of identity between nonelite settlers and natives. Above all, the low level of immigration limited encroachments on the stability of African societies. Between 1820 and 1867, only some nineteen thousand American blacks arrived in Liberia. For more than two decades, one-fifth of the immigrants died during their first year in Africa. By 1843, largely as a result of malaria and other infectious diseases, 4,571 immigrants had left a surviving Americo-Liberian population of only 2,388.[32]

Considering the imperialistic control exercised by this minuscule group, which by 1880 claimed sovereignty over six hundred miles of the African coast and over territory extending inland as far as the Niger River, one wonders what might have occurred if the settlers' appalling mortality had been quickly overcome. What if white colonizationists had succeeded in their goal of transporting a million or more African Americans to a Greater Liberia, or had even matched the British government's efforts in assisting the immigration between 1820 and 1850 of over 200,000 Europeans to Australia? It is clear that the objectives of the Liberian government were continually thwarted by the nation's failure to attract a significant number of immigrants, particularly experienced farmers and skilled artisans, teachers, sanitarians, and engineers. But one can only speculate about the effects of massive immigration in a country of limited resources and even more limited technology, a country whose expansion would inevitably collide in the late nineteenth century with the European Scramble for Africa.[33]

This emphasis on underdevelopment and black imperialism, however justified by the continuing disfranchisement and exploitation of the vast majority of Liberia's population, obscures the symbolic importance of the settlers' achievement. The Americo-Liberians, one must remember, were all former slaves or the descendants of slaves. Even the elite Johnsons, Robertses, Shermans, and Tubmans belonged to the most degraded and persecuted caste in North America, a caste that increasing numbers of whites thought incapable of self-government or of anything but the most menial labor. From the very outset, Liberia's racial and ideological mission was defined by Western criteria of historical progress. It is clearly unrealistic to judge the Americo-Liberians' treatment of aborigines by higher standards than those applied to white colonists from the sixteenth to the twentieth century.[34] And it was the white demand for cocoa, rubber, coffee, gold, and other products that Liberia's coerced labor was intended to serve.

Despite a shortage of capital, labor, and political experience, the Americo-Liberians established a constitutional republic in 1847 and maintained relative political stability for more than a century. Against overwhelming odds, they also preserved their national independence during a prolonged period when Britain and France were gnawing at their borders and when massive foreign debt and economic dependency increased the dangers of annexation. Competing in a capitalist world market with the most exploited, colonialized regions of the tropics, Liberia developed small but successful rice, sugar, and coffee plantations. Unfortunately, the perils of this route became evident in the late nineteenth century, when the global agricultural depression gave a decisive advantage to Cuba, Brazil, and other countries that profited from superior infrastructures and from more plentiful or more easily regimented labor.[35]

If Liberia's modest achievements failed to abate the rising intensity of racism in the Euro-American world, the very survival of the nation made an important though belated contribution to black pride and hope. The relationship between Liberia and black nationalism was always complicated by the American free black community's vehement hostility to the American Colonization Society. Early Liberian settlers such as Daniel Coker, Lott Cary, and John Russwurm, who might have been remembered as Pan-African pioneers, have traditionally been depicted as misguided accomplices in a racist conspiracy. Lewis Woodson, James M. Whitfield, and other early contributors to a black nationalist perspective advocated separate black settlements within the United States as a way of breaking the bonds of racial dependency while avoiding the taint of African colonization. After the financially troubled ACS forced Liberia to become independent in 1847, Martin Delany was prepared to admit that the nation had "thwarted the design of the original schemers, its slaveholding founders." At the same time, he excoriated President Roberts for having forfeited all the honor he had won on a diplomatic mission to Europe by giving an official report, "like a slave, 'cap in hand,' " to Anson G. Phelps, a wealthy American merchant and colonizationist.[36]

As we shall see in later chapters, this central concern with racial self-respect and the psychological hazards of dependency on whites was clearly a prerequisite for black liberation. But it also became a political weapon, used for various motives, that stimulated suspicion and bitter discord among black leaders. The fear of becoming an unwitting agent of white racism tended to dim the points upon which various factions of black abolitionists agreed. Frederick Douglass epitomized the first of these basic beliefs in 1854, when, after deploring the degraded and servile occupations of most free blacks, he asserted that "the free colored man's elevation is essential to the slave colored man's emancipation." If this principle extended to the condition of free blacks wherever they resided, especially where they had escaped the effects of discriminatory laws, Liberia could hardly be ignored.[37]

A second point of agreement by the 1850s was that conditions and prospects for free blacks in the United States were worsening, not improving. The Fugitive Slave Law brought despair and physical insecurity not only to such prominent fugitives and foreign lecturers as Garnet, Pennington, William Wells Brown, Samuel Ringgold Ward, and William and Ellen Craft, but to the most obscure American free blacks, who were now vulnerable to seizure and enslavement without due process of law. The Dred Scott decision confirmed the fact that Southern slavery, far from being weakened by the "elevation" of free blacks, was eroding that population's last remnants of civil rights. If virtually all black spokesmen still clung to the hope of regenerating America's corrupted institutions, most of them showed a growing interest in external influence and alternatives to domestic political action: in the British free produce movement, which might weaken or destroy the market that poisoned the American economy; in related proposals for free black agricultural settlements in the Caribbean, South America, or Africa, which would serve as models of African American self-determination; and in efforts to restore Africa's ancient leadership and promise by equipping its natives with the techniques and knowledge of Christian civilization. Liberia was intimately connected with all these aspirations. Indeed, President Roberts warmly encouraged plans for free-labor cotton and welcomed, along with Christian missionaries, agents sent by English textile firms.[38]

As early as January 1849, Henry Highland Garnet broke ranks with Frederick Douglass and black abolitionist tradition on the issue of emigration. Clearly influenced by the attacks of white land reformers on monopoly and aristocratic privilege in the eastern states, Garnet advocated black emigration to the West and Southwest as a "source of wealth, prosperity, and independence." After cleverly associating aid to fugitive slaves with other forms of uplift and geographic mobility, he informed Douglass

that my mind, of late, has greatly changed in regard to the American Colonization scheme. So far as it benefits the land of my fathers,

I bid it God speed; but so far as it denies the possibility of our elevation here, I oppose it. I would rather see a man free in Liberia, than
a slave in the United States.[39]

Garnet still felt it necessary to denounce the forcible expatriation
of blacks from the United States, although by the mid-1840s, ACS
officials were insisting that emigration to Liberia would have to be
selective as well as voluntary and that the Society wanted to help
small numbers of aspiring blacks to "rise above their present level,"
to Christianize Africa, and to abolish the slave trade at its source.
Garnet applauded these objectives, when detached as far as possible from the ACS, and predicted that the new Liberian Republic
would become the "Empire State of Africa."[40] In England he continued to expose the hypocrisy of the Clays and Websters, "who made
the laws and would then transport the black man, that he might be
freed from their operation!" But Garnet also assured a large meeting of the British and Foreign Anti-Slavery Society that Americans
"were a people who did things rapidly and earnestly . . . in right and
in wrong." There was still hope, therefore, that America would fulfill its Revolutionary promise and abolish slavery "almost instanta-
neously" if British public opinion constantly spoke out, reminding
"the Americans of that sacred declaration, whereon their constitution
as a nation was based, that declaration which declared that all men
are equal." Garnet quickly added that such arguments on consistency
must be reinforced by economic pressure, especially capital investment in free-grown cotton in Africa and other regions.[41] This goal of
undermining the Southern slave economy became a centerpiece of
Garnet's later African Civilization Society and similar black emigration projects.

The black emigrationists made every effort to differentiate their
aims and motives from those of white colonizationists. Although
Alexander Crummell became an ardent Liberian nationalist, Delany,
Garnet, Holly, and most other emigrationists looked for separate and
more healthful asylums in Central America, Haiti, or the Niger Valley. With some justice they angrily denied the charge made by Frederick Douglass and other antiemigrationists that their projects were
no more than fronts for the despised ACS. They could not conceal,
however, the assumptions they shared with the more philanthropic
white colonizationists nor their financial dependence on such figures

as Benjamin Coates, a Quaker merchant and longtime supporter of the ACS. Despite their continuing suspicion of the ACS, black abolitionists became increasingly attuned to the symbolic meaning of Liberia.

For early black nationalists like Edward Wilmot Blyden, a young West Indian immigrant to the United States who was inspired by the Reverend John B. Pinney and by William Coppinger and other Northern white colonizationists, Liberia gave substance to a growing faith that Africa's ancient glories—the glories of Egypt, Nubia, and Carthage—could be restored. After landing on Liberian soil late in 1850, Blyden described in the official journal of the ACS "the delight with which I gazed upon the land of Tertullian, ancient father in the Christian Church; of Hannibal and Henry Diaz, renowned generals; yes, and the land of my forefathers." White colonizationists had actually helped to popularize the views of the Comte de Volney, James C. Prichard, and other European writers who had affirmed that the Egyptians and eminent North Africans of antiquity were Negroid.[42]

Alexander Crummell experienced a similar sense of exaltation in 1853 when he and his family arrived in Monrovia from England and beheld a nation governed and populated by blacks. With his friend Henry Highland Garnet, Crummell had been educated at the African Free School in New York City, at Noyes Academy in New Hampshire (where they were attacked and driven away by an armed mob), and at Oneida Institute in upstate New York; after being denied admission to the Episcopal Theological Seminary because of his race, he then studied mathematics, classics, and theology at Cambridge University. Like Blyden, he was confident that "the days of Cyprian and Augustine shall again return to Africa." As a missionary he hailed Liberia as the site of a new and more glorious civilization: "The world needs a higher type of true nationality than it now has: why should not we [Liberians] furnish it? . . . Why not make ourselves a precedent?"[43]

In 1859, even Martin Delany made his peace with Liberia, while declaiming this theme of black nationality. Having earlier shifted his sights from New World emigration to a plan for exploring and colonizing the Niger Valley, Delany compromised his principles and sought financial aid from ACS officials, some of whom were already supporting Garnet's rival African Civilization Society. Although Delany had always been one of Liberia's harshest critics, he sailed to Monrovia on a Liberian bark, accompanied by three prosperous black entrepreneurs and thirty-three emigrants selected by the ACS. During the ten weeks he spent in the Republic, before moving on to Lagos and Abeokuta, Delany admired the neat brick houses and coffee plantations, met the president, traveled with Crummell, and insisted that he had never "spoken directly 'against Liberia.' " He assured the white colonizationist John B. Pinney that he was highly pleased with the Liberians, "a noble, struggling people, who only require help from the intelligent of their race, to make them what they desire and should be." He proclaimed to enthusiastic crowds that "Your country shall be my country," and that "the desire of African nationality has brought me to these shores."[44]

Ironically, these phrases of Blyden, Crummell, and Delany almost precisely echoed the famous letter written by George Harris, the fictional runaway slave in *Uncle Tom's Cabin,* which had outraged abolitionists from the moment the novel was published in 1852. Stowe's character, it should be emphasized, had studied for four years at a French university; he and his family were light enough in complexion to pass for white, had his sympathies been inclined toward his "father's race." But, as Harris explains:

> It is with the oppressed, enslaved African race that I cast in my lot; and, if I wished anything, I would wish myself two shades darker, rather than one lighter.
>
> The desire and yearning of my soul is for an African nationality. I want a people that shall have a tangible, separate existence of its own; and where am I to look for it? . . . On the shores of Africa I see a republic,—a republic formed of picked men, who, by energy and self-educating force, have, in many cases, individually raised themselves above a condition of slavery. Having gone through a preparatory stage of feebleness, this republic has, at last, become an acknowledged nation on the face of the earth,—acknowledged by both France and England. There it is my wish to go, and find myself a people.[45]

In Harris's apotheosis of nationality, in his acknowledgment that Liberia had "subserved all sorts of purposes, by being played off, in the hands of our oppressors, against us . . . as a means of retarding our emancipation," and in his affirmation that blacks as a nation could best serve the cause of their race, Harriet Beecher Stowe conveyed to millions of readers the central concerns of black nationalists of the 1850s.

It was not in a work of fiction, for example, that Hilary Teague, the wealthy editor of the *Liberia Herald,* informed an enthusiastic gathering of Liberians that "upon you . . . depends, in a measure you can hardly conceive, the future destiny of the race. You are to give the answer whether the African race is doomed to interminable degradation . . . a libel upon the dignity of human nature; or whether they are capable to take an honourable rank amongst the great family of nations."[46] This was one "answer" to the crucial issue of black dehumanization that we examine throughout this book. Nor were such thoughts confined to a privileged elite. Grandville B. Woodson, a former slave from Mississippi who emigrated to Liberia at age sixteen, wrote in 1853 from the isolated and poverty-ridden Greenville settlement:

This is the land of our fore fathers, the land from which the children went, back to the land they are Returning. Liberia is now spreading her rich perfume roun and about the big valleys of the World and introducing and calling out to her suns and Daughters to rise and come up out of the Valley of ignorance and Heathenism.[47]

5

Colonizing Blacks, Part III: From Martin Delany to Henry Highland Garnet and Marcus Garvey

NATIONALISM

The profound sense of mission and deliverance brings us unavoidably to the relationships between nationalism, assimilation, and Westernization (or modernization, if one prefers the less troubling term). These concepts, extraordinarily slippery in any context, have been further complicated by the explosive debates and sloganeering of the past century. Revolts against political, economic, and cultural dependency have long "assimilated" and exploited the rhetoric of the West's own disenchantment with civilization and its discontents. It has long been fashionable to romanticize the authenticity, conviviality, and lack of inhibitions of premodern ways of life. But attacks on Eurocentric uplift and "civilizationism" were more appropriate for the twentieth century's arrogant beginning than for its somber end. Whatever evils Westernization may have brought the world, only the most die-hard primitivist or cynic can dismiss the benefits of abolishing slavery, improving public health, promoting economic growth, pursuing the ideals of individual equality and self-fulfillment, and cultivating a respect for cultural and religious diversity. Nevertheless, a bias against professionalism, technocracy, improvement, and moral respectability has often prevented historians from appreciating the aspirations and genuine accomplishments of Westernized black nationalists who understood the world they faced, as well as the kind of skills and knowledge needed to empower the powerless, to break through the constricting coils of dependency, including those cultivated by well-meaning whites in search of authentic emotion or an antimodernist soul.

Assimilation is often thought of in the passive sense of being absorbed: in the nineteenth century, for example, various "unified" nation-states sought to assimilate ethnic and national minorities by eroding their distinctive identities. But one can actively and selectively assimilate foreign ideas and methods, as the history of numerous peoples has shown, in order to strengthen collective identity. For most black leaders in antebellum America, the key question was whether their people could obtain the freedom and power to make significant choices—especially the choice to assimilate and syncretize whatever they needed to develop their full human potentialities. That is why there is a certain artificiality to the conventional dichotomy between assimilationists and separatists, both of whom were intent on overcoming the deeply entrenched obstacles to economic opportunity for blacks. Most advocates of racial separation wanted to gain control over the purposes and goals of assimilation.[1]

For many American liberals of our time, haunted by accounts of the origins of two world wars, horrified by outbursts of superpatriotism, terrorism, and religious fanaticism in a thermonuclear age, nationalism has long seemed as repugnant as a dangerous disease. The term is confusing because it can refer to a sense of national solidarity shared by many diverse groups within a nation-state, such as the Basques, Bretons, Flemings, Savoyards, and Alsatians of France, or the scores of ethnic and linguistic groups that make up modern India. But nationalism also applies to similar feelings confined to a specific ethnic or religious group, such as the Sikhs, Magyars, Shiites, Czechs, Catholic Irish, or modern Palestinians. Nationalism does not necessarily include the demand for a national territory—Simon Dubnow, for example, can be termed a major figure in the history of Jewish nationalism even though he envisioned cultural autonomy within existing political territories, not a separate Jewish state. What various nationalists share is a determination to resist being persecuted or made subservient as a people, a sense of loyalty to their own traditions and culture, and a commitment to some kind of collective and historical mission. The first of these concerns, while preeminent for British North American colonists in 1776 and for later subjects of the Austro-Hungarian, Turkish, and Russian empires, has become a pretext for war or oppression when nationalism has merged with the consolidation and expansion of nation-states. "The paradox of nationalism," E. J. Hobsbawm points out, "was that in forming its own nation it automatically created the counter-nationalism of those whom it now forced into the choice between assimilation and inferiority."[2] The world has repeatedly seen how the nationalism or national liberation of one group can lead to the political, social, and economic enslavement of another.

The Age of Emancipation, which witnessed the eradication of legal chattel slavery in the Western Hemisphere, was also the age when European nation-states became unified and industrialized; when militant nationalistic movements emerged, from Ireland to the Turkish empire; and when elites in parts of the future Third World first became conscious of their societies' "underdevelopment" and need for both modernization and ultimate independence. As various scholars have shown, nationalist leaders generally fabricated historical myths and traditions to encourage ideological cohesiveness and belief in some kind of manifest destiny, as white Americans termed it in the 1840s. Thus France, whose first revolution provided the model for both nationhood and world liberation, became in the words of the Saint-Simonians "the Christ of the nations." According to Giuseppe Mazzini, the torch of freedom had passed from France to Italy; according to Adam Mickiewicz, to Poland. For the radical Hegelians it was Germany's mission to redeem the world.[3] America's black nationalists were well aware of the effervescent dreams rising from Europe's "springtime of peoples" and that were personified in such touring celebrities as Louis Kossuth.

The ideal of solidarity, of subordinating individuals to the supposed interests of an ethnic group or nation, can obviously open the way to demagoguery and tyranny. A small elite, such as the one that ruled Liberia, may even arrogate to itself the right to define the interests of an entire race. This strategy has often been used to legitimate privilege and exploitation within an oppressed social class or ethnic group. The appeal for solidarity has also helped to perpetuate simplistic and monolithic stereotypes, which then become attached to anyone who belongs to the class, group, or so-called nation. These familiar dangers must be balanced, however, against other considerations. In view of the growing disparities in wealth and power in the nineteenth-century world, coupled with the racism that increasingly consigned non-western peoples to a status of permanent inferiority, one must draw a clear distinction between nationalisms mobilized for regional or global dominance and nationalisms designed to protect or restore a nucleus of human dignity.

When Henry Highland Garnet advocated selective emigration to Africa as a means of creating a "negro nationality," he was not envisioning a mass withdrawal from the United States or even asserting a claim to a particular territory. For Garnet and other black nationalists of his time, the crucial goal was to free individual blacks from the subservience, dishonor, and persecution they suffered simply by virtue of being black—of belonging, like the ancient Israelites, to an enslaved nation. In 1859 Garnet tried to clarify the goals of his African Civilization Society in a speech to a large audience in Boston. After affirming his faith that blacks could advance toward equal rights in the United States while also helping to civilize Africa and undermine the Southern slave economy, he spoke of establishing "a grand centre of negro nationality, from which shall flow the streams of commercial, intellectual, and political power which shall make colored people respected everywhere." The key issues were power and respect. In response to a hostile, anticolonizationist question about the location of such a center, Garnet did not rule out Africa but expressed a hope that it would be in the Southern United States, "especially if they reopen the African slave trade." "In Jamaica," he pointed out, "there are forty colored men to one white; Hayti is ours; Cuba will be ours soon, and we shall have every island in the Caribbean Sea."[4]

There is no need here to review the history of black nationalism except as it illuminates the antebellum controversies over colonization and slave emancipation to which we will later turn. It should be stressed that black nationalism was not necessarily linked with emigration and that American blacks who moved to Canada, Africa, or the Caribbean had not necessarily abandoned hope of winning citizenship and equality within the United States. If nationalism is equated with racial pride and the determination of a people to shape their own lives and not pass on an irreversible heritage of degradation, dependency, and humiliation, virtually all American black writers and speakers were nationalists—and here this historical term is needed to draw a contrast with the many mulattoes in West Indian societies who tried to dissociate themselves from the interests of blacks and slaves. In the United States black nationalism, in this very general sense, was closely wedded to the ideals of uplift, enterprise, and respectability preached with special fervor by the black clergy, whose profession offered one of the few channels open for black leadership. This rhetoric of moral improvement has often repelled modern antielitist intellectuals who can afford to disdain the aspirations and self-discipline of their own forebears (or own youth) and romanticize styles of life that men like Richard Allen, Garnet, Pennington, David Ruggles, Douglass, Crummell, and Delany tried to overcome. Today it is difficult to comprehend that courageous radicalism was once thoroughly compatible with calls for moral discipline as defined by a self-appointed elite. This fusion of protest and self-help was as characteristic of the emigrationists as it was of the so-called assimilationists.

Despite their hatred for the ACS, black nationalists became increasingly inclined in the 1850s to accept the argument that the elevation of blacks depended on removing at least some of their population from a malignantly prejudiced environment. By 1852, Martin Delany had concluded:

> We are politically, not of them, but aliens to the laws and political privileges of the country. . . . Our descent, by the laws of the country, stamps us with inferiority—upon us has this law [the Fugitive Slave Law] worked corruption of blood. We are in the hands of the General Government, and no State can rescue us.[5]

Like the Poles in Russia, the Hungarians in Austria, and the Jews throughout Europe, Delany wrote, America's blacks were "a nation within a nation," but far more debased in condition than any other population. White prejudice and oppression had paralyzed the "energies" of blacks; instead of thinking of business or self-improvement, young men willingly accepted servile positions that offered "the best opportunity to dress and appear well." In every town and city, men of superior talent wasted their lives as barbers and hotel waiters. William Whipper, a black lumber dealer and abolitionist, had defined the problem in a vivid phrase that Delany quoted: " 'They cannot be raised in this country, without being stoop shouldered.' " Yet the daily arrival of Irish and German immigrants showed what physiological and psychological changes a land of promise, a land of "unrestricted soil," could produce. To prove "that there are circumstances under which emigration is absolutely necessary to [a people's] political elevation," Delany cited among several examples "the Exodus of the Jews from Egypt to the land of Judea," and "the ever memorable emigration of the Puritans, in 1620, from Great Britain, the land of their birth, to the wilderness of the New World."[6]

I have suggested that the African colonization movement contributed to this nationalistic hope not only by founding Liberia and prophesying the messianic achievements of an Americo-Liberian civilization but by dwelling on the futility of individual progress for blacks living in a society dedicated to white supremacy. While conveying this message, the ACS bitterly alienated blacks by its equivocations on slave emancipation, its use of racist language and racist threats, and its refusal to respect black organizations and leadership. Perhaps because God spared the United States from devastating plagues, at least until 1861, the ACS showed little interest in finding or negotiating with a black Moses. Yet there was a complex dynamic between racist contempt and black pride, between the white desire to expel and the black quest for independence, between white nationalism and black nationalism. It was no accident that in later years Edward Blyden and Marcus Garvey both welcomed incidents of racial oppression that might enable more blacks to perceive the true character of American society and thus make them want to emigrate to Africa. Blyden, who worked closely with the ACS in the 1880s, rejoiced when the Supreme Court struck down the Civil Rights Act of 1875. As he wrote William Coppinger, the secretary-treasurer and most active leader of the ACS: "I think that God who has His hands both upon Africa and America will deepen the prejudice against the Negro in the United States. He will continue to harden Pharaoh's heart, until the oppressed shall be driven from the house of bondage, as Israel was from Egypt, to do his work in the land of his fathers." Thirty-six years later, Marcus Garvey defended Jim Crow laws, thanked white Southerners for having "lynched race pride into the Negroes," and held a two-hour conference in Atlanta with Edward Clarke, the second-ranking national leader of the Ku Klux Klan.[7]

When all these emigration or "repatriation" movements are viewed over time, from the height of a mountaintop, two features stand out: the continuity of their arguments and their repeated failures. By 1861 even Frederick Douglass, the archenemy of all previous emigration schemes, had become so discouraged by the Republican party's extreme caution regarding slavery that he agreed to join James Theodore Holly and James Redpath on an exploratory trip to Haiti, which once again was inviting black settlers from the United States.[8]

As the Civil War began, virtually every prominent black leader had shown a willingness to accept aid from the ACS or from other white colonizationists, such as the Republican politicians who advocated "homesteads" for black settlers in Central America. Yet at no time in the nineteenth or twentieth centuries did a significant proportion of the black population seem willing to leave the United States. Historians may well have underestimated the number of antebellum free blacks who would have emigrated had they been offered adequate transportation and reasonable opportunities abroad. This point applies with greater force to rural freedmen in parts of the South following the grim failures of Reconstruction.[9]

The fact remains that references to "emigration fever" or "Liberia fever" are based on the inquiries or expressed interest of a few thousand people, not tens of thousands or hundreds of thousands. However disillusioned they may have become, too many American blacks knew at least vaguely of the genuine malarial fever and yellow fever that decimated the Americo-Liberians. As Edwin S. Redkey also points out, the American blacks who emigrated to Liberia did not send money back to friends and relatives to help them reach the Promised Land, as often happened among Europeans who scouted out America; instead, the Americo-Liberians asked for money to help them return home.[10]

Redkey, Moses, and other historians have traced the threads of continuity that led from the antebellum emigrationists to the "back-to-Africa" projects of Henry McNeal Turner, a bishop in the African Methodist Episcopal Church, and on to Marcus Garvey. While the appeal of such projects is remarkable, they would have been far more successful if it had not been for the Great Northern Migration, which lasted five decades and saw some 6 million blacks flee the former Confederate states, seeking new lives in the North.[11] Bearing in mind the earlier doctrinaire hostility to the ACS, one is first struck by the widespread acceptance of the ACS coupled with the growing importance of black initiatives. It was the Liberian missionary Alexander Crummell who first converted Turner, a South Carolinian, to the idea of African repatriation. After the collapse of Reconstruction, when Southern freedmen were deprived of the hope of land, political power, or economic improvement, Turner revived the old arguments of the ACS, invoking the example of the Plymouth Pilgrims, declaiming on the immutability of white prejudice, and finding the hand of God in the American blacks' mission to redeem their African fatherland—following their providential enslavement, emancipation, and gradual absorption of Christianity and civilization. The enfeebled ACS, now happy to make use of eloquent black nationalists, elected Turner an honorary lifetime vice-president and in 1889 invited Edward Blyden to return from Liberia and address blacks throughout the South.[12]

No doubt the abolition of slavery helped to make the ACS more palatable for black leaders who had long insisted that the organization was part of a proslavery conspiracy. From this standpoint, it is noteworthy that white interest in black colonization declined precipitously in the decades following the Civil War despite the persistence of racism and a marked increase in lynching and other kinds of antiblack violence. Racial prejudice, in other words, was not sufficient to overcome an understood need for cheap black labor and resistance to the expense of subsidizing massive emigration. Weakened by falling revenues, the ACS was thus unable to meet the requests for aid from former enemies like Martin Delany, to say nothing of thousands of Southern sharecroppers and farmworkers. While keeping in close touch with the ACS, Delany and Turner both supported independent black ventures, such as the Liberian Exodus Joint Steamship Company, which in 1878 sent a bark jammed with more than two hundred emigrants on a disastrous voyage from Charleston to Monrovia. After sending more than two thousand blacks to Liberia in the four years following the Civil War, the ACS recorded declining receipts and a mere trickle of colonists during the next three decades; emigration projects were increasingly taken up by poorly funded and sometimes fraudulent black organizations.[13]

The number of blacks who sailed to Liberia and other African destinations is not nearly so significant as the way emigration movements continued to nourish the desire for black economic and political self-determination. When Bishop Turner visited Liberia in 1891, at the beginning of a decade of persecution and catastrophic defeats for American blacks, he wrote that "one thing the black man has here, and that is manhood, freedom and the fullest liberty; he feels like a lord and walks the same way."[14] This "one thing" had been the objective of the early black ship captain, Paul Cuffe, who had transported the first American blacks to Sierra Leone; it had been the reward promised by the ACS; the goal sought by a long succession of male and female black nationalists who vacillated over the course of a century, in response to changing conditions, on the possibility of achieving genuine freedom within a white society.[15] Finally, in the 1920s, it was this vision that ignited the first mass movement in African American history.

We may pass over the politics and internal contradictions of the Garvey movement, limiting our attention to the light it casts, like the final act in a play, on the preceding century's colonization debates. In 1834, abolitionists of both races would have been dumbfounded to know that in 1924 America's most charismatic black leader, speaking in New York's Liberty Hall, would talk of fulfilling the vision of the American Colonization Society! As he prepared to send off to Liberia an advance party of "civil and mechanical engineers" to set up camps for some twenty to thirty thousand families who were supposed to arrive in the fall, Garvey, who had been deeply influenced by Edward Blyden, eulogized Liberia's founders and rulers: "They have been able," he said, "to arouse the sleeping consciousness of the 400 million Negroes of the world to go to the rescue, to help build Liberia and make her one of the greatest nations of the world. And we are going to do it." In a newspaper advertisement appealing for funds to

DEVELOP COLONIES IN LIBERIA AS PEACEFUL HOMES FOR
NEGROES—SIMILAR TO HOMELAND IN PALESTINE FOR JEWS,

Garvey tacitly repudiated the long struggle of American abolitionists to discredit the ACS, applauding what he called "the white friends of the Negro in America" who "over a hundred years ago" had helped establish "the only independent nation on the West Coast of Africa." The ACS, according to Garvey, had anticipated the glorious hour when American blacks would liberate and repossess the African continent.[16]

Garvey had founded the Universal Negro Improvement Association in Jamaica, in 1914, after working in Costa Rica as a timekeeper on a United Fruit Company plantation, taking courses at Birkbeck

College in London, and doing miscellaneous jobs in the office of Dusé Mohamed Ali's *African Times* and *Orient Review.* Impressed by Booker T. Washington's achievements at Tuskegee Institute, Garvey was primarily concerned with racial uplift and self-improvement, the key issues we will focus on in chapter 8. The entire world, he pointed out, looked down upon blacks as inferior and degraded beings, as a people devoid of national, commercial, or social status. In 1914 Garvey called on the sons and daughters of Africa to defy

> the scornful designation of "nigger" uttered even by yourselves, and be a Negro in the light of the Pharaohs of Egypt . . . Hannibals of Carthage, L'O[u]ve[r]tures and Dessalines of Hayti, Blydens, Barclays and Johnsons of Liberia, Lewises of Sierra Leone, and Douglas's [*sic*] and DuBois's of America, who have made, and are making history for the race, though depreciated and in many cases unwritten.

Despite this litany of prominent leaders, Garvey castigated the "representative and educated negroes" who set themselves apart and who thought it degrading and ignominious to identify themselves with the masses of the people who "are still ignorant and backward; but who are crying out for true and conscientious leadership, so that they might advance into a higher state of enlightenment whence they could claim the appreciation and honest comradeship of the more advanced races who are to-day ignoring us simply because we are so lethargic and selfish."[17]

After attacking the privileged blacks for shirking their responsibility, Garvey pointedly observed that this same elite, for all their pretensions, "are snubbed and laughed at just the same as the most menial of the race, and only because they are Negroes."[18] This need for racial solidarity was the very heart of Garvey's early message, although his proposed solutions soon changed, especially after his move to Harlem in 1916. Like earlier black nationalists—and, for that matter, like white colonizationists—he accepted a theory of historical decline. In antiquity, black Africans had created a "glorious civilization" and had dispensed it to the world. White men, including the Israelites, had once been the servants and subjects of black Egyptians. But in what Garvey termed the "process of time," the African "reverted into savagery," and "subsequently became a slave even to those whom he once enslaved."[19] This set of beliefs had an obvious bearing on Garvey's views of Liberia and the mission to civilize Africa. It also helps to explain his sense of affinity and competition with Jews.

We have already taken some note of the extraordinary significance American slaves and free blacks found in the biblical Exodus narrative, which was dramatized in sermons and such spirituals as "Go Down Moses," and even read aloud by slave mothers to impressionable children like Booker T. Washington.[20] From the pre–Civil War decades to the 1890s, when few American blacks had ever seen a Jew, such diverse figures as Douglass, Delany, Washington, and Blyden not only drew frequent parallels between the persecution of modern Jews and blacks but urged their fellow blacks to emulate the Jews' unity, pride, and quest for knowledge and achievement. In 1899 Booker T. Washington summarized the message repeated for many decades by the black elite: "Unless the Negro learns more and more to imitate the Jew in these matters, to have faith in himself, he cannot expect to have any high degree of success."[21]

From the National Negro Convention at Rochester in 1853 to the horror Booker T. Washington expressed over Russia's pogroms and his affirmation in 1904 that "my heart goes out to our Hebrew fellow-sufferers across the sea," blacks often specified Jews as the single group that had suffered more oppression historically than they had. For a time this example was immensely reassuring, since it proved that prejudice could be conquered. As Douglass put it in 1863, "The Jews were treated with every species of indignity, and not allowed to learn trades, nor to live in the same part of the city with other people. Now kings cannot go to war without the consent of a Jew. The Jew has come up, and the negro will come up by and by." A generation later a black Cleveland lawyer, John P. Green, compared the bloodstained path Jews had traversed since the Roman destruction of Jerusalem with their present attainments in science, art, literature, and finance, concluding, "we may well cheer up and persevere along the same lines until victory crowns our efforts."[22]

While blacks and Jews naturally absorbed some of the negative stereotypes that prevailed in the surrounding culture, it would be a serious mistake to project later conflicts backward into the early twentieth century. As hundreds of thousands of Jewish immigrants arrived in Northern cities that were already beginning to attract a massive black migration from the South, the Yiddish press devoted an extraordinary amount of space to black cultural achievements, glowing biographies of black leaders, attacks on Jim Crow laws and racial discrimination, denunciations of lynching and race riots, and parallels between the Jewish and black experience. Although Yiddish and English-language Jewish newspapers represented a wide spectrum of religious and political views, they took a common stand against whites (including Jews) who victimized blacks, and devoted far more space to blacks than to the Irish, Italians, Greeks, Germans, or Chinese. Where earlier immigrant groups had often established their "Americanism" by joining in the common white ridicule of blacks, Jews tended to affirm their special American identity by invoking the ideals of Lincoln and the Founding Fathers and by launching a united campaign against racism and anti-Semitism.[23]

Most surprising, perhaps, was the Jewish connection with black nationalism as well as with "assimilationist" institutions. Much has been written about the enormous philanthropic support that Jews gave to the National Urban League, the NAACP, and Tuskegee Institute, to say nothing of innumerable black schools, artists, musicians, writers, and future leaders of the "Talented Tenth." Less well known is the fact that Edward Blyden had concluded by the end of the nineteenth century that blacks and Jews, allied by divine guidance and "a history almost identical of sorrow and oppression," were destined to become the spiritual leaders of the world.[24]

Emphasizing the African origins of Moses and much of Judaism, Blyden hailed "that marvellous [*sic*] movement called Zionism," which so closely resembled the mission of former black slaves to return to their African homeland. Significantly, Theodore Herzl, the "father" of modern Zionism, affirmed in a utopian novel of 1902 that only a Jew could understand what blacks had endured or wish, having "lived to see the restoration of the Jews," "to pave the way for the restoration of the Negroes." For his part, Blyden made a statement that seems astoundingly naive for a man who had learned Arabic and traveled to Egypt, Syria, and Jerusalem:

There is hardly a man in the civilized world—Christian, Mohammedan, or Jew—who does not recognize the claim and right of the Jews to the Holy Land; and there are few who, if the conditions were favourable, would not be glad to see them return in a body and take their place in the land of their fathers as a great—a leading—secular power.[25]

Marcus Garvey and his followers found somewhat similar inspiration in both the biblical and Zionist sense of mission, though by Garvey's time the relations between Jews and blacks were becoming more strained and complex.[26] For Henrietta Vinton Davis, International Organizer of the UNIA, Garvey was "the reincarnation of King Solomon." More frequently he was perceived as the black Moses who faced even more stupendous obstacles than a hardhearted Pharaoh. Garvey himself noted that "we have been as much enslaved mentally, spiritually and physically as any other race and a fair comparison is the race that Moses led out of Egyptian bondage."[27] In 1924, Dr. George Alexander McGuire recalled the "solemn awe" that swept the throngs at New York's Liberty Hall, four years earlier, when the UNIA ratified its Declaration of Rights: "It was as though we were standing at the foot of Sinai when the Decalogue was pronounced."[28] Garvey repeatedly compared his tribulations to those of Moses, who endured similar recalcitrance, slander, and backsliding; it was reassuring, at least, to see the intrinsic parallels between the proposed liberation of Africa and the Israelites' recovery of their Promised Land.

As Garvey became more radical in his demands for black power, he was no less attuned to the Zionist and Irish struggles for national independence. In 1919, he admonished blacks to be as determined to reclaim Africa and found a government there as modern Jews had been to recover Palestine. The alternative—to "live everlastingly under the domination of a white man . . . [to] bequeath to my children white overlordship"—would be a fate worse than death. UNIA speakers referred frequently to the sufferings of Jews who had been carried away into captivity, who had been deprived in their Diaspora of statehood and respect, and who had finally learned that freedom was inseparable from power. For hundreds of years, Garvey pointed out, blacks had cried out for liberty, justice, and equal opportunities. Their appeals had been no more successful than those of the Jews. Now, at last, the Negro "refuses to admit that he is a cringing sycophant." The time had arrived for blacks to found their own factories, banks, and steamship lines that would link together the colored peoples of the world.

These objectives were related to Garvey's remarkable interpretation of Jewish achievements, an interpretation that combined anti-Semitic mythology with more than a touch of admiration. In a speech in 1921 Garvey informed his listeners that for centuries Jews had been a despised race in Europe, "buffeted worse than the Southern Negro today." Even in the United States "it was a disgrace to be a Jew." "What did the Jews do?" Garvey asked. They were too few in number to carry out any physical conquest. Therefore, they had devised a master plan for the financial conquest of the world. Jewish financiers had brought on the First World War, presumably as a profit-making venture, and had then abruptly stopped the war when they were promised the possession of Palestine. In Russia, where pogroms had slaughtered millions of Jews, Trotsky and the financiers had engineered a revolution that had destroyed the Czar and put a Jew in command. "The Jew has gone back to Palestine," Garvey concluded, "and the Jew it is that has the world in the palm of his hand." While much of this sounded like Henry Ford and other contemporary anti-Semites, Garvey conveyed no sense of outrage. On the contrary, he was exhorting his followers to learn from the Jewish example. Given their overwhelming numbers, blacks did not need to think in terms of financial conquest. They already had the power needed for the physical conquest of Africa. And since Jews in Palestine had already enhanced the prestige and opportunities for Jews in England, one could be assured that self-governing blacks in Africa would help to liberate blacks in all parts of the world.[29]

This particular speech omits the sense of prophetic fulfillment that gave Garveyism much of its appeal. As Dr. McGuire put it, "After ages of almost forlorn hope the Jews are rejoicing in the triumphs of Zionism and the repossession of the land of their forefathers. Their fullness of time has come. So will ours, for, in the Eternal Volume of Truth it is predicted that 'Princes shall come out of Egypt.' "[30] McGuire reported that when Garvey was convicted of mail fraud, he delivered the simple, reverberating sentence: "Gentlemen of the jury, this is a spiritual movement." McGuire added, "the Jews made of Zionism a spiritual movement and today the goal is achieved, the fact accomplished. Africanism must become a universal spiritual movement among Negroes." In actuality, when Garvey heard the jury's verdict, he cursed "the Jews" and shouted anti-Semitic remarks that may have affected the sentence delivered by Judge Julian W. Mack, a

Jew who had been praised by a black journalist and friend of Garvey's as a model of understanding and fairness.[31]

By any material measurement, Garveyism was an even more disastrous failure than the earlier colonization movement. The Black Star Line and Negro Factories Corporation quickly sank in a sea of incompetence and corruption. Although Garvey attracted thousands of West Indian immigrants, who were derisively called "the black Jews of Harlem" because of their clannishness, enterprise, and business skills, many American blacks were repelled by his megalomania, obsession with racial purity, and contempt for African American culture. Far from unifying the American black community, his movement spawned dissent and became an easy target for infiltration by the federal government's Bureau of Investigation. The Liberian elite, though initially interested in attracting productive settlements in the Cape Palmas region, soon became alarmed by the prospect of losing its own monopoly of power and acquiring militants bent on expelling Britain, France, Belgium, and other colonial nations from Africa. Victimized and betrayed by some of his followers, Garvey was finally imprisoned, pardoned, and deported to Jamaica. But regardless of the size of his following and the practicability of his program, which are still in dispute, Garvey became a hero and a powerful symbol in Africa, the Caribbean, and the United States.[32]

Without considering tributes by such figures as Kwame Nkrumah, Jomo Kenyatta, Norman Manley, Elijah Mohammed, and Malcolm X, it is sufficient to turn to a less likely leader. In 1965, Martin Luther King Jr. laid a wreath at Garvey's shrine in Kingston, Jamaica. Before an audience of some two thousand, King summed up Garvey's meaning for nonseparatist blacks: "Garvey was the first man of color in the history of the United States to lead and develop a mass movement. He was the first man on a mass scale and level to give millions of Negroes a sense of dignity and destiny and make the Negro feel he was somebody."[33] This, we should recall, was the professed goal of Liberia's founders—although Martin Luther King and the civil rights movement, to say nothing of Malcolm X and the Black Power movement, were precisely what the ACS wanted to prevent. In pre–Civil War America, no one could foresee the circuitous route by which the example of Liberia would help to nourish black nationalism, which would nourish, in its turn, the domestic demand for equal civil rights.

How do these reflections affect our evaluation of the colonization movement? No doubt early colonizationists of both races would feel vindicated if we allowed them a *selective* glimpse of the past century and a half: a panorama that included the fratricidal Civil War, in which President Lincoln long supported various colonizationist plans and in which some 200,000 black soldiers and sailors helped to ensure a Union victory;[34] the crushed hopes of Reconstruction; the suffering inflicted by the Ku Klux Klan and Jim Crow; the lynching between 1889 and 1946 of nearly four thousand blacks; the growth of festering urban ghettos; the persistence of white racism and black deprivation; the report that in 1980, a half century after the predicted termination of the most gradual emigration plans, blacks constituted 12 percent of the nation's population but 45 percent of the inmates of state and federal prisons; that in family income blacks ranked thirteenth out of fourteen American ethnic groups, earning on average 60 percent of the income of whites, 50 percent of the income of Asian-Indians, and only 46 percent of the income of Japanese-Americans; but that in 2012 Americans would reelect a black president.[35]

With respect to the intractability of prejudice and racial conflict, the colonizationists were clearly better prognosticators than the abolitionists. Edward Blyden and Marcus Garvey acknowledged this point. The glaring defect in the colonizationist ideology was the refusal to recognize the vital contributions that blacks had made and would continue to make to American civilization.[36] Even the best-intentioned white reformers and missionaries remained obstinately blind to the fact that from the beginnings of American history, the lives of blacks and whites had been intertwined on the most complex social, cultural, economic, and psychological levels.[37] America, that mythic amalgam of hope, abstract principles, and mission, was as much black as white.

This reasoning brings us at last to the true and insidious meaning of the colonization movement, which was never dependent on the number of blacks shipped off to Liberia. It was sufficient to use philanthropic language to expatriate the entire race, to wall blacks off as an extraneous and dangerous presence that someday, somehow would disappear and no longer affront white vision. Psychologically and ritualistically, the ACS "deported" blacks while affirming their capacity to flourish in a distant, tropical clime. This strategy, which simply assumed new forms in the twentieth century, is deceptive precisely because it is seldom cynical and has often been combined with genuine goodwill.

For example, in his annual message to Congress in 1862, Lincoln described his unsuccessful efforts to find sites for voluntary black colonization in which emigrants would be protected "in all the rights of freemen" and ensured conditions "which shall be equal, just, and humane." Liberia and Haiti, Lincoln observed, are "the only countries to which colonists of African descent from here, could go with certainty of being received and adopted as citizens." Unfortunately, the president added, few of the blacks contemplating emigration were willing to go to either Liberia or Haiti. For Lincoln, a man of goodwill who thought he knew the blacks' best interest, the problem seemed insoluble. While historians debate the timing of Lincoln's abandonment of colonization, Eric Foner convincingly argues that it occurred by mid-1864, well after his Emancipation Proclamation.[38]

As the war progressed, Lincoln ultimately abandoned colonization and saw the necessity of combining racial coexistence with equal protection of the law. Two months before Lincoln was killed, William Henry Channing, the abolitionist chaplain of the House of Representatives, invited Henry Highland Garnet to deliver a sermon to Congress commemorating the recent congressional passage of the Thirteenth Amendment, which Lincoln had strongly supported. Garnet, who had been born a slave and had in 1843 exhorted America's slaves to rebel, who had become an expatriate in Jamaica and had then become an ardent supporter of the Union cause, was the first black to address Congress.[39]

Taking as his text the twenty-third verse of St. Matthew, Garnet first denounced the modern scribes and Pharisees who ruled the state. Professing to believe in principles of righteousness passed down from Moses, Socrates, Plato, the early church fathers, the Magna Carta, and the Declaration of Independence, America's leaders had continued to defend or tolerate an institution that embodied the "concentrated essence of all conceivable wickedness," "snatching man from the high place to which he was lifted by the hand of God, and dragging him down to the level of the brute creation, where he is made to be the companion of the horse and the fellow of the ox." If slavery had finally been destroyed merely from necessity, in the course of war, as Garnet acknowledged, he exhorted Congress to enfranchise every class "at the dictation of justice. Then we shall have a Constitution that shall be reverenced by all."[40]

What is most striking, in view of the themes we have pursued, is the way Garnet merged freedmen's rights with a powerful transfiguration of the Exodus trope. The amendment abolishing slavery, he noted, could not escape divine notice:

> The nation has begun its exodus from worse than Egyptian bondage; and I beseech you that you say to the people, "that they go forward." With the assurance of God's favor in all things done in obedience to his righteous will, and guided by day and by night by the pillars of cloud and fire, let us not pause until we have reached the other and safe side of the stormy and crimson sea. Let freemen and patriots mete out complete and equal justice to all men, and thus prove to mankind the superiority of our Democratic, Republican Government.
>
> Favored men, and honored of God as his instruments, speedily finish the work which he has given you to do. Emancipate, Enfranchise, Educate, and give the blessings of the gospel to every American citizen.[41]

As Garnet envisioned a modern day of jubilee, quoting from a poem that called for "our" Aaron, Miriam, and Joshua, it was not only the slaves or the African Americans who stood in need of deliverance from Egyptian bondage. In the United States whites themselves were yoked to the blacks they had enslaved. The nation as a whole, modeled on ancient dreams of deliverance and fulfillment, could march no further forward than all the victims of its self-betrayal.

6

———❖———

Colonizationist Ideology:
Leonard Bacon and
"Irremediable Degradation"

Colonizationists and abolitionists agreed that the insuppressible problem originated with the African slave trade, which Congress had outlawed in 1807. Since the federal government had been able to achieve this significant reform, colonizationists reasoned that national support could be mobilized to undo the evil consequences of the slave trade by instituting a kind of counter slave trade that would return the victims and their descendants to their native land. By reversing an unfortunate stream of history, Americans could bypass a question some abolitionists had posed since the eighteenth century: was not every buyer and keeper of slaves, as Theodore Dwight Weld maintained, a "joint partner in the original sin" of man stealing, making it "the business of every moment to perpetrate it afresh, however he may lull his conscience by the vain plea of expediency or necessity?"[1] For colonizationists, this rhetoric of moral condemnation (when not confined to the Atlantic slave trade) could only be counterproductive: it would obviously alienate and embitter Southerners as well as many Northerners and thus prevent any effective action from being taken.

The fear that disputes over slavery would lead to disunion and civil war was greatly aggravated by the congressional crisis of 1819–21

over admitting Missouri as a slave state. But in 1823 the British abolitionist movement, well publicized in America and long dedicated to
eradicating all branches of the African slave trade, launched a parliamentary campaign for the amelioration and gradual abolition of
slavery in the British colonies. The flood of literature generated by
this struggle suggested that the monarchical mother country, which
Americans had blamed since the 1760s for imposing on them the
unwanted curse of slavery, was at last putting the young republic to
shame. Like the British abolitionists, the American colonizationists
were confident that a movement led by distinguished political figures,
appealing to the highest moral concerns of the nation but also attuned
to the need for compromise and skilled at merging diverse interests
in a common cause, could eventually find a solution for a seemingly
insoluble problem.

In the United States, however, the problem of slavery—the growing conflict between a modern ideology of individual freedom and
a system of exploitative labor that served the interests of millions
of landholders, producers, and especially consumers—had become
fatally intertwined with the problem of race. Since the West Indian
slaves lived thousands of miles from Britain, British abolitionists were
relatively free from the issue of racial "amalgamation." But, as we
will see later, antiblack racism increased in America as the emergence
of abolitionism raised the image of hundreds of thousands or even
millions of blacks bursting free from the chains of slavery and assimilating in some way with white society. Ironically, and not acciden-
tally, the focus on race as the major obstacle to emancipation diverted
attention from the economy's parasitic dependence on an immensely
profitable labor system.

According to the growing consensus, it was the African Americans' alleged incapacity for freedom and responsible citizenship, not
their indispensable role in the economy as productive field hands, that
stood as the major roadblock to slave emancipation. The way problems are conceived and structured reveals much about unexamined
assumptions and the issues, such as the economic benefits American
whites received from black slave labor, that cannot be faced. While
the colonization movement tried to build a national following by
appealing to diverse sectional interests, its approach to the problem
of race rested on two widely shared but highly questionable assumptions: first, that the nation would become more prosperous and secure

if free white workers replaced black slaves; second, that even though America's emancipated blacks were mired in poverty and deprived of education and elemental civil rights, they were capable of creating a civilized, prosperous, and respected society in Africa. Though it is important to keep these assumptions in mind, we should also move beyond contemptuous exclamations over the colonizationists' "inconsistencies." If we wish to know why the movement attracted so many intelligent and sensitive white Americans who detested slavery and who genuinely wanted to improve the condition of African Americans, we must look more closely at their understanding of social evil and the human ability to overcome evil. We can gain some insight into these matters and into the connections that well-intentioned colonizationists drew between slavery and race by examining in some detail Leonard Bacon's 1823 "Report on Colonization," which helped to marshal the antislavery sentiment of New England Congregationalists behind the national movement. The space I devote to Bacon does not mean that I consider him a more important figure than such supporters of colonization as Henry Clay or Abraham Lincoln. Rather, I think that Bacon will help illuminate a much-neglected state of mind held by a significant number of white Northerners, as well as crucial connections between slavery and historical conceptions of original sin that I have discussed in earlier books.

The son of a Connecticut missionary and a graduate of Yale College and Andover Theological Seminary, Bacon became at age twenty-three the minister at New Haven's Center Church, whose congregation included such notable figures as Eli Whitney, Noah Webster, and Senator James Hillhouse, as well as many members of the Yale faculty. In the 1840s, after Bacon had become nationally prominent as a clerical leader, critic of slavery, and advocate of African American education and uplift, he recalled that in 1823 he had strongly endorsed the views of the British abolitionists and had learned much from their reports and pamphlets. In his own influential "Report" of 1823, written when he was still a student at Andover on behalf of a committee appointed by the Society of Inquiry Respecting Missions, he clearly identified himself with the cause of Wilberforce and Clarkson, whose "unwearied labors" and "cry against the wrongs of Africa" had led not only to the abolition of the slave trade by "every Christian power in both continents" but to "a total revolution in public sentiment" regarding "the most high-handed outrage that ever was practiced by fraud and power against simplicity and weakness."[2]

In 1823, Bacon called on American philanthropists to "summon up their energies to a like effort," and predicted that "the same spirit which answered to the plea of Wilberforce" would enable benevolent Americans to arouse the nation, alleviate great evils, and delay "if not utterly prevent" some ominous "final catastrophe" related to "the evils attendant on the circumstances of our black population." This vague and awkward phrasing reveals Bacon's uncertainty over the precise nature of "the evils" and the people responsible for them, as well as the tension he felt as he struggled to find a formula that would "excite" public opinion and lead to effective reform without evoking a "feverish, half-delirious excitement like that produced by the agitation of the Missouri question."[3] Aside from the aftershocks left by the Missouri confrontation, Bacon was proposing active clerical involvement in a social and political movement at a transitional moment in the history of the so-called benevolent empire of missionary and reform societies. The official Congregationalist establishment, challenged and weakened by Unitarians in Massachusetts, had been unseated in Connecticut in 1818 by a coalition of religious and political dissidents. A vast network of Congregationalist-Presbyterian moral societies, long committed to using coercive methods in their campaigns against Sabbath-breaking, drunkenness, and sexual immorality, had also collapsed.[4] But as young ministers like Bacon came to terms with religious toleration and the power of public opinion, they could draw comfort from the growing success of religious revivals and the apparent conquest of atheistic "infidelity"; from the public enthusiasm for missionary enterprises and for such national institutions as the American Bible Society; and from theological innovations that made increasing room for individual initiative even within the bleak cellblock of Calvinism.[5]

For all his circumlocutions, Bacon depicts black slavery in America as the prime evil, the nation's fatal defect, the cause from which racial degradation "is only a single necessary consequence." To understand Bacon's approach to race, we must first consider the particular evils he finds in American slavery and the connection between such evils and the doctrine of sin. According to Bacon, Andover's ministers and missionaries needed to convince the public that slavery in America was far more iniquitous than the slavery of antiquity or of modern

Asia and Africa. In no pagan, Islamic, or Christian country, with the single exception of the West Indies, was slavery "so terrible in its character, so pernicious in its tendency, so remediless in its anticipated results, as the slavery which exists in these United States." Bacon hastens to explain that the evil he has in mind had nothing to do with physical well-being or even with floggings and bodily suffering. For the most part, he is willing to concede, the material standard of living of American slaves—their "mere animal existence"—presented no grounds for complaint. Allowing for some exceptions, "the condition of a slave, in most parts of the United States, is generally as much superior to that of a slave in the West Indies, as the condition of an American farmer is to that of an Irish peasant."[6]

One explanation for the pernicious and ominous character of slavery in the United States, according to Bacon, lay in the blatant contradiction between human bondage and "the primary principles of our republican government." Although Bacon was hardly a moral relativist, he concludes that slavery was perfectly consistent with the tyrannical systems of government in the Old World and even with the more democratic principles of ancient Greece and Rome. If slavery was a shocking anachronism in the United States, as Bacon indicates, it had become a political evil only in modern times. A similar point extends to stages of economic development. Ignoring the economic benefits of slave labor to the nation as a whole, Bacon likens slaves to "the degraded serfs of a Polish aristocracy" and suggests that Virginia might rival New England's enterprise and wealth if only her 425,000 slaves were replaced by a free and independent yeomanry who "in blood and complexion, as well as in immunities and enjoyments, should be one with the proudest of her children."[7] Even apart from the desire for racial homogeneity, most American commentators shared this republican conviction that slavery subverted the nation's prospects for balanced economic growth and prosperity, at least in the longer term.

Much as slavery itself was antithetical to America's political principles and economic enterprise, Bacon argues, so the black victims of bondage were alien to American society and, unlike the freedmen of Greece, Rome, and most other nations, were "all marked out and stigmatized with the brand which nature has stamped upon them." As a consequence, they could never be "amalgamated with the rest of the community" and gain open access to wealth, honor, and office. It was this racial aspect of American slavery that Bacon finds particularly alarming, precisely because it appeared to preclude amelioration and gradual emancipation. The individual slave could not reasonably hope for an act of manumission or eventual integration into a homogeneous society.[8]

Racial difference could help to rationalize hierarchical domination but it also intensified fear. Writing less than a year after the exposure of Denmark Vesey's alleged but highly publicized conspiracy to seize Charleston, South Carolina, Bacon underscores the terror of slave plots and insurrections, quoting Jefferson's famous lines about "trembling for his country when he reflects that God is just, that his justice cannot sleep forever," and that "the Almighty has no attribute which can take side with us in such a contest."[9] Although Bacon thinks that Jefferson exaggerated a bit when he proclaimed that "the whole commerce between master and slave, is a perpetual exercise of the most boisterous passions, the most unremitting despotism on the one part, and degrading submission on the other," he echoes Jefferson's fears when he predicts that America's slaves, "surrounded by the memorials of freedom," will inevitably learn "something of their own power" and "that freedom is the birthright of humanity."

It is only a matter of time, then, before "that righteous Providence, which never wants instruments to accomplish its designs, whether of mercy, or of vengeance, shall raise up a Touissaint [*sic*], or a Spartacus, or an African Tecumseh." While Bacon can envision the destruction of Southern cities and plantations, he feels certain that within the next century any general insurrection would lead to the near extermination of the "ill-fated Africans" by the united efforts of Northern and Southern whites: "there is hardly an enterprize [*sic*] to which the militia of Vermont or Connecticut would march with more zeal, than to crush a servile rebellion (if such an event should ever take place with all its cruelties and horrors) in Virginia." Blacks would have to wait a longer time to acquire the numerical force sufficient to win total emancipation and a Haitian-like empire. As a colonizationist writing after the Missouri crisis and eager to find means of uniting slaveholding and nonslaveholding states, Bacon was far more conciliatory toward the South than his Connecticut antislavery predecessors had been in the 1790s.[10]

The specter of racial warfare, often exemplified by Bacon's accompanying image of "rivers of blood," was always a central ingredient of the colonizationist mentality, and the fear led Bacon at times to compromise or restrict the ideal of African American education. He appears to have regarded the political and economic evils of slavery as less iniquitous than the institution's "moral tendency" and "moral influence" on both blacks and whites. Here he has in mind, in language that verges on abolitionism, the way the presence of slaves silenced and deadened the conscience of most Southerners, who failed to lift up their voices against "a system which permits all the atrocities of the domestic slave-trade, which permits the father to sell his children as he would his cattle—a system which consigns one half of the community to hopeless and utter degradation." No less shocking, for Bacon, were the laws that "exist in nearly all the slaveholding States, prohibiting [the blacks'] instruction, and even driving them from Sunday schools, because it is supposed that the public safety requires them to be kept in perfect ignorance."[11] As we shall see, nothing could be more disturbing to the New England evangelical mind than such barriers to the instruments of divine grace. Yet the version of Bacon's "Report" reprinted in the *Christian Spectator* and the ACS Annual Report of 1824 contained a new passage that sharply curtailed the activities of any national movement "for the benefit of the blacks":

> Nor may it aim directly at the instruction of the great body of the blacks. . . . [T]he prejudices and terrors of the slave-holding States would be excited in a moment; and with reason too, for it is a well-established point, that the public safety forbids either the emancipation or the general instruction of the slaves. It requires no great skill to see that the moment you raise this degraded community to an intellectual existence, their chains will burst asunder like the fetters of Sampson [*sic*], and they will stand forth in the might and dignity of manhood, and in all the terrors of a long injured people, thirsting for vengeance.[12]

The image of Samson, we should note, affirmed the capacity of the most "degraded" slaves to recover the source of their strength, honor, and human dignity, but only at the cost of pulling down the temple, of bringing "down the same ruin on the master and the slave."[13]

For Bacon, who preached on "the vast designs of that Eternal Providence which will rescue humanity from darkness and misery and death, and renovate our world in the image of heaven," nothing could blight America's hopes more decisively than the predicament that allowed a fear for public safety to convince white Americans that blacks must be kept "in perfect ignorance." Unlike George Bourne and a few other early radical abolitionists, Bacon did not denounce slaveholding as a personal sin or as an inexcusable evil in itself. He did not rail against the master's usurpation of God's authority or the sin of defining a human being as chattel property. Bacon's attention focused on the subjective effects of slavery's "degradation," particularly within a cosmic framework of redemptive theology.[14] In "A Plea for Africa," delivered in 1824 as the annual Fourth of July address at Park Street Church in Boston and repeated the following year in New Haven, Bacon posed the question "And what is it to be a slave? We know what it is to be free. We know what it is to walk forth in the consciousness of independence and to act with the feeling that we are responsible only to our God and to the community of which we are equal members. . . . But we know not what it is to be a slave." One could picture, he continued, the whippings, the toil, the physical captivity. These would correspond, in his theology, to partial constraints on man's natural ability to choose virtue and justice. But try to imagine, he asked his listeners, what it would be like to have your spirit broken, your intellect dulled, your moral sense blinded:

> [A]nd you may thus be able faintly to imagine the degradation of the slave, whose mind has scarcely been enlightened by one ray of knowledge, whose soul has never been expanded by one adequate conception of his moral dignity and moral relations, and in whose heart hardly one of those affections that soften our character, or those hopes that animate and bless our being, has been allowed to germinate.

In this image of a ravaged mind and withered soul, of a human being rendered incapable of moral choice or benevolent feeling, Bacon constructed a concrete exemplification of original sin, a helpless victim of an evil system who, paradoxically, has become the sinner.[15]

While Bacon could not explore these connections in any manifest way, his concern with the "moral influence of the system on the blacks" reflected his struggle with a central theological issue that preoccupied the Congregationalist followers of Jonathan Edwards. The issue, quite simply, was how to reconcile the basic doctrines of Calvinism with the evangelical methods needed to Christianize

America and the world. Although Bacon and his famous mentors Lyman Beecher and Nathaniel W. Taylor thought of themselves as Calvinists, they could not believe that God had brought sinners into the world in order to condemn them for Adam's fall or for predetermined actions they could not help taking. A parallel issue, which was beginning to attract increasing attention in the secular sphere, was whether victims of oppression could be held accountable for criminal, immoral, or socially dysfunctional behavior that was the direct result of their oppression. From the time of the American Revolution, the evangelical clergy, both Calvinist and Arminian, had searched for social correlates for sin, repentance, and redemption, in part to dramatize the meaning and urgency of religious issues to a populace preoccupied with politics and skeptical of traditional authority. The sudden outburst of evangelical attacks on the sin of slaveholding, in the Revolutionary era, typified the shifting boundaries between sacred and secular concerns and also suggested that denunciations of black slavery could be a means of testing and objectifying changing concepts of original sin.[16] Ironically, as Orlando Patterson has shown, the Pauline and Augustinian conceptions of original sin and spiritual freedom had been modeled on actual experiences with Roman slavery and manumission. A large number of early Christian leaders were either freedmen or the children of liberated slaves who understood the literal meaning of redemption. According to Patterson, "Paul's theology miraculously transposed this secular experience of slavery-into-freedom, or the intense expectation of a rebirth into social life, into a doctrine of spiritual freedom from which the Western mind would never be released."

Augustine, who presented himself as a "disillusioned freedman," depreciated the value of personal liberty and magnified the importance of spiritual liberty as the unmerited gift of a totally free and sovereign master. Ideas derived from ancient slavery and Roman slave law were "encoded" in Christian theology, which became for future centuries, as Patterson puts it, "a cultural memory bank of ancient knowledge."[17] Obviously there was much diversity and complexity in Christian views of slavery and sin. But a brief summary of some of the linkages between slavery and sin, which were deeply embedded in Western culture, will help to clarify the intellectual framework that Bacon applied to the evils of slavery and racial prejudice.

From the time of the Stoics and early Christians, the institution of slavery had been associated with the regrettable but unavoidable imperfections of the world, eventually epitomized in the doctrine of original sin. Christian authorities, particularly Augustine, viewed human bondage as one of the penalties for man's fall from grace and as part of a system of hierarchical discipline and governance made necessary by human sin. The need to punish and control the species as a whole, however, did not imply any correlation between an individual's outward condition and his inward spiritual state. The conventional dualism of body and soul meant that a particular slave, no matter how degraded, might be spiritually free and even a Christian saint; a master or a king might be "enslaved" to greed, pride, sensuality, or to sin in general. Nevertheless, secular bondage inevitably took on a burden of guilt by association as Christians repeatedly described spiritual salvation as a redemption from bondage to sin, a liberation that drew on and transmogrified the Hebrews' journey out of Egypt.[18]

This use of slavery and emancipation as a paradigm for the central religious experience went well beyond analogies and figures of speech. Experience with chattel slavery was a precondition for the idea of physical and spiritual freedom; for devout Christians, sin was not only genuine slavery but slavery in the profoundest sense—slavery viewed, indeed, from eternity. Like chattel servitude, original sin was innate and hereditary, subjecting each victim to the absolute dominion of law, death, or Satan's will. Binding and constricting, it deprived the individual, at least in the Calvinist version, of any ability to choose the good, just, or honest. It therefore alienated its victims from their fellows and brethren by promoting deception, self-indulgence, envy, and violence. Like slavery, sin degraded and dishonored human beings, rendering them contemptible in God's eyes. Sin, to expand a point made by Orlando Patterson, was both a *condition* that contained no seeds for transformation and a *master* whose resistance could only be overcome by divine grace. Such a state of social and spiritual death could be sublated only by "the death of death," the negation of death itself as the sinner-slave partook in the death and resurrection of Jesus.[19]

In the eighteenth century, Calvinists like Jonathan Edwards confronted a broad movement to repudiate the traditional doctrine of original sin. They struggled to find ways to reinforce belief in the absolute sovereignty of God and to combat the widespread tendency to exalt the powers and moral ability of individuals, as if human destiny were determined by human valuations of merit. Edwards, who was much esteemed by William Wilberforce and the British Evangelicals as well as by his New England disciples, drew a crucial distinction between the natural and moral ability of unregenerate humans. Edwards and his followers rejected the notion of a natural or physically innate depravity—analogous to the belief in inherent racial inferiority—that prevented the unregenerate from choosing the good, just, and honest. For the Edwardseans it was not natural inability but a *moral inability*—the inability of the unregenerate will to break free from self-serving inclinations that led to sin. This subtle shift in emphasis reaffirmed human dependence on divine grace while also opening a window of incentive as Christians searched for the stirrings of grace in their own subjective inclinations.[20]

Samuel Hopkins, Edwards's most influential disciple and one of New England's earliest champions of slave emancipation and African colonization, took further steps to vindicate God's justice and equate virtue with "disinterested benevolence," later epitomized, for Hopkins's followers at Andover Seminary, by Christian missionaries in Asia and Africa.[21] At Yale and Andover, Leonard Bacon was exposed to repeated efforts on the part of "New Divinity" theologians to expand the limits of human moral ability without abandoning the need for divine grace. No one went further in this project than Nathaniel W. Taylor, whom Bacon replaced as minister at New Haven's Center Church when Taylor was appointed Dwight Professor of Didactic Theology at the new Yale Divinity School. Drawing particularly on Scottish commonsense philosophy, Taylor held that depravity always consists of sinful actions that are freely chosen; depravity should never be thought of as a sinful state of being or as an inherited propensity that is part of God's creation. "There can be no sin in choosing evil," Taylor affirmed, "unless there be power to choose good." However inevitable the choice of sin without the aid of divine grace, individual responsibility was premised, according to Taylor, on a "power to the contrary." This New Haven theology, of which Bacon became a champion, aroused bitter controversy and eventually contributed to the great Presbyterian schism of 1837. In 1823 and 1824, however, Bacon was still feeling his way toward a more liberating view of sin and moral responsibility.[22]

THE PARADOX OF SIN AND "IRREMEDIABLE DEGRADATION"

The existence of slavery and the presence in Boston and New Haven of an oppressed race descended from slaves presented Bacon with a tangible model for grappling with the problems of evil and moral responsibility. The moral "inability" of African Americans, as a discrete, identifiable group, conveyed by contrast a presumption of "ability" to white Americans, who could take comfort in their freedom from insurmountable deprivations. Physically marked off by nature and stamped with what Bacon termed a visible "brand," blacks had little freedom of choice and appeared to lack any "power to the contrary"; like Jonathan Edwards's sinners, they were only free to obey their strongest inclinations.

While Bacon did not explicitly apply such moral philosophy to his case study, he made it clear that the African American could not be raised "from the abyss of his degradation."[23] Not in the United States, that is, where as we have seen the force of prejudice was infinitely magnified by the fear of Samson "thirsting for vengeance" and bursting his chains asunder. But as this very fear attested, the psychological damage of slavery, like the debilities of sin, was not irreversible. From the perspective of New Divinity theology, the most alarming aspect of the American dilemma was the way it cut blacks off from all the "means" of grace—from the preaching, Sunday schools, benevolent societies, and what Horace Bushnell would later call "Christian nurture"—that softened the heart, expanded the soul, cultivated the moral sense, and prepared the way for an "active conversion" to spiritual freedom. What inspired Bacon and other missionary types was the realization that the "black cloud" provided white Americans with an opportunity to prove that they could transcend the national evil of slavery by removing its victims to a missionary world where the victim-beneficiaries could save themselves while also Christianizing and saving Africa.

The question of the slave's degradation and impaired moral and intellectual capacities led inescapably to the effects of emancipation. To what degree did liberation within the supposedly free American environment negate the "depraved" condition produced by enslavement? Significantly, the issue that led to the appointment of Bacon's committee of 1823 was not slavery but whether the Society of Inquiry "ought at present to make any exertions in favor of the black population of our country." In 1816, before the American Colonization Society was formed, the Society of Inquiry had listened to a discourse on "the condition of the black population of our country," and Bacon's committee was later appointed "to inquire respecting the black population of the United States." The "Report" does not begin with slavery or the slave trade but with the degraded condition of 1,769,000 black people within the United States, a "strange anomaly of a large part of the nation that loves to call itself the freest, happiest, and most enlightened nation on the globe."[24]

Even in the Northern states, Bacon points out, everyone was familiar to some extent with the barrier of "Caste"—a word Robert A. Warner retained 117 years later in his classic 1940 study *New Haven Negroes*—that cut blacks off "from all that is valuable in citizenship" and condemned them to wander "like foreigners and outcasts, in the land which gave them birth." After comparing the inequalities of blacks and whites with those of the Sudra and Brahman, Bacon concludes that American racial prejudice was even more insuperable than the institution of caste in India. In infancy the Negro "finds himself, he knows not why, the scorn of his playmates, from the first moment that their little fingers can be pointed at him in derision. In youth, he has no incentive to prepare for an active and honorable manhood. No visions of usefulness, or respectability, animate his prospects." The thousands of blacks in New England, far from contributing to "the good order and happiness of society," added more to the parish poor rates than they did to the government's revenue. Throughout the free states, blacks were mired in "irremediable degradation."[25]

The latter term, which Bacon repeatedly uses to describe the condition of slaves and free blacks, connotes a lowering in grade, rank, status, or honor, a dragging down in moral and intellectual character. Yet Bacon, who on this topic favors the passive voice, never identifies or describes the degraders. He never specifically acknowledges that Northern whites prevented black children from attending the common schools; denied unwealthy blacks the right to vote (a statutory prohibition in Connecticut and Rhode Island); excluded them from most skilled trades, thereby confining blacks to the most menial forms of employment; forced them to ride on the outside of stagecoaches and to live in squalid, segregated districts in proximity to crime and vice. If the Negro was "always degraded in the estimation of the community," Bacon seems purposefully vague about the laws and customs that actively deprived and humiliated the Negro, so that "the deep sense of that degradation enters into his soul and makes him degraded indeed." Although Bacon had rejected the Calvinists' deterministic theory of original sin, he adopted a resigned and passive posture toward the no less deterministic social forces which, in his view, transformed Northern free blacks into paradigms of moral inability, salvageable only by the shock therapy of physical removal.

Like most other colonizationists (including Abraham Lincoln), Bacon refrains from censuring white racial prejudice, though as a minister he would take prudent steps to weaken it. Prejudice, he suggests, is the inevitable response to a physiognomic difference made "by the God of nature." The crucial point, in modern terms, was the way an ethnic division, which often appears between competing but roughly equal groups, coincided with an extreme form of superordination and subordination in a society that increasingly professed equality as a norm.[26] Well-to-do whites in cities like New Haven were happy to mix as superiors with the black barbers and servants who shaved their faces, cut their hair, washed and pressed their clothes, cleaned their houses and stables, and cooked and served their food. But no members of such a servant race were allowed to interact with whites as social equals.[27] This merger of class and somatic barriers to "amalgamation" meant, as Bacon puts it, that "a slave cannot be really emancipated. . . . You may call him free, you may enact a statute book of laws to make him free, but you cannot bleach him into the enjoyment of freedom." In these and other passages Bacon merges physical characteristics—the "brand" of skin color or other features— with the effects of social degradation: free blacks are "as a body, ignorant and vicious," "more vicious and miserable than slaves can be." Although Bacon sincerely wishes to alleviate the misery and rescue blacks from "the scoffs and the scorn to which they are exposed," he cannot, when faced with a racially defined "other," conceal his own distaste, contempt, and fear.[28]

Clearly Bacon did not think that some racial defect explained the omnipresence of blacks "in our penitentiaries, and jails, and poor-houses . . . [in] the abodes of poverty, and the haunts of vice." Nor does he appear to blame African Americans for not appearing "in the society of the honest and respectable"—in the sanctuaries of God and in "the schools in which it is our boast that the meanest citizen can enjoy the benefits of instruction." Unfortunately, blacks were "separated by obstacles which they did not create, and which they cannot surmount, from all the institutions and privileges to which the other portions of the community owe their superiority." In other words, their own physical difference cut them off from educational and moral influences from which they would otherwise benefit. Bacon admits that a few exceptional blacks had overcome every obstacle to moral and social improvement. But the "peculiar circumstances or powers" of such individuals could not weaken Bacon's convictions about the constraints of race or what later writers would call "the Negro problem." His views on this subject are particularly revealing since they are uncontaminated by any notion of inherent inferiority; indeed, as a young clergyman Bacon sought to mitigate the depravity of New Haven's black community precisely because he knew that whites would behave the same way if subjected to the same conditions.[29]

Although we should not minimize the power and utility of racial symbolism, it is important to note that concerns and anxieties similar to those of the colonizationists could appear in a nonracial setting. At the time of the colonization debates, Bacon's counterparts in Europe were beginning to discover "dangerous classes" multiplying on what the historian John M. Merriman terms "the urban frontier"—the faubourgs that ringed the growing cities of France and other countries. These marginal people, including ragpickers, hawkers, Gypsies, peddlers, vagabonds, and prostitutes, were described in precisely the same terms as America's free blacks. Addicted to poverty and vice, they lived for the present moment only, giving no thought to the future or to familial or social obligations. They were, in the words of Antoine-Honoré Frégier, "the vicious and delinquent agglomerations which agitate the metropolises and in the substantial cities of countries other than France."[30]

"Vicious," with its connotations of vice, ferocity, and animality, seems to have been the favorite term used by both the American colonizationists and the European officials who voiced alarm over the "new barbarians" who imperiled civilization and who were therefore removed as far from the urban centers as possible. The American moral societies at the beginning of the nineteenth century revealed a similar, nonracial concern over premonitions of urban vice and disorder. But, as George M. Fredrickson has discovered, the first annual report of the Boston Prison Discipline Society, "an organization for penal reform, pointed out . . . [in 1826] that Negroes constituted a disproportionately large percentage of the prison population of the Northeastern states and concluded that 'the first cause existing in society of the frequency and increase of crime, is the degraded character of the colored population.' " In 1828, Leonard Bacon made a similar point about New Haven's blacks. Despite the extremely low percentage of blacks in the Northern population, racism was so deeply entrenched that it overrode other ways of interpreting and simplifying the disruptions of urban life.[31]

New Haven's notorious Liberian Hotel, owned by William Lanson, a wealthy black contractor, and located in a factory section east of town known as "New Liberia," fulfilled the long-standing fantasies of an interracial counterculture. Rumors of lewd entertainment, cheap whisky, prostitution, and a black man who kept three white mistresses, prompted raids by self-constituted posses that "arrested" whites of both sexes but apparently left the blacks undisturbed. The very name "New Liberia" was a mocking reminder that New Haven's blacks were already "colonized" in a region off-limits to whites.[32] Although few people blamed blacks for all the crime, delinquency, and vulgar behavior that preoccupied various reform societies, colonizationists suggested that the removal of blacks would go far toward restoring order and moral values. One further observation will underscore the complexity of this racial displacement. Some Europeans, particularly in England, may have indulged in fantasies about the benefits of deporting the dangerous or marginal classes to a Botany Bay. For Europeans, however, it would have been inconceivable to think of such unwanted people as redeemable victims who deserved compensation for past wrongs, as potential missionaries who would be restored, as Bacon put it, "to a real freedom in the land of their fathers," as exemplars whose achievements abroad would even "elevate, in some degree, the character of those who remained."[33]

For colonizationists like Bacon, the racial problem absorbed the issues of urban depravity and of imposing discipline on a threatening and potentially disruptive underclass. But, as we have seen, for Bacon and his associates blacks represented something more than a dangerous underclass. They embodied sin—paradoxically, as victims of "the most high-handed outrage that ever was practiced by fraud and power against simplicity and weakness"; as agents and examples of human behavior when the faculties have been totally "degraded"; and as a providential challenge to white Americans, who could thereby prove their "moral ability" to atone for past wrongs, to escape the retribution of racial or civil war, and to unite in "a great enterprise" that Bacon compares to "a river whose broad, deep, peaceful streams are supplied by perennial fountains, and whose pure waters, like the waters of Jordan, shall wash away from our national character this foul and loathsome leprosy."[34]

Bacon's wording may have been deliberately ambiguous: he presumably means that "our national character" will be cleansed of a particularly grievous sin; "loathsome leprosy," like his more explicit use of "the black cloud," can refer to the institution of slavery, since he expresses confidence that the ACS "will ultimately be the means of exterminating slavery in our country [and] will eventually redeem and emancipate a million and a half of wretched men."[35] Yet in view of the negative imagery Bacon applies to blacks, coupled with the traditional association of leprosy with Africans, the passage also conveys the joyous sense of relief and purification that America can expect when the nation has been purged of nonwhites. The context suggests that Bacon sees no conflict between these readings. He is not proposing that America's "leprosy," blight, or sin be transferred to Africa. To grasp Bacon's meaning, one must take seriously his faith in the stupendous promise of salvation in history. Loathsome sin, far from being the ground for despair, was the launching pad for redemption. For American blacks colonization would be a genuine emancipation, a "death" of social death and moral inability, a rebirth into a world in which the yearning for freedom was not nullified by white mockery and prejudice.[36]

Bacon's faith in such a glorious transfiguration may have been no more miraculous than William Lloyd Garrison's later faith that white racial prejudice would be quickly overcome by moral suasion. Bacon does express some skepticism regarding the "entire success" of the colonization plan and insists on the necessity of establishing, preferably in New England, "a Seminary for the education of blacks previously to their leaving the country." While he stresses the need for state and federal financial support, he relies above all on a popular movement that will take on the holy character of the Bible Society and Missionary Society. Here Bacon is following the revered path of Samuel Mills, one of Andover's recent heroes and martyrs, a missionary and fund-raiser for various benevolent societies who began working for the ACS in 1816, collecting donations to train black missionaries and magistrates, and in 1817 sailed off on a "mission of inquiry" to England and Sierra Leone, only to die at sea the following year from a disease contracted in Africa.

Bacon was strongly tempted to follow the missionary calling of his father and of close friends and classmates like Samuel Worcester. Knowing how each letter from a missionary awakened "a higher joy, and a livelier interest" among supporters, he can imagine how communications from Liberia, reporting tangible progress in eradicating the slave trade and Christianizing Africa, would bring Americans a sense of "increasing brightness," until "the kingdoms of this world shall become the kingdoms of our Lord."[37] Bacon's reasoning and imagery tell us a great deal about the way race and class were conceptualized within a framework of secularized theology, a framework that was angrily rejected and denounced by immediate abolitionists like Elizur Wright, who had played with Bacon as a child and who had then been instructed by him and Nathaniel Taylor at Yale.[38] On an instrumental level, Bacon soon became aware of the woeful inadequacies of the ACS management: as a result of the "Report," he and an Andover classmate received a free trip to Washington to meet and be courted by the national leaders of the Society, whom Bacon accused of inept administration and the "want of that energy and business-like regularity of operations" that explained the success of other benevolent societies.[39]

Even in the "Report," Bacon casually acknowledges that the colonization plan, while "practicable," would depend on achieving the consent and agreement of three groups. First, the consent of blacks themselves. Second, judging by the estimates of the ACS, the government would need to appropriate each year at least $250,000 to transport the annual increase of free blacks, or $2 million, "or a capitation tax of less than twenty-five cents on all the citizens of the United States," to transport "the whole annual increase of bond and free." Reports from the legislatures of Virginia, Maryland, and Tennessee were at least encouraging, and Bacon notes that a federal tax on the "fatal poison" of liquor would more than suffice, thereby allowing the nation's two greatest evils "to counteract and destroy each other."[40]

A third hurdle would be the willingness of Southern slaveholders to free their slaves if they were assured that all blacks, including the potential Spartacus or Toussaint, could be removed to a safe and distant refuge. Since Bacon was blind to the economic importance of slave (and free black) labor and assumed that large numbers of masters were eager to manumit their bondsmen, especially in northern Virginia, he theorizes that the power of example will spread once it is realized that emancipation is "no longer useless and dangerous," and that public opinion will eventually "declare itself louder and louder against the practice of slavery till at last the system should be utterly abolished." National unity on the subject would also be promoted if New Englanders talked "less of the guilt of slavery, and more of the means of counteracting its political and moral tendencies; or if, when they speak of its guilt, they would acknowledge that New England is a partaker; if they will remember that it was their ships and sailors that carried the African in chains across the ocean."[41]

SOME BLACK RESPONSE

Yet, even assuming that national unity could transform the ACS into a powerful and effective agency of benevolence, a modern crusade inspired by the knowledge that colonization had been the vehicle for extending civilization from ancient Egypt to Greece, from Greece to Rome, from Rome to the rest of Europe, from Europe to America and eventually to Hindustan and Hawaii, would American blacks themselves agree to carry the torch back to Africa in order to disperse "the shadows of heathenism" and "see Ethiopia waking, and rising from the dust, and looking abroad on the day, and stretching out her hands to God till all the fifty millions of Africa are brought into the 'glorious light and liberty of the sons of God' "? Bacon wastes no words on this vital question of black consent. In meeting the objection that "free blacks cannot be induced to go," he simply states that some have gone and "hundreds are waiting to go."[42]

Because colonizationists almost always dismissed this question as quickly as Bacon did, it has been generally assumed that they paid no attention to the views of African Americans and were long unaware of the bitter hostility to the ACS that finally found expression between 1827 and 1830 in Samuel Cornish's *Freedom's Journal,* David Walker's *Appeal to the Coloured Citizens of the World,* and the black national convention movement (to which we will later turn). But early in 1825 Bacon received a long and informative report on black opinion from Samuel H. Cowles, one of the three other members of the Andover

Society of Inquiry's committee on colonization, who had traveled through New York, Philadelphia, and Baltimore on his way to meet with ACS officials in Washington. Cowles was interested in promoting the idea of a black seminary or college, which Bacon and Solomon Peck, another member of the original Andover committee, had presented to the ACS in 1823. During days of heated debate with Samuel Cornish and James Forten, Cowles also struggled in vain to vindicate the colonizationist cause in the eyes of influential black leaders.[43]

Cornish, who in two years would launch the first African American newspaper, presided as minister over the debt-ridden First Colored Presbyterian Church of New York. He had been given special training at the Philadelphia Presbytery, had served as a missionary to slaves in Maryland, and had then worked as an evangelist with impoverished blacks in one of the worst slums of New York. At the time Cowles met Cornish and talked so late into the night that he got little sleep, the black pastor could take pride in his new brick church and congregation of several hundred. But Cornish, whom Cowles considered "a good and intelligent though of course imperfectly educated man," was anything but happy or deferential to a white colonizationist whose own education was incomplete. As Cowles informed Bacon, this black man expressed himself without inhibition and "with more national and manly feeling than I was exactly prepared for":[44]

He said that his people had borne their full share of the toils and hardships[,] the fears and sufferings that had been endured in order to make this country what it is. He thought they had therefore a good righ[t] to enjoy it. But this was denied to them while at the same time as if to render the injustice with which they were treated more cutting and to show the extent of their degradation[,] all the privileges of the most favored were with ostentatious generosity offered to the offscourings of Europe. For himself he was so hurt by this injustice[,] he was so sensible of the utter degradation that he should hail with a joy he had never felt—the breaking of that day when the whites[,] impelled by no cause which should involve his people in guilt[,] should rise and destroy them—every living soul—thus terminating at once their own uneasiness and the miseries of the blacks. Such a day he never expected to see but he often sighed for it when he pondered on the condition of himself and his people. [45]

This sense of despair, dramatized by the fantasy of an unprovoked genocide, no doubt confirmed Cowles and Bacon in their conviction that only a separation of the races could prevent further injustice and open genuine opportunities for blacks. One of Bacon's other colleagues, who felt that whites owed an enormous debt to African Americans, had written in anguish over the difficulty of arousing interest and making white people care: "But Alas! What can make white men sympathetic with black men—freemen with their own slaves? They can feel for the Hindoo for the Greek and for the black Hottentot, if he is at as great a remove the distance gives a kind of dignity in which the commonness and disgust of seeing and receiving a black man at their own door is lost."[46]

But for Cornish, blacks could hardly be expected to welcome the offer of distance or to see any dignity in being colonized. As Cowles paraphrased him:

> [T]he whites it seemed were about to take another step in injustice. Such were the feelings of disgust and contempt with which they regarded the blacks that they could not rest so long as the possibility remained of [the blacks] rising to their own level and mingling with them in the various scenes of life. Since then they were not likely to be of any further service on the whole and although they were so much attached to this country and so much accustomed and wedded to civilization that they must suffer much by the change[,] yet they had formed a Soc. for the purpose of transporting them all to the barbarous and horrible land of their fathers.[47]

Cornish assured Cowles that "he knew that some men who were connected with the C.S. [ACS] were actuated by very different feelings and such as entitled them to the highest gratitude of the blacks"; yet the popularity of the ACS "depended on the contempt and disgust with which negroes were commonly regarded. It was hard to be the object of such feelings." One can only wonder whether Cowles and Bacon got Cornish's point about colonizationists treating individuals as members of an impersonalized class. No doubt they separated their own motives from the repellent motives they needed to accept if the ACS were to succeed. Cornish told Cowles that blacks would be content "to oppose passive resistance" to the efforts of the colonizationists, but it was too much to expect "that they would voluntarily yield to it when it required that they should suffer the treatment of convicts."[48]

On Cornish's recommendation, Cowles called on James Forten when he reached Philadelphia. It is a mark of Cowles's and presumably Bacon's ignorance of the black community that Cowles had not previously heard of Forten and misspelled his name, while noting that he was "said to be worth from [$]1 to 200.000 00, He is proud of his money and vain of his abilities which have enabled him to get it and withal possesses a great deal of information."[49] A prosperous sailmaker, Forten was nearing sixty and had long been the leader of Philadelphia's black elite. For a decade he had been at the center of controversies over colonization, at first cooperating with the business and African emigration ventures of Paul Cuffe, the black shipowner who transported American blacks to Sierra Leone, and then strengthening his own position as a racial leader by chairing public meetings to denounce the ACS. According to Cowles, his sentiments were very nearly those of Cornish "unmodified and unrestrained by religion." Indeed, Cowles regretted that his lengthy and exhausting visit with Forten had prevented him from seeing James Cassey, a barber and financier "of less fortune but more liberality," whom Cornish had recommended "with more confidence."[50]

Forten had long been interested in selective emigration to Haiti, and he shocked Cowles by praising "the great men of Hayti [as] the defenders and the avengers of his race." Forten's views on the outcome of racial conflict differed sharply from those of Bacon:

> [H]e said repeatedly, that reasoning from the righteousness of God and from the manifest tendency of events[,] he was brought to the conclusion that the time was approaching and to judge from his manner, was already at the door when the 250,000,000 who had for centuries been the oppressors of the remaining 600,000,000 of the human race would find the tables turned upon them and would expiate by their own sufferings those which they had inflicted on others. When they had done this[,] he could hear proposals for placing all men on the same level and not till then.

While Forten may simply have intended to shake up his youthful white visitor, his menacing words must have strengthened the convictions of Cowles and of New Haven's newly appointed Congregational leader. Cowles concluded, however, that the anti-ACS sentiments he had encountered in New York and Philadelphia were shared by "all the blacks north of the Potomac." And in Baltimore he was disheartened by the "very tedious" talk of the ACS's General Robert Goodloe Harper, whose tacit disapproval of the New Englanders' educational plan "was a good preparation for what I was to find in Wash."

In the nation's capital, Cowles discovered that the ACS was "certainly a strange matter." Elias Caldwell, the Society's first secretary, "never distinguished for his abilities," was now superannuated and near death. One of the officers seemed attached to the cause "but has everything else to do"; another "sputters in your face a moment and then is off with whew." Although Cowles found much to admire in Ralph R. Gurley, the young Connecticut Yankee who really ran the society and who was about to succeed Caldwell as secretary, Gurley's ingenuousness was "a great defect in a man of business." Judge Bushrod Washington, the most celebrated name on the ACS roster, in reality "had nothing to do [with the society] and cares nothing about it."[51]

As we have seen, in the antebellum period a large majority of whites continued to believe that slave emancipation was unthinkable without some form of colonization, a fact reflected in Lincoln's support of the idea in the first years of the Civil War. By the late 1850s, even most black leaders had shifted their hopes to some kind of racial emigration, and those very temporary hopes resurfaced as late as the 1920s with the surprising support for Marcus Garvey's "Back to Africa" movement. But in the 1820s, slaveholders in the Deep South were instrumental in blocking the political goals of the ACS, and despite their continuing oppression, the great majority of American blacks always resisted pressures for emigration or colonization. As we will see in the next chapter, it was such black resistance that thwarted any significant merger of antislavery and colonization and that led to the emergence in the early 1830s of a new biracial movement for the "immediate" emancipation of all American slaves.

From Opposing Colonization
to Immediate Abolition

PAUL CUFFE AND EARLY PROPOSALS FOR EMIGRATION

Before the American Colonization Society was formed in 1816, evoking strong black protest, the connections between emigration, colonization, and genuine antislavery sentiment seemed much clearer. That could even be true when the proposed colonization involved some coercion. For example, in 1715 the Quaker John Hepburn appended to his own pioneering abolitionist tract an anonymous article, "Arguments Against Making Slaves of Men," which countered almost every conceivable defense of human bondage. Yet this seemingly radical author argued that before being emancipated, all blacks should be given a Christian education and then returned to Africa, where they could further the causes of religion and civilization. Slaves would have to choose between this form of liberation with free transportation or remain as slaves in America. The author drew on the example of white Christians who had been enslaved by Moors or Turks and who longed to be redeemed and returned to Europe. Significantly, even this early proposal included a suggestion of missionary work in Africa, an idea that would attract some black emigrationists and eventually become a central theme of the ACS.[1]

Clearly the idea of returning slaves to Africa had a very different meaning in the colonial period, when a majority of American slaves had been born in Africa and transported westward in the Middle

Passage.[2] In 1773 a group of Massachusetts slaves petitioned the legislature, appealing not only for their natural right to freedom but for an opportunity to obtain funds to transport themselves to some part of the African coast where they would found a "settlement." African-born blacks in Rhode Island expressed a desire to return to a more agreeable warm climate, free from racist oppression.[3]

Nevertheless, the parallel with rescuing Christian slaves in Muslim regions was highly misleading, even apart from the fact that West Africans were not trying to redeem their enslaved brethren in America. As the petition of the Massachusetts slaves indicated, it was difficult to find a homelike destination in Africa. Even if an African-born slave managed to return to his or her native region, there could be a genuine danger of reenslavement. For this reason philanthropists also began to think in terms of founding slave-free settlements, which led Granville Sharp and other British reformers to establish Sierra Leone in 1787 as an African refuge for blacks freed during the American Revolution, who had begun to crowd the streets of London. If African American slaves had actually been in a position similar to that of English slaves in Tripoli, there would have been no ambiguity about returning to a homeland. Or if, like slaves in ancient Rome, they had not been racially differentiated and could have become genuine citizens after being manumitted, there would have been no need to seek a homeland. But as whites even in colonial Virginia made clear, slaves could not ordinarily be manumitted without having to leave the colony. As we have now repeatedly seen, emancipation thus involved powerful pressures for removal but no clear location to which to move—except a vague sense of Africa, symbolized by the problematic and at times lethal British colony of Sierra Leone.[4]

It is significant that New England, which witnessed the most important early antislavery agitation in the Revolutionary period, also became the site of the first black interest in emigration to Africa. In the North, Vermont in 1777 became the first government in the world to outlaw slavery by constitutional fiat, and to the south, the Congregationalist minister Samuel Hopkins, a disciple of the slave-owning Jonathan Edwards, became the father of an abolitionist theology that connected the First Great Awakening of the 1740s with the second great period of religious revivalism in the 1820s and beyond. It can be argued that Hopkins's linkages of slavery with divine punishment and a new conception of original sin and "disinterested benevolence" had a profound influence on nineteenth-century abolitionists and even Harriet Beecher Stowe. But it was in 1770, when he moved to Newport, Rhode Island, that Hopkins directly confronted the slave trade and a population of African-born blacks and began writing key abolitionist works. After attempting to establish a school for black missionary work in Africa, he continued to advocate free transport for freed slaves who wanted to return to Africa.[5]

Beginning in the 1780s, when African Americans started forming their first social organizations such as the African Masonic Lodge in Boston, the African Free Society in Philadelphia, and (with the support of Hopkins) the African Union Society in Newport, their response to colonization ideas fluctuated according to situation and changing conditions. This can be seen in the different response between blacks in New England and Philadelphia to the arrival in 1786 of William Thornton, the Quaker son of a wealthy Antiguan planter who had been educated at the University of Edinburgh before joining the London founders of Sierra Leone in an effort to free and colonize slaves, including those he had inherited.[6]

After only a few weeks in America, Thornton claimed that he had found two thousand freedmen ready to go to Africa. It was especially in Newport and Boston that African-born blacks expressed an interest in returning to "ancestral lands," though the Boston group wrote that they much preferred to charter a vessel of their own. Philadelphia's blacks gave Thornton a much cooler reception, despite his glowing description of Sierra Leone. Later communications between Philadelphia's African Free Society (AFS) and the Newport group suggested that the latter believed in a divine mission to evangelize Africa and that blacks in Newport and Boston felt they were "strangers and outcasts in a strange land, attended with many disadvantages and evils which are likely to continue on us and our children, while we and they live in this country." In contrast, members of the AFS had all been born in America and were convinced that some whites were dedicated to improving the condition of blacks.[7]

Through the 1790s and early nineteenth century, Sierra Leone became a model for various black and white discussions of emigration, though there were also numerous negative reports of terrible voyages, emigrants being stranded in ships at port, nearby slave trading, and conflict with natives. Various plans also failed as a result of lack of funding, bureaucratic obstacles, and uneven black support. But then in 1811, Paul Cuffe, the famous seafaring black captain and probably the wealthiest black in the country, made his first trip to Sierra Leone and was much taken with the idea of establishing a small African American settlement (though the British administrators told him he would need more official backing from America or Britain, which he did his best to seek).

Cuffe was the son of an African-born father and Wampanoag Indian mother. His father, who died when Paul was thirteen, had been the slave of a Quaker master who had then apparently allowed him to work for his freedom.[8] Cuffe himself became a devout Quaker and at age sixteen began working on a whaling ship and as a sailor, learning the arts of navigation and commerce before creating a shipping empire. Building his own ships, Cuffe traded with great success from his home in Massachusetts along the coast to the Carolinas, staffing his boats with black sailors. His Quaker connections and transatlantic travel made him the best-known African American of his time. His later activities were even covered by newspapers in most major cities. He corresponded with such figures as Thomas Clarkson and William Allen in Britain, and in London, after his first voyage to Sierra Leone, he won support for his ideas about black emigration from leaders of the important African Institution. Thanks to his network of influential friends, Cuffe's colonization ideas even received strong personal support from President James Madison and Albert Gallatin, secretary of the treasury, before being totally blocked by the outbreak of the War of 1812. Cuffe was the first black guest known to have been received by an American president, and Madison, addressed as "James" by Cuffe, in Quaker fashion, interviewed him with great cordiality.[9]

It should be stressed that Cuffe was not interested in finding a refuge for the black poor or in a mass migration to Africa. He hoped to recruit a small number of men of some property whose good character and sobriety would ensure a commercial settlement in Africa that would bring in profits, serve as a model, and enhance the image of all persons of African descent. No less important, the kind of economic development Cuffe had in mind would help obviate the need for the slave trade and create a black society free from both slavery and racial prejudice. Ironically, although Cuffe had a strong desire to join a settlement in Sierra Leone, his Pequot wife refused to leave the land of her ancestors.[10]

With the end of the War of 1812, Cuffe finally transported thirty-eight carefully selected black colonists to Africa, landing in Sierra Leone on February 3, 1816. While not greeted as warmly as he expected, Cuffe remained highly optimistic over the future prospects of his settlers. Most of all, his timing coincided with and helped nourish an immense upsurge of interest in colonization, epitomized by the founding of the American Colonization Society in December 1816 by a group that included antislavery clergy, missionaries, and slaveholders intent on exporting as many free blacks as possible. But then Cuffe's health suddenly deteriorated and he died on September 7, 1817, at age fifty-eight.[11]

JAMES FORTEN AND BLACK REACTIONS TO THE AMERICAN COLONIZATION SOCIETY

Largely as a result of the gradual but total slave emancipation in the North, the free black population increased dramatically in the early nineteenth century, an event that stimulated white racism on all levels.[12] Despite the patriotic praise given to black Philadelphians for their assistance against the British in the War of 1812, race relations deteriorated rapidly after the war. Expressions of Negrophobia became commonplace in print and on the street, and in Philadelphia, even Bishop Richard Allen became the victim of a kidnapper who, as was the custom, swore that he had recently purchased Allen as a slave, until Allen was able to call witnesses to testify about his identity.[13] This virulent racism aroused new interest in emigration proposals— at least among black leaders like Allen and Philadelphia's wealthy sailmaker and inventor, James Forten. Forten asserted many times that he saw no future for blacks "until they come out from amongst the white people."[14]

By 1816, Paul Cuffe had established close ties with Forten and with the eminent black ministers Richard Allen and Absalom Jones, who assured him there was strong support for colonization in Philadelphia.[15] When Cuffe corresponded with the white missionary Samuel Mills and Robert Finley (the Presbyterian minister who played the leading role in conceptualizing and founding the ACS), he urged them to make use of black organizations, such as the African Institutions he had helped establish in the Northern cities. He also warned Finley that the Cape of Good Hope would be far more suitable than Sierra Leone for a massive resettlement of blacks. But, like Cuffe, Mills and Finley also soon died (Mills had rushed to Cuffe's bedside after learning he was ill, and after Cuffe's death, took off on an ACS trip to Sierra Leone, where he contracted a disease that killed him on his return). This loss of three key figures destroyed important potential connections between black leaders and the more benevolent-minded leaders of the ACS.[16]

Because James Forten (1766–1842) became such a central figure in the history of black opposition to colonization—as we will see, he played an important role in converting and then financially supporting William Lloyd Garrison and thus in launching the radical biracial abolitionism of the 1830s and beyond—a bit more should be said about his background. Born free in Philadelphia, he attended the Quaker African School run by the pioneer abolitionist Anthony Benezet, but after his father died, he left school at age nine in order to work full-time. After the Revolution, when for a time he was a prisoner of the British, Forten was apprenticed as a sailmaker and invented a device to handle ship sails. That breakthrough helped him succeed in a major way when he started his own sail making company and became one of the wealthiest blacks in the country. Forten married Charlotte Vandine, and they raised a large family devoted to abolitionism, philanthropy, temperance, and women's rights. But in January 1817, Forten assured Robert Finley that even his own spectacular success could not overcome the oppression of American racism: "observing that neither riches nor education could put them [blacks] on a level with the whites, and the more wealthy and the better informed any of them became, the more wretched they were made; for they felt their degradation more acutely. *He* [Forten] gave it as his decided opinion that Africa was the proper place for a colony."[17]

James Forten, Richard Allen, and the black ministers Absalom Jones and John Gloucester—inspired in part by Cuffe—took a strongly positive view of colonization when they responded to the waves of fear and even panic that spread among Philadelphia's black population in January 1817 in reaction to the recent founding of the ACS.[18] As a result of extensive press coverage, which included racist statements made by ACS leaders in the Washington meeting—Henry Clay declaring that free blacks "are a dangerous and useless part of the community"—many blacks quickly accepted rumors that the most powerful whites had met in the nation's capital to devise a plan for deporting all free African Americans to Africa, in part to protect and strengthen the institution of slavery. As Forten put it, "the People of Colour here was very much fritened." It is unclear exactly who called for the great meeting of some three thousand of Philadelphia's black men, around January 15, 1817, in Bishop Allen's Bethel Church. No formal record of the meeting has survived. But Forten chaired the meeting and he, Allen, Jones, and Gloucester all sought to appease the fears and respond to what they saw as the popular overreaction to proposals for colonization. Forten believed that despite some unfortunate statements made in Washington, the main founders of the ACS were well-intentioned and he tried to assure the audience that no one planned to round them up and ship them off to Africa against their will.[19]

After the four leaders had done their best to convey such reassurance, Forten looked out at the thousands of blacks who jammed the main floor and packed the balcony and called for a vote of "ayes" from those who favored colonization. There was total silence. When Forten called on those who opposed colonization, there was a tremendous "No" that seemed, Forten wrote some years later, "as it would bring down the walls of the building."[20] As he explained to Paul Cuffe, "there was not a soul that was in favor of going to Africa." Fearful that free blacks would be compelled to leave in a massive deportation scheme, they doubted that white ACS members wished "a great good" for a group that they both hated and feared. They were unanimous in the opinion that "the slaveholders want to get rid of them so as to make their property more secure."[21]

Forten and the other black leaders were clearly stunned by this response, which challenged their status as a wise elite capable of representing and directing the masses. Abandoning any pretense of paternalism, they immediately adopted a resolution endorsing the views of the black public, appointed a committee of eleven to correspond with their congressional representative, and in August issued a more detailed and eloquent Address to the Inhabitants of the City and County of Philadelphia, attacking all aspects of colonization. But, as Forten's few letters to Cuffe make clear, a gap remained between his public statements and private views. On January 25, 1817, Forten described the Bethel Church meeting to his "esteemed friend" Cuffe, concluding that "as the majority is decidedly against me I am determined to remain silent, except as to my opinion which I freely give when asked."[22] He did not mention the crucial anticolonization resolution he had signed as chairman. It took some months, perhaps reinforced by Cuffe's death, for Forten to become an ardent opponent of colonization—and, given their sensitivity to the power of white racism, black leaders were usually open to thoughts about emigration to the West, Canada, and in the 1820s, to Haiti.

Here is the substance of the Philadelphia meeting's resolution, which Garrison reprinted in 1832 in his extremely influential *Thoughts on African Colonization* (Forten no doubt provided Garrison with copies of both the Resolution and the longer Address to the Inhabitants of Philadelphia, which Garrison also reprinted):

Whereas our ancestors (not of choice) were the first successful cultivators of the wilds of America, we their descendants feel ourselves entitled to participate in the blessings of her luxuriant soil, which their blood and sweat manured; and that any measure or system of measures, having a tendency to banish us from her bosom, would not only be cruel, but in direct violation of those principles, which have been the boast of this republic.

Resolved, That we view with deep abhorrence the unmerited stigma attempted to be cast upon the reputation of the free people of color, by the promoters of this measure, "that they are a dangerous and useless part of the community," when in the state of disfranchisement in which they live, in the hour of danger they ceased to remember their wrongs, and rallied around the standard of their country [in the American Revolution and War of 1812].

Resolved, That we never will separate ourselves voluntarily from the slave population in this country; they are our brethren by the ties of consanguinity, of suffering, and of wrong; and we feel that there is more virtue in suffering privations with them, than fancied advantages for a season.

Resolved, That without arts, without science, without a proper knowledge of government, to cast into the savage wilds of Africa the free people of color, seems to us the circuitous route through which they must return to perpetual bondage.

Resolved, That having the strongest confidence in the justice of God, and philanthropy of the free states, we cheerfully submit our destinies to the guidance of Him who suffers not a sparrow to fall, without his special providence.[23]

The later Address to the Inhabitants of Philadelphia by the city's free people of color, also signed by Chairman Forten, is far more deferential, as the blacks "humbly and respectfully lay before you this expression of their feelings and apprehensions." Relieved from the miseries of slavery, the free blacks are now reportedly happy and contented with their present situation and condition, but dedicated to the improvement and education of their children and to the benefits and blessings "which industry and integrity in this prosperous country assure to all its inhabitants." Since this law-abiding and Christian people "have no wish to separate from our present homes, for any purpose whatever," it is a tremendous shock to learn that some of "the wisest, the best, and the most benevolent of men, in this great nation," have proposed a plan for colonizing the free people of color on the coast of Africa.[24] It should be noted that even Garrison, the outspoken radical, conceded that many supporters of the ACS were "men of piety, benevolence, and moral worth," and affirmed that "Little boldness is needed to assail the opinions and practices of notoriously wicked men; but to rebuke great and good men for their conduct, and to impeach their discernment, is the highest effort of moral courage."[25]

The authors of the Address, speaking for the city's black population, want to assure the general public that if the plan of colonization is meant for the blacks' benefit, that "with humble and grateful acknowledgements to those who have devised it, [we] renounce and disclaim every connexion [*sic*] with it; and respectfully but firmly declare our determination not to participate in any part of it."[26]

Along with the superficial deference, the authors succeed in subtly exposing the most threatening aspect of colonization by turning to the seemingly benevolent argument that a colony would also "provide a refuge and dwelling for a portion of our brethren, who are now held in slavery in the south." Indeed, the authors' strongest concern is the way colonization could block, rather than aid, what they see as the otherwise inevitable progress toward "the ultimate and final abolition of slavery in the United States":[27]

> Nor do we view the colonization of those who may become emancipated by its operation among our southern brethren, as capable of producing their happiness. Unprepared by education, and a knowledge

of the truths of our blessed religion . . . those who will thus become colonists will themselves be surrounded by every suffering which can afflict the members of the human family.

Without arts, without habits of industry, and unaccustomed to provide by their own exertions and foresight for their wants, the colony will soon become the abode of every vice, and the home of every misery. Soon will the light of Christianity, which now dawns among that portion of our species, be shut out by the clouds of ignorance, and their day of life be closed, without the illuminations of the gospel.

To those of our brothers, who shall be left behind, there will be assured perpetual slavery and augmented sufferings. Diminished in numbers, the slave population of the southern states, which by its magnitude alarms its proprietors, will be easily secured. Those among their bondmen, who feel that they should be free . . . and who thus may become dangerous to the quiet of their masters, will be sent to the colony; and the tame and submissive will be retained, and subjected to increased rigor. Year after year will witness these means to assure safety and submission among their slaves, and the southern masters will colonize only those whom it may be dangerous to keep among them. The bondage of a large portion of our brothers will thus be rendered perpetual. . . .

Nor ought the sufferings and sorrows, which must be produced by an exercise of the right to transport and colonize such only of their slaves as may be selected by the slaveholders, escape the attention and consideration of those whom with all humility we now address. Parents will be torn from their children—husbands from their wives—brothers from brothers—and all the heart-rending agonies which were endured by our forefathers when they were dragged into bondage from Africa, will be again renewed, and with increased anguish. The shores of America will, like the sands of Africa, be watered by the tears of those who will be left behind. Those who shall be carried away will roam childless, widowed, and alone, over the burning plains of Guinea.[28]

THE SEARCH FOR BLACK IDENTITY
AND EMIGRATION TO HAITI

The 1817 Philadelphia Resolution and Address, quoted in the future by many prominent blacks, including Frederick Douglass, became part of the anticolonizationist African American culture.[29] They also raised issues of defining black identity at the beginning of a period when the vast majority of blacks had no memory of Africa or connection with a given African ethnic group.[30] In fact, the period following the War of 1812–1815 marked a new search for identity on the part of the American population as a whole. By 1820, nearly half the white population was under the age of sixteen and barely 12 percent over age forty-three—old enough perhaps to remember the Battle of Yorktown, only thirty-seven years earlier. There was thus a national obsession, shared by many African Americans, over keeping knowledge of the American Revolution alive and relevant.[31] Black identity was of course shaped in a context of rising racism, of being negatively defined by whites as an unwanted group that did not belong. Partly in reaction against this, black spokesmen idealized the Declaration of Independence and the principles upon which the nation was founded, and affirmed an American identity based on the patriotism of their parents or grandparents who had fought in the Revolution or the War of 1812. As we have seen, they also stressed the physical labor of their ancestors who had helped create America.

On the other hand, large numbers of black churches and secular organizations and institutions adopted the moniker "African" beginning in the late eighteenth century.[32] The black physician James McCune Smith later wrote that "It was in after years, when they set up protest against the American Colonization Society and its principles that the term 'African' fell into disuse and finally discredit."[33] Among blacks as well as whites, there was profound ignorance concerning Africa, a continent associated with stereotypes of ignorant and barbarous heathen living in uncultivated jungles. There was also a tradition, exploited by the ACS, of celebrating ancient Egypt as a "black" civilization. And of course African Americans, whose genealogy provided some word-of-mouth traditions, were involved in the discovery and settlement of Liberia. The main point, however, is that by the 1820s, black churches, organizations, and communication networks—including a newspaper—were contributing to a new black American identity that centered on the abolition of slavery and opposition to the ACS.[34] Yet a large number of free blacks—some historians estimate as many as 20 percent—remained open to various opportunities for emigration.[35]

As we noted at the end of chapter 2, Haiti became a major site for free black emigration in the 1820s. The image of the country was transformed when President Jean Pierre Boyer, a mulatto veteran of the Haitian Revolution, united the North and South in 1820, invaded Santo Domingo and united all of Hispaniola under one government in 1821, and then won recognition from France by making a staggering indemnity payment of 150 million francs. Eager to attract productive workers, Boyer offered American black immigrants thirty-six acres of land, four months of provisions, and other perks in the hope of stimulating the nation's economy. No less important, he sent some highly effective agents to the United States to recruit black immigrants. Jonathan Granville, in particular, attracted crowds of free blacks in New York, Baltimore, Boston, and especially Philadelphia, with the establishment of the Haitian Immigration Society in 1824. By 1826, more than six thousand American blacks had emigrated to Haiti, and it is estimated that by the end of the decade the number ranged from eight to thirteen thousand.[36]

But the experiment was probably doomed to failure from the start. Even apart from Haiti's poverty and dismal economy (weakened by the indemnity payment to France), there were formidable barriers of language and religion, and many urban American blacks sold or abandoned their homesteads and headed for towns when they faced the realities of farming and the lack of quick success. Haitian animosity toward the Americans, and even accusations of criminality, led Boyer to reconsider the scheme. By 1826, one-third of the immigrants had returned to America, many complaining that the rural work was equivalent to plantation slave labor.[37]

Yet this disillusion had little effect on continuing African American pride in the Haitian Revolution and even on later proposals for black emigration to Haiti. In 1826, when John Brown Russwurm became the third black to graduate from an American college, he gave the graduation address, on "The Condition and Prospects of Haiti." At Bowdoin, where Russwurm's fellow students included Nathaniel Hawthorne and Henry Wadsworth Longfellow, it seemed appropriate for the first black graduate to celebrate both the Haitian Revolution and the future prospects of the republic:

> Thirty-two years of their independence, so gloriously achieved, have effected wonders. No longer are they the same people. They had faculties, yet were these faculties oppressed under the load of servitude and ignorance. With a countenance erect and fixed upon

Heaven, they can now contemplate the works of divine munificence. Restored to the dignity of man to society, they have acquired a new existence; their powers have been developed; a career of glory and happiness unfolds itself before them.[38]

We find a similar optimism thirty-five years later in the *Weekly Anglo-African* magazine:

> Hayti cannot but command the most lively sympathies of all men of African descent. It is the only nationality of our race in the Western Continent; it is the only land in which we have conquered our liberty by the sword against the bravest white warriors in the world. IT HAS A HISTORY OF EXTRAORDINARY INTEREST, ABOUNDING IN THE INCIDENTS THAT NONE OF US CAN READ WITHOUT A GLOW OF PRIDE OF RACE.[39]

RUSSWURM, CORNISH, AND WALKER

As historian Richard S. Newman has emphasized, the refusal of early white antislavery organizations to condemn colonization pushed black reformers, who were excluded from such groups as the Pennsylvania Abolition Society, "into the national spotlight."[40] Richard Allen, James Forten, and John Gloucester continued to hold protest meetings in the 1820s against the ACS in and around Philadelphia, with Allen declaring that "The land we have watered with our tears and our blood is now OUR MOTHER COUNTRY." While there was no clear-cut continuity, black organizations opposing slavery and colonization appeared in the 1820s throughout the Northeast and Midwest. Talk of forming national organizations led in 1830 to the first meeting of the American Society for Free Persons of Color in Philadelphia. Under the tutelage of Allen and Forten, the American Society affirmed the blacks' "firm and settled conviction" that the problems of slavery and racism could be addressed only on American soil.[41]

The late 1820s have been seen as the beginning of a black Renaissance, with the launching of two black newspapers, *Freedom's Journal* and *The Rights of All*, as well as the publication of David Walker's famous *Appeal to the Coloured Citizens of the World* (which we will discuss in detail in chapter 8).[42] The newspapers were the creations of John

Brown Russwurm and Samuel Eli Cornish, whose lives deserve a brief summary.

A mulatto, Samuel Cornish was born in 1795 to free colored parents, probably farmers, in Delaware. After attending a small female-run Methodist school, he moved to Philadelphia, where, thanks to the guidance of black Presbyterian minister John Gloucester, Cornish underwent the lengthy and rigorous ordination process to become a Presbyterian minister. He probably attended and was certainly very familiar with the 1817 anticolonization meeting at the Bethel Church. He then worked as a missionary in Maryland and as a reformer in the slums of New York City before founding New York's first black Presbyterian church. But it was as a journalist—no doubt the most important black journalist before Frederick Douglass—that Cornish made his major contribution. In March 1827 he became the senior editor, with Russwurm as junior editor, of the first African American newspaper, *Freedom's Journal;* in 1829 he founded and edited *The Rights of All,* and from 1836 to 1842, the *Colored American.* A devoted abolitionist, Cornish was one of the founding members of the biracial American Anti-Slavery Society and held high-ranking positions in the American Missionary Association and American Bible Society.[43]

John Brown Russwurm was born in 1799 in Jamaica, the son of a white American merchant and his black, no doubt slave, mistress. The father not only accepted his paternity but brought John up in his household as a privileged mulatto son and sent him off to a boarding school in Quebec; the father subsequently moved to Portland, Maine, and settled down with a white wife. The father seemed proud of John, introduced him to the best society in Portland, and continued to send him to the best schools in preparation for his later admission to Bowdoin.[44]

Though his father died when he was sixteen, Russwurm continued to live with his stepmother, with whom he had a continuing close relationship. It was not until he went to Boston to look for work and experience that Russwurm encountered the shock of racial poverty and discrimination. Since he had long lived apart from a normal American racial identity, it was doubtless easier for him to think of leaving it. In 1826, the year of his Bowdoin graduation speech celebrating Haiti, he expressed some interest in emigrating to Haiti and also thought it "advisable," after talking with friends, to turn down a "liberal offer" from the ACS to take a post in Liberia—perhaps in anticipation of his defection from the anticolonization cause and decision in 1829 to migrate and spend the rest of his life in Liberia, where he initially worked as colonial secretary for the ACS.[45]

By March 1827, when a number of prominent New York ministers and other blacks met at the home of Boston Crummell (father of Alexander Crummell) to found *Freedom's Journal*, a number of pressing issues faced the black community. The Missouri Crisis of 1819–21 had suddenly exposed slavery as a critically divisive issue that could threaten the very existence of the nation, reinforcing desires to repress and avoid the subject as much as possible. There was also an inevitable tendency to blame blacks for the country's most dangerous problem.[46] The nature and future of antislavery were therefore much in doubt. Since Britain had shown that the mobilization of public opinion, largely on moral grounds, could lead to legislation outlawing the Atlantic slave trade, there was a strong inclination to look to Britain as a model, especially given the stature of such towering figures as Thomas Clarkson and William Wilberforce. But by the late 1820s, the British movement for the amelioration and very gradual ending of slavery, begun in 1823, was clearly not succeeding. In both Britain and America, a decline of faith in gradualism was marked in the mid-1820s by enthusiasm for a boycott of slave produce, a movement that promised to give a cutting edge to the moral testimony of individuals. It is a striking coincidence, as we will see, that both the British and American antislavery movements shifted toward "immediatism" by 1830.[47]

Meanwhile, *Freedom's Journal* was launched when the ACS was in some ways at its peak, receiving strong clerical support and endorsement from much of the press and from most white opponents of slavery, including prominent future abolitionists. But if most opponents of slavery assumed that abolition was unfeasible in America without some form of colonization, the ACS was officially committed to voluntary emigration and therefore assumed that most blacks could be converted and made to see their own self-interest, especially if they were made more aware of how unwelcome they were in a white society (and assuming that the mortality and other difficulties in Liberia were as temporary as those associated with the founding of Jamestown and Plymouth, a repeated argument).

In other words, African American opinion was ultimately essential. But, as the ACS struggled with the problem of recruiting reluctant black volunteers, for ten years most of the white press cooperated by refusing to print resolutions passed by gatherings of blacks rejecting the ACS program.[48] All of which highlights the extraordinary importance of the first black newspaper, which under Cornish respectfully but lucidly rejected colonization as a plan that would actually strengthen and perpetuate slavery. Even more important, *Freedom's Journal* provided a voice for blacks, even for a very short period, on a variety of issues related to human dignity and the overcoming of negative stereotypes related to the growing white consensus that the nation would immensely benefit from the blacks' total removal. According to historian David Swift, "If there were roughly 1,300 black subscribers by the summer of 1827, it can be concluded that several thousand black people read at least parts of a weekly issue."[49]

In the initial issue of *Freedom's Journal*, Cornish and Russwurm (who as junior editor took the backseat to the more dominant voice of Cornish)[50] affirmed the central purpose of the journal:

> From the press and the pulpit we have suffered much by being incorrectly represented. Men, whom we equally love and admire have not hesitated to represent us disadvantageously, without . . . discerning between virtue and vice among us. The virtuous part of our people feel themselves sorely aggrieved under the existing state of things—they are not appreciated. Our vices and our degradation are ever arrayed against us, but our virtues are passed by unnoticed. And what is still more lamentable, our friends, to whom we concede all the principles of humanity and religion . . . seem to have fallen into the current of popular feeling and are imperceptibly floating on the stream—actually living in the practice of prejudice, while they abjure it in theory, and feel it not in their hearts. Is it not very desirable that such should know more of our actual condition, and of our efforts and feelings, that in forming or advocating plans for our amelioration, they may do it more understandingly? In the spirit of candor and humility we intend by a simple representation of facts to lay our case before the publick, with a view to arrest the progress of prejudice, and to shield ourselves against the consequent evils. We wish to conciliate all and to irritate none, yet we must be firm and unwavering in our principles, and persevering in our efforts.[51]

During Cornish's crucial six months as editor, *Freedom's Journal* focused on such matters as colonization, racial prejudice, poverty, economic opportunity, uplift, and temperance, interspersed with curiosity pieces and items of public interest. In the discussion of political subjects, Cornish, in contrast to the later Garrisonians, affirmed, "we shall ever regard the constitution of the United States as our polar star." Also in contrast to Garrison, Cornish assured his readers that "It ever has been our object to use the most pacific measures, studiously avoiding every thing that might tend to irritate the feelings of any." As a Presbyterian minister and a transitional figure in the history of black abolitionists, Cornish was deferential to whites who had shown a long-standing concern for the black community, and he professed a desire to consider facts and give colonization a fair hearing—even while stressing his opposition to colonization "in principle, object, and tendency."[52] Black historian Benjamin Quarles concluded that Cornish's newspapers "generally furnished an accurate barometer of Negro thought,"[53] and he won great plaudits from such figures as David Walker in 1829 and Theodore S. Wright in 1837.[54]

Despite evidence of rising antiblack sentiment and racist responses to *Freedom's Journal,* Cornish held firm to his central conviction that "We are unwavering in our opinion that the time is coming (though it may be distant) in which our posterity will enjoy equal rights."[55] But Russwurm, who took over editorship when Cornish left, had increasing doubts on this point and ultimately became convinced that the depth and immutability of white racism presented a permanent obstacle to slave emancipation—unless some way could be found to remove free blacks. Under his editorship, *Freedom's Journal* printed more announcements for colonization, including emigration plans for Haiti, and became less vituperative toward the ACS. Nevertheless, Cornish was greatly surprised by Russwurm's decision to move to Liberia and his parting defense of colonization in March 1829 in *Freedom's Journal.*[56]

Russwurm assured readers that though he supported universal emancipation as ardently as ever, the goal was impossible "unless some door is opened whereby the emancipated may be removed as fast as they drop their galling chains, to some other land besides the free states." Cornish and others had called for an objective consideration of the facts, and for Russwurm the facts were clear. If a state like

Virginia freed its slaves, it would require their removal; in which case Northern states would pass laws prohibiting their entry. This barrier to emancipation could only be overcome by getting rid of "present prejudices," but "It will never be in our power to remove or overcome them." Indeed, "So easily are these prejudices imbibed, that we have often noticed the effects on young children who could hardly speak plainly, and were we a believer in dreams, charms, &c we should believe that they imbibed them with their mother's milk."[57]

Despite Russwurm's attempt to placate opponents by reminding them of his long, hard work opposing the ACS, he was seen by many blacks as a traitor. The shock and vituperative responses from the paper's subscribers indicate strong anticolonizationist sentiment among the black elite and probably the black community in general. After Russwurm's defection to Liberia, the backers of *Freedom's Journal* solicited Cornish to take back the editorship and continue the paper as a weekly. Cornish accepted, but given the furor over Russwurm's last issues, the title was changed to *The Rights of All* (published monthly). Cornish now dealt in more strongly critical terms with what he termed the "chimerical plans" of colonization,[58] assuring his readers that Russwurm had not had any effect except in inducing a need for reforming the quality of the paper. Yet much space was devoted to the racial crisis in Cincinnati, where Black laws and the violent persecution of free blacks led to a mass migration to Canada, an event that Russwurm could have used to his advantage if he had remained as an editor.[59]

But as mentioned, 1829 also marked the publication of David Walker's *Appeal*, which Richard Newman has termed "an exclamation point after this decade of anticolonizationist black activism." In Boston, Walker served as the local agent for *Freedom's Journal* and *The Rights of All*.[60] While dealing with a broad range of issues involving slavery and the concerns of people of African descent throughout the world, Walker's *Appeal* paid tribute to *The Rights of All* and emphasized "the absolute necessity" of helping to circulate the paper:

> I adopt the language of the Rev. Mr. S. E. Cornish, of New York, editor of the Rights of All, and say: "Any coloured man of common intelligence, who gives his countenance and influence to that colony, further than its missionary object . . . should be considered as a traitor to his brethren, and discarded by every respectable man of colour.

And every member of that society [ACS], however pure his motive, whatever may be his religious character and moral worth, should in his efforts to remove the coloured population from their rightful soil, the land of their birth and nativity, be considered as acting gratu- itously unrighteous and cruel.[61]

BLACKS AND GARRISON

Cornish and Walker were not only vocal black opponents of coloni- zation but represent a broadening faith on the part of literate blacks in print culture and the effectiveness of the written word in elevating and mobilizing people of color and also overcoming white prejudice. As we have seen, by 1829 this belief already had a fairly long tradition and was related to the history of black churches and secular orga- nizations in the Eastern cities. Walker was highly unusual in writ- ing a pamphlet that actually reached the hands of Southern slaves, thus igniting a national furor, especially after Nat Turner's allegedly related slave rebellion of 1831. But the words of Cornish and Walker were also read by important whites, such as the young William Lloyd Garrison,[62] a would-be reformer who, in the words of historian David Blight, "came hungry and angry and in need of his own liberation as he learned about the desperation of millions that had been caused by slavery in America."[63]

Cornish and Walker were by no means the only or the most influ- ential blacks who interacted with Garrison, though Garrison's refusal to identify such influence makes it difficult to reconstruct the exact connections between black and white reformers. As historian Julie Winch has shown, it was James Forten and his fellow black leaders in Philadelphia, including the family of his wealthy and nearly white son-in-law, Robert Purvis, who kept radical abolitionism and oppo- sition to the ACS alive during the 1820s. Aided by the wandering but persistent white Quaker abolitionist Benjamin Lundy, they also helped Garrison emerge in the early 1830s as the central if highly con- troversial figure in American abolitionism—the man who launched *The Liberator* in 1831, published an all-out attack on colonization in 1832, founded the New-England Anti-Slavery Society in 1832, and cofounded the American Anti-Slavery Society in 1833.[64]

While it was Lundy, a longtime friend of Forten's, who converted Garrison to the abolitionist cause, it was Garrison's repudiation of colonization, which Lundy supported in various forms, that won him the devotion of Forten. Forten's continuing flow of monetary contributions kept Garrison's *The Liberator* alive (it then ran for thirty-five years), helped Garrison make his fund-raising trip to England in 1833, and prepared the way for the creation of the American Anti-Slavery Society. Forten also played a major part in persuading the extremely wealthy merchant Arthur Tappan, who bailed Garrison out of jail in Baltimore, to sever his ties with the ACS. And Forten played a crucial role in rounding up the black subscribers, who made up some 75 percent of *The Liberator*'s subscription list in 1834. Without that continuing black support the paper could not have survived. Forten also wrote countless letters, some containing confidential and negative information on Liberia, which Garrison printed in *The Liberator.* Forten's home in Philadelphia became a stopping place for scores of abolitionists of both races.[65]

Garrison was born in Newburyport, Massachusetts, late in 1805 and was only two when his father deserted the family, putting his upbringing entirely in the hands of a strong and deeply religious mother. He was an apprentice at a local newspaper, began writing at an early age, and by 1828 was editing a Boston paper promoting temperance. That year he met Benjamin Lundy, who since 1821 had been editing *The Genius of Universal Emancipation,* the first important American abolitionist paper. Lundy was in Boston to gain subscriptions to his paper and raise support for his cause—during his extensive travels he promoted manumissions in the South and assisted black emigrants to Haiti, even sailing to the island a number of times. Lundy in many ways embodied Garrison's ideal of the reformer-editor, and their meeting opened Garrison's eyes to the need for an all-out crusade to expose and combat the sins of slavery.

Garrison agreed to move to Baltimore in 1829 and become assistant editor of *The Genius of Universal Emancipation,* freeing Lundy for other priorities. There is much ambiguity regarding the influences and timing that led him to fuse a commitment to immediate emancipation with an unmitigated attack on colonization during the Baltimore years, from 1829 until his return to Boston in 1831 when he launched *The Liberator.*

While still in Boston, Garrison had expressed support for the ACS, while adding doubts about the efficiency of its plan, at a Fourth of July fund-raising ACS meeting. In his first edition as assistant editor of

Lundy's paper, he expressed similar sentiments, praising Liberia and hoping to see the funds for the ACS "as exhaustless as the number of applicants for removal," while also stressing the shortcomings and inadequacies of a plan that should be viewed and supported as an "auxiliary," not a "remedy."

Yet even in Boston, where he had had some personal contacts with blacks, Garrison had been impressed by black opposition to colonization and was influenced in 1829 by an outdoor black celebration of the British abolition of the slave trade. He had far more interaction with blacks in Baltimore, where he lived in a boardinghouse also occupied by William Watkins, a black reformer with whom Garrison discussed colonization and abolition. Lundy also took Garrison to Philadelphia, where he met both black and white abolitionists. In addition, in Philadelphia Garrison witnessed for the first time some of the cruelties of slave markets and the physical punishment of slaves, while on a more abstract level, he absorbed the radical attacks on "moderation" in such works as George Bourne's 1816 *The Book and Slavery Irreconcilable* and the English Quaker Elizabeth Heyrick's 1824 *Immediate, Not Gradual Abolition*. The latter, reprinted by Lundy in *The Genius of Universal Emancipation*, called for "a holy war,—an attack upon the strong holds, the deep intrenchments [*sic*] of the very powers of darkness," and eventually had a profound impact in both Britain and America.[66]

The phrase "immediate emancipation" has long evoked confusion and controversy. To the general public in the 1830s it meant simply the abolition of black slavery without delay or preparation. But the word "immediate" may denote something other than closeness in time; to many abolitionists it signified a rejection of intermediate agencies or conditions, a directness or forthrightness in action or decision. In this sense immediatism suggested a repudiation of the various media, such as colonization or apprenticeship, that had been advocated as remedies for the evils of slavery. To many reformers the phrase mainly implied a direct, intuitive consciousness of the sinfulness of slavery and a sincere, "immediate" commitment to work for its abolition. In this subjective sense the word "immediate" was charged with religious overtones and referred more to the moral disposition of the reformer than to a particular plan for emancipation. Thus, some reformers confused immediate abolition with an immediate personal decision to abstain from consuming slave-grown produce; and a person might be considered an immediatist if he or she was genuinely convinced that slavery should be abolished absolutely and without compromise, though not necessarily without some preparation. Such a range of meanings led unavoidably to misunderstanding. The ambiguity, however, was something more than semantic confusion. The doctrine of immediatism, in the form it took in both Britain and America in the 1830s, was at once a logical culmination of the antislavery movement and a token of a major shift in intellectual history, as abolitionists reacted against continuing slaveholder recalcitrance as well as a generation of unsuccessful "gradualism."[67]

Garrison's conversion in Baltimore to immediatism was visceral and total and had more to do with his own unrestrained, uninhibited language and actions than with any specific program for emancipation. For example, he was jailed for libel because he published a list indicting local merchants and community leaders for sinful ties with slavery. The meaning of immediatism for Garrison is exemplified by his famous rhetoric in the first issue of *The Liberator*:

> I am aware that many object to the severity of my language; but is there not cause for severity? I will be as harsh as truth, and as uncompromising as justice. On this subject, I do not wish to think, or to speak, or write, with moderation. No! No! Tell a man whose house is on fire to give a moderate alarm; tell him to moderately rescue his wife from the hands of the ravisher; tell the mother to gradually extricate her babe from the fire into which it has fallen;—but urge me not to use moderation in a cause like the present. I am in earnest—I will not equivocate—I will not excuse—I will not retreat a single inch—AND I WILL BE HEARD. The apathy of the people is enough to make every statue leap from its pedestal, and to hasten the resurrection of the dead.[68]

Such language was far more extreme than that of early black abolitionists, except for some passages in David Walker's *Appeal*. But the blacks' writing presupposed a kind of immediatism, and 20 percent of the nearly two hundred articles published in *The Liberator*'s first year came from black writers. In order to counteract the claims of slavery's apologists, many white abolitionists began appending black "testimony" to their essays condemning black slavery. One antiabolitionist declared that Garrison was nothing but a "white Negro." And black abolitionist William Watkins wrote in *The Liberator* in 1831: "We recognize, in *The Liberator* . . . a FAITHFUL REPRESENTATIVE OF OUR sentiments and interests; and an uncompromising advocate of OUR indefensible rights."[69] As Richard Newman concludes, "Whites were the newcomers to the more radical abolitionist strategy of declaring a moral war against bondage; black activists had been using it for decades."[70]

Thanks to this connection, Garrison's gratitude to his "colored brethren" was more than matched by immense loyalty and affection on the part of blacks.[71] If Garrison's attacks on slavery and colonization conveyed little that was new, they served to mobilize the black community. As James Forten put it in a letter to Garrison, "Upon the colored population in the free states, it has operated like a trumpet call. They have risen in their hopes and feelings to the perfect stature of men; in this city [Philadelphia], every one of them is as tall as a giant."[72] Theodore Wright later echoed the same message: "At that dark moment we heard a voice;—it was the voice of GARRISON, speaking in trumpet tones! It was like the voice of an angel of mercy! . . . The signs of the times began to indicate brighter days."[73]

While Garrison never directly gave credit to blacks for converting him on the subject of colonization, he did emphasize that blacks had long opposed the idea and strongly refuted opponents' claims that he himself was responsible for anticolonizationist sentiment in the black community:

> From the organization of the American Colonization Society, down to the present time, the free people of color have publicly and repeatedly expressed their opposition to it. They indignantly reject every overture for their expatriation. It has been industriously circulated by the advocates of colonization, that I have caused this hostility to the African scheme in the bosoms of blacks; and that, until the Liberator was established, they were friendly to it. This story is founded upon sheer ignorance. It is my solemn conviction that I have not proselytized a dozen individuals; for the very conclusive reason that no conversions were necessary.[74]

Following this statement, in his *Thoughts on African Colonization,* Garrison printed sixty-eight pages on "Sentiments of the People of Color," documenting black protests against colonization. But strangely enough, while he began with the two Philadelphia resolutions of 1817, signed by James Forten, Garrison overlooked *Freedom's Journal* and other sources and jumped to a large number of documents from 1831 and 1832. Despite his claims of near universal black opposition to colonization, this gap in dates seemed to undermine his denial of his own influence.

In *Thoughts on Colonization,* as in his other writings, Garrison reveals an unmitigated religious faith that he can overcome the lies and misrepresentations that had enabled the ACS to win support from much of the clergy, media, and even state legislatures, to say nothing of the general public. His model, quite simply, was the kind of religious conversion that begins by exposing sin and guilt and leads to immediate repentance and change of behavior—a "teetotal" abandonment of alcohol, in the terms of temperance. He clearly hoped that the widespread belief in ultimate divine judgment or retribution would reinforce this kind of war on sin.

As we have seen, John Russwurm became convinced that since no such "conversion" could possibly end or even mitigate America's profound racism and discrimination against blacks, colonization became the only solution. In contrast, Garrison *documented* the racial discrimination and blamed it on the ACS—as part of their efforts "to render the situation of the free blacks intolerable" and thus coerce people like Russwurm into leaving. Determined to create and nourish "the bitterest animosity against the free blacks," the ACS kept warning the free states, "Your colored population can never be rendered serviceable, intelligent or loyal; they will only, and always, serve to increase your taxes, crowd your poor-houses and penitentiaries, and corrupt and impoverish society!" At the end of *Thoughts on Colonization,* Garrison took the risk of printing colonization documents claiming that in Connecticut blacks comprised only a thirty-fourth of the population, and yet furnished one-third of all convicts, and that in Vermont 24 of the 918 blacks were in the penitentiary.[75]

Yet Garrison thought he could convince his readers that with the defeat and removal of colonization, the way would be open for the uplift and improvement of the free black population, for an all-out campaign against racial prejudice and discrimination, and for the crusade to convince slaveholders of their sins. It is significant that in his survey of racism, Garrison concentrates on discriminatory state laws and says little about the public opinion he is confident he can help transform. And with respect to that goal, given the public's generally negative views of slavery, he again and again highlights the proslavery aspects of the ACS, arguing that their main and ultimate objective is to strengthen and perpetuate the slave system by removing from the South the great bulk of the country's free black population, which, he and the colonizationists agree, presents an increasingly corruptive and dangerous influence on the slaves.

Since people supported colonization for quite diverse and even conflicting reasons, it was not difficult to dismiss many criticisms as applying to others and not oneself. But that was not easy when it came to a central contradiction. As Garrison put it:

> In one breath, colonization orators tell us that the free blacks are pests in the community; that they are an intemperate, ignorant, lazy, thievish class; that their condition is worse than that of the slaves; and that no efforts to improve them in this country can be successful, owing to the prejudices of society. In the next breath we are told what mighty works these miserable outcasts are to achieve—that they are the missionaries of salvation, who are to illumine all Africa—that they will build up a second American republic—and that our conceptions cannot grasp the result of their labors. Now I, for one, have no faith in this instantaneous metamorphosis. I believe that neither a sea voyage nor an African climate has any miraculous influence on the brain.[76]

This passage, while devastating as criticism of the ACS, raises the crucial issue, to be explored in the next chapter, of how to "improve and uplift" the free black population. Even though Garrison and the abolitionists rejected the portrayal of an "intemperate, ignorant, lazy, thievish class," and especially the argument that free blacks in the North were worse off than slaves in the South, they recognized the dismal and depressing effects of generations of profound discrimination. Garrison stressed the intellectual and social deprivations of slavery and accused the ACS of thwarting the education of free blacks.

Yet there were some significant differences between white and black abolitionists. As David Blight has observed, "For blacks especially, many of whom were former slaves who wore the scars of bondage on their backs and in their psyches, the emergencies of freedom, security, and basic rights did not permit them the luxury of debate over ideological or strategic purity that sometimes occupied white abolitionists."[77] Garrison's free black supporters were even more focused on the issues of education and improvement and much more concerned with social equality and civil rights. They were also far more pragmatic in their approach to reform and would become impatient and sometimes mystified by the white abolitionists' ideological debates and divisions. But these differences would become more apparent in the 1840s and 1850s, after the division of the American Anti-Slavery Society and the emergence of political activism.

8

Free Blacks as the Key to Slave Emancipation

RECOGNITION OF THE ISSUE

On March 8, 1853, Frederick Douglass wrote a long and highly detailed response to Harriet Beecher Stowe, now world famous as the author of *Uncle Tom's Cabin*, who had requested information that "would permanently contribute to the improvement and elevation of the free coloured people in the Unites States." Nearly twenty years after the founding of the American Anti-Slavery Society, Douglass emphasized a point that had dominated early relations between black and white American abolitionists but had then declined as a priority: "The most telling, the most killing refutation of slavery, is the presentation of an industrious, enterprising, thrifty, and intelligent free black population." He also stressed that "the most powerful arguments now used by the Southern slaveholder, and the one most soothing to his conscience, is that derived from the low condition of the free coloured people in the North."[1]

As already implied in our discussions of the Haitian Revolution and the option of colonizing freed American slaves, the ongoing status of blacks who had *already* been emancipated, whether in Haiti, the Northern American states, or the British West Indies, had a crucial bearing on debates over the immediate or gradual liberation of millions of African American slaves whose future place in society was difficult to predict. Indeed, it is worth underscoring the obvious but often neglected point that for the general public, especially in America, the key issue raised by abolitionism was the status and condition of freed slaves. Stowe's and Douglass's interest in the "permanent . . . improvement and elevation" of the free black population also ties in with our earlier central theme of dehumanization and animalization as part of the process of reducing a human to the status of chattel property, an instrument to serve the needs of an owner. Ideally, for the master or mistress, a slave is a person who has internalized a consuming desire to please and flatter the owner, like a loving pet. As we have seen, according to Northerners like the eminent and procolonizationist New England clergyman Leonard Bacon, writing in 1823, slavery had so completely dehumanized the African American that he could never safely be raised "from the abyss of his degradation" without being colonized in a much less racist environment.

Unfortunately, in 1853, seventy-three years after Pennsylvania first led the Northern states toward gradual emancipation, twenty-six years after New York State celebrated the liberation of its last slaves, reformers like Douglass and Stowe realized that the plight of free blacks in the North had in some ways continued to deteriorate, a point dramatized by the African Americans' own testimony, by proslavery arguments and statistics on black incarceration in the North, and especially by the dangers imposed by the Fugitive Slave Law of 1850. Even in 1846 Douglass had acknowledged, after a Philadelphia mob had attacked a black temperance society parade of 1,200 marchers and then rampaged against blacks and their homes for two days:

> The colored man in the United States has great difficulties in the way of moral, social, and religious advancement. Almost every step he takes towards mental, moral, or social improvement is repulsed by the cold indifference or the active mob of the white. He is compelled to live an outcast from society . . . and the very fact of his degradation is given as a reason why he should be continued in the condition of a slave.[2]

Yet, as we shall see, many free blacks had overcome formidable barriers to great achievement, and countless black and white abolitionists had struggled to educate and elevate the free black community in ways that would counteract the parasitical abuse of institutional racism, by which whites gained pride and a sense of superiority from the blacks' alleged "incapacity" and loss of self-respect—a form of psychological exploitation that depended on "keeping Negroes in their place."

The complexities of this struggle, especially involving such issues as black gratitude and reaction to white paternalism, demand special imaginative efforts on the part of both author and reader. We must try at the start to imagine what it would have been like to have been both a free black abolitionist and a white abolitionist in the antebellum North.

As free "Negroes" in the mid-1840s, we abolitionists and most other blacks are always conscious that most of our brethren are chattel slaves in the South and that we can easily be kidnapped, or officially arrested, and sold in the South, suddenly deprived of our family members and our very names. But in some ways free blacks are better off in the Deep South. New laws have been passed to keep us from entering or settling in states north of the Ohio River, and many towns in the North have passed ordinances requiring us to register or even post bond for good behavior. Most states deny us the right to vote, sit on juries, or even testify against whites in court. Most free blacks are illiterate and even our children have little chance of attaining a grade school education. Perhaps most important, we are surrounded by white supremacy and are constantly viewed as inferior people in our daily interactions with whites— who sometimes verbally curse or ridicule us or even spit on us on the street, and whose egos climb when we bow or step off the walk to let them pass. No matter how close we might become to a white friend, we cannot accompany him or her to most restaurants, hotels, stores, libraries, lectures, concerts, and public places (except in a few radical communities).

It is true, there have been many breakthroughs since 1830, when the vast majority of our brethren regarded all whites as our enemies. Black and white abolitionists changed this stereotype. Now, we "can witness the labors and sacrifices of white men and women in a cause inseparably linked with our own." At abolitionist meetings, we speak to racially mixed audiences of both men and women. In short, white abolitionists have heightened our optimism and our quest for self-improvement and self-respect, though most of us feel that despite their hatred of slavery, they care far too little about the true social equality of the two races.[3]

Beginning in the 1830s, with the rise of "immediatism" or "modern" abolitionism, we worked closely with white abolitionists, convincing them to repudiate the American Colonization Society. Gradually we saw the need for some independence as they focused on abstractions and became embroiled in needless and distractive conflicts. We are of course immensely grateful to those very few who speak out on our behalf, but we are no less conscious of the traces of condescension and superiority conveyed, often unconsciously, even by most of our ardent white supporters.

No one has exposed the meaning of that prejudice more eloquently than our brother Theodore S. Wright (1797–1847), minister of New York's black Presbyterian Church, who in 1837 declared that while we free colored people are spared many of the evils of slavery, "But sir, still we are slaves— everywhere we feel the chain galling us":

> *This spirit is withering all our hopes, and ofttimes causes the colored parent as he looks upon his child, to wish he had never been born. . . . This influence cuts us off from everything; it follows us from childhood to manhood; it excludes us from all stations of profit, usefulness and honor; takes away from us all motive for pressing forward in enterprises, useful and important to the world and to ourselves. . . . A colored man can hardly learn a trade, and if he does it is difficult for him to find any one who will employ him to work at that trade. . . . In most of our large cities there are associations of mechanics who legislate out of their society colored men. And in many cases where our young men have learned trades, they have had to come to low employments for want of encouragement in those trades.[4]*

As white abolitionists, we are committed in principle to racial equality and believe that slaves, like captives illegally held by force, have an "immediate" right to be freed. We may even pride ourselves on having close personal ties with a few black coworkers, with whom we have faced hostile white mobs. Yet, as devout Christian reformers intent on ideals of moral improvement, we are appalled when we view the state of urban black society.

Most whites wrongly believe that the black urban population keeps increasing, in part because lowly black workers are so visible from the earliest morning, when street sweepers kick up clouds of disagreeable dust. Then in New York the streets are filled with black vendors noisily peddling their goods. Unemployed blacks crowd the docks searching for work, black performers appear on the roofs, many black men drink through the day at local dram shops, and under cover of darkness, criminal gangs assemble in back alleys. After midnight, black "tubmen" empty the privies and move about the city dumping the city's personal waste into the Hudson River. Even our fellow

*black abolitionists are deeply disturbed by the number of young blacks in
the city, including tradesmen, domestics, artists, and performers, who are
indifferent to efforts for the kind of community uplift and moral improvement
that is essential for overcoming racial prejudice.[5]*

*Like most of the radical white abolitionists of the 1830s, we earlier
supported the American Colonization Society as the only hope of overcoming
deeply entrenched white racism and securing some realistic solution to
the problem of slave emancipation. We then learned, mainly from blacks
themselves, that the ACS actually promoted and reinforced racism. While we
are committed to racial equality in the long run, some colleagues stress that
promoting that cause will antagonize many potential supporters and greatly
delay slave emancipation, a measure that will depend on converting public
opinion. But, while the challenges are momentous (and this will be difficult
for our descendants to grasp), we fervently believe that God is dedicated to
humanity's historical progress as well as to the retributive punishment of
nations that reject all chances to reform.*

(A white abolitionist's last note, looking ahead to the twenty-first
century: Belief in divine intervention and collective punishment
was absolutely central to abolitionism in Britain as well as America.
Unfortunately, a later modern and secular failure to understand the
radical potentialities of evangelical religion has distorted interpretations of our commitment to racial equality. Some students and even a
few historians have been inclined to view the entire white abolitionist approach to free blacks as condescending, patriarchal, and even
racist.)

ABOLITIONIST ADDRESSES TO FREE AFRICAN AMERICANS

Two official *Addresses*—letters to the free people of color from abolitionist leaders reveal a great deal about the campaign for racial uplift
as an instrument for slave emancipation. Since whites dominated the
biracial antislavery organizations, there is good reason to read the
words as expressions of a white mentality. But, except for some passages that convey a special white identity, the main arguments, values, and assumptions resemble those in an address to the free black
population from a black convention held in Philadelphia in June 1832,
as well as those in numerous other black publications.[6]

The first *Address*, directed to some twenty thousand blacks of New

York City, in October 1834, by the Executive Committee of the newly formed American Anti-Slavery Society (AASS), was signed by the white abolitionists Arthur and Lewis Tappan, Joshua Leavitt, Simeon Jocelyn, John Rankin, Elizur Wright Jr., and A. L. Cox. It begins with much praise for the blacks' "wonderful forbearance, and peaceful endurance" in responding to a recent race riot in which "an infuriated mob" attacked people of color, destroyed their property, and reduced their churches to "scenes of sacrilege, pillage, and ruin." According to the abolitionists, the blacks' behavior aroused the sympathy and respect of the public and now presents a favorable opportunity for blacks to unite with the AASS, which is officially pledged to "the improvement and civil elevation of the Free People of Color" in overcoming racial prejudice; to secure the "rights and immunities" to which blacks are entitled "as men and citizens"; and to remove obstacles "to the emancipation of two millions of our countrymen in bondage at the south."[7]

Note that the blacks' peaceful response to the racist mobs seemed to remove the fear of revenge and Haitian-like violence that Bacon had associated with the rehumanization of freed slaves. And the abolitionist authors' later examples of black achievement—such as the acceptance "on terms of perfect equality" of two black delegates at a convention called for the nomination of a new governor for the state of Maine—challenged the belief in black incapacity. The goal of the *Address* was to urge people of color to work with the new biracial Phoenix Society, founded by black reformers and dedicated to "your improvement in morals, literature, and the mechanic arts, and thereby to secure to you all other important privileges." But the success of this enterprise—which planned to register every colored person in the city, to enroll their children in schools, "to induce the adults also to attend school and church on the Sabbath," to establish circulating libraries and lyceums for lectures, and in every way to encourage blacks "to improve their minds and abstain from every vicious and demoralizing practice"—depended most of all on "personal effort."[8]

After stressing that the white abolitionists would never underrate the virtues of the colored people, the authors wrote that "it would be folly in us to deny that there are numbers of colored persons, who are helping to swell the amount of degradation, infamy and ruin, which so fearfully abounds in this great city." It was therefore in the spirit of "real friendship" that the abolitionists turned to some specific causes and remedies of "human wretchedness." Surprisingly, nothing is said of crime. Even unemployment is dismissed as a "rare" problem that can be solved by having urban blacks seek work on farms in the countryside and by training youth in the "mechanic arts."[9] The crucial issues involved Christian piety, responsibility, and respectability, which were above all threatened by intemperance, gambling, and Sabbath-breaking:

> We perceive . . . with great pain, several Porter Houses and dram shops, not a few of which are open on the Sabbath, and are kept by colored persons, which are resorted to by many of the youth and other persons of color. The number of these places appears to increase with the population of the city. The awful consequences attending such establishments, to youth, to families, and to the community, cannot be described. It is lamentable that any persons who profess any respect for themselves, should enter these gates of destruction.[10]

Hence, the black man who could pull himself away from the dram shops, refuse to sell or buy lottery tickets, and then regularly attend church and whatever school or lectures were available, would cast a crucial vote for the emancipation of "your and our enslaved brethren."

It should be noted that according to one study, the total per capita consumption in 1830 of distilled liquor in what was then our "alcoholic republic" came to 4.7 gallons, or 2.6 times the amount drunk in the 1970s. The striking increase in drinking in the early nineteenth century helped to fuel in the 1820s a massive and vibrant temperance movement that preceded and then overlapped with the abolition movement. By 1840, the consumption of hard liquor had fallen to an estimated 3.1 gallons per capita, and by the 1850s to 2.2.[11]

In his 1846 lecture on temperance and antislavery, given in Scotland, Frederick Douglass affirmed that "The [American] blacks are to a considerable extent intemperate, and if intemperate, of course vicious in other respects, and this is counted against them as a reason why their emancipation should not take place." Yet, by the 1830s, Northern free blacks had become deeply involved in the temperance crusade, and since they were barred from membership in most of the white organizations, they founded numerous and thriving colored temperance societies. Virtually all of the major black leaders, including Douglass, became ardent proponents of Prohibition.[12]

The second letter, *An Address to Free Colored Americans*, published in New York in 1837 by the newly formed and biracial Anti-Slavery Convention of American Women, carefully avoided paternalistic admonitions and complaints. Despite the fact that the organization included such notable figures as Lucretia Mott, the Grimké sisters, and Lydia Maria Child, the thirty-two-page *Address* has been neglected by historians even though it is one of the most eloquent and sophisticated abolitionist calls for racial equality. It also bears directly on both the dehumanization of slaves and the issue raised by Stowe and Douglass. But many modern readers would be troubled by the fact that the wording is saturated with Christian passion and based on the widely shared abolitionist conviction that racial slavery and emancipation were all part of God's master plan for human redemption.[13]

The four-day convention opened in New York City on May 9, 1837, and included some two hundred women, perhaps twenty of them black, from nine states. Since men were excluded, it was the first major public political meeting of women in American history and provided an opportunity to discuss and debate "almost every major theme concerning women's rights that would be explored a full decade later at the 1848 Seneca Falls Women's Rights Convention."[14] This is a matter of some importance, given the fact that the move for gender equality has become the greatest social revolution in modern history.

But the purpose of the organizers was to enable women to participate in a national campaign to collect 1 million signatures on petitions to Congress calling for the abolition of slavery in the District of Columbia and in Florida Territory (it was assumed that the Constitution prohibited direct federal intervention against slavery in the existing states). This was a time when American abolitionists hoped to follow the remarkably successful British model of bombarding government with antislavery petitions. Congressman John Quincy Adams, for example, to whom the Convention addressed a special letter of gratitude, was challenging a "gag rule" preventing any consideration or discussion of any antislavery petitions.

The Convention succeeded in raising funds, coordinating the petition campaign, and preparing six pamphlets and "open letters" including a "Letter to the Women of Great Britain," "An Appeal to the Women of the *Nominally* Free States," drafted by Angelina Grimké, and the "Address to the Free Colored Americans," drafted by Angelina's sister, Sarah Grimké. The last two important documents were each prepared by a committee of three and then referred to a committee of nine for revision and publication. Nevertheless, they brought much fame to the Grimké sisters and it is more convenient to refer to the sisters as the authors.[15]

The Grimké sisters were born and reared in South Carolina, the daughters of a rich plantation owner who as an attorney and judge ardently supported the slave regime as well as the subordination of women. Sarah, twelve years older than Angelina, resented the inferiority of her own education as well as her father's fury over her attempts to teach her personal slave to read. Having accompanied her ill father to Philadelphia for medical care, Sarah moved there upon his death and became a Quaker convert. She persuaded Angelina to become a Quaker and move to Philadelphia in 1829. While the antislavery traditions of the Society of Friends encouraged the sisters to develop and express their own radical abolitionism, they soon clashed with the Quaker establishment over issues of slavery, racism, and especially women's rights, which the Grimkés saw as essential, since it would free women to help achieve slave emancipation. According to the sisters' friend Catherine H. Birney, the pamphlets they wrote at the Convention led the way to their becoming the most famous women speakers of the abolitionist movement and among the first women to speak publicly to mixed (then termed "promiscuous") audiences of women and men.[16]

The Anti-Slavery Convention of American Women evoked much public criticism and ridicule concerning the proper role of women and the standards governing the relationship between blacks and whites. Some white delegates, like the Grimkés, who were acutely sensitive to racial prejudice among abolitionists, recognized that the black women delegates always confronted *both* racism and sexism wherever they turned. While the the Convention was engaged in "animated discussion" of "the province of women," Angelina Grimké decried the indifference with which American churches had regarded the sin of slavery and implored every woman to reject

the circumscribed limits with which corrupt custom and a perverted application of Scripture have encircled her; therefore that it is the duty of woman, and the province of woman, to plead the cause of the oppressed in our land, and to do all that she can by her voice, and her pen, and her purse, and the influence of her example, to overthrow the horrible system of American slavery.[17]

This challenge to institutional religion, implying that individual women could wholly reinterpret Scripture, shocked many delegates and of course invited clerical denunciation, which would persist as the Grimkés launched their fairly brief campaign as abolitionist speakers. The delegates were also divided over whether women should continue to pursue a separate course, as antislavery activists, or demand equality and join men in integrated societies. By 1840, this issue would lead to the major division and split in the national antislavery societies.

While Lydia Maria Child opposed the emphasis on women's rights, she joined the Grimkés in denouncing racism and proposed specific measures to encourage whites to hire more blacks and to avoid segregation by sitting next to blacks in churches and other gatherings. Angelina viewed racism as a kind of "demon" that whites must struggle to "root out." She told the Convention that "it is a solemn duty for every woman to pray to be delivered from such an unholy feeling and to act out the principles of Christian equality by associating with them [blacks] as if the color of the skin was of no more consequence than that of the hair, or the eyes." Only such dedicated personal efforts could remove "one of the chief pillars of American slavery."[18]

Turning now to the *Address to Free Colored Americans*, toward the end of the document Sarah Grimké pays passionate tribute to their beloved colored "Brethren and Sisters" for exposing the racism and criminality of the American Colonization Society and for probably preventing America from adding

> to her manifold transgressions against the descendants of Africa, the transcendent crime of banishing from her shores those whom she has deeply injured . . . You saw that the root of the evil was in our own land, and that expatriation of the best part of our colored population, so far from abolishing slavery, would render the condition of the enslaved tenfold more hopeless. . . .

After quoting the eloquent resolutions proclaimed by Philadelphia's blacks soon after the ACS was founded, Grimké makes clear that future generations should honor America's free blacks for initiating and making possible an abolitionist movement "on which heaven has smiled (for it could have success only from the great Master)."[19]

Endorsing the blacks' view that "the Colonization Society originated in hatred to the free people of color," Grimké then turns to the issue of white "supercilious prejudice" and "arrogant pretensions of unfounded superiority." She acknowledges that many whites who have "a kind of sentimental desire for your welfare" are nevertheless "anxious to keep you as they term it, in your proper place." Grimké even admits that the women can understand this denial to blacks of full social equality, since "most, if not all of us have had to combat these feelings, and such of us as have overcome them, have abundant cause to sing hallelujah to our God, and bless his holy name for our abolition principles; they have opened a source of heavenly joy in our bosoms, which we would not exchange for all the gold of Ophir."[20]

This extraordinary candor, based on a millennial faith in "that blessed and glorious era, when the brother of low degree will rejoice in that he is exalted, and the brother of high degree in that he is made low," encouraged Grimké to persuade black readers that the women were true friends and sisters who understood the dilemmas of race in antebellum America. In particular, they had learned that racism—"the unfounded calumny that the people of color are unfit for freedom"—had been "designed, on the part of slaveholders, as a salve for their consciences, and a plea for the continuation of slavery, and is used . . . for the diabolical purpose of shielding from merited infamy the system of American slavery."[21]

Christian empathy also offered a possible solution to the great problem of reconciling slave dehumanization with black capability. The *Address* begins with an effort to persuade black readers that abolitionists grasp the very worst aspects of human bondage. " 'THE WORST IS NOT GENERALLY KNOWN,' " one Southerner is quoted as saying, after describing the institution's well-known physical cruelties: "the nakedness of some [slaves], the hungry yearnings of others, the wailings and wo[e], the bloody cut of the keen lash, and the frightful scream that rends the very skies—and all this to gratify lust, pride, avarice, and other depraved feelings of the human heart." Grimké then stresses that it is much easier for all people, who are "alive to bodily pain," to apprehend the slaves' *physical* sufferings. Only a comparative few appreciate the slaves' "mental and spiritual degradation"—that is, the effects of dehumanization:

Slavery seizes a rational and immortal being crowned by Jehovah with glory and honor, and drags him down to a level with the beasts that perish. It makes him a thing, a chattel personal, a machine to be used to all intents and purposes for the benefit of another. . . . It would annihilate the individual worth and responsibility conferred upon man by his Creator. It deprives him of the power of self-improvement. . . . It prevents him from laboring in a sphere to which his capacities are adapted. It abrogates the seventh commandment, by annulling the obligations of marriage, and obliging the slaves to live in a state of promiscuous intercourse, concubinage, and adultery. . . . It dooms its victims to ignorance, and consequently to vice.

The *Address* then quotes Southerner Samuel McDowell Moore, who delivered a blistering attack on slavery during the debate over emancipation and deportation in Virginia's House of Delegates, in January 1832, in response to Nat Turner's revolt:

I think I may safely assert that ignorance is the inseparable companion of slavery, and that the desire of freedom [evidenced by Nat Turner] is the inevitable consequence of implanting in the human mind any useful degree of intelligence: it is therefore the policy of the master that ignorance of his slaves should be as profound as possible; and such a state of ignorance is wholly incompatible with the existence of any moral principles or exalted feeling in the breast of the slave.[22]

So depicting slavery "at its worst" creates a huge dilemma. Grimké is now calling for the emancipation of dehumanized humans whose supposed ignorance and lack of foresight would seem to preclude any capability of becoming responsible free citizens or participants in the social compact. Grimké clearly recognized the danger of slipping into a racist conclusion, a circular, self-perpetuating argument in which the dehumanization of slavery leads to an Aristotelian view of the docile "natural slave," of men *born* to be bondsmen.

It was doubtless Sarah Grimké's stroke of brilliance to add the citation, "(Speech of Mr. Moore, House of Delegates, Va., 1832)," following the passage above that "such a state of ignorance is wholly incompatible with the existence of any moral principles or exalted feeling in the breast of the slave." Nat Turner's bloody insurrection was still a vivid memory, especially in the minds of many free blacks and white Southerners such as Grimké.[23] If the Executive Committee of the AASS had earlier seen the wisdom of praising the "peaceful endurance" of New York City blacks when confronting a racist mob, this was now an occasion, for Grimké, to refer very obliquely to the slaves' desire for freedom and capacity for armed resistance—to the slaveholders' failure at achieving full dehumanization.

Later on there is another significant reference to the Nat Turner–inspired Virginia legislative debate, following an appeal to Northern free blacks to consider abstaining, "as far as practicable," from the products of slave labor. After stressing that friends of emancipation were increasingly interested in such a boycott and in finding free labor substitutes, Grimké affirms that the Southern slave will rejoice at the news that his Northern friends "feel a sympathy so deep for his sufferings, that they cannot partake of the proceeds of his unrequited toil." But how could supposedly ignorant, dehumanized chattel be aware of Northern abolitionists? One answer came from "Mr. Goode," whose resolution produced "the celebrated debate" in the Virginia legislature, and who reminded planters who were in a state of near panic over Turner's rebellion that many slaves were "'wise and intelligent men, constantly engaged in reflection, informed of all that was occurring, and having their attention fixed upon the Legislature.'" Grimké also cites evidence of slaves who "spent many a midnight hour in discussing the probable results of the abolition movements," to say nothing of the fact that every Northern fugitive slave "who is carried back, bears to his unhappy countrymen an account of all that is doing."[24]

But how can one reconcile the view that slavery transforms a human into "a thing, a chattel personal, a machine to be used . . . for the benefit of another" with the image of recaptured fugitives secretly conveying the latest news about Northern abolitionists to highly alert slaves who also converse about Nat Turner and the Virginia legislative debates? Of course we now know that the desires and goals of slaveholders were considerably limited by the slaves' resistance, negotiation, subcultures, and by the realities of human nature. The slave community also included a broad spectrum, ranging from lowly field workers to a few highly privileged bondspeople who sometimes had extraordinary power and responsibilities. And we discussed earlier the historians' debates inspired in part by Stanley Elkins's 1959

"Sambo" stereotype, and examined the complexities of slave dehumanization, white psychological parasitism, and the effects of such racism on black self-esteem.

For Grimké and the women abolitionists, however, the crucial and overriding premise came with their declaration that "the people of color are not in any respect inferior to the white man, and that under favorable circumstances they would rise again to *the rank they formerly held.*" If the minds of the American slaves, "who are writhing under the lash of worse than Egyptian taskmasters . . . are beclouded by ignorance and enfeebled by suffering," we are assured that they "need only to have the same advantages which Europeans and their descendants have enjoyed, [in order] triumphantly to refute the unfounded calumny that they are inferior in powers of intellect, and less susceptible of mental improvement."[25]

Given these assumptions, one can imagine a "modern" reformer proposing a massive Freedman's Bureau rehabilitation program, working to convey equal "advantages," to accompany slave emancipation. In very limited ways, the British plan of "apprenticeship," inaugurated in 1834 with slave emancipation, was *advertised* as a step in this direction of "preparation" for freedom. But, given America's tradition of mistrusting government power (and before the era of Social Security or even support for high-school education), any widespread agreement that slave emancipation *required* an expensive program of rehabilitation would have been seen as a fatal barrier to emancipation. As it happened, Congress had to override President Andrew Johnson's veto in order to permit the unpopular Freedman's Bureau to continue its valuable work for three more years. It is true that after the Civil War the federal government spent over $4 million in launching a huge grassroots campaign to reinter the bodies of some 303,536 Union soldiers who were left in the South and vulnerable to vengeful former Confederates. However, historian Drew Gilpin Faust stresses that this reburial program "would have been unimaginable before the war" and, significantly, that the U.S. Colored Troops were especially targeted and segregated in death as well as in life.[26]

Like Frederick Douglass, Sarah Grimké saw that the best answer to the dilemma of slave dehumanization and black capability lay in what Douglass termed "the presentation of an industrious, enterprising, thrifty, and intelligent free black population," though Grimké put far greater emphasis on religious values like piety and humility.

Religion reinforced the women abolitionists' faith that local and private efforts could be effective and that the Northern free blacks could become a model for a grassroots campaign led by literate, knowledgeable, and educated blacks aided by white abolitionists and religious or charitable organizations.

As the *Address* puts it, speaking to the women's black "brethren and sisters":

> Nothing will contribute more to break the bondman's fetters, than an example of high moral worth, intellectual culture and religious attainments among the free people of color—living epistles known and read of all men—a standard of exalted piety, of dedication to the works of righteousness, of humble-mindedness, of Christian charity; to which abolitionists may confidently point . . . and demand of them [slaveholders], in view of what their slaves might be, to restore their victims to themselves, to the human family, and to God.[27]

To convince readers of the possibility of such *restoration*, Grimké then presents many pages of evidence of black achievement and capability, starting with ancient Africa (especially Egypt) and including the current testimony of teachers regarding the intellectual progress of black students. The *Address* even underscores the attainments of black "Generals, Physicians, Philosophers, Linguists, Poets, Mathematicians, and Merchants." Noted for their kindness and generosity, most free blacks were even in some ways in a more favorable situation for "the growth of piety," since being in "the furnace of adversity" they were less corrupted by prosperity and "the love of money, which is the root of all evil."

The *Address* finally turns to the sensitive issue of offering some advice before making a final appeal. Nothing is said of the supposed "vices" traditionally associated with black degradation. Invoking the model of Christ's humility, Grimké recommends simplicity and frugality with regard to clothing and physical appearance and warns against attending the theater, a "sink of vice" that made use of the racist stereotypes of the blacks' oppressors. Since many of the presumed readers worked as servants for white families, "who have been educated with deep-rooted prejudices against you," the blacks had the opportunity "of proving that these prejudices are as unfounded as they are unjust—of exhibiting in your deportment, that moral loveliness which will constrain those who regard themselves as your superiors, to acknowledge that worth can neither be determined by the color of the skin, nor by the station occupied." Along with this optimism, the blacks are warned to carefully avoid "families which pay little or no respect to the Sabbath, that you may escape the contamination arising from such intercourse."[28]

Even house servants are exhorted to save money for the education of their children, and "every exertion" is urged for the establishment of good schools to aid "in the great work of moral and intellectual elevation":

> On the rising generation depends in a great measure the success of that enterprise, which aims at establishing Christian and Republican equality among the citizens of these United States. Let us then labor to implant in the minds of our children a love for useful learning, to imbue them thoroughly with religious feeling, to train them to habits of thinking, of industry and economy, to lead them to the contemplation of noble and benevolent objects, that they may regard themselves as responsible beings upon whom high and holy duties devolve.[29]

The ultimate and crucial goal of such education is to prepare the rising black generation to participate in "the great moral conflict between light and darkness, which now agitates our guilty country." While enthusiastically praising African Americans for launching a true abolition movement by repudiating the ACS, Grimké now calls on blacks to unite, "whenever you can," with such white organizations (and she is well aware of racist exclusion) as antislavery societies, peace societies ("based on the principle that all war is inconsistent with the gospel"), temperance societies, moral reform societies, maternal associations, and other groups dedicated to "the great work of Reformation." Such racial integration will have "reciprocal benefit," because it will tend to remove that unchristian prejudice which "bites like a serpent, and stings like an adder." Yet Grimké, as a member of the somewhat racially integrated Anti-Slavery Convention of American Women, was well aware that blacks "may have to suffer much in thus commingling, but we entreat you to bear hardness as good soldiers of

Jesus Christ that your children, and your children's children, may be spared the anguish you are compelled to endure on this account."[30]

In a final call for cooperation in abolishing slavery, racial prejudice, and inequality, Grimké proclaims that the women

> are sensible that our brethren of color have a more difficult and deli-
> cate part to act in this reformation, than their white fellow-citizens;
> but we confidently believe, that as their day is, so their strength will
> be; and we commend them and the cause of human rights, in which
> we are engaged, to Him [Jesus] who is able to save unto the uttermost
> all who come unto God by Him. May he strengthen us to pursue
> our holy purposes with the zeal of the Apostles and the spirit of the
> Martyrs.[31]

DAVID WALKER AND OVERCOMING
SLAVE DEHUMANIZATION

David Walker's famous and radical *Appeal To the Coloured Citizens of the World*, published in 1829, would seem to have come from a different world than Sarah Grimké's *Address*. Calling on the colored population of the world to unite and resist slavery and racial oppression, by violence if necessary, Walker's *Appeal* was smuggled into the slaveholding South where it evoked a sense of panic and defensive legislation and was blamed, along with other "inflammatory" works, for helping to incite Nat Turner's insurrection of 1831. But as we shall see, Walker and Grimké shared many of the same central concerns and values, including a passionate desire to solve the problems of black dehumanization and white racism, a religious aspiration to uplift the black population, and the goal of finally integrating blacks and whites as equal human beings in a democratic republic.

Walker, who was born to a free mother and slave father in Wilmington, North Carolina, grew up surrounded by slaves and a few other free blacks.[32] Like Sarah Grimké, as a Southerner he had the opportunity to view slavery "at its very worst," especially as he traveled around the South and lived for some years in Charleston, South Carolina, where he probably had some contact with Denmark Vesey's conspiracy of 1822. Even as a child Walker managed to receive a highly exceptional education, no doubt related to black religious organizations, with which he remained in contact when he moved to Boston in the mid-1820s. In Wilmington and Charleston, Walker interacted with free blacks who were highly skilled and well educated and he developed a deep devotion to the African Methodist Episcopal Church. In the *Appeal,* Walker pays passionate tribute to Philadelphia's bishop Richard Allen, even quoting a long letter from Allen attacking the colonization movement and declaring that "we are an unlettered people, brought up in ignorance, not one in a hundred can read or write, not one in a thousand has a liberal education; is there any fitness for such to be sent into a far country, among heathens, to convert or civilize them, when they themselves are neither civilized or Christianized?"[33] Like other free blacks in the anticolonization and emerging antislavery movement, Walker expressed pride in the Haitian Revolution, which blacks in Boston began celebrating in the mid-1820s, and was keenly aware of a tradition of rebellion that extended from the American slave conspiracies of 1800 and 1802 to Denmark Vesey.

In Boston, Walker started a used clothing store, a business blacks were beginning to dominate. He married in 1826, and by 1830, a year after the publication of his *Appeal,* had three children. In August 1830, the Boston Index of Deaths reported that Walker had died of consumption at the age of thirty-three, shortly after the death of a daughter from the same illness. Various stories immediately emerged, however, claiming that he had been murdered by Southern bounty hunters or other enemies.[34] By 1830 there were some 1,875 free blacks in Boston and Walker lived and worked next to self-employed barbers, tailors, bootblacks, and other small businessmen. As a rising member of Boston's African Lodge of Prince Hall Masonry, Walker also gained access to many of the most prominent men in the city's black community, including a few ministers, teachers, and lawyers. Black Freemason lodges, extending to New York, Philadelphia, Baltimore, Washington, and even Alexandria, Virginia, were part of the urban networks that enabled a systematic correspondence among black leaders and helped create a black abolitionist movement, which, based on fervent opposition to the ACS, revolutionized white abolitionism by the early 1830s. This development was also aided by two other institutions to which David Walker had close connections: the Massachusetts General Colored Association and the first black newspaper, *Freedom's Journal.*

Black opposition to being colonized in Africa coincided, as we have seen, with rising and virulent white racism and discrimination. Thus the efforts of blacks like Walker to unite and change the world around them were in part a response to daily threats and insults and to the ridicule in animalizing cartoons and posters that declared them unfit for freedom. Historian Peter Hinks is surely right when he argues that Walker and other black reformers, from Maria Stewart to the Negro Convention Movement of the 1830s, were not kowtowing to whites when they set the highest priority on black uplift and moral improvement. When they called for education, industry, temperance, self-confidence, ambition, regular work habits, and Protestant religion, they were seeking black *empowerment*—equipping blacks to compete and succeed in a society based on those values. Walker "knew full well that an integral part of white America's oppression of blacks was to deprive them of the opportunity to acquire knowledge" and to discourage behavior, such as diligence, enterprise, and temperance, that generated individual and collective respect.[35]

Although Sarah Grimké and the antislavery women approached the subject from a different angle than Walker died, they all agreed on the need to counter racism and discrimination by uplifting and empowering the free black population. Both black and white reformers were themselves empowered and motivated by a broad evangelical movement, the so-called Second Great Awakening, that nourished reforms ranging from public schools to temperance, universal male suffrage, and slave emancipation. However, as Hinks points out when considering divisions in the black community, many of Boston's African Americans "were neither church-going nor temperate, and they were not committed to study and displayed little interest in adopting the reformers' prescriptions for self-improvement."[36]

Grimké's *Address* and Walker's *Appeal* differ dramatically in style and approach. Unlike Grimké, Walker was appealing to slaves as well as to the literate free black minority who, he clearly hopes, would read his passionate words to their illiterate brethren. As he seeks to arouse and unite the entire black population, even outside the United States, he becomes highly emotional, in what amounts to a stream-of-consciousness sermon and at times seems close to losing control. Walker's pamphlet evoked much condemnation from white readers, and even the pioneer abolitionist Benjamin Lundy wrote that Walker "indulges himself in the wildest strain of fanaticism" and censured his "attempt to rouse the worst passions of human nature."[37] Yet Walker and Grimké share the same central concerns, assumptions, and even hopes and ideals. Both focus on "slavery at its worst," and Walker devotes many pages to the passionate argument that black slavery in the Americas is by far the worst form of oppression known in human history, worse even than that suffered by the ancient Israelites, Sparta's Helots, and slaves of the Romans. For Walker it is this fact, coupled with the intransigence of white racism, that justifies violent resistance—though he hopes for other possibilities.

Even more than Grimké, Walker expresses a deep concern over the way "slavery at its worst" has dehumanized American slaves and even many free blacks. On the issue of "incapacity," Walker anticipates Grimké in repeatedly emphasizing the word "ignorance" but then conveys fury over the slaves' subservience and complicity in aiding slaveholders. In one of the most memorable passages in the *Appeal*, Walker stops on the street in Boston to talk to a free black "with a string of boots on his shoulders," and remarks,

> "what a miserable set of people we are!" He asked why?—Said I, "we are so subjected under the whites, that we cannot obtain the comforts of life, but by cleaning their boots and shoes, old clothes, waiting on them, shaving them &c." Said he, (with the boots on his shoulders) "I am completely happy ! ! ! I never want to live any better or happier than when I can get a plenty of boots and shoes to clean! ! !"

Walker then explains that he is not troubled by such low employments as a reality of life but by the thought that whites will conclude "our Creator made us to be an inheritance to them for ever, when they see that our greatest glory is centered in such mean and low objects . . . My objections are, to our glorying and being happy in such low employments."[38]

Far worse for Walker was the way white oppression and dehumanization had led to submissiveness and even complicity on the part of black slaves. As Hinks puts it, Walker became convinced of "some significant degree of internal assent within black individuals to the supposed naturalness of white dominion over blacks."[39] What had happened, as Hinks interprets Walker's basic understanding, was that blacks failed to see their own oppression since they had internalized the whites' definition of their own identity and even felt a sense of duty and indebtedness to their more paternalistic masters. Walker provides numerous examples of slave docility and complicity, coupled with emotional outbursts:

> O, my God!—in sorrow I must say it, that my colour, all over the world, have a mean, servile spirit, They yield in a moment to the whites, let them be right or wrong—the reason they are able to keep their feet on our throats. Oh! my coloured brethren, all over the world, when shall we arise from this death-like apathy?—and be men! !⁴⁰

We read of an American slave woman who, being led south for sale with some sixty other slaves, enabled the white trader to recapture all the other blacks after they had escaped. Then we turn to the West Indies and South America, where "there are six or eight coloured persons for one white. Why do they not take possession of those places? . . . The fact is, they are too servile, they love to have Masters too well! !" In one passage, especially surprising in a supposedly revolutionary work, Walker claims that such evidence "shows at once, what the blacks are":

> we are ignorant, abject, servile and mean, and the whites know it— they know that we are too servile to assert our rights as men—or they would not fool with us as they do. Would they fool with any other peoples as they do with us? No, they know too well, that they would get themselves ruined. Why do they not bring the inhabitants of Asia to be body servants to them? They know they would get their bodies rent and torn from head to foot. Why do they not get the Aborigines of this country to be slaves to them and their children, to work their farms and dig their mines? They know well that the Aborigines of this country, or (Indians) would tear them from the earth. . . . But my colour, (some, not all,) are willing to stand still and be murdered by the cruel whites.⁴¹

In a number of such passages, Walker seems momentarily to doubt the innate equality of races or at least to accept the Stanley Elkins view that the extreme oppression of American slavery had led to compliant and brainwashed "Sambos" who had internalized the aims and goals of the master class.[42]

Given these uncertainties, Walker is understandably drawn to and becomes almost obsessed with Thomas Jefferson's infamous lines on black inferiority in *Notes on the State of Virginia*. Walker tells his readers that Jefferson "was one of [the] great[est] characters as ever lived among the whites" and "a much greater philosopher the world never afforded." As a result of his stature, Jefferson's verdict on blacks "has in truth injured us more, and has been as great a barrier to our emancipation as any thing that has ever been advanced against us."[43]

Nevertheless, Walker leads up to Jefferson's key statement with his own exclamation: "Oh! coloured people of these United States, I ask you, in the name of that God who made us, have we, in consequence of oppression, nearly lost the spirit of man, and in no very trifling degree, adopted that of brutes [i.e., become domesticated animals]? Do you answer, no?—I ask you, then, what set of men can you point me to, in all the world, who are so abjectly employed by their oppressors, as we are by our *natural enemies*?" After further examples of black dehumanization, Walker asks,

> How could Mr. Jefferson but say, "I advance it therefore as a suspicion only, that the blacks, whether originally a distinct race, or made distinct by time and circumstances, are inferior to the whites in the endowments both of body and mind?" . . . [H]ow could Mr. Jefferson but have given the world these remarks respecting us, when we are so submissive to them, and so much servile deceit prevail among ourselves—when we so *meanly* submit to their murderous lashes, to which neither the Indians nor any other people under Heaven would submit?[44]

Having argued that the blacks' dehumanized behavior had given Jefferson strong grounds for such a conclusion, Walker underscores the frightening implications of Jefferson's crucial question, "'What further is to be done with these people?'" Jefferson suggests that this question embarrasses many white advocates of emancipation who are then inclined to join "those who are actuated by sordid avarice only [in defending slavery]." And as a matter of fact, even late in the Civil War proslavery Democrats continued to prod Republicans with the question, "What is to be done with the negroes who may be freed?"[45] Walker agrees with Jefferson, arguing that white abolitionists are constantly betrayed by "our treachery, wickedness, and deceit." Blacks cannot therefore count on their white friends but must take a lesson from Jefferson and realize that nothing will count until they unite and prove "that we are MEN."[46]

If Walker's own examination of black dehumanization could lead him, with tears in his eyes, to "exclaim to my God, 'Lord didst thou make us to be slaves to our brethren, the whites?' " then it was all the more certain that "Mr. Jefferson's remarks respecting us, have sunk deep into the hearts of millions of the whites, and never will be removed this side of eternity." Walker must thus struggle with Jefferson's words—even at one point cleverly turning them around, when he advances his "suspicion," backed by historical evidence, whether whites are *"as good by nature as we are or not."* But above all he responds by exhorting his fellow blacks, especially the more educated "men of sense," to disprove Jefferson and resolve his own anxieties and doubts by overcoming the dehumanizing and bestializing effects of slavery and racial prejudice. It is primarily faith in God's support and providence that leads Walker to proclaim, "You have to prove to the Americans and the world, that we are MEN, and not *brutes,* as we have been represented, and by millions treated."[47]

It is this theme, especially including Walker's crucial faith in God's power to help change the hearts and minds of people, that brings us back to Grimké's *Address.* Like Walker, Grimké is much concerned with what she terms the slaves' "mental and spiritual degradation," though she never mentions the slaves' passivity and complicity. But like Walker, she would have passionately agreed with Frederick Douglass's assertion, quoted at the beginning of this chapter, that "The most telling, the most killing refutation of slavery, is the presentation of an industrious, enterprising, thrifty, and intelligent free black population."[48] Indeed, this was the central goal in both Grimké's and Walker's pamphlets, along with a racially integrated and harmonious society of black and white Americans, free from prejudice. And both ultimately rely on God to support a revolutionary transformation in both black and white consciousness—a transformation that would transcend the ordinary progression of time and history.[49]

Walker's despair over the behavior of his fellow blacks is at least partly countered by his prophetic voice—Hinks rightly states that he "virtually equated his pronouncements with the word of God." After proclaiming that England is the blacks' great friend, he ends one chapter with the declaration: "O Americans! Americans!! I call God— I call angels—I call men, to witness, that your DESTRUCTION *is at hand*, and will be speedily consummated unless you REPENT." He affirms that God has a special love for the colored people of the world, who are destined to be the ones who finally Christianize the world. While determined to undermine the psychological foundations of blacks' individual self-deception and, as in a religious conversion, to free the repressed but "unconquerable disposition" in their breasts, Walker speaks ultimately of a collective mission founded on a special, "chosen," relationship with God. A millennial vision pervades his work.[50]

But Hinks rightly notes that Walker's "stature as an architect of black nationalism has been overstated, and his commitment to a racially integrated society in which racial distinctiveness would play little role has been relatively ignored."[51] Despite his extremely acute sense of black victimization, Walker several times strikes the note of Christian forgiveness for the past if only whites could recognize black humanity. And he clearly believed that a change in black behavior could help facilitate that goal. Notwithstanding his few threats of black violence and divine retribution, Walker tried in the end to convey a very simple message:

> Treat us like men, and there is no danger but we will all live in peace and happiness together. . . . Treat us like men, and we will be your friends. And there is not a doubt in my mind, but that the whole of the past will be sunk into oblivion. . . . The whites may say it is impossible, but remember that nothing is impossible with God.[52]

JAMES MCCUNE SMITH AND JEFFERSON'S "WHAT FURTHER IS TO BE DONE WITH THESE PEOPLE?"

In many ways James McCune Smith became the fulfillment of David Walker's dreams of the educated and fully liberated African American leader. Despite their difference in age and formal education, Walker's and McCune Smith's interests overlapped—from major issues regarding slavery and race to the use of violence, the significance of a contented black bootblack, and the need to respond to

Jefferson's "Fourteenth Query" in his *Notes on the State of Virginia*. Only recently rescued from amazing obscurity (by historian John Stauffer), McCune Smith was "the foremost black intellectual in the nineteenth century," an ardent abolitionist who "with his polymath curiosity . . . aimed to elevate his race."[53]

Born a slave in New York City in 1813 (his unknown father was white), McCune Smith was formally freed in 1827 by the final Emancipation Act of New York State. As a boy McCune Smith became a star student at the New York African Free-School No. 2, an institution run by whites that was also attended by some of the most famous blacks of the next decades. Thanks to his early learning of foreign languages, McCune Smith became fluent in Greek, Latin, and French and proficient in German, Spanish, Italian, and Hebrew. Though turned down by American medical schools because of his race, McCune Smith was accepted by the highly prestigious University of Glasgow. During his five years abroad, always scoring near the top of his class, he won B.A., M.A., and M.D. degrees and became well read in the classics and humanities as well as in mathematics, statistics, and science. When he returned to New York in 1837, the year of Sarah Grimké's *Address,* McCune Smith was the most educated African American before W. E. B. DuBois, and welcomed as a celebrity by the leaders of the city's African American community. In Glasgow, McCune Smith had joined with Scottish abolitionists, living in an environment relatively free from racism, and had become deeply aware of the effects of American racial prejudice, which he considered a system of "caste."[54]

In New York, McCune Smith established a successful medical practice, treating both blacks and whites, and also ran a pharmacy. He won respect from white physicians for both his successful practice and his scientific writings. After marrying a woman from an esteemed black family, McCune Smith lived in a spacious house in Manhattan and helped raise his own family. Though somewhat reserved and private in personality, he became active in black literary and reform societies and gave lectures that ranged from highly empirical praise for and justification of the Haitian Revolution to a scientific rebuttal of the phrenological argument that skulls could be used to prove the inferiority of the brains of black people. McCune Smith also found time to become a highly prolific writer on a vast range of subjects. Along with publishing pieces in leading medical journals, he became the New York correspondent for *Frederick Douglass's Paper* and in 1855 wrote the introduction to Douglass's famous *My Bondage and My Freedom*. Douglass termed McCune Smith the "foremost black influence" in his life. Along with friends Douglass, Gerrit Smith, and John Brown, McCune Smith helped to found a new political party, the Radical Abolitionists, and chaired its inaugural convention in Syracuse in June 1855. The party accepted the possible need for violence, exemplified in John Brown's later plan at Harpers Ferry, and in many ways fulfilled David Walker's dreams.

Like Grimké and Walker, McCune Smith's overriding concerns were the elevation of the free black population, transforming the hearts as well as minds of white people, slave emancipation, and the eventual goal of a society of integrated equals. Like Walker, McCune Smith became deeply troubled over the passivity and complicity of blacks who had internalized a racist identity, but unlike Walker, he overcame this concern in a way that greatly reinforced his millenarian faith in African American destiny: "I freely confess that I long feared the case to be otherwise and almost admitted as true the bitter saying of those who branded us as a pusillanimous and unmanly people, tamely bearing the lash and apparently fit for slavery. But at length that error has exploded."[55] By 1843, when McCune Smith gave this lecture on "The Destiny of the People of Color," abolitionism and black resistance had created more grounds for optimism than in 1829, when Walker wrote his *Appeal*. McCune Smith was especially encouraged by the blacks' success in defeating the colonization movement's hopes and expectations, the achievements of black Methodism, and the way blacks in Ohio had responded to the Black laws that "dehumanized [them] as far as laws could reach." Amazingly, he concluded with a prophecy that the African Americans' struggle for liberty would lead to a revolutionary contribution to American culture:

> For we are destined to write the literature of this republic, which is still, in letters, a mere province of Great Britain. We have already, even from the depths of slavery, furnished the only music which the country has yet produced. We are also destined to write the poetry of the nation; for as real poetry gushes forth from minds embued with a lofty perception of the truth, so our faculties, enlarged in the intellectual struggle for liberty, will necessarily become fired with

glimpses at the glorious and the true, and will weave their inspiration into song.[56]

This deep commitment to the idea of historical progress shaped McCune Smith's landmark response, in 1859, to the Fourteenth Query of Thomas Jefferson's *Notes on the State of Virginia*. Like David Walker, McCune Smith saw the essence of American racism in Jefferson's "suspicion" "that the blacks, whether originally a distinct race, or made distinct by time and circumstances, are inferior to the whites in the endowments both of body and mind," and in Jefferson's crucial question, "What further is to be done with these people?" That question would never have been asked, according to McCune Smith, if Jefferson "had been acquainted with the philosophy of human progress." If he had possessed the wisdom for which he is celebrated, Jefferson would have welcomed the presence of blacks "as one of the positive elements of natural progress," as McCune Smith had shown in an earlier article, "Civilization: Its Dependence on Physical Circumstances," which drew on the writings of Henry Thomas Buckle and John Stuart Mill. On at least two occasions, McCune Smith also underscored Jefferson's hypocritical inconsistency by referring to his long affair with Sally Hemings and his legacy of black grandchildren—"living testimony" "that there is nothing essentially hideous or distinctly deformed in a black complexion."[57]

McCune Smith fulfills Walker's hopes by presenting a scientific analysis of the physical differences between whites and blacks—bones, muscles, texture of hair, color of skin—designed to show there were no true barriers that would prevent the two races from living together "in harmony under American institutions, each contributing to the peace and prosperity of the country." In 1859 McCune Smith could cite the equality of laws in Maine, Massachusetts, and Rhode Island as an example of democratic progress, enabling all men, "including black and white," to live "in peace and harmony."[58]

This detailed exercise followed his challenge to the idea of any "standard" occupied by the whites that was *elevated* above that occupied by the black population: "Is it [the standard] ingenuity in constructing machinery? Is it in morals? Is it in physical courage? Or is it to be measured by the tone a 'shop-keeping gentility?' " "Who is the more elevated?" McCune Smith asks, the master "with a slave-whip in his hand—or the poor Christian slave, his breast heaving, his eyes raining tears, his flesh rooted up, quivering beneath the lash, whilst he prays to God to soften the heart of the accomplished torturer." Given the ambiguity of the word "elevated," the real question was whether "there is anything in the races themselves" that would prevent "a harmonious dwelling together."[59]

We may recall that when Leonard Bacon gave a strongly affirmative answer to this question, he cited the repugnant Indian caste system and argued that the gap between American whites and blacks was even deeper and more immutable. As McCune Smith took a global view of human skin color, he noted that in India the "Tiars," "free cultivators" who were only one-third below the top caste ranking, "must not come within thirty-six steps of a Brahmin, or within twelve of a Nayr"—hardly a more egalitarian picture than that of race in America. More to the point, he observed that "In India there are not only many Hindoos with complexion perfectly black, but what is more singular, the Brahmins, even of the highest caste, vary in complexion from nearly white to perfectly black. Darkness of skin and hair, far from being exceptional or inherently derogatory, was "part and parcel of the great original stock of humanity—of the rule, and not of the exception." True whiteness, on the other hand, was a mark of defect, evidenced by the albino children born of all races. Above all, McCune Smith argued that differences in complexion originated as a result of climatic and environmental influences, and, given constant racial intermingling, there were more differences within a race than between races.[60]

McCune Smith finds final and dubious grounds for hope in the fact that newspapers, in the fifty years since Jefferson wrote, have adopted the term "colored people" instead of "black" or "negro." "The class is the same, the name is changed; they are no longer blacks, bordering on bestiality; they are 'colored,' and they are a 'people.'" McCune Smith is convinced that this means "a lessening of the distance—a step towards harmony and reciprocal kindness between man and his fellow man—between the black and the white man in this Republic."[61]

McCune Smith displayed similar questionable optimism regarding historical progress in his brilliant and scientifically reasoned but faulty essay on the dependence of civilization on "physical circumstances." At that time, when little was known about the effects of culture, it appeared that racist ethnology could best be overcome by an extreme form of environmentalism. With great erudition, McCune Smith examines the peoples of the world and not only correlates levels of civilization with climate and geographical location but argues that the dark races of the tropics quickly gain in both physical vigor and mental abilities as they move into temperate zones. While nature had given them dark skin as a protection against heat, civilization—and McCune Smith stresses that the term means "coming together"—is restricted to temperate climes. As black Africans became "colored Americans," however, they soon equalled whites in the "physical and mental peculiarities" that supposedly distinguish all American peoples. Refuting any notion of innate racial superiority or inferiority, McCune Smith affirms that so-called Anglo-Saxons were in fact a mixture of all Indo-European races, who owed their success to the fortunate accidents of climate and a favorable geographic position. McCune Smith especially stresses the evils of human isolation, the benefits of intermixture, and the unique duty and opportunity facing "colored Americans" who for the first time in recorded history have the chance of becoming part of "civilization."[62]

Throughout his writing McCune Smith seems almost obsessed with the theme that physical and intellectual labor should go hand in hand, an idea embodied in the manual labor schools that were popular at that time. It was a theme that could counteract the conviction that slaves and freed slaves, like McCune Smith himself, were destined to mindless labor of the lowest sort. That fear, as we have seen, was exemplified in David Walker's outrage over the happiness and contentment of the bootblack he confronted on a Boston street: "My objections are, to our glorying and being happy in such low employments."

McCune Smith may have had Walker's passage in mind when he chose to include a happy and highly successful bootblack in his ten biographical sketches, "Heads of the Colored People," published in *Frederick Douglass's Paper* from 1852 to 1854.[63] As Professor Stauffer puts it, these witty and ironic pieces, on such figures as a Washerwoman, Sexton, News-Vender, and Steward, "portray with subtlety and dignity the lives and careers of New York City's black working class, and in so doing offer an antidote to the general malaise felt by New York City blacks at the time."[64]

Portraying the human achievements and intellectual abilities of mostly illiterate former slaves had a special meaning at a time when, as Stauffer points out, a severe but "hidden" economic depression impacted skilled urban workers, especially blacks, who also faced rising competition from white immigrant workers, an upsurge of racist theories from eminent scientists, and the acute danger of being seized by Southern "slave-catchers" as a result of the 1850 Fugitive Slave Law.[65]

McCune Smith's unnamed and illiterate bootblack exemplifies the connections between manual and intellectual efforts as he struggles upward from childhood slavery to become a highly successful boot-cleaning entrepreneur. Aided by his wife, who hires out as a washerwoman, and as a result of hard work and religious faith, the bootblack finally acquires fine property and makes sure that his daughters acquire a good education and end up as teachers in their own private school. Though always aware that his calling is "looked down upon," the happy and vigorous bootblack has nothing but scorn for those who would rather starve than "handle a shoe-brush." And McCune Smith concludes by affirming that boot blacking "is the calling which has produced the best average colored men, and has made men of *character,* not of *wealth.*"[66]

Ironically, while Frederick Douglass was willing to publish these portraits illuminating the "heads" of working-class blacks, he echoed David Walker's sentiments in his criticism of such "faithful pictures of contented degradation" and his wish for examples of far more elevated and "respectable" black achievement that would do more to flatter black pride.[67]

McCune Smith's faith in the potentialities of combining physical and intellectual labor as a way of elevating the North's freed slave population found its grandest promise in a vast project for settling thousands of mainly urban black workers on land donated by the wealthy land baron Gerrit Smith in New York's Adirondacks. We have noted the desire of some white reformers to encourage urban blacks to migrate to the countryside. The ideal of family land ownership later embodied in the federal Homestead Act of 1862 merged with the hope of enabling inhabitants of black urban ghettos to live and work like white farmers. Such land ownership would presumably provide not only economic independence but political power by meeting New York's controversial $250 property qualification for black suffrage. This answer to Jefferson's question on what to do with them would go far, in Smith's eyes, in changing the hearts of whites and undermining the racism that lay at the core of caste.[68]

McCune Smith was dumbfounded and believed that God himself must have been the inspiration when Gerrit Smith announced
on August 1, 1846, that he was donating 120,000 acres of land in order
to provide 40-acre plots to 3,000 poor blacks from New York State,
and then asked McCune Smith to serve as the principal trustee and
help select and compile a list of recipients. When he returned from
Scotland in 1837, McCune Smith had joined William Lloyd Garrison's American Anti-Slavery Society, but by 1840, with the movement
sharply divided, he had become disillusioned with white abolitionists
and their organizations and had drawn apart. Gerrit Smith's extraordinary gift, despite its impulsiveness and lack of rational planning,
changed everything. As Stauffer puts it, McCune Smith took on his
duties "with the zeal of a recent convert" and the two men established
"an intimate and rich friendship." Indeed, Gerrit Smith's project of
building a black community in North Elba (also called Timbucto)
led to a crucial alliance between the two Smiths, Frederick Douglass,
and John Brown, in what Stauffer terms a radical "Bible politics" that
ultimately endorsed violence and ended with John Brown's famous
raid at Harpers Ferry.[69]

Gerrit Smith's contributions to the abolitionist movement help
illustrate the insuperable obstacles it faced, including the strength and
depth of racism and the power of the slaveholding interests. He helped
found and finance the Liberty Party and its more radical successors.
But the Liberty Party's presidential compaign in 1844 may well have
led to the defeat of the moderate Whig Henry Clay and the election
of the Democrat James K. Polk and thus to the Mexican War and the
further expansion of slavery. One can of course argue that by moving abolitionism into the political realm and away from Garrison's
nonresistance and disunionism, Gerrit Smith helped prepare the way
for the Republican Party, Civil War, and slave emancipation. Yet he,
James McCune Smith, Frederick Douglass, and John Brown, whose
commitment to racial equality led increasingly to an acceptance of
violence, took a path in the 1850s that sharply diverged from that of
Lincoln and the other Republicans whose commitment to prohibiting
the spread of slavery benefited from the deep and longtime racist fear
of a westward migration of blacks. On the other hand, I would argue
that Lincoln and the Republicans succeeded by offering a middle
path between the radicals and the antipolitical Garrisonians. As we
will see in the epilogue, Lincoln and the Republicans created a more

moderate road that countered and withstood the virulent racism of the Democrats and that remained committed to the ultimate abolition of American slavery.

But Gerrit Smith's contributions to the cause—up to or even over a billion dollars in today's currency—freed many slaves and made possible a harmonious model of interracial community in his home town of Peterboro, New York.[70] Nevertheless despite McCune Smith's attempts to select, advise, and prepare poor blacks for settlement in North Elba, only about one hundred managed to move there and deal with the problems of poor soil, harsh climate, and exploitative whites who posed as surveyors and cheated some of the blacks out of their land. Most of all, Gerrit Smith had been hard hit by the economic depression (in 1842 he owed creditors $600,000 and became delinquent on part of it) and lacked the cash to pay the poor settlers for the needed wagons, horses, oxen, tools, and supplies.[71]

At times Gerrit Smith became disillusioned over the overpowering effects of racism, which led to the loss of self-respect among free blacks and to the internalization of what he termed "self-contempt," even among whites like himself.[72] Yet a small number of black survivors did create an animated community at North Elba that served as a base for John Brown, whom the settlers accepted as if he were black. Brown succeeded in getting supplies from Gerrit Smith and planned his revolutionary raid in conjunction with various white conspirators, though he was especially close to the two Smiths and to Frederick Douglass.[73] As Stauffer has brilliantly shown, the radical four developed a new faith in individual and national liberation based on the dissolution of such traditional boundaries as black and white, rich and poor, sacred and profane.

By the 1850s, the achievements of McCune Smith, Frederick Douglass, and numerous other free blacks who were mostly former slaves had at least proved that colored Americans were capable of overcoming the most formidable obstacles and matching whites on professional and entrepreneurial levels. By 1860, according to one historian, blacks had "developed enterprises in virtually every area important to the pre–Civil War business community, including merchandising, manufacturing, real estate speculation and development, the construction trades, transportation, and the extractive industries." At least twenty-one had acquired assets exceeding $100,000, interpreted as a mark of true wealth. One of those, James Forten, the

Philadelphia sailmaker whom McCune Smith celebrated for having helped launch the abolitionist movement, had achieved that worth by the 1830s. Ironically, most of the wealthiest blacks lived in the South, especially Louisiana, as slaveholders. The sole millionaire, William Leidesdorff, made his fortune in San Francisco.[74]

Unfortunately, the deprived, degraded status of most African Americans long obscured the remarkable individual successes as well as the vibrancy of black churches and community organizations. Most whites, along with the media, totally ignored or falsified the free blacks' achievements and focused only on their degradation. Even the 1840 census, as exposed by McCune Smith, presented false and highly exaggerated statistics on black insanity and other forms of institutionalized deformities. The national racist bias had a continuing effect on black self-contempt. Thus, as we have seen, Theodore Wright noted in 1837 that colored parents often wished their children "had never been born," and sixty years later, in *Souls of Black Folk*, W. E. B. Du Bois described his feelings of racial gladness when his firstborn son died: "Well sped, my boy, before the world had dubbed your ambition insolence, had held your ideals unattainable, and taught you to cringe and bow."[75]

9

————⫸•⫷————

Fugitive Slaves, Free Soil,
and the Question of Violence

FREDERICK DOUGLASS AS A FUGITIVE

In 1834, only months after the founding of the American Anti-Slavery Society, Frederick Bailey, a sixteen-year-old Maryland slave who was aware of Northern abolitionism, repeatedly looked out over what he called the "broad bosom" of Chesapeake Bay, where the sun glinted on the sails of countless ships headed north. As an overworked field hand, subject to almost daily whippings, Bailey felt like a caged animal staring at the free movement of humans who, without carrying a "required pass," could head for the legendary region of free soil. Frederick—who as a fugitive fearful of recapture changed his name to Frederick Douglass—had recently been "broken in body, soul, and spirit" by "nigger-breaker" Edward Covey, whose techniques of dehumanization had transformed the young slave, as he later claimed, "into a brute!"[1]

As a result, the young Douglass sometimes viewed the white sails, "so delightful to the eye of freemen," as "shrouded ghosts, to terrify and torment me with thoughts of my wretched condition." But as he thought of God and longed to swim or fly to the ships, Douglass also resolved to run away:

> I have only one life to lose. I had as well be killed running as die standing. Only think of it; one hundred miles straight north, and I

am free! Try it? Yes! . . . This very bay shall yet bear me into freedom. The steamboats steered in a north-east course from North
Point. I will do the same; and when I get to the head of the bay, I
will turn my canoe adrift, and walk straight through Delaware into
Pennsylvania. . . . Meanwhile, I will try to bear up under the yoke.
I am not the only slave in the world. Why should I fret? . . . Thus I
used to think, and thus I used to speak to myself; goaded almost to
madness at one moment, and at the next reconciling myself to my
wretched lot.[2]

Four years later, when he finally achieved his dream of running
away, only to become the archetypal fugitive slave, Douglass took a
somewhat different course. But his fluctuation between longing to
escape and reconciling himself to his lot reflected the extraordinary
range and diversity of his experience as a slave. Born in 1818, the son
of a slave woman and an unknown white man, Douglass spent his
relatively happy first years in his elderly grandmother's isolated cabin,
not really conscious that he was the property of an absentee master,
Aaron Anthony, who served as a steward for one of the largest plantations on Maryland's Eastern Shore. Separated from his mother, Douglass's life as a child was disrupted by moves that placed him under
different authorities, but in many ways he was a highly privileged
slave.[3]

After moving to the Wye House plantation at age six, Douglass
witnessed the cruelties and brutality of the slave system but played
with and established close ties with the older son of the plantation's
owner. As a gifted and remarkably intelligent child, he attracted
the interest and empathy of his aging owner's daughter, Lucretia Anthony, and then of her husband, Thomas Auld. As a result,
Thomas Auld became the unlikely owner of Douglass following the
death of Anthony and then, suddenly, of Lucretia. Douglass's brother,
sisters, and grandmother, on the other hand, were all inherited by the
"dreaded" Andrew Anthony, a gambler and alcoholic who sold Douglass's sister Sarah to Mississippi. Douglass looked back upon Thomas
Auld, who may well have been his father, with much hostility—
"When I lived with Capt. Auld I thought him incapable of a noble
action."[4] But while Auld intimated at times that he might sell a mis-
behaving Douglass to the South, he also clearly wanted to develop
Douglass's talents and spoke of freeing him at age twenty-five.[5]

Douglass saw it as a blessing when Thomas Auld sent him at age nine to live for five and a half years with Thomas's brother Hugh, a shipwright in Baltimore. Here, thanks largely to Sophia Auld, Hugh's wife, who served for a time as a surrogate mother, Douglass developed skills and capabilities denied to the vast majority of slaves in adolescence. As he later described this temporary relationship,

> I hardly knew how to behave toward "Miss Sophia," as I used to call Mrs. Hugh Auld. I had been treated as a *pig* on the plantation; I was treated as a *child* now. . . . How could I hang down my head, and speak with bated breath, when there was no pride to scorn me, no coldness to repel me, and no hatred to inspire me with fear? I therefore soon learned to regard her as something more akin to a mother, than a slaveholding mistress.[6]

Above all, Sophia put Douglass on the course to literacy, and may have taught him more than he later admitted, before she accepted the rule prohibiting slaves from learning to read. At age twelve Douglass was able to purchase, read, and deeply absorb a copy of *The Columbian Orator*, a collection of famous speeches defending liberty, including an attack on black slavery, which would remain a basic source for Douglass of Enlightenment and American Revolutionary ideas and rhetoric.[7]

As Douglass became a tall, strong teenager, he also became more surly and rebellious, spending time among young men along Baltimore's docks and shipyards, and undergoing religious conversion after attending a new Sabbath school for black children at a Methodist Church. For a variety of reasons, the Auld brothers decided that it would be safer to remove the fifteen-year-old Frederick from Baltimore and transfer him to Thomas on Maryland's Eastern Shore. According to Douglass's biographer William S. McFeely, Frederick and Thomas loved each other at this time and Frederick was eager to promote his master's religious conversion—his later indictment of Auld being a necessary repudiation of "the possibility of such a relationship" given Douglass's "absolute condemnation of slavery."[8] Yet whatever affection Auld had for Douglass, he would not allow him to construct a "little Baltimore," in the form of a Sabbath school for young men, on the Eastern Shore. On the contrary, in January 1834 he hired Douglass out as a field hand to Edward Covey, an ambitious man known for his ability to break the will of unruly slaves, who was trying to create a farm on rented land. Understandably, Douglass felt much bitterness over the torment and physical abuse he received from Covey. While downplaying the aid he received from Bill and Caroline, two fellow slaves who refused to help Covey, Douglass presented his decision to fight Covey as the turning point in his life, the beginning of his journey toward freedom. But his time with Covey was relatively brief and, perhaps because of Auld's intervention, Covey never beat him again. The exposure to the brutalities of field work was clearly crucial in equipping Douglass, as the preeminent fugitive, to testify later on the meaning of dehumanization and the slave's longing for freedom.

In 1835 Thomas Auld reassigned Douglass as a field hand to a more lenient master, William Freeland. After establishing a close friendship with two of Freeland's slaves, Douglass became ringleader of a plot with four others to escape to the North. But the conspiracy was uncovered, Douglass was thrown in jail, and Thomas Auld faced severe pressure to sell him to the Deep South, the common fate of would-be runaways. While it is no proof of his fatherhood, Auld let Douglass suffer and worry in jail for a week, and then put him on board a boat bound for Baltimore, destined again for the home of Hugh Auld. According to biographer Dickson J. Preston, "As they parted, Auld told Frederick earnestly that he wished him to learn a trade, and promised that if Frederick behaved himself properly he would be emancipated at the age of twenty-five."[9]

Studies of fugitives have emphasized the surprising increase in the nineteenth century of the Southern practice of hiring or renting out slaves to various kinds of employers, and even of paying such slaves a portion of their earnings. According to John Hope Franklin and Loren Schweninger, "In towns and cities or in the South's growing industries—hemp, textiles, tobacco, iron—a large proportion of the workforce was hired."[10] This system clearly added to the increasing profits, productivity, and economic growth of the slave system, even though hired slaves obtained more independence and were more likely to find ways to escape.

Like most other privileged slaves, Douglass at age twenty welcomed the chance to become an apprenticed shipbuilder-caulker back in Baltimore, to learn a trade, and then finally to live by himself, find his own employment, and pay Hugh Auld three dollars of his wages each week. But Thomas and Hugh Auld's offerings and promises never eradicated Douglass's dream of escaping to free soil, following the sailboats he had watched so longingly at age sixteen. When his delay in making a weekly payment infuriated Hugh, who then demanded that he return to his former controlled status, Douglass decided that the time had come for him and Anna Murray, a free black housekeeper he had recently met and courted, to plan an escape to New England. As with many fugitives, it was a specific event, such as the breakup of a family or the death of an owner, that tipped the balance between his desire for freedom and reconciling himself to his "wretched lot."[11]

Douglass had helped other runaways plan such trips and was aware of the risks as well as the active network of antislavery people who helped fugitives along well-established routes, such as rail and water transports from Baltimore to Philadelphia and New York. Since all free blacks were required while traveling to carry proof that they were not slaves, Douglass either purchased or was given the papers of a free seaman (which might well have been insufficient). Anna loaned him money for a train ticket, agreeing to meet him in New York after he succeeded in getting there.[12]

His trip, beginning September 3, 1838, exemplified in extreme form the fortuity that had governed Douglass's early life. It should be stressed that only a small number of runaways succeeded in obtaining their freedom, and many from Maryland were either captured at the beginning and then put on the auction block, or were later seized in the streets of Philadelphia or New York. For Douglass the traumatic moment came when, disguised as a sailor, he explained to the train conductor that as a sailor he never carried his free papers but offered his seaman's papers as a substitute. The conductor paused, but said "all right," enabling Douglass to pay his fare. There were other close calls, but Douglass finally found himself in New York, "gazing upon the dazzling wonders of Broadway." "A free state around me, and a free earth under my feet!" Suddenly, he "was a FREEMAN."[13]

For the fugitive, standing on free soil could bring a certain sense of "rehumanization," of achieving human capacities that slaveholders attempted to destroy. In the introduction and first chapter of this book, we noted that both slaves and domesticated animals were "tamed" by being totally confined in *spaces* that were subject to an owner's control. While some slaves used temporary escape as a way of bargaining over freedom of movement, it was the lack of control over space and movement that epitomized slavery, from the original slave trade from Africa to the auctions and sale of slaves to the Deep South. But once a slave like Douglass escaped, who then was in control? European traditions of free soil, going back to the medieval German *Stadtluft macht frei,* and reinforced by England's Somerset decision, suggested that the runaway could obtain true freedom within a city or nation like France or England. In America, though, the U.S. Constitution— while not specifically recognizing the property rights of slaveholders— specifically required nonslaveholding states to return fugitives, an obligation spelled out by congressional legislation.

Douglass was soon overcome by this reality when he met a fellow black Baltimorean who told him that slaveholders hired other blacks for a few dollars to spot runaways, and warned Douglass not to go into any colored boardinghouse or look for a job on the wharves, since "all such places were closely watched." Hungry and afraid to ask for directions, Douglass wandered the streets for some time before he was aided by a black sailor and finally found the house of the great David Ruggles, the black head of New York's Vigilance Committee. We will later look more closely at such vigilance committees, which gave indispensable help in protecting fugitives and enabling them to fit into the free black communities of the North. With Ruggles's aid, Douglass wrote to Anna, who then succeeded in making use of the three trains and four boats needed to get to New York. The bride and groom were married by W. C. Pennington—himself a runaway who had become a Presbyterian minister and abolitionist—then the couple left New York and took off for New Bedford, Massachusetts.[14]

David Ruggles provided essential help in giving Douglass contacts with Quaker New Englanders who helped pay his fare to New Bedford and then took him in while he looked for day jobs (Anna was pregnant). When Douglass decided to change his name, one Quaker host even suggested "Douglas," from Walter Scott's *Lady of the Lake.* Thanks to the whaling industry, New Bedford was at that time a rich and thriving small town of 12,354, of whom 1,051 were black. Despite some prejudice against black workers, Douglass found employment and spoke out at a church meeting in March 1839 against colonizing blacks in Africa, recounting his own experience with slavery. The next month he was electrified when he heard a speech by William Lloyd Garrison, which clearly augmented his own ambition, going back to *The Columbian Orator,* to become a public speaker. He even succeeded in getting a free trial subscription to *The Liberator,* which he read avidly.[15]

The great event that transformed Douglass's life and launched him as the first fugitive slave to become a major orator occurred in Nantucket in August 1841. The Massachusetts Anti-Slavery Society had planned a great midsummer meeting on this lovely island, a center of Quaker-led abolitionism. It was William C. Coffin, a New Bedford Quaker bookkeeper with strong family connections in Nantucket, who urged Douglass to attend. When Coffin spotted Douglass in the Nantucket throng, he invited the escaped slave to stand up and speak, if so moved, according to the Quaker tradition. With considerable anxiety, Douglass chose to do so, and gave an account of his life as a slave. The huge, mostly white audience, including stellar figures such as Garrison, Wendell Phillips, and Samuel J. May, was spellbound. In response, Garrison rose to exclaim: "Have we been listening to a thing, a chattel personal, or a man?" The audience shouted, "A man! a man!" As Garrison continued, "Shall such a man ever be sent back to bondage from the free soil of old Massachusetts?" Now the audience rose and shouted, "No! No! No!" As McFeely eloquently puts it, though Douglass was not the first former slave to make such a speech, on this Nantucket night, "it was clear that a powerful new voice had been raised, one that demonstrated how high a former slave could stretch in a demonstration of his humanity."[16]

THE UNDERGROUND RAILROAD AND RUNAWAY SLAVES

The celebration and romanticizing of the Underground Railroad has at best been a way of publicly recognizing the humanity of slaves and the dehumanizing effects of permanently confining people in times and spaces chosen by masters.

David Blight has noted, in an insightful essay, that despite all that has been learned about slavery in recent decades, the average American is still likely to encounter the subject "first, and most often, through the *lore* of the Underground Railroad." Throughout the North, tourists encounter countless "stations" where "conductors" supposedly protected runaway slaves, many on their way to Canada. Cincinnati's Underground Railroad and Freedom Center has long been one of the nation's leading centers for learning about slavery. This long history of congratulatory commemoration is deeply embedded in American literature and film—it celebrates one of the few prideful historical moments in racial relations before the civil rights movement.[17]

In 1872, William Still, the leader of the Philadelphia Vigilance Committee and an active "operator" of the Underground Railroad, published a book on the subject based on extensive interviews and correspondence, as well as on such personal recollections as the arrival of an elderly slave, Daniel Payne, "infirm and well-nigh used up," who had escaped so that he could "die on free land." Important scholarly work began in 1892, when Wilbur Sieburt, a historian at Ohio State University, started collecting resources that led to thirty-eight bound volumes, organized by state, as well as the publication of his *The Underground Railroad* (1898), which included a map of the detailed "routes" slaves took as they entered a supposedly highly rationalized system heading to freedom. Having interviewed former slaves who had escaped, Sieburt offered readers the chance to put themselves in the slaves' place and did much to create the mythology of the Underground Railroad that has persisted to the present.

David Blight is careful in acknowledging the many revisions historians have brought to the subject, especially since Larry Gara's landmark study, *The Liberty Line: The Legend of the Underground Railroad* (1961), while insisting on the need to respect the local lore and mythology as a way of understanding the extraordinary "hold of the Underground Railroad on Americans' historical imagination."[18]

It should be added that the fugitive slave issue was absolutely central in bringing on the Civil War, especially after the North's hostile response to the Fugitive Slave Law of 1850, with large crowds of Northerners attempting to give aid to captured blacks. The popularity of the Underground Railroad is especially remarkable in view of the widespread fear, popularized by the South, that any significant freeing of slaves would lead to a mass migration to the North, where blacks would take jobs away from the higher-paid whites, especially immigrants. Given the profound depth of Northern racism, it's clear that many whites who were thrilled over the slaves' escape would not have wanted runaways settling next door or sending their children to the neighborhood school. But the assumption that most fugitives were headed for Canada helped remove some of that concern; the actual numbers of fugitives, as we will see, were not large; and the very fact that slaves were willing to take such risks undermined the Southern propaganda regarding paternalistic treatment and happy, contented bondspeople. The fugitive slave narratives enlisted crucial religious themes of redemption, exodus, and salvation, which fell into already well established tropes regarding American conceptions of freedom. As one correspondent wrote, the Underground Railroad would "thrill the heart and quicken the pulse of the eager student of the grand progressive movement of human liberty in the past," offering " 'hairbreath [sic] escapes, perilous journeys by land and water, incredible human suffering for a wide readership.' "[19]

Moreover, given the constitutional structure of the Union, it was very difficult to take direct action that could have any effect on the nation's "problem of slavery." That point was exemplified in 1833, when the British Parliament passed a sweeping law for the gradual emancipation of colonial slaves. In America, abolitionists saw the need to limit petitioning to the supposedly constitutional abolition of slavery in the District of Columbia, ending the interstate slave trade, or prohibiting the admission of Texas as a slave state (and for many years a "gag law" suppressed all antislavery petitions). From 1856 to 1861, Lincoln and the Republicans restricted their antislavery policy to excluding any further slave states or territories. Therefore, helping fugitives became a vital and popular way of enabling even thousands of Northerners to participate personally in an activity that could give freedom to individual slaves while also renouncing national complicity in the slave system. Indeed, by projecting all of slavery's evil on slaveholders and slave catchers, there could be a denial of national complicity and complexity and a reassuring assumption that the entire problem would be resolved as soon as individual slaves were freed in the way that runaways were. One of the defects Blight finds in the Underground Railroad lore and mythology is that it reinforces the conviction that America's racial issue would end and did end with slave emancipation.[20]

Two other major shortcomings concern the omission of the predominant role of free blacks in the Underground Railroad, and an exaggerated view of the system's organization and, especially, of the number of fugitives transported. We now know that the great Harriet Tubman was not exceptional in being a black conductor and that most fugitives preferred finding refuge in black homes or quarters. Blacks in effect ran the Underground Railroad, and black conductors often worked at occupations connected with transportation, as river men, railroad porters, or coach owners. Nevertheless, it was the white involvement—in particular the enthusiastic white response to the fugitive slave issue—that alarmed and infuriated Southerners and helped lead to secession and war. As Benjamin Quarles noted, "Slavery was weakened far less by the economic loss of the absconding blacks than by the antislavery feeling they evoked by their flight and the attempts to reclaim them."[21]

This point ties in with the small number—according to one historian, "only a trickle"—of the millions of Southern slaves who actually escaped to freedom in the North or Canada. Ironically, the most authoritative and deeply researched book, John Hope Franklin and Lauren Schweninger's *Runaway Slaves: Rebels on the Plantation,* underscores the frequency of slaves escaping *locally* to avoid work, to encourage concessions, to see members from broken-up families, or to avoid punishment. While precise numbers are impossible to determine, advertisements for runaways and slaveholder journals, diaries, and records make it clear that few masters could boast that none of their slaves had absconded. There can be no doubt that tens of thousands of slaves ran away each year "into the woods, swamps, hills, backcountry, towns, and cities of the South."[22]

This fact, documented in great detail by Franklin and Schweninger, was related to a general pattern of preceived resistance that included theft, damaging equipment, mocking whites while seeming to flatter, playing on conflicts between masters and their white overseers, and lightening unending work with moments of song, intimacy, slowdowns, and relaxation. As human beings, most slaves had one overriding objective: self-preservation at a minimal cost of degradation and loss of self-respect. For most, the goal of "freedom" was simply unrealistic, given the rarity of manumissions, the mechanisms and institutions of social control, and the distance to the North, Canada, or Mexico (small numbers of American slaves did escape to Spanish Florida, Mexico, and even Cuba).

According to a very conservative estimate, the total number of annual runaways in the 1850s would have exceeded 50,000 (1.26 percent of the 1860 slave population; about 5 out of every 400 slaves). But the vast majority of these slaves remained fairly close to their farms or plantations and either returned or were captured within days or weeks. It is probable that between 1830 and 1860, no more than 1,000 or 2,000 fugitives annually made it to the North and achieved freedom.[23]

Since an average of 1,500 would be only .0375 percent of the 1860 slave population, totaling only 45,000 over a thirty-year period—far fewer than the number of slaves who escaped behind British lines during the American Revolution—it is clear that the Underground Railroad and the flight of fugitives to the North posed no serious demographic threat to the Southern slave system.

The extraordinary attention devoted to the fugitive issue between Frederick Douglass's *Narrative of the Life of Frederick Douglass, an American Slave* (1845) and Harriet Beecher Stowe's *Uncle Tom's Cabin* (1852) gives the impression that it was a new phenomenon. But slaves have fled their owners throughout human history. In seventeenth-century Virginia and Maryland, Native American slaves found it easy to abscond, and planters then struggled to prevent African slaves from colluding and escaping with white indentured servants. By the eighteenth century, urbanization contributed to the problem, because cities like New York, as in medieval Europe, could provide refuge for slaves from the countryside as well as hiding places and supporters for urban slaves who had fled their owners. But, as in the Caribbean, it was wars—especially the French and Indian War and the American Revolution—that led to the large-scale exodus of slaves from their owners' control. It is especially remarkable that the massive departure of slaves behind British lines in the Revolution—some were sold in British colonies; most were freed and sent to Nova Scotia and eventually Sierra Leone—did not lead to any longer-term weakening of the American slave system.[24]

Also in the eighteenth century, the first maroon communities took shape in unsettled and difficult-to-access regions in the South. These refuges for runaway slaves were never as large or strong as the maroon communities in Brazil and parts of the Caribbean. But in some bogs and wild areas of the Deep South, and the Great Dismal Swamp on the border shared by Virginia and North Carolina, fugitives founded communities that depended in part on raiding and trading with local plantations for food and supplies.[25] Historian Steven Hahn has imaginatively argued that all of the free black communities, including those in the North and Midwest, were essentially maroon settlements made up by freed or escaped slaves and their descendants, whose identity and political orientation was defined by the national character of American slavery. This is part of a larger thesis that extends from the supposed political activism and resistance of slaves to the flight of tens of thousands of slaves behind Union lines during the Civil War, a kind of self-emancipation that Hahn terms "the greatest slave rebellion" in human history. Apart from the theory's exaggerations and omissions, the maroon aspect provides an interesting perspective on the overall relationship between fugitives, free blacks, and slavery.[26]

As for slaveholders, their immediate loss was both economic and ideological. When one or more slaves absconded, there was an immediate loss of labor that could be difficult or impossible to replace. Hardly less important was the example set and the destabilization of discipline on plantations and small farms. Yet as we have seen, most runaways returned after a fairly short period, so there were strong incentives for masters to bargain for such a return when that was possible. The slaves who actually sought or achieved true freedom threatened a major loss of capital, which increased in the 1840s and 1850s as slave prices soared. Moreover, when a recaptured runaway was sold there could be a considerable loss in value if it became clear to buyers that the slave had left repeatedly or had headed north. On the other hand, the cost of retrieval amounted to a small percentage of the slave's value. In the 1850s, when some average slave prices rose from $900 to $1,800, the cost of retrieval when successful never usually rose above $75. As we will see, Northern resistance to the Fugitive Slave Law could greatly increase the cost in some highly publicized individual cases. But in general, the most expensive expeditions after slaves—if the slave had a good head start—cost $150 to $200, even counting extensive hiring of slave catchers.[27] Once again, the South clearly overreacted to the supposedly disastrous threat of the fugitive slave issue.

An important clue to the underlying reasons for this overreaction can be seen in the slaveholders' psychological and ideological reaction to slaves' running away, a reaction made explicit in thousands of printed advertisements for individual fugitives. Today, following a long but revolutionary shift in moral perception that has stigmatized slavery as a crime, it is very difficult to see the world through slaveholders' eyes. One famous fugitive expressed the complexity it is so easy for us to miss: "The relation between master and slave is even as delicate as a skein of silk: it is liable to be entangled at any moment."[28] Convinced of the moral legitimacy of the system, most slave owners sincerely believed that their own best interests were identical with their slaves' best interests, though most masters admitted that the institution, like any other, was capable of being abused. The desire for profit and personal power could be mitigated by the desire to be thought of, especially by fellow planters, as good Christians and decent fellows. Moreover, it made good economic sense to keep the slaves' morale as high as possible and to encourage them to do willingly and even cheerfully the work they would be forced to do in the last resort. Like their Roman predecessors, Southern planters expected gratitude for their acts of kindness, indulgence, and generosity, and even for their restraint in inflicting physical punishment. Several travelers noted that American masters wanted above all to be *"popular"* with their slaves—a characteristically American need that was probably rare in Brazil or the Caribbean.[29]

While numerous ads for runaway slaves complain that the escape was triggered by too much generosity, confirming the adage "give-'em-an-inch-and-they'll-take-a-mile," many others reveal an almost pathetic faith that a given slave, who was said to have been very friendly and wanting to please, would accept an offer of forgiveness and "come home" like an errant son. Most masters desperately sought a consensual element, a sign of consent and gratitude on the part of at least some slaves. Ads and plantation records also reveal an overriding psychological response of anger.

> Again and again, slave owners used the same word to describe runaways: ungrateful. They had been treated well and humanely; they had been given proper food and clothing; they had been well housed and provided with other necessities; their families had been kept together. Yet, at the first opportunity they had set out on their own. They had neither honor nor gratitude; as a race, they were deceptive and deceitful.[30]

HARRIET JACOBS AS A FEMALE FUGITIVE

While the story of Harriet A. Jacobs exhibits some striking parallels with Frederick Douglass (whom she got to know in Rochester), more significant is what it reveals about the profound vulnerabilities of slave women and mothers and about the psychological obsessions of masters like Dr. James Norcom, who was determined to use his slaveholder powers as a means of obtaining some kind of "consensual" sex with the teenage Jacobs.[31] Southerners continued to deny the key abolitionist claim that slaveholding led to the ubiquitous sexual exploitation of slave women. In response, abolitionists needed only to point to travelers' accounts and to the growing ubiquity in the South of mulatto slave children. Jacobs's *Incidents in the Life of a Slave Girl, Written by Herself* was published in 1861 under the pen name "Linda Brent," and was long thought to be the work of a white abolitionist, especially Lydia Maria Child, who edited the work but denied authorship. Even as a supposedly "inauthentic" slave narrative, *Incidents* became the most widely read and persuasive account of a fugitive slave woman's struggle to maintain some control over her body, her children, and her human values. Thanks to the prodigious research of historian and biographer Jean Fagan Yellin, who has confirmed Jacobs's authorship, we now even know the historical identity of the characters, such as Dr. Norcom ("Dr. Flint" in the narrative).[32]

Like Frederick Douglass, Jacobs was a very privileged slave, compared to the mass of field hands—but, given her situation, she was even more miserable than Douglass. Both of these slaves had happy early childhoods, lost contact with mothers, and became close to grandmothers. Harriet's first owner, Margaret Horniblow, taught her to read and write. Both slaves were sent to plantations as a kind of punishment and both overcame their masters' efforts to break their rebellious spirits. Both attempted in different ways to escape— Harriet by hiding for seven years in a cramped space not far from her master—and both succeeded in reaching free soil in the North, in changing their names, and in avoiding recapture until supporters actually purchased their freedom.[33]

Jacobs was born a slave in North Carolina in 1813 (five years before Douglass). At age twelve, upon the death of Margaret Horniblow, she became the property of Horniblow's three-year-old niece—Dr. James Norcom's daughter. Before long, Jacobs attracted the libido of Norcom, who became her de facto master. Jacobs was as determined to resist his sexual advances, originally in the form of notes and whispers, as Douglass had been determined to resist Edward Covey's assault upon his manhood. Norcom's wife, Mary, became intensely jealous of Jacobs's hold on her husband's sexual attention, and Jacobs would awaken in the middle of the night to find Mrs. Norcom leaning over the bed to make sure her husband was not there. Because Mary

Norcom was so eager to get Jacobs out of the house, she was able to move and live with her nearby grandmother, who had been freed and had purchased a house thanks to her sales of prepared foods.[34]

As Norcom's sexual advances continued, Jacobs concluded at age fifteen or sixteen that the only way to prevent an inevitable end to these solicitations would be to agree to an affair with a friendly and eminent local lawyer, later a U.S. Congressman, Samuel Tredwell Sawyer.

> I knew nothing would enrage Dr. Flint [Norcom] so much as to know that I favored another; and it was something to triumph over my tyrant even in that small way. I thought he would revenge himself by selling me, and I was sure my friend, Mr. Sands [Sawyer's pseudonym] would buy me.[35]

Jacobs's affair with Sawyer led to the birth of two children, Joseph and Louisa Matilda. Sawyer eventually purchased both, as well as Jacobs's younger brother, John S. Jacobs, and allowed all three to continue living with Jacobs's grandmother. But while Sawyer was of much help in enabling Jacobs to have contact with her children and free herself from Norcom, the affair caused her to struggle with a sense of guilt, given her religious commitment to Victorian standards of female morality, which she answered with the claim that slave women must be judged by a different set of moral standards. Her editor, Lydia Maria Child, realized that the sexual content of *Incidents* might offend Victorian sensibilities and defended lifting the "veil" "for the sake of my sisters in bondage, who are suffering wrongs so foul, that our ears are too delicate to listen to them."[36]

Although Norcom was infuriated by the continuing affair, he was still obsessed with having sex with Jacobs, without actually raping her: "You are mine; and you shall be mine for life. There lives no human being that can take you out of slavery. I would have done it; but you rejected my kind offer."[37] Norcom finally issued a clear-cut ultimate demand: Jacobs could either live in a cottage as his concubine, with the promise that her children would be freed; or he would send her to his son's plantation in Auburn, North Carolina, a place, she heard, "to break us all in to abject submission to our lot as slaves."[38] When Jacobs rejected the cottage, Norcom's fury was too extreme to be printed: " 'Very well. Go to the plantation, and my curse go with you,' he replied. 'Your boy shall be put to work, and he shall soon be sold; and your girl shall bee [*sic*] raised for the purpose of selling well. Go your own ways!' He left the room with curses, not to be repeated."[39]

Jacobs was spared from field work on the plantation, but worked endless hours as a house maid for Norcom's son's new wife. Above all, she concluded that unless she took some drastic step, such as running away, Norcom would use the treatment of her children as a device for abusing her, even sending them to the plantation to be "broken" as slaves. If she did escape, she thought he might well sell Joseph and Louisa to their father, who might free them. As it happened, contrary to Norcom's wishes, Sawyer did secretly purchase the children and her brother by means of a slave speculator, after she became a fugitive. But it took him a long time to free even his own children, perhaps because he feared that doing so would harm his political ambitions.[40]

Meanwhile, one midnight, Jacobs prayed to God for guidance and protection, jumped from a high window into the rain, and then, aided by her uncle, hid for some time in various local refuges, including a swamp, before moving to a cupboard or garret above her grandmother's storehouse, seven feet wide and sloping down to a height of three feet, with a small trapdoor through which family members could give her food and other necessities. Incredibly, she lived in that cramped space, undetected, for seven years. Since she could stand up at one end of the garret, she bored holes in the cupboard for air and light, and was able to sew cloth and read the Bible and other works. Surrounded by mice and rats, she baked in the summer and had frostbite in the winter. Nevertheless, she considered this choice far better than the life of most slaves:

> I was never cruelly over-worked; I was never lacerated with the whip from head to foot; I was never so beaten and bruised that I could not turn from one side to the other; I never had my heel-strings cut to prevent my running away; I was never chained to a log and forced to drag it about, while I toiled in the fields from morning till night; I was never branded with hot iron, or torn by bloodhounds. On the contrary, I had always been kindly treated, and tenderly cared for, until I came into the hands of Dr. Flint. I had never wished for freedom till then. But though my life in slavery was comparatively devoid of hardships, God pity the woman who is compelled to lead such a life![41]

Predictably, the news of Jacobs's disappearance infuriated Norcom, who advertised a reward of $100 for the apprehension and delivery of his "light mulatto" "Servant Girl HARRIET," who "will probably appear, if abroad, tricked out in gay and fashionable finery." Warning all persons "under the most rigorous penalties of the law" against harboring her or helping her escape, Norcom stressed that since "this girl absconded from the plantation of my son without any known cause or provocation, it is probable she designs to transport herself to the North."[42] Locally, he searched countless locations and terrorized her family and friends, even confining some of them in jail. Norcom now transferred his sexual obsession into an obsession for tracking down this rebellious fugitive and recovering his power as a master. In Yellin's words, Norcom "angrily marshaled the entire resource of the slave power—sheriff, patrols, courts, and the press—to catch her." He even traveled three times to New York City in search of his once-desired concubine and during the rest of his life (he died in 1850) pursued various schemes for her recapture.[43]

Samuel Tredwell Sawyer, who was elected to Congress in 1837 and married the next year, saw Jacobs in hiding and promised that he would free their children and try to get Jacobs sold to him. Communicating through her grandmother, Jacobs agreed that Louisa should be sent north to live with Sawyer's cousin in Brooklyn, since Norcom was claiming that the sale of the children to the slave speculator was illegal.[44]

By 1842, Jacobs became convinced that she needed to get north in order to see Louisa and send for Joseph, in part because she feared that Louisa was being treated as a slave. After a friend told her grandmother about a ship she could board, she succeeded in fleeing to New York, receiving help on the way from the Vigilance Committee in Philadelphia. In New York she became a nurse to a prominent family and was able to spend time with Louisa, who, to her distress, had not been freed and was not being sent to school as promised.[45]

Jacobs's life during the next years became extremely complicated, as a result of the continuing danger of her being apprehended, her relations with her children and brother, and her ties with her wealthy New York employer, the Willis family. Attempts to capture Jacobs, which led to moves between New York and Boston, even involved her legal owner, Norcom's grown daughter and her husband, who traveled to the North in search of her (and eventually sold her, thanks to the Willis family's intervention). Jacobs's brother John S. (probably for "Sawyer") ran away from Sawyer in 1838, served as a sailor for two years, and ended up in Boston and then Rochester as an abolitionist speaker. Jacobs and her children built a flourishing life in Boston and interacted closely with the black community there. But after tending Mary Stace Willis's baby daughter in New York, Jacobs retained close ties with that family. When Mary died in childbirth in 1845, her husband traveled to Boston and persuaded Jacobs to accompany him on a trip to England, to take care of the daughter as they visited his wife's grieving family.[46]

In 1849, John S. Jacobs succeeded through his abolitionist contacts in obtaining his niece Louisa's entrance as a "colored female" into the exclusive Young Ladies Domestic Seminary in Clinton, New York, and he prepared a move to Rochester and an itinerary with Frederick Douglass. Harriet Jacobs understandably chose to move to Rochester so that she could be nearer her daughter's boarding school and could work with her brother on his new project of running the Anti-Slavery Reading Room, above the offices of Douglass's new newspaper, the *North Star*. Since her brother was often away on lecture tours, Jacobs in effect ran the reading room. She lived with noted Quaker abolitionists, Amy and Isaac Post, and was surprised to find herself feeling at home with this white family. The Posts were pillars of the Western New York Anti-Slavery Society and strong supporters of the *North Star* and of Douglass's challenge to school segregation. Amy Post had recently attended the Seneca Falls Women's Rights Convention and according to one historian, she and her circle "reshaped the landscape of female activism in Rochester."[47]

Jacobs developed an intimate friendship with Amy Post, to whom she slowly and bit by bit confided her personal history as a slave. It was Amy Post, reinforced by Jacobs's brother, who finally overcame Jacobs's strong reluctance to contribute to the abolitionist cause by writing and publishing a full account of the "incidents" in her life as a slave. As Post later recalled, Jacobs could not think of divulging her secrets to strangers "when it was all she could do to sob them into her friend's ear": "Though impelled by a natural craving for human sympathy, she passed through a baptism of suffering, even in recounting her trials to me. . . . The burden of these memories lay heavily upon her spirit."[48]

In 1853, a year after a recapture scare and after Cornelia Grinell Willis solicited funds to purchase her freedom, Jacobs decided to begin to write her story. (She had earlier rejected an offer to have it included in Harriet Beecher Stowe's *A Key to Uncle Tom's Cabin*.) At one crucial moment, she heard that her beloved but judgmental grandmother had died in North Carolina. This removed the last psychological obstacle to revealing her troubled sexual history. A few months earlier she had published three letters in the *New York Tribune*, signed "A Fugitive Slave," describing the kind of sexual crimes masters committed against their female slaves.[49]

Working mostly at night, after caring for the children and family with whom she lived, Jacobs completed the manuscript in 1858. Despite Lydia Maria Child's offer to edit the work and write an introduction, there were fortuitous problems in getting it published. Two Boston publishers accepted the manuscript but then went bankrupt. In 1861, it was published by a Boston printer "for the author," but the book sold widely in bookstores and by antislavery agents and was even pirated by a publisher in England. When Jacobs went off to Washington early in the Civil War to do relief work among the so-called contrabands who had fled from slavery—and she would continue to work for Quakers in distributing clothing, teaching, and providing health care—she was well recognized by abolitionists as the author of the most vivid and compelling account of the anguish, suffering, and dilemmas slave women faced as they lost real control over their "owned" bodies.[50]

FUGITIVE SLAVES AND THE LAW

Frederick Douglass and Harriet Jacobs achieved remarkably free and successful lives after escaping to free soil, but the hazards they faced are indicated by the fact that both achieved true liberty only after friends purchased their *legal* freedom. The boundaries fugitives faced involved both physical space and the law, and free soil was defined by law. We turn now to the conflict between North and South over the meaning of free soil—a nonissue before 1777, when racial slavery was legal and relatively unchallenged in all the North American colonies.

The American Revolution led to the emancipation of the small number of slaves in Vermont in 1777 and in Massachusetts in the 1780s and to laws providing for the gradual freeing of slaves in Pennsylvania in 1780 and in four other northeastern states by 1804. In 1787, the Northwest Ordinance seemed to ensure that the institution was doomed in the vast Northwest Territory north of the Ohio River. These measures were very slow to take effect. Slavery remained legal if in diminishing importance in New York until 1827, in Connecticut and Illinois until 1848, and in New Jersey until the Civil War. But as early as the Constitutional Convention of 1787, a meeting in a state then committed to future freedom, it became clear to Southerners that the new nation would be divided between "free" and "slave" states and that this division would affect various crucial issues in the Constitution, ranging from national representation to the African slave trade. Although the Constitution significantly avoided use of the terms "slave" and "slavery," South Carolinians in particular were successful in gaining a provision regarding fugitive slaves:

> No Person held to Service or Labour in one State, under the Laws thereof, escaping into another, shall, in Consequence of any Law or Regulation therein, be discharged from such Service or Labour, but shall be delivered up on Claim of the Party to whom such Service or Labour may be due.[51]

Even by 1793 there were enough fugitives to motivate Congress to pass a Fugitive Slave Law implementing this constitutional provision. The law saddled local legal authorities in the North, such as circuit or district judges, with the responsibility of delivering runaways to their masters or slave-catcher representatives. In states like Pennsylvania and Ohio, bordering slaveholding Maryland, Virginia, and Kentucky, this put free blacks in constant danger of being kidnapped, since many officials equated blackness with slavery and readily believed the claims of slaveholders. Yet with the passage of time, the flagrant injustice of such invasive captures led most Northern states to pass personal liberty laws, often mandating jury trials, to prevent kidnappings, and Northern magistrates showed less and less interest in helping to recover fugitives—a development that finally evoked the South's counterproductive Fugitive Slave Law of 1850.[52]

Even in the South, runaway slaves often headed for cities and towns, where they could more easily avoid detection, solicit help from free blacks, and find work. The smaller number who headed north ended up in Baltimore, Philadelphia, New York, Cincinnati, or even Boston. Many slaves manumitted during or after the Revolution assembled in Baltimore, which also became an obvious place for rural slaveholders to look for fugitives. The resulting vulnerability of free blacks led, as early as 1819, to the creation of a vigilance committee, which soon became the Baltimore Society for the Protection of Free People of Color. Full-fledged vigilance committees, dedicated to the assistance of fugitives and populated by the best-known African American leaders of the time, emerged in Philadelphia and New York in the 1830s and in Boston in 1846.[53] The New York Vigilance Committee boasted that after a single year it had enlisted one hundred members and had "protected from slavery" a total of 335 persons. No less important was that by publishing the stories of fugitives, the committee made it increasingly necessary for slave catchers to procure warrants and begin hearings, instead of just seizing a supposed fugitive.[54]

Vigilance committees would continue to face the somewhat controversial issue of paying money to free a fugitive. In some cases, collections were raised for such a purpose, but there was seldom any organized effort to free more than a single individual, after the failure of other efforts, since abolitionists hated giving any sanction to the principle of human ownership. Often a payment was seen as "paying ransom" to recover a family member or a recently returned fugitive.

One sees a blend of solutions in the formal and informal efforts to free George Latimer in Boston. A fugitive from Norfolk, Virginia, Latimer was arrested in Boston in October 1842; his owner's lawyer had avoided getting a warrant and had enlisted the local police. After a crowd of angry blacks tried without success to rescue Latimer, abolitionists failed to free him legally through a writ of habeas corpus. Frederick Douglass and other dignitaries then addressed mass meetings, and local black churches helped raise money to pay for his freedom. His owner, after receiving threats of violence, finally agreed to sell Latimer to the abolitionists.[55]

The fugitive slave issue provided opportunities for increasing cooperation between black and white abolitionists, who were divided on other matters, such as true social equality for blacks. Yet blacks dominated the vigilance committees and led the way not only in the Underground Railroad efforts to help fugitives escape and avoid recapture, but in "Upperground" assistance in helping them find homes, employment, and a social place within the United States.[56]

The unification of these goals can be seen in David Ruggles, the fearless and scrappy founder of the New York Vigilance Committee.

Born in Connecticut to free parents, Ruggles moved to New York City in 1827, opened and ran a grocery store, and then delighted Samuel Cornish and other black reformers when he became a temperance man and stopped selling alcohol. As the full-time agent for *The Emancipator,* Ruggles traveled in the Mid-Atlantic states, lecturing, getting subscriptions, and making connections with Underground Railroad stations. He then rapidly rose within the ranks of New York's black abolitionist community and exemplified the movement for black uplift and improvement we examined in chapter 8 (he played a crucial part in the Phoenix High School for Colored Youth; wrote articles and pamphlets calling for black education and enhancement; and opened the first African American–owned bookstore and library). As the founding officer of the New York Vigilance Committee, Ruggles did his best to assist fugitives, prevent kidnappings, and help runaways move farther north or to Canada. Working with black veterans such as Samuel Cornish and Peter Williams, he helped solicit funds from wealthy white abolitionists, such as Gerrit Smith and the Tappan brothers. Ruggles published a kind of black list of merchants and others who were complicit in supporting slavery or the internal slave trade, and helped educate the city's black community on the legal issues surrounding the seizure of blacks—on how the burden of proof for their freedom was upon them and that the courts were not to be relied on, "where every advantage is given to the slaveholders and to the kidnappers."[57]

Ruggles's service in aiding fugitives was relatively brief, because he had a conflict with Cornish and other abolitionists, and he was forced to resign as an officer from the Vigilance Committee. He went on to establish a successful Water-Cure Hospital in Massachusetts, where he treated Garrison and Sojourner Truth, before dying at age thirty-nine. But Ruggles succeeded in combating New York's slave catchers—he was dragged out of his house at night and beaten by enemies, and suffered long-term injuries—and, according to his modern biographer, "Unlike any activist before, Ruggles brought ordinary blacks into the struggle by empathizing with the plight of families damaged by kidnappers or by tapping into the anger of young blacks in the street."[58]

Given the physical confrontation between blacks and slave catchers, it is surprising that there were not more violent attempts in major cities to seize and free fugitives who were held by authorities. Such efforts did occur, especially in smaller towns, and in Boston a group of blacks liberated two fugitives in 1836, and in 1851 an interracial mob stormed the courthouse and freed Shadrach Minkins, a fugitive from Virginia. But, while hundreds of abolitionists poured into the Boston streets to protest the capture and reenslavement of Thomas Sims in 1851 and Anthony Burns in 1854, no serious effort was made to physically free them. In part, this was because they were protected by armed guards and the U.S. Marines as they were tried and taken for deportation. Moreover, many of Boston's blacks were themselves fugitives who were fearful of recapture and increasingly intent on escaping the Fugitive Slave Law by fleeing to Canada.[59] But especially in view of the Garrisonian abolitionists' commitment to pacifism, there was a very slow and gradual acceptance of violence, in the 1850s, on the part of black and even white abolitionists. It was only as the Civil War approached, exemplified by John Brown's raid, that increasing numbers of abolitionists concluded that a slave system undergirded by violence required violence to topple it.

This point is illustrated by the black response to Henry Highland Garnet's "Address to the Slaves," or "Call for Rebellion," given at the 1843 National Convention of Colored Citizens at Buffalo. Born a slave in the South, Garnet escaped as a child to Pennsylvania with his fugitive family, attended black schools in New York, and became a Presbyterian minister and radical abolitionist. He was much taken with David Walker's *Appeal*, which he reprinted with a brief account of Walker's life. His Buffalo speech was the first important call on American slaves to rebel since Walker's *Appeal*. Slaveholders, Garnet proclaimed, "endeavor to make you as much like brutes as possible." And "TO SUCH DEGRADATIOIN IT IS SINFUL IN THE EXTREME FOR YOU TO MAKE VOLUNTARY SUBMISSION." Like Walker, Garnet coupled his endorsement of violence with a startling condemnation of slave docility and complicity, a recognition of at least some success on the part of Southern paternalists. Thus his praise for Denmark Vesey, Nat Turner, Cinque, and Madison Washington was coupled with the image of brain-washed ("Elkins-like") Sambo slaves:

It is in your power so to torment the God cursed slaveholders that they will be glad to let you go free. If the scale was turned, and black men were the masters and white men the slaves, every destructive agent and element would be employed to lay the oppressor low. Danger and death would hang over their heads day and night. Yes, the tyrants would meet with plagues more terrible than those of Pharaoh. But you are a patient people. You act as though you were made for the special use of these devils. You act as though your daughters were born to pamper the lusts of your masters and over-seers. And worse than all, you tamely submit while your lords tear your wives from your embraces and defile them before your eyes. In the name of God, we ask, are you men? Where is the blood of your fathers? Has it all run out of your veins? Awake, awake; millions of voices are calling you! Your dead fathers speak to you from their graves. Heaven, as with a voice of thunder, calls on you to arise from the dust.[60]

By 1843, there was much skepticism even among white abolitionists over the Garrisonian commitment to pacifistic "moral suasion," but in view of influencing public opinion, there was still much sensitivity to the dangerous Southern "narrative" that the French Amis des noirs had instigated the Haitian Revolution, that American abolitionists were responsible for Nat Turner's uprising, and that abolitionists in general always threatened to incite a major slave insurrection with its predicted bloodshed and raping of white women. The fear of the persuasiveness and possible truth of such accusations surely prompted a negative white reaction to Garnet's call for slave revolt—there was virtually no white interest or support—and may well have influenced the black assembly's voting down an adoption of his address (by a vote of 19 to 18). James Gillespie Birney, who ran as the Liberty Party's candidate for president in 1840, remarked in 1838 that he did not know a single abolitionist who would incite slaves to insurrection. Garnet himself had disavowed slave violence in a speech a year and a half before his 1843 address. Aside from issues of Christian nonviolence, much of the discussion at the Buffalo convention centered on questions of practicality—in the aftermath of Nat Turner's bloody uprising of 1831, even slaves themselves came to recognize the almost inevitable self-destructive outcome of armed resistance.[61] Yet the Fugitive

Slave Law of 1850, coupled with a number of judicial decisions, helped to persuade many abolitionists, blacks especially, that slavery could not be ended without some kind of violence. Frederick Douglass and Charles Lenox Remond, who both spoke out against Garnet's address in Buffalo, also moved in that direction.[62]

The Fugitive Slave Law of 1850 greatly magnified the issue of fugitives and free soil. The law was counterproductive and self-defeating for the South, since the number of fugitives who escaped to the North was never large enough to endanger the Southern economy, and the provisions of the law increasingly outraged Northern public opinion, as a kind of gift to the abolitionists. There was of course much initial support for the law in parts of the North, given the concern for the union and strong ties with the South. The North received some gains from the Compromise of 1850, and it was argued that the fugitive slave measure was simply a way of carrying out a provision in the Constitution.[63] Nevertheless, it was Daniel Webster's defense of the law that ruined his political career, and Northern opposition to the law increased over time, thanks in part to Harriet Beecher Stowe's *Uncle Tom's Cabin* and the growing fear of "the Slave Power" and its expansion of slavery in the West. It can well be argued that resistance to the Fugitive Slave Law, declared unconstitutional in 1854 by the Wisconsin Supreme Court, later reinforced by resistance to the Kansas-Nebraska Act and Dred Scott Decision, prepared the way for Northern acceptance of Civil War.[64]

The Fugitive Slave Law was part of Henry Clay's large Compromise of 1850, an omnibus of measures intended to pacify the country by meeting and balancing the demands of North and South in the aftermath of the Mexican-American War. Although the effort was initially voted down by Congress, Stephen A. Douglas guided the measures through Congress as separate bills. Thus the North achieved the ending of the slave trade in the District of Columbia and the admission of California as a free state. The South won the Fugitive Slave Law and the organization of the rest of the land ceded by Mexico into two territories, New Mexico and Utah, without any federal restriction on slavery.

The Fugitive Slave Law, which required federal agents to recover fugitive slaves from sanctuaries in the North, directly challenged the North's integrity and its new self-image as an asylum of liberty.

Increasing numbers of former moderates, especially religious believers in God's punishment of national sins, now echoed Garrison's rhetoric of disunion, and an increasing number of former nonresistants called for a slave uprising or predicted that the streets of Boston might "yet run with blood." As abolitionists in effect declared war on the so-called Slave Power, the Western territories would become the crucial testing ground that would determine whether America would stand for something more than selfish interest, exploitation, and rule by brutal power.

The new Fugitive Slave Law radically strengthened the law of 1793, which had not provided for any government support for the removal of a slave. Federal commissioners could now be appointed by Circuit Courts throughout the United States, where they could issue warrants, certificates of removal, and hold hearings. Suspected fugitives were not allowed to testify, there were no juries, and if no attorney volunteered or was hired by the defendant, only the commissioner and the claimant (the master or master's agent) could speak. Even more alarming, the law required any citizen to become a "deputy of the law" and help in the task of apprehending fugitives. Anyone who interfered in such apprehensions, or who assisted a fugitive, could be fined as much as $1,000 or sentenced to six months in jail. Finally, commissioners were to be paid ten dollars if they returned the supposed fugitive to his or her owner, and only five dollars if they acquitted the accused black—the difference being justified on the basis that convicted fugitives required more paperwork and thus more labor.[65]

As for effectiveness, census figures suggest that some ten thousand fugitives were living in the North at the time the law was enacted, and at least that number probably escaped in the remaining years before the Civil War. Yet the major study of the enforcement of the law counted only 332 fugitive cases heard under the new law, and only 298 slaves returned to slavery by the end of 1860. This was far more than all the fugitive slaves returned from 1793 to 1850. But it hardly affected the loss that Southerners felt over the decade. The ideological and political cost of those returns, in terms of the alienation of the North, enormously outweighed any benefit. Moreover, the monetary cost of returning a fugitive, while ordinarily low, could be exorbitant. It cost the federal government and the city of Boston as much as $20,000 to return the fugitive slave Thomas Sims, not to mention the direct retrieval costs incurred by his master, the salaries of those enlisted to keep the peace, and the fortifications put up around the courthouse.[66]

It would be misleading to think of the conflicting views over the Fugitive Slave Law as just another example of strong partisan conflicts over contentious political issues. Abolitionists were not alone in viewing the 1850 law as a total violation of basic religious and legal principles—thus justifying open defiance of the law—and as authorization for Southern invasions of the North that could lead to the seizure and kidnapping of free people. This was sometimes seen as a repetition of the original seizure and enslavement of free people in Africa, which now endangered the entire American free black population and the very meaning of emancipation. Southerners like John C. Calhoun, on the other hand, saw the law as a final test of the willingness of the North to deal fairly with the South and support the basic principles of the Constitution and the founding, or face the inevitability of disunion. For this reason, it is enlightening to print some representative quotations.[67]

First, consider a somewhat paranoid Southern response to Northern resistance to the Fugitive Slave Law, coupled with a sense of impending conflict, taken from *The Nashville American:*

> The constitutional authorities are all on the side of free negroes and abolitionists against the Southerners. They run Southerners who are overpowered from the watering places, and if a Southerner goes amongst them to catch his fugitive slave, his life is endangered at every step by ungoverned mobs of abolitionists and free negroes. He is treated as a man-stealer, a land pirate, who deserves death at the hands of all persons. This is so in almost every part of the Northern States. The Constitution, so far as the capture of fugitive slaves is concerned, is at the end, no one now goes into a free State to get his slave, who does not go armed to the teeth, prepared to risk his life, and who is not prepared at every step of his progress to encounter gangs of dissolute and desperate abolitionists, and crowds of runaway slaves and free negroes, sent on by prominent and leading citizens. How many under these circumstances will go? An actual state of war on a small scale already exists.[68]

Next, an excerpt from a speech given by Luther Lee, a prominent Wesleyan Methodist minister and theologian in Syracuse, New

York, who became an abolitionist and supporter of the Underground Railroad. He is recounting an address he made to a meeting called in response to news of the arrest of two persons under the Fugitive Slave Law:

> I affirmed that slavery is wrong—a moral wrong, a violation of every commandment of the decalogue, that no law can make it right to practice it, support it, or to in any way aid and abet it; that the Fugitive Slave Law is a war upon God, upon his law, and upon the rights of humanity; that to obey it, or to aid in its enforcement, is treason against God and humanity, and involves a guilt equal to the guilt of violating every one of the ten commandments. I never had obeyed it—I never would obey it. I had assisted thirty slaves to escape to Canada during the last month. If the United States authorities wanted any thing of me my residence was at 39 Onondaga-street. I would admit that they could take me and lock me up in the Penitentiary on the hill; but if they did such a foolish thing as that I had friends enough in Onondaga County to level it with the ground before the next morning. The immense throng rose upon their feet and shouted, "We will do it! we will do it!" and I have no doubt at that moment they thought they would.[69]

Finally, here is the way William Lloyd Garrison describes the state of the country in a letter to a prominent English merchant, reformer, and philanthropist, to whom he is recommending an African American friend who is considering moving to England:

> Never has this nation been so convulsed on the subject of slavery as at the present time. The Fugitive Slave Bill, (so called), which has passed at the late session of Congress, granting unlimited facilities as it does to slave-hunters in quest of their prey,—and striking down, as it does, the writ of habeas corpus, trial by jury, and all the safeguards of liberty, in the non-slaveholding States of this Union,—is producing a tremendous sensation, and rousing up all the human, moral and religious elements in the land against it, and against the foul system it is designed to strengthen and protect.[70]

The issue of fugitive slaves leads directly to John Brown's 1859 abortive raid at Harpers Ferry. According to historian John Stauffer,

"In John Brown's mind the decision to raid Harpers Ferry was a natural extension of his plan to run slaves north through his 'Subterranean Pass Way' in the Alleghenies."[71] The mountains surrounding Harpers Ferry had been regularly used by runaways as escape routes, including those aided by Harriet Tubman, who helped Brown plan the raid. It was now Brown's hope that instead of helping fugitives move northward to freedom, his capture of the federal arsenal and its supply of arms would arouse the slaves and free blacks in the region, who were already prepared to join him and launch an insurrection that would spread through the South and bring freedom to the heartland of bondage.[72]

On October 16, 1859, Brown and twenty-one men, including five blacks, invaded and captured the federal arsenal at Harpers Ferry. Though initially successful, no slaves rose in rebellion and the local militia and residents surrounded the armory. Brown took some captives and several townspeople were killed before Colonel Robert E. Lee, of later Civil War fame, arrived with the U.S. Marines. Ten of Brown's raiders, including two of his sons, were killed in the struggle. After being finally captured, Brown was taken to a local courthouse, convicted of treason against the commonwealth of Virginia, and hanged on December 2. It was his conduct during the trial, however, that elevated him to the status of a martyr.

Brown had established very close ties with Frederick Douglass and had been a major influence in Douglass's break with Garrisonian "moral suasion" and endorsement of the need for violence in ending slavery. But when Brown invited Douglass to participate in the raid in the summer of 1859, Douglass refused, believing that the venture was doomed to failure. Nevertheless, in an address in 1881 at Harpers Ferry, Douglass affirmed, "His zeal in the cause of my race was far greater than mine—mine was bounded by time, his stretched away to the boundless shores of eternity. I could live for the slave, but he could die for him."[73] In the words of Ralph Waldo Emerson, "[John Brown] was that new saint . . . who, if he shall suffer, will make the gallows glorious like the cross."[74] Or, as Henry David Thoreau put it, "Some 1800 years ago Christ was crucified. This morning Captain Brown was hung. He is not Old Brown any longer, he is an angel of light." Before long Union soldiers marching into the South would be singing, "John Brown's body lies a mouldering in the grave."

The Civil War gave a wholly new meaning to the fugitive issue. Like the American Revolution and other previous wars, it provided slaves with the opportunity to escape behind "enemy" military lines. Soon after hostilities began, Union general Benjamin F. Butler accepted three fugitive slaves at Union-controlled Fort Monroe, in Virginia. Violating the Fugitive Slave Law, he presciently declared that the fugitives were "contrabands" of war, since if they had remained on the Confederate side, they would be economically assisting the enemy's war effort. If President Lincoln had little desire at this point to make the war "about" slavery, Butler had provided the administration with a means of undermining the enemy's economy and further troubling Southern society by encouraging more runaways. While the flow of contrabands could slow Union army movements, they were used in Union camps to do a variety of tasks, and paid a wage.[75] Even more important, some 250,000 of the men took up arms on the Union side. Of the 4 million slaves in the South, approximately half a million had crossed Union lines as contrabands by the end of the war. The issue of contrabands had a profound impact on the Lincoln administration's evolving stance toward blacks and slavery.[76] The Union army became, in effect, an army of liberation, extending freedom—as John Brown had desired—into the South; and hundreds of thousands of slaves responded by fleeing, like the earlier fugitives, into the new "free soil." Their legal status remained unclear for a time but was eventually determined by Lincoln's Emancipation Proclamation and especially by the Thirteenth Amendment, which later for Cuba and Brazil became an early culmination of the Age of Emancipation.

10

The Great Experiment:
Jubilee, Responses, and Failure

AN ESCHATOLOGICAL EVENT AND AMERICA'S BARRIERS

The British Parliament's slave emancipation act of 1833, like its earlier abolition of the slave trade in 1807, was hailed as a moral triumph of unprecedented importance. Officially and repeatedly celebrated in Britain, as in 1933 and 2007, these events raised crucial questions about how a nation that had profited immensely from a system of massive dehumanizing exploitation could seemingly renounce greed and self-interest and abolish not only the trade in slaves but slavery itself. For some time the dominant interpretation stressed the importance of prayer and Providence, canonized William Wilberforce, and played down the more radical implications, such as the influence of the great Jamaican slave insurrection, or "Baptist War," of 1831. Despite the initial misgivings of most abolitionists over the issues of compensation and apprenticeship, on which the actual passage of emancipation depended, the day of "liberation," August 1, 1834, was celebrated in Britain as a biblical Jubilee, a millennial turning point in human history.

In one of the most significant of the hundreds of sermons delivered on August 1, 1834, Ralph Wardlaw showed how a seemingly political and secular act helped to fulfill the eschatological promise of Christianity, prefiguring an era of universal freedom and harmony. If slavery exemplified the human conflict and oppression that had permeated modern societies, its abolition would open the way to a new kind of harmony. A prominent reformer in Glasgow, Wardlaw was a devout evangelical who also subscribed to the principles of the eighteenth-century Scottish Enlightenment. In hailing emancipation as a literal Jubilee, Wardlaw drew on the doctrine that the ancient Hebrew Jubilee prefigured Christ's mission "to proclaim liberty to the captives, and the opening of the prison to them that are bound," a passage from Isaiah that, according to Saint Luke, Jesus "stood up to read" in the synagogue at Nazareth. For Wardlaw, Parliament's political decision was nothing less than the harbinger of Christ's final salvation of the world:

> The trumpet has sounded through all the colonial dependencies of our country, which proclaims "liberty to the captives."—O! what heart is there so cold, so seared, so dead, as to feel no thrill of exulting emotion at the thought, that on the morning of this day, eight hundred thousand fellow-men and fellow-subjects, who, during the past night, slept bondmen, awoke freemen![1]

Wardlaw claimed that Britain had averted "a gathering storm of divine retribution" for a national sin, and that the first day of a Jubilee year would inaugurate continuous progress in the cause of freedom, including the Christianization of the former slaves, some of whom would become missionaries in Africa. Above all, he rejoiced that "Britain's trans-Atlantic daughter" had already caught the spirit of British philanthropy; and that once America joined Britain in setting "the united example of the entire, peaceful, and final extinction of slavery,—the world will be shamed into imitation."[2] Yet it is crucial to note that Wardlaw and his audience could simply take it for granted that West Indian blacks would and should continue to perform the same kinds of labor for the same former masters.

Despite highly conflicting reports in America concerning the response of West Indian blacks to emancipation, Ralph Waldo Emerson echoed Wardlaw's optimism in an influential speech commemorating the tenth anniversary of the Jubilee on August 1, 1844. For Emerson, British emancipation was "an event singular in the history of civilization; a day of reason; of the clear light; of that which makes us better than a flock of birds and beasts; a day, which gave the immense fortification of a fact,—of gross history,—to ethical abstractions." It especially impressed Emerson that "the negro population was equal in nobleness to the deed." Meeting in churches and chapels on the night of July 31, they had welcomed their emancipating moment with prayers and tears of joy, "but there was no riot, no feasting" and, according to one report, "not a single dance . . . nor so much as a fiddle played." The next morning, Emerson assured his listeners, "with very few exceptions, every negro on every plantation was in the field at work." Since the much criticized apprenticeship was also abolished on August 1 in 1838, the second emancipation was easily subsumed in the first. Like Wardlaw, Emerson stressed that "other revolutions have been the insurrection of the oppressed; this was the repentance of the tyrant," the harbinger of a new era, when "the masses" would awaken and apply an absolute moral standard to every public question.[3]

For most free African Americans, the First (or Second) of August soon became a national holiday replacing the Fourth of July, a day of promise when both black and white abolitionists could deliver orations and sermons that not only condemned the evils of slavery and racial discrimination but reminded the world that Britain, the tyrant symbolically overthrown every Fourth of July, must still teach white Americans the meaning of freedom.

Frederick Douglass, who frequently spoke on such holidays, elaborated on this theme in a long address delivered to some three to four thousand blacks and whites in Poughkeepsie, New York, on August 2, 1858:

> How long may we ask, shall it be the standing reproach and shame of the American Government that while England is exerting her mighty power, and her all-pervading influence, to emancipate mankind from Slavery, and to humanize the world, the American Government is taxing its ingenuity, and putting forth its power, to thwart and circumvent this policy of a great and kindred nation?[4]

For Douglass, the profound goal was to make "this ever memorable day" the means of awakening the American people "in the cause of the fettered millions in our own land." Douglass emphatically argued that the British emancipation act was not an "experiment," contrary to the views of Britain's colonial secretary Edward Stanley and the other framers of the law. Instead, according to Douglass, the act "naturally addresses itself to the highest and most ennobling attributes of human nature." Unequaled in "the annals of the world," it was "a manifestation of Christian virtue . . . a confession and a renunciation of profitable sin at great expense, on a grand and commanding scale, by a great nation." This victory was far from easy or undemanding; Douglass underscored the power of the selfish and "Satanic" interests and the repeated earlier defeats in Parliament and out of Parliament.[5]

What finally made success possible was the spread of abolition sentiment "from individuals to multitudes all over the United Kingdom of Great Britain and Ireland." In response to this united voice of the nation, the British Parliament "calmly" proceeded "to dissolve the relation of master and slave," and "on the morning of the 1st of August 1834, eight hundred thousand colored members of the human family were instantly declared free, emancipated." "They had been ranked, as our slaves are, with the beasts of the field, rated with bales of goods and barrels of rum, driven before the taskmaster's lash." "But all at once they learn that their bondage is ended, the taskmaster is dismissed, the whips and chains are buried, they are no longer slaves." Douglass accepted abolitionist reports that the freed slaves had then "staggered and fell down, rose up, ran about, shouted, laughed, cried, sung."[6]

But in 1858, as America moved toward the Civil War, Douglass was especially concerned with including a response to the widespread British and American consensus that British West Indian emancipation had been a shocking economic failure. The London *Times* had editorialized in 1857,

> Confessedly, taking that grand summary view of the question which we cannot help taking after a quarter of a century, the process was a failure: it destroyed an immense property, ruined thousands of good families, degraded the Negroes still lower than they were, and, after all, increased the mass of Slavery in less scrupulous hands.[7]

Employing irony, Douglass "admitted" that "in some respects" (from the slaveholders' perspective) it had failed—that is, the British had failed to impose a repressive substitute for slavery and had failed to prevent former slaves and their descendants from creating their own farms and employments and from achieving civil rights or even becoming jurors and legislators.[8]

Douglass was here responding to the undeniable fact that emancipation had led to a sharp decline in the production of West Indian plantations, especially in larger colonies like Jamaica, where many freed blacks were able to obtain their own land and depend on at least subsistence agriculture. He even acknowledged Britain's dependence on the importation of thousands of so-called East Indian Coolies to replace the ex-slaves who had left the plantations. But for Douglass the preservation of the plantation system was not a priority. The priority was the condition and welfare of the former slaves, which had clearly been vastly improved in the twenty years since the abolition of apprenticeship.

Douglass was well aware that even by 1858 antislavery was still far from becoming a "united voice" of the Northern American states and that this contrast with Britain had raised immense obstacles to the idea of America simply following the British example. Apart from public opinion, the British Parliament had had almost complete control over the colonies. The American Congress was bound by a Constitution that protected states' rights, and slaveholders retained immense power in the executive, legislative, and judicial branches of government. Moreover, a deep tradition of Anglophobia played into the hands of opponents of abolitionism, who were able to portray the reformers as subversive agents of a British plot to divide and destroy the antimonarchic republic.

When noted British abolitionists like Charles Stuart and George Thompson came to the North in the 1830s, hoping to rally popular support by applying the successful British lecturing techniques, they were often met by hostile and even dangerous mobs—which also victimized many American abolitionist speakers. According to Thompson, in "this heaven-favored, but mob-cursed land," public opinion had by the mid-1830s become a *"demon of oppression."*[9]

Thus, in 1834, not long before British Emancipation Day, Charles Stuart joined an abolitionist meeting in Middletown, Connecticut, which *The Liberator* described as "cogent, temperate, and solemn." Stuart had converted Theodore Dwight Weld, a chief architect of the American antislavery movement, to the abolitionist cause, and was celebrated on both sides of the Atlantic for such seminal works as *The West India Question: Immediate Emancipation Safe and Practical.* But after an angry mob confronted and interrupted the meeting, a U.S. Navy lieutenant challenged Stuart to a duel and proclaimed him a liar and coward. Then the mob threw eggs, attacked and injured some speakers, and threatened to tar and feather Stuart and a colleague before aid finally came from a sheriff and some members of the nearby Wesleyan college.

As Stuart and Thompson discovered, the "public sphere" of the United States was drastically different from that in Britain, where abolitionists faced little if any public hostility and had for decades succeeded in mobilizing mass support from a spectrum of social classes. Nevertheless, the British and American antislavery movements were intricately interconnected, and speakers like Stuart and Thompson did travel widely and make an impression. The American reformers' obsession with petitioning Congress, despite no likelihood of success, was largely the result of the highly successful British petition campaigns to end the slave trade, emancipate British slaves, and end the apprenticeship system. American abolitionists greatly benefited from the vibrant transatlantic abolitionist print culture and also found significant British financial, moral, and religious support for their cause from the 1830s to the Civil War. And this tradition of popular antislavery support, some of it even from the British working class, played a key role in preventing Britain from following its economic self-interest by intervening in the war and recognizing the cotton-producing Confederacy.

THE ENACTMENT OF BRITISH EMANCIPATION

Perceptions of British emancipation involved a kind of double vision of historical change. On the one hand, as we have seen, the freeing of some 800,000 slaves was viewed as an eschatological event, an event related to the Hebrew Jubilee, the millennium, the Last Judgment, and the ultimate destiny of mankind. Such sharp breaks in history did not occur in a continuous line with the events before and after them. According to the apocalyptic rhetoric, Providence had revealed itself through a new human ability, the ability of an enlightened and righteous public to control events.

On the other hand, British political leaders feared abrupt or revolutionary change. In addition to the examples of the French and Haitian revolutions and subsequent slave insurrections, the British public seemed on the verge of revolt in the early 1830s as democratic dreams clashed with a highly undemocratic political order. Moreover, the

West India lobby was still powerful enough to gain crucial concessions. Even after years of public petitioning, the Jamaican slave revolt
of 1831, and the parliamentary Reform Act of 1832, it took many long
months for Thomas Fowell Buxton, Lord Howick, Edward Stanley,
the younger James Stephen, and other government officials to ham-
mer out a compromised emancipation bill. Thus British slave emancipation could also be seen as another result of pragmatic political
negotiation.

But the eschatological achievement confirmed the evangelical
faith of Wilberforce and others that the very existence of slavery had
provided Protestant Christianity with an epic stage for vindicating
itself as the most liberating force in human history. Abolishing slavery
became a way for a nation to accumulate "moral capital," overcoming self-centered materialism and responding to the Enlightenment's
sweeping attacks on institutional religion.[10] One of the French phi-
losophes' most damning charges had been that Christians, with the
exception of a few Quakers, had continued to defend colonial slavery.
But the same Enlightenment had furthered scientific racism, and the
French Revolution had led to Napoleon's reinstituting slavery and
the slave trade in 1801–2. The elder James Stephen, who exploited
this French moral regression, exemplified the double vision when he
called on the British public to chant in unison a demand as "simple"
as that of Jehovah's messenger to Pharaoh, "LET THE PEOPLE
GO," and then leave the practical means to Parliament.[11]

Government leaders as well as abolitionists accepted this conceptual demarcation between the formal act or command of emancipation, with all its religious overtones, and the "practical" regulations to
give the command effect.[12] There was a parallel dichotomy between
the "voice" of the British public, seen as a pure and spontaneous
expression of Christian morality, and the political arts of compromise
that were needed to balance contending interests and advance the
common good. Even within the Stephen family, the younger James,
who drafted the final emancipation act, sought to ensure ordered,
sequential progress, whereas his father and his brother George
invoked the imagery of holy warriors annihilating a demonic power.[13]

While many British economists and legislators urged caution and
delay in any even gradual attempt to convert slaves into free laborers, British abolitionists were blessed, compared to their American
or even French counterparts, in the fact that defenders of the status

quo hardly ever claimed that blacks were racially inferior in capability, even if they exhibited some of the backward traits of "savages." Seymour Drescher has made the extraordinary discovery that despite the racist writings of such eighteenth-century figures as Edward Long and even David Hume, defenders of slavery in Parliament ignored racial arguments and for some sixty years appeals to race played almost no role in the government's discussions of the slave trade, slavery, and apprenticeship. In fact, when attacking the slave trade and then slavery, Wilberforce quoted Long's comparison of Africans with apes, "assured that his audience, in or out of Parliament, would react to such arguments 'with astonishment as well as with disgust.' " Since even Britain had become infected with various forms of racism by the late 1840s and 1850s, Wilberforce, Clarkson, Buxton, and their colleagues were very fortunate in finding a time when white legislators and much of the public were quite free of racial prejudice.[14]

The British movement against slavery itself began around 1814 in a very reserved, conservative way, exemplified by the amelioration acts of 1823 and 1826, and then changed dramatically by 1830 with demands for "immediate" emancipation. We have already examined the role of free blacks in steering the American movement toward immediatism by 1830. While Quaker reformers maintained connections between the British and American movements—the American Benjamin Lundy, for example, reprinted in his *Genius of Universal Emancipation* Elizabeth Heyrick's 1824 radical British pamphlet, *Immediate, Not Gradual Abolition*—it is still remarkable that the two movements, facing entirely different situations, developed along parallel lines and reached a crucial turning point by 1830.[15] When it became clear that ending the slave trade in 1807 was not encouraging planters to reform and "ameliorate" the institution, Wilberforce led a parliamentary campaign for his brother-in-law James Stephen's ideal of a central Registry of all British colonial slaves, which would not only reveal illegal importations but also provide data on mortality rates and thus serve as an entering wedge for British reform legislation.[16] In 1816, the parliamentary debates helped trigger a major slave uprising in Barbados, which, unlike the Jamaican revolt of 1831–32, set back further significant discussions of slavery for some years.

Following the lead of Liverpool's wealthy Quaker merchant James Cropper, the London abolitionists formed in 1823 the Society for the Mitigation and Gradual Abolition of Slavery. The word "mitigation" reflected the earlier hope and expectation that ending the slave trade would induce West Indian planters to improve the treatment of slaves and begin to transform them into a self-reproducing peasantry, thereby obtaining the supposed economic advantages of free labor. The abolitionists confronted the powerful Society of West Indian Planters and Merchants, which claimed that much moral progress had already transformed British colonial slavery into a humane and highly paternalistic institution. The owners of the majority of West Indian estates lived as absentee landlords in England, where, united with wealthy merchants, they purported to favor their own ameliorative measures, including the religious instruction of slaves, something strongly resisted in the colonies.

In 1823, Thomas Fowell Buxton, who replaced the aging Wilberforce as the abolitionist leader in Parliament, presented resolutions that included freeing all slave children born after a fixed date and measures to prepare the other slaves for freedom by slow degrees. To the delight of the planters and merchants, who had conferred with the government, George Canning, leader of the House of Commons, then seized the initiative and presented the government's own ameliorative resolutions, which were adopted without opposition. While Canning vaguely committed the government to future emancipation, he made it clear that planters themselves would be the agents for slow, step-by-step change. And by 1830 it was clear that planters had successfully resisted any major amelioration, and, by castigating even gradual abolitionism as a dangerous threat to security, had begun convincing many reformers that Elizabeth Heyrick had been right in proclaiming in her subtitle that immediate emancipation was *The Shortest, Safest, and Most Effectual Means of Getting Rid of West Indian Slavery.*[17]

The efforts of the abolitionists' new Agency Committee of paid lecturers, who beginning in the summer of 1831 adopted the methods of religious revivalists as they circulated petitions and traveled from town to town elaborating on the sins of slavery, were immensely enhanced by a great slave insurrection in Jamaica, soon known as the Baptist War.[18] On the night of December 27, 1831, a white Presbyterian missionary described the clusters of fire as estates were consumed and "then the sky became a sheet of flame, as if the whole country had become a vast furnace." Yet he added that "amid the wild excitement of the night, not one freeman's life was taken, not one freewoman molested by the insurgent slaves."

As some sixty thousand Jamaican slaves joined the monthlong rebellion—led by a slave elite including drivers, carpenters, coopers, and blacksmiths—planters and Jamaican legislators agreed that English missionaries and their slave converts, especially Baptists, were the cause of the upheaval. While the missionaries opposed such violence and insisted that they had coupled their campaign to Christianize and uplift the blacks with admonitions against disobedience, a large number of the rebel leaders were Christian converts who were well aware of the political agitation over slavery in Britain. Many domestic slaves had even concluded from the overheard ranting and raving of Jamaican whites that the English king or government wished to free them.[19]

It was doubtless this consciousness of an English antislavery public, along with the influence of missionaries, that explains the slaves' extraordinary determination to prevent the slaughter of whites, both in Jamaica and in the earlier 1823 three-day uprising in Demerara (part of later British Guiana). In the latter colony, where missionary John Smith was sentenced to be hanged after being wrongly tried for inciting the slaves to rebel, many of the ten to twelve thousand rebels carried guns, cutlasses, or knives, and more than 255 blacks were killed or wounded by colonial troops in the confrontations. Yet the slaves, who slapped and whipped some captured masters and overseers, killed no more than two or three white men. This amazing self-discipline helped British missionaries to defend the slaves and dramatize Demerara as a godless colony where Christian missionaries were violently persecuted. (Smith, who died in jail of consumption, was soon celebrated in Britain as the "Demerara Martyr.") In the much larger and longer (by more than a factor of ten) Jamaican war, slaves burned hundreds of plantation houses, destroyed fields of sugarcane and other crops, and engaged in virtual battles that led to a final death toll of some 540 blacks. But throughout the month, no more than fourteen whites were killed.[20]

If Jamaican blacks had killed hundreds of whites, preaching abolition to thousands of Britons would have been much more difficult for William Knibb and other refugee missionaries in 1832 and 1833. The issue of religious persecution greatly strengthened abolitionism as missionaries testified before the Select Committee of the House of Commons, and played a central role in depicting the cruelty of godless planters and the virtues and victimization of slaves.[21]

Following the Jamaican rebellion, about a dozen refugee missionaries returned to England, where they were hailed as heroes. In response to the strict rules of the established Anglican Church, the English public had long struggled for the rights of nonconformist sects, such as the Baptists and Methodists, who had greatly expanded their memberships. By 1832, religious dissenters, who were strongly inclined toward abolitionism, represented about 21 percent of the English electorate. Large crowds listened to missionaries' accounts of being jailed, tarred and feathered, and threatened with death as Jamaican mobs destroyed dozens of chapels. One missionary, Henry Whitely, published an account of his persecution and of the brutal treatment of slaves, excerpts of which Thomas Fowell Buxton read to a very receptive audience. Hatchard's bookstore in Piccadilly sold 200,000 copies of the work within two weeks.[22] The missionaries were careful to underscore their own innocence with respect to any instigation of the rebellion and even to wrongly insist that most black Christians had tried to protect their masters' property and had refused to participate in the rebellion. Their vivid descriptions of the evils of slavery had an immense impact on British public opinion.

In America, the news of a massive Jamaican slave rebellion had a very different and alarming meaning. The seeming connection between British abolitionist activity and the Jamaican slave insurrection greatly enhanced Southern fears and the argument that even news of antislavery agitation would almost certainly lead to slave uprisings. Yet the Northern religious press, traditionally sensitive to Southern opinion, now disregarded past boundaries in depicting the Jamaican persecution of missionaries. The *Boston Recorder* frankly reported, in 1831, "the [British] religious newspapers and magazines that we receive are unanimous in favor of immediate adoption of [abolitionist] measures by Parliament. . . . the treatment of the Jamaica Missionaries . . . has awakened a spirit throughout the kingdom, that will not soon sleep."[23]

The issue of immediate slave emancipation arose in Britain at a time of protracted public struggle for a wide range of political and social rights. It was the parliamentary Reform Act of 1832 that revolutionized the prospects of slave emancipation, which would not have been possible under the traditional system of political representation. Proposed by the Whigs and led by Prime Minister Lord Grey, the reform granted seats in the House of Commons to the large cities that had grown during the early Industrial Revolution, and cut representation from the so-called rotten boroughs, where Tories had benefited from very small electorates. Despite a significant increase in the size of the electorate, voting was still limited to less than 17 percent of adult males. But the West India interest lost many seats in the House of Commons. Following the next election, they could count on only thirty-five MP Representatives, as opposed to well over one hundred who had pledged in the campaign to support immediate emancipation. In the fall of 1832, Buxton joyfully concluded that "things are ripe for obtaining nearly the full extent of our wishes." Confident that the Whig administration would introduce a satisfactory bill, he even cautioned abolitionists to avoid militant agitation that might alarm conservatives, especially in the House of Lords.[24]

But the British cabinet faced a complex problem. By 1833, the ratio of British petition signatures calling for immediate emancipation, compared to those in opposition, came to more than 250 to 1. The abolitionists' extraordinary mobilization led some 20 percent of all British men, many religious dissenters, to sign antislavery petitions that year. Yet concessions would have to be won from the West Indians, who had the active sympathy of the king and of powerful Tories (and some Whigs), who were above all worried about the violation of established rights to private property. Since a defining feature of chattel slavery was the inheritable and transferable claim of ownership in human beings and their offspring, how could such claims be challenged without challenging the very principle of hereditary private property? Lord Grey, the prime minister, made it clear that no measure for emancipation could be proposed without first obtaining the West Indians' consent.[25]

By late March, Buxton changed his mind and saw the need to encourage the militant public crusade for immediate emancipation. Even the elderly Wilberforce, who had opposed inciting public agitation, was persuaded to publicly initiate a petition to Parliament. In 1833, Parliament received more than five thousand antislavery petitions, containing some 1.3 million signatures (roughly 30 percent signed by women). Most notable, perhaps, was a monstrous document, the largest single antislavery petition in British history, sewn and pasted together by a team including Buxton's daughter Priscilla, and signed by 187,000 women. Buxton expressed temporary despair when he first read the plan drafted by the colonial secretary, Edward Stanley, which included compensation to slaveholders and a long apprenticeship for slaves. But after Stanley presented the plan to the House of Commons, Buxton exclaimed to Priscilla that "Emancipation is effected, the thing is done."[26]

Young Viscount Howick, who had devoted intensive study to the issue of slave emancipation, had a far less optimistic view regarding the ability of Parliament to delete or significantly modify objectionable provisions like apprenticeship, which was intended to provide continuity and prepare slaves for freedom. In a speech on May 14, he asked the MPs to imagine the effect on the mind of the slave "when he is told that he is free, but finds that, for so long a period [twelve years], his freedom is to make no difference whatever in his condition—that he is to go on laboring as before, without any remuneration for his toil, beyond his accustomed and scanty supply of necessaries?" Howick shrewdly added that masters, with no investment in human property, would want for twelve years to extract the maximum amount of labor from apprentices, without any regard for mortality.[27]

Ironically, at a meeting on May 10, the Standing Committee of West India Planters and Merchants professed "a loss for adequate terms to express their feelings of disappointment and dismay" over Stanley's plan. They saw "nothing in the measure now submitted to them, but the confiscation of property, and the prospect of all those calamities which must result from a dissolution of the ties which connect the Colonies with the British Empire." The West India Committee was especially troubled by the provision that an apprentice would need to work for his master only three-fourths of his time and could then "employ himself elsewhere" or receive wages for this extra time. This clause, according to the West Indians, would for twelve years deprive the master of "at least one-fourth of the gross production of his property" and would give the Negro the choice of working in periods when labor would be lightest and leaving when his services would be most valuable.

No less troubling was the provision that compensation should be in the form of a loan, and in the "quite inadequate" amount of £15 million. After many pages of specific complaints, the Committee concluded that the proposed measure "involves an unparalleled violation of the rights of property—of spoliation of the weaker by the stronger party," that "it is not even calculated to advance the comforts and well-being of the negro," and that it "utterly destroys the possibility of productive cultivation." Moreover, the destruction of the British colonies "will have the direct effect of giving an irresistible impulse to the *Slave Trade* to supply this deficiency from foreign countries."[28]

Despite the struggles and revisions of the next three months, George Stephen was prescient in late May when he told Daniel O'Connell, the pro-abolitionist popular champion of Irish rights, that if Stanley succeeded in committing the Commons to his broad resolutions, "no dexterity in committee will mend his odious scheme."[29] The West India representatives won most of the major concessions and revisions, above all raising a £15 million loan into a direct grant of £20 million compensation for the loss of slave property. Equal to roughly 40 percent of the national budget, this enormous payment pleased British financial interests, since the absentee owners of a large percentage of plantations lived in Britain and many plantations were mortgaged and their London creditors ultimately received much of the money.[30] In contrast to this generosity, an allowance of only £300 per person a year was to be paid to the absurdly small corps of 130 special magistrates, who were supposed to enforce the law and protect the apprentices from being treated like slaves, but who would now be especially dependent on planter hospitality. Moreover, the final law gave colonial legislatures the power to define the duties of the special magistrates as well as the details regarding the apprentices' labor, discipline, maintenance, and contractual obligations. The House of Lords even empowered colonial authorities to punish any so-called willful absence of an apprentice by requiring additional work for a period as long as seven years after the end of apprenticeship.[31]

The abolitionists succeeded with great difficulty in reducing the term of apprenticeship from twelve to seven years for agricultural workers and from six to five years for nonagricultural workers. They also persuaded Stanley to abandon one extremely unfair idea of compensation. While apprentices were obliged to devote three-quarters of their time to work for their former masters, they were to be paid a fixed rate of wages for any work done in the remaining quarter, and in theory could use some of that money to achieve full freedom. But the original plan required them to make a direct monetary contribution to the fund for slaveholders' compensation—when many abolitionists argued that it was the *slaves* who deserved compensation. In actuality, the apprentices' years of uncompensated labor were a form of compensation and the apprentices were therefore required to subsidize a large share of the cost of their own emancipation.[32]

William Lloyd Garrison, who had arrived in England in late May on a mission to raise money and expose the evils of the American Colonization Society, was elated to learn that "slavery has received its death-blow." But he was outraged that leading British abolitionists had accepted the "heresy" of monetary compensation to planters, rewarding those who for years had been "whipping, starving, plundering, brutalizing, and trafficking their own species," those who deserved only "punishment proportionate to their crimes." "The slaves," Garrison affirmed, "and the slaves only, are entitled to remuneration." Some abolitionists later tried to reassure Garrison that the measure "excites universal reprobation among the people." But except for a few radical members of the Agency Committee, British abolitionists, including even Thomas Clarkson, realized that emancipation without some form of compensation was politically inconceivable.[33]

The government had essentially disarmed its opponents by endorsing and absorbing two ideologies. First, the abolitionist ideology that called for the total eradication of an ancient and deeply implanted institution, for a wholly new dispensation attuned to moral principles revealed by the collective voice of the Christian public. Second, the proprietor ideology, which insisted on gradual change, minimal interference with local self-government, and compensation for pecuniary losses. This unstable mixture inevitably led to continuing conflict, notably the abolitionists' final major crusade, in the mid-1830s, against the barbarities of apprenticeship. By 1835, Buxton had compiled a volume of evidence against apprenticeship, documenting instances of murder, torture, overwork, and the infliction of more corporal punishment than in the days of slavery.[34] But it was the more radical Quaker and Agency Committee member Joseph Sturge who took the lead in the campaign against apprenticeship, who traveled to the West Indies and compiled and then published much evidence that helped move the public and government toward abolishing the system. Convinced that this was soon inevitable, the colonial legislatures avoided further parliamentary interference and ended apprenticeship on their own in 1838. Still, some abolitionists continued to protest police and vagrancy acts—similar to those in America's post–Civil War South—designed to curtail the freedom and movement of black workers. But, as we have already seen, this need for renewed agitation in no way diminished the heroic public image of slave emancipation in 1833.

SOME AMERICAN RESPONSES TO BRITISH EMANCIPATION

News of Britain's nearly "immediate" emancipation hit slaveholding America like a political and social tsunami. While Britons saw the abolition of the slave trade as a first step toward an eventual eroding of slavery, British abolitionists had not worked for even a very gradual ending of the institution until 1822. People still spoke of the way Christianity had supposedly taken centuries to wear away slavery and serfdom in medieval western Europe. Despite the commitment to emancipation by Northern American states during or following the American Revolution, slavery was still legal in Connecticut until 1848, and a form of involuntary apprenticeship survived in New Jersey until the passage of the Thirteenth Amendment. The unexpected British law not only became a precedent but focused attention, like the Haitian Revolution, on the *consequences* of emancipation—on what happens *after* slaves are freed. For some abolitionists this meant an emphasis on free labor ideology—on stressing the moral virtues and productivity of physical labor when wages replaced the lash, and when both workers and employers supposedly profited from a natural harmony of interests. But since white Americans lived in a biracial society and most of them regarded blacks as in some way "less than human," Britain's sudden freeing of 800,000 black slaves evoked a good bit of alarm.

In April 1833, both the *New Orleans Bee* and Baltimore's *Niles' Register* printed an article from a London paper on the "intention" of the British government to introduce a bill for the immediate emancipation of slaves, noting that the government was prepared to send "an imposing force" of fifteen thousand troops to protect white colonists from the "probable consequence" if the intentions of Parliament were "prematurely announced." The Southern press had given limited coverage to the Jamaican slave rebellion, out of fear that such news could spread rebellious tendencies by word of mouth among their own slaves. But the three major slave revolts in the British Caribbean, coupled with the uproar over the Denmark Vesey conspiracy in South Carolina and Nat Turner's slaughter of whites in Virginia, had greatly reinforced the conviction, originally disseminated by Bryan Edwards's argument on the antislavery origins of the Haitian Revolution, that abolitionist agitation or legislative debates over slavery would inevitably lead otherwise docile and contented slaves to insurrection. And it is true that in all five of the Anglo-American events, one could point to the slaves' and free blacks' almost certain awareness of antislavery protest.

In late July 1833, after covering the parliamentary debates, the *New Orleans Bee* made a direct allusion to the Haitian Revolution: "in agitating the question of emancipation," Britain's ministers "must have forgotten the consequences to a neighboring nation produced by similar measures adopted with equal imprudence." Some weeks later the paper reprinted a letter from a Barbadian planter who not only prayed that Providence would protect the islands from "the scenes of horror" that had devastated Saint-Domingue, but warned Southerners to take serious steps with respect to their own safety, since proximity and shared interests doomed the United States to "participate . . . in the deep and fatal results" of the British colonies' imminent destruction.[35]

These very thoughts were uppermost in the minds of Southern journalists like Duff Green, whose *United States Telegraph* became the Washington news voice for Senator John C. Calhoun. Green not only covered the British parliamentary debates over slave emancipation, but linked this detailed news with the way it inspired and encouraged the emerging abolition movement in the North. Like other Southern editors, Green greatly exaggerated the strength and influence of American abolitionism—the American Anti-Slavery Society would not even be formed until December 1833, partly in response to British emancipation. And, according to Green's "spy" in New York, American abolitionists were convinced that British abolition would help them overcome the "strong barriers" that protected slavery in the United States. Green dramatized a possible consequence of such an abolitionist victory by reprinting a letter from the U.S. consul in Jamaica, who reported that the white population lived in fear for their lives, since the slaves were dissatisfied with the British plan and threatened to "emancipate themselves, the effect of which would be the destruction of every white inhabitant."[36]

As historian Edward Bartlett Rugemer points out, in his comprehensive study of the subject, "Americans of every political stripe looked to the West Indies, making press descriptions of emancipation an essential factor in the development of public opinion on slavery in the United States." Virginians, who had recently considered and debated gradual emancipation, could now view the actual results of such a measure. Abolitionists, inspired by the political success of their British counterparts, awaited news of continuing progress, and defenders of slavery eagerly seized on the exaggerated early news of violence and rebellion that dominated the American press. But, as Rugemer makes clear, newspapers throughout the country, representing diverse political and sectional perspectives, portrayed a decidedly negative view of British emancipation: "Of the forty-six newspaper reports examined from the moment of emancipation through 1835, only seven characterized emancipation as a success."[37]

Initially this interpretation focused on black violence in the form of arson, riots, and the need for martial law. Reports dwelled upon a rebellion on the north coast of Jamaica and on a mob of a thousand apprentices tearing down a jail in Trinidad and rescuing a prisoner. When the expected major insurrections failed to appear, attention turned to the failure of apprentices to work as well as slaves. Drawing on free labor ideology, many British abolitionists had assured the public that, despite the common view that blacks were somewhat lazy because they were still "savages," freed blacks would quickly develop proper work incentives and produce more sugar and other products than slaves had done. This expectation was reinforced by the conviction that divine Providence rewards virtue and punishes evil. However, by October 1834, two and a half months after emancipation, even a Boston newspaper reprinted a report that apprentices in Jamaica were performing only "one fourth of their former labor," and that the Special Magistrates from Britain showed undue favor to the workers. Even though some papers carried reports from British journals attacking the harshness of the apprenticeship system, with its savage "military flogging" of workers, readers throughout the country encountered repeated examples of "lazy and indolent" apprentices who resisted orders and refused to work long hours. By the spring of 1835, estates in Grenada were supposedly producing only half the hogsheads of sugar they had produced under slavery.[38]

This negative view of British emancipation was strongly disputed, especially by American abolitionists and their supporters like Ralph Waldo Emerson. Eminent economist Robert William Fogel has pointed to a great moral paradox that persists to this day: the belief "that 'events' reward virtue and punish evil," the theory that "immoral economic systems cannot be productive, for that would reward evil, and moral systems cannot be unproductive, for that would punish virtue." It was only in the mid-1960s that scholars *began* to discover that "slavery was profitable, efficient, and economically viable in both the United States and the West Indies when it was destroyed . . . [that] its death was an act of 'econocide,' a political execution of an immoral system at its peak of economic success." But while American reformers were extremely reluctant to accept mounting empirical evidence that West Indian productivity had deteriorated after emancipation, Southerners seized on that evidence as proof that abolitionists posed a fatal threat to their increasingly prosperous and expanding society.[39]

It is true that in the first years after British emancipation, there were legitimate arguments over the temporary effects of apprenticeship and the sharp differences between a small island like Antigua, which rejected apprenticeship and where the immediately freed slaves faced hardly any opportunities besides plantation field work, and large islands like Jamaica and Trinidad, where many of the eventually freed apprentices could find land for their own subsistence agriculture.[40]

By 1837, the Executive Committee of the American Anti-Slavery Society decided it was time to obtain a detailed and authoritative report on the effects of emancipation in the British Caribbean. They commissioned James A. Thome and J. Horace Kimball to gather "facts and testimony" to prove the safety, efficiency, and profitability of immediate emancipation, by exposing "the truth." As Thome and Kimball make clear in the introduction to their 1838 book, *Emancipation in the West Indies. A Six Months' Tour in Antigua, Barbadoes, and Jamaica*, the ultimate goal was to "present the work to our countrymen who yet hold slaves, with the utmost confidence that its perusal will not leave in their minds a doubt, either of the duty or perfect safety of *immediate emancipation*, however it may fail to persuade their hearts—which God grant it may not!"[41]

Backing up such confidence was the book's recorded testimony of numerous former slaveholding planters and political leaders in the Caribbean, "island authorities [who] are as unchallengeable on the score of previous leaning towards abolitionism as Mr. [George] McDuffie, or Mr. [John C.] Calhoun would be two years hence, if slavery were to be abolished throughout the United States to-morrow." As Thome and Kimball interviewed countless authorities and common people, especially in Antigua, and dined with members of the Antiguan assembly, proprietors, managers of estates, and missionaries, they only rarely encountered someone who retained "some old prejudices of slavery." The governor, who stressed that "he had never found such a peaceable, orderly, and law-abiding people as those [the freed slaves] of Antigua," also affirmed that "the planters all conceded that emancipation had been a great blessing to the island, and he did not know of a single individual who wished to return to the old system."[42]

By concentrating on the effects of immediate emancipation in Antigua, as opposed to their briefer treatment of apprenticeship in Jamaica and Barbados, Thome and Kimball tried to prove that "the bad reports of the newspapers, spiritless as they have been compared with the [alarming] predictions, have been traceable, on the slightest inspection, not to emancipation, but to the illegal continuance of slavery, under the cover of its legal substitute [apprenticeship]."[43]

James A. Thome, the son of a Kentucky slaveholder, had a genuine understanding of slaveholding culture. Like James G. Birney and a number of other Southerners, he was converted to abolitionism in 1834 by the famous debates at the Lane Theological Seminary, near Cincinnati, led by Theodore Dwight Weld. Thome became an agent of the American Anti-Slavery Society and in 1836 convinced his father to manumit the family's slaves, an achievement that enhanced his faith in "moral suasion," the abolitionists' early belief that following the model of religious conversion, Southern Christians could be peacefully persuaded to recognize the sin of slaveholding.[44]

Benjamin David Weber has brilliantly compared Thome's massive handwritten manuscript with the published book, showing that Theodore Dwight Weld edited the work in a way that deemphasized religion and moral suasion and focused on the economic superiority of free labor within a context of laissez-faire individualism and harmony of interests. With Southern slaveholding readers clearly in mind, Weld welcomed the passages that demonstrated "the safety and profitability for the masters and the new mechanisms of discipline focused on inculcating inward self-control and industriousness." The issue of the freed slaves' incentives to work had been especially crucial in Britain. But, given Weld's pragmatism, this also meant the deletion of Thome's paragraphs noting the great desire of some workers to escape field labor and describing the way Antigua restricted the blacks' employment options in order to keep sufficient field labor on the estates. Since Kimball, an antislavery editor from New England, became seriously ill during their West Indian tour and died soon thereafter, it was Thome who really reported on their interviews and discoveries.[45]

In their introduction, Thome and Kimball summarized the "established facts," the crucial points "beyond the power of dispute or cavil" that emerged from their investigation of British emancipation in Antigua, Jamaica, and Barbados. First, that the immediate emancipation in Antigua "was not attended with any disorder whatever." Second, that the emancipated slaves "have readily, faithfully, and efficiently worked for wages from the first" (elsewhere they stressed that free labor was less expensive and more productive, and that land values had risen). Third, that apprenticeship, which planters had never wanted as a "preparation" for freedom, was the source of the only serious difficulties, and that any "disturbance in the working of apprenticeship" was "invariably" the fault of the masters or officers charged with administering it. Fourth, that "the prejudice of caste" was "fast disappearing in the emancipated islands." Fifth, that the planters "who have fairly made the 'experiment,' now greatly prefer the new system to the old." And sixth, that the emancipated people "are perceptibly rising in the scale of civilization, morals, and religion."[46]

This glowing vision of the British precedent, of life after slavery, becomes darker when Thome and Kimball actually turn to Jamaica, a "half-way house between slavery and freedom." In Kingston, where Kimball would become confined because of illness, the attorney general gave them letters of introduction to influential planters. They also interviewed the solicitor general, merchants, and newspaper editors, and concluded that despite the failures of apprenticeship, there had been no sign of revolt, defiance of law, or increase in crime. Thome and Kimball later found that planters differed on the industriousness of the apprentices.[47] Yet the apprentice system perpetuated or even magnified the cruelties of slavery, as when an apprentice would be sent to a house of correction and tortured on a treadmill for the crime of being late to work. In discussing the complexities of this partial dismantling of the slave system, Thome and Kimball could only predict that Jamaica would move toward the Antiguan model once apprenticeship was abolished.[48]

FROM JOSEPH JOHN GURNEY TO THE ISSUE OF FAILURE

While Weber shows that Thome and Kimball's work helped change the meaning of immediatism for American abolitionists—and some nonabolitionist Northerners like Governor Edward Everett of Massachusetts wrote that Thome and Kimball's evidence *"sealed the fate of slavery throughout the civilized world"*[49]—it was British Quaker Joseph John Gurney who directly conveyed a positive view of British emancipation to America's most prominent leaders in Washington, in 1840.[50]

A member of a famous and prosperous Quaker banking and philanthropic family, Gurney was the brother-in-law of Thomas Fowell Buxton (not a Quaker) and the brother of the eminent reformer Elizabeth (Gurney) Fry. Gurney was a banker, reformer, philanthropist, and evangelical Quaker minister (his preaching in the United States contributed to a schism in the Society of Friends), and his three-year mission to America in 1837–40 enabled him to travel throughout the country, visiting colleges, prisons, and asylums, and even conducting a religious service in January 1838 in the House of Representatives, which was attended by President Martin Van Buren, Senator Henry Clay, and Congressman John Quincy Adams, all of whom Gurney had previously interviewed.

Though committed to abolitionist principles, Gurney had an incredible network of connections that made it possible, after his later tour of the West Indies, to have a private audience concerning the effects of British emancipation not only with Secretary of State John Forsyth, but with President Van Buren (whom he visited at least four times), John C. Calhoun, Henry Clay, Daniel Webster, John Quincy Adams, and the British ambassador Henry Fox. Hardly less amazing, when Gurney stopped in Savannah, Georgia, on his way from the Caribbean to Washington, he succeeded in addressing nearly two thousand people, in two public meetings, despite the diffusion of reports that he was an "anti-slavery spy." By 1840 the Lower South was becoming notorious for its often violent suppression of antislavery writings and speeches. Yet Gurney left Savannah "under feelings of sincere regard and affection towards many of its inhabitants," and also reported that "we are bound to acknowledge that they treated us with great civility and kindness."[51]

Given the Southerners' intense hostility to Northern abolitionists, Gurney's warm reception in Savannah and especially by slaveholders like Clay and Calhoun in Washington is difficult to understand. He was one of the most remarkable of all the advocates of slave emancipation, in part because his approach differed so strikingly from that of the most prominent American abolitionists. Said to be tall, handsome, and cordial, he was clearly at age fifty a very agreeable and appealing man, capable of establishing close ties not only with a moderate opponent of slavery like William Ellery Channing but also with a moderate slaveholder like Henry Clay, the president of the American Colonization Society who had argued for gradual emancipation in Kentucky in the late 1790s.

Scrupulous in avoiding any public censure of slaveholders (he was well aware that another English "foreign" abolitionist, George Thompson, had been vilified, mobbed, and threatened with death), Gurney succeeded in presenting some of the clearest and most concise critiques of racial slavery in the American South, Cuba, and the other slaveholding colonies he visited.

It is also important to note that even by 1840 and later, some antislavery views persisted in the Upper South, and many Southerners still expressed some ambivalence and internal misgivings over the institution, in part because of their deep devotion to the ideal of "liberty."[52] Many slaveholders still believed that slavery, like medieval serfdom, was doomed by history to disappear. They were eager to hear a report on the consequences of British emancipation, even from a strong advocate of freedom, if he embodied the prestige and reputation of Joseph John Gurney. Gurney himself emphasized, in a later published letter to his "brother" Buxton, that many American slaveholders were "increasingly disposed to enter upon a fair consideration of the subject." Expressing his deep-rooted optimism, he added that if such slaveholders were "wisely dealt with" (he condemned the use of "harsh epithets and violent language" toward slaveholders), they could hardly fail to arrive at conclusions that would lead them "to openly support the cause of emancipation."[53]

As a Quaker evangelist, Gurney saw "preaching the gospel" as the main purpose of his travels in America and the West Indies. But in England he had also been an ardent reformer, like his sister Elizabeth Fry, and had engaged in various causes, including the improvement of prison discipline and criminal codes, and of course the abolition of British colonial slavery. As a young man, Gurney had worked with Wilberforce and Clarkson, and had then helped his brother-in-law

Buxton by writing, speaking, and offering funds to promote the final emancipation act. In America, he continued his efforts regarding the treatment of criminals and the insane, and since his visit coincided with the massive westward "removal" of Indians, he addressed many political leaders regarding this cruel act of oppression, which he regarded as "one of the foulest blots on the character of the nations of Christendom."[54]

In Quaker meetings, Gurney spoke out more openly against the immense immorality of slavery, especially the laws banning the education of slaves and the cruelty of the internal slave trade. He felt free to present the Friends' views on "the oppressed negro population" to the governor of Virginia, who responded by attacking the Northern abolitionists for barring progress toward emancipation.[55] Gurney also felt free to publish a "friendly" response to a major speech Clay gave to the U.S. Senate, defending the legal rights of slaveholders. Gurney pointed out that aside from its other faults, Clay's colonization scheme diverted attention from the need to abolish slavery by constitutional means, and from the need for the civil and moral improvement of the blacks. Gurney must have been pleased and surprised when Clay later told him that this widely read piece was the best of all the reviews of his speech.[56]

Although Gurney saw his West Indian trip as primarily a religious mission that might additionally improve his health, he also planned to study and record the effects of British slave emancipation. Before leaving he took the time to visit the office of the American Anti-Slavery Society, where he conversed about the West Indies with abolitionists James G. Birney and Joshua Leavitt. (He also gave them $200 to finance an uncut version of Buxton's *The African Slave Trade*, which documented America's continuing complicity with the illegal trade to Cuba and Brazil, a subject Gurney would investigate further in Cuba.) In late November 1839, Gurney and a young Quaker companion set sail for a five-month tour of the islands. Since Henry Clay had urged him to publish the results of his inquiries and observations in the West Indies, Gurney later drew on his diaries and wrote and published in 1840 an account of his trip as a series of "familiar letters" addressed to "Henry Clay, of Kentucky," with Clay's permission. Since the book is especially directed to the self-interest of Southern slaveholders, Gurney's emphasis on the economic superiority of free labor is notable.[57]

Gurney's first letters compare the situation in the slaveholding Danish Virgin Islands with British Dominica, St. Christopher's, and especially Antigua, where he more than confirms the buoyant views of Thome and Kimball. In the Danish colonies he is repeatedly struck by the "dead weight" of the slave system, as evidenced by land exhaustion, the decline in sugar exports, and the transfer of heavily mortgaged estates from the hands of original owners to managers. Despite Danish efforts at amelioration, Gurney is shocked by the "low physical, intellectual, and moral condition of the slaves," especially when compared with the liberated blacks he would later see in the British islands.[58]

Like the governor of Antigua, a high official in St. Christopher's assured Gurney that not a single person on the island wished that slavery would be restored. As Gurney held large religious gatherings for whites and blacks in Methodist and Moravian meetinghouses, he also learned that on both islands imports and land values had vastly increased and that black workers were performing a far greater quantity of work in a given time than under slavery. In Antigua he was told that in the first five years of freedom, exports of sugar and molasses had significantly increased, despite two years of drought, and that in the sixth year, 1839, exports of sugar were almost double the average during the last five years of slavery.[59]

As one planter pointed out, only one-third of the slaves had really been "operative" at one time, since planters had to support the nonworking children and the elderly, the infirm, the sick, and those who shammed illness. Paid-wage labor by freedpeople was thus "incalculably cheaper," according to the Speaker at the Antiguan assembly. Planters had a savings of at least 30 percent when every man, black and white, was thrown upon his own exertions, and the "cooperation" of employer and employee enhanced the community's wealth. No less important, emancipation had brought an increase in black marriage and a decrease in black crime, along with other evidence of a striking "moral improvement of the Negro population."[60]

Like Thome and Kimball, Gurney struggled to reconcile some deeply disturbing facts in Jamaica with the premises of free labor ideology and the wholly positive expectations derived especially from Antigua. Indeed, Gurney's letters to Clay, coupled with a brief introductory letter to Buxton and a letter at the end of the book addressed to Jamaican planters, contain an embarrassing contradiction. On the one hand, Gurney repeatedly gives optimistic assurances that Jamaica was on the "road to prosperity" and could not, "when duly inspected and fairly estimated, furnish any exception" to the highly positive results of slave emancipation. On the other hand, he continues to express deep concern over signs of economic failure.[61]

These signs of trouble are scattered throughout the letters, separated by reassuring arguments, and thus have less collective impact. Worst of all, according to Gurney, Jamaica suffered from the fact that the great majority of estates belonged to absentee proprietors and were thus under the care of young attorneys, often of "immoral character," who often managed numerous estates at one time and who merged the payment of wages with the blacks' payment of rent in a highly exploitive way. Gurney repeatedly emphasizes that when the workers, or "peasants," are fairly and humanely treated, and paid weekly in cash—which promotes everyone's best economic interest—they happily continue working on the property of their old masters, which is most familiar to them and nearest their homes.[62]

Unfortunately, immediately after the end of apprenticeship and the award of full freedom in 1838, workers throughout the island faced a payment of rent, which was often doubled or tripled and extracted from expected wages. When workers protested or complained, there were threats of ejection, some cottages were demolished, and family provision grounds were despoiled, all of which amounted, according to Gurney, to "a new form of slavery." This oppression explained why many of the freedpeople, who were conscious of their rights and interests, began deserting the estates on which they had been unfairly treated and succeeded in establishing their own small freeholds near or on Jamaica's mountains—an option not available on the smaller islands.[63]

Gurney noted that the "impolitic attempts to force the labor of freemen" had angered the peasants and led to the desertion of many estates and thus to the decline in the labor force. He was deeply troubled by some of the resulting new penal laws against vagrancy and indebtedness, similar to those in the postwar American South, that restricted freedom and endangered the "peace and prosperity of the colony." But he tended to downplay the decline in sugar and coffee exports and affirmed that evidence of improved understandings between planters and workers gave reason to expect increased production in the near future.[64]

Moreover, the freed slaves who had left the estates were by no means idle. Gurney happily asserted that the old notion that blacks were inherently lazy and would work only by compulsion was "now for ever exploded." The freed Jamaican blacks were now busy cultivating their own grounds and building stone walls, houses, roads, ditches, and even villages that would have been inconceivable before emancipation. Many were also engaged in fishing or producing handicrafts. And the employers of blacks were now freed from the necessity of paying for their clothing, bedding, food, and medicines, to say nothing of whips, a fact that helped explain the increase in imports, land values, and urban trade. Gurney stressed that even if some planters had been deprived of their profits, emancipation had brought a marked increase in black schools, literacy, marriages, church attendance, and a decrease in crime. And his firm faith in the natural laws of progress confirmed his belief that the ultimate prosperity of the proprietors "is linked by an indissoluble tie to justice, mercy, and wisdom, which ensures well-being of the population at large."[65]

As we have seen, Gurney was very confident of his ability to interact successfully with American slaveholders and West Indian former slaveholders—he informed Clay that he had had "much satisfaction" in relating the story of West Indian emancipation to "a political rival of thine," John C. Calhoun, for whom he had "sincere personal esteem," and who "listened with the greatest attention to the narrative." According to Gurney, Calhoun then "admitted his belief not only in the accuracy of the relation itself," but in the pecuniary, physical, and moral points Gurney made regarding "the favorable working of freedom."

Of course Calhoun then felt compelled, with an "eagle eye" fixed on Gurney, to argue that in America, which lacked the strong military arm of Britain, abolition would lead to Haitian-like racial violence and war. Gurney refrained from countering this fallacy, but assured Clay that Britain's military arm had been needed only under slavery and that the freed blacks harbored no desire for revenge or antipathy for whites. And it was with similar confidence that he addressed the urgent letter to Jamaican planters on the theme of racial reconciliation.[66]

Having dined with Jamaican planters as well as with the governor and other officials, Gurney knew that it was crucial to address issues of self-interest to "persons habituated to slaveholding throughout their lives." He assured the planters that by 1840 the eyes of such slavery-supporting nations as France, Denmark, Spain, Portugal, Brazil, and the United States were fixed on the British West Indies, and especially Jamaica. These regions should now prove that free labor was more economical and productive than slave labor, and that the just and equal liberty of all citizens of a state had "an unfailing tendency to increase its wealth." But this goal required all Jamaicans to unite in promoting the island's prosperity. And such unity, Gurney stressed, could be achieved only by "reconciliation," by overcoming misunderstandings between planters and workers, especially concerning fair work for fair wages. Fortunately, he noted, as in Antigua and Dominica, task or piece work, as opposed to day wages, was becoming more prevalent even in Jamaica, and the decline in production was supposedly easing.[67]

But the most central and urgent point, as Gurney also made clear in his letter to Buxton, was the need for British and West Indian unity on the threatening issue of a proposed equalization of duties on sugar.[68] By 1840, free-trade ideology was gaining much strength in Britain as representatives of the consumer public called for a repeal of the Corn Laws and other measures that created high monopolistic prices for wheat, sugar, and other commodities by maintaining protective tariffs that cut off free-market imports. In general, the kind of liberals who believed in the superiority of free labor also favored free trade.

But Britain's emancipation of colonial slaves in 1834 and 1838 created a new conflict between advocates of free trade and many defenders of free labor. The abolition of Britain's slave trade in 1807 had put Britain's plantation colonies at a great disadvantage in competing with such booming slave-importing regions as Cuba and Brazil. In virtually all parts of the New World, except the United States, slave societies depended on slave imports to maintain population growth. While the British colonies were slowly weakened by a declining slave population, they also suffered when the abolition movement frightened domestic investors and creditors. By 1833, as Seymour Drescher notes, a parliamentary committee found that the British West Indies "were in severe distress. Large portions of the sugar plantations were currently turning little or no profit, and many were running multiyear losses." Moreover, "the share of the British slave colonies in the trade and income of the metropolis had been measurably declining for more than fifteen years." Accordingly, despite the faith of some MPs in the superiority of free labor, the emancipation law of 1833 strongly raised the duties on imports of foreign sugar, in part to protect planters, freed workers, and what Colonial Secretary Stanley termed the "mighty experiment." The import duties also provided funds for compensating slave owners.[69]

Nevertheless, the British colonies were still producing enough sugar to supply the domestic market and also sell a small surplus in the Atlantic market. In 1836, the price of sugar sold in Britain was still equal to the world price. But, as even Gurney acknowledged, slave emancipation led to a decline in production, especially in colonies like Jamaica. By 1841—three years after the end of apprenticeship—domestic demand had risen and the supply had fallen. Londoners who yearned for sugar in their tea now paid twice the price they would have paid in Paris. Not surprisingly, it became necessary that year for MPs who were concerned over the fate of the emancipation experiment to join the West India interest and vote down a fervently debated bill to equalize duties and promote the importation of slave-grown sugar.[70]

The parliamentary debates in 1841 also reflected an important transformation in the British abolitionist movement. Having achieved emancipation in most British colonies (but not in India, where slavery was an indigenous institution),[71] British abolitionists now focused on the goal of a universal, global ending of slavery. They strongly supported the prohibitive levy on foreign sugar, despite the high price of sugar for the British poor, since importing duty-free sugar from Cuba and Brazil would greatly stimulate the Atlantic slave trade and increase the exploitation of slaves in those regions. When charged by free traders with inconsistency regarding the importation of slave-grown American cotton, they lamely replied that there was no alternative to American cotton, unlike the sugar from the now free British colonies.[72]

Given the powerful free-trade movement that led to the repeal of the Corn Laws in 1846, it is not surprising that Parliament passed a Sugar Duties Act the same year, equalizing duties on British colonial and foreign sugar and initiating a gradual process of removing all protections by the early 1850s. Given the state of public opinion, abolitionists did not dare to make an appeal to the people on behalf of the freed slaves. But they privately feared that "free trade" would lead to the expansion of the slave trade and the failure of Britain's great experiment. Despite the optimistic predictions of free traders concerning the "union of prosperity and morality," the new Sugar Duties Act had a devastating effect on the British Caribbean colonies. They could not compete with slaveholding Cuba and Brazil and also faced the rise of European beet sugar as a cheap alternative to sugarcane. The sharp decline in British sugar prices wiped out dozens of merchant houses in the West Indies and Britain. A European economic depression in 1847–48 also contributed to the failure of the West India Bank and to the growing inability of planters to pay their debts or provide adequate wages for their workers.[73]

In 1848, a "select" parliamentary committee gathered a vast amount of data on the crisis of the British colonies and the production of sugar from China to Peru. Given the evaporation of credit and the fact that the price of sugar had fallen below the cost of production, the manager of one of Jamaica's most profitable and efficient estates now reported that his plantation was operating at a loss. Even Antigua, once the model of emancipation's economic success, now expressed doubt about the island's ability to continue commercial cultivation. According to Seymour Drescher, the media's widespread publication of such dramatic examples of failure gave a Tory like Benjamin Disraeli a strong "stick" with which to beat the free-trade Whigs: "The great experiment, the greatest blunder in the history of the English people, had simultaneously ruined the British colonies, encouraged the African slave trade, and revealed 'the quackery of economic science.' "[74]

Even well before the impact of the Sugar Duties Act, the growing shortage of productive West Indian labor had been signified by British efforts to transport "free" black contract labor from West Africa to the Caribbean, efforts abolitionists successfully countered as a disguised revival of the slave trade. Then, in 1843, the British government sent a minister, Edward Fox, to meet secretly in Washington with Secretary of State Abel Upshur to convey the conservative Peel ministry's startling proposal to recruit and pay transportation costs for large numbers of American free blacks to migrate to the British West Indies, where they would do the contract work that former slaves were now either unable or refusing to do. Upshur, an ardently proslavery Virginian, rejected Fox's proposal on grounds of states' rights (at a time when the Underground Railroad was aiding slaves to escape to British Canada, he could hardly imagine allowing British agents to recruit free blacks in the South). Still, because of the labor shortage from 1839 to 1845, Trinidad did import some 1,300 subsidized free blacks from the United States.[75]

Fox's admission that the British colonies were "suffering severely" from "a dearth of agricultural laborers" had a decisive impact on Upshur and especially on John C. Calhoun, who replaced Upshur as secretary of state immediately after Upshur was killed by the explosion of a cannon on a warship. Upshur had ordered Robert Monroe Harrison, the American consul in Jamaica, to present a comprehensive report on the results of British emancipation. Harrison sent back material to support his conclusion that "England has ruined her own colonies, and like an unchaste female wishes to see *other* countries, where slavery exists, in a similar state." Southerners could claim that Lord Aberdeen, the Tory foreign secretary, confirmed the latter point when he declared in 1843 that "Great Britain desires, and is constantly exerting herself to procure, the general abolition of slavery throughout the world." Upshur's State Department substantiated the first point by publishing Harrison's statistics claiming that by 1843 the price of freeholds in Jamaica had declined by half, coffee and sugar production had declined by as much as 50 percent, and some large plantations were worth less than 10 percent of their preemancipation value.[76]

It is doubtful that Calhoun had ever been really convinced by Gurney's reports on the success of British emancipation. In any event, he and other Southern leaders would now interpret British policy as an effort to undermine successful foreign slavery, as a means of counteracting the disastrous failure of their own experiment with emancipation. Calhoun rightly predicted that Britain would try to restore plantation production in the Caribbean by importing huge numbers of only nominally free "coolie" labor from India. Yet he affirmed that such investment could never succeed unless Britain also destroyed the rival slave societies that "have refused to follow her suicidal policy" and that could therefore keep the prices of tropical staples "so low as to prevent their cultivation with profit, in the possessions of Great Britain, by what she is pleased to call free labor." Examples of Lord Aberdeen's professed antislavery policy could be seen in Britain's interference in Cuba (which expelled the British consul and abolitionist David Turnbull for supposedly plotting a slave insurrection) and most alarmingly in the new Republic of Texas, a site Britons feared could promote the reestablishment of the African slave trade. Calhoun's deep concern over Britain's antislavery pressures on Texas helped lead to America's annexation of the slaveholding republic in 1845 and thus to the Mexican-American War and the extraordinary expansion of the American West.[77]

With slavery expanding in the United States and thousands of African slaves being imported into Cuba each year, the prospects seemed increasingly dim that the world would follow the example of British emancipation, as abolitionists and statesmen had hoped in 1833. As the London *Times* put it in 1857,

> Our own colonies are impoverished, but the sum of slavery is not diminished, it has only been transferred from us to more grasping pitiless and unscrupulous hands. Never was the prospect of emancipation more distant than now that foreign slave-owners are establishing a monopoly of all the great staples of tropical produce. [The old islands] . . . are going out of cultivation, while Cuba, the United States, and Brazil are every day extending the area of their cultivation and the number of their slaves.

The views of academic social scientists were no more hopeful. In the words of Nassau W. Senior, one of Britain's most venerable political economists, noting in 1855 that American slaveholders were now coveting Cuba and thinking of annexing Jamaica, "We do not venture to hope that we or our sons or grandsons, will see American slavery extirpated from the earth."[78]

On the other hand, the importation of thousands of indentured Indian coolie laborers into Trinidad, British Guiana, and Mauritius (in the Indian Ocean) helped to restore some levels of sugar production and prevent a total collapse of free produce imports into Britain. In the decade following the 1846 Sugar Duties Act, British consumption of slave-grown sugar rose from virtually nothing to 40 percent of British supply, but it could have been much more. Similarly, from 1831 to 1857, British sugar imports from the British West Indies dropped from 4 million to only 3 million hundredweight. That British emancipation was not a total economic failure can be seen in the fact that it served as a model for the Dutch in 1863 (reinforced by the American Civil War). Having ended their slave trade in 1814, the conservative Dutch now established an apprenticeship system that lasted more than twice as long as the British system. They also paid much more compensation to colonial planters and introduced Asian indentured labor immediately after the end of apprenticeship, so that in the West Indian colony of Suriname, laborers from India and Java outnumbered ex-slaves within a decade. And none of these measures prevented a postemancipation decline in Dutch sugar exports.[79]

By the 1850s, even the British proponents of free labor ideology had revised their assumptions to take account of the supposedly *temporary* success of slave economies when competing with newly freed plantation labor. But, as Seymour Drescher imaginatively argues, a rather sudden upsurge of racial ideology beginning in the late 1840s served as the most important way of reconciling—for *white* people— the West Indian economic failure with belief in the superiority of free labor. This is all the more remarkable in view of the relative absence of racist arguments in the earlier British debates over the slave trade and slave emancipation. But Thomas Carlyle's notorious 1849 essay, *Occasional Discourses on the Negro* [later *Nigger*] *Question*, coincided with the blossoming of scientific racism in Europe and especially America. The rise of British resentment against abolitionists' "privileging" West Indian blacks carried over to the widespread but by no means universal view that blacks were so inherently lazy and lacking in ambition and incentive that they would never do much work unless compelled to do so. As the *Times* put it in 1848:

> [A] day's work is seldom done except the African ambition has been stimulated by recollections of rum or roused by the attractions of some outrageously red piece of calico. One day's labour in a week will supply the necessities which negro nature owns. . . . they squat and vegetate in groups, working only lazily, and at rare intervals, till their condition becomes far more brutish than it was on their landing.[80]

But despite much talk of "inferior races" and agreement that it was "the slow, indolent temperament of the African race," as *The Economist* put it, that explained the economic failure of British emancipation, there were no calls for reenslavement. The immense popularity in the 1850s of Harriet Beecher Stowe's *Uncle Tom's Cabin*, which sold a million copies in Britain, pointed to the limits of racist ideology.

And as we have seen, when Frederick Douglass spoke at an American celebration of British emancipation in 1858, he responded to the widespread belief in West Indian economic failure by celebrating black achievement and the "failure" of whites to keep free blacks "in their place":

It [emancipation] has failed to keep Slavery in the West Indies under the name of Liberty. It has failed to change the name without changing the character of the thing. The negroes have really been emancipated, and are no longer slaves. Herein is the real failure. Emancipation has failed to keep negroes out of civil office, it has failed to keep them out of the jury box, off the judge's bench, and out of the Colonial Legislature, for colored men have risen to all these stations since Emancipation. It has failed to keep the lands of Jamaica in the hands of the few and out of the hands of the many. It has failed to make men work for a planter at small wages, when they can work for themselves for larger wages. . . . You cannot get men to work on plantations for a lordly proprietor when they can do as well, and better, for themselves in other ways. I will not assume that Yankees are a lazy, good-for-nothing set, because we are compelled to import Irishmen to dig our canals and grade our railroads.[81]

It is important to stress that Britain remained the world's leading supporter of antislavery policies—from the nation's success in finally stopping the slave trade to Brazil in 1850 to Europe's often Machiavellian embrace of antislavery in the 1880s' Scramble for Africa. As philosopher Kwame Anthony Appiah has shown, much of this central moral commitment emerged as a matter of Britain's national *honor*, regardless of expense and ordinary self-interest. And, as Drescher and others have made clear, the expense of Britain's emancipation of slaves and of its prolonged efforts to abolish oceanic slave trading was prodigious.[82]

Yet, when judging the expense of slave emancipations—and America's emancipation as the result of a civil war was doubtless the costliest of all—one must consider the prolonged human costs of exploitive slave regimes. It would be difficult to calculate that expense if Britain's 800,000 slaves or America's 4 million slaves had not been freed for one or two or three more generations. In some respects there was an element of "failure" in all the emancipations, from Haiti to the Northern American states, the British and French colonies, the American Civil War, and on to Cuba and Brazil in the 1880s. In no case did emancipation lead to a prosperous, racially egalitarian society. Yet as Gurney observed in 1840 and as Frederick Douglass argued eighteen years later, the freed slaves in the British colonies were immensely better off than under slavery.

As the British celebrated and redefined their great historical event, as at the Jubilee meeting on August 1, 1884, they radically divorced the moral achievement from any economic issues. Their goal, as expressed by the Prince of Wales, was "to carry on this civilizing torch of freedom until its beneficent light shall shed abroad over all the earth." As Drescher concludes, "The great experiment was in fact a great improvisation. The true taproot of antislavery lay in its successful mass political mobilization around a fundamental uneconomic proposition."[83] Drescher and Appiah both note that this antislavery commitment helped prevent Britain from following its best economic interest and recognizing the Confederacy in the American Civil War. One should add that it was the Civil War, Lincoln's Emancipation Proclamation, and the Thirteenth Amendment that transformed the global meaning of Britain's "mighty experiment." While a war costing 750,000 military lives signified an opposite "solution" to the problem of slavery, it helped redefine Britain's parliamentary act of 1833 as the launching of what W. E. H. Lecky termed an "unwearied, unostentatious, and inglorious crusade" to exterminate slavery from the earth.[84]

11

<hr/>

The British Mystique:
Black Abolitionists in Britain—
the Leader of the Industrial Revolution
and Center of "Wage Slavery"

FREDERICK DOUGLASS CONFRONTS THE WORLD

On August 16, 1845, some three months after the publication of his best-selling and highly acclaimed *Narrative of the Life of Frederick Douglass, An American Slave,* the twenty-seven-year-old Frederick Douglass boarded the *Cambria,* a Cunard paddle steamer, and sailed from Boston toward Liverpool. During his antislavery lecture tours, Douglass had long been absent from his wife, Anna, and four children, but his ongoing decision to spend nearly two years in Britain represented a drastic tradeoff in values. While reluctant to leave his family, Douglass became increasingly aware that the spectacular sales and reviews of his book magnified the risk of his being recaptured as a fugitive slave. Massachusetts provided very limited protections, and Douglass's owners, Hugh and Thomas Auld, furious over the way Douglass had portrayed them, reportedly vowed to reenslave him. Britain not only provided a safe haven, but British abolitionists finally succeeded in raising funds and negotiating with Hugh Auld for Douglass's legal manumission.[1]

Given his success in America as a lecturer and author, Douglass was also strongly attracted by the prospect of touring Britain and Ireland as a lecturer, exposing the evils of American slavery to audiences that were receptive and amazingly free from racial prejudice, according to the testimony of earlier black abolitionist visitors like the Reverend Nathaniel Paul and Charles Lenox Remond. The success of British abolitionists in mobilizing the public and emancipating 800,000 slaves drew increasing numbers of African Americans to this capital of abolitionism and reinforced the contrast between Americans and the British people, who, as Samuel Ringgold Ward later told a Southampton audience, "were looked upon by the Negro as his especial friends and guardians, and surely the actions and sacrifices of the British people in the Negro's behalf fully justified this idea."[2]

Douglass boarded the *Cambria* with a white friend, James N. Buffum, a wealthy abolitionist and future mayor of Lynn, Massachusetts, who had earlier helped Douglass fight off a mob. Buffum had failed, despite its being a British ship, to obtain a cabin passage for Douglass on the *Cambria*, having been told that this "would give offense to the majority of American passengers." Accordingly, Buffum also took a steerage compartment. But, after two days at sea, Douglass found that "one part of the ship was about as free to me as another," and he even visited the first-class section at the invitation of fellow passengers, who often called on him in steerage.[3]

As Douglass wrote to his friend and mentor, William Lloyd Garrison, the ship's population could hardly have been more diverse. The famous fugitive slave now confronted the transatlantic world of the mid-1840s:

> [O]ur passengers were made up of nearly all costs [*sic*] of people, from different countries of the most opposite mode of thinking on all subjects. We had nearly all sorts of parties in morals, religion, and politics, as well as trades, callings, and professions. The Doctor and the Lawyer, the soldier and the sailor were there. The scheming Connecticut wood clock maker, the large, curly New York lion-tamer, the solemn Roman Catholic Bishop, and the Orthodox Quaker were there. A minister of the Free Church of Scotland, and a minister of the Church of England—the established Christian and the meandering Jew, the Whig and the Democrat, the white and the black, were there. There was the dark-visaged Spaniard, and the light-visaged Englishman—the man from Montreal, and the man from Mexico. There were slaveholders from Cuba,

and slaveholders from Georgia. We had anti-slavery singing and pro-slavery grumbling; and at the same time that Governor Hammond's Letters were being read, my Narrative was being circulated [and copies sold to passengers]. In the midst of the debate going on, there sprang up quite a desire, on the part of a number on board to have me lecture to them on slavery.[4]

Douglass knew that Garrison would be pleased to learn that "from the moment we first lost sight of the American shore till we landed at Liverpool," there was an "almost constant discussion of the subject of slavery—commencing cool but growing hotter every moment as it advanced." "If suppressed in the saloon, it broke out in the steerage; and if it [repealed?] in the steerage, it was reversed in the saloon; and if suppressed in both, it broke out with redoubled energy high upon the saloon deck, in the open, refreshing, free ocean air."[5]

During most of the voyage, Douglass expressed delight in the way that "the sunshine of free discussion" enabled antislavery truths to triumph over the attempts to defend and justify slavery. However, on the night of August 27, as they approached the Irish coast and after Douglass had accepted the captain's invitation to deliver an address on slavery, about a half dozen proslavery militants were determined to prevent him from speaking.[6] They had concluded that "reason, morality, humanity, and Christianity" were all against them and that "argument was no longer any means of defense." They therefore reverted to the use of brute force and made "bloody threats" to Douglass if he attempted to speak. Although the captain urged Douglass's opponents to move to a different space, they "actually got up a mob—a real American, republican, democratic, Christian mob—and that, too, on the deck of a British steamer."

The captain succeeded temporarily in quieting the mob and introducing Douglass, but after he spoke a few words on the condition of slaves, Northerners from Connecticut and New Jersey shouted out, "That's a lie!" and appeared anxious to strike him. Another called out, "Down with the Nigger!" One slaveholder from Cuba shook his fist in Douglass's face, and said, "O, I wish I had you in Cuba!" "Ah!" said another, "I wish I had him in Savannah! We would use him up!" When Douglass tried to substantiate his claims by reading some passages from American slave laws, "the slaveholders, finding they were now to be fully exposed, rushed up about me with hands clenched, and swore I should not speak. They were ashamed to have American laws read before an English audience." But such opponents were countered by antislavery supporters. When one mobster called for help in throwing Douglass overboard, a "noble-spirited" Irishman "assured the man who proposed to throw me overboard, that two could play at that game, and that, in the end, he might be thrown overboard himself." Nevertheless, the disruption prevented Douglass from speaking and was only silenced when the captain "told the mobocrats if they did not cease their clamor, he would have them put in irons; and he actually sent for the irons, and doubtless would have made use of them, had not the rioters become orderly."[7]

Douglass would repeatedly describe this event in his speeches in Britain and Ireland, dramatizing the boundary between slaveholding America and Europe. As he summarized his feelings to Garrison:

> I declare, it is enough to make a slave ashamed of the country that enslaved him, to think of it. Without the slightest pretensions to patriotism, as the phrase goes, the conduct of the mobocratic Americans on board the Cambria almost made me ashamed to say I had run away from such a country. It was decidedly the most daring and disgraceful, as well as wicked exhibition of depravity, I ever witnessed, North or South.[8]

AFRICAN AMERICANS EMBRACE THE MOTHER COUNTRY

The relationship between Britain and the United States in the antebellum decades was infinitely complex. England provided most of the manufactures that America imported, and American cotton provided the basis for the textile factories that empowered England's Industrial Revolution. British banks and citizens invested heavily in American securities and state and municipal bonds, while a host of churches and reform movements in both countries maintained intimate connections.[9]

As Frederick Douglass told an audience in Belfast, America was indebted to Britain for her literature, religion, judicial system, and social institutions. Yet he stressed to other listeners that while the British had set a glorious model by emancipating 800,000 slaves, they were the ones who had originally introduced slavery to their colonies and now continued to support the institution by purchasing enormous amounts of slave-grown cotton and other products. Like most American abolitionists, Douglass was committed to democratic ideals and principles that sharply conflicted with Britain's monarchy, aristocracy, and treatment of industrial workers. On the other hand, in his speeches Douglass sometimes likened his journey to Britain with his earlier escape from bondage to freedom, and could write to Garrison that "instead of a democratic government, I am under a monarchical government. . . . I breathe, and lo! the chattel becomes a man."[10]

The sense of a common heritage had long been personified in familial imagery—"mother country," "our American cousins," "parent and offspring." But the American Revolution and War of 1812 greatly polarized this sense of family, as did continuing conflicts over the Canadian border and America's expansion into Florida, Texas, and the Far West, conflicts that sometimes threatened war but were resolved by treaty. American presidents from Jefferson to Polk and Buchanan tended to see monarchial Britain as America's "natural enemy," dedicated to the humiliation and subjugation of her rebellious and increasingly democratic former colonies. Anglophobia had brought a fairly rapid death to the Federalist party. Hatred of England was further nourished by contemporaneous anti-American essays in British periodicals and unflattering descriptions by English travelers that were widely reprinted in the United States.[11]

Historian Marcus Cunliffe noted long ago that both the British and Americans used the other as a negative reference group, "evoking the desired ideal of one's own society by describing opposite characteristics in the other." Uncle Sam and John Bull embodied the supposed worst qualities of republicanism and monarchy. According to the more hostile British accounts, "American republicanism entailed strident vulgarity, abject conformity, demagoguery, corrupt politics, and endemic violence. Its values were superficial. It treasured quantity rather than quality, and pursued the 'Almighty Dollar' with joyless intensity." American critics focused attention on the extraordinarily expensive and superfluous monarchy, which "cost the British taxpayer as much as the entire outlay of the United States government," and even worse, the aristocracy, "with their hereditary titles and their vast estates," who cooperated with the bishops of the Church of England in exploiting and dominating the working poor, who were kept in a state of near destitution. As American writer John C. Cobden put it in his 1853 book, *The White Slaves of England,* "In no country are the few richer than in England, and in no country are the masses more fearfully wretched."[12]

According to Cunliffe, Americans increasingly blamed the repugnant traits of Irish immigrants on centuries of British mistreatment and also accused the British of deliberately dumping its paupers across the Atlantic, thus filling America's urban streets with poverty and crime:

> [T]he apparent evidence convinced a remarkable number of sober citizens of the United States, first, that wage slavery was an inherent element in the British economy at home and throughout the British empire; second, that the antislavery propaganda of the aristocracy, the church, and the manufacturing and mercantile interest was a calculated device to divert attention from British forms of slavery; and third, that this propaganda concealed a diabolic plot to undermine and even destroy the American Union.[13]

As we saw in chapter 10, such a view of British conspiracy was highly compatible with the official doctrines of Secretary of State Calhoun and many other Southern leaders regarding the motives and strategy of British promoters of antislavery. According to this theory, British leaders had responded to the economic disaster of West Indian emancipation by planning to undermine slavery in all other nations in order to improve the competitive advantage of her own colonies, including India. Calhoun succeeded in publicizing the private statement of Lord Aberdeen, the British foreign secretary, that "Britain desires, and is constantly exerting herself to procure, the general abolition of slavery throughout the world." This helped Calhoun to identify even Northern efforts to block America's annexation of slaveholding Texas—and antislavery movements in general—as part of a British plot to destroy the Union.[14]

But Lord Aberdeen's declaration of a national commitment to destroy human bondage only magnified the appeal and magnificence of Britain in the eyes of American abolitionists, especially black abolitionists. Yet, as we will see later, even black abolitionists would eventually need to respond to the issue of British "wage slavery"—to the fact that abolitionism reached unique success in the world's first industrialized nation, the center of free labor ideology and a nation that became notorious for overworking women and even young children, in dismal, dehumanizing factories.

W. Caleb McDaniel has recently published a brilliant book that dramatizes the profound paradox that the world's leading model and advocate of democracy also defended an expanding system of racial slavery, while the world's leading champion of antislavery was still a monarchic and highly aristocratic nation that, as the leader of the Industrial Revolution, also presented shocking examples of so-called wage slavery. McDaniel insightfully explores the way that Garrisonian abolitionists coped with this anomaly, as transatlantic reformers dedicated to both democracy and slave emancipation. The book is especially illuminating with respect to Garrisonians and the British Chartist efforts to blame poverty and low wages on political disempowerment and the need for universal manhood suffrage. Garrison at one point found it necessary to reassure the "working men" in his audience that in denouncing slavery, "I do not denounce democracy."[15]

Although the shocking conditions of the working poor were publicized in the press, novels, and parliamentary reports, capitalist Britain was seen by the 1840s and early 1850s as "the moral arbiter of the western world"—the home for democratic and radical exiles from Italy, Poland, Hungary, Russia, Germany, and Scandinavia, including such figures as Lajos Kossuth, Giuseppe Mazzini, Giuseppe Garibaldi, and Karl Marx. Beginning in the early 1830s, virtually every important African American leader followed a similar path, hoping to gain British support for specific causes and to build what R. J. M. Blackett, quoting Frederick Douglass, terms a "moral cordon" around the United States, so that slaveholders would be overwhelmed wherever they went by denunciations of their so-called peculiar institution. African Americans' affection for Britain was deepened immensely by its abolition of slavery in 1834 and of apprenticeship in 1838, supplemented by the World Antislavery Conventions in London in 1840 and 1843, while earlier black antislavery publications, such as *Freedom's Journal* and David Walker's *Appeal*, had expressed very positive views of the British, in part because of Canada's reception of fugitive slaves. And we will remember that when James McCune Smith found himself barred from American universities, he enrolled in 1831 in the University of Glasgow and became a distinguished American physician.[16]

Nathaniel Paul, a Baptist minister originally from Albany, New York, became the first major black abolitionist to travel to Britain to raise funds and promote the African American cause. In a speech at Glasgow, in 1834, Paul pointed to young McCune Smith, who was sitting on the platform, as an example of Britain's lack of prejudice in providing for the education of a black man of "the highest respectability and intelligence."[17] Having founded the Albany African Church Association, a school for black children, and an Albany society for "the Improvement of the Colored People in Morals, Education, and the Mechanic Arts," and having contributed regularly to *Freedom's Journal* and then *Rights of All,* Paul joined the agrarian Wilberforce Colony in Ontario not long after it was established by blacks who fled the terrible racist laws and 1829 race riots in Cincinnati. Then early in 1832, he departed for England on a mission to raise money for the Canadian colony and for a proposed black manual labor college in New Haven, Connecticut, which the white community soon prohibited.[18]

When Paul arrived in Britain, abolitionists had obtained enormous public support for immediate West Indian emancipation, and British interest in the United States had turned to debates over the alleged antislavery character of the American Colonization Society and African American colonization. Distressed by the growing attacks from American abolitionists, led as we have seen by African Americans, the ACS in 1831 shrewdly commissioned Elliott Cresson, a Quaker philanthropist and ardent supporter of colonization, to visit Britain and persuade abolitionists and humanitarians that the ACS represented the most realistic path to slave emancipation in America. Like even William Lloyd Garrison, Nathaniel Paul had originally been somewhat open to the missionary and antislavery potentialities of African colonization, but by 1832 he had come to see the ACS as a barrier to slave emancipation and a vicious source of racial prejudice. He therefore joined the passionate British abolitionist Charles Stuart in trying to counter Cresson's crusade to raise funds and validate the colonization cause.[19]

Captain Charles Stuart, a retired British officer who had served in India and had then become principal of the Utica Academy in upstate New York, became extremely influential in the Anglo-American antislavery cause. The work he wrote in his initial campaign against

Elliott Cresson helped inspire Garrison to write his 1832 landmark, *Thoughts on African Colonization.*[20]

Along with his crucial role in finally overcoming Cresson, whose arguments in 1831 had greatly impressed Wilberforce and even persuaded Thomas Clarkson to write a commendation of the ACS and its work in Liberia, Stuart was instrumental in converting to the antislavery cause a man who would become one of the foremost American abolitionists. When living in New York's "Burned-Over District" in the 1820s, during Charles Grandison Finney's Great Religious Revival, Stuart, a devout Presbyterian, became a loving father figure for Theodore Dwight Weld, who would later become a leading abolitionist lecturer, author of the most important abolitionist book, and an adviser to John Quincy Adams's congressional campaign against "gagging" antislavery petitions. In March and June of 1831, Stuart helped to transform "his beloved Theodore" by sending him letters and publications imploring him to engage his soul "in the Sacred cause of Negro emancipation" and expressing profound gratitude to God "that as we continue guilty of [slavery], he can refrain from fairly breaking up the world beneath our feet, and dashing us into sudden hell."[21]

By the time Garrison arrived in Britain in the summer of 1833, Cresson had been so damaged by the attacks of Stuart, Paul, and James Cropper, a pioneer British abolitionist and wealthy Liverpool merchant, that he was writing desperate letters to the ACS complaining about their proslavery statements (exposed in Stuart's pamphlets) and lack of response to Garrison's book. Paul, who as a minister had easy access to pulpits throughout the British Isles, quickly discovered that his dark skin color was a key asset and that British humanitarians would look upon blacks as the most legitimate, convincing, and knowledgeable proponents of American abolition. Indeed, Cresson soon pleaded with the leaders of the American Colonization Society to find a black man who could counteract Paul's impact. Moreover, Paul represented a black colony in Canada that was in some ways a competitor with Liberia, but that was also a refuge from the kind of militant racism fostered by white colonizationists. Paul even played a crucial role in getting the current leadership of the British abolition movement to sign a document condemning the ACS; he even helped persuade Wilberforce to sign the "Protest" just before he died. According to Garrison's account of their meeting, Paul's evidence of free-black opposition finally convinced Clarkson to declare his neutrality on colonization after realizing he had been misled by Cresson.[22]

In 1833, Paul married an Englishwoman, a fact which, coupled with his enthusiastic response to British slave emancipation and the appeal of working with other abolitionists, encouraged him to remain in Britain until 1836. Paul no doubt realized that when he and his wife returned to the United States, they would be subjected to great prejudice as an interracial couple. As it turned out, they were unable to find a place to live together, and Garrison arranged for Mrs. Paul to live in Northampton, at the home of Garrison's father-in-law, for one year, while Nathaniel was on a speaking tour.[23] Though Paul succeeded in raising thousands of dollars in Britain and even lent money to Garrison, he outraged the Wilberforce community by spending and charging even more than he received. He therefore returned to Albany, where he became the pastor of a Baptist church and continued to condemn racial prejudice and call for black moral uplift and improvement until he died in 1839 at age forty-six.[24]

In April 1833, after a year of successful lecturing in Britain, Paul wrote an important letter to William Lloyd Garrison. By the time the letter appeared in *The Liberator*, Garrison had arrived in Britain and joined Paul on an extensive tour to defeat Cresson, who finally returned to America in the fall of 1833. In his letter, Paul could joyfully report that "the voice of this nation is loud and incessant against the system of slavery. Its death warrant is sealed, so far as it relates to the British West Indies." He modestly concluded by saying that his lecture tours had been successful and that his arguments had received "decided approbation from all classes of people." He had even had breakfast twice with "the venerable Wilberforce" and had met "the patriotic Clarkson," both "Angels of liberty." But the decisive point related to Britain's answer to America's "hypocritical pretenders to humanity and religion, who are continually crying out, 'What shall we do with our black and colored people?'"[25] Since Paul felt a deep bond to America, based in part on the fact that his father had been a Revolutionary War veteran and an eminent leader and Baptist minister in Boston, he rejoiced, while also expressing anger, in the discovery that Britain presented a spectacular answer to America's great racist question "what shall we do with them?"

[T]o contrast the difference in the treatment that a colored man receives in this country, with that which he receives in America, my soul is filled with sorrow and indignation. I could weep over the land of my nativity! . . . Here, if I go to church, I am not pointed to the 'negro seat' in the gallery; but any gentleman opens his pew door for my reception. If I wish for a passage in a stage, the only question that is asked me is, 'Which do you choose, sir, an inside or an outside seat?' If I stop at a public inn, no one would ever think here of setting a separate table for me; I am conducted to the same table with other gentlemen. The only difference that I have ever discovered is this, I am generally taken for a stranger, and they therefore seem anxious to pay me the greater respect.[26]

Like large numbers of future African American visitors, Paul was astonished and immensely gratified by the British treatment of a man of color. The widespread acceptance in America of some form of colonization depended on the conviction that white prejudice was so strong and entrenched that the two races could never live together with any prospect of peace or equality. Yet, for Paul and his successors, the tolerance they encountered in England, Ireland, and Scotland not only exposed the hollow hypocrisy of American claims of freedom and democracy but seemed to prove that the crushing white prejudice they met at home could be overcome. With this in mind, they continued to dramatize the contrast between America and Britain as thousands of Britons flocked to hear their rapturous odes to British tolerance, compassion, and humanitarianism. Just as Britain took the momentous and risky step of emancipating some 800,000 colonial slaves, Nathaniel Paul and subsequent black speakers, including many fugitive slaves, reinforced the righteousness of the cause. Even as increasing doubts arose about the economic consequences of emancipation, black abolitionists could continue to reassure British audiences concerning the justice of freeing human beings like themselves. And Paul's list of situations in which he was treated as an equal, as a "gentleman," implied a kind of democratic acceptance that cloaked the issue of social class. In America, race had long superseded class. In Britain, despite a highly structured class system that included levels of respect and contempt, African American abolitionists, even fugitive slaves, received remarkable respect apart from class, even as racism began to emerge in the late 1840s and 1850s.

After Garrison arrived in Britain in 1833, he joined Nathaniel Paul on a tour, rebutting the claims of Elliot Cresson that the ACS was primarily dedicated to slave emancipation. Paul and Garrison often spoke together, as at a public meeting held in London's Exeter Hall on July 13, attended by two thousand people and featuring speeches by prominent abolitionists intended "to expose the real character and objects of the American Colonization Society and to promote the cause of universal emancipation."

Cresson, called "an apostate Quaker" by Paul, had tried to defame Garrison as a "convicted libeler" who had been convicted and thrown into prison in the United States. Paul, first emphasizing the importance of his own dark complexion, contended that Garrison had "suffered forty-nine days incarceration in a prison in the city of Baltimore, in the State of Maryland, because he had the hardihood to engage in defence of the suffering slaves in that State." Paul then noted that in a supposed "land of freedom and equality," the laws of America were so "exceedingly liberal" that they allowed a thriving trade in "the souls and bodies of our fellow creatures." "Mr. Garrison had the impudence, the unblushing effrontery to state, in a public newspaper, that this traffic was a direct violation of the laws of God, and contrary to the principles of human nature. (Cheers) This was the crime of which he was convicted." Indeed, Paul went on, Wilberforce, Clarkson, Buxton, and the abolitionists present in the room would all have been "indicted, convicted, and thrown into prison if they had resided in Maryland and "pursued the course they have adopted in this country." As a final stab against Cresson and the ACS, before turning to a detailed denunciation of the racism and hypocrisy of colonization, Paul added that the "Court and Jury would have convicted the whole Anti-Slavery Society of this country, and would have transported them all to Liberia as the punishment of their crimes (Laughter and loud cheers)."[27]

As R. J. M. Blackett shows, Nathaniel Paul's role in overcoming British support of the ACS prepared the way for succeeding African American abolitionists' efforts in Britain to build a cordon or "anti-slavery wall" around the United States, so that, as Frederick Douglass put it, "wherever a slaveholder went, he might be looked down upon as a man-stealing, cradle-robbing, and woman-stripping monster, and that he might see reproof and detestation on every hand."[28] The blacks' goal of exposing the evils of American slavery and racism brought a unity to their otherwise diverse interests as well as to the fractured Anglo-American abolitionist movement, enabling some supporters and opponents of political abolitionism (Garrisonians) to work together. As Blackett observes, the building and preservation of the antislavery cordon for more than thirty years required a pragmatic mentality as well as "skill, determination, and consummate diplomacy on the part of black Americans. As products of American slavery and discrimination, they brought an authenticity, a legitimacy, to the international movement that their white co-workers could never claim. They were the bona fide representatives of millions of oppressed human beings."[29]

If the African American abolitionists gave a certain unity to Anglo-American antislavery movements, they also provided a certain unity to their highly diversified audiences. When fugitive slave Samuel Ringgold Ward toured Britain in the mid-1850s, he found that within a month of his arrival "I had been upon the platforms of the Bible Tract, Sunday School, Missionary, Temperance, and Peace, as well as the Anti-Slavery Societies."[30]

One must remember that British abolitionists achieved their *goals* of colonial slave emancipation in 1834 and of ending apprenticeship in 1838. But the spectacular success of the British abolitionist movement then furnished a model and incentive for a wide range of other causes. Joseph Sturge, the wealthy Quaker who helped found the radical Agency Committee in 1831 and then led the campaign against apprenticeship, went on in 1839 to help found the British and Foreign Anti-Slavery Society (today known as Anti-Slavery International), dedicated to worldwide slave emancipation. Officials in the BFASS also served in the British Peace Society, the Aborigines Protection Society, and other reform organizations. Sturge himself, a pacifist and teetotaler, supported the liberal Anti-Corn Law League and radical workers' Chartist movement, helped found the National Complete Suffrage Union for universal male enfranchisement, and tried to broker an alliance between the bourgeois Anti-Corn Law League and the Chartists—a movement born as an alliance of factory workers, artisans, and middle-class radical reformers determined to democratize the British political system.[31]

In short, the sympathetic crowds that cheered the black American abolitionists, including crowds of working-class laborers, arrived with highly diverse interests. But they all opposed "slavery" and were reassured by the African Americans that their own nation had not only achieved a high level of racial tolerance but had set a model for the world in abolishing a deeply rooted social evil. Later questions about the economic failure of that action only highlighted the national achievement of moral justice. But there was clearly a conflict or at least tension between Sturge's merging of antislavery with Chartist outrage over domestic suffering and injustice, and the way African American abolitionists celebrated a monarchic nation that treated them as equal human beings and that led the world in abolishing a unique and unparalleled evil. As we will see later, Frederick Douglass repeatedly stressed the uniqueness of chattel slavery, arguing that there was no more similarity between examples of British domestic oppression and American slavery "than there was between light and darkness." We will later need to examine the fact that British abolitionism could exercise this dual character, both promoting broader moral progress and unintentionally supporting the status quo.

THE PROBLEMS OF RACE, DEHUMANIZATION, AND WAGE SLAVERY

As noted in the introduction and chapter 1, black abolitionist Henry Highland Garnet focused on the issue of dehumanization and animalization when he assured American slaves, in 1843, that the ultimate goal of slaveholders was "to make you as much like brutes as possible," and when he told the U.S. Congress, in 1865, that the Thirteenth Amendment should put an end to an institution based on "snatching man from the high place to which he was lifted by the hand of God, and dragging him down to the level of brute creation, where he is made to be the companion of the horse and the fellow of the ox."[32] We also saw that these statements about treating slaves as animals were confirmed by the testimony of countless slaves and former slaves, including those recorded in the WPA narratives of the 1930s.

Dehumanization and its implications—the need of African Americans to confront and counteract the kind of white psychological exploitation that would deprive them of the respect and dignity needed for acceptance as equals in a white society—has been the central theme of this book. I have long interpreted "the problem of slavery" as centering on the impossibility of converting humans into the totally compliant, submissive, accepting chattels symbolized by Aristotle's ideal of "the natural slave." On the other hand, Garnet acknowledged that brutal treatment could lead to some internalization, some acceptance or contentment "with a condition of slavery," even if no genetic domestication took place. In chapter 8 we noted David Walker's anger over numerous examples of slaves' docility, subservience, and complicity, and his appeal to blacks to prove to Americans "that we are MEN, and not *brutes*, as we have been represented, and by millions treated." Even the relatively privileged Frederick Douglass recalled that after he had been "tamed" by interminable work and countless whippings, "Mr. Covey succeeded in breaking me. I was broken in body, soul, and spirit. My natural elasticity was crushed, my intellect languished, the disposition to read departed . . . the dark night of slavery closed in upon me; and behold a man transformed into a brute!"[33]

As we have seen, it was the kind of perceived animalization implied by Walker and Douglass that led to widespread views of vicious, animal-like Haitian blacks intent on "revenge"; of the supposed incapacities of freed American slaves and the need for their colonization; and of the urgency of black "uplift" and civilization in the North. These issues reached a climax in Britain when black abolitionists helped destroy support for the ACS and basked in the public recognition of their full humanity. As Walker had predicted, despite his frequent despair, "Treat us like men, and there is no danger but we will all live in peace and happiness together."

In chapter 1 we also noted the ways in which a white pathology of racial exploitation, of dehumanizing blacks, led to the theme of self-hatred and sense that "You don't really belong here" in African American literature. Thus, for blacks as well as whites, the essential issue was how to recognize and establish the full and complete humanity of a "dehumanized people."

While black abolitionists found new self-esteem and acceptance as full humans in Britain, they struggled with their own sense of identity as they felt compelled to inform the British regarding the unique evils of dehumanization in supposedly democratic America. How could an escaped slave like Frederick Douglass, whose extraordinary eloquence, intelligence, and decorum made him a great celebrity, convince thousands of Britons that he had fairly recently been a brute? Paradoxically, as Douglass soon came to understand, the more he focused his attention in lectures on his own and even other slaves' dehumanizing treatment, the more he would narrow the boundaries of his own humanity.

Yet British audiences, many of whom had never heard a slave or ex-slave speak, usually expected to hear shocking accounts of cruelty and torture. Many white abolitionists assumed, with some condescension, that Douglass should evoke horror and sympathy by limiting his speeches to accounts of cruel and savage treatment. Douglass soon became extremely sensitive to the paternalistic and implicitly racist approach of some white American abolitionists who felt he was not competent to handle his own financial affairs and who sought to restrict his desire to assert his own intelligence and capabilities—to develop his own "manhood."[34] But, for a time, Douglass was willing to talk of his own scarred back, to hold up actual whips and chains as examples of torture, and to describe seeing a slave woman have her ear nailed to a post for attempting to run away, adding, "but the agony she endured was so great, that she tore away, and left her ear behind. (Great sensation.)"[35] Yet Douglass soon toned down his descriptions and even publicly admitted that despite mistreatment, he had been a relatively privileged slave who had escaped the worst evils of the institution.

Some historians have criticized Douglass and other black abolitionists for not expressing more concern over the plight of English industrial workers and the suffering of the Irish at the start of the Great Potato Famine of the 1840s. The question might seem even more meaningful in view of the strong ties between a few leading radical British abolitionists like Joseph Sturge and the Chartist movement, as well as the large number of working-class supporters who attended many of Douglass's lectures. But, as historian Marcus Cunliffe makes clear, the comparison between American chattel slavery and British "wage slavery" was part of a much larger cultural contest. There is doubtless some truth to Cunliffe's conclusion that the abolitionist crusade "would have been altered out of all recognition if they had endeavored to direct a dual assault, on both chattel slavery and wage slavery." Douglass, who called himself a "man of one idea," was not unusual in concentrating his efforts on the evils of chattel slavery while expressing occasional sympathy for the victims of other forms of oppression. And as Cunliffe shows, some British and American abolitionists, such as Richard Oastler and Charles Edwards Lester, became wholly preoccupied with the evils of British wage slavery. In

Yorkshire, a mass meeting congratulated Oastler, a Chartist and MP who held that the bondage of children working in English cotton mills was "more horrid" than colonial slavery, for exposing "the conduct of those pretended philanthropists and canting hypocrites who travel to the West Indies in search of slavery, forgetting that there is a more abominable and degrading system of slavery at home."[36]

The contest between the two systems of oppression began in the later eighteenth century, when West Indian planters and supporters of the British slave trade claimed that black slaves were much happier and better treated than English industrial workers. In 1788 Gilbert Francklyn, a Tobago planter and propagandist for the West India Committee, compared the horrors of Britain's emerging industrial factories with a preposterously idyllic picture of West Indian slavery. In response to Thomas Clarkson's celebrated essay attacking the slave trade, which won a prize at Cambridge University, Francklyn asked: Why did the two great universities not offer prizes "for the best dissertation on the evil effects which the manufactures of Birmingham, Manchester, and other great manufacturing towns, produce on the health of the lives of the poor people employed therein?"[37]

The subsequent spread of highly regimented and large-scale manufacturing, long hours of work, and increasing use of female and child labor gave strong ammunition to nineteenth-century Southern American defenders of racial slavery, such as George Fitzhugh and John C. Calhoun, who contended that American slavery was infinitely more humane than British industrial bondage. Since America was soon flooded with evidence of British working-class suffering and exploitation—from parliamentary reports, articles in the *Edinburgh Review* and London *Times,* to the writings of Engels, Carlyle, and Dickens—the belief that British wage slavery was at least as dehumanizing as American chattel slavery was by no means confined to proslavery Southerners. A famous British traveler to America like geologist Sir Charles Lyell could report, "The Negroes, so far as I have yet seen them, whether in domestic service or on the farms, appear very cheerful and free from care, better fed than a large part of the labouring class of Europe."[38]

Of course, the majority of British writers condemned American slavery as a barbarous anachronism. And, as we have already seen, Cunliffe shows that the opposing views played into the hands of critics of America and Britain as opposing "reference groups"—an

arrogant democratic republic dependent on viciously exploited black
slave labor, and an aristocratic monarchy in which thousands of
poor factory children worked up to thirteen hours or more a day.
Even in the North, many Americans became convinced that British
abolitionism, with its increasing attacks on American slavery, was a
part of a massive plot, led by the aristocrats, Church, and manufac-
turers, to divert attention from British forms of slavery. Even worse,
the antidemocratic conspiracy supposedly aimed to undermine the
American Union by exploiting sectional divisions and sending British
abolitionists like George Thompson to America to foment discord.
Cunliffe cites the extremely hostile, violent response to Thompson,
even in Massachusetts, as evidence of this Anglophobia and commitment to patriotic unity.[39]

This background provides some context and perspective for the
way Frederick Douglass addressed the subject of wage and chattel
slavery, which he did on various occasions during his first time in
Britain. Since brief summaries can't begin to do justice to the profun-
dity and eloquence of his talks or the importance of his arguments,
I will devote some space to the text of his extraordinary speech at
Bristol, where he and William Lloyd Garrison both addressed a fairly
select audience on August 25, 1846. Repeating many points made in
earlier talks, Douglass concentrated on the unique nature of American slavery—whose central evil lay not in whipping and other physical abuse, but in a total domination that closed down the brain and
soul of every dehumanized individual.[40]

After asking the audience to attribute his possible lack of refine-
ment to his experiences as a slave, Douglass stressed that he was not
there "to trouble them with any horrible details" of his life as a slave,
which could be found in his autobiography. His purpose was rather
to examine "the wrongs of three millions of his fellow-countrymen
in the United States," where slavery "assumed a more horrible form"
than had ever existed in any other nation. Like David Walker, Henry
Highland Garnet, Angelina Grimké, and James McCune Smith,
Douglass made it clear he was referring to "the moral condition of
the slaves" more than to "the lashing, branding, cathauling, hunting,
imprisoning":

> In the first place he [the slave] was denied all intellectual improve-
> ment. It was made by the laws punishable with death, for a sec-

ond offence, to teach a slave his letters. In the next place, there was . . . an utter abolition of the institution of marriage. A slave was not protected in that relation. He might be separated from his partner at any time at the will or caprice of his master. His own wishes or will were never consulted—he lived only for his master's interest, and his master might do whatever he liked with him.[41]

Throughout his speech Douglass noted some reasons that a British audience might find it difficult or impossible to grasp the full horrors of American slavery. In the United States, there was a "class of philosophers" who denied blacks "equal humanity with the whites, and who spoke of them as being the connecting-link between humanity and the brute creation." In Britain, various writers and others regarded American slavery with some indifference "on account of the political disadvantages under which some portion of the subjects of this country were said to labour." This was a clear reference to the Chartist demand for universal male suffrage as an antidote to economic exploitation. Showing that he was well aware of the larger debate, Douglass noted he had heard some individuals say, " 'Why talk to us of American slavery—why speak to us of slavery 3000 miles off? We have slavery in England!' " Largely as a result of ignorance, according to Douglass, some writers diminished the horrors of American slavery by speaking "of slavery in the army, slavery in the navy, and looking upon the labouring population [contemplating] them as slaves." One reformer had exclaimed, " 'Why does not England set the example by doing away with these forms of slavery at home, before it called upon the United States to do so?' "

Yet was he there boldly to proclaim that there was no more similarity between slavery, as existing in the United States, and any institution in this country, than there was between light and darkness. Only look at the condition of the slave, stripped of every right—denied every privilege, he had not even the privilege of saying "myself"—his head, his eyes, his hands, his heart, his bones, his sinews, his soul, his immortal spirit, were all the property of another. He might not decide any question for himself—any question relating to his own actions. The master—the man who claimed property in his person—assumed the right to decide all things for him—what he should eat, how he should eat, what he should drink;

to whom he should speak, what he should speak; for whom he should work and under what circumstances; when he should marry, to whom he should marry, and how long the marriage covenant should continue, for they claimed the power of separating those who considered themselves joined together before God (hear). They took upon themselves to determine for the slave what was right and what was wrong, and they had a very different code of morals from that contained in the decalogue.

Douglass had already stressed that he had "not one word to say in defence of any form of oppression on earth—not a sentence in extenuation of the conduct of any tyrant on earth." He wished and prayed "that tyranny and oppression of every kind might have an end (cheers)." Yet in the United States "there were three millions of human beings who were denied the right to improve themselves; the more like brutes they could be made, the more beastly in their habits they could be made, the better were the wishes of the master accomplished— for his desire was to break up as far as possible all likeness to mankind on the part of the slave." For this purpose, Douglass continued, masters divided families, took the infant from the mother, made it penal for the slave to be taught his letters, or for a woman "to defend her person from the brutal outrage of an unfeeling master."

In short, the slave was "a mere thing":

—a human brute, dragged down from the condition of a man and ranked with the brute creation. Were there any such in this country? No—not one (hear). They had their rags and their poverty, their hard toiling for a subsistence, as also they had in the Northern states of America, but they had not slavery (cheers). No man could assert over another the right of property—he was free to act— free to go and free to come; but the slave was bound in unending chains—he could not improve, progress was annihilated with him.

Despite his reassuring words about opposing all forms of tyranny and oppression (and, as we will see, he supported and lectured with various Chartists), Douglass's analysis of American chattel slavery and his protest against extending the concept of slavery to British forms of labor implied some support for the British status quo. According to Douglass, *ignorance* of the true evils of American chattel slavery prevented many good-hearted Britons from understanding that there was no more similarity between British and American systems of labor than "between light and darkness." Britain, in his view, had not only succeeded in emancipating their colonial slaves, but British workers were free from owners intent on their total dehumanization; they were free to act or to come and go as they wished. Though Douglass ignored crucial aspects of British "wage slavery," the audience seemed to approve with "cheers." Douglass's long lecture, like a somewhat later one in Sheffield that made similar points, ended with "long-continued cheering" or "much applause"[42]

There is much conflicting evidence regarding working-class and radical reform group support for British abolitionists, and this question fits into a long-term past debate among historians over the degree to which abolitionism stimulated and reinforced domestic reform or provided "moral capital" for the ruling classes, unintentionally diverting attention from domestic issues like "wage slavery." In briefly examining this issue, which provides the larger context for Douglass's efforts to differentiate chattel slavery from other types of oppression, it is essential to draw a distinction between the period after 1830 in Britain, which was marked by domestic turbulence and a protracted public struggle for a variety of political and economic rights, and the earlier conservative decades, beginning in the late 1790s, when British leaders were obsessed with the radical French Revolution and Napoleonic Wars. For William Wilberforce, James Stephen, and the other "Saints" and government leaders who succeeded in abolishing the slave trade and moving toward very gradualist antislavery policies, it was essential to maintain a sharp distinction between the evils of the colonial slave world and the ostensibly free institutions that had been imperiled both by French tyranny and English "Jacobins." The constant comparisons in early abolitionist literature between the agony of black slaves and the smiling, contented life of English "husbandmen" was not fortuitous. Abolitionists repeatedly reminded Britons that the Somerset decision of 1772 had outlawed slavery in England.[43]

There was clearly a dramatic change in the 1830s, especially following the Reform Act of 1832 and the harsh New Poor Law of 1834, as numerous progressive organizations tried to copy the techniques of the incredibly successful abolition movement. Pamphlets, broadsides, and petitions for various causes often included some words opposing slavery or apprenticeship, although antislavery publications seldom reciprocated. Historians Betty Fladeland and Seymour Drescher long ago provided conclusive evidence of strong ties between British abolitionism and movements to expand suffrage, aid the poor, and reduce the hours of workers, especially children, in factories.[44]

But even Fladeland acknowledges that in the early decades of the nineteenth century abolitionists were "constant targets of the radical press," which portrayed abolitionist leaders as "pious hypocrites who wrung their hands over the plight of far-off black slaves while at home they eased their consciences by supplying the poor with Bibles instead of bread."[45] Fladeland begins a different essay, which emphasizes the later strong links between abolitionists and Chartists, by stressing that a reader of workingmen's newspapers and journals for the 1820s and 1830s "might easily conclude that the working classes' worst enemies were the members of anti-slavery societies who were dedicated to freeing black slaves in far-off colonies while being blindly insensitive to the exploitation of white workers at home." Historian Patricia Hollis argues that from 1823 to the 1840s, "the abolitionist cause attracted little working-class support, much working-class indifference, and considerable working-class hostility." She adds that "the major labor reform leaders, William Cobbett, Richard Oastler, and Bronterre O'Brien, [despite their opposition to slavery], all excoriated abolitionists as hypocrites, indifferent to poverty and suffering at home . . . [who] financed their philanthropy abroad by increasing the exploitation of their white 'slaves' at home." From one radical perspective, Britain's traditional abolitionists sought to impose a Christian, moralistic ethic upon black slaves who would merely be converted into more servile wage slaves in a capitalist society. Such abolitionists were said to be guilty not only of ignoring the worse plight of British "wage slaves," but of philosophically and even politically supporting the domestic status quo, a fact dramatized by the well-known emancipationists who supported the incredibly oppressive 1834 Poor Law, which separated family members within the new workhouses.[46]

This prejudice against certain aspects of the traditional antislavery movement gave added justification to the Chartists' widespread efforts to raid, disrupt, and take over abolitionist meetings. Following the large-scale armed rebellion at Newport in 1839, which led to the government's arrest of hundreds of Chartists, three of whom were convicted of high treason and sentenced to death (later commuted to transportation for life), the group adopted a policy of attending and interrupting public gatherings of many kinds, ranging from meetings of parish churches to those of the Anti-Corn Law League, in attempts to focus public attention on the plight of the poor and disfranchised. But, given their major desire to build on the successful abolitionist movement, Chartists were especially eager to interrupt and gain some control over such abolitionist meetings as the Glasgow Emancipation Society in 1840 and the 1840 World Anti-Slavery Convention in London. These struggles to obtain resolutions on "wage slavery" and manhood suffrage involved bitter disputes and nearly violent confrontations.[47]

When William Lloyd Garrison came to Britain to attend the 1840 World Convention, he was horrified by the terrible condition of the poor and the oppressive character of a monarchical, aristocratic society, but he was also deeply troubled by the Chartist efforts "to take violent possession of meetings convened expressly for anti-slavery purposes, and to transform their character and design." As Garrison wrote in *The Liberator*, "In their struggle to obtain those rights and privileges which belong to them as men, and of which they are now ruthlessly deprived, I sympathize with all my heart, and wish them a speedy and complete victory!" But the Chartists' behavior at the antislavery meetings "is both dastardly and criminal, and certainly most unwise and impolitic for themselves."[48]

Despite these reservations, Garrison's relations with the Chartist movement in 1840 and 1846 shed light on the ways that Frederick Douglass's desire to maintain and preserve the unique evil of chattel slavery could be combined with efforts to relieve the suffering and degradation of other oppressed peoples. In a speech in Glasgow in 1840, Garrison anticipated Douglass's defense of the unique evil of American chattel slavery:

Although he expressed sympathy for oppressed labor, he insisted that there was a basic and essential difference between a so-called white slave and a real black slave—the difference between oppression and slavery. Whereas the white laborer may be impoverished and exploited, he nevertheless had freedom to work for his employer or to seek work elsewhere. The slave had to do his master's bidding or suffer the consequences—perhaps even death itself.[49]

Yet Garrison called for the support of Chartist goals, though in 1840 he was surprised to find little support for the movement. For the first time Garrison was struck by the way narrow-minded abolitionists ignored the suffering and degradation of British workers, and by the fact that "nine-tenths of mankind are living in squalid poverty and abject servitude in order to sustain in idleness and profligacy the one-tenth!" If England "*looked* beautiful," he told Samuel J. May upon his return, it was "sitting on a volcano," as evidenced by the anger evoked by the Chartists.[50]

When Garrison entered the chapel in Glasgow to speak to a large audience assembled by the Glasgow Emancipation Society, a Chartist handed him a placard entitled "*Have we no white slaves?*" and signed "A WHITE SLAVE." Garrison put it in his pocket and resolved to read it to the meeting, without even consulting his close friend George Thompson, who introduced him, who led the British wing of Garrisonians, and who in 1842 publicly joined the Chartists. After first emphasizing that "not a single *white* SLAVE can be found" in all the possessions of Great Britain, Garrison went on to ask whether it was not true that there were thousands of British workers both at home and abroad "who are deprived of their just rights—who are grievously oppressed—who are dying, even in the midst of abundance, of actual starvation?" After the audience shouted "YES!" he called on British abolitionists to prove themselves the true friends of suffering humanity abroad "by showing that they were the best friends of suffering humanity at home." But when he asked whether the abolitionists were in fact carrying out this dual obligation, the response from various parts of the chapel was "No! no! no!" Garrison then expressed deep regret, a hope that this was not true "of all of them," and gave his reasons for reading the Chartist placard signed "A White Slave." This support for Chartist goals was then later interrupted by a well-known Chartist from the audience who outraged the audience by trying to make a speech. Garrison wrote that "I, for one, should have had no objection to his being heard; yet he was clearly out of order, and had no just cause to complain of the meeting."[51]

Six years later, when Garrison returned to Britain and often spoke in company with Douglass, he sent his wife an account of his addressing a large meeting of "Moral Suasion Chartists" (also called Moral Force Chartists, as opposed to Physical Force Chartists), who responded with thunderous and protracted applause that "made

the building quake" and "adopted by acclamation a highly flatter-
ing resolution." Since he did not appear in his "official capacity as
an abolitionist," Garrison felt free to fully identify himself with "all
the unpopular reformatory movements in this country," even if that
would alienate some "good society folks." As he talked to "the workingmen of England," he knew "that the cause of my enslaved countrymen cannot possibly be injured by my advocacy of the rights of all
men, or by my opposition to all tyranny."[52]

In retrospect, it appears that the earlier great success of the British
antislavery movement depended first on a concentrated focus on the
British slave trade, then on emancipating British colonial slaves and
apprentices. However, by the late 1830s, when antislavery had permeated British culture, the government was intensifying its efforts to end
the international slave trade and some abolitionists had turned not
only to global slavery but to domestic oppression of various kinds, a
development that foreshadowed the delayed concerns over all forms
of coerced labor that arose after the complete outlawing of chattel
slavery in the Americas in 1888 and then, aided by the United Nations
in 1962, in the world.

JOSEPH STURGE, FREDERICK DOUGLASS, AND THE CHARTISTS—THE DECLINE AND EXPANSION OF ANTISLAVERY IN THE 1850S

We have already taken note of Joseph Sturge, the wealthy Quaker
corn merchant and abolitionist leader who probably best dramatizes
the later connections between antislavery and radical reform. Having
supported a variety of causes as a young man, Sturge in effect retired
from work before age forty and devoted his full time to antislavery,
temperance, adult education, abolishing the Corn Laws, ending capital punishment, advocating universal manhood suffrage, and aiding
the poor in his home city of Birmingham. In London he was instrumental in founding and managing the World Anti-Slavery Conventions of 1840 and 1843; he traveled to the West Indies and testified
before parliamentary committees as part of the successful campaign
to abolish apprenticeship; and in 1841 he even toured the United
States, wanting especially to reinvigorate Quaker antislavery activity and promote more unity among the divided American abolitionists. With respect to the effects of political democracy, Sturge was

impressed by the relative comfort and prosperity of America's white workers. After being rebuffed by proslavery president John Tyler, he sent a protest to every member of Congress.[53]

But it was in 1838 that the British abolitionists' final triumph of ending apprenticeship coincided with the founding of the radical Chartist movement. As the Chartists fought for universal male suffrage—some of them threatening violence, partly in response to violent government repression—they drew constant analogies between the condition of British laborers and chattel slaves. Though totally committed to pacifism and nonviolence, Sturge supported and worked with the Chartists, believing that universal male voting provided the key to solving the larger problem of class discrimination and oppression.[54]

While there are numerous other instances of progressive unions between antislavery and domestic reform, especially in the 1830s and 1840s, Joseph Surge was exceptional in having the time, energy, wealth, and motivation to combine having a leading role in the abolitionist movement with such activities as founding a pacifist newspaper and helping to launch the Complete Suffrage Movement. And though Frederick Douglass was still a "Garrisonian," and the Garrisonians were in sharp conflict with Sturge's British and Foreign Anti-Slavery Society, Douglass interacted with Sturge and acquired much respect for him. In December 1845, Douglass visited Birmingham in order to address Sturge's local temperance society. As noted in chapter 8, temperance was the only other major reform movement that really attracted Douglass, in part because he had witnessed the ways slaveholders used alcohol to pacify slaves, and later became deeply disturbed by the amount of alcohol consumed by free African Americans and the poverty-stricken Irish. In Birmingham, Douglass was a dinner guest at Sturge's home, and on May 18, 1846, the two men met again in London, when the anti-Garrisonian BFASS somewhat surprisingly invited Douglass to lecture, as well as demanded that the Free Church of Scotland "send back the money" that had been donated by American slaveholders. Disappointed by the small turnout, Sturge not only arranged another meeting for Douglass, crowding Finsbury chapel "almost to suffocation" on May 22 with 2,500 to 3,000 people, but immediately raised $500 after hearing that Douglass might remain in the British Isles if he could afford to bring over his wife and children. While Douglass decided to return to America, he repeatedly praised Sturge, despite their different views of British industrial labor.[55]

For Douglass and other black American abolitionists, representing a country in which slavery was expanding, not shrinking, the first priority was to mobilize British public opinion behind efforts to cut off all supportive ties with American slavery. As Douglass exhorted the large London audience assembled by Joseph Sturge on May 22, 1846:

> To tear off the mask from this abominable system, to expose it to the light of heaven, aye, to the heat of the sun, that it may burn and wither it out of existence, is my object in coming to this country. . . . What would I have you then do? I would have the church, in the first place— Methodist, Baptist, Congregationalist, all persuasions—to declare, in their conventions, associations, synods, conferences . . . "*no Christian fellowship with slave holders.*" (Loud cheers.)
>
> I want the slave holder surrounded, as by a wall of anti-slavery fire, so that he may see the condemnation of himself and his system glaring down in letters of light. I want him to feel that he has no sympathy in England, Scotland, or Ireland; that he has none in Canada, none in Mexico, none among the poor wild Indians. . . . I would have condemnation blaze down upon him in every direction, till, stunned and overwhelmed with shame and confusion, he is compelled to let go the grasp he holds upon the persons of his victims, and restore them to their long-standing rights (Loud cheers.)[56]

This goal of global expansion, of recruiting antislavery support in ways that would isolate, disgrace, and dishonor American slave-holders, reinforced American abolitionism and proved to be compatible with Chartist concerns for the disfranchised and oppressed British workers. Other black Americans, such as Charles L. Remond and Henry Highland Garnet, could also identify with such workers since, as blacks, they were deeply aware of their own deprivations and inequalities, including disfranchisement, even when legally free. Remond was repeatedly asked "what Americans were prepared to do to help oppressed British workers in return for help received to abolish American slavery." Garnet promised to work to unify the causes of slaves and poor whites, and Douglass supposedly even called himself "a Chartist."[57] In 1846 Garrison, Douglass, Henry Clarke Wright, and many other American visitors seemed committed to Chartist principles and worked closely with such "moral suasion" Chartist leaders as William Lovett and Henry Vincent, both long committed to the antislavery cause. Of course, for most Americans in the 1840s, there was nothing especially radical about such demands in the People's Charter of 1838 as total manhood suffrage, a secret ballot, no property requirement of members of Parliament, and payment for MPs. Yet Britain did not reach these goals until well after the American Civil War. The 1840s, a great decade of reform agitation, culminated in the failed revolutions of 1848 in Europe, the death of Chartism in Britain, and proslavery triumphs in the United States.

Some events in Britain in the 1850s seemed to encourage the expansion of slavery in America and confirm the American slaveholders' symbols of progress from the Fugitive Slave Law of 1850 to the Dred Scott Decision of 1857 (see chapter 10). The rise of antiblack and "scientific" racism supported the broad consensus that British slave emancipation had been a disastrous economic failure and that the prospect of further emancipation, as the London *Times* put it in 1857, was "never more distant than now."[58] Yet, on May 11, 1853, when Frederick Douglass delivered a long speech to the anti-Garrisonian British and Foreign Anti-Slavery Society, regarding "the future prospects of the whole colored people in the United States," he moved from proslavery victories, such as the Compromise of 1850, to the slaveholders' decisive failure in suppressing "discussion":

> Why, Sir, look all over the North; look South—look at home—look abroad—look at the whole civilized world—and what are all this vast multitude doing at this moment? Why, Sir, they are reading *"Uncle Tom's Cabin,"* and when they have read that, they will probably read *"The Key to Uncle Tom's Cabin"*—a key not only to the Cabin, but, I believe to the slave's darkest dungeon. A nation's hand, with that "key," will unlock the slave prisons to millions. Then look at the authoress of "Uncle Tom's Cabin." There is nothing in her reception abroad which indicates a declension of interest in the great subject which she has done so much to unfold and illustrate. The landing of a Princess on the shores of England would not have produced the same sensation. . . .
>
> Herein, sirs, is our hope. Slavery cannot bear discussion; it is a monster of darkness.[59]

Despite his enthusiasm, Douglass did not exaggerate the impact of the most influential novel ever written by an American. After being published serially in the *National Era*, *Uncle Tom's Cabin* sold some

310,000 copies within a year in the United States (about three times the number of the two previous record-setting American novels), a million copies in the United Kingdom (also three times the record), and more than 2 million copies worldwide. Given the absence of international copyright, there were many pirated editions. The book was translated into French, German, Spanish, Italian, Danish, Swedish, Flemish, Polish, and Magyar, and then into Portuguese, Welsh, Russian, Arabic, and other languages. Since the novel was widely read aloud in families and literary groups, Garrison's *The Liberator* estimated some 10 million total readers.[60]

Frederick Douglass, who as we have seen had later close ties and correspondence with Harriet Beecher Stowe (she wrote to him in 1851 requesting information on cotton plantations), was well aware of her triumphant tour of Great Britain in the spring and summer of 1853, where as historian David Reynolds points out, she was "feted, cheered, and praised" wherever she went. In London she met such notables as Prime Minister Palmerston and Mr. and Mrs. Charles Dickens. Three years later she met Queen Victoria and Prince Albert, and succeeded in obtaining funds and a petition signed by 562,800 British women urging American women to work for the abolition of slavery. Reynolds emphasizes that Stowe's influence on Western culture was extended by "Uncle Tomitudes," representations of characters or scenes from the novel in plays, paintings, engravings, and countless other popular media, usually with an antislavery message. He adds that the book thus paved the way for the North's openness to an antislavery presidential candidate like Lincoln, and "stiffened the South's resolve to defend slavery and demonize the North."[61]

Nevertheless, while Stowe stimulated an antislavery revival in Britain, and though Prime Minister Palmerston, a lifelong enemy of slavery and the slave trade, allegedly read her novel from cover to cover three times,[62] he and other leaders refused to see Abraham Lincoln as a genuine enemy of slavery and were at times prepared (as I shall show in the epilogue) to recognize and support the Confederacy and intervene to put an end to the American Civil War.

Epilogue

1

Many years ago, when I was writing my book *Slavery and Human Progress*, I was surprised to discover that in Britain a few leading liberals like John Stuart Mill and John Elliott Cairnes attempted to respond to a sudden and unexpected upsurge of opinion hostile to the Northern cause early in the American Civil War. "Why is it," Mill asked in 1862, "that the nation which is at the head of abolitionism, not only feels no sympathy with those who are fighting against the slave holding conspiracy, but actually desires its success? Why is the general voice of our press, the general sentiment of our people, bitterly reproachful to the North, while for the South, the aggressors in the war, we have either mild apologies or direct and downright encouragement?"[1]

Since Mill and Cairnes sought to refute the prevalent but false British view that even early in the war the Lincoln administration had no interest in ending slavery, one would assume that the British would have responded initially with great enthusiasm to Lincoln's Preliminary Emancipation Proclamation of September 22, 1862, and the Emancipation Proclamation of January 1, 1863. It is true that the Confederate defeat at Antietam and Lincoln's related proclamations did check the greatest chance of British and French intervention to end the war and recognize Confederate independence. But most traditional accounts downplay or ignore the way the British press widely denounced both proclamations as "a cynical and desperate ploy."

As the London *Times*, which represented the views of the wealthier classes, put it on January 15, 1863:

> It must also be remembered that this act of the PRESIDENT, if it purposed to strike off the fetters of one race, is a flagrant attack on the liberties of another. The attempt to free the blacks is a flagrant attack on the liberties of the whites. Nothing can be more unconstitutional, more illegal, more entirely subversive of the compact on which the American Confederacy rests, than the claim set up by the PRESIDENT to interfere with the laws of individual States by his Proclamation. . . . It is preposterous to say that war gives these powers; they are the purest usurpation. . . . [T]he President well knows that not a slaveholder in the South will obey his Proclamation, that it can only be enforced by violence, and that if the negroes obtain freedom it will be by the utter destruction of their masters. . . . LINCOLN bases his act on military necessity, and invokes the considerate judgment of mankind and the judgment of ALMIGHTY GOD. . . . Mankind will be slow to believe that an act avowedly the result of military considerations has been dictated by a sincere desire for the benefit of those who, under the semblance of emancipation, are thus marked out for destruction, and HE who made man in His own image can scarcely . . . look with approbation on a measure which, under the pretence of emancipation, intends to reduce the South to the frightful condition of Santo Domingo.[2]

Outrage over the massacre of British whites in the Indian Sepoy Mutiny of 1857–58 gave new force to the traditional fear of provoking another Haitian-like uprising of slaves, a fear now infused by the racism that developed in the 1850s. The *Times*, along with other papers, accused Lincoln of inciting Southern slaves to kill their owners: "[He] will appeal to the black blood of the African; he will whisper of the pleasures of spoil and the gratification of yet fiercer instincts; and when the blood begins to flow and shrieks come piercing through the darkness, Mr. Lincoln will wait till the rising flames tell that all is consummated, and he will rub his hands and think that revenge is sweet."[3]

In chapter 10 I stressed that it was the British public's traditional hostility to slavery that played a key role in preventing their government from intervening in the American Civil War and recognizing the independence of the cotton-producing Confederacy. But while the spokesmen for the middle and working classes were more pro-American and generally supported the Union, Charles Francis Adams, America's minister in England, emphasized that "the great body of aristocratic and wealthy commercial classes are anxious to see the United States go to pieces." By 1860, America symbolized democratic social and political reforms that the British establishment abhorred and that British progressives would struggle to achieve for many decades.[4] Nevertheless, when historian Amanda Foreman began research on her comprehensive book *A World on Fire: Britain's Crucial Role in the American Civil War*, she was shocked to find evidence of support of the Confederacy among some people generally considered as belonging to the "progressive" classes in Britain—"journalists, writers, university students, actors, social reformers, even the clergy."[5] Even liberal newspapers like the *Morning Advertiser* were stunned by Lincoln's Preliminary Emancipation Proclamation: "We can give no credit to President Lincoln. . . . the motive was not any abhorrence of Slavery in itself, but a sordid, selfish motive." Many writers complained that if Lincoln had really opposed slavery, he would not have exempted the slaveholding Border States. They thus ignored Lincoln's constitutional restrictions and his crucial need to prevent Maryland, Delaware, Kentucky, and Missouri from joining the Confederacy. Thus according to the antislavery *Spectator*, "the principle asserted is not that a human being cannot own another, but that he cannot own him unless he is loyal to the United States."[6] In Britain there was widespread misunderstanding of the American government and its constitutional limitations.

This negative response to the American government's prosecution of the war—matched by the strong hostility of the Northern public to Britain—was clearly related to decades of Anglo-American conflict going back to the War of 1812 and the American Revolution. At the very beginning of the Civil War, Britain led other nations in recognizing the Confederate states as a belligerent power and declaring its own neutrality in the conflict, an act that outraged Secretary of State William H. Seward, who kept warning of war if Britain took the next step of recognizing the South as a nation. Given Britain's deep dependence on cotton from the Southern states and the war's effect in paralyzing the cotton textile industry, bringing mass unemployment to Lancashire, Southern leaders were initially very confident that the need for cotton would make British and wider European intervention inevitable. The South even imposed an informal embargo on cotton exports, which ironically reinforced the limited effects of the Northern naval blockade on the South. Even some British antislavery writers were convinced that a Northern victory would continue to jeopardize Lancashire's main supply of cotton and result in permanent tariff barriers on British manufactures.[7]

Many Britons even believed that Confederate independence would actually hasten emancipation by separating the South from the racist and antiabolitionist North, and exposing the Confederacy to pressure from "progressive" free-labor nations. Confederate agents and propagandists did their best to confirm such expectations, and spread lies to a gullible British public about the Confederacy's intent to abolish slavery after winning independence. Late in the war, some British leaders expressed great regret that Confederate president Jefferson Davis had not emancipated the slaves in 1863, when the successes of Robert E. Lee's army had reached its highest point.[8]

As news arrived in England in September 1862 that Lee's army was marching north and had invaded Maryland, Lord Palmerston, the seventy-seven-year-old prime minister, revived plans for intervention. Though long committed to antislavery, Palmerston had experienced bitter conflicts with the United States when he was foreign secretary. Fearing, with some reason, the American goal of annexing Canada, he complained that Yankees were "disagreeable fellows," "totally unscrupulous and dishonest and determined somehow or other to carry their Point." Such negativity was reinforced during the war by a succession of conflicts with the Union that on occasion threatened the possibility of Britain's entry into the war. As late as December 1864, Lord John Russell, Britain's foreign secretary, told Charles Francis Adams that the responsibility for preventing an Anglo-American war depended on the two of them finding "a safe issue from this, as we had from so many other troubles that had sprung up during this war."[9]

By early September 1862, Confederate victories not only seemed to fulfill Palmerston's criteria for recognizing Southern nationhood, but convinced the French foreign secretary that "not a reasonable statesman in Europe" believed the North could win the war. As Palmerston anticipated news of "a great battle" north of Washington (Antietam), he proposed having a cabinet meeting, where he would present a mediation plan that he would offer to both North and South. If the North accepted, and Palmerston stressed that a "thorough" defeat would "bring them to a more reasonable state of mind," Britain would recommend an armistice, an end to blockades, and a negotiated separation. If only the South accepted, Palmerston concluded, "we should then, I conceive, acknowledge the independence of the South."[10]

Lord John Russell and William E. Gladstone, chancellor of the exchequer and son of a West India merchant and slaveholder, were far more enthusiastic about intervening to end the war and the terrible bloodshed. The battle at Antietam (25,000 casualties in a single day) convinced Gladstone that only Britain had the power "to stop the humanitarian crisis unfolding in America." Even after the news of what he termed "Lincoln's lawless proclamation," Gladstone urged forming an alliance with France and Russia to force the Union and Confederacy to agree to an armistice. And Russell not only urged the cabinet to intervene and settle the war, but made a somewhat successful overture to Napoleon III via the British ambassador in Paris.[11]

But Palmerston was shaken by the wholly unexpected news of Lee's rout and retreat at Antietam, which raised new questions about the weakness of his army and the outcome of the war. He also feared that any involvement might lead Britain into the war (given Seward's warnings), and felt a strong need to wait before making any decision. Though Russell and Gladstone continued to press for intervention, on November 11 the cabinet endorsed Palmerston's argument against moving beyond the position of neutrality.

In addition, despite initial negative press reaction, by early 1863, Lincoln's Emancipation Proclamation aroused growing public support for the North. An outflowing of pamphlets and books coincided with widespread "Emancipation Meetings" celebrating the antislavery goals of the Union. The British and Foreign Anti-Slavery Society abandoned its pacifist stance and endorsed the Union's emancipationist cause, which, given the bleak views of British West Indian emancipation in the 1850s, put British historical leadership in an entirely new perspective. This point was powerfully confirmed by the Thirteenth Amendment, which permanently freed all American slaves and evoked enthusiastic British support.[12]

Although British responses to the war continued to fluctuate, given the complexities of the transatlantic relationship, liberal leaders became increasingly aware that a Union defeat would shatter prospects for electoral reform in Britain. As the war progressed, an increasing number of intellectuals, evangelicals, and labor reformers agreed with Goldwin Smith "that the union cause was not that of the negro alone, but of civilization, Christian morality, the rights of labour, and the rights of man."[13]

2

The changing British responses to the American Civil War underscore two broad points. First, the extreme fortuity and contingency of the final stage of the Age of Emancipation. Second (as we will see in part 3), the fact that America's Emancipation Proclamation and especially the Thirteenth, Fourteenth, and Fifteenth Amendments represent the climax and turning point of the Age of Emancipation, with the sudden liberation of some 4 million slaves—far more than had ever been amassed in one part of the New World—followed by their award of citizenship and the right to vote.

Turning first to the issue of contingency, it is now clear that New World bondage was not a retrograde or economically backward institution that, without war or abolition movements, was headed for natural extinction. In Cuba and Brazil as well as the American South, slave labor was not only profitable and productive but was deeply intertwined with transatlantic industrial capitalism and had become compatible with the latest technology, from steamboat transportation to sugar mills. New World slavery actually anticipated the efficiency and productivity of factory assembly lines, and in the American South exhibited enough flexibility to put slaves to work in mines, building canals and railroads, and even manufacturing textiles and other industrial products. By 1860, two-thirds of the wealthiest Americans lived in the South, where the value of slaves continued to soar along with a major export economy. Many slaveholders dreamed of annexing an expanding tropical empire ranging from Cuba to Central America, and it is conceivable that an independent Confederacy might have moved in that direction.

In a very important recent work, historian Walter Johnson points out that our standard accounts of the coming of the Civil War focus on the territorial spaces that resulted from the war and overlook the plans for territorial expansion before the war. Such accounts not only minimize the growing significance of the Mississippi River's great "Cotton Kingdom," but ignore the fact that slaveholders in that region had a vision of a proslavery empire in which Cuba, Nicaragua, and the reopening of the African slave trade were far more crucial than congressional debates over slavery in Kansas. Many of these concerns were shared in other parts of the Deep South and should be kept in mind when considering the contingencies of a Confederate victory or of continued peace.[14]

Johnson shows that the Mississippi Valley, centered on New Orleans and containing more millionaires per capita than any other part of the nation, was a highly distinctive part of the South. Since steamboats could sail up as well as down the Mississippi (by 1860, more than 3,500 arrived at the levee in New Orleans), since the hundreds of millions of acres of upriver land were especially fertile, and since New Orleans long exported most of the cotton used in the British textile industry and brought in much of the financial credit that America absorbed from Europe, it's not surprising that the region took in most of the million slaves transported from the Upper South (especially Virginia and Maryland) to the Deep South from 1820 to 1861.[15]

Slaveholders in the Mississippi Valley were especially alert to the Northern antislavery strategy of building a wall or "cordon" of freedom around all slaveholding territory—a vision eloquently expressed, as we have seen, in Frederick Douglass's lectures in Britain. This strategy to contain and demoralize slaveholding would also become central for Lincoln's Republican administration from 1860 well into the Civil War. It is therefore highly significant that in an 1857 article in *DeBow's Review*, William Walker defended his war in Nicaragua as a struggle for "whiteness" that involved "the question whether you will permit yourselves to be hemmed in on the South as you already are on the North and West—whether you will remain quiet and idle while impassible barriers are being built [especially by the British] on the only side left open for your superabundant energy and enterprise."[16]

Walker's focus on Nicaragua was preceded by a number of filibustering efforts to overthrow the Spanish regime in Cuba, which even John Quincy Adams and other national leaders viewed as a "natural" and inevitable part of the United States, given Cuba's location and the long decline of the Spanish New World empire. But whereas the American government relied on diplomacy with Spain, and outlawed military expeditions against countries at peace with the United States, Southern expansionists were deeply concerned with the need to revitalize an economy overinvested in land, slaves, and steamboats. They were also alarmed by Britain's anti-slave-trade interventions in slaveholding Cuba, following the emancipation of British colonial slaves.[17] Cuba was said to be "the Sentinel of the Mississippi" and "the Mistress of the Gulf of Mexico"—the stepping-stone from New Orleans to the Atlantic and the Pacific. But since Central America provided the only short, noncontinental access to the Pacific, a matter of even greater importance before the completion of the first transcontinental railroad in 1869, Nicaragua offered an added attraction in terms of trade. Moreover, if Walker had succeeded in permanently restoring both slavery and the slave trade, control of Nicaragua would destroy any cordon of freedom.[18]

William Walker graduated *summa cum laude* at age fourteen from the University of Nashville; he spent two years in Europe and obtained both law and medical degrees.[19] He became a popular figure throughout the South and drew financial and military support from Mississippi Valley slaveholders. In 1856 he became "a more or less self-appointed president" of Nicaragua after intervening in a civil war with a group of mercenaries and briefly establishing a filibuster government that evoked for the South the vision of a proslavery Latin American empire. Walker's government restored Nicaraguan slavery and also reopened the African slave trade at a time when states in the Deep South were calling for such a measure to meet the growing demand for slave labor and, in view of the rising price of slaves, to enable the growing and mistrusted population of nonslaveholding whites (some 40 percent of the white population) to become part of the slaveholding elite. Walker also addressed this concern by arguing that nonslaveholding whites would be able to migrate to places like Nicaragua, where they could become members of the ruling white master class.[20]

While Upper South leaders in states like Virginia and Maryland naturally opposed any reopening of the African trade, which would undercut their own internal slave trade with the Deep South, Mississippi Valley and South Carolina planters expressed growing fears that the internal trade was "draining" the Upper South of slaves and thus threatening the solidarity of the South as a whole. Walker's forces were defeated in 1857 by a coalition of Central American armies, and he was then executed in 1860 after another filibustering expedition. Yet he had continuing influence on Confederate scenarios of securing a southern frontier against abolitionist encirclement.[21]

Among countless contingencies, if we keep in mind America's conquest of Cuba and Puerto Rico in the Spanish American War of 1898, as well as the hypothetical removal of the crucial impact of America's Civil War on Cuban and Brazilian emancipation in the 1880s, it seems quite possible that, despite British opposition, a victorious Confederacy might have acquired Cuba and Puerto Rico and created at least a minor slaveholding empire. This effort to present a wholly "modernized" version of racial slavery would have been reinforced by the shocking rise and spread of "scientific racism." The article on "Negro" in the renowned 1911 edition of *Encyclopaedia Britannica* underscored the semiofficial consensus that "mentally the negro is inferior to the white."[22] It is certainly clear that without a Civil War, American slavery would probably have persisted well into the twentieth century, significantly setting back "the century of New World emancipation." As for any argument that slavery is wholly incompatible with "modernized" nations, in the 1940s the productive Nazi and Soviet economies became dependent on more enslaved people than ever existed at one time in the New World.[23]

3

The second broad point I mentioned, that America's Emancipation Proclamation and especially the Thirteenth, Fourteenth, and Fifteenth Amendments represent the climax and turning point of the Age of Emancipation, is illuminated by James Oakes's recent revisionist book on the destruction of slavery in the American Civil War.[24]

Oakes shows, contrary to many standard accounts, that Lincoln's Emancipation Proclamation did not appear as a sudden, radical action, totally out of the blue. For more than a year, Lincoln's Republican administration did remain committed to a supposed constitutional ban on interference with slavery in the *existing* slaveholding states. But they were determined from the first to move toward the ultimate extinction of slavery, first by establishing an antislavery "cordon of freedom" around the South that would contain and undermine the institution; and second, by using the doctrine of "military necessity" to free tens of thousands of slaves—so-called contrabands—who fled behind Union lines. Republican leaders drew upon the antislavery arguments of John Quincy Adams as well as leading abolitionists and were convinced that since chattel bondage violated natural and international law and was unrecognized by the Constitution, which defined slaves as "persons held in service," not property, it was restricted within the boundaries of specific Southern states. In 1862 they thus banned slavery on the high seas and in all territories "where the national government has exclusive jurisdiction." And in early 1862, while applying pressure on the four slaveholding Border States that remained within the Union, they required a new state, West Virginia, to abolish slavery as a condition for admission to the Union.

Contrary to many conventional accounts, the Republicans' First and Second Confiscation Acts freed enormous numbers of slaves and led directly to Lincoln's Preliminary Emancipation Proclamation of September 22, 1862. While the First Confiscation Act was originally intended to apply only to those fugitives "employed in hostility to the United States," under the War Department's instructions of August 8, 1861, "military necessity" meant the freeing of *all* slaves who voluntarily entered Union lines from any Confederate state. Despite some debate over "loyal" and "disloyal" masters, no freed people were to be reenslaved. While Union generals acted in different ways, they were influenced by the fact that runaway slaves often provided Northern troops with important military intelligence regarding the location of rebel forces. Within a year of passage, the law had liberated tens of thousands of slaves, and it is difficult to imagine how emancipation could have begun any sooner.

The Second Confiscation Act, or "The Emancipation Bill" as it was frequently called, was debated for seven months and aimed at completely destroying slavery in the seceded states. Signed by Lincoln on July 17, 1862, it immediately freed thousands of slaves in parts of Louisiana and the lower Mississippi Valley occupied by Union troops. Most surprising, a "prospective" clause called upon Lincoln to issue a proclamation freeing all rebel-owned slaves in areas not yet occupied by Union forces. Lincoln acknowledged this by quoting verbatim Section 9 of the Act in his Preliminary Emancipation Proclamation, which he finally felt free to release following the Union victory at Antietam on September 17, and which promised to call for slave emancipation on January 1, 1863, if the South continued to rebel. One should note that Democratic and Border State congressmen were outraged by the success of the Second Confiscation Act, and declared that Republican fanatics had destroyed all prospects of restoring the Union.

Unfortunately, Oakes's emphasis on the antislavery unity of the Republican Party obscures the crucial importance of Abraham Lincoln as a leader of the Union. Everything would have been different if Lincoln had not possessed the extraordinary "capacity for growth" documented in Eric Foner's Pulitzer Prize–winning *The Fiery Trial: Abraham Lincoln and American Slavery*. Though Lincoln hated slavery from his earliest reflections and stressed in 1858 that the natural rights of the Declaration of Independence applied to blacks and that Democrats were attempting to "dehumanize the negro," he had no adequate reply to Steven Douglas's persistent repetition of Jefferson's famous question, "what shall be done with the free negro?"[25] Indeed, despite his impressive growth on other fronts, such as treating Frederick Douglass as a genuine equal, Lincoln advocated colonization and helped plan for voluntary black removal even after his Emancipation Proclamation of January 1, 1863. Yet Lincoln also played a central role in helping to shape public opinion toward the radical goal of emancipation and in helping to pass the Thirteenth Amendment.

Oakes refutes the myth that Lincoln's Emancipation Proclamation did not free a single slave as well as the myth that it shifted the purpose of the war from the restoration of the Union to the abolition of slavery—the war to restore the Union had always been a conflict over slavery. He also highlights other aspects of the Proclamation, such as the importance of recruiting 180,000 black troops to join the Union army, which became indispensable for a Union victory. The Proclamation not only converted the Union army into a true army of liberation but helped lift the ban on the "enticement" of slaves, so that countless Union soldiers now coaxed slaves to leave, spread word of the Proclamation, or even delivered talks on plantations, reducing fears of flight and adding to the huge number of blacks who followed invading Union forces. Above all, the Proclamation gradually helped convince a large number of voters that total slave emancipation was a necessary condition for the restoration of the Union, a prerequisite for passage and ratification of the Thirteenth Amendment.

Yet military emancipation could never free most of the slaves in the South, and the Union army could hardly deal with the hundreds of thousands who flocked behind their lines. Of the nearly 4 million slaves in the South in 1860, no more than 14 percent of those in the eleven Confederate states had been freed by war's end (approximately 474,000 in the Confederate states and another 50,000 in the Border States). Lincoln and the Republican leaders long expressed faith in both military emancipation and the effects of a "cordon of freedom," especially for Border States, but the major military victories at Gettysburg and Vicksburg in 1863 showed that the war might end without any assurance that even the emancipated blacks would not be reenslaved. How could Lincoln guarantee his proclamation that freed slaves would be "forever free" when Confederate leaders promised they would be reenslaved after the war? In early 1864 Republicans arrived at a consensus that the full and permanent destruction of slavery would require a Thirteenth Amendment to the Constitution.

Whereas Northern Democrats were still making a full-scale defense of slavery in June 1864, Republicans drew on a tradition going back to Jefferson's failed bill of 1784 banning slavery from all the western territories. Like the authors of the Northwest Ordinance of 1787, banning slavery north of the Ohio River, they used Jefferson's words in the amendment: "neither slavery nor involuntary servitude, except as a punishment for crime" before ending with "shall exist within the United States, or any place subject to their jurisdiction." Since the Republicans dominated the Senate, they easily approved the amendment, 38 to 6. But on June 15, Democrats won the necessary one-third of the votes in the House of Representatives to block the measure, to the dismay of Lincoln and the Republicans.

In the November election Republicans gained more than enough seats in the House of Representatives to secure passage of the Thirteenth Amendment in the next Congress. But that would be many months away and Lincoln and his associates feared that an impending Union victory would remove a major justification for the amendment— the wartime need to suppress a slaveholder rebellion. As a result, they saw the need for an intense lobbying campaign in the final lame-duck session of the Thirty-Eighth Congress. After much arm-twisting, bribing, and patronage, Republican leaders succeeded on January 31, 1865, in converting enough Border State and Democratic congressmen (a change of three votes would have reversed the outcome). The House erupted in jubilation; spectators wept and danced. In a speech the next day Lincoln stressed that slavery was the only thing that ever threatened to destroy the Union and praised the Thirteenth Amendment for freeing all slaves, everywhere, for all future time, "a King's cure for all the evils" that had not been cured by the Emancipation Proclamation.

But of course the measure could not become part of the Constitution until three-fourths of the states had ratified it. Despite bitter Democratic opposition, by February 3, New York, Illinois, Rhode Island, Michigan, Maryland, and West Virginia had ratified the amendment, and eleven more state legislatures followed by the end of the month. But after Lincoln's assassination on April 14, progress slowed considerably and it was not until December 18 that Secretary of State Seward officially certified that the requisite twenty-seven states had ratified the amendment—the same day that Delaware and Kentucky finally abolished slavery. This meant that during most of the year 1865, slavery was still legal in most of the Southern states and that more slaves may have been freed in December 1865 than in the four preceding years of war. But, by the year's end, freedom was truly "national."

While the implementation of the amendment and the meaning of freedom would long be problematic, this culmination of Anglo-American emancipation had been totally unforeseen and unanticipated at the beginning of the war. Even more astonishing, from a prewar perspective, was the award of citizenship and suffrage by the Fourteenth Amendment in 1868 and the Fifteenth Amendment in 1870. And while major attention has long and rightly focused on the failure of Reconstruction and the emergence of a Southern penal system that was "worse than slavery,"[26] few slave emancipations in history have been followed by anything equivalent to America's first civil rights legislation and the Constitutional amendments that for a limited time in the Reconstruction Era led a significant number of African Americans to vote, to serve in state legislatures, and even to serve in the U.S. Senate (two) and House of Representatives (twenty).[27]

4

In 1788, the first French abolitionist society (the Société des Amis des Noirs) was formed and entered into correspondence with the recently established abolitionist societies in London, Philadelphia, and New York. At that time Vermont and Massachusetts, containing very few slaves, were the only places in the New World that had taken effective steps to outlaw the kind of racial slavery that extended from Canada to Chile and Argentina. A century later, in 1888, Brazil celebrated the immediate and uncompensated emancipation of the only slaves remaining in the hemisphere, concluding an extraordinary century of emancipation. Since most of this abolition of the Atlantic slave trade and chattel slavery was contrary to economic self-interest,[28] it probably stands, despite the U.S. Civil War and other heavy costs, as the greatest landmark of willed moral progress in human history.

In all three volumes of my *Problem of Slavery* trilogy I have addressed both slavery and its abolition as essentially moral issues while of course recognizing the economic functions of the institution. The very concept of chattel slavery has always embodied a profound moral contradiction, exemplified in this volume by my emphasis on the efforts to dehumanize and animalize fellow human beings. The true slave, as Aristotle put it, could have no will or interests of his own; he was merely a tool or instrument who could only affirm his consciousness by partaking of his master's consciousness and by becoming one with his master's desires. Yet, as Hegel later observed, the master's identity depends on having a slave who recognizes him as master: the truth of the master's independent consciousness lies in the dependent and supposedly unessential consciousness of the slave. And while some freed slaves like David Walker and Frederick Douglass agreed that slaves sometimes internalized their master's desires, no masters, whether in ancient Rome, medieval Tuscany, or seventeenth-century Brazil, could forget that the obsequious servant might also be a "domestic enemy" bent on theft, poisoning, arson, or rebellion.

My first volume, *The Problem of Slavery in Western Culture*, dealt with this "problem" first by analyzing the ways in which Western culture explained and rationalized slavery as part of a necessarily imperfect social system. The book then explored the cultural heritage that provided the framework for a profound transformation in moral perception in the late seventeenth and eighteenth centuries that led a growing number of Europeans and Americans to see the full horror of a social evil to which mankind had been blind for centuries. This attack on the most extreme form of labor exploitation was related to the "discovery" and celebration of free labor, which was virtually unknown outside of Western Europe during most of history.

The second volume, *The Problem of Slavery in the Age of Revolution, 1770–1823*, deals with the consequences of this revolution in moral perception, centered in the Enlightenment and evangelical revivals, at a time when any serious attack on slavery carried momentous implications, since the institution was not only thriving economically in this period but had long been interwoven with other widely accepted forms of domination and submission. After reviewing "what the abolitionists were up against," the book analyzes the early history of antislavery movements in Britain and America, and ends with a discussion of legal and theological issues, and an imaginary confrontation between Napoleon and the black Haitian leader Toussaint Louverture.

In the present volume I have stressed that even many abolitionists recognized two major barriers to any "immediate" emancipation. Since for millennia slaves had been defined as private property, freeing them without some form of compensation to owners would set a dangerous precedent in societies in which property rights had become transcendent. Second, before the sudden rise of "immediatism" among British and American abolitionists around 1830, it was taken for granted that slaves would need some kind of "preparation" for freedom. Contrary to the wishes of the leading radicals, the famous British emancipation act of 1833 provided for both generous compensation to owners and a period of "apprenticeship" for freed slaves. Earlier, five of the Northern American states had enacted emancipation measures that freed only the children born of slaves, in their twenties, thus combining some supposed preparation with compensation through youthful labor. Various forms of gradual emancipation followed the Spanish American wars of independence.

Holland and some other countries followed Britain's example, but as I have strongly emphasized in this volume, white Americans, who thought they faced the prospect of living together with millions of freed blacks who were totally "unprepared" for equal citizenship, clung to the "solution" of colonization as the only possible route to slave emancipation. This white consensus about the exile of blacks evoked a powerful response on the part of free African Americans who were determined to counter racism and launch a radical abolition movement as well as elevate and uplift their own population. Such figures as Frederick Douglass and James McCune Smith exemplified some success in achieving respect, dignity, and acceptance as equals in a white society.

Douglass's response to Chartism and so-called wage slavery in Britain illustrates the complexity of comparing chattel slavery with other forms of exploitation and servitude. Because slavery has long epitomized the most extreme form of domination and oppression, it has served as a metaphor for rejecting almost every deprivation of freedom (including "enslavement" to sex, greed, drugs, ignorance, and even ambition). More important, as with Douglass's acceptance of the Chartists' assault on local bondage, despite his insistence on the uniqueness of chattel slavery, the comparison has provided a way of extending the historically successful moral condemnation of slavery to other forms of coerced labor and exploitation, ranging from the traditional sexist oppression of women to modern human trafficking.

While the historical ownership of slaves as property meant that even a highly privileged slave could suddenly be sold as a field hand, the fact that property in slaves represented a financial investment provided a certain protection totally lacking among workers in modern concentration camps. When we read of a highly privileged slave in charge of boiling sugar on a Jamaican sugar plantation, a head man who reports only to an overseer and attorney, or an enslaved Mississippi River boatman who hires free workers as he transports cotton to New Orleans, we realize that a few New World chattel slaves were considerably better off than the millions of coerced laborers in Nazi and Soviet camps, or even many modern sex slaves.[29]

Careful historical comparisons could modify the view that chattel slavery was a wholly unique social evil and also draw on the strong positive legacies of Anglo-American abolitionism. From the 1890s to the 1930s, radical American reformers like Daniel DeLeon, Eugene Debs, Jack London, Upton Sinclair, Clarence Darrow, and members of the Industrial Workers of the World (the IWW) continually expressed their indebtedness to the abolitionists, who had also been treated as public enemies but who had found ways to mobilize and transform public opinion. "We are the modern abolitionists," exclaimed the Wobbly leader James Thompson, "fighting against wage slavery."[30] Somewhat similar tributes to the abolitionist model were made by feminists and black leaders of the NAACP.

The issue of legacies is complex. Despite the dismal failure of American Reconstruction, the succeeding century of Jim Crow discrimination, and the legacy of racism even in the Caribbean and South America, Anglo-American emancipation had a profound influence on the freeing of slaves in the French, Dutch, and Danish colonies, and especially in Cuba and Brazil. We should also note that in the twentieth century the legacy of New World emancipation extended, thanks in part to the League of Nations and the United Nations, to the outlawing of chattel slavery throughout the world.

When thinking of the earlier Age of Emancipation as a model for the future, one can of course point to the extraordinary contingency I have emphasized, especially involving the American Civil War and the goals of an independent Confederacy, as well as what Seymour Drescher has termed the amazing "reversion" to mass forced labor in Nazi and Soviet Europe in the 1930s and 1940s. Yet when viewed in retrospect, influenced by today's public opinion and social values, many people would no doubt regard the outlawing of New World and even global slavery as inevitable. But I would conclude, given the overall findings of my trilogy, that the outlawing of New World slavery was both astonishing and, at times, even foreseeable. Astonishing in view of the institution's antiquity and modern economic strength, resilience, and importance. Foreseeable, if not from what I term the revolutionary shift in moral perception, then from the time in the early 1830s when British abolitionists, having triumphed in their mobilization of public opinion, began demanding the "immediate" ending of bondage around the world, and in 1833 achieving a compromise that soon led to the freeing of 800,000 colonial slaves. If even New World slave emancipation might have required another fifty years or more, one is also impressed by how limited in time the Soviet and Nazi "reversion" really was.

The global outlawing of chattel slavery has already become an important precedent for abolishing human trafficking and other forms of coerced labor—as we read the shocking estimates of the number of women and men held today in different kinds of bondage. But as for any inevitable moral "progress," when we view the present state of the world with respect to human nature, there is less cause for optimism. Many humans still love to kill, torture, oppress, and dominate. Moral progress seems to be historical, cultural, and institutional, not the result of a genetic improvement in individual human nature. One needs only to note what happened in a highly "civilized" country like Germany in the 1930s and 1940s. If we imagine a worst-case scenario in which future climate change or nuclear war breaks up modern nations as we know them, antimodernists and ultraconservatives might well restore chattel slavery on a large scale, especially in the Middle East.[31] If my friends and I were suddenly stripped of our twentieth-century conditioning and plummeted back to Mississippi in 1860, we would doubtless take for granted our rule over slaves. So an astonishing historical achievement really matters. The outlawing of chattel slavery in the New World, and then globally, represents a crucial landmark of moral progress that we should never forget.

Acknowledgments

This project concludes a three-volume scholarly enterprise that began in 1958 when a Guggenheim Fellowship supported my initial research in Britain that led to my book *The Problem of Slavery in Western Culture* (1966). This prefatory volume explores the historical background that provided a framework for the great struggles over slavery in modern times. It is addressed essentially to a problem of moral perception—why it was that at a certain moment of history a small number of men and women not only saw the full horror of a social evil to which people had been blind for centuries, but felt impelled to attack it through personal testimony and cooperative action.

The next volume, *The Problem of Slavery in the Age of Revolution, 1770–1823* (1975), moves on to the social, economic, and political contexts that shaped an antislavery ideology and which defined the implications and consequences of early antislavery protests in Britain, France, and the United States. Like the preceding work, the second volume suggests that any serious challenge to slavery carried momentous implications precisely because slavery had long symbolized the most extreme model of treating human beings as exploitable objects. To question such a model of domination that had been accepted for millennia could lead to the questioning of most forms of domination and submission.

During the long period between the publication of the second volume and the completion now of this third volume of the trilogy, I wrote nine other books, many of them on related topics involving slavery and emancipation. From the very start I realized that this final volume of the project, on the "Age of Emancipation," would present the most formidable problems of coverage, selectivity, organization, and method. Accordingly, when I began envisioning the third volume, soon after the publication of the second, I decided to first write an exploratory pilot study that would put the "Age of Emancipation" within a broad historical survey of slavery and antislavery from antiquity to the modern United Nations. Therefore, when I was awarded a priceless National Endowment for the Humanities–Henry E. Huntington Library Fellowship in 1976, I concentrated my efforts on the pilot study, or what would become *Slavery and Human Progress* (1984). While I had earlier done research for the second volume of the trilogy at the wonderful Huntington Library in San Marino, California, I was now able to make use of the library's invaluable resources for both *Slavery and Human Progress* and *The Problem of Slavery in the Age of Emancipation*.

As I explained in a report to the National Endowment for the Humanities, my goal at that time was to use history as a source for disciplined moral reflection on the ironies, achievements, tragedies, and unintended consequences of human idealism and self-interest, unraveling some of the complex historical ties between human exploitation and liberation, ties that give a multitude of meanings to notions of human "progress." In many ways *The Problem of Slavery in the Age of Emancipation* benefited from the discoveries and decisions I made when writing *Slavery and Human Progress*. And as I have indicated in the preface to this volume, both *Slavery and Human Progress* and then *Inhuman Bondage: The Rise and Fall of Slavery in the New World* (2006) helped to free me from trying to cover too much material in the final volume of the trilogy.

Much of my writing on slavery during the past third-of-a-century was made possible by the assistance of further generous research grants to Yale University from the National Endowment of the Humanities, beginning in 1980. While the grants were primarily intended for *The Problem of Slavery in the Age of Emancipation,* the invaluable research also made it possible to treat British West Indian emancipation and related subjects in much greater depth in *Slavery and Human Progress.*

Since I had agreed to teach and hold the first chair in American Civilization at the École des Hautes Études en Sciences Sociales in Paris for the academic year 1980–81, I was fortunate as the project director in having Loueva F. Pflueger, an administrative assistant in the Yale Department of History, oversee the budget and work with Joan Binder, a full-time associate in research who managed the project in the United States while I was abroad. Ms. Pflueger and Ms. Binder also worked with Dr. Fiona E. Spiers, my full-time, highly experienced researcher in Britain. I could not be more grateful to Joan Binder and Fiona Spiers for the outstanding work they did in gathering, sorting, and organizing a vast collection of largely primary source materials. While I was in Paris, Ms. Binder also did research on her own from Boston to Washington and supervised the work of quite a few student researchers, including Amy Dru Stanley and Donna Dennis. Dr. Spiers, whom I visited many times from Paris when I did research in Britain, examined primary sources in Dublin, London, Glasgow, Oxford, Cambridge, Manchester, Leeds, Hull, and Durham. When I returned to Yale to teach in the academic year 1981–82, Joan Binder presented me with enormous well-organized files of source material.

There was increasingly a strong interconnection between this research, my writing, and my teaching. In both lecture courses and high-level new seminars, I distributed hundreds of pages of Xeroxed primary sources— often material that placed slavery within a broad context of antebellum American culture. Above all, I learned a great deal from seminar discussions and student papers, and was very pleased by the way many of my NEH-grant student researchers received personal intellectual benefits by basing some of their own papers on this same research. Unfortunately, given the passage of time I apologize that I cannot begin to thank by name everyone who contributed, including the students whom Joan Binder was able to recruit.

It is crucial to understand that most of this book was written *after* the publication in 2006 of *Inhuman Bondage: The Rise and Fall of Slavery in the New World.* The path that led to *Inhuman Bondage* was related to my new and long professional relationship, beginning in 1994, with the philanthropists Richard Gilder and Lewis E. Lehrman. My founding of Yale's Gilder Lehrman Center for the Study of Slavery, Resistance, and Abolition, and the annual summer courses I taught for New York City high school teachers, sponsored by the Gilder Lehrman Institute of American History, helped me create a new lecture course at Yale on the origins and significance of New World slavery. My work at the center, the summer courses, and the new Yale lecture course then led to my book *Inhuman Bondage.*

There is much in the acknowledgments of *Inhuman Bondage,* as in *Slavery and Human Progress,* which also applies to *The Problem of Slavery in the Age of Emancipation.* Here I will only mention the international libraries listed in *Slavery and Human Progress.* And once again I express my eternal gratitude to Stanley L. Engerman, probably the world's leading expert on comparative slavery, who carefully read all three of my books in manuscript, including this one, and penned in invaluable corrections and suggestions.

Turning to the final phase of production of this volume, I am most grateful to Patricia Dallai, executive director of Yale's Henry Koerner Center for Emeritus Faculty, for helping me receive an Andrew W. Mellon Foundation Emeritus Fellowship, which helped pay for indispensable research assistance as I wrote seven new chapters of the book and revised those already completed. I am also very appreciative of the annual research fund of my Sterling Professorship that supplemented the Mellon grant. I am extremely grateful to the librarians at Yale who gave such effective help to my research assistants.

I briefly benefited from the excellent help of Joseph Yannielli and Christopher Bonner, graduate students at Yale. My immense thanks to Philipp Peter Ziesche, who as a graduate student had been a major contributor to my work on *Inhuman Bondage,* and for this volume continued to play a leading role tracking down materials and offering his own insights. Even after receiving a Ph.D., publishing his own book, and working full-time as a top editor of the Benjamin Franklin Papers project, he helped me update the older chapter on the Haitian Revolution. Immense thanks also go to Christopher Allison, now a doctoral student at Harvard, who for years not only found crucial sources for this project at every step of the way but had such an imaginative grasp of the material that he was able to help me plan and envision the arguments of many of the chapters.

I am immensely grateful to the following historians for reading and commenting on parts of this book: Harold Brackman, Peter Hinks, David P. Geggus, David Blight, Michael G. Kammen, Seymour Drescher, Malick Ghachem, and Matt Spooner. As so often in the past, I am especially indebted to John Stauffer, Steven Mintz, Sean Wilentz, and William Casey King, former students and now distinguished historians and friends who provided essential comments and corrections on all or parts of the book.

Since my work on this book began so long ago, I fear I have inevitably omitted the names of some of the people who gave me important help, an error for which I deeply apologize. It is also crucial to exempt everyone named from any blame for any errors, misconceptions, and omissions— shortcomings for which I take full responsibility.

Finally, let me emphasize my indebtedness to my literary agent, Wendy Strothman, who in 2007 arranged a publishing agreement with Alfred A. Knopf and who continued to advise and assist me. My thanks to my superb editor at Knopf, Andrew Miller, who improved my prose, who continued to give me encouragement, and who in countless ways facilitated the publication of this book. Thanks also to his able assistant, Mark Chiusano, who helped with countless details.

Since the completion of this trilogy, at age eighty-six, in many ways marks the fulfillment of a career, it is appropriate to emphasize the *central* parts of a life that balance and compensate for a career. I am immensely grateful to such close personal friends as Howard and Sylvia Garland, Mal and Jane Rudner, and Sam and Judy Sprotzer because they enhance and deepen my life. When they express real interest in how my book is coming along, it is because we are deeply interested in one another's lives, not because they are historians.

I have dedicated this book to my sons Adam and Noah and their wonderful families because they and their future lives are far more important to me than any books I write. When I read to little Jonah or Tola, or hold baby Elena in my arms, I am forming a connection with a beloved family that will hopefully last long after my death. My profound love and interest in the lives of Adam and Noah and their families, and their love for me, forms part of a center that has given enormous meaning to my life.

Throughout the past forty-four years my wonderful and beloved wife, Toni Hahn Davis, has helped create that balancing center, and I am above all indebted to her. She has not only read and improved much of my work, supported my efforts as a teacher and writer, but has really made possible my continuing career as a historian. Above all else, she has enriched my life in infinite ways.

Notes

INTRODUCTION

1. Laurent Dubois, *Colony of Citizens: Revolution and Slave Emancipation in the French Caribbean, 1787–1804* (Chapel Hill: University of North Carolina Press, 2004); Dubois, *Avengers of the New World: The Story of the Haitian Revolution* (Cambridge, Mass.: Harvard University Press, 2006); Madison Smartt Bell, *Toussaint Louverture: A Biography* (New York: Pantheon, 2007); Julius S. Scott, "The Common Wind: Currents of Afro-American Communication in the Era of the Haitian Revolution" (Ph.D. diss., Duke University, 1986); Robert L. Paquette, *Sugar Is Made with Blood: The Conspiracy of La Escalera and the Conflict between Empires over Slavery in Cuba* (Middletown, Conn.: Wesleyan University Press, 1988), 15, 26, 36,42, 76–77, 123–24, 211; Alfred N. Hunt, *Haiti's Influence on Antebellum America: Slumbering Volcano in the Caribbean* (Baton Rouge: Louisiana State University Press, 1988); Douglas R. Egerton, *Gabriel's Rebellion: The Virginia Slave Conspiracies of 1800 and 1802* (Chapel Hill: University of North Carolina Press, 1993), ix, 45–48, 160–61, 168–72. For simplicity I use here the term "free blacks," but there was often a significant division between free blacks like Toussaint Louverture and the lighter-skinned "free coloreds" or mulattoes.

2. Bryan Edwards, *The History Civil and Commercial, of the British Colonies in the West Indies,* 4 vols. (Philadelphia, 1806), IV, 68–80, 98. Edwards went to Saint-Domingue shortly after the slave insurrection of 1791 and later gathered much information from the British expeditionary force that made extensive use of black troops. By "Philanthropy" he means the antislavery movement.

3. James Madison to the Marquis de Lafayette, November 25, 1820, Gilder Lehrman Collection, New-York Historical Society.

4. William W. Freehling, *The Road to Disunion: Secessionists at Bay, 1776–1854* (New York: Oxford University Press, 1990), Part III.

5. [Leonard Bacon], *Christian Spectator,* 5 (Oct. 1, 1823), 544; [Bacon], "Report to the Committee appointed February 18, 1823, to inquire respecting the black population of the United States," in *Memoirs of American Missionaries, Formerly Connected with the Society of Inquiry respecting Missions, in the Andover Theological Seminary . . .* (Boston, 1823), 300–301. For more on Bacon, see chapter 6.

6. David Brian Davis, *The Problem of Slavery in the Age of Revolution, 1770–1823* (New York: Oxford University Press, 1999), p. 303. As George M. Fredrickson has pointed

out, with respect to race and racism, in a culture dedicated to the ideal of equality, a particular group like blacks can be denied the prospect of equal status "only if they allegedly possess some extraordinary deficiency that makes them less than fully human." *Racism: A Short History* (Princeton, N.J.: Princeton University Press, 2002), 12.

7. From 1780 to 1804, Pennsylvania, Connecticut, Rhode Island, New York, and New Jersey enacted laws for the gradual emancipation of all slaves. Largely because there were so few slaves in northern New England, Vermont was able to outlaw slavery with a constitution of 1777; in Massachusetts and New Hampshire judicial decisions had a somewhat similar effect in the 1780s, although a few slaves remained in New Hampshire for many decades.

8. Despite the continuing fluctuations between "nature" and "nurture," these hereditary and environmental versions of dehumanization would sometimes seem to merge.

9. [Theodore Dwight Weld], *American Slavery as It Is: Testimony of a Thousand Witnesses* (New York: American Anti-Slavery Society, 1839), 110.

10. Adrian Desmond and James Moore, *Darwin's Sacred Cause: How a Hatred of Slavery Shaped Darwin's Views on Human Evolution* (Boston: Houghton Mifflin, 2009), 182. Quoted from Darwin's *Journal of Researches* (1845; repr., 1860).

11. Henry Highland Garnet, *A Memorial Discourse; by Rev. Henry Highland Garnet, Delivered in the Hall of the House of Representatives, Washington City, D.C. on Sabbath, February 12, 1865*, with an introduction by James McCune Smith, M.D. (Philadelphia, 1865), 69–74. I am grateful to Seth Moglen for calling this work to my attention.

It should be noted that chattel slavery has not *always* been the worst form of human oppression, even though slaves have usually occupied the lowest rung of social hierarchies. In addition to genocidal death camps and twentieth-century gulags and prison farms, there are such examples as the Chinese "coolies" shipped in the mid-nineteenth century to the coast of Peru, where they died in appalling numbers from the lethal effects of shoveling seabird manure for the world's fertilizer market. What distinguished slaves was the fact that their subjugation—their vulnerability to nearly unchecked power and lack of familial support—arose from their being *owned* (like domestic animals), a status that could often provide at least a degree of protection. Moreover, most slaves became slaves involuntarily, whereas many other forms of coerced labor involved a degree of initial choice.

12. Winthrop D. Jordan, *White Over Black: American Attitudes Toward the Negro, 1550–1812* (Chapel Hill: University of North Carolina Press, 1968), 232.

13. Here one thinks, for example, of the modern Sudanese Janjaweed, who have used repeated gang raping and even so-called rape camps for the ethnic cleansing of blacks in Darfur and eastern Chad. It would often be difficult to distinguish this military raping from the gang raping of modern sex slaves, such as the young women in Cambodia who report having been raped by as many as twenty-five men in a row.

14. The issue is somewhat complicated by the fact that in rare situations, such as Thomas Jefferson's relationship with Sally Hemings, family ties could become quite close over a long period of time. Yet whatever affections Jefferson may have felt for his enslaved chambermaid and her four surviving children, he never failed to include her and her children in his plantation inventory, along with their market value. As Jefferson himself acknowledged:

> The whole commerce between master and slave is a perpetual exercise of the most boisterous passions, and the most unremitting despotism on the one part, and degrading submission on the other. Our children see this and learn to imitate it; for man is an imitative animal. . . . The man must be a prodigy who can retain his manners and morals undepraved by such circumstances.

Annette Gordon-Reed, *The Hemingses of Monticello* (New York: W. W. Norton, 2008), passim; Thomas Jefferson, *Notes on the State of Virginia*, ed. William Peden (Chapel Hill: University of North Carolina Press 1955), 162.

15. Mia Bay, *The White Image in the Black Mind: African-American Ideas about White People, 1830–1925* (New York: Oxford University Press, 2000), 119.

16. Ibid., 127–28.

17. This remark would seem to be exceptional or at least unusual in view of the nineteenth-century efforts of Southern slave owners to encourage the Christianization of their slaves. But the belief that religion would make slaves more obedient and dutiful did not mean that whites anticipated a racially integrated heaven. Bay's quotations from ex-slaves show that even household servants were repeatedly denied, like household pets, any sense of communion within the white churches.

18. Bay, *The White Image in the Black Mind,* 124, 129–31.

19. Ibid., 131–32.

20. See especially Walter Johnson, *Soul by Soul: Life Inside the Antebellum Slave Market* (Cambridge, Mass.: Harvard University Press, 1999).

I. SOME MEANINGS OF SLAVERY AND EMANCIPATION: DEHUMANIZATION, ANIMALIZATION, AND FREE SOIL

1. Frederick Law Olmsted, *The Cotton Kingdom: A Traveller's Observations on Cotton and Slavery in the American Slave States,* ed. Arthur Schlesinger, Sr. (New York: Modern Library, 1984), 452.

While I have focused attention in chapter 1 on North America, it is important to stress that the animalization of black slaves was widespread throughout the world. Charles Darwin, for example, was continually shocked by the examples of slavery he witnessed during his time in South America in the early 1830s: "Near Rio de Janeiro I lived opposite to an old lady, who kept screws to crush the fingers of her female slaves. I have stayed in a house where a young household mulatto, daily and hourly, was reviled, beaten and persecuted enough to break the spirit of the lowest animal." Olivia Judson, "The Origin of Darwin," *The New York Times,* February 12, 2009, A35; see also Adrian Desmond and James Moore, *Darwin's Sacred Cause: How a Hatred of Slavery Shaped Darwin's Views on Human Evolution* (Boston: Houghton Mifflin, 2009), 68–110.

2. Since surprisingly few scholars have explored this important subject, I want to express my gratitude and admiration for David Livingstone Smith's *Less Than Human: Why We Demean, Enslave, and Exterminate Others* (New York: St. Martin's Press, 2011).

3. Saul Friedländer, *The Years of Extermination: Nazi Germany and the Jews, 1939–1945* (New York: Oxford University Press, 2007), 335; Hugh Raffles, "Jews, Lice, and History," in *Public Culture: An Interdisciplinary Journal of Transnational Cultural Studies* 19, no. 3 (Fall 2007), online. I should emphasize that animalization was only one part of a much broader Nazi, anti-Jewish ideology and culture.

4. For many examples of genocidal animalization, see Ben Kiernan, *Blood and Soil* (New Haven, Conn.: Yale University Press, 2007), 357–58, 440, 549, 558–59, 660.

5. Kwame Anthony Appiah, *Experiments in Ethics* (Cambridge, Mass.: Harvard University Press, 2008), 144, 247.

6. Joel Williamson, *The Crucible of Race: Black-White Relations in the American South Since Emancipation* (New York: Oxford University Press, 1984), 185–86.

7. Smith, *Less Than Human,* 25.

8. In war, combatants often escalate dehumanizing measures by responding to sadistic acts of the other side. In World War II the Japanese invited brutalizing retaliation by starving, bayoneting, beheading, raping, and even vivisecting prisoners of war, according to Evan Thomas's review of Max Hastings's *Retribution: The Battle for Japan, 1944–45, The New York Times Book Review,* March 30, 2008, online. But there was also much racism in the Western portrayal of the Japanese; the British general Sir William Slim "captured the mood of the time: the Japanese soldier, Slim said, 'is the most formidable fighting insect in history.' "

9. I will later try to clarify the relationship between animalization and racism.

Ironically, the Slavic root for "slave," *rab,* as in *rabotat,* to work, made its way into "robot" (actually the old Czech word for serf). The likening of a slave to a robot or inhuman machine parallels in some ways the comparison of the slave to an animal or a permanent child. My friend Harold Brackman informs me that the current "transhumanist movement" is focusing increasing attention on the ethical implications of such things as implanting micro nanorobots in the brains of Alzheimer patients. It would appear that the issue of humanized machines might well replace in many ways the issue of animalization.

10. Winthrop D. Jordan imaginatively develops this important theme, with regard to white attitudes toward black Africans and African American slaves, in *White Over Black: American Attitudes Toward the Negro, 1550–1812* (Chapel Hill: University of North Carolina Press, 1968). According to Jordan, racial slavery as it developed in colonial North America was a system of psychological exploitation, or cultural parasitism, that allowed the whites to achieve a sense of communal solidarity and purpose through the systematic debasement of African Americans. After surveying a vast Anglo-American literature regarding Africans and African Americans, Jordan concluded that American society became functionally based on a rationale of racial superiority.

11. Reinhold Niebuhr, *The Nature and Destiny of Man: A Christian Interpretation, One Volume Edition, I. Human Nature* (New York: Charles Scribner's Sons, 1948), 3.

12. Montaigne, *Essays,* II; Sardanapalus, iv. i., "Sonnet to Chillon." The dilemma of being human also prompted poets and other writers to satirize human failings by stressing the advantages of being an animal. Thus Walt Whitman: "They do not sweat and whine about their condition;/They do not lie awake in the dark and weep for/their sins;/They do not make me sick discussing their duty to God."

There is abundant evidence that many people feel far closer to their animal pets than to other humans. In 2008 Leona Helmsley left up to $8 billion in a charitable trust solely for the care and welfare of dogs, and some $12 million for the care and support of her own pet Maltese dog Trouble—far more than she bequeathed to her grandchildren. *New York Times, Week in Review,* July 6, 2008, 5.

13. As we saw in the introduction, slaveholders could have it both ways. They could enhance their self-esteem by projecting their animalistic attributes on slaves, but white males could also indulge their "Id" by sexually exploiting slave women.

14. David Brion Davis, review of Winthrop D. Jordan, *White Over Black,* in *William and Mary Quarterly* (January 1969): 110–14.

15. David Brion Davis, *The Problem of Slavery in Western Culture* (New York: Oxford University Press, 1966), 255–61. Since even free blacks were barred from testifying in court, such laws were obviously difficult to enforce.

16. It is significant that the word had been exterminated well before an African American became president.

17. Williamson, *Crucible of Race,* 122–30.

18. Margaret Abruzzo's *Polemical Pain: Slavery, Cruelty, and the Rise of Humanitarianism* (Baltimore: Johns Hopkins University Press, 2011) brilliantly shows how an eighteenth-century Anglo-American transformation in public responses to cruelty and pain shaped the nature of the antislavery movements and also contributed to a new sensitivity to animal cruelty.

19. A few examples: gods pictured with animal faces or heads; people wearing animal masks or simulating animal behavior; pretended animals talking like people in folktales or children's literature; actual animals dressed like people or trained to do human-like actions (often considered cute, or comic, or wondrous); various forms of animal sacrifice, sometimes as a substitute for human sacrifice; bestiality, in the sense of human sex with animals, and legends of mixed offspring.

20. Laurence Urdang, *The Oxford Thesaurus, American Edition* (New York: Oxford University Press, 1992), 14; *Webster's Dictionary of Synonyms,* 1st ed. (New York: G. & C. Merriam, 1942), 53; *Free Online Thesaurus,* www.thefreedictionary.com/animalization.

21. Keith Thomas, *Man and the Natural World: A History of the Modern Sensibility* (New York: Pantheon Books, 1983), 40–41.

22. http://www.emory.edu/LIVING_LINKS/ourinnerApe/pdfs/anthropo denial.html; http://asc.nhc.rtp.nc.us/2007/conference/session_one.html; Frans de Waal, *Good Natured: The Origins of Right and Wrong in Humans and Other Animals* (Cambridge, Mass.: Harvard University Press, 1996).

23. Genesis 1:20–28 (King James Version). My italics.

24. Ibid., 2:19–20; 8:20; 9:2–3.

25. Thomas, *Man and the Natural World*, 15–21.

26. Paul Freedman, *Out of the East: Spices and the Medieval Imagination* (New Haven, Conn.: Yale University Press, 2008), 35.

27. Seymour Drescher reminds me that the Eastern religions did not condemn human slavery or organize movements to abolish it. He raises the interesting question whether a much earlier Western equation between animal and human rights would have increased or diminished the abolitionist appeal.

28. Thomas, *Man and the Natural World*, pp. 33–35. Of course there are numerous examples of animals arousing sympathy and romantic feeling, or becoming a vantage point for criticizing human folly.

But David Hume said that some animals were endowed with thought and reason, and Montesquieu made the fairly common point that animals knew nothing of our hopes and fears, especially the fear of death. According to Voltaire, "they don't hear the clock strike."

29. Paul Freedman, *Images of the Medieval Peasant* (Stanford: Stanford University Press, 1999), 133–73, 300–303. Because peasants were an indispensable, food-producing majority of the population, writers often balanced the serfs' or rustics' alleged filth, stupidity, and bestiality with occasional tributes to their piety, simplicity, and closeness to God.

30. Burke, *Reflections on the Revolution in France,* in Oxford Quotations, iii,14; On the other hand, when Thomas Jefferson was living in France in the 1780s, he could speak of "the cloven hoof" of the aristocracy Jefferson in France sees Elkins & McKitrick, 315.

31. Yvon Garlan, *Slavery in Ancient Greece,* trans. Janet Lloyd, rev. ed. (Ithaca, N.Y.: Cornell University Press, 1988), 46.

32. Leviticus 25:44–46. I have used a modern translation that gives a more accurate translation of the Hebrew. The King James Bible generally avoids the word "slaves," using instead "bondmen" and "bondmaids" who will nevertheless remain "bondmen for ever."

33. Jean Barbot, a French slave-ship captain, claimed that he had observed the Golden Rule and that other traders should treat African slaves the way they would want to be treated if captured by Algerians. *A Description of the Coasts of North and South-Guinea . . . ,* in John Churchill, *A Collection of Voyages and Travels,* vol. 5 (London, 1732), 47, 100.

34. Even in medieval and early modern Russia, where slaves and serfs belonged to the same ethnic group as their masters, some Russian noblemen invented a theory claiming a separate historical origin, in effect making these subalterns "outsiders." Like slaves in other cultures, serfs were said to be intrinsically lazy, childlike, licentious, and incapable of life without authoritative direction. It was even said that they had black bones! Peter Kolchin, *Unfree Labor: American Slavery and Russian Serfdom* (Cambridge, Mass.: Harvard University Press, 1987), 170–73.

35. Charles Verlinden, *"L'Origine de 'sclavus—esclave,' " Archivum latinitatis medii aevi,* XVII (1943), 97–128.

36. In the 1580s, Sir Francis Drake found and freed Turks, North African Moors, and even a few Frenchmen and Germans among the Spanish galley slaves in Santo Domingo and Cartagena, the great center of trade and transshipment of African

slaves in what is today Colombia. Michael J. Guasco, "The Idea of Slavery in the Anglo-Atlantic World before 1619," p. 26, Working Paper No. 00–28, International Seminar on the History of the Atlantic World, 1500–1800, Harvard University, August 17, 2000. I am much indebted to Dr. Guasco for letting me cite his paper.

37. A fascination with the black African's penis extended from ancient times to later European explorers and scientists. In 1799, the English geologist Charles White wrote: "That the Penis of an African is larger than that of a European has I believe been shown in every anatomical school in London. Preparations of them are preserved in most anatomical museums, and I have one in mine." Charles White, *An Account of the Regular Gradation in Man, and in Different Animals and Vegetables; and from the Former to the Latter* (London, 1799), 237. See also Jordan, *White Over Black*, 30, 34–35, 158–59, 163, 464, 501.

38. Jordan, *White Over Black*, 29–35.

39. As I will soon note, an exception can probably be made for at least parts of later fifteenth-century Iberia, where Muslim racist traditions coincided with Portugal's importation of large numbers of slaves from West Africa.

40. John Hunwick, "Arab Views of Black Africans and Slavery," paper given at Yale's Gilder Lehrman Center Conference on Collective Degradation: Slavery and the Construction of Race, November 7, 2003, 10–12. Ibn Khaldūn, who found similar defects in Slavs and other "northern Europeans," attributed this inferiority to zones of climate, but also affirmed, like many ancient and medieval writers, that such traits were in effect hereditary. He did later admit that some West Africans were more civilized, and could be redeemed by Islam. Ibid., 14–15.

41. Gernot Rotter, *Die Stellung des Negers in der islamisch-arabischen Gesellschaft bis zum XVI. Jahrhundert* (Bonn: Rheinische Friedrich-Wilhelms-Universität, 1967), 162–63; Bernard Lewis, *Race and Color in Islam* (New York: Harper & Row, 1971), 38.

42. Over the ages, Jews, Muslims, and Christians engaged in highly imaginative efforts to interpret the enigmatic "Curse" in Genesis 9:18–27, and the increasing enslavement of black Africans totally transformed biblical interpretation. In the Bible, Ham views and perhaps mocks his naked, drunken father, Noah, who upon waking curses Ham's son Canaan and condemns him and his descendants to the lowest form of slavery. While the Canaanites were the enemies of the ancient Israelites, there was long no mention of skin color. Medieval Arabs tended to shift attention from Canaan to Ham, who eventually came to be seen as the ancestor of black Africans. Despite continuing confusion over Ham's sin and the fact he was not cursed, the story provided many nineteenth-century Americans with divine sanction for racial slavery. See David Brion Davis, *Inhuman Bondage: The Rise and Fall of Slavery in the New World* (New York: Oxford University Press, 2006), 64–70.

43. Lewis, *Race and Slavery*, 57–58. It should be noted that Ahmad Baba felt it necessary to make this eloquent point in order to contest an opposite view.

44. It should be stressed that while Muslim corsairs enslaved hundreds of thousands of Christians by raiding the coasts of Europe and capturing ships, Christians and Jews living under Muslim rule were defined as "protected persons" (*dhimmīs*) who could not legally be enslaved unless they violated the terms of the contract that defined their status. Ibid., 7.

45. James H. Sweet, "The Iberian Roots of American Racist Thought," *William and Mary Quarterly*, 3rd ser., vol. 54, "Constructing Race" (Jan. 1997): 159, 166. Imanuel Geiss makes essentially the same point in *Geschichte des Rassismus* (Frankfurt am Main: Suhrkamp Verlag, 1988), 84–88. I have written in more detail concerning the Iberian origins of antiblack racism, stressing the importance of the originally anti-Semitic concept of "purity of blood," in Davis, *Inhuman Bondage*, 70–73.

46. Edmund S. Morgan, *American Slavery, American Freedom: The Ordeal of Colonial Virginia* (New York: W. W. Norton, 1975), passim.

47. Marcel Trudell, *L'Esclavage au Canada français; histoire et conditions de l'esclavage*

(Québec: Presses Universitaires Laval, 1960), 20–35. Of course, slave labor was not the major source of economic growth in New York and New England, but it was more important than many historians have realized.

48. George M. Fredrickson, *Racism: A Short History* (Princeton, N.J.: Princeton University Press, 2002), 6.

49. These and many similar antiblack and anti-Semitic quotations can be found on the Web, geocities.com/ru00ru00/racismhistory/18thcent.html.

50. Ironically, Linnaeus's classification of human types along with all animals overturned the effect of Adam's biblical *naming* of the animals. By including humans as part of the animal kingdom, he also inadvertently opened the way to a theory of polygenesis.

51. Fredrickson, *Racism*, 56–58.

52. Jordan, *White Over Black*, 499–502.

53. *Politics*, books 1 and 2, in Thomas Wiedemann, *Greek and Roman Slavery* (London: Routledge, 1981), 18–20. Plato brought the concept of slavery into his cosmology, positing a dualism between the primary cause, which was intelligent and divine, and the mechanical or slave cause, which was irrational, disorderly, and lacking in both freedom and conscious purpose. Like a wise master, the *Demiurge* guided the *ananke* of the material universe toward the good. Gregory Vlastos, "Slavery in Plato's Republic," *The Philosophical Review* 50 (1941): 289–304. Plato also associated slavery with the unruly multitude as well as the chaotic material world devoid of *Logos*. And he spoke of a "slavish people" who lack the capacity for self-government and higher pursuits of virtue and culture. For Plato, a slavish mind might hold a true belief but could not know the truth of this belief. The human institution of slavery thus reflected basic structures of the universe. Davis, *Problem of Slavery in Western Culture*, 67–68.

54. Gerda Lerner, *The Creation of Patriarchy* (New York: Oxford University Press, 1986), 76–100.

55. Davis, *Problem of Slavery in Western Culture*, 167–73.

56. Karl Jacoby, "Slaves by Nature? Domestic Animals and Human Slaves," *Slavery & Abolition: A Journal of Slave and Post-Slave Studies* 15 (April 1994): 89–97. This article originated as a paper in my graduate seminar at Yale. Keith Bradley, probably the leading expert on Roman slavery, has drawn on the work of Karl Jacoby and myself to show in a brilliant article that "animalization" was a central feature of even nonracial slavery in antiquity: "Animalizing the Slave: The Truth of Fiction," *Journal of Roman Studies* 90 (2000): 110–25.

57. Jared Diamond, *Guns, Germs, and Steel: The Fates of Human Societies* (New York: Norton, 1999), 157–75.

58. Jacoby, "Slaves by Nature?," 89–97; Stanley L. Engerman, "Labor Incentives and Manumission in Ancient Greek Slavery," in *Essays in Economic Theory, Growth, and Labour Markets: A Festschrift in Honor of E. Drandakis*, ed. George Bitros and Yannis Katsoulacos (Cheltenham, UK: Edward Elgar, 2002), 213–17.

59. Theoretically, Aristotle's ideal slave, like a genetically engineered subhuman, would be as content and submissive as a trained dog, but better capable of understanding his owner's ideas and wishes. Aristotle clearly assumed this would lead to relative harmony between the citizens of the city-state and their compliant force of slave workers. But, even aside from the ways humans have exploited domestic animals, there would still appear to be a flaw in the ideal. If the natural slave became capable of carrying out many of the more skilled and humanly sensitive tasks ordinary slaves were expected to do, they would also be capable of the pride, sensitivity, envy, resentment, and rebellion of human beings. In short, "the problem of slavery" would remain.

60. Henry Highland Garnet, *Walker's Appeal, With a Brief Sketch of his Life. By Henry Highland Garnet. And also Garnet's Address to the Slaves of the United States of America* (New York, 1848), 92.

61. Orlando Patterson, *Slavery and Social Death: A Comparative Study* (Cambridge,

Mass.: Harvard University Press, 1982), 96–97, 299–333. The quotation describing the Sambo stereotype in the American South comes from Stanley Elkins, *Slavery: A Problem in American Institutional and Intellectual Life* (Chicago: University of Chicago Press, 1959), 82. Without implying any biological or hereditary change, Elkins argued that slavery in the United States was so distinctively harsh that it produced a psychological transformation in slaves, similar to that of many inmates in Nazi concentration camps, and thus actually created many Sambos.

62. Patterson, *Slavery and Social Death*, 12, 97, 299–333, 367n41.

63. John Stauffer, *Giants: The Parallel Lives of Frederick Douglass and Abraham Lincoln* (New York: Twelve, Hachette Book Group, 2008), 24.

64. [Frederick Douglass], *Narrative of the Life of Frederick Douglass, an American Slave*, ed. Benjamin Quarles (Cambridge, Mass.: Harvard University Press, 1960), 66–67, 95; Waldo E. Martin, *The Mind of Frederick Douglass* (Chapel Hill: University of North Carolina Press, 1984), 29.

65. Terence Collins, "Phillis Wheatley: The Dark Side of the Poetry," *Phylon*, 36 (1975): 80; James Baldwin, "An Open Letter to My Sister, Angela Davis," *New York Review of Books*, January 7, 1971 (http://www.nybooks.com/articles/10695; James Baldwin, *James Baldwin's Notes of a Native Son* (New York: Bantam Book, 1964), 4.

66. Toni Morrison, "Afterword," *The Bluest Eye* (New York: Alfred A. Knopf, 2000).

67. Barack Obama, *Dreams from My Father: A Story of Race and Inheritance* (New York: Times Books, Random House, 1995), 177–84. The issue of self-esteem is doubtless related to the fact that more than one-half of all black males still drop out of high school.

68. Daryl Michael Scott, *Contempt and Pity: Social Policy and the Image of the Damaged Black Psyche, 1880–1996* (Chapel Hill: University of North Carolina Press, 1997). Some of the social scientists who focused attention on "the damaged black psyche" were in effect repeating the kind of argument made by Leonard Bacon, discussed in the introduction, that the "degradation" of slavery had rendered blacks incapable of freedom in America.

2. THE FIRST EMANCIPATIONS: FREEDOM AND DISHONOR

1. *Chicago Tribune*, January 3, 1893; Frederick Douglass, "Lecture on Haiti," in *The Life and Writings of Frederick Douglass*, ed. Philip S. Foner, vol. 4 (New York: International Publishers, 1955), 484. The speech recorded in the *Chicago Tribune* differs substantially from the text preserved in the Library of Congress and reprinted by Foner; I have drawn on both versions. The *Tribune* noted that the dedication ceremony, which was planned to commemorate the eighty-ninth anniversary of Haitian independence, had not been "advertised to any extent" and was apparently attended by only one exposition official, who rushed to the scene just in time to make a speech. Douglass had been involved in an uphill struggle at the exposition to win some recognition of black achievements. See Elliott M. Rudwick and August Meier, "Black Man in the 'White City': Negroes and the Columbian Exposition, 1893," *Phylon* 26 (Winter 1965): 354–61; Robert W. Rydell, *All the World's a Fair: Visions of Empire at American International Expositions, 1876–1916* (Chicago: University of Chicago Press, 1984), 52–55.

2. Douglass, "Lecture on Haiti," 485–86.

3. Although Waldo E. Martin Jr. emphasizes the centrality of the Haitian Revolution in Douglass's mind, he relies on the 1893 Chicago speech and on some passages in a West Indian Emancipation Day address of August 2, 1858. *The Mind of Frederick Douglass* (Chapel Hill: University of North Carolina Press, 1984), 50–52, 269, 271. But these passages do not appear in the text that was printed in *Frederick Douglass's Paper*, *The New York Times*, the *Rochester Democrat and American*, and other newspapers. John Blassingame's edition of Douglass's speeches and debates from 1841 to 1863 does not

contain a single positive reference to the Haitian Revolution except for occasional praise of Toussaint Louverture. John W. Blassingame, ed., *The Frederick Douglass Papers, Series One, Speeches, Debates, and Interviews,* vols. 1–3 (New Haven, Conn.: Yale University Press, 1979; 1982; 1985). It seems probable that Douglass avoided the subject for tactical reasons, especially when addressing white audiences.

4. Douglass, "Lecture on Haiti," 486; *Chicago Tribune,* Jan. 3, 1893. For colonial sources of North Atlantic sugar imports, see Seymour Drescher, *Econocide: British Slavery in the Era of Abolition* (Pittsburgh: University of Pittsburg Press, 1977), p. 48, table 11.

5. Katherine Plymley Diaries, 1066/1, book 5: 10–15, County Record Office, Shire Hall, Abbey Fossgate, Shrewsbury. Clarkson was in close touch with his coworkers Joseph and Katherine Plymley, and kept them fully up-to-date on abolitionist activities. In March 1792, Katherine noted that the abolitionists were being blamed for the bloodshed in Saint-Domingue; the West Indians were complaining that their own slaves were aware of the abolitionist agitation in England and were already showing signs of unrest, although Joseph had obtained a letter from a planter who affirmed that "the Negroes never were more peaceful & quiet, no disturbances of any kind nor the least appearance of a revolt. . . ." (March 5 to 20, 1792, book 7: 10–11). By November 1793, Clarkson was convinced that the upheavals in the French colonies had convinced even the British merchants that "nothing but ameliorating the condition of the slaves in the other West India islands can save the inhabitants from revolts & insurrections, & the proportion of blacks to whites is now greater than ever" (Nov. 9 to 15, 1793, book 21: 1–2). But Clarkson overestimated this fear and also underestimated the fear on the part of more conservative abolitionists that his sympathies with the French Revolution would harm the cause.

6. This point was stressed by W. E. B. DuBois in his classic study of 1896, *The Suppression of the African Slave-Trade to the United States of America, 1638–1870* (1986; repr., New York: The Social Science Press, 1954), 70–93; it is reaffirmed in more recent works, such as Alfred Nathaniel Hunt, "The Influence of Haiti on the Antebellum South, 1791–1865" (Ph.D. diss., University of Texas, 1975), 127, published as Alfred N. Hunt, *Haiti's Influence on Antebellum America: Slumbering Volcano in the Caribbean* (Baton Rouge: Louisiana State University Press, 1988), 108–10. A slew of new work has sought to trace the influence of the Haitian Revolution and its figures, such as Toussaint, in the United States. A sampling includes Gordon S. Brown, *Toussaint's Clause: The Founding Fathers and the Haitian Revolution* (Jackson: University Press of Mississippi, 2005); Matthew J. Clavin, *Toussaint Louverture and the American Civil War: The Promise and Peril of a Second Haitian Revolution* (Philadelphia: University of Pennsylvania Press, 2009); Maurice Jackson and Jacqueline Bacon, eds., *African Americans and the Haitian Revolution: Selected Essays and Historical Documents* (New York: Routledge, 2010); Jeremy D. Popkin, *You Are All Free: The Haitian Revolution and the Abolition of Slavery* (Cambridge, UK: Cambridge University Press, 2010). Edward Bartlett Rugemer, *The Problem of Emancipation: The Caribbean Roots of the American Civil War* (Baton Rouge: Louisiana State University Press, 2008); Ashli White, *Encountering Revolution: Haiti and the Making of the Early Republic* (Baltimore: Johns Hopkins University Press, 2010).

7. Drescher, *Econocide,* 167–70. On the arming of slaves by the British, and other European powers in the West Indies, see Christopher Leslie Brown and Philip D. Morgan, eds., *Arming Slaves: From Classical Times to the Modern Age* (New Haven, Conn.: Yale University Press, 2006).

8. David Geggus, "The Cost of Pitt's Caribbean Campaigns, 1793–1798," *The Historical Journal* 26, no. 3 (1983): 699–706; Geggus, *Slavery, War, and Revolution: The British Occupation of Saint-Domingue, 1793–1798* (New York: Clarendon Press, 1982), 212, 383. Geggus estimates that from 1793 to 1798 12,695 British troops died in Saint-Domingue, about one-third of the total mortality in the Caribbean theater. His estimate for deaths of seamen ranges from 12,500 to a maximum of 20,000. To this figure he adds 5,740 deaths among foreign regiments in British pay. These estimates have been updated in

Michael Duffy, *Soldiers, Sugar, and Seapower: The British Expeditions to the West Indies and the War Against Revolutionary France* (Oxford, UK: Clarendon Press, 1987), 366.

9. See sources cited in David Brion Davis, *The Problem of Slavery in the Age of Revolution, 1770–1823* (Ithaca, N.Y.: Cornell University Press, 1975), 159–60, 441–43; and Davis, *Slavery and Human Progress* (New York: Oxford University Press, 1984), 173–74, 345; David Geggus, "British Opinion and the Emergence of Haiti, 1791–1805," in *Slavery and British Society, 1776–1846*, ed. James Walvin (Baton Rouge: Louisiana State University Press, 1982), 134–36, 142–49. It is significant that in 1798, when Toussaint finally triumphed over the British in Saint-Domingue, Georgia became the last American state to close off the slave trade and even Southern congressmen agreed to a prohibition of any slave from outside the United States into Mississippi Territory. As a result of the British abolition of the African slave trade and restriction of the intercolonial slave trade, which would otherwise have more than made up for heavy mortality, the slave population of the new sugar colonies, such as Trinidad, Dominica, Saint Vincent, and Guiana, declined by 25.3 percent between 1807 and 1834. B. W. Higman, *Slave Populations of the British Caribbean, 1807–1834* (Baltimore: Johns Hopkins University Press, 1984), 72–85.

10. J. Philmore [pseud.], *Two Dialogues on the Man-Trade* (London, 1760), 54; David Brion Davis, *The Problem of Slavery in Western Culture* (Ithaca, N.Y.: Cornell University Press, 1966), 418. Diderot also defended the right of bondsmen to use any possible means to regain their freedom.

11. The importance for American blacks of the Haitian Revolution has been explored in much recent scholarship, in particular see White, *Encountering Revolution*, 145–46; and the essays in Jackson and Bacon, *African Americans and the Haitian Revolution.*

12. Douglass, "Lecture on Haiti," 486.

13. Eugene D. Genovese, *From Rebellion to Revolution: Afro-American Slave Revolts in the Making of the Modern World* (Baton Rouge: Louisiana State University Press, 1979), xviii–xx, 82–125. Black slaves staged a massive uprising in Iraq as early as 869 CE and were not suppressed for fourteen years. See Davis, *Slavery and Human Progress*, 5–8. But no slaves in history had supplanted their masters and created a state based in principle on universal freedom. Yet, as much as the Haitian Declaration of Independence positioned Haiti among the "world's free peoples," it was clear that its claims of freedom against enslavement were for Haitians. The document officially rejected a "missionary spirit" in spreading the revolution, and shirked from being "the lawgivers of the Caribbean," or letting their "glory consist of troubling the peace of the neighboring islands." The other islands, unlike Haiti, the Declaration claimed, had not been "drenched in the innocent blood of its inhabitants . . . they have no vengeance to claim from the authority that protects them." "The Haitian Declaration of Independence, January 1, 1804," in *Slave Revolution in the Caribbean, 1789–1804: a Brief History with Documents*, ed. Laurent Dubois and John D. Garrigus (Boston: Bedford/St. Martin's, 2006), 188. Despite the assurances in the Declaration, British officials in London and in Jamaica perceived Haiti as a troubling precedent, and worried that a spirit of rebellion would emanate from the island. Julia Gaffield, "Haiti and Jamaica in the Remaking of the Early Nineteenth-Century Atlantic World," *William and Mary Quarterly* 69, no. 3 (July 1, 2012): 583–614. And even for Haitians, the ideal of universal freedom was circumscribed in the new republic—there was no right of public assembly or of association, and the Catholic faith remained the state religion, not to mention the aggressive disciplinary regime set up within the constitution aimed at shoving the new republic back onto the road to prosperity. Carolyn E. Fick, "The Saint-Domingue Slave Revolution and the Unfolding of Independence, 1791–1804," in *The World of the Haitian Revolution*, ed. David Patrick Geggus and Norman Fiering (Bloomington: Indiana University Press, 2009), 177, 183–84.

14. Orlando Patterson has argued that the "Sambo" stereotype is "an ideological

imperative of all systems of slavery, from the most primitive to the most advanced," and is "simply an elaboration of the notion that the slave is quintessentially a person without honor," totally lacking in "manhood." While rightly insisting, contrary to Stanley Elkins, that slaves retained "the irrepressible yearning for dignity and recognition," Patterson seems to underestimate the degree to which many oppressed peoples internalize the standards and values of their oppressors. *Slavery and Social Death: A Comparative Study* (Cambridge, Mass.: Harvard University Press, 1982), 96–97. Michael Walzer, drawing on centuries of commentary on Exodus, emphasizes the extreme difficulty of transforming slaves into freemen (the lesson of the forty years in the wilderness), and holds that in Egypt the bulk of slaves "admitted into their souls the degradation of slavery." He adds, however, that at least some of the Israelite slaves were ready to fight and thought of themselves as free or potentially free. *Exodus and Revolution* (New York: Basic Books, 1985), 43–66. The tension between the slave's internalized degradation and his "irrepressible yearning for dignity and recognition" has been central to the continuing debate over both slavery and the human condition; it was precisely because so many slaves degraded themselves in order to please their masters that the example of Haiti was so inspiring to blacks like Denmark Vesey and David Walker.

15. There has always been confusion and controversy over the terms used to designate persons of African and mixed African and European ancestry. In the United States the term "Negro" usually included "colored" persons of mixed ancestry (usually lumped together as "mulattoes"), and there was no widely accepted terminology to denote the varying degrees of racial intermixture or phenotypic distinctions such as lighter skin and Caucasoid hair. In the Caribbean, usage varied from one island to another and was never entirely consistent. In the French colonies, the legal category "free men of color" (*hommes de couleur libres* or *gens de couleur*) included free blacks; some British officials extended the term "free colored" to include blacks as well as browns. But in the Caribbean, both whites and freedmen drew sharp distinctions based on color and accorded higher status to persons with diminishing degrees of African ancestry. As far as possible I will follow the usage that best fits the region being discussed. When referring to the United States, I will use the term "black" or "African American" in general, except where the context indicates a more specific phenotype. When discussing the West Indies, "free coloreds," "*gens de couleur,*" and "*anciens libres*" will usually refer to people of mixed racial ancestry but will sometimes include, especially in Saint-Domingue, free blacks. Following the practice of recent historians of the Caribbean, I will use the convenient term "freedmen" to refer to African Americans of both sexes, whether colored or black, who were either manumitted or born free.

16. Lyman L. Johnson, "Manumission in Colonial Buenos Aires, 1776–1810," *The Hispanic American Historical Review* 59, no. 2 (May 1, 1979): 261. Frank "Trey" Proctor III, "Gender and the Manumission of Slaves in New Spain," *Hispanic American Historical Review* 86, no. 2 (May 2006): 309–36.

17. Roger Norman Buckley, *Slaves in Red Coats: The British West India Regiments, 1795–1815* (New Haven. Conn.: Yale University Press, 1979), 79.

18. Patterson, *Slavery and Social Death*, chapters 8–10.

19. For a useful comparative survey, see David W. Cohen and Jack P. Greene, eds., *Neither Slave nor Free: The Freedmen of African Descent in the Slave Societies of the New World* (Baltimore: Johns Hopkins University Press, 1972).

20. Elsa V. Goveia, *Slave Society in the British Leeward Islands at the End of the Eighteenth Century* (New Haven, Conn.: Yale University Press, 1965), 222; Ira Berlin, *Slaves Without Masters: The Free Negro in the Antebellum South* (New York: Oxford University Press, 1974), 89, 95–96. For the evolving responses by white refugees to the causes of the Haitian Revolution while in the United States, see Ashli White, "The Saint-Dominguan Refu-

gees and American Distinctiveness in the Early Years of the Haitian Revolution," in Geggus and Fiering,*The World of the Haitian Revolution*, 248–58.

21. Robert Stein, "The Free Men of Colour and the Revolution in Saint Domingue, 1789–1792," *Histoire sociale—Social History* 14 (May 1981): 7–28; Davis, *Problem of Slavery in the Age of Revolution*, 137–48.

22. Jerome S. Handler, *The Unappropriated People: Freedmen in the Slave Society of Barbados* (Baltimore: Johns Hopkins University Press, 1974), 80; Berlin, *Slaves Without Masters*, 191.

23. David Geggus, "The Enigma of Jamaica in the 1790s: New Light on the Causes of Slave Rebellions," *William and Mary Quarterly*, 3rd series (April 1987); 288–99. For Toussaint's status as a freedman, see note 53, infra.

24. Gad J. Heuman, *Between Black and White: Race, Politics, and the Free Coloreds in Jamaica, 1792–1865* (Westport, Conn.: Greenwood Press, 1981), 24; Richard B. Sheridan, "The Maroons of Jamaica, 1730–1830: Livelihood, Demography and Health," *Slavery and Abolition: A Journal of Comparative Studies* 6, no. 3 (Dec. 1985): 152–70; Geggus, "Enigma of Jamaica," 275–85; Ellen Gibson Wilson, *The Loyal Blacks* (New York: Capricorn Books, 1976), 393–97.

25. Benjamin Quarles, *The Negro in the American Revolution* (Chapel Hill: University of North Carolina Press, 1961), 14–18, 51–67; Donald L. Robinson, *Slavery in the Structure of American Politics, 1765–1820* (New York: Harcourt Brace Jovanovich, 1971), 114–21; Phillip Morgan and Andrew Jackson O'Shaughnessy, "Arming Slaves in the American Revolution," in Brown and Morgan, *Arming Slaves: From Classical Times to the Modern Age* (New Haven: Yale University Press, 2006), 180–208.

26. Buckley, *Slaves in Red Coats*, passim. Also see the comparative essay of Christopher Leslie Brown, "The Arming of Slaves in Comparative Perspective," in Brown and Morgan, eds., *Arming Slaves*, 330–53.

27. Cohen and Greene, *Neither Slave nor Free*; Berlin, *Slaves Without Masters*; Herbert S. Klein and Clotilde Andrade Paiva, "Freedmen in a Slave Economy: Minas Gerais in 1831," *Journal of Social History* 29, no. 4 (July 1, 1996): 933–62. Jerome S. Handler and John T. Pohlmann, "Slave Manumissions and Freedmen in Seventeenth-Century Barbados," *William and Mary Quarterly* 41, no. 3 (July 1, 1984): 390–408.

28. Population statistics for the early nineteenth century are usually unreliable, especially for the Caribbean, and there are many discrepancies in the censuses and other standard sources. I have used the tables in Higman, *Slave Populations*, 77; B. W. Higman, *Slave Population and Economy in Jamaica, 1807–1834* (Cambridge, UK: Cambridge University Press, 1976), 61–62; Berlin, *Slaves Without Masters*, 46–47; Cohen and Greene, eds., *Neither Slave nor Free*, 4, 10, 194; Handler, *Unappropriated People*, 18–19; Heuman, *Between Black and White*, 7–8; Orlando Patterson, *The Sociology of Slavery: An Analysis of the Origins, Development and Structure of Negro Slave Society in Jamaica* (London: MacGibbon & Kee, 1967), 95–97; Bureau of the Census, *Historical Statistics of the United States, Colonial Times to 1970*, 2 vols. (Washington, D.C.: U.S. Printing Office, 1975), 1:22–36; Bureau of the Census, *Negro Population, 1790–1915* (Washington, D.C.: Government Printing Office, 1918), 53–57.

29. Douglas Hall, "Jamaica," in Cohen and Greene, *Neither Slave nor Free*, 196; Edward Brathwaite, *The Development of Creole Society in Jamaica, 1770–1820* (Oxford, UK: Clarendon Press, 1971), 167–75. For the criteria used in listing color in the West Indian slave registrations from 1813 to 1832, see Higman, *Slave Populations*, 19–21.

30. Frederick P. Bowser, "Colonial Spanish America," in Cohen and Greene, *Neither Slave nor Free*, 55; Philip D. Curtin, *Two Jamaicas: The Role of Ideas in a Tropical Colony, 1830–1865* (Cambridge, Mass.: Harvard University Press, 1955), 44–45.

31. See especially Carl N. Degler, *Neither Black nor White: Slavery and Race Relations in Brazil and the United States* (New York: Macmillan, 1971). Stuart B. Schwartz, "The Manumission of Slaves in Colonial Brazil: Bahia, 1684–1745," *The Hispanic American Historical Review* 54, no. 4 (Nov. 1, 1974): 603–35.

32. White, *Encountering Revolution*, 87–123. See also Larry Koger, *Black Slaveowners: Free Black Slave Masters in South Carolina, 1790–1860* (Columbia: University of South Carolina, 1994); Juliet E. K. Walker, "Racism, Slavery, and Free Enterprise: Black Entrepreneurship in the United States Before the Civil War," *The Business History Review* 60, no. 3 (Autumn 1986): 343–82; Thomas N. Ingersoll, "Free Blacks in a Slave Society: New Orleans, 1718–1812," *William and Mary Quarterly* 48, no. 2 (April 1, 1991): 173–200.

33. Michael P. Johnson and James L. Roark, *Black Masters: A Free Family of Color in the Old South* (New York: W. W. Norton, 1984), 3–29, 127–29.

34. Handler, *Unappropriated People*, 98–99, 190–94, 201–04.

35. Berlin, *Slaves Without Masters*, passim; Barbara Jeanne Fields, *Slavery and Freedom on the Middle Ground: Maryland during the Nineteenth Century* (New Haven, Conn.: Yale University Press, 1985), 29–32, and passim.

36. In the United States, "free black" has replaced "free Negro," even though the latter term more clearly indicated people of mixed black and white descent. In the Caribbean and elsewhere, "free colored" remains the appropriate term for a population in which people of mixed descent predominated.

37. Berlin, *Slaves Without Masters*, 46–49, 136–37; Bureau of the Census, *Historical Statistics*, 1: 8–9, 24–36; Bureau of the Census, *Negro Population*, 53–57; Fields, *Slavery and Freedom*, 1–15. Leonard P. Curry, *The Free Black in Urban America, 1800–1850: The Shadow of the Dream* (Chicago: University of Chicago Press, 1981), 1–14.

38. Yvan Debbasch, *Couleur et liberté: le jeu du critère ethnique dans un ordre juridique esclavagiste*, vol. I: *L'affranchi dans les possessions françaises de la Caraïbe, 1635–1833* (Paris: Dalloz, 1967), 80; Geggus, *Slavery, War, and Revolution*, 405n3; Cohen and Greene, *Neither Slave nor Free*, 4, 6, 10, 194, 218–20; Heuman, *Between Black and White*, 7. Popkin, *You Are All Free*, 12.

39. Berlin, *Slaves Without Masters*, 46–47, 136–37; Richard S. Dunn, "Black Society in the Chesapeake, 1776–1810," in *Slavery and Freedom in the Age of the American Revolution*, ed. Ira Berlin and Ronald Hoffman (Charlottesville: University Press of Virginia, 1983), 74–82. In Virginia the proportion of blacks who were free reached 10 percent in 1840; in Louisiana the proportion declined from 18 percent in 1810 to 13.2 percent in 1820 and 5.3 percent in 1860. In Maryland the figure rose gradually to 49.1 percent in 1860, but there was a large difference between the northern and southern counties of the state. In Jamaica the proportion of blacks who were free rose from 3 percent in 1800 to something over 10 percent in 1834. In Barbados the comparable increase was from 3 percent to over 7 percent.

40. Quarles, *Negro in the American Revolution*, 39, 43–45; Sidney Kaplan, *The Black Presence in the Era of the American Revolution, 1770–1800* (Greenwich, Conn.: Greenwood Press, 1973), 11–14, 26–27, 186–90; Arthur Zilversmit, *The First Emancipation: The Abolition of Slavery in the North* (Chicago: University of Chicago Press, 1967), 101–02, 110–17; Winthrop D. Jordan, *White Over Black: American Attitudes Toward the Negro, 1550–1812* (Chapel Hill: University of North Carolina Press, 1968), 291; William Alan Muraskin, *Middle-Class Blacks in a White Society: Prince Hall Freemasonry in America* (Berkeley: University of California Press, 1975), 31–34; Floyd J. Miller, *The Search for a Black Nationality: Black Emigration and Colonization, 1787–1863* (Urbana: University of Illinois Press, 1975), 3–6; Sheldon H. Harris, *Paul Cuffe: Black America and the African Return* (New York: Simon & Schuster, 1972), 159–61.

41. Jordan, *White Over Black*, 328–30, 409; Heuman, *Between Black and White*, 23–24; Annals of Congress, 6th Cong., 1st Sess. (1800), 229–45. The debate took place on January 2 and 3, 1800. After much dispute over wording, the motion to refer the petition to a committee was passed but amended with the following sentence: "And that the parts of the said petition which invite Congress to legislate upon subjects from which the General Government is precluded by the Constitution, have a tendency to create disquiet and jealousy, and ought therefore to receive no encouragement or

countenance from this House." George Thatcher argued that the petition contained no such propositions; he cast the only negative vote against the amendment.

42. Geggus, *Slavery, War, and Revolution,* 6; Robert I. Rotberg, with Christopher K. Clague, *Haiti: The Politics of Squalor* (Boston: Houghton Mifflin, 1971), 32.

43. Debbasch, *Couleur et liberté,* 53–59, 97–98, 118–22; Pierre de Vaissière, *Saint-Domingue: la société et la vie créoles sous l'ancien régime, 1629–1789* (Paris: Perrin, 1909), 221–24; C. L. R. James, *The Black Jacobins: Toussaint L'Ouverture and the San Domingo Revolution,* 2nd rev. ed. (New York: Vintage Books, 1963), 36–42; Geggus, *Slavery, War, and Revolution,* 20–22; John D. Garrigus, *Before Haiti: Race and Citizenship in French Saint-Domingue* (New York: Palgrave Macmillan, 2006), 40–41; Laurent Dubois, *Avengers of the New World: The Story of the Haitian Revolution* (Cambridge, Mass: Belknap Press of Harvard University Press, 2004), 60–71.

44. Davis, *Problem of Slavery in the Age of Revolution,* 110–12; Gabriel Debien, *Les colons de Saint-Domingue et la révolution: essai sur le club Massiac, Août 1789-Août 1792* (Paris: Librairie Armand Colin, 1953), 63–78, 140–52; Debbasch, *Couleur et liberté,* 134–50.

45. Mitchell Bennett Garrett, *The French Colonial Question, 1789–1791* (Ann Arbor, Mich.: G. Wahr, 1918), 19–26; Debbasch, *Couleur et liberté,* 123–24, 149–51. Dubois, *Avengers of the New World,* 75–82.

46. Ruth F. Necheles, *The Abbé Grégoire, 1787–1831: The Odyssey of an Egalitarian* (Westport, Conn.: Greenwood Press, 1971), 53–66; Davis, *Problem of Slavery in the Age of Revolution,* 111; Debbasch, *Couleur et liberté,* 154–55.

47. [Henri-Baptiste] Grégoire, *Mémoire en faveur des gens de couleur ou sang-mêlés de St.-Domingue, et des autres Isles françoises de l'Amérique, adressé à l'Assemblée Nationale* (Paris, 1789), 34–35. According to the abolitionists' journal, *Patriote françois,* it was the freedmen's enemies who constantly confused freedmen's rights with slave emancipation; the freedmen sympathized with the plight of the slaves but fully understood the danger of innovative action. *Patriote françois,* no. 594 (March 25, 1791): 319–20.

48. Clarkson told the Plymleys that Ogé had returned to Saint-Domingue to report the National Assembly's actions "to his constituents," that he had then been attacked by the whites and had been treacherously given up by the Spaniards after he had fled to the Spanish part of the island. Both Clarkson and Grégoire defended Ogé as a martyr who had fought for the freedmen's legitimate rights. Katherine Plymley Diaries, Feb. 9 to 24, 1792, book 5: 13–14; *Archives parlementaires* 25 (May 11, 1791): 737–41. See also Thomas O. Ott, *The Haitian Revolution, 1789–1804* (Knoxville: University of Tennessee Press, 1973), 36–39. But, as John Garrigus has shown, colonial whites had good reasons to think that the abolitionists had a hand, at least, in Ogé's rebellion. For example, two ceramic (presumably Wedgwood) medallions depicting a chained African were found in Ogé's bags by colonial authorities, likely a gift from Clarkson, which seemed ample proof of premeditation and an abolitionist conspiracy. Garrigus argues, however, that Ogé's preeminent revolutionary act was to bring the new Parisian idea of militiaman-as-citizen to Saint-Domingue, forcing the colonial authorities either to bring more regulars to replace the free coloreds, or to extend citizenship across the color line. John Garrigus, " 'Thy coming fame, Ogé! is sure': New Evidence on Ogé's Revolt (1790) and the Beginnings of the Haitian Revolution," in *Assumed Identities: Race and Identity in the New World,* ed. John Garrigus and Christopher Morris (College Station: Texas A&M University Press, 2010), 37–38.

49. Davis, *Problem of Slavery in the Age of Revolution,* 140–41; Debbasch, *Couleur et liberté,* 172–82; Julien Raymond, *Réflexions sur les véritables causes des troubles et des désastres de nos colonies, notamment sur ceux de Saint-Domingue* (Paris, 1793), 33–35; James, *Black Jacobins,* 72–75. For the rebellious, buccaneer spirit of Saint-Domingue's whites, see Charles Frostin, *Les révoltes blanches à Saint-Domingue aux XVIIe et XVIIIe siècles* (Paris: l'École, 1975).

50. Popkin, *You Are All Free,* 36–37.

51. Davis, *Problem of Slavery in the Age of Revolution*, 142–44; Debbasch, *Couleur et liberté*, 61–62, 184–86; Theodore Lothrop Stoddard, *The French Revolution in San Domingo* (Boston: Houghton Mifflin, 1914), 119–27; Debien, *Les colons de Saint-Domingue*, 262–90.

52. Geggus, *Slavery, War, and Revolution*, 122. See also Genovese, *From Rebellion to Revolution*, 87–88; and Ott, *Haitian Revolution*, 47–52.

53. J. P. Martin [Abraham Bishop], *American Museum* 12 (Nov. 1792): 299–300; Davis, *Problem of Slavery in the Age of Revolution*, 327; Tim [*sic*] Matthewson, "Abraham Bishop, 'The Rights of Black Men,' and the American Reaction to the Haitian Revolution," *Journal of Negro History* 67 (Summer 1982): 148–53. Matthewson prints the text of Bishop's articles, which appeared originally in the Boston *Argus* in November and December 1791. White, *Encountering Revolution*, 57.

54. Timothy M. Matthewson, "George Washington's Policy Toward the Haitian Revolution," *Diplomatic History* 3 (Summer 1979): 321–36; Donald R. Hickey, "America's Response to the Slave Revolt in Haiti, 1791–1806," *Journal of the Early Republic* 2 (Winter 1982): 364–65; Hunt, "Influence of Haiti," 27–30. Hamilton did object to subsidizing French radicalism with funds set aside to pay the American debt to France. The Washington administration would probably have given much more aid to the French planters if it had not had to deal with the intrigue of the French ministers, Jean-Baptiste de Ternant and Edmond Genêt. The American army, as Matthewson points out, was preoccupied with hostile Indians on the western frontier.

55. *Columbian Centinel*, Sept. 2, 1791, 10; Geggus, "British Opinion," 124. Some antislavery papers attributed the revolt to the slave system and used it as an argument against the continuation of the slave trade.

56. Davis, *Problem of Slavery in the Age of Revolution*, 146–47; J. Saintoyant, *La colonisation française pendant la révolution, 1789–1799*, 2 vols. (Paris: La Renaissance du Livre, 1930), 2:115–36; Geggus, *Slavery, War, and Revolution*, 42–65; James, *Black Jacobins*, 126–29; Ott, *Haitian Revolution*, 69–72; Popkin, *You Are All Free*, 376.

57. Geggus, *Slavery, War, and Revolution*, 39–41, 68, 70, 105, 114, 126.

58. Ibid., 84–85, 124–29; James, *Black Jacobins*, 164–66.

59. Geggus, *Slavery, War, and Revolution*, 150–61, 182–84, 313–23, 388–90. Many of the blacks who joined the British evacuation were over sixty, under fifteen, or disabled.

60. Gabriel Debien, Jean Fouchard, and Marie Antoinette Menier, "Toussaint Louverture avant 1789, légendes et réalités," *Conjonction, Revue Franco-Haitienne* 134 (June–July 1977), 67–77.

61. Mats Lundahl, "Toussaint L'Ouverture and the War Economy of Saint-Domingue, 1796–1802," *Slavery and Abolition: A Journal of Comparative Studies* 6 (Sept. 1985): 130.

62. Constitution de la colonie française de Saint-Domingue, du 17 Aout 1801 (29 Thermidor an 9), reprinted in *La révolution française et l'abolition de l'esclavage* (Paris, n.d.), 11, no. 18. Though Toussaint had conquered Spanish Santo Domingo and won complete power over the island, he refrained from proclaiming independence from France, partly because of waning British and American support. Ott, *Haitian Revolution*, 119–20.

63. Ott, *Haitian Revolution*, 139–61. David Geggus estimates that the French sent a total of 44,000 troops to Saint-Domingue (private communication to author). Further work on estimating the numbers on both sides of the conflict has been done by Phillipe Girard. Girard puts the number of French soldiers sent to Saint-Domingue at 43,800, but "only 7,000 made it to the pontoons of Jamaica." The death toll topped 50,000, and even more if you add the people of color who fought for France. And these losses are staggering compared to the 10,000 French deaths early in the Haitian Revolution. Bonaparte, Girard notes, was utterly oblivious to loss of life and treasure in his attempt to restore the colony to absolute French control. As for the Haitians, the numbers are even more sobering. Girard notes that "there is good reason to believe that the coun-

try's population which had neared six hundred thousand in 1789, had dropped by half by 1804, and that the Leclerc expedition itself is responsible for the deaths of one hundred thousand Haitians. The rebellious slaves of 1791 had pledged to live free or die; in the end, they did both in roughly equal numbers." Philippe R. Girard, *The Slaves Who Defeated Napoleon: Toussaint Louverture and the Haitian War of Independence, 1801–1804* (Tuscaloosa: University of Alabama Press, 2011), 343–44.

64. James, *Black Jacobins*, 322–62; Stoddard, *The French Revolution in San Domingo*, 303–46; Ott, *Haitian Revolution*, 170–82.

65. Quoted in Geggus, "British Opinion," 136.

66. One should note, however, that in 1816, Alexandre Pétion furnished arms and supplies to Simón Bolívar on the secret condition that Bolívar would promote the cause of slave emancipation in South America. Although Bolívar offered freedom to slaves willing to fight the royalists, at the Congress of Panama in 1825, from which Haiti was excluded, he called for ruling-class unity in freeing Latin America from the fear of "this tremendous monster which has devoured the island of Santo Domingo." Quoted in David Nicholls, *From Dessalines to Duvalier: Race, Colour and National Independence in Haiti* (Cambridge, UK: Cambridge University Press, 1980), 63. Also, more recent scholarship has looked at the more expansive diplomatic vision of Dessalines, in particular, and his attempt to maintain links in diplomacy, labor, and capital across the Atlantic world. Philippe R. Girard, "Jean-Jacques Dessalines and the Atlantic System: A Reappraisal," *William and Mary Quarterly* 69, no. 3 (July 1, 2012): 549–82.

67. Geggus, "Enigma of Jamaica," 282–84, 292–99. David Geggus, "Slave Rebellion During the Age of Revolution," in *Curaçao and the French and Haitian Revolutions,* ed. Wim Klooster and Gert Oostindie (Leiden: KITLV, 2011). Geggus presents convincing evidence that British slaves were aware of the strength of colonial military garrisons during the prolonged period of warfare with France and that insurrections were most likely when the garrisons were reduced.

68. Michael Craton, *Testing the Chains: Resistance to Slavery in the British West Indies* (Ithaca, N.Y.: Cornell University Press, 1982), 260–61; Hunt, "Influence of Haiti," 39, 41–78, 114, 118, 123–29; Berlin, *Slaves Without Masters*, 124–25.

69. Berlin, *Slaves Without Masters*, 38–41; Hunt, "Influence of Haiti," pp. 128–30. Hunt reports that in Virginia some ads for runaways said that the fugitive might try to head for the West Indies (243n49).

70. Matt D. Childs, *The 1812 Aponte Rebellion in Cuba and the Struggle against Atlantic Slavery*, Kindle Edition (Chapel Hill: University of North Carolina Press, 2006), loc. 2522–2555.

71. Gwendolyn Midlo Hall, *Social Control in Slave Plantation Societies: A Comparison of St. Domingue and Cuba* (Baltimore: Johns Hopkins University Press, 1971), 55, 125–26; Brathwaite, *Development of Creole Society*, 246–48, 251–59; Mavis Christine Campbell, *The Dynamics of Change in a Slave Society: A Sociopolitical History of the Free Coloreds of Jamaica, 1800–1865* (Cranbury, N.J.: Fairleigh Dickinson University Press, 1976), 32–33; Heuman, *Between Black and White*, 33–41. In 1829, the Colonial Office extended legal equality to all freedmen in the crown colonies; hoping to unite the entire free population against slave emancipation, the Jamaican Assembly granted equal civil rights in 1830. See also Childs, *1812 Aponte Rebellion in Cuba*.

72. Robert S. Starobin, ed., *Denmark Vesey: The Slave Conspiracy of 1822* (Englewood Cliffs, N.J.: Prentice Hall, 1970); Richard C. Wade, "The Vesey Plot: A Reconsideration," *Journal of Southern History* 30, no. 2 (1964): 143–61; John Lofton, *Denmark Vesey's Revolt: The Slave Plot That Lit a Fuse to Fort Sumter* (Kent, Ohio: Kent State University Press, 1983); Robert L. Paquette and Douglas R. Egerton, "Of Facts and Fables: New Light on the Denmark Vesey Affair," *The South Carolina Historical Magazine* 105, no. 1 (Jan. 1, 2004): 8–48; James O'Neil Spady, "Power and Confession: On the Credibility of the Earliest Reports of the Denmark Vesey Slave Conspiracy," *William and Mary Quarterly* 68, no. 2 (April 1, 2011): 287–304.

73. Julie Winch, "The Leaders of Philadelphia's Black Community, 1787–1848" (Ph.D. diss., Bryn Mawr College, 1982), 12–13, 235; Berlin, *Slaves Without Masters*, 314–15; David Walker's *Appeal, in Four Articles; Together with a Preamble, to the Coloured Citizens of the World, but in Particular, and Very Expressly, to Those of the United States of America*, ed. Charles M. Wiltse (1829; repr., New York: Hill and Wang, 1965), 20–21; Iain McCalman, "Anti-Slavery and Ultra-Radicalism in Early Nineteenth-Century England: The Case of Robert Wedderburn," *Slavery and Abolition: A Journal of Comparative Studies* 7 (Sept. 1986): 100–115. Walker associated Haiti with ancient Carthage and with "that mighty son of Africa, HANNIBAL," but the lesson he drew from both histories was that internal division led to the slaughter of blacks by their "natural enemies."

74. Geggus, "British Opinion," 137–39.

75. Brown, *Toussaint's Clause*, 151.

76. Ibid., 140–49; Geggus, "Haiti and the Abolitionists: Opinion, Propaganda and International Politics in Britain and France, 1804–1838," in *Abolition and Its Aftermath: The Historical Context, 1790–1916*, ed. David Richardson (London: F. Cass, 1986), 113–17. While I have borrowed extensively from Geggus's masterly studies, I am skeptical about his conclusion that the British abolitionists won the argument regarding Haitian violence. They may have persuaded the public that emancipation in the British colonies would not lead to Haitian-like massacres, but they hardly overturned the dominant images of the Haitian Revolution. In the 1830s, French officials, American observers, and even Thomas Fowell Buxton expressed surprise that British emancipation proceeded without undue violence.

77. Nicholls, *From Dessalines to Duvalier*, 65.

78. See especially Geggus, "Haiti and the Abolitionists," 117–37; Hunt, "Influence of Haiti," 166–83.

79. See, for example, *The Liberator*, April 25, 1845, 67. See also White, *Encountering Revolution*, 207–11.

80. Nicholls, *From Dessalines to Duvalier*, 45; Pompée Valentin de Vastey, *Réflexions sur une lettre de Mazères, ex-colon français* (Cap-Henri, Haiti, 1816), 14. Contrary to Nicholls, Vastey's text does not explicitly point to Haiti "as the first fruit of a great colonial revolution"; he rather quotes Rousseau and asserts that all Europe repudiates the racist aspersions of the former French colonists.

3. COLONIZING BLACKS, PART I: MIGRATION AND DEPORTATION

1. E. W. Blyden to the Rev. John B. Pinney, July 29, 1859, *New York-Colonization Journal* 9 (Oct. 1859): 3. Delany had bitterly denounced the American Colonization Society and belittled Liberia for more than twenty years. When greeted with enthusiasm by the Liberian people, however, he dramatically changed his views. See Richard Blackett, "Martin R. Delany and Robert Campbell: Black Americans in Search of an African Colony," *Journal of Negro History* 62 (Jan. 1977): 15. It should be noted that the ACS, which had always publicly disavowed coercion, had also come to accept the black emigrationists' goal of limited, selective emigration.

2. More recent works on the ACS, which have shed light on the movement's complexity while still taking a critical view, include Beverly C. Tomek, *Colonization and Its Discontents: Emancipation, Emigration, and Antislavery in Antebellum Pennsylvania* (New York: New York University Press, 2011); Nicholas Guyatt, " 'The Outskirts of Our Happiness': Race and the Lure of Colonization in the Early Republic," *Journal of American History* 95 (March 2009): 986–1011; Eric Burns, *Slavery and the Peculiar Solution: A History of the American Colonization Society* (Gainesville: University Press of Florida, 2005); Kenneth C. Barnes, *Journey of Hope: The Back-to-Africa Movement in Arkansas in the Late 1800s* (Chapel Hill: University of North Carolina Press, 2004); Lamin O. Sanneh, *Abolitionists Abroad: American Blacks and the Making of Modern West Africa* (Cambridge, Mass.: Harvard University Press, 2006).

3. 2 Kings 17. Except where otherwise indicated, biblical quotations are from the Jewish Publication Society translation, *Tanakh: A New Translation of the Holy Scriptures According to the Traditional Hebrew Text* (Philadelphia: Jewish Publication Society, 1985); John Bright, *A History of Israel*, 3rd ed. (Philadelphia: Westminster Press, 1981), 269–76; Hayim Tadmor, "The Period of the First Temple, the Babylonian Exile and the Restoration," in *A History of the Jewish People*, ed. H. H. Ben-Sasson (Cambridge, Mass.: Harvard University Press, 1976), 133–38; William W. Hallo and William Kelly Simpson, *The Ancient Near East: A History* (New York: Harcourt Brace Jovanovich, 1971), 131–38. The prophet Hosea's rendering of God's castigation of Israel's sins and threats of terrible punishment became a central homiletic theme in Jacobean England and a main source of the so-called puritan Jeremiad. Michael McGiffert, "God's Controversy with Jacobean England," *American Historical Review* 88 (December 1983): 1151–74.

4. Michael Walzer, *Exodus and Revolution* (New York: Basic Books, 1985), 36–37, 73.

5. Numbers 16:12–13.

6. Gary B. Nash, *Forging Freedom: The Formation of Philadelphia's Black Community, 1720–1840* (Cambridge, Mass.: Harvard University Press, 1988), 189–90.

7. George B. Cheever, *The Guilt of Slavery and the Crime of Slaveholding, Demonstrated from the Hebrew and Greek Scriptures* (Boston: John P. Jewett, 1860), 191–95.

8. Exodus 14:12.

9. Daniel Coker, *Journal of Daniel Coker* (Baltimore: Edward J. Coale, 1820), 15–17, 27, 31; Tom W. Shick, *Behold the Promised Land: A History of Afro-American Settler Society in Nineteenth-Century Liberia* (Baltimore: Johns Hopkins University Press, 1980), 22; Robert A. Hill, ed., *The Marcus Garvey and Universal Negro Improvement Association Papers*, vol. 5 (Berkeley: University of California Press, 1986), 291. John B. Russwurm, the Bowdoin College graduate who edited *Freedom's Journal* and then emigrated to Liberia in 1829, also compared himself to Moses and referred to the Americo-Liberians as Israelites. Penelope Campbell, *Maryland in Africa: The Maryland State Colonization Society, 1831–1857* (Urbana: University of Illinois Press, 1971), 172. Although Garvey denied that he had ever called himself a Moses, he referred continually to the biblical Exodus and to Jewish history in general, including the rise of Zionism. When quoting letters of Coker and other historical figures, I have retained the spelling and punctuation of the specified text, without inserting *sic*.

10. McGiffert, "God's Controversy with Jacobean England," 1153, 1157. McGiffert, who sees John Downame's Lectures upon the Four First Chapters of the Prophecy of Hosea (1608) as a crucial preparatory step toward the revolution of the saints, disputes the distinctions that Sacvan Bercovitch (see note 11, infra) and others have made between the themes of American and European Jeremiads.

11. Sacvan Bercovitch, *The American Jeremiad* (Madison: University of Wisconsin Press, 1978); Jan Shipps, *Mormonism: The Story of a New Religious Tradition* (Urbana: University of Illinois Press, 1985); Edwin S. Redkey, *Black Exodus: Black Nationalist and Back-to-Africa Movements, 1890–1910* (New Haven, Conn.: Yale University Press, 1969); Nell Irvin Painter, *Exodusters: Black Migration to Kansas after Reconstruction* (New York: Alfred A. Knopf, 1977); Edmund David Cronon, *Black Moses: The Story of Marcus Garvey and the Universal Negro Improvement Association* (Madison: University of Wisconsin Press, 1969); Hollis R. Lynch, *Edward Wilmot Blyden: Pan-Negro Patriot, 1832–1913* (New York: Oxford University Press, 1970), 117, 121. In his two-volume history of religious refugees from antiquity to the 1960s, Frederick A. Norwood pictures Exodus as the paradigmatic event. *Strangers and Exiles: A History of Religious Refugees*, 2 vols. (Nashville: Abingdon Press, 1969). But for Christians, the Mosaic Exodus could also prefigure or "typify" a decisive change in an individual's life; for example, this is the way John Bunyan interpreted the publication of his own *Grace Abounding to the Chief of Sinners*. Linda H. Peterson, *Victorian Autobiography: The Tradition of Self-Interpretation* (New Haven, Conn.: Yale University Press, 1986), 103.

12. Walzer, *Exodus and Revolution*, 16–17, 120, 134; Revelation 21:1; 2 Peter 3:13.

13. Walzer, *Exodus and Revolution*, 77–80, 115, 120–22; Jeremiah 42–44. Egypt fought together with Judah against the Babylonian invasion and even tried to break the Babylonian siege of Jerusalem.

14. Jeremiah 31:31–34; Walzer, *Exodus and Revolution*, 115–20; Bright, *History of Israel*, 269–76, 350; Peter R. Ackroyd, *Exile and Restoration: A Study of Hebrew Thought of the Sixth Century B.C.* (London,: S.C.M. Press, 1968), 17–24.

15. Walzer, *Exodus and Revolution*, pp. 119–20. It should be stressed that Western perfectionism and utopianism also drew on Classical and Eastern sources.

16. Ibid., 122–25.

17. Abraham Lincoln was a notable exception. In a speech eulogizing Henry Clay and praising the goals of the American Colonization Society, Lincoln warned, "Pharaoh's country was cursed with plagues, and his hosts were drowned in the Red Sea for striving to retain a captive people who had already served them more than four hundred years. May like disasters never befall us! If as the friends of colonization hope, the present and coming generations of our countrymen shall by any means, succeed in freeing our land from the dangerous presence of slavery; and, at the same time, in restoring a captive people to their long-lost father-land, with bright prospects for the future; and this too, so gradually, that neither races nor individuals shall have suffered by the change, it will indeed be a glorious consummation." "Eulogy on Henry Clay," July 6, 1852, in *The Collected Works of Abraham Lincoln*, ed. Roy P. Basler (New Brunswick, N.J.: Rutgers University Press, 1953), pp. 2, 132.

18. Thomas Jefferson, *Autobiography*, in *The Life and Selected Writings of Thomas Jefferson*, ed. Adrienne Koch and William Peden (New York: Modern Library, 1944), 51; [Jesse Burton Harrison], *Review of the Slave Question, Extracted from the "American Quarterly Review," Dec. 1832; Based on the Speech of Th. Marshall, of Fauquier: Showing that Slavery is the Essential Hindrance to the Prosperity of the Slave-Holding States . . .* (Richmond: T. W. White, 1833), 25. On September 10, 1786, Thomas Barclay had written to Jefferson and John Adams from Tangier, attributing the origin of Moroccan piracy to "the expulsion of the Moors from Spain in the reign of Phillip the 3d. when 700,000 were banish'd from that Country." Julian P. Boyd, ed., *The Papers of Thomas Jefferson*, vol. 10 (Princeton: Princeton University Press, 1954), 346–47. J. H. Elliott estimates that after the edict of 1609, approximately 275,000 Moriscos left Spain (out of a Morisco population of some 300,000). Between 120,000 and 150,000 Jews were expelled from Spain in 1492. J. H. Elliott, *Imperial Spain, 1469–1716* (London: E. Arnold, 1963), 95–98, 301; Léon Poliakov, *The History of Anti-Semitism*, vol. 2, *From Mohammed to the Marranos*, trans. Natalie Gerardi (New York: Vanguard Press, 1973), 199. About 160,000 Huguenots fled from France between 1680 and 1690. Jon Butler, *The Huguenots in America: A Refugee People in New World Society* (Cambridge, Mass.: Harvard University Press, 1983), 3. In 1824 Jefferson was privately proposing the deportation of 60,000 blacks a year, "the whole annual increase," for a period of twenty to twenty-five years. Jefferson to Jared Sparks, Feb. 4, 1824, in *The Writings of Thomas Jefferson*, ed. Paul Leicester Ford, 10 vols. (New York: G. P. Putnam's Sons, 1892–1899), 10: 289–93.

19. Cecil Roth, *A History of the Jews in England* (Oxford, UK: Clarendon Press, 1941), 68–90; Robert C. Stacey, "Royal Taxation and the Social Structure of Medieval Anglo-Jewry: The Tallages of 1239–1242," *Hebrew Union College Annual* 56 (1985): 201, 205; Elliott, *Imperial Spain*, 98, 299–303; Henry Charles Lea, *The Moriscos of Spain: Their Conversion and Expulsion* (Philadelphia: Lea Bros., 1901), 292–343. Many of the Jewish physicians who did leave Spain acquired great prestige and influence in Turkey. Heinrich Graetz, *History of the Jews*, vol. 4 (New York: G. Dobsevage, 1927), 401. From the time of Constantine, Christian efforts to expel Jews or force them to convert were partly mitigated by a recognition of their mercantile, financial, and scientific services.

20. Thomas Jefferson to Jean Nicolas Démeunier, June 26, 1786, in Boyd, *Papers of Thomas Jefferson*, 10, 63.

21. John Boswell, *The Royal Treasure: Muslim Communities under the Crown of Aragon in the Fourteenth Century* (New Haven, Conn.: Yale University Press, 1977), 293–307; Robert Ignatius Burns, *Islam under the Crusaders: Colonial Survival in the Thirteenth-Century Kingdom of Valencia* (Princeton, N.J.: Princeton University Press, 1973), 16, 334, and passim.

22. Lea, *Moriscos of Spain*, 292–365; Elliott, *Imperial Spain*, 227–34, 299–303.

23. Graetz, *History of the Jews*, vol. 4, 334–422; Haim Hillel Ben-Sasson, "The Middle Ages," in *History of the Jewish People*, 568–71, 583–90, 620–21; Poliakov, *History of Anti-Semitism*, 2:147–233; E. H. Lindo, *The History of the Jews of Spain and Portugal* (1848; repr., New York: B. Franklin, 1970, 325–26. During the fourteenth and fifteenth century, Jews were also expelled from France and parts of Germany. In 1496, after Portugal had received a massive influx of Jewish refugees from Spain, King Emanuel I ordered them to leave the country but then enabled most of them to stay by forcing their conversion to Christianity.

24. Poliakov, *History of Anti-Semitism*, 2:198–99; Norwood, *Strangers and Exiles*, 2:30–54; Charles M. Weiss, *History of the French Protestant Refugees*, trans. Henry William Herbert (New York, 1854), vol. 1, passim; Bona Arsenault, *History of the Acadians* (Québec: Le Conseil de la vie française en Amérique, 1966), 105–242; Lawrence Henry Gipson, *The Great War for the Empire: The Years of Defeat, 1754–1757* (New York: Alfred A. Knopf, 1960), 243–57; Mary Beth Norton, *The British-Americans: The Loyalist Exiles in England, 1774–1789* (Boston: Little, Brown, 1972), 8–41, 244–47; Ellen Gibson Wilson, *The Loyal Blacks* (New York: Capricorn Books, 1976).

25. Jane Kamensky, "Limits of Resistance: The Uncertain Legacy of Ernst von Weizäcker and the Final Solution" (unpublished senior history essay, Yale University, 1985); Eugene Havesi, "Hitler's Plan for Madagascar," *Contemporary Jewish Record* 4 (August 1941): 381–94; Karl A. Schlevnes, *The Twisted Road to Auschwitz: Nazi Policy toward German Jews, 1933–1939* (Urbana: University of Illinois Press, 1970), 184–85; Celia Heller, *On the Edge of Destruction: Jews of Poland Between the Two World Wars* (New York: Columbia University Press, 1977), 136–37; Harry M. Rabinowicz, *The Legacy of Polish Jewry: A History of Polish Jews in the Inter-War Years, 1919–1939* (New York: Y. Yoseloff, 1965), 191–92; Howard Morley Sachar, *The Course of Modern Jewish History* (New York: Dell, 1977), 267–79, 355–61, 510–11; Gerald Reitlinger, *The Final Solution: The Attempt to Exterminate the Jews of Europe, 1939–1945*, 2d ed. (London: Valentine Mitchell, 1968), 79–82; Gordon A. Craig, "Schreibt un Farschreibt!" *New York Review of Books*, April 10, 1986; David Vital, *Zionism: The Crucial Phase* (Oxford, UK: Clarendon Press, 1987), 173–74. There had been a long history of Jewish colonization projects. In the mid-nineteenth century, a number of Jewish writers began envisaging a return to the ancestral homeland in Palestine; in the 1890s, as conditions worsened in the Russian Pale of Settlement and as increasing numbers of Eastern European Jews found a refuge in the United States, Baron Maurice de Hirsch's Jewish Colonization Association advocated a mass migration to Argentina; even Theodor Herzl, the organizer of the First Zionist Congress, accepted as an "emergency measure" Britain's proposal in 1903 for a Jewish settlement in Uganda, a concession that brought a bitter though temporary division in the Zionist movement. David Vital, *The Origins of Zionism* (Oxford, UK: Clarendon Press, 1975); Vital, *Zionism: The Formative Years* (Oxford, UK: Clarendon Press, 1982).

26. For the deportation of the French Acadians, see John Mack Faragher, *A Great and Noble Scheme: The Tragic Story of the Expulsion of the French Acadians from Their American Homeland* (New York: W. W. Norton, 2005).

27. Lindo, *Jews of Spain and Portugal*, 248–351; Graetz, *History of the Jews*, 4:387–88; Lea, *Moriscos of Spain*, 343–65; Butler, *Huguenots in America*, passim; Gipson, *Great War for the Empire*, 289–96.

28. Lea, *Moriscos of Spain*, 328–31.

29. Poliakov, *History of Anti-Semitism* 2: 199; Graetz, *History of the Jews,* 4: 387, 400.

30. Pierre Jurieu, *The Last Efforts of Afflicted Innocence* (London, 1682), 62–71, 136; Isaac Minet, epigraph to Part I of Butler, *Huguenots in America;* Jurieu, *Lettres pastorales* (Rotterdam: Abraham Acher, 1688), 89–91, 120; Jurieu, *Monsieur Jurieu's pastoral letters, Directed to the Protestants in France . . .* (London: Jo. Hindmarsh, 1688), 15 and passim; Jurieu,*The Reflections of the Reverend and Learned M. Jurieu upon the Strange and Miraculous Extasies of Isabel Vincent* (London: Richard Baldwin, 1689), 38–39; Jurieu, *Lettres pastorales,* 89–91, 120.

31. American Colonization Society [hereafter ACS], *Second Annual Report of the American Society for Colonizing the Free People of Colour of the United States* (Washington, D.C.: Davis and Force, 1819), 193; P. J. Staudenraus, *The African Colonization Movement, 1816–1865* (New York: Columbia University Press, 1961), 17; Shick, *Behold the Promised Land,* 8–9; Deuteronomy 1:19–45.

32. Deuteronomy 7:1–2, 22–24; 20:16–18; Joshua 6:21. At Sinai, God had already promised to annihilate the Amorites, Hittites, Perizzites, Canaanites, Hivites, and Jebusites (Exodus 23:23–31).

33. William W. Hallo, "Deuteronomy and Ancient Near Eastern Literature," in *The Torah: A Modern Commentary,* ed. W. Gunther Plaut (New York: Union of American Hebrew Congregations, 1981), 1381; Walzer, *Exodus and Revolution,* 143–44.

34. Historians long assumed that the early "Calvinistic" Afrikaners invoked the Israelite model of a chosen people to legitimate their divine commission, based on Deuteronomy, to "smite" and enslave the black heathen, to flee "Egypt" in the Great Trek, and to establish a Promised Land of white supremacy. André du Toit has carefully traced the origins of this historical interpretation, which appears to be a myth largely created by the missionary David Livingstone but which was then appropriated, in the early twentieth century, by the Afrikaners themselves. André du Toit, "No Chosen People: The Myth of the Calvinistic Origins of Afrikaner Nationalism and Racial Ideology," *American Historical Review* 88 (October 1983): 920–52.

35. For some of the historical distinctions drawn between blacks and Indians, see David Brion Davis, *The Problem of Slavery in Western Culture* (Ithaca, N.Y.: Cornell University Press, 1966), 4–5, 10, 167–75, 177–81, 192–94; Winthrop D. Jordan, *White Over Black: American Attitudes toward the Negro, 1550–1812* (Chapel Hill: University of North Carolina Press, 1968), 21–11, 89–91, 162–63, 239–40.

36. I am aware that the eastern Indians who were removed west of the Mississippi were also placed in the role of "colonists" living in regions already inhabited. But even the Cherokees were not expected to civilize and regenerate the entire West. Apart from criticism from opponents of removal that civilized tribes would be surrounded by violent "savages," little thought seems to have been given to the specific cultural implications of westward removal.

37. *The Papers of Benjamin Franklin,* ed. Leonard W. Labaree, vol. 4 (New Haven, Conn.: Yale University Press, 1961), 227–34. Franklin's prejudiced remarks about German immigrants, blacks, and people of "a swarthy Complexion" were omitted from reprinted editions of the essay in the 1760s but were publicized by his political enemies.

38. There were precedents for such colonization in the European plantations in Palestine, Cyprus, Crete, Sicily, and especially in the Canary Islands, the Cape Verde, Madeira, and São Tomé. See David Brion Davis, *Slavery and Human Progress* (New York: Oxford University Press, 1984), 53–63. But Irish and New World colonization was on a larger scale and involved the new objective of obtaining land for sizable European settlements.

39. T. W. Moody, F. X. Martin, and F. J. Byrne, eds., *A New History of Ireland,* vol. 3, *Early Modern Ireland, 1534–1691* (Oxford, UK: Clarendon Press, 1976), 69–141, 187–232; Karl S. Bottingheimer, *Ireland and the Irish: A Short History* (New York: Columbia University Press, 1982), 73–140.

40. Thomas More, *Utopia,* ed. Edward Surtz (New Haven, Conn.: Yale University

Press, 1964), 76, as quoted in Edmund S. Morgan, *American Slavery, American Freedom: The Ordeal of Colonial Virginia* (New York: Norton, 1975), 23.

41. James Monroe, "First Annual Message, December 2, 1817," in *A Compilation of the Messages and Papers of the Presidents,* ed. James D. Richardson, vol. 2 (New York: Bureau of National Literature, ca.1917), 585–86.

42. Perry Miller, *The New England Mind: The Seventeenth Century* (1939; repr., Cambridge, Mass.: Harvard University Press, 1954), 475, 477; Alan Heimert, "Puritanism, the Wilderness, and the Frontier," *New England Quarterly* 26 (Sept. 1953): 361–69, 376–77, 382; David D. Hall, *The Faithful Shepherd: A History of the New England Ministry in the Seventeenth Century* (Chapel Hill: University of North Carolina Press, 1972), 86–89; Andrew Delbanco, "The Puritan Errand Re-Viewed," *Journal of American Studies* 88 (December 1984): 343–60; John Cotton, *God's Promise to His Plantations* (London, 1630), reprinted in *Old South Leaflets* 3, no. 53 (Boston, n.d.): 4–16; 2 Samuel 7:10 (King James Version). English claims to land in North America were not based on biblical precedents but on royal grants and charters. Wilcomb E. Washburn, "The Moral and Legal Justifications for Dispossessing the Indians," in *Seventeenth-Century America: Essays in Colonial History,* ed. James Morton Smith (Chapel Hill: University of North Carolina Press, 1959), 16–18. It should be stressed that the parallels drawn between New England and ancient Israel generated increasing anxiety as clerical leaders contemplated the corruptions and punishments of ancient Israel. Robert Middlekauff, *The Mathers: Three Generations of Puritan Intellectuals, 1596–1728* (New York: Oxford University Press, 1971), 22–23, 105–12.

43. Cotton, *God's Promise,* 5–7; Karen Ordahl Kupperman, *Settling with the Indians: The Meeting of English and Indian Cultures in America, 1580–1640* (Totowa, N.J.: Rowman and Littlefield, 1980), 166–68. Cotton quoted many other biblical passages that suggested a divine appointment for settling New England, such as Exodus 15:17: "when he plants them in the holy Mountaine of his Inheritance."

44. Cotton, *God's Promise,* 6.

45. Genesis 21:25; 33:18–19; 34; Cotton, *God's Promise,* 14–15; Wilcomb E. Washburn, ed., *The Indian and the White Man* (Garden City, N.Y.: Anchor Books, 1964), 176–77. Jacob's only response to Simeon and Levi, who had murdered the males of the city, was to complain that the act would make him "odious" among the Canaanite and Perizzite inhabitants, and provoke retaliation. But much later, in his final blessing and prophecy, Jacob cursed their anger and violence (Genesis 49:5–7).

46. Morgan, *American Slavery, American Freedom,* 47. The English, like other European colonizers, always expressed a desire to convert the Indians to Christianity. But since professions of fairness and goodwill were coupled with fear and brutal violence against "savages" who were seen as the agents of Satan, historians continue to debate the meaning of Indian-white relations. See especially Francis Jennings, *The Invasion of America: Indians, Colonialism, and the Cant of Conquest* (Chapel Hill: University of North Carolina Press, 1975); Kupperman, *Settling with the Indians*; Peter N. Carroll, *Puritanism and the Wilderness: The Intellectual Significance of the New England Frontier, 1629–1700* (New York: Columbia University Press, 1969), 11–13, 123–24, 137–39, 147–53; Alden T. Vaughan, *New England Frontier: Puritans and Indians, 1620–1675* (Boston: Little, Brown, 1965); Richard Slotkin, *Regeneration Through Violence: The Mythology of the American Frontier, 1600–1860* (Middletown, Conn.: Wesleyan University Press, 1973); Yasuhide Kawashima, *Puritan Justice and the Indian: White Man's Law in Massachusetts, 1630–1763* (Middletown, Conn.: Wesleyan University Press, 1986).

47. Adam J. Hirsch, "The Collision of Military Cultures in Seventeenth-Century New England," *Journal of American History* 74 (March 1988): 1187–1212; Kupperman, *Settling with the Indians,* 31–32, 81–86, 184; Richard Slotkin and James K. Folsom, eds., *So Dreadfull a Judgment: Puritan Responses to King Philip's War, 1676–1677* (Middletown, Conn.: Wesleyan University Press, 1978), 3, 34–35, 38–39; Slotkin, *Regeneration through Violence,* 38, 55, 83–93. While Adam J. Hirsch presents an original and convincing

argument concerning the fortuitous and degenerating interaction of European and Indian "military cultures," one must also take account of European religious culture, especially with respect to the treatment of unrepentant heathen.

4. COLONIZING BLACKS, PART II: THE AMERICAN COLONIZATION SOCIETY AND AMERICO-LIBERIANS

1. W. E. B. Du Bois, "Little Portraits of Africa," *The Crisis* (April 1924), 273–74; Du Bois, *Dusk of Dawn: An Essay toward an Autobiography of a Race Concept* (New York: Schocken Books, 1968), 124–26; Rayford W. Logan, ed., *W. E. B. Du Bois: A Profile* (New York: Hill and Wang, 1971), 225–27. It should be stressed that Du Bois was not endorsing African colonization or a movement "back to Africa," as was his contemporary Marcus Garvey. M. P. Akpan suggests that Du Bois, who was known to be Garvey's "most formidable Afro-American opponent and critic," was sent to Liberia to help sever that country's links with the Universal Negro Improvement Association. Judith Stein argues convincingly that there is no evidence to support this view, and that Liberia's ruling class needed no American encouragement to torpedo the UNIA. M. P. Akpan, "Liberia and the Universal Negro Improvement Association: The Background to the Abortion of Garvey's Scheme for African Colonization," *Journal of African History* 14, no. 1 (1973): 123–26; Judith Stein, *The World of Marcus Garvey: Race and Class in Modern Society* (Baton Rouge: Louisiana State University Press, 1986), 213–14. Although Du Bois dreamed of an African civilization "without coal, without noise, where machinery will sing and never rush and roar, and where men will sleep and think and dance. . . ," he urged the State Department to provide the Liberian government with expert advice on economic development, education, transportation, and sanitation. He never visited the hinterland, where President King's officials were involved in the brutal oppression and virtual enslavement of native peoples. Du Bois, "Little Portraits," p. 274.

2. W. W. Schmokel, "Settlers and Tribes: The Origins of the Liberian Dilemma," in *Western African History*, ed. Daniel F. McCall, Norman R. Bennett, and Jeffrey Butler, Boston University Papers on Africa, vol. 4 (New York, 1969), 158. In 1842, missionaries at Maryland's colony at Cape Palmas charged that the settlers, having been removed from the wholesome restraints of the United States, had lapsed into vices that set the worst example for Africans and thwarted missionary work. Penelope Campbell, *Maryland in Africa: The Maryland State Colonization Society, 1831–1857* (Urbana: University of Illinois Press, 1971), 138.

3. See, for example, the letter of Richard Allen to *Freedom's Journal*, November 2, 1827, 134.

4. It is worth noting that J. L. Watson, a black abolitionist who in 1849 opposed proposals for emigration, argued that "our 'Pilgrim Fathers' " who first came to this country were not colonizers. Philip S. Foner and George E. Walker, eds., *Proceedings of the Black State Conventions, 1840–1865*, vol. 1 (Philadelphia: Temple University Press, 1979), 223.

5. Tyler, an ardent defender of slavery and president of the Virginia Colonization Society, is quoted in Katherine Harris, *African and American Values: Liberia and West Africa* (Lanham, Md.: University Press of America, 1985), 61. Lawrence J. Friedman, "Purifying the White Man's Country: The American Colonization Society Reconsidered, 1816–40," *Societas* 6 (Winter 1976): 1–23, presents a fascinating psychological analysis of "the parallel between the colonizationist's underlying quest for purity and the human defecation process" (16); he fails, however, to give adequate attention to the theme of racial elevation and redemption, or to the concern of many colonizationists for the practical consequences of slave emancipation.

6. Andrew Delbanco, "The Puritan Errand Re-Viewed," *Journal of American Studies* 18 (Dec. 1984): 343–60; Theodore Dwight Bozeman, "The Puritans' 'Errand into

the Wilderness' Reconsidered," *New England Quarterly*, 59 (June 1986): 231–51; Karen Ordahl Kupperman, "Errand to the Indies: Puritan Colonization from Providence Island through the Western Design," *William and Mary Quarterly*, 3rd ser., 45 (January 1988): 70–99. As Karen Kupperman points out, there was no consensus among emigrants that New England was the Promised Land; many English Puritans advocated Caribbean colonization as a more effective means of challenging the Roman Catholic Antichrist and thus of carrying out God's design.

7. *African Repository and Colonial Journal* [hereafter *African Repository*] 13 (Oct. 1837): 310. While this claim was clearly an attempt to answer accurate charges that many colonizationists fanned the flames of racism, it is still remarkable that colonizationists would admit that racial prejudice could be overcome, a belief that would appear to undermine the very raison d'être of the ACS.

8. George M. Fredrickson, *The Black Image in the White Mind: The Debate on Afro-American Character and Destiny, 1817–1914* (New York: Harper & Row, 1971), 12. My own research confirms Fredrickson's conclusion, which I reread only after thinking I had made an original discovery.

9. Letter of Robert Goodloe Harper to Elias B. Caldwell, August 20, 1817, ACS, *First Annual Report* (Washington, D.C.: R. Rapine, 1818), 20–21; ACS, *Seventh Annual Report* (Washington, D.C.: Davis and Force, 1824), 14; *African Repository* 13 (Oct. 1837): 310; *African Repository* 14 (January 1838): 20.

10. Daniel Coker, *Journal of Daniel Coker* (Baltimore: Edward J. Coale, 1820), 48; ACS, *Third Annual Report* (Washington, D.C.: Davis and Force, 1820), 121. Kizzel was born on Sherbro Island, off Sierra Leone, and taken to America as a slave; in 1792 he joined the 1,190 black refugees who chose to leave Nova Scotia and accompany John Clarkson's expedition to Sierra Leone. In 1811, Paul Cuffe, the black American shipowner and merchant, induced Kizzel to help organize a mutual aid society to promote commerce and immigration to Sierra Leone or Sherbro Island. In 1818 Kizzel welcomed the first ACS agents to Sherbro Island. He soon proved, however, to be a misleading interpreter and intermediary with the local chiefs. In 1820 he helped to lead the first American settlers to their deadly encounter with African disease and then charged them extortionist rent for their flooded huts and distributed their supplies to Sherbro kings. Lamont D. Thomas, *Rise to Be a People: A Biography of Paul Cuffe* (Urbana: University of Illinois Press, 1986), 53, 62, 66, 70, 80, 84, 91; P. J. Staudenraus, *The African Colonization Movement, 1816–1865* (New York: Columbia University Press, 1961), 59–62; Charles S. Johnson, *Bitter Canaan: The Story of the Negro Republic*, with an introductory essay by John Stanfield (New Brunswick, N.J.: Transaction Books, 1987), 22, 23, 35, 36, 41.

11. ACS, *Third Annual Report*, 19; ACS, *Fourth Annual Report* (Washington, D.C.: Davis and Force, 1821), 62.

12. Tom W. Shick, *Behold the Promised Land: A History of Afro-American Settler Society in Nineteenth-Century Liberia* (Baltimore: Johns Hopkins University Press, 1980), 61; Staudenraus, *African Colonization Movement*, 234–36; Schmokel, "Settlers and Tribes," 167.

13. Christopher Fyfe, *A History of Sierra Leone* (London: Oxford University Press, 1962), 24–25, 89–92; A. P. Kup, *Sierra Leone: A Concise History* (London: Cambridge University Press, 1975), 123, 164–66.

14. Howard Temperley, "African-American Aspirations and the Settlement of Liberia," *Slavery & Abolition*, 21, no. 2 (2000): 67–68; Lamin O. Sanneh, *Abolitionist Abroad: American Blacks and the Making of Modern West Africa* (Cambridge, Mass.: Harvard University Press, 1999), 41–45; Svend E. Holsoe, "A Study of Relations between Settlers and Indigenous Peoples in Western Liberia, 1821–1847," *International Journal of African Historical Studies* 4, no. 2 (1971): 331–56; Paul E. Lovejoy, *Transformations in Slavery: A History of Slavery in Africa* (Cambridge, UK: Cambridge University Press, 1983), 135–36, 159–70; Philip Curtin, Steven Feierman, Leonard Thompson, and Jan Vansina, *African History* (Boston: Little, Brown, 1978), 231–34, 369–76.

15. Shick, *Behold the Promised Land*, 44–45, 65; Staudenraus, *African Colonization Movement*, 62–68, 88–90; Richard West, *Back to Africa: A History of Sierra Leone and Liberia* (London: Cape, 1970), 114–22; C. Abayomi Cassell, *Liberia: History of the First African Republic* (New York: Fountainhead Publishers, 1970), 67–78; Johnson, *Bitter Canaan*, 55–57; Holsoe, "Study of Relations," 336–40. Holsoe shows there was much division among the indigenous chieftains over the acceptability of the settlement. Sao Boso, ruler of the powerful Condo confederation, who came down to the coast from Bopolo, favored peace and amicable commerce. But after Sao Boso returned home, the Dei chiefs began plotting an attack. Sao Boso's death in 1837 led to several years of heightened disorder and conflict. Ibid., 337–51.

16. Shick, *Behold the Promised Land*, 73.

17. Harris, *African and American Values*, 18–22, 33–36. Although the United States continued to maintain an informal presence in Liberia as well as an official agency for disposing of recaptives, these intimations of colonialism were more than counterbalanced by a Jacksonian hostility to federal spending and by a racist refusal, from 1847 to 1862, to recognize a government ruled by blacks. American colonizationists were forced to rely on private philanthropy and intermittent support from state governments. Even in the late nineteenth century, Liberia was unable to arouse the interest of either the United States government or private financiers in projects for building roads and railways to the interior, a fact that casts doubt on claims of American imperialism, as distinct from Americo-Liberian imperialism. See M. B. Akpan, "Black Imperialism: Americo-Liberian Rule over the African Peoples of Liberia, 1841–1964," *The Canadian Journal of African Studies* 7, no. 2 (973): 224.

18. *African Repository* 21 (Feb. 1845): 42. Ralph R. Gurley, the leading agent and fund-raiser for the ACS, argued that biblical and secular history showed that God's "usual mode of civilizing a country is, by planting there, colonies of civilized men, with whom the natives may amalgamate, or before whom they must disappear, as their own character and conduct shall decide." Gurley admitted that most colonies had been guilty "of more or less injustice to the aborigines around them," a fact that aroused some prejudice against colonization itself. He insisted, however, that "a rigidly impartial examination of facts would generally show that the natives themselves are not blameless; that they unjustifiably provoke the treatment under which they suffer." Ibid., 25 (April 1849): 103.

19. Schmokel, "Settlers and Tribes," 157–58; Harris, *African and American Values*, 60–63; Akpan, "Black Imperialism," 219–21, 225–26; Shick, *Behold the Promised Land*, 53–59; Gary B. Nash, *Forging Freedom: The Formation of Philadelphia's Black Community, 1720–1840* (Cambridge, Mass.: Harvard University Press, 1988), 190–211, 218–33, 246–79.

20. Harris, *African and American Values*, 63, 66–68; Apkan, "Black Imperialism," 218–19, 225–29; Schmokel, "Settlers and Tribes," 162–66; Shick, *Behold the Promised Land*, 13, 31–59; Tom W. Shick, "A Quantitative Analysis of Liberian Colonization from 1820 to 1843, with Special Reference to Mortality," *Journal of African History* 12, no. 1 (1971): 45–59; Wally Genser, "Relations between Settlers and Indigenous Peoples in Liberia, 1821–1880" (unpublished paper, Program in American Culture, University of Michigan, April 21, 1986). (I am much indebted to Mr. Genser for allowing me to use this illuminating study.)

21. In 1843, more than half the population of Monrovia was illiterate. Shick, *Behold the Promised Land*, 37. The rate of literacy was of course much higher among freeborn blacks than among manumitted slaves.

22. Bell I. Wiley, ed., *Slaves No More: Letters from Liberia, 1833–1869* (Lexington: University Press of Kentucky, 1980). John Stanfield points out that Charles S. Johnson was struck by the fact that "Americo-Liberian oppressors, like their White American counterparts, used the term 'boy' to simultaneously signify the degradation of natives and reinforce their disenfranchised status in the social order." See introduction to Johnson, *Bitter Canaan*, lii.

23. Peyton Skipwith to John H. Cocke, April 22, 1840, in Wiley, *Slaves No More*, 52–54.

24. Sion Harris to Samuel Wilkeson, April 16, 1840, in Wiley, *Slaves No More*, 220–23, 332. Wiley notes that the passages concerning mutilations were crossed out in the manuscript and omitted from the ACS's published version of the letter. For an account of the origins of the conflict, see Holsoe, "A Study of Relations," 350–51.

25. Skipwith to Cocke, in Wiley, *Slaves No More*, 53.

26. Wiley, introduction to *Slaves No More*, 4; Shick, *Behold the Promised Land*, 29–30, 109; Akpan, "Black Imperialism," 220–23; Genser, "Relations between Settlers and Indigenous Peoples." It should be noted that Blyden was one of the few Liberian leaders who developed a deep respect for African customs and institutions, which he hoped to preserve. See Hollis R. Lynch, *Edward Wilmot Blyden: Pan-Negro Patriot, 1832–1913* (New York: Oxford University Press, 1970), chapter 4.

27. Shick, *Behold the Promised Land*, 106–07; Johnson, *Bitter Canaan*, 115–24.

28. *Proceedings of the Colored National Convention, held in Rochester July 6th, 7th and 8th, 1853* (Rochester, N.Y.: Frederick Douglass, 1853), 47–49, 55–56. Pennington claimed that in 1798, an American naval officer had urged the government to colonize America's free blacks in southern Africa in order to head off Britain's colonization schemes and encourage white immigration to the United States. When this plan failed, "the Americans then turned their eyes to Western Africa." For a fascinating account of Pennington's life, see R. J. M. Blackett, *Beating Against the Barriers: Biographical Essays in Nineteenth-Century Afro-American History* (Baton Rouge: Louisiana State University Press, 1986), 1–84.

29. Johnson, *Bitter Canaan*, 73, 81, 89–90, 129–31; Shick, *Behold the Promised Land*, 66–72, 113; Akpan, "Black Imperialism," 227; Schmokel, "Settlers and Tribes," 159.

30. Shick, *Behold the Promised Land*, 65–72, 96, 98–100; Johnson, *Bitter Canaan*, 5–9, 72–73, 79–81, 89, 130–40, 175–97, 223–26. In 1930 it would have been difficult to find a more reliable and perceptive investigator than Charles S. Johnson, who was chosen by President Herbert Hoover as America's representative on the League of Nations Commission. After doing graduate work in sociology with Robert E. Park at the University of Chicago, Johnson had become director of research and investigations at the National Urban League and editor of the League's publication, *Opportunity*. He belonged to the small group of black intellectuals, including James Weldon Johnson, Alain L. Locke, and Arthur A. Schomburg, who nurtured and publicized the Harlem Renaissance. Before embarking on his seven-month tour of Liberia, Johnson visited the International Institute of African Languages and Cultures in London and conferred with Bronislaw Malinowski and other anthropologists. It was Johnson who wrote the International Commission's lengthy report, which led to the resignation of Liberia's president King and vice president Allen Yancy. Although he began drafting *Bitter Canaan* in 1930, Johnson soon became distracted by other duties and responsibilities, culminating with the presidency of Fisk University. By 1945, when Johnson finally submitted the manuscript for publication, it had become apparent that a devastating critique of Liberian history and society might be detrimental to the emerging nationalist independence movements in Africa and the Caribbean. Although various motives dissuaded Johnson from publishing what he considered to be his best work, the views of Eric Williams, Charles Thompson, and Claude Barnett, all of whom read the manuscript, were probably decisive. The sociologist John Stanfield deserves much credit for finally making available this brilliantly written account of Liberian society.

31. Akpan, "Black Imperialism," 229–34; Johnson, *Bitter Canaan*, 5–9, 90–91, 135, 138–40, 175–97; Ibrahim K. Sundiata, *Black Scandal: America and the Liberian Labor Crisis, 1929–1936* (Philadelphia: Institute for the Study of Human Issues, 1980), passim; Sundiata, "The Black Planters: African Environment and Ecology in the Bight of Biafra in the Era of Abolition, 1827–1930," part 3. (I am much indebted to Professor Sundiata for sending me a copy of this manuscript.) British naval patrols had used Fernando Po,

in the Bight of Biafra, as a base for intercepting slave ships. Some of the recaptives and their descendants became successful cocoa planters.

32. Shick, *Behold the Promised Land*, 26–27, 50; Shick, "Quantitative Analysis of Liberian Colonization," 45–59; Wiley, *Slaves No More*, 311n2. Wiley calculates a total by 1866 of 13,136 immigrants sent under the auspices of the ACS and the Maryland State Colonization Society. This number was augmented by 5,722 "repatriated" African captives who were freed by the United States Navy and taken to Liberia; 4,701 of these recaptured Africans landed in Liberia in a single year, 1860. The ACS also listed 346 immigrants from Barbados, and 9 from Indian Territory. Shick, *Behold the Promised Land*, 68, table 16; ACS, *Fifteenth Annual Report* (Washington, D.C.: James C. Dunn, 1867), 95.

33. Despite the official goal of assimilation, only a few hundred Africans, together with two or three favored tribes, had become Liberian citizens after the first twenty years of settlement. In 1884, tribal delegates were given the right to speak in the legislature on matters concerning their respective tribes, but this reform provided natives with little power. It was not until the administration of President William V. S. Tubman (1944–71) that the government adopted a serious "Unification Policy." Schmokel, "Settlers and Tribes," 171, 172; Akpan, "Black Imperialism," 228, 234–35. African resentment toward the continuing dominance of the small minority of Americo-Liberians (no more than 5 percent of the population) contributed to Samuel K. Doe's bloody coup of 1980. Despite the survival of American traditions and institutions, Charles S. Johnson found in 1930 that at least 95 percent of the population was illiterate; before World War II, more than 95 percent of all trade was controlled by foreigners, most of the food consumed by Liberians was imported, there were no technicians available to repair broken engines and machinery, and in Monrovia there was not a single qualified physician "apart from those supplied by the missions, Firestone, Pan American Airways, and those connected with American military installations." *Bitter Canaan*, 129–33. In the early 1980s, Liberia had a per capita income ($400) below that of Ghana, Zambia, Zimbabwe, and Egypt; from 1971 to 1984 life expectancy at birth had risen from 44 to 54 (compared to 65 in Jamaica); in 1984 literacy stood at 24 percent (compared to 76 percent in Jamaica). *The World Almanac and Book of Facts, 1987*.

34. Tom W. Shick touches on this question when he briefly compares the nineteenth-century development of Liberia, South Africa, Australia, and Argentina. See *Behold the Promised Land*, 135–43.

35. Ibid., 114–18, 141–42.

36. Floyd J. Miller, *The Search for a Black Nationality: Black Emigration and Colonization, 1787–1863* (Urbana: University of Illinois Press, 1975), 94–102, 138; *The North Star*, March 2, 1849, in *Black Abolitionist Papers*, microfilm edition, ed. Peter C. Ripley et al. (hereafter *BAP*), reel 5, 992–93.

37. Douglass is quoted in Wilson Jeremiah Moses, *The Golden Age of Black Nationalism, 1850–1925* (Hamden, Conn.: Archon Books, 1978), 92. In Martin Delany's earlier phrasing of this idea, which had long been advanced by many white colonizationists, "we believe it to be the duty of the Free, to elevate themselves in the most speedy and effective manner possible; as the redemption of the bondman depends entirely upon the elevation of the freeman." *The Condition, Elevation, Emigration, and Destiny of the Colored People of the United States. Politically Considered* (Philadelphia: printed by author, 1852), 205. But in his famous 1843 Address to the Slaves, Henry Highland Garnet had nearly inverted the argument: "While you have been oppressed, we have also been partakers with you; nor can we be free while you are enslaved. We therefore write to you as being bound with you." *An Address to the Slaves of the United States of America* (New York: printed by author, 1848), 90. And in 1856, John Gains pointed out that the existence of Haiti had not diminished American racial prejudice or "removed one unholy law"; he concluded that "a Negro Republic, on the coast of Africa, the Caribee Islands, or South America, will never induce the haughty Saxon to respect us at home, unless it be a

power physically as strong as Russia, and morally [as strong] as England or France." Quoted in Jane H. Pease and William H. Pease, *They Who Would Be Free: Blacks' Search for Freedom, 1830–1861* (New York: Atheneum, 1974), 266–67.

38. Richard MacMaster, "Henry Highland Garnet and the African Civilization Society," *Journal of Presbyterian Church History* 48 (Summer 1970): 99–100; Joel Schor, *Henry Highland Garnet: A Voice of Black Radicalism in the Nineteenth Century* (Westport, Conn.: Greenwood Press, 1977), 154. The argument that even black radicals were committed to the redemption of American institutions is admirably documented in a 1987 Yale senior essay by Matthew A. Lamberti, "'Mismatched Messiahs': Black Abolitionists and the Redemption of American Institutions, 1829–1860."

39. Garnet to Douglass, *The North Star,* Jan. 26, 1849, *BAP,* reel 5, 959–60.

40. *African Repository* 22 (November 1846): 347; Schor, *Henry Highland Garnet,* 101–3.

41. *The Patriot,* May 22, 1851, *BAP,* reel 6, 942. For guidance to Garnet's writings, I am much indebted to a brilliant Yale senior essay written in 1986 by Seth Moglen, "Henry Highland Garnet and the Problem of Black Nationalism in Antebellum America."

42. Hollis R. Lynch, "Pan-Negro Nationalism in the New World, before 1862," in *The Making of Black America: Essays in Negro Life and History,* ed. August Meier and Elliott Rudwick (New York: Atheneum, 1969), 51, 52, 58; Lynch, *Edward Wilmot Blyden,* 3–6; Anthony J. Barker, *The African Link: British Attitudes to the Negro in the Era of the Atlantic Slave Trade, 1550–1807* (London: F. Cass, 1978), 96, 192–93; Robert O. Collins, ed., *Problems in African History* (Englewood Cliffs, N.J.: Prentice-Hall, 1968), 7–55; ACS, *Tenth Annual Report* (Washington, D.C.: Way & Gideon, 1827), 8–10; ACS, *Fourteenth Annual Report* (Washington, D.C.: James C. Dunn, 1831), vii–xi. It was not until the 1840s that the "American school of ethnology," led by Dr. Samuel George Morton and George R. Gliddon, asserted the view that ancient Egyptians were Caucasians and that blacks had been held as slaves in antiquity just as in modern times. William Stanton, *The Leopard's Spots: Scientific Attitudes Toward Race in America, 1815–59* (Chicago: University of Chicago Press, 1960), 39, 50–51, 97. For a discussion of blacks in Hannibal's army and in antiquity in general, see Frank M. Snowden Jr., *Blacks in Antiquity: Ethiopians in the Greco-Roman Experience* (Cambridge, Mass.: Harvard University Press, 1970); Snowden, *Before Color Prejudice: The Ancient View of Blacks* (Cambridge, Mass.: Harvard University Press, 1983).

43. Gregory U. Rigsby, *Alexander Crummell: Pioneer in Nineteenth-Century Pan-African Thought* (Westport, Conn.: Greenwood Press, 1987), 65–66, 71–73; Wilson J. Moses, "Civilizing Missionary: A Study of Alexander Crummell," *Journal of Negro History* 60, no. 2 (April 1975): 233–39; Moses, *Golden Age of Black Nationalism,* 63–68.

44. Miller, *Search for a Black Nationality,* 182–205; Lynch, *Edward Wilmot Blyden,* 24–25.

45. Harriet Beecher Stowe, *Uncle Tom's Cabin: or, Life among the Lowly* (Boston: Houghton and Mifflin, 1888), 482–84. For Delany's hostility toward Mrs. Stowe for approving the "dependent colonizationist settlement of Liberia," see Cyril E. Griffith, *The African Dream: Martin R. Delany and the Emergence of Pan-African Thought* (University Park, Pa.: Pennsylvania State University Press, 1975), 20–21.

46. Lynch, "Pan-Negro Nationalism in the New World," 52; *African Repository* 14 (Jan. 1838): 20.

47. Wiley, *Slaves No More,* 162; Jo M. Sullivan, "Mississippi in Africa: Settlers Among the Kru, 1835–1847," *Liberian Studies Journal* 8, no. 2 (1978–79): 79–94.

5. COLONIZING BLACKS, PART III:
FROM MARTIN DELANY TO HENRY HIGHLAND GARNET
AND MARCUS GARVEY

1. Wilson Jeremiah Moses perceptively shows that assimilation and nationalism were not mutually exclusive and that black nationalism should not be equated with territorial separation. However, his hostility to "civilizationism" brings a tone of contempt to his treatment of black nationalists, whom he regards as "conservatives."

With the exception of Crummell, they were not seen as conservatives by their contemporaries, and it can be argued that the true conservatives were those who opposed "elevation" and improvement and who idealized dysfunctional traditions. Moses, *The Golden Age of Black Nationalism, 1850–1925* (Hamden, Conn.: Archon Books, 1978).

2. E. J. Hobsbawm, *The Age of Capital, 1848–1875* (New York: Scribner, 1975), 97.

3. Robert M. Berdahl, "New Thoughts on German Nationalism," *American Historical Review*, 77 (1972): 65–80; G. Eley, "Nationalism and Social History," *Social History* 6 (1981): 83–107; E. J. Hobsbawm, *The Age of Revolution, 1789–1848* (New York: New American Library, 1962), 164; François Fejtö, "Europe on the Eve of the Revolution," in *The Opening of an Era: 1848: An Historical Symposium*, ed. François Fejtö (New York: H. Fertig, 1948, 1966), 41–42. Hobsbawm, who also notes the messianic claims of "the Russian Slavophils with their championship of Holy Russia," maintains that it was "rational" to look only to Paris: "But in those days there had been only one great and revolutionary nation and it made sense (as indeed it still did) to regard it as the headquarters of all revolutions, and the necessary prime mover in the liberation of the world" (*Age of Revolution*, 164). Such reasoning, which seems to accept the possible messianic role of a nation-state, could apply with even greater force to the United States, whose revolution had led to a kind of political stability and economic growth that was attracting hundreds of thousands of immigrants.

4. "Henry Highland Garnet's Speech at an Enthusiastic Meeting of the Colored Citizens of Boston," *The Weekly Anglo-African*, September 19, 1859, reprinted in Sterling Stuckey, *The Ideological Origins of Black Nationalism* (Boston: Beacon Press, 1972), 183. Garnet's ideal of "a grand centre of negro nationality" was strikingly similar to Ahad Ha-'Am's view of Zionism in 1912, as summarized by David Vital: "The true aim of Zionism, namely the fostering of a new national life and a new national consciousness in all parts of scattered Jewry, was not the achievement of 'a secure refuge for the people of Israel,' but of 'a fixed centre for the spirit of Israel.'" Vital, *Zionism: The Crucial Phase* (New York: Oxford University Press, 1987), 60.

5. Martin Robison Delany, *The Condition, Elevation, Emigration, and Destiny of the Colored People of the United States. Politically Considered* (Philadelphia: printed by author, 1852), 158.

6. Ibid., 12–13, 159, 203–08. Although Delany's book denounced both the ACS and Liberia, he reprinted a long extract from the *First Annual Report of the Trustees of Donations for Education in Liberia*, which presents a rather glowing picture of the Republic; he also defended the colonizationist Benjamin Coates, who reported that he had recently left the ACS. Ibid., 35, 162–68.

7. Hollis R. Lynch, *Edward Wilmot Blyden, Pan-Negro Patriot, 1832–1913* (New York: Oxford University Press, 1970), 117–18; Judith Stein, *The World of Marcus Garvey: Race and Class in Modern Society* (Baton Rouge: Louisiana State University Press, 1986), 154–56. Both Blyden and Garvey were West Indians who favored black "racial purity," who were deeply prejudiced against mulattoes, and who lacked the respect for American institutions that was so pronounced among even radical American blacks such as Henry Highland Garnet.

8. Floyd Miller, *The Search for a Black Nationality: Black Emigration and Colonization, 1787–1863* (Urbana: University of Illinois Press, 1975), 236–40. Douglass changed his mind and canceled the trip when the outbreak of war offered new opportunities, as he put it, to "serve the cause of freedom and mankind."

9. See especially Nell Irvin Painter, *Exodusters: Black Migration to Kansas after Reconstruction* (New York: Alfred A. Knopf, 1977), 71–145.

10. Edwin S. Redkey, *Black Exodus: Black Nationalist and Back-to-Africa Movements, 1890–1910* (New Haven, Conn.: Yale University Press, 1969), 298. Redkey also points out that there was little commercial trade between the United States and West Africa and consequently little cheap transport, in contrast to the shipping facilities between the United States and Europe (299).

11. See Isabel Wilkerson, *The Warmth of Other Suns: The Epic Story of America's Great Migration* (New York: Random House, 2010).

12. Ibid., 23–58; Moses, *Golden Age of Black Nationalism*, 76, 197–219; Joel Williamson, *After Slavery: The Negro in South Carolina During Reconstruction, 1861–1877* (Chapel Hill: University of North Carolina, 1965), 110–11; James E. Turner, "Historical Dialectics of Black Nationalist Movements in America," *Western Journal of Black Studies* 1, no. 3 (Sept. 1977): 164–80.

13. Redkey, *Black Exodus*, 22–35, 150–286; P. J. Staudenraus, *The African Colonization Movement: 1816–1865* (New York: Columbia University Press, 1961), 251. In 1868 Delany urged blacks to sail to Liberia on the ACS-sponsored *Golconda*; he continued to correspond with William Coppinger, seeking appointment as U.S. minister to Liberia, a post that was actually conferred on Garnet. Miller, *Search for a Black Nationality*, 266.

14. Redkey, *Black Exodus*, 44.

15. Much further attention needs to be given to the writings of black women, who are almost wholly ignored in the standard historical accounts but whose views are becoming accessible in such collections as Henry Louis Gates, ed., *The Schomburg Library of Nineteenth-Century Black Women Writers*, 30 vols. (New York: Oxford University Press, 1988), and in such studies as Jacqueline Jones, *Labor of Love, Labor of Sorrow: Black Women, Work, and the Family from Slavery to the Present* (New York: Basic Books, 1985).

16. *Marcus Garvey and UNIA Papers*, vol. 5 (Berkeley: University of California Press, 1986), 586–87, 610. Garvey, who hoped to use Liberia as a base for expelling white imperialists from Africa, had earlier claimed that Liberia was founded "for the purpose of helping the refugee slave and the exiled African to re-establish a foothold in his native land; therefore, no Liberian, neither at home nor abroad, has any moral or other right preventing Negroes to return to their home to do the best they can for its development." *Marcus Garvey and UNIA Papers*, vol. 4 (Berkeley: University of California Press, 1985), 632–33. But his praise of Liberia's founders and leaders did not prevent President King's government from forbidding on June 30, 1924, the entry of any UNIA members into the country. Garvey's advance party, which arrived in July, was promptly seized and deported. "Press Release by Ernest Lyon, Liberian Consul General in the U.S., July 10, 1924," in ibid., vol. 5, 611; Stein, *World of Marcus Garvey*, 210–13.

17. *Marcus Garvey and UNIA Papers*, vol. 1 (Berkeley: University of California Press, 1983), 25–27, 55–57.

18. Ibid., 56.

19. Ibid., 56–57; ibid., vol. 5, 531. As early as 1829, David Walker, in his famous *Appeal, in Four Articles; together with a Preamble, to the Coloured Citizens of the World*, had played with this inversion, noting that the Egyptians who enslaved the Israelites "were Africans or coloured people, such as we are—some of them yellow and others dark—a mixture of Ethiopians and the natives of Egypt—about the same as you see the coloured people of the United States at the present day." Yet, aside from emphasizing the relative mildness of the Israelites' bondage compared to that of the American blacks, Walker was religious enough to side with God and identify his cause with that of Moses. Reprinted in Stuckey, *The Ideological Origins of Black Nationalism*, 47, 50, 104, 111.

20. Lawrence W. Levine, *Black Culture and Black Consciousness: Afro-American Folk Thought from Slavery to Freedom* (New York: Oxford University Press, 1977), 23, 50–52, 137; Dena J. Epstein, *Sinful Tunes and Spirituals: Black Folk Music to the Civil War* (Urbana: University of Illinois Press, 1977), 244–51; Louis R. Harlan, "Booker T. Washington's Discovery of Jews," in *Region, Race, and Reconstruction: Essays in Honor of C. Vann Woodward*, ed. J. Morgan Kousser and James M. McPherson (New York: Oxford University Press, 1982), 274. For black celebrations of deliverance, see William H. Wiggins Jr., *O Freedom! Afro-American Emancipation Celebrations* (Knoxville: University of Tennessee Press, 1987).

21. Waldo E. Martin Jr., *The Mind of Frederick Douglass* (Chapel Hill: University of

North Carolina Press, 1984), 109–10, 123, 201; *The Frederick Douglass Papers,* Series One, *Speeches, Debates, and Interviews,* ed. John W. Blassingame, vol. 3, *1855–63* (New Haven: Yale University Press, 1985), 556; Delany, *Condition,* 18–19; Lynch, *Edward Wilmot Blyden,* 63–65; August Meier, *Negro Thought in America, 1880–1915: Racial Ideologies in the Age of Booker T. Washington* (Ann Arbor: University of Michigan Press, 1963), 248; Arnold Shankman, "Friend or Foe? Southern Blacks View the Jew, 1880–1935," in *Turn to the South: Essays on Southern Jewry,* ed. Nathan M. Kaganoff and Melvin I. Urofsky (Charlottesville: American Jewish Historical Society by the University Press of Virginia, 1979), 109–14; Harlan, "Booker T. Washington's Discovery of Jews," 268–75. For a broad overview of early Jewish-black relations, nothing can rival Harold David Brackman's unpublished diss., "The Ebb and Flow of Conflict: A History of Black–Jewish Relations Through 1900" (Ph.D. diss., University of California Los Angeles, 1977). A few American blacks had encountered Jews as Southern planters and slaveholders (one of whom, Judah P. Benjamin, became the second most powerful leader of the Confederate States of America), and as Northern merchants and abolitionists. For different approaches to the history of Jewish-black relations, beginning with the Iberian and Caribbean background, see David Brion Davis, *Slavery and Human Progress* (New York: Oxford University Press, 1984), 82–101; Robert G. Weisbord and Arthur Stein, *Bittersweet Encounter: The Afro-American and the American Jew* (Westport, Conn.: Greenwood Press, 1970); David Levering Lewis, "Parallels and Divergences: Assimilationist Strategies of Afro-American and Jewish Elites from 1910 to the Early 1930s," *Journal of American History* 71, no. 3 (Dec. 1984): 543–64; and Hasia R. Diner, *In the Almost Promised Land: American Jews and Blacks, 1915–1935* (Westport, Conn.: Greenwood Press, 1977). Despite some historical errors, Lenora E. Berson's *The Negroes and the Jews* (New York: Random House, 1971) contains important information and insights, but it is almost useless to scholars because it lacks notes, any reference to sources or bibliography, and an index.

22. Herbert Aptheker, ed., *A Documentary History of the Negro People in the United States,* vol. 1 (New York: The Citadel Press, 1969), 349, 456; Blassingame, *Frederick Douglass Papers,* 3:556; Harlan, "Booker T. Washington's Discovery of the Jews," 277n10. Compare these statements by blacks to the jurist Louis Marshall's boast to the 1926 annual convention of the NAACP: "We were subjected to indignities in comparison with which to sit in a 'Jim Crow' car is to occupy a palace." Quoted in Lewis, "Parallels and Divergences," 546.

23. Diner, *Almost Promised Land,* 28–81, 89–115. The Yiddish newspapers Diner analyzes had a readership of more than 550,000 by 1925. For examples of ethnic jokes and stereotypes, see Levine, *Black Culture,* 302–06; Diner, *Almost Promised Land,* 92–93.

24. Diner, *Almost Promised Land,* 118–91; Harlan, "Booker T. Washington's Discovery of the Jews," 271–74; Lewis, "Parallels and Divergences," 546–62; Lynch, *Edward Wilmot Blyden,* 63–65. Blyden, like Douglass before him, felt an affinity with Arabs and Islam. Yet, apart from the Jewish homeland in Palestine, he wanted to admit Jews to Africa while excluding whites. His views drew on an African American tradition of "Ethiopianist" biblical interpretation, according to which Jethro, an Ethiopian priest, was the divinely appointed religious mentor of Moses, who married a black Cushite.

25. Lynch, *Edward Wilmot Blyden,* 64–65; Diner, *Almost Promised Land,* 22–23.

26. An investigation of the complex sources of discord between blacks and Jews, which became increasingly apparent in the 1930s, lies beyond the scope of this study. It is worth emphasizing, however, that in addition to concrete conflicts between ghetto-imprisoned blacks and Jewish landlords and merchants, the long-standing advice "to emulate the Jews" was bound to backfire as the disparities in education, wealth, and power between the two groups continued to widen. Few Jews or blacks were sensitive to the cultural differences that prepared Jews for the competitive struggles of urban life and that made the success of the black "Talented Tenth" irrelevant to the needs of the black masses. Many blacks were angered by the condescending and

patronizing counsel of wealthy Jews who kept insisting that they had endured much worse discrimination and suffering than blacks had. For some blacks, traditional anti-Semitic dogma furnished the easiest explanation. Much valuable information on this subject, especially for the 1960s, can be found in Weisbord and Stein, *Bittersweet Encounter*. But the deteriorating relationship between the two groups requires further comprehensive and dispassionate study.

27. *Marcus Garvey and UNIA Papers*, vol. 5, 127.

28. Ibid., 621.

29. Ibid., vol. 2 (Berkeley: University of California Press, 1983), 245, 317, 466; ibid., vol. 3 (Berkeley: University of California Press, 1984), 215–16; ibid., vol. 5, 127–28.

30. Ibid., vol. 5, 621.

31. Ibid., 627; Stein, *World of Marcus Garvey*, 200–204. Some of Garvey's followers, such as Arthur L. Reid, became active anti-Semites in the 1930s (Weisbord and Stein, *Bittersweet Encounter*, 46). There are obviously echoes of Garvey's ambivalent rhetoric in Malcolm X's outburst in a 1963 *Playboy* magazine interview: "The Jew never went sitting-in and crawling-in and sliding-in and freedom-riding, like he teaches and helps Negroes to do. The Jew stood up and stood together, and they used their ultimate power, the economic weapon. That's exactly what the Honorable Elijah Muhammad is trying to teach black men to do. The Jews pooled their money and bought the hotels that barred them." Quoted in ibid., 97.

32. For a time, Garvey enjoyed a considerable revival, symbolized by the naming of Marcus Garvey Park in Manhattan and by the publication of such works as Amy Jacques's *Garvey and Garveyism* (1963; repr., New York: Collier Books, 1970), and the reprinting by Arno Press of *Philosophy and Opinions of Marcus Garvey*, ed. Amy Jacques (New York, 1968). I am indebted to Professor Clarence Walker for sending me a sample of his current and devastating reevaluation, "The Virtuoso Illusionist: Marcus Garvey," now published in Walker, *Deromanticizing Black History: Critical Essays and Reappraisals* (Knoxville: University of Tennessee Press, 1991), 34–55.

33. David J. Garrow, *Bearing the Cross: Martin Luther King, Jr., and the Southern Christian Leadership Conference* (New York: William Morrow, 1986), 428.

34. For the searing and at times liberating experience of black soldiers in the Civil War, see Ira Berlin et al., eds., *Freedom: A Documentary History of Emancipation, 1861–1867*, The Black Military Experience, 2nd series (Cambridge, UK: Cambridge University Press, 1982).

35. Andrew Hacker, "Black Crime, White Racism," *New York Review of Books* (March 3, 1988): 36–41. Puerto Ricans are the only designated ethnic group whose family income falls below that of blacks.

36. There were occasional exceptions to this generalization. In the mid-1840s, when the ACS had virtually given up hope of winning government support and sought to persuade the clergy to raise funds for selective emigration, Ralph Randolph Gurley sounded the theme of moral obligation: "Let us reflect for a moment how much we are indebted to the colored race. How much have they toiled for us? How many of our blessings have come to us through their daily labors? How much of our wealth have they poured into our coffers? How many of our children have been nursed by them? How much of our present prosperity is the result of their joyless and untiring industry! . . . They have a claim upon us from which we never can shrink, without violating some of our most solemn and imperative obligations!" *African Repository* 21 (June 1845): 163–64.

37. See, for example, Mechal Sobel, *The World They Made Together: Black and White Values in Eighteenth-Century Virginia* (Princeton, N.J.: Princeton University Press, 1988).

38. "Annual Message to Congress," Dec. 1, 1862, in *The Collected Works of Abraham Lincoln*, ed. Roy P. Basler, vol. 5 (New Brunswick, N.J.: Rutgers University Press, 1953), 520–21; Phillip W. Magness and Sebastian N. Page, "Lincoln and Colonization: Navi-

gating the Evidences," http://www.hnn.us/articles/137542.html; Eric Foner, *The Fiery Trial: Abraham Lincoln and American Slavery* (New York: W. W. Norton, 2010), 257–63.

39. Henry Highland Garnet, *A Memorial Discourse; by Rev. Henry Highland Garnet, Delivered in the Hall of the House of Representatives, Washington City, D.C. on Sabbath, February 12, 1865,* with an introduction by James McCune Smith, M.D. (Philadelphia: Joseph M. Wilson, 1865).

40. Ibid., 69–74, 86–87. In a sermon in December 1862, anticipating the forthcoming Emancipation Proclamation, Garnet pictured Lincoln as a new Saul: "But God be praised, one has been chosen, and anointed by the people, who is greater than Saul, and to him, it would seem is committed the work of destroying the power that has occasioned our national wrong." However, Garnet warned, "if after the First of next January, the lowing and bleating of the enemy's herds and flocks are heard in our camps, we shall meet the displeasure of the Almighty, and our gallant leader, whose name has hitherto been a tower of strength, may fall on the hights [*sic*] of some Gilboa, a victim of his forbearance." *National Principia*, December 11, 1862, *BAP*, reel 14, 611.

41. Garnet, *Memorial Discourse*, 89–91.

6. COLONIZATIONIST IDEOLOGY: LEONARD BACON AND "IRREMEDIABLE DEGRADATION"

1. Theodore Weld to William Lloyd Garrison, January 2, 1833, in *Letters of Theodore Dwight Weld, Angelina Grimké Weld, and Sarah Grimké, 1822–1844,* ed. Gilbert H. Barnes and Dwight L. Dumond (1934; repr., Gloucester, Mass.: Peter Smith, 1965), 1:98.

2. Leonard Bacon, *Slavery Discussed in Occasional Essays, from 1833 to 1846* (New York, 1846), p. iii; [Bacon], "Report of the Committee appointed February 18, 1823, to inquire respecting the black population of the United States," in *Memoirs of American Missionaries, Formerly Connected with the Society of Inquiry Respecting Missions, in the Andover Theological Seminary* . . . (Boston, 1823), 303. Copies of Bacon's "Report" were widely distributed in New England; a slightly revised version was also incorporated into a review essay in the *Christian Spectator,* which was then reprinted in the *Seventh Annual Report of the American Society for Colonizing the Free People of Colour of the United States* (Washington, D. C., 1824), 87–104 (hereafter ACS). See "Review of the Reports of the American Colonization Society," *Christian Spectator* 5 (Sept. 1, 1823): 485–94; (October 1, 1823): 540–51 ; Leonard Bacon to Alice Bacon, May 27, 1823, series 1, box 1, folder 14; Thomas F. Davies to Leonard Bacon, July 28, 1823, ibid., folder 15, Bacon Family Papers, Yale University Library.

3. [Bacon], "Report of the Committee," 302–04. Even Bacon was surprised by the effectiveness of his formula; as he wrote his mother, when the "Report" was first read, "a very great and unexpected degree of interest was excited in the members of the Society. They accepted the Report unanimously and adopted the measures recommended by the Committee with a view to keep the subject permanently before them. . . . [Some professors] recommended that we should first consult with the managers of the Colonization Society at Washington on the best means of producing an excitement at the North, and therefore were of the opinion that during the vacation we ought not only to write to them on the subject, but if possible to send an agent to see them and talk with them and lay before them our own views and feelings." Bacon was chosen as the principal agent, and he wrote the above lines in Philadelphia, on his way to Washington. Leonard Bacon to Alice Bacon, May 27, 1823.

4. Joel Bernard, "Between Religion and Reform: American Moral Societies, 1812–1821" (unpublished paper). I am much indebted to Joel Bernard, who years ago drew my attention to Bacon's 1823 "Report" and who provided a critique of the paper from which this chapter is adapted.

5. My discussion of New England theology and benevolent societies draws on

George M. Marsden, *The Evangelical Mind and the New School Presbyterian Experience* (New Haven, Conn.: Yale University Press, 1970); H. Shelton Smith, *Changing Conceptions of Original Sin* (New York: Charles Scribner's, 1955); Joseph A. Conforti, *Samuel Hopkins and the New Divinity Movement: Calvinism, the Congregational Ministry, and Reform in New England Between the Great Awakenings* (Grand Rapids, Mich.: Christian University Press, 1981); Oliver W. Elsbree, *The Rise of the Missionary Spirit in America, 1790–1815* (Williamsport, Pa.: The Williamsport Printing and Binding Co., 1928); Charles I. Foster, *An Errand of Mercy: The Evangelical United Front, 1790–1837* (Chapel Hill: University of North Carolina Press, 1960); Sidney Earl Mead, *Nathaniel William Taylor, 1786–1858* (Chicago: University of Chicago Press, 1942); Mark A. Noll, *America's God: From Jonathan Edwards to Abraham Lincoln* (New York: Oxford University Press, 2002); Earl A. Pope, *New England Calvinism and the Disruption of the Presbyterian Church* (New York: Garland, 1987); Douglas A. Sweeney and Allen C. Guelzo, eds., *The New England Theology: From Jonathan Edwards to Edwards Amasa Park* (Grand Rapids, Mich.: Baker Academic, 2006); Douglas A. Sweeney, *Nathaniel Taylor, New Haven Theology, and the Legacy of Jonathan Edwards* (New York: Oxford University Press, 2002); Claude Welch, *Protestant Thought in the Nineteenth Century*, vol. 1, *1799–1870* (New Haven, Conn.: Yale University Press, 1972); William K. B. Stoever, "The Calvinist Theological Tradition," in *Encyclopedia of the American Religious Experience*, ed. Charles H. Lippy and Peter W. Williams, 3 vols. (New York: Scribner's, 1988), 2:1039–56.

6. [Bacon], "Report of the Committee," 298. A number of historians have drawn a similar distinction between the relatively good material conditions and the moral evils of American slavery. See especially Robert William Fogel, *Without Consent or Contract: The Rise and Fall of American Slavery* (New York: W. W. Norton, 1989).

7. [Bacon], "Report of the Committee," 298–99. Congregationalist ministers and New England Federalists had long pointed to slavery as an explanation for the South's supposedly backward economy and low state of morals. See James D. Essig, *The Bonds of Wickedness: American Evangelicals against Slavery, 1770–1808* (Philadelphia: Temple University Press, 1982), 98–103; David Brion Davis, *The Problem of Slavery in the Age of Revolution, 1770–1823* (Ithaca, N.Y.: Cornell University Press, 1975), 336–42. Yet as Alison Goodyear Freehling has shown, the views Bacon expressed were also widely shared in Virginia. *Drift Toward Dissolution: The Virginia Slavery Debate of 1831–1832* (Baton Rouge: Louisiana State University Press, 1982).

8. [Bacon], "Report of the Committee," 300–301.

9. Ibid., 299, 301–2. Curiously, Bacon omitted the following passage from Jefferson's Query XVIII in *Notes on the State of Virginia*: " . . . that considering numbers, nature and natural means only, a revolution of the wheel of fortune, an exchange of situation [between whites and blacks] is among possible events: that it may become probable by supernatural interference!" Paul Leicester Ford, ed., *The Writings of Thomas Jefferson*, 10 vols. (New York: 1892–99), 3:267.

10. [Bacon], "Report of the Committee," 302, 305. Theodore Dwight, for example, when addressing the Connecticut Society for the Promotion of Freedom in 1794, affirmed that when slave rebellions erupted in the South and whites appealed for military support, "Surely, no friend to freedom and justice will dare to lend them his aid," and quoted the prophet Jeremiah on the Lord's proclamation of liberty and bloody destruction of transgressors. *An Oration Spoken before The Connecticut Society, for the Promotion of Freedom and the Relief of Persons Unlawfully Holden in Bondage* (Hartford, Conn. 1794), 19–20.

11. [Bacon], "Report of the Committee," 299–300.

12. "Review of New Publications," *Christian Spectator* 5 (Oct. 1, 1823): 544; ACS, *Seventh Annual Report* (Washington, D.C.: R. Rapine, 1818), 94. There is no way of knowing whether Bacon wrote the inserted passage, but the editor of the *Christian Spectator*, Thomas F. Davies, seemed eager to print whatever Bacon submitted, even though Davies expressed skepticism "with respect to the possibility of materially diminish-

ing the black population of our country by means of the Colonization Society," and stressed instead "the great benefit" that would result from "the civilization of knowledge which the colony may impart to the [African] tribes surrounding it." Davies to Bacon, July 28, 1823, Bacon Family Papers. I suspect that Bacon had been impressed by the need for greater caution after his visit in 1823 to the ACS headquarters in Washington. None of the versions of the "Report" lists Bacon as the author.

13. [Bacon], "Report of the Committee," 300.

14. Leonard Bacon, *A Plea for Africa, Delivered in New Haven, July Fourth, 1825* (New Haven, Conn., 1825), 13–14.

15. Ibid.

16. Davis, *Problem of Slavery in Age of Revolution*, 285–99; Essig, *Bonds of Wickedness*, 14–52, 106–08, 113; David Brion Davis, *Slavery and Human Progress* (New York: Oxford University Press, 1984), 116–29.

17. Orlando Patterson, *Freedom*, vol. 1, *Freedom in the Making of Western Culture* (New York: Basic Books, 1991), 316–44, 376–80. See also Dale B. Martin, *Slavery as Salvation: The Metaphor of Slavery in Pauline Christianity* (New Haven, Conn.: Yale University Press, 1990).

18. David Brion Davis, *The Problem of Slavery in Western Culture* (New York: Oxford University Press, 1988), 75–90.

19. Patterson, *Freedom*, 1:326, 329–34.

20. In addition to sources cited in note 5, I have drawn on Paul Ramsey, introduction to Jonathan Edwards, *The Works of Jonathan Edwards*, vol, 1, *Freedom of the Will*, (New Haven, Conn.: Yale University Press, 1957), 11–47, and passim, Nathaniel Niles, *Two Discourses on Liberty, Delivered in the North Church, in Newburyport* (Newburyport, Mass., 1774); Perry Miller, *Jonathan Edwards* (New York: W. Sloane, 1949), 235–63; George M. Marsden, *Jonathan Edwards: A Life* (New Haven, Conn.: Yale University Press, 2003) 255–58, 465–71, 498–501.

21. Noll, *America's God*, 271–77.

22. Theodore Bacon, *Leonard Bacon*, 31–80, 100–43; Marsden, *Evangelical Mind*, 43–52; Mead, *Nathaniel William Taylor*, 24–53, 62–63, 101–27, 225–26; Welch, *Protestant Thought*, 127–37; Stoever, "The Calvinist Theological Tradition," 1048–50.

23. [Bacon], "Report of the Committee," 301.

24. "Committee on Colonization," in *Memoirs of American Missionaries*, 29–34; [Bacon], "Report of the Committee," 296–97.

25. [Bacon], "Report of the Committee," 296–97, 303, 311.

26. See especially Donald L. Horowitz, *Ethnic Groups in Conflict* (Berkeley: University of California Press, 1985).

27. Robert Austin Warner, *New Haven Negroes: A Social History* (1940; repr., New York: Arno Press, 1969), 3–4, 11, 19–25, 27, 46–47.

28. [Bacon], "Report of the Committee," 301, 311.

29. Ibid., 296–97; Warner, *New Haven Negroes*; Theodore Bacon, *Leonard Bacon*, 81, 164, 182; Bacon, *Plea for Africa*, 10.

30. John M. Merriman, *The Margins of City Life: Explorations on the French Urban Frontier, 1815–1851* (New York: Oxford University Press, 1991), 3–23, 27–29.

31. George M. Fredrickson, *The Black Image in the White Mind: The Debate on Afro-American Character and Destiny, 1817–1914* (New York: Harper & Row, 1971), 5; Theodore Bacon, *Leonard Bacon*, 182.

32. Warner, *New Haven Negroes*, 21, 28–29, 58. In 1810–11, William Lanson built on contract the last, stone section of New Haven's Long Wharf. In October 1831, a mob seized four white women and fourteen white men in "New Liberia." Earlier, mobs had assaulted blacks in New Haven and had torn down "a Negro hut on 'Sodom Hill.' "

33. [Bacon], "Report of the Committee," 311. For contrasting and roughly contemporary efforts to deport and make use of criminal classes, see Robert Hughes, *The Fatal Shore* (New York: Alfred A. Knopf, 1987), 1–42; Joanna Waley-Cohen, *Exile*

in Mid-Qing China, 1758–1820 (New Haven, Conn.: Yale University Press, 1991), 1–32, 78–102.

34. [Bacon], "Report of the Committee," 303–4, 309.

35. Ibid., 309–10.

36. In the 1820s, American free blacks became increasingly aware that emigration to Liberia had resulted in the literal death of many of their brethren.

37. *Memoirs of American Missionaries*, 13–14, 217–19; P. J. Staudenraus, *The African Colonization Movement, 1816–1865* (New York: Columbia University Press, 1961), 18–19, 28, 37–47; [Bacon],"Report of the Committee," 307, 309, 312, 316.

38. Lawrence B. Goodheart, *Abolitionist, Actuary, Atheist: Elizur Wright and the Reform Impulse* (Kent, Ohio: Kent State University Press, 1990), 37, 44, 46, 56, 80. Wright, who like most abolitionists of his generation had once supported the colonization movement, wrote to Bacon in 1837: "I put it to your inmost soul Bacon: you know you were wrong in that whole miserable humbug of colonization. . . . Now take my advice and come out like a man—a true Christian—and confess your sin." Ibid., 37.

39. Theodore Bacon, *Leonard Bacon*, 187; Staudenraus, *African Colonization Movement*, 77–78, 117.

40. [Bacon], "Report of the Committee," 313.

41. Ibid., 306, 312.

42. Ibid., 307, 314–15.

43. Samuel H. Cowles to Leonard Bacon, Feb. 9, 1825, part 1, box 1, folder 19, Bacon Family Papers.

44. Cowles to Bacon, Feb. 9, 1825; David E. Swift, *Black Prophets of Justice: Activist Clergy before the Civil War* (Baton Rouge: Louisiana State University Press, 1989), 19–23.

45. Cowles to Bacon, Feb. 9, 1825; D. Greene to Leonard Bacon, April 25, 1824, part 1, box 1, folder 16, Bacon Family Papers.

46. Greene to Bacon, April 25, 1824.

47. Cowles to Bacon, Feb. 9, 1825.

48. Ibid.

49. Ibid.

50. Ibid.; Julie Winch, *Philadelphia's Black Elite: Activism, Accommodation, and the Struggle for Autonomy, 1787–1848* (Philadelphia: Temple University Press, 1988), 29–38.

51. Cowles to Bacon, February 9, 1825.

7. FROM OPPOSING COLONIZATION TO IMMEDIATE ABOLITION

1. John Hepburn, *The American Defence of the Christian Golden Rule, or An Essay to Prove the Unlawfulness of Making Slaves of Men* (Philadelphia: Andrew Bradford, 1714), 23–43.

2. Yet, some eighty years before Congress outlawed the slave trade in 1808, America's slave population began to benefit from rapid natural growth. North America absorbed no more than 5 percent of the African slaves transported to the New World.

3. Gary B. Nash, *Forging Freedom: The Formation of Philadelphia's Black Community, 1720–1840* (Cambridge, Mass: Harvard University Press, 1988), 101. James Oliver Horton and Lois E. Horton, *In Hope of Liberty: Culture, Community, and Protest Among Northern Free Blacks, 1700–1860* (New York: Oxford University Press, 1997), 179. George E. Brooks, "The Providence African Society's Sierra Leone Emigration Scheme, 1794–1795: Prologue to the African Colonization Movement," *The International Journal of African Historical Studies* 7, no. 2 (1974): 185–86.

4. This vague sense of Africa and the importance of the Sierra Leone model is demonstrated in a recently discovered source. See Richard S. Newman, Roy E. Finkenbine, and Douglass Mooney, "Philadelphia Emigrationist Petition, circa 1792: An Introduction," *William and Mary Quarterly* 64, no. 1 (Jan. 2007): 162.

5. For the Edwardsean antislavery tradition, see Kenneth P. Minkema and Harry S. Stout, "The Edwardsean Tradition and the Antislavery Debate, 1740–1865," *Jour-*

nal of American History 92, no. 1 (June 2005): 52–55, and passim. For Hopkins and his role in Providence among the black population, see Brooks, "The Providence African Society's Sierra Leone Emigration Scheme," 185–86; Horton and Horton, *In Hope of Liberty*, 179. For a general account of Hopkins's life, see Joseph A Conforti, *Samuel Hopkins and the New Divinity Movement: Calvinism, the Congregational Ministry, and Reform in New England Between the Great Awakenings* (Grand Rapids, Mich: Christian University Press, 1981).

6. Nash, *Forging Freedom*, 101.

7. Ibid.; Brooks, "The Providence African Society's Sierra Leone Emigration Scheme," 187; Horton and Horton, *In Hope of Liberty*, 179.

8. Sheldon H. Harris, *Paul Cuffe: Black American and the African Return* (New York: Simon & Schuster, 1972), 15–17.

9. Ibid., 58.; Lamont Thomas, *Rise to Be a People: A Biography of Paul Cuffe* (Urbana: University of Illinois Press, 1986), 4, 73–74, 88–91.

10. Horton and Horton, *In Hope of Liberty*, 186.

11. I rely heavily on Julie Winch's excellent biography of James Forten, *A Gentleman of Color: The Life of James Forten* (New York: Oxford University Press, 2002), 177–97; Horton and Horton, *In Hope of Liberty*, 177–87.

12. From 1800 to 1810, the free black population increased by 72 percent. Calculated from the table in *Remarks on the Colonization of the Western Coast of Africa by the Free Negroes of the United States, and the Consequent Civilization of African and Suppression of the Slave Trade* (New York: W. L. Burroughs Steam Power Press, 1850), 9. For a thorough and modern demographic analysis of free black population patterns in the major cities of the United States see Leonard P. Curry, *The Free Black in Urban America, 1800–1850: The Shadow of the Dream* (Chicago: University of Chicago Press, 1981).

13. Nash, *Forging Freedom*, 242.

14. Quoted in Horton and Horton, *In Hope of Liberty*, 188.

15. Winch, *A Gentleman of Color*, 182.

16. Thomas, *Rise to Be a People*, 118, 118n18.

17. Winch, *A Gentleman of Color*; Isaac Van Arsdale Brown, *Biography of Robert Finley* (Philadelphia, 1819), 99–102, quoted in William Loren Katz, introduction to William Lloyd Garrison, *Thoughts on African Colonization* (New York: Arno Press and the New York Times, 1968), vii.

18. As early as January 10, 1817, a meeting of blacks in Georgetown expressed their unwavering opposition to African colonization but indicated a willingness to consider a settlement on the Missouri River. Winch, *Gentleman of Color*, 189–90.

19. Ibid., 189–91.

20. Nash, *Forging Freedom*, 237.

21. Quoted in ibid., 237–38.

22. Katz, introduction to Garrison, *Thoughts on African Colonization*, ix.

23. William Lloyd Garrison, *Thoughts on African Colonization: Or, an Impartial Exhibition of the Doctrines, Principles and Purposes of the American Colonization Society. Together with the Resolutions, Addresses and Remonstrances of the Free People of Color* (Boston: Printed and published by Garrison and Knapp, 1832), Part 2, 9.

24. Ibid. Part 2, 10.

25. Ibid., Part 1, *Introductory Remarks*, 40, 6.

26. Ibid., Part 2, 11.

27. Ibid.

28. Ibid., 11–12.

29. In fact, many black abolitionists would subsequently remember the anticolonization protest as the "Spirit of 1817." Julie Winch, *Philadelphia's Black Elite: Activism, Accommodation, and the Struggle for Autonomy, 1787–1848* (Philadelphia: Temple University Press, 1988), 38.

30. Between 1804 and 1808, there was a significant increase in the number of Afri-

can slaves imported into the South, mainly South Carolina. Most of the 40,000-plus imports were legal and were brought in response to the demand created by the Louisiana Purchase and the knowledge that importations would soon be prohibited.

31. David Brion Davis, *Challenging the Boundaries of Slavery* (Cambridge, Mass.; Harvard University Press, 2003), 35–36.

32. For a discussion of why this occurred, and the meanings surrounding "African" see Ira Berlin, "Time, Space, and the Evolution of Afro-American Society on British Mainland North America," *The American Historical Review* 85, no. 1 (Feb. 1980): 53; Craig Steven Wilder, *In the Company of Black Men: The African Influence on African American Culture in New York City* (New York: New York University Press, 2005), 158.

33. Quoted in ibid.

34. This opposition to the ACS had the unintended effect of opening black lines of communication from Canada, the West Indies, Africa, and all along the Eastern Seaboard of the United States. These new international connections were further strengthened as black denominations, such as Richard Allen's African Methodist Episcopal Church, began to conduct missionary activity abroad. Laurie F. Maffly-Kipp, *Setting Down the Sacred Past: African-American Race Histories* (Cambridge, Mass: Belknap Press of Harvard University Press, 2010), 50–51.

35. Daniel Walker Howe, *What Hath God Wrought: The Transformation of America, 1815–1848* (New York: Oxford University Press, 2007), 263.

36. Horton and Horton, *In Hope of Liberty*, 194.

37. Ibid., 195.

38. John Brown Russwurm, "Condition and Prospects of Haiti," John Brown Russwurm Papers, Bowdoin College Archives, Brunswick, Maine.

39. *Weekly Anglo-African*, Jan. 12, 1861. The staying power of affection for Haiti throughout the antebellum period and beyond is rather phenomenal given the numbers of returned emigrants. The symbolism of what Haiti represented to American blacks clearly outweighed the setbacks of emigration. For a thorough analysis of this "legacy" in the nineteenth century, see Philip N. Edmondson, "The St. Domingue Legacy in Black Activist and Antislavery Writings in the United States, 1791–1862" (Ph.D. diss., University of Maryland, College Park, 2003).

40. Richard S. Newman, *The Transformation of American Abolitionism: Fighting Slavery in the Early Republic* (Chapel Hill: University of North Carolina Press, 2002), 96.

41. Ibid., 99, 103.

42. Bella Gross, "Freedom's Journal and the Rights of All," *The Journal of Negro History* 17, no. 3 (July 1932): 245.

43. For Cornish's early life and work I rely heavily on Christopher Allison, "Floating on the Stream of Prejudice: The Making of the Religious Activism of Samuel Cornish" (M.A. thesis, Yale University, 2010); the first significant biographical treatment is Howard Nathaniel Christian, "Samuel Cornish: Pioneer Negro Journalist" (M.A. thesis, Howard University, 1936). A concise and critical chapter (with a few biographical errors) is "The Negro Conservative: Samuel Eli Cornish" in Jane H. and William H. Pease, *Bound with Them in Chains; a Biographical History of the Antislavery Movement*, Contributions in American History, no. 18 (Westport, Conn: Greenwood Press, 1972), 140–61. For an excellent analysis of Cornish's interactions with other abolitionists and reformers, white and black, see David E. Swift, "Black Presbyterian Attacks on Racism: Samuel Cornish, Theodore Wright and Their Contemporaries," *Journal of Presbyterian History* 51 (Dec. 1, 1973): 433–70; Swift, *Black Prophets of Justice: Activist Clergy Before the Civil War* (Baton Rouge: Louisiana State University Press, 1989), especially chapters 3, 4, and 5.

44. Sandra Sanford Young, "John Brown Russwurm's Dilemma: Citizenship or Emigration?" in *Prophets of Protest: Reconsidering the History of American Abolitionism*, ed. Timothy P. McCarthy and John Stauffer (New York: New Press, 2006), 92 and passim.

45. Ibid.

46. For a good exposition of antiblack sentiment, in print and in public in the 1820s, leading up to the publication of *Freedom's Journal*, see Shane White, *Stories of Freedom in Black New York* (Cambridge, Mass: Harvard University Press, 2002), 46–51; Swift, *Black Prophets of Justice*, 32.

47. David Brion Davis, "The Emergence of Immediatism in British and American Antislavery Thought," in Davis, *From Homicide to Slavery: Studies in American Culture* (New York: Oxford University Press, 1984), 238–57; previously published in *Mississippi Valley Historical Review* 49, no. 2 (September 1962): 209–30.

48. The result of this refusal to print black protest meant that most whites were largely ignorant of the fact that there was significant black opposition to colonization. Thus, when Garrison published *The Liberator*, accusations that Garrison had tainted the people of color against colonization were natural. There would only be pockets of whites who were aware of black opposition prior to the 1830s. Swift, *Black Prophets of Justice*, 26.

49. Ibid., 40. Cornish and Russwurm seemed to have been substantially more optimistic about the exposure of the *Journal* among the black populace, despite the obvious barriers of literacy: "interesting fact that there are FIVE HUNDRED THOUSAND free persons of colour, one half of whom might peruse, and the whole be benefited by the publications of the Journal." *Freedom's Journal*, March 16, 1827.

50. The assessment that Cornish was the more dominant voice during the first six months of *Freedom's Journal* has been affirmed by most close observers of Cornish's life and *Freedom's Journal*. See Swift, *Black Prophets of Justice*, 30; Christopher Allison, "Floating on the Stream of Prejudice," 32; Gross, "Freedom's Journal and the Rights of All," 247–48. Timothy Patrick McCarthy, " 'To Plead Our Own Cause': Black Print Culture and the Origins of American Abolitionism," in McCarthy and Stauffer, *Prophets of Protest*, 131. Also, in Cornish's departure note he indicates his dominance as well: "Six months of our Editorial labours having expired; by mutual consent, and good wishes for the prosperity and usefulness of each other, our connection in the 'JOURNAL,' is this day dissolved, and the right and prerogatives exclusively vested in the Junior Editor, J.B. RUSSWURM." "To Our Patrons," *Freedom's Journal*, Sept. 14, 1827.

51. "To Our Patrons," *Freedom's Journal*, March 16, 1827.

52. Allison, "Floating on the Stream of Prejudice," 2.; "Colonization Society," *Freedom's Journal*, June 8, 1827. In this same article he expresses his careful deference, but firm disagreement: "There are many friends of colonization, whom we respect, and for no consideration, would we be guilty of treating their opinions lightly. Their objects are emancipation; the salvation of Africa; and the extermination of the slave trade. Nothing could be more worthy the philanthropist, and the Christian. . . . In soliciting patronage to our Journal among Colonizationists, we expressed ourselves to many of them, as opposed to colonization in any shape, unless it be merely considered as a missionary establishment; yet, if we were wrong, our minds were open to conviction, and we wished to see the subject discussed; they were generally pleased with the idea. If the Colonization Society possess any merits, it cannot lose by investigation; but if the motives of its founders will not bear investigation, it ought to sink: every good man will say the same."

53. Benjamin Quarles, *Black Abolitionists* (New York: Oxford University Press, 1969), 184.

54. Walker's *Appeal* reserves his praise for two individuals in *The Appeal*, Cornish and Richard Allen. Theodore Wright: "The press came out against us, and we trembled. Maryland passed laws to force out the colored people. It was deemed proper to make them go, whether they would or not. Then we despaired. Ah, Mr. President, that was a dark and gloomy period. The united views and intentions of the people of color were made known, and the nation awoke as from slumber. The 'Freedom's Journal,' edited by Rev. Sam'l. E. Cornish, announced the facts in the case, our entire

opposition. Sir, it came like a clap of thunder!" ADDRESS. of the Rev. Theodore S. Wright, "Before the Convention of the New York State Anti-Slavery Society, on the Acceptance of the Annual Report, Held at Utica, Sept. 30," *Colored American,* Oct. 14, 1837.

55. "Colonization Society," *Freedom's Journal,* June 8, 1827.

56. Allison, "Floating on the Stream of Prejudice," 33. Cornish writes of his response to Russwurm's departure: " . . . the sudden change of the late Editor of 'Freedom's Journal' in respect to colonization, has excited much astonishment, and led to many inquiries; to me the subject is equally strange as to others, and I can only dispose of it, by classing it with the other novelties of the day." He encouraged his readers to "dispose" of their feelings over what had transpired and support the new venture. See "To Our Patrons, and the Publick Generally" *Rights of All,* May 29, 1829. Others were less civil: "This John B. Russworm is known, I presume, to every one of us; his ingratitude is but too deeply stamped on the minds of many . . . which neither time nor space will obliterate. After he subverted the pledge he made to his colored brethren, he left, to our satisfaction, his country—suffused with shame—and branded with the stigma of disgrace—to dwell in that land for which the temptor MONEY caused him to avow his preferment. . . . we will pray God, that his notions of nobleness may never enter our hearts, and that we will not be contented with our condition, but will make it better in this our native home." "To the Editor of the Liberator" *The Liberator,* April 16, 1831, quoted in *The Mind of the Negro as Reflected in the Letters Written During the Crisis,* ed. Carter G. Woodson (New York: Russell & Russell, 1969), 161.

57. "Colonization," *Freedom's Journal,* March 14, 1829.

58. "The Old Hobby Colonization," *Rights of All,* Sept. 18, 1829.

59. Russwurm's defection to Liberia haunted *The Rights of All* from the start. *The Rights of All* was initially supposed to be a continuation of *Freedom's Journal,* with Cornish back at the helm. But Cornish was forced to change the name to distance himself from the scandal and to incur a lot of debt to keep the paper going; he was apologetic to his readers in the inaugural edition of *The Rights of All* over both the slippage in quality of *Freedom's Journal* and the opinions of its late editor. By October of 1829, recurrent sickness and insurmountable financial obstacles led to the closure of Cornish's second paper; once again Cornish was finished after only six months. Allison, "Floating on the Stream of Prejudice," 32–33.

60. Newman, *Transformation of American Abolitionism,* 97.

61. David Walker, *Walker's Appeal, in Four Articles; Together with a Preamble to the Coloured Citizens of the World, but in Particular, and Very Expressly, to Those of the United States of America, Written in Boston, State of Massachusetts, September 28, 1829,* Third and Last Edition with additional notes, corrections, &c. (Boston, Mass.: David Walker, 1830), 76.

62. Garrison acknowledged *The Rights of All* and called Cornish "a colored gentleman of intelligence and spirit." See *Genius of Universal Emancipation,* Feb. 5, 1830, vol. 4, issue 22. He reprinted original pieces from *Freedom's Journal* (a Lundy tribute from the March 21, 1828, issue) in the *Philanthropist,* though it is unknown if he read any of the journal in 1827 when Cornish was senior editor. Henry Mayer, *All on Fire: William Lloyd Garrison and the Abolition of Slavery,* 1st ed. (New York: St. Martin's Press, 1998), 54. Garrison called Walker's *Appeal* one of the most "remarkable productions of the age" with an "impassioned and determined spirit." He thought Walker's call for retributive justice was "injudicious" but recognized that his call to resistance was the right of a free people. "Walker's Appeal No. I," *The Liberator,* January 8, 1831, 1:2.

63. David W. Blight, "Garrison's Legacy for Our Time," in *William Lloyd Garrison at Two Hundred: History, Legacy, and Memory,* ed. James B. Stewart (New Haven, Conn.: Yale University Press, 2008), 5.

64. Winch, *A Gentleman of Color,* passim; Newman, *Transformation of American Abolitionism,* 112–16.

65. Newman, *Transformation of American Abolitionism,* 112–16; Mayer, *All on Fire,* 101, 110, 116, 147, 173. While Mayer gives some recognition to Forten's aid and names James G. Barbadoes as Garrison's "chief black ally" in Boston, Winch shows that Forten's support and influence were considerably stronger than previous historians have recognized. On the essential black support of Garrison and *The Liberator,* see Donald M. Jacobs, "William Lloyd Garrison's *Liberator* and Boston's Blacks, 1830–1865," *The New England Quarterly* 44, no. 2 (June 1971): 261.

66. Elizabeth Heyrick, *Immediate, Not Gradual Abolition* (London, 1824), 36; Davis, "Emergence of Immediatism," 248–57. In 1829 there were still slaves in Philadelphia, even though Pennsylvania had passed a gradual emancipation act in 1780.

67. This paragraph is a revised version of the opening paragraph in Davis, "Emergence of Immediatism," 238–39.

68. "TO THE PUBLIC," *The Liberator,* January 1, 1831.

69. Newman, *Transformation of American Abolitionism,* 105.

70. Ibid., 105–6.

71. For black gratitude towards Garrison in Boston, see James Oliver Horton and Lois E. Horton, *Black Bostonians: Family Life and Community Struggle in the Antebellum North* (New York: Holmes & Meier, 1979), 84.

72. Quoted in Jacobs, "William Lloyd Garrison's *Liberator* and Boston's Blacks," 260.

73. "ADDRESS of the Rev. Theodore S. Wright . . . ," *Colored American,* Oct. 14, 1837.

74. Garrison, *Thoughts on African Colonization,* Part 2, 8.

75. Ibid., Part 1, 104–05; Part 2, 14.

76. Ibid., Part 1, 155–56.

77. Blight, "Garrison's Legacy for Our Time," 7.

8. FREE BLACKS AS THE KEY TO SLAVE EMANCIPATION

1. Carter G. Woodson, ed., *The Mind of the Negro as Reflected in Letters Written During the Crisis, 1800–1860* (Westport, Conn.: Greenwood Press, 1969), 654, 658.

2. Frederick Douglass, "Temperance and Anti-Slavery: An Address Delivered in Paisley, Scotland, on 30 March 1846," *The Frederick Douglass Papers,* Series One, *Speeches, Debates, and Interviews,* ed. John W. Blassingame, vol. 1: *1841–46* (New Haven, Conn.: Yale University Press, 1979), 206.

3. For the more positive view, see Benjamin Quarles, *Black Abolitionists* (New York: Oxford University Press, 1969), 40–41.

4. Carter Godwin Woodson, *Negro Orators and Their Orations* (Washington, D.C.: Associated Publishers, 1925), 93.

5. This paragraph draws on Christopher Mark Brady Allison, "Floating on the Stream of Prejudice: The Making of the Religious Activism of Samuel Cornish" (M.A. thesis, Yale University, May 2010), 24, 29.

6. "Address by Abraham D. Shadd, William Hamilton, and William Whipper, 13 June 1832," in *The Black Abolitionist Papers,* vol. 3, *The United States, 1830–1846,* ed. C. Peter Ripley (Chapel Hill: University of North Carolina Press, 1991), 109–15.

7. *Address to the People of Color of the City of New York, by Members of the Executive Committee of the American Anti-Slavery Society* (New York, 1834), 3–7.

8. Ibid.; *Objects of the Phoenix Society of New York,* 8. Led by prominent black and white figures, the Phoenix Society grew rapidly and founded a high school for colored youth as well as Ward Societies with lending libraries, reading rooms, and lecture series devoted to history and science as well as "morals, literature, and the mechanic arts." Much effort was given to the promotion of temperance and wholesome evening activities for black youth. Samuel Cornish, cofounder of the first black newspaper, played a key role in raising funds (often from women) to build up the

Society's library holdings. Dorothy B. Porter, "The Organized Educational Activities of Negro Literary Societies, 1828–1846," *The Journal of Negro Education* 5, no. 4 (Oct. 1936): 565–67.

9. While the financial crisis and depression of 1837 lay ahead, there would be continuing efforts to induce urban blacks to find employment in the countryside.

10. *Address to the People of Color,* 4.

11. W. J. Rorabaugh, *The Alcoholic Republic: An American Tradition* (New York: Oxford University Press, 1979), 237–40. According to Rorabaugh's charts, per capita consumption of distilled spirits was much higher in Scotland and Sweden than in the United States. In America the consumption of beer rose rapidly after 1881.

12. Douglass, "Temperance and Anti-Slavery," 206; Donald Yacovone, "The Transformation of the Black Temperance Movement, 1827–1854: An Interpretation," *Journal of the Early Republic* 8, no. 3 (Fall 1988): 281–97. Douglass also drew on personal experience to argue that slaveholders used alcohol to mollify and subdue their slaves. For reformers, the parallels and metaphors between slavery and intemperance were endless.

13. Anti-Slavery Convention of American Women, *An Address to Free Colored Americans* (New York, 1837).

14. Quotation from Ruth Bogin and Jean Fagan Yellin, introduction to *The Abolitionist Sisterhood: Women's Political Culture in Antebellum America,* ed. Jean Fagan Yellin and John C. Van Horne (Ithaca, N.Y.: Cornell University Press, 1994), 12; Dorothy Sterling, ed., *Turning the World Upside Down: The Anti-Slavery Convention of American Women, Held in New York City, May 9–12, 1837* (includes the Minutes of the Convention) (New York: CUNY Feminist Press, 1987), passim; Carolyn L. Karcher, *The First Woman in the Republic: A Cultural Biography of Lydia Maria Child* (Durham, N.C.: Duke University Press, 1994), 244–48; Gilbert Hobbs Barnes, *The Antislavery Impulse, 1830–1844* (1933; repr., Gloucester, Mass.: Peter Smith, 1957), 142–44; Julie Roy Jeffrey, *The Great Silent Army of Abolitionism: Ordinary Women in the Antislavery Movement* (Chapel Hill: University of North Carolina Press, 1998), 93–95.

15. "Ladies' Anti-Slavery Convention," *The Liberator* (1831–65), June 2, 1837, 7, 23 (American Periodicals Series Online, 90); Sterling, *Turning the World Upside Down,* 4. *The Liberator* lists the Grimkés as the main authors of the two pamphlets. The women's *Address* should not be confused with a piece that appeared in the June 3, 1837, *Colored American,* "For the Colored American. An Address," which had been delivered before the Female Branch Society of Zion, by William Thompson, at Zion's Church, on April 5.

16. Gerda Lerner, *The Grimké Sisters from South Carolina: Pioneers for Women's Rights and Abolition* (New York: Oxford University Press, 1998), passim; Catherine H. Birney, *Sarah and Angelina Grimké: The First American Women Advocates of Abolition and Women's Rights* (New York: Lee and Shepard, 1885), 172–73. In 1838, Sarah Grimké published *Letters on the Equality of the Sexes,* the first comprehensive statement of feminism to appear in America. According to Birney, who lived with the sisters toward the end of their lives, the two pamphlets distributed by the Convention made the sisters so widely known, and so increased the desire to hear them speak, "that invitations poured in upon them from different parts of the North and West, as well as from the New England States. It was finally decided that they should go to Boston first, to aid the brave, good women there, who, while willing to do all that women could do for the cause in a private capacity, had not yet been persuaded to open their lips for it in any kind of public meeting. It was not contemplated, however, that the sisters should address any but assemblies of women. Even Boston was not yet prepared for a greater infringement of the social proprieties" (173).

17. Sterling, *Turning the World Upside Down,* 13; Karcher, *First Woman in the Republic,* 246.

18. Sterling, *Turning the World Upside Down,* 14, 30–31; Karcher, *First Woman in the*

Republic, 244–47. In 1838 a larger number of women joined the Convention in Philadelphia, but a hostile mob attempted to disrupt the meeting and then burned down Pennsylvania Hall, driving the group to another location. The local press blamed the abolitionists for provoking the violence by seating blacks and whites side by side, a step toward the much feared racial "amalgamation."

19. Anti-Slavery Convention of American Women, *Address to Free Colored Americans*, 21.

20. Ibid., 30–31.

21. Ibid., 31, 5–6.

22. Ibid., 4. Sarah Grimké had been exposed to the realities of slavery from the time she was a small child. The most knowledgeable abolitionists, like Theodore Dwight Weld, who married Angelina Grimké, emphasized the same point. Weld wrote that from personal observation in the South, he knew that "atrocious cruelty" "is the rule, not the exception; that those who hold human beings as property will inflict upon them greater cruelties than they do upon their brutes." Yet such treatment was only "an appendage of slavery" that could turn the public mind "from the crowning horror of slavery." "At the *present crisis*, the inflictions of slavery on mind—its prostration of conscience—its reduction of accountability to a chattel—its destruction of personality—its death-stab into the soul of the slave—should constitute the main prominence before the public mind" (Weld to J. F. Robinson, May 1 (?), 1836, in *Letters of Theodore Dwight Weld, Angelina Grimké Weld, and Sarah Grimké, 1822–1844*, ed. Gilbert H. Barnes and Dwight L. Dumond, 2 vols. (1934; repr., Gloucester, Mass.: Peter Smith, 1965), 1:296–97.

23. Nat Turner's revolt began on August 22, 1831, in Southampton County, Virginia. As they moved through the countryside, Turner and some fifty to sixty mounted insurgents killed nearly sixty whites, most of them women and children. While Virginia's militia and vigilantes killed well over one hundred suspected insurrectionists, Turner eluded searchers for sixty-eight days and was not hanged until November 11, 1831, when he spoke of receiving divine revelations and demanded, "Was not Christ crucified?" The traumatic slaughter of so many white families underscored the risks and costs of an allegedly paternalistic institution, and in January 1832 it enabled legislators from the largely nonslaveholding western counties of Virginia to launch a unique and futile debate in the legislature over the future of a labor system that greatly favored the tidewater region. Samuel McDowell Moore, one of the delegates from the west, "blamed slavery for the loose morals, ignorance, and lack of industry that he believed characterized too much of the state's white population." David Brion Davis, *Inhuman Bondage: The Rise and Fall of Slavery in the New World* (New York: Oxford University Press, 2006), 208–10; Lacy K. Ford, *Deliver Us from Evil: The Slavery Question in the Old South* (New York: Oxford University Press, 2009), 369.

24. Anti-Slavery Convention of American Women, *Address to Free Colored Americans*, 17–18. Toward the end of the document, the women implore Northern blacks to resist using violent means to rescue their "brethren" from being seized as fugitive slaves. But the language strongly recognizes the free blacks' desire and motivation to counter violence with violence as well as God's own needed intervention: "We marvel, as we behold these reproachful scenes, that the God of Justice has held back his avenging sword. . . . [H]e will assuredly visit this nation in judgment unless she repent." Aside from their devotion to Jesus's model of nonresistance, the women argue pragmatically that any violent attempts at rescue "can only end in disappointment; they infuriate public sentiment still more against you, and furnish your blood-thirsty adversaries with a plausible pretext to treat you with cruelty . . . and render doubly difficult the duties of those who have been called by Jehovah to assert the colored man's right to freedom, and to vindicate his character from those calumnies which have been heaped upon him" (29).

25. Ibid., 6 (my italics).

388 Notes to Pages 206–215

26. Drew Gilpin Faust, *This Republic of Suffering: Death and the American Civil War* (New York: Alfred A. Knopf, 2008), 236–37. The fact that Southerners mutilated the bodies of Union troops and demanded segregated cemeteries and burial grounds for the Confederate dead fits in with the glorification of the Lost Cause and all-out resistance to Radical Reconstruction, which underscores the impossibility of any effective educational and rehabilitation program for emancipated slaves.

27. Anti-Slavery Convention of American Women, *Address to Free Colored Americans*, 6.

28. Ibid., 12–15.

29. Ibid., 16.

30. Ibid.

31. Ibid., 32.

32. My treatment of Walker relies heavily on Peter P. Hinks, *To Awaken My Afflicted Brethren: David Walker and the Problem of Antebellum Slave Resistance* (University Park, Pa.: Pennsylvania State University Press, 1997), a book based on a doctoral dissertation I directed.

33. David Walker, in *Appeal, in Four Articles; Together with a Preamble To the Coloured Citizens of the World, but in Particular, and Very Expressly, to those of THE UNITED STATES OF AMERICA*, ed. Charles M. Wiltse (New York: Hill & Wang, 1965), 56–59.

34. There has long been debate, even among historians, over the causes of Walker's death. While it is probable that no certain answer will ever be found, Hinks presents a convincing argument "that available sources shed no light on the shadowing of Walker, while they strongly support a natural death from a common and virulent urban disease of the nineteenth century." Hinks, *To Awaken My Afflicted Brethren*, 269–70.

35. Ibid., 86, 111.

36. Ibid., 85. Hinks adds, "A number of them preferred the dance halls of the North end or the gambling, dog fights, drinking, and sexual carousing that also flourished there and on the north slope."

37. Ibid., 213. William Lloyd Garrison was an exception. He wrote: "We deprecate the spirit and tendency of this Appeal. Nevertheless, it is not for the American people, as a nation, to denounce it as bloody or monstrous. Mr. Walker but pays them in their own coin, but follows their own creed, but adopts their own language. We do not preach rebellion—no, but submission and peace." *The Liberator,* January 8, 1831.

38. Walker, *Appeal*, 29.

39. Hinks, *To Awaken My Afflicted Brethren*, xvi.

40. Walker, *Appeal*, 62.

41. Ibid., 62–63.

42. Hinks even affirms that Walker "would rush to agree with Stanley Elkins's basic assessment that the experience of enslavement in America deeply affected and often damaged most blacks' sense of self and hindered their ability to create a core identity based on autonomy and entitlement." Hinks, *To Awaken My Afflicted Brethren*, 217–18n34.

43. Walker, *Appeal*, 15, 27.

44. Ibid., 26.

45. Eric Foner, *The Fiery Trial: Abraham Lincoln and American Slavery* (New York: W. W. Norton, 2010), 317 and passim.

46. Walker, *Appeal*, 27.

47. Ibid., 28, 17, 30.

48. Woodson, *Mind of the Negro*, 654, 658.

49. With respect to time, both authors imply a religious sense of *kairos*, defined by Paul Tillich as "a decisive moment" of qualitative change that must be distinguished from *chronos*, that is, chronological or "watch time." See David Brion Davis, *Slavery and Human Progress* (New York: Oxford University Press, 1984), 128.

50. Hinks, *To Awaken My Afflicted Brethren*, 228; Walker, *Appeal*, 43, 25, passim.

51. Hinks, *To Awaken My Afflicted Brethren*, 249.

52. Walker, *Appeal*, 70.

53. John Stauffer, ed., *The Works of James McCune Smith, Black Intellectual and Abolitionist* (New York: Oxford University Press, 2006), xiii. In addition to producing this invaluable collection of McCune Smith's writings, Stauffer has included much biographical information in his prize-winning *The Black Hearts of Men: Radical Abolitionists and the Transformation of Race* (Cambridge, Mass.: Harvard University Press, 2002). As Stauffer points out, one of the reasons McCune Smith fell into obscurity soon after his death in 1865 was that he wrote no book and his essays, published on cheap newsprint, had little popular appeal. More important, his descendants soon passed for white and "wanted him erased from the historical record" (ibid., xvi–xvii). My account of McCune Smith is almost wholly dependent on Stauffer, including e-mails from him, but I have also drawn on David Blight's early essay, "In Search of Learning, Liberty, and Self-Definition: James McCune Smith and the Ordeal of the Antebellum Black Intellectual," in *Afro-Americans in New York Life and History* 9, no. 2 (July 1985): 7–17.

54. Stauffer, *Works of James McCune Smith*, xiii, xix–xxiii, and passim; Stauffer, *Black Hearts of Men*, 65–66, 86–88, and passim.

55. Stauffer, *Works of James McCune Smith*, 55.

56. Ibid., 59.

57. Ibid., 274.

58. Ibid., 265.

59. Ibid., 264–65.

60. Ibid., 275–78.

61. Ibid., 279. Curiously, at other times McCune Smith seems to have preferred "black" to "colored."

62. Ibid., 245–63.

63. Ibid., 195–99. In 1865, McCune Smith referred to Walker's *Appeal*, in James McCune Smith, quoted from *A Memorial Discourse; by Rev. Henry Highland Garnet, Delivered in the Hall of the House of Representatives, Washington City, D.C. on Sabbath, February 12, 1865*, with an introduction by James McCune Smith, M.D. (Philadelphia: Joseph M. Wilson, 1865), 52.

64. Stauffer, *Works of James McCune Smith*, 195–99.

65. Ibid., 187.

66. Ibid., 199.

67. Ibid., 189.

68. Stauffer, *Black Hearts of Men*, 135–44. Stauffer points out that despite its failure, the North Elba enterprise was a "dress rehearsal for the project of distributing land during Reconstruction."

69. Ibid., 144, 117, and passim.

70. Stauffer, *Works of James McCune Smith*, xxiv.

71. Stauffer, *Black Hearts of Men*, 127.

72. Ibid., 157–58. Despite their continuing friendship, Gerrit Smith's disillusion led him to make an impulsive remark in an 1857 letter to Horace Greeley's *Tribune*, which infuriated McCune Smith. Gerrit stated that "the mass of blacks are ignorant & thriftless," words that conformed with Greeley's own racism. In an angry letter to Gerrit, on April 9, 1858, McCune Smith retorted that "the heaviest blow we blacks could possibly receive came from your hand" (Stauffer, *Works of James McCune Smith*, 319–20). Gerrit Smith's disillusion reached a climax in his reaction to the results of John Brown's raid at Harpers Ferry, which led to his temporary insanity and commitment to an insane asylum at Utica, New York.

73. Stauffer, *Black Hearts of Men*, 168–74.

74. Juliet E. K. Walker, "Racism, Slavery, and Free Enterprise: Black Entrepreneurship in the United States before the Civil War," *Business History Review* 60 (Autumn,

1986): 344–58. Leidesdorff was born in the West Indies to a black mother and Danish father, became a sea captain in New Orleans, and then passed as a Californian Mexican as he developed an import-export business, ship chandlery shop, lumberyard, and shipyard before provisioning the U.S. Army in the Mexican-American war.

75. I am indebted to an e-mail from John Stauffer for this ending of the chapter.

9. FUGITIVE SLAVES, FREE SOIL, AND THE QUESTION OF VIOLENCE

1. Frederick Douglass, *My Bondage and My Freedom*, in *Frederick Douglass: Autobiographies*, ed. Henry Louis Gates Jr. (New York: Library of America, 1994), 268.

2. Frederick Douglass, *Narrative of the Life of Frederick Douglass, an American Slave, Written by Himself*, ed. Benjamin Quarles (Cambridge, Mass.; Belknap Press of Harvard University Press, 1960), 95–96.

3. Dickson J. Preston, *Young Frederick Douglass: The Maryland Years* (Baltimore: Johns Hopkins University Press, 1980), 31–40.

4. Douglass, *My Bondage and My Freedom*, 215, and *Life and Times of Frederick Douglass*, 544, in Gates, *Frederick Douglass: Autobiographies*.

5. Preston, *Young Frederick Douglass*, 41–82; William S. McFeely, *Frederick Douglass* (New York: W. W. Norton, 1991), 11–41.

6. Douglass, *My Bondage and My Freedom*, in Gates, *Frederick Douglass: Autobiographies*, 215.

7. McFeely, *Frederick Douglass*, 26–41.

8. Ibid., 41.

9. Preston, *Young Frederick Douglass*, 140–41. It should be stressed that there is no agreement among historians regarding Douglass's father. Preston devotes a chapter to Aaron Anthony as "Father Image."

10. John Hope Franklin and Loren Schweninger, *Runaway Slaves: Rebels on the Plantation* (New York: Oxford University Press, 1999), 4.

11. McFeely, *Frederick Douglass*, 69.

12. Ibid., 70.

13. Ibid., 71–72.

14. Ibid., 72–73. For an excellent study of Ruggles, see Graham Russell Hodges, *David Ruggles: A Radical Black Abolitionist and the Underground Railroad in New York City* (Chapel Hill: University of North Carolina Press, 2010).

15. Ibid., 74–80, 83–85.

16. Ibid., 87–89.

17. David W. Blight, "Why the Underground Railroad, and Why Now? A Long View," in *Passages to Freedom: The Underground Railroad in History and Memory*, ed. David W. Blight (Washington D.C.: Smithsonian Books, 2004), 234.

18. Ibid., 247.

19. Quoted in ibid., 239.

20. Ibid., 242.

21. Benjamin Quarles, *Black Abolitionists* (New York: Oxford University Press, 1969), 143–48, 143.

22. Franklin and Schweninger, *Runaway Slaves*, 367.

23. Ibid., 367n49. They point out that not all of the one to two thousand slaves traveled along the routes of the Underground Railroad.

24. Ira Berlin, "Before Cotton: African and African American Slavery in Mainland North America during the Seventeenth and Eighteenth Centuries," in Blight, *Passages to Freedom*, 24–25; James Oliver Horton and Lois E. Horton, *In Hope of Liberty: Culture, Community, and Protest Among Northern Free Blacks, 1700–1860* (New York: Oxford University Press, 1997), 50–51. Historian Gary Nash has notably made the assessment that "In reality, the American Revolution represents the largest slave uprising in our history." Yet it was "obvious soon after the new federal government was in place, that

slavery was not going to wither in the United States." Gary B. Nash, *Race and Revolution* (Madison, Wisc.: Madison House, 1990), 57–59.

25. Franklin and Schweninger, *Runaway Slaves*, 86–89.

26. Steven Hahn, *The Political Worlds of Slavery and Freedom* (Cambridge, Mass.: Harvard University Press, 2009), 13, 24, 27–38, 55–58. On the political mobilization of slaves, see also Steven Hahn, *A Nation Under Our Feet: Black Political Struggles in the Rural South from Slavery to the Great Migration* (Cambridge, Mass.: Belknap Press of Harvard University Press, 2003), especially Part 1. When discussing slave resistance, Hahn omits the complicity of many slaves in supporting their masters, as well as the growing economic success of the slave system and the way self-interest motivated planters to extend privileges of various kinds. When treating free blacks in the North, he ignores their frequent pride in an American identity, extending back to their participation in the American Revolution, and their desire for racial integration.

27. Franklin and Schweninger, *Runaway Slaves*, 279–81.

28. James, W. C. Pennington, *The Fugitive Blacksmith; or, Events in the History of James W. C. Pennington*, 3rd ed. (Westport, Conn.: Negro Universities Press, 1971), v.

29. Eugene D. Genovese, *Roll, Jordan, Roll: The World the Slaves Made* (New York: Pantheon Books, 1974), 89–91.

30. Franklin and Schweninger, *Runaway Slaves*, 30.

31. Harriet Ann Jacobs, *Incidents in the Life of a Slave Girl*, in *Slave Narratives*, ed. William L. Andrews and Henry Louis Gates Jr., Library of America 114 (New York: Library of America, 2000); Jean Fagan Yellin, *Harriet Jacobs: A Life* (New York: Basic Civitas Books, 2004). My understanding of Jacobs has also been broadened by Gloria T. Randle, "Between the Rock and the Hard Place: Mediating Spaces in Harriet Jacobs's Incidents in the Life of a Slave Girl," *African American Review* 33, no. 1 (Spring 1999): 43–56; Ann Taves, "Spiritual Purity and Sexual Shame: Religious Themes in the Writings of Harriet Jacobs," *Church History* 56, no. 1 (March 1987): 59–72; and Kimberly Drake, "Rewriting the American Self: Race, Gender, and Identity in the Autobiographies of Frederick Douglass and Harriet Jacobs," *MELUS* 22, no. 4 (Winter 1997): 91–108.

32. Yellin, *Harriet Jacobs*, xv–xxi.

33. Yellin guesses that Harriet may have first used the surname Jacobs when she met the family of the vigilance committee member who met her at the Philadelphia wharf after her escape. The name came from her grandfather, Henry Jacobs. Her father Elijah, a carpenter, used the last name Knox and was the slave of Dr. Andrew Knox, but was probably the son of a white farmer named Henry Jacobs. Ibid., 66, 67.

34. Jacobs on the effects of her jealous mistress's nightly vigils: "At last I began to be fearful for my life. It had often been threatened; and you can imagine, better than I can describe, what an unpleasant sensation it must produce to wake up in the dead of night and find a jealous woman bending over you. Terrible as this experience was, I had fears that it would give place to one more terrible." Jacobs, *Incidents*, 780.

35. Jacobs, *Incidents*, 801.

36. Ibid., 801–2, 747–48. As Gloria T. Randle puts it: "This mother at once deeply loves and sincerely regrets her children, since their existence constitutes a visible sign of her degradation, an irrefutable marker of her transgression, and the prospect of her children's eventual judgment against her." Randle, "Between the Rock and the Hard Place," 51. But this point is qualified by Kimberly Drake: "Jacobs sets the cult of true womanhood, with its moral expectations, against cultural ideals for motherhood, underlining the limitations of the former as she describes her achievement of the latter. She attempts to change her status from sexual object to sacred mother . . . [hoping] that her maternity, despite its illegitimacy, will provide an appeal to mothers of the North and enable her to form a bond with them." Drake, "Rewriting the American Self," 101.

37. Jacobs, *Incidents*, 826.

38. Ibid., 840.

39. Ibid., 830.

40. Ibid., 830–40. Harriet learned while on the plantation that her children were going to be sent to the plantation as well: "They thought that my children's being there would fetter me to the spot, and that it was a good place to break us all in to abject submission to our lot as slaves."

41. Ibid., 860.

42. Quoted in Yellin, *Harriet Jacobs,* 45.

43. Ibid., 44.

44. Ibid., 59.

45. Jacobs, *Incidents,* 911, 914.

46. Yellin, *Harriet Jacobs,* 83, 114–16, and passim.

47. Yellin, *Harriet Jacobs,* 96, 131–32. Issac and Amy Post's activist circle in Rochester has garnered significant scholarly attention, for more on the Post circle of activism and spiritualism, see Nancy A. Hewitt, *Women's Activism and Social Change: Rochester, New York, 1822–1872* (Ithaca, N.Y.: Cornell University Press, 1984); and Ann Braude, *Radical Spirits: Spiritualism and Women's Rights in Nineteenth-Century America,* 2nd ed. (Bloomington: Indiana University Press, 2001). Harriet Jacobs would be influenced by the Posts' interest in the spirit world, so far that she consulted spirits to find out about the welfare of her son and brother who were chasing gold in Australia.

48. Ibid., 104.

49. Ibid., 118–41.

50. Ibid., 129–31, 140–43, 190–201.

51. U.S. Constitution, Article IV, Section 2.

52. For a concise and detailed explanation of the history of fugitive slaves and American law, see Stanley W. Campbell, *The Slave Catchers: Enforcement of the Fugitive Slave Law, 1850–1860* (Chapel Hill: University of North Carolina Press, 1970), 3–25. The threat of kidnapping is often mentioned in studies of free black life and abolitionism in the nineteenth century, but deserves more study as a subject of its own. The issue gains considerable attention in antislavery newspapers prior to the war, free black community organizations, not to mention its frequent inclusion in the numbers of injustices cited by black and white abolitionists on their speaking tours. The only work devoted to the issue is the short book by Carol Wilson, *Freedom at Risk: The Kidnapping of Free Blacks in America, 1780–1865* (Lexington: University Press of Kentucky, 1994).

53. Leonard P. Curry, *The Free Black in Urban America, 1800–1850: The Shadow of the Dream* (Chicago: University of Chicago Press, 1981), 229.

54. David Everett Swift, *Black Prophets of Justice: Activist Clergy Before the Civil War* (Baton Rouge: Louisiana State University Press, 1989), 83. The late historian David Swift notably argued that the New York–based *Colored American,* the important black antislavery paper of the late 1830s and early 1840s, was formed primarily to serve the ends of the New York Vigilance Committee. Although the theme of the paper moved well beyond issues of fugitives and kidnapping during its run, the paper nonetheless retained a sense of collective effort and assertive public presence that characterized the vigilance committees of the North.

55. James Oliver Horton and Lois E. Horton, *Black Bostonians: Family Life and Community Struggle in the Antebellum North* (New York: Holmes & Meier, 1979), 99.

56. Quarles, *Black Abolitionists,* 150.

57. Hodges, *David Ruggles,* 94 and passim.

58. Ibid., 204.

59. Curry, *The Free Black in Urban America,* 230–31.

60. Henry Highland Garnet, "Address to the Slaves of the United States," in *A Memorial Discourse; by Rev. Henry Highland Garnet, Delivered in the Hall of the House of Representatives, Washington City, D.C. on Sabbath, February 12, 1865,* with an introduction by James McCune Smith M.D. (Philadelphia: J. M. Wilson, 1865), 44–51.

61. Steven H. Shiffrin, "The Rhetoric of Black Violence in the Antebellum Period: Henry Highland Garnet," *Journal of Black Studies*, vol. 2, no. 1 (Sept. 1971): 45–49. As Kenneth Stampp, the great historian of slavery, put it long ago: "The Turner story was not likely to encourage slaves to make new attempts to win their freedom by fighting for it. They now realized that they would face a united white community, well armed and quite willing to annihilate as much of the black population as might seem necessary," (ibid. 47).

62. Ibid., 52.

63. Stanley W. Campbell convincingly argues that while most Northerners were opposed to slavery, "only a few citizens in isolated communities engaged in active opposition to enforcement of the Fugitive Slave Law." But his work tends to underplay the strength and importance of Northern opposition to the law as well as the failure of the South to recover between 1850 and 1860 more than three hundred fugitives (*The Slave Catchers*, xvii–xviii, and passim).

64. In a study of Methodist newspapers, Ralph A. Keller argues that for churchmen and much of the North's religious population, it was the Fugitive Slave Law that brought tensions to the highest level at mid-century, and that even conservative editors who ordinarily avoided political issues were outraged by the law. Hence the supposed period of calm following the Compromise of 1850 "might better be understood as a time of smoldering bitterness which, in turn, can help explain the magnitude of the Kansas-Nebraska explosion of 1854." Keller, "Methodist Newspapers and the Fugitive Slave Law: A New Perspective for the Slavery Crisis in the North," *Church History* 43, no. 3 (Sept. 1974): 320–27.

Despite the fact that the biblical Paul was willing, but reluctant, to send the escaped slave Onesimus back to his master, Philemon, in Philemon 1:8–21, the Fugitive Slave Law directly violated Deuteronomy 23:15: "Thou shalt not deliver unto the master his servant which has escaped unto thee. . . . Thou shalt not oppress him." Because of this direct violation, the verse was seized upon in literature opposing the Fugitive Slave Law. Whereas abolitionists had to typically rely on the "spirit of the law" in arguing for the Bible's opposition to slavery, in this case the letter of the law could more or less serve their ends.

65. Campbell, *The Slave Catchers*, 23–25.

66. Ibid., 207; James Oliver Horton and Lois E. Horton, "A Federal Assault: African Americans and the Impact of the Fugitive Slave Law of 1850," in *Slavery and the Law*, ed. Paul Finkelman (Lanham, Md.: Rowman and Littlefield, 2002), 144–45, 148–51; Leonard W. Levy, "Sims' Case: The Fugitive Slave Law in Boston in 1851," *The Journal of Negro History* 35, no. 1 (Jan. 1950): 72 and passim. Paul Finkelman states that the whole Sims retrieval cost as much as $100,000 if you count salaries and other peripheral expenses. Paul Finkelman, "Fugitive Slave Law of 1850" in *Encyclopedia of African American History, 1619–1895: From the Colonial Period to the Age of Frederick Douglass*, ed. Paul Findelman (New York: Oxford University Press, 2006), 74–78.

67. Calhoun's famous speech, read on the floor of the Senate by Senator James Mason from Virginia (due to Calhoun's sickly state) on March 4, 1850, illustrates the testlike atmosphere offered by Calhoun and like-minded Southern congressmen: "But will the North agree to do this [compromise]? It is for her to answer this question. But, I will say, she cannot refuse, if she has half the love of the Union which she professes to have. . . . At all events, the responsibility of saving the Union rests on the North, and not the South. The South cannot save it by any act of hers, and the North may save it without any sacrifice whatever, unless to do justice, and to perform her duties under the Constitution. . . . If you, who represent the stronger portion, cannot agree to settle them on the broad principle of justice and duty, say so; and let the States we both represent agree to separate and part in peace. If you are unwilling we should part in peace, tell us so, and we shall know what to do, when you reduce the question to submission or resistance." John Caldwell Calhoun, "Speech on the Slavery Question,"

in *The Papers of John C. Calhoun, 1849–1850,* vol. 27, ed. Clyde N. Wilson and Shirley B. Cook (Columbia: University of South Carolina Press, 2003) 210–11.

68. "From the Nashville American: ABOLITIONISTS AND FREE NEGROES," *The Liberator,* October 18, 1850.

69. Luther Lee, *Autobiography of the Rev. Luther Lee* (New York: Phillips & Hunt, 1882), 335–36. Such views were by no means limited to radical clergymen. According to Ralph Waldo Emerson, the law was one that "everyone of you will break on the earliest opportunity—a law which no man can obey, or abet obeying, without loss of self-respect and forfeiture of the name of a gentleman." Quoted in Campbell, *Slave Catchers,* 50.

70. *The Letters of William Lloyd Garrison,* ed. Louis Ruchames, vol. 4: *From Disunionism to the Brink of War, 1850–1860* (Cambridge, Mass.: Belknap Press of Harvard University Press, 1975), 41.

71. John Stauffer, *The Black Hearts of Men: Radical Abolitionists and the Transformation of Race* (Cambridge, Mass: Harvard University Press, 2002), 255.

72. Ibid., 170–73, 236, 255.

73. Frederick Douglass, "John Brown: An Address at the Fourteenth Anniversary of Storer College" in *Meteor of War: The John Brown Story,* ed. Zoe Trodd and John Stauffer (Maplecrest, N.Y.: Brandywine Press, 2004), 206.

74. Stauffer, *Black Hearts of Men,* p. 37. Stauffer notes that Emerson borrowed the words from his friend Mattie Griffith.

75. Hahn, *A Nation Under Our Feet,* 68–78.

76. Hahn, *Political Worlds of Slavery and Freedom,* 57–61.

10. THE GREAT EXPERIMENT: JUSTICE, RESPONSES, AND FAILURE

1. Ralph Wardlaw, *The Jubilee: A Sermon Preached in West George-Street Chapel, Glasgow, on Friday, August 1st 1834, the Memorial Day of Negro Emancipation in the British Colonies* (Glasgow, 1834), 13, 16–27, 20.

2. Ibid., 26–37.

3. Ralph Waldo Emerson, "Address Delivered in Concord on the Anniversary of the Emancipation of the Negroes in the British West Indies, August 1, 1844," in *Complete Works of Emerson* (New York: Houghton Mifflin, 1903–04), 11:99, 115–16, 135.

4. Frederick Douglass, "Freedom in the West Indies: An Address Delivered in Poughkeepsie, New York, on 2 August 1858," *The Frederick Douglass Papers,* Series One, *Speeches, Debates, and Interviews,* ed., John W. Blassingame, vol. 3, *1855–63* (New Haven, Conn.: Yale University Press, 1985), 217–21.

5. Ibid., 215–17.

6. Ibid., 216–17.

7. Seymour Drescher, *The Mighty Experiment: Free Labor versus Slavery in British Emancipation* (New York: Oxford University Press, 2002), 202–3. For a detailed analysis of the astounding costs of Britain's campaign against both the slave trade and slavery, see Chaim D. Kaufmann and Robert A. Pape, "Explaining Costly International Moral Action: Britain's Sixty-Year Campaign Against the Atlantic Slave Trade," *International Organization* 53, no. 4 (Autumn 1999): 631–68. Drescher points out that even Kaufmann and Pape overlook the cost of depreciating plantation values from 1808 to the 1850s. Drescher, *Mighty Experiment,* 285n4.

8. Douglass, "Freedom in the West Indies," 219–21.

9. *Letters and Addresses of George Thompson, during his Mission in the United States* (Boston, 1837), 107.

10. Reginald Coupland, *Wilberforce: A Narrative* (Oxford, 1923), 240–41.

11. James Stephen, *The Slavery in the West Indian Colonies Delineated, as It Exists Both in Law and Practice, and Compared with Slavery in Other Countries, Ancient and Modern* (London, 1824–30), 2:401–2.

12. Of course, many abolitionists opposed specific measures, such as compensation and apprenticeship, while still accepting and celebrating the British emancipation act.

13. David Brion Davis, *Slavery and Human Progress* (New York: Oxford University Press, 1984), 174–77.

14. Drescher, *Mighty Experiment,* 75–86, 125. Some proponents of slave "amelioration" did argue that African savages needed time to overcome the indolence and licentiousness of uncivilized men (108). It should be added that Wilberforce devoted some attention to refuting racist arguments in his 1807 book on the abolition of the slave trade. William Wilberforce, *A Letter on the Abolition of the Slave Trade; Addressed to the Freeholders and Other Inhabitants of Yorkshire* (London, 1807), 57–85, 127–33.

15. David Brion Davis, "The Emergence of Immediatism in British and American Antislavery Thought," in Davis, *From Homicide to Slavery: Studies in American Culture* (New York: Oxford University Press, 1986), 238–57.

16. Davis, *Slavery and Human Progress,* 176–77. By 1814, James Stephen, in the Colonial Office, became convinced that many slaves were being smuggled into the British West Indian colonies, and he succeeded in obtaining local slave registrations in a number of the colonies. But in 1815 Wilberforce failed to get a central registry intended to open the way to ameliorative measures. (I am indebted to Stanley L. Engerman for sending me a copy of his paper in 2011, "Monitoring the Abolition of the International Slave Trade: Slave Registration in the British Caribbean and the Recording of Slaves in the United States.")

17. *Substance of the Debate in the House of Commons, on the 15th May, 1823, on a Motion for the Mitigation and Gradual Abolition of Slavery throughout the British Dominions . . .* (London, 1823), 1–21. J. R. Ward shows that West Indian planters did respond to abolitionist demands for amelioration and succeeded in raising the slaves' standard of living and productive efficiency, but failed to change the dehumanizing aspects of the institution that greatly troubled reformers. Ward, *British West Indian Slavery, 1750–1834: The Process of Amelioration* (New York: Oxford University Press, 1988).

18. Agency Committee speakers focused attention on religious and moral themes as opposed to questions of free labor and economic outcomes. Drescher, *Mighty Experiment,* 122.

19. Michael Craton, *Testing the Chains: Resistance to Slavery in the British West Indies* (Ithaca, N.Y.: Cornell University Press, 1982), 291–303, 315.

20. Ibid., 267–90, 300–302, 312–21.

21. Mary Turner, *Slaves and Missionaries: The Disintegration of Jamaican Society, 1787–1834* (Chicago: University of Chicago Press, 1982), 20–21, 171–73.

22. Betty Fladeland, *Men and Brothers: Anglo-American Antislavery Cooperation* (Urbana: University of Illinois Press, 1972), 202; Robert William Fogel, *Without Consent or Contract: The Rise and Fall of American Slavery* (New York: W. W. Norton, 1989), 230. Fogel argues that the Grey government was eager to gain the support of the religious dissenters, especially Methodists, as a "main counterweight to the radicals," who among other things "viewed the abolitionist campaign with deep suspicion, denouncing it as an instrument intended to divert attention from the plight of the English workers" (30–31).

23. Edward Bartlett Rugemer, *The Problem of Emancipation: The Caribbean Roots of the American Civil War* (Baton Rouge: Louisiana State University Press, 2008), 132.

24. Davis, *Slavery and Human Progress,* 200.

25. For details regarding the negotiations that led to emancipation, see ibid., 198–219; and Seymour Drescher, *Abolition: A History of Slavery and Antislavery* (New York: Cambridge University Press, 2009), 248–66.

26. Davis, *Slavery and Human Progress,* 202–03; Drescher, *Abolition,* 250.

27. Davis, *Slavery and Human Progress,* 203.

28. *Proceedings and Resolutions of the West India Body, Consequent on Mr. Secretary Stan-*

ley's Communication of the Outline of the Intended Measure Respecting Slavery, May 1833, Public Record Office London, (London, 1833), 3–12.

29. George Stephen to Daniel O'Connell, May 29, 1833. George Stephen Papers (unidentified when I consulted them), the Hull Museums, UK.

30. Adam Hochschild, _Bury the Chains: Prophets and Rebels in the Fight to Free an Empire's Slaves_ (Boston: Houghton Mifflin, 2005), 347; Drescher, _Mighty Experiment_, 136. Since this compensation came to 40 percent of the government's average annual income and three times the expenditure on the Poor Law, it required additional public borrowing. Nicholas Draper has recently provided a comprehensive analysis of the extent and importance of the absentee owners who received a large share of the compensation. _The Price of Emancipation: Slave-Ownership, Compensation, and British Society at the End of Slavery_ (Cambridge, UK: Cambridge University Press, 2010).

31. Davis, _Slavery and Human Progress_, 204–5.

32. Ibid., 205. When the apprentices' uncompensated labor is added to the £20 million compensation, it appears that slave owners received nearly full compensation for the value of their slaves.

33. _The Letters of William Lloyd Garrison_, ed. Walter M. Merrill, vol. 1, _I Will Be Heard, 1822–1835_ (Cambridge, Mass.: Harvard University Press, 1971), 230–31, 237–38; Thomas Clarkson to "Mr. Buxton," from Playford Hall, September 25, 1833, Clarkson Papers, Huntington Library, San Marino, California. After rejoicing over the abolition of slavery, even with compensation paid to planters, Clarkson expressed hope that a society would be formed to see that the intentions of Parliament were actually carried out, as the African Institution was founded to monitor the enforcement of the ending of the slave trade. Such a society, Clarkson added, would start correspondence with all the islands.

34. MS Brit. emp. S.444, XXIV, Buxton Papers, Rhodes House, Oxford. (In view of possible changes in classification, I did this research many years ago.)

35. Rugemer, _The Problem of Emancipation_, 117, and passim. Rugemer shows in great detail how Bryan Edwards's writing on the Haitian Revolution influenced later developments of the theory that antislavery agitation was responsible for specific slave revolts.

36. Ibid., 118, 120, 122.

37. Ibid., 156–60.

38. Ibid.

39. Howard Temperley, _British Antislavery, 1833–1870_ (Columbia: University of South Carolina Press, 1972), 119–20; Fogel, _Without Consent or Contract_, 406–11. Fogel argues that slavery was "intrinsically evil because its productive efficiency arose directly out of the oppression of its laborers," and concludes that "Whatever the opportunity for a peaceful abolition of slavery along British lines before 1845, it surely was nonexistent after that date" (411–12).

40. Stanley L. Engerman has documented the striking differences between the British slave colonies with regard to sugar production before and after emancipation in "Economic Change and Contract Labor in the British Caribbean: The End of Slavers and the Adjustment to Emancipation," _Explorations in Economic History_ 21 (1984): 133–50.

41. James A. Thome and J. Horace Kimball, _Emancipation in the West Indies. A Six Months' Tour in Antigua, Barbadoes, and Jamaica, in the Year 1837_ (New York: The American Anti-Slavery Society, 1838), iii–vi.

42. Ibid., 7, 12.

43. Ibid., iii.

44. Benjamin David Weber, "_Emancipation in the West Indies_: Thome and Kimball's Interpretation and the Shift in American Antislavery Discourse, 1834–1840" (essay written as candidate for honors in history at Oberlin College, Professor Carol Lasser, Advisor, Spring 2007), 7–23.

I am much indebted to this brilliant and highly original essay. A published version can be seen in "Emancipation in the West Indies and the Freedom to Toil: Manual Labor and Moral Redemption in Transatlantic Discourse," *Journal of the Oxford University History Society* 6, no. 1 (Feb. 2009).

45. Ibid., 1–3, 24, 28, 33–34, 39–40, 49, 61–68.

46. Thome and Kimball, *Emancipation in the West Indies,* vi.

47. Ibid., 108.

48. Ibid, 90–91.

49. Rugemer, *The Problem of Emancipation,* 170.

50. For Gurney's life, I have drawn on *Memoirs of Joseph John Gurney; with Selections from his Journal and Correspondence,* ed. Joseph Bevan Braithwaite, 4th ed. Two Volumes Complete in One (Philadelphia, 1857).

51. Ibid., 2:118–20, 220–32.

52. Charles Grier Sellers Jr., "The Travail of Slavery," in *The Southerner as American,* ed. Charles Grier Sellers Jr. (Chapel Hill: University of North Carolina Press, 1960), 40–71.

53. Joseph John Gurney, "Prefatory Letter to Thomas Fowell Buxton," in *A Winter in the West Indies, Described in Familiar Letters to Henry Clay, of Kentucky* (London, 1840), xii–xiii.

54. James A. Rawley, "Joseph John Gurney's Mission to America, 1837–1840," *Mississippi Valley Historical Review,* 49, no. 4 (March 1, 1963): 664.

55. Ibid., 666.

56. Ibid., 669–70.

57. Braithwaite, *Memoirs of Joseph John Gurney,* 2:129–30, 164–218, and passim.

58. Gurney, *Winter in the West Indies,* 19–21.

59. Ibid., 44–46, 67–69.

60. Ibid., 44–46, 54–58, 61–62, 67, 69.

61. Ibid., 143–44, 178.

62. Ibid., 100–101, 109.

63. Ibid., 100–101, 113, 117,

64. Ibid., 100–102, 117, 148, 166, 171–73.

65. Ibid., 111, 143–44, 151–52, 178–79, 183.

66. Ibid., 195–97. Gurney also describes his conversation with Calhoun in Braithwaite, *Memoirs of Joseph John Gurney,* 1:223–24. Except for Gurney's highly optimistic account, there seems to be no evidence that Calhoun accepted his very positive view of the economic success of British emancipation, which Gurney himself qualifies in his descriptions of Jamaica.

67. Gurney, *Winter in the West Indies, Appendix B: Reconciliation Respectfully Recommended to all Parties in the Colony of Jamaica, in a Letter Addressed to the Planters,* 181–95.

68. Ibid., 183–85; Gurney, "Prefatory Letter to Thomas Fowell Buxton," ibid., xiv–xvi. Gurney tried to counter any implication that slave labor was cheaper than free labor. He tried to give reasons for the temporary advantages of slaveholding Cuba and Brazil, and assured Buxton that in the future free labor in the West and East Indies and Africa would produce sugar and coffee in such abundance and at such a low price that slave-grown produce "will be driven from every market, even without the aid of prohibitory duties."

69. Drescher, *Mighty Experiment,* 126–27.

70. Ibid., 121–27. Back in Britain, Gurney continued to publicly oppose such measures.

71. It was not until 1860 that Britain outlawed the formal owning of slaves in India, which was exempted in the 1833 emancipation act. This was largely because Britain faced in India a complex and deeply rooted indigenous and largely domestic system of slavery and caste.

72. C. Duncan Rice, "'Humanity Sold for Sugar!' The British Abolitionist

Response to Free Trade in Slave-Grown Sugar," *The Historical Journal* 13, no. 3 (1970): 404–12; Richard Huzzey, *Freedom Burning: Anti-Slavery and Empire in Victorian Britain* (Ithaca, N.Y.: Cornell University Press, 2012), chapter 5.

73. Drescher, *Mighty Experiment*, 176–83.

74. Ibid.

75. David Brion Davis, *Inhuman Bondage: The Rise and Fall of Slavery in the New World* (New York: Oxford University Press, 2006), 283–85; I have drawn mainly on Steven Heath Mitton, "The Free World Confronted: The Problem of Slavery and Progress in American Foreign Relations, 1833–1844" (Ph.D. diss., Louisiana State University, 2005), 133–45 and passim; and more recently on Mitton, "The Upshur Inquiry: Lost Lessons of the Great Experiment," *Slavery and Abolition* 27 (April 2006): 89–124. I am also indebted to Stanley L. Engerman for the information about Trinidad.

76. Mitton, "Free World Confronted," passim; Mitton, "Upshur Inquiry," 89–124; Rugemer, *Problem of Emancipation*, 204–21; Drescher, *Mighty Experiment*, 169–72. For the Southern response to Lord Aberdeen's famous statement, see *The Southern Literary Messenger: Devoted to Every Department of Literature and the Fine Arts* (Richmond, Virginia) 10 (Oct. 1844): 584.

77. William W. Freehling, *The Road to Disunion*, vol. 1, *Secessionists at Bay, 1776–1854* (New York: Oxford University Press, 1991), 355–452; Drescher, *Abolition*, 318–21; Rugemer, *Problem of Emancipation*, 210–21.

78. Quoted in Drescher, *Mighty Experiment*, 200–201. I have relied heavily on this work because of its extraordinary scholarship and detail.

79. Ibid., 204–205, 217.

80. Ibid., 217–25.

81. Douglass, "Freedom in the West Indies," 219–21.

82. Kwame Anthony Appiah, *The Honor Code: How Moral Revolutions Happen* (New York: W. W. Norton, 2010), 103–36. See also my review, David Brion Davis, "Honor Thy Honor," *New York Review of Books* 58, no. 16 (Oct. 27, 2011): 46–48; Drescher, *Mighty Experiment*, 231–37; Kaufmann and Pape, "Explaining Costly International Moral Action," 631–68.

83. Drescher, *Mighty Experiment*, 236–37.

84. W. E. H. Lecky, *A History of European Morals: From Augustus to Charlemagne*, 2 vols. (1869, New York, 1876), 1:161.

II. THE BRITISH MYSTIQUE:
BLACK ABOLITIONISTS IN BRITAIN—THE LEADER OF THE
INDUSTRIAL REVOLUTION AND CENTER OF "WAGE SLAVERY"

1. *The Frederick Douglass Papers*, Series One, *Speeches, Debates, and Interviews*, 3 vols.: 1841–46, ed. John W. Blassingame (New Haven: Yale University Press, 1979; 1982; 1985), 1:252n4; 401n3; 481–82n4.

2. R. J. M. Blackett, *Building an Antislavery Wall: Black Americans in the Atlantic Abolitionist Movement, 1830–1860* (Baton Rouge: Louisiana State University Press, 1983), 8. For some insightful essays regarding Douglass's time in Britain, see Alan J. Rice and Martin Crawford, eds., *Liberating Sojourn: Frederick Douglass and Transatlantic Reform*, (Athens: University of Georgia Press, 1999).

3. Blassingame, *Frederick Douglass Papers*, Series One, 1:62–63nn5–6.

4. Frederick Douglass to William Lloyd Garrison, Dublin, Sept. 1, 1845, in Frederick Douglass Papers, General Correspondence, Library of Congress, Washington, D.C.

5. Ibid.

6. Blassingame, *Frederick Douglass Papers*, Series One, 1:63.

7. Douglass to William Lloyd Garrison, Dublin, Sept. 1, 1845, in Frederick Douglass Papers.

8. Ibid. For Douglass's later accounts of the *Cambria* events, see Blassingame, *Frederick Douglass Papers*, Series One, 1:62–66, 82–84, 90–92, 138–42. I have drawn a couple of points from these summaries, but since Douglass's detailed letter to Garrison was written four or five days after his attempted lecture, it is probably the most accurate account.

9. Marcus Cunliffe, *Chattel Slavery and Wage Slavery: The Anglo-American Context, 1830–1860* (Athens: University of Georgia Press, 1979), 32.

10. R. J. M. Blackett, *Building an Antislavery Wall*, 13; Benjamin Soskis, "*Heroic Exile*: The Transatlantic Development of Frederick Douglass, 1845–1847" (senior essay, Yale University, April 13, 1998), 8. (When writing this outstanding essay, which I directed and which won the 1998 Wrexham Prize for the best senior essay in the humanities, Mr. Soskis did extensive research in the UK and in the Frederick Douglass Papers. The essay, to which I am deeply indebted, is now available on line: www.yale.edu/glc/soskis/index.htm.)

11. David Brion Davis, *The Great Republic: A History of the American People*, 3rd ed., vol. 1 (Lexington, Mass.: D.C. Heath, 1985), 388.

12. Cunliffe, *Chattel Slavery and Wage Slavery*, 34–35, 38, 44.

13. Ibid., 56.

14. For the publicizing of Lord Aberdeen's statement, see *The Southern Literary Messenger: Devoted to Every Department of Literature and the Arts* (Richmond, Virginia), 10 (Oct. 1844): 584, which also affirmed that the abolition societies in the North were encouraged and incited by those in London (581).

15. W. Caleb McDaniel, *The Problem of Democracy in the Age of Slavery: Garrisonian Abolitionists and Transatlantic Reform* (Baton Rouge: Louisiana State University Press, 2013), 147.

16. Blackett, *Building an Antislavery Wall*, ix–xi, 3–4.

17. "Speech by Nathaniel Paul, Delivered at the Trades' Hall, Glasgow, Scotland, 2 December 1834," *The Black Abolitionist Papers*, ed. C. Peter Ripley, vol. 1, *The British Isles, 1830–1865* (Chapel Hill: University of North Carolina Press, 1985), 56. For a brief biography of Paul, see ibid., 42–43.

18. Blackett, *Building an Antislavery Wall*, 4, 18, 52–53, 213.

19. Ibid., 51–55; *Black Abolitionist Papers*, 1:41–43.

20. *The Liberator*, October 1, 1831. 158.

21. Blackett, *Building an Antislavery Wall*, 53, 55–57; *Letters of Theodore Dwight Weld, Angelina Grimké Weld, and Sarah Grimké, 1822–1844*, ed. Gilbert H. Barnes and Dwight L. Dumond, 2 vols. (1934; repr., Gloucester, Mass.: Peter Smith, 1965), 1:6–7, 21–22, 25, 29–30, 35–36, 43, 48–49, 509; 2:562; Robert H. Abzug, *Passionate Liberator: Theodore Dwight Weld and the Dilemma of Reform* (New York: Oxford University Press, 1980), 32–34, 86–87, 140. Like many other white abolitionists, it took Weld a bit longer to reject colonization, in part because of his awareness of the depth of white racial prejudice and the difficulties of achieving racial equality, to say nothing of the dangers of black retribution, signified by the Haitian Revolution and the recent Nat Turner revolt.

22. Blackett, *Building an Antislavery Wall*, 58–67; Betty Fladeland, *Men and Brothers: Anglo-American Antislavery Cooperation* (Urbana: University of Illinois Press, 1972), 217; on October 24, 1833, Clarkson wrote a private letter to a Mr. Crisp that "I am truly sorry, that after my last letter to you in which I expressed to you my desire to have no further concern with the discussion relating to the American Colonization Society, you should have written me again upon that subject." He told of a recent four-hour visit with Garrison, and his determination to keep an open mind and examine Garrison's views closely, "having much important American intelligence in our possession." (Thomas Clarkson papers, Huntington Library, San Marino, California.)

23. James Oliver Horton and Lois E. Horton, *Black Bostonians: Family Life and Community Struggle in the Antebellum North* (New York: Holmes & Meier Publishers, 1979), 85.

24. *Black Abolitionist Papers*, 1:42–43.

25. Ibid., 1:38–39.

26. Ibid.

27. Ibid., 44–46.

28. Blackett, *Building an Antislavery Wall*, 6.

29. Ibid., 195.

30. Richard Huzzey, *Freedom Burning: Anti-Slavery and Empire in Victorian Britain* (Ithaca, N.Y.: Cornell University Press, 2012), 76–77.

31. Ibid., passim; Betty Fladeland, *Abolitionists and Working-Class Problems in the Age of Industrialization* (Baton Rouge: Louisiana State University Press, 1884), 49–73. As Fladeland shows, Sturge worked for a variety of reform causes, including abolitionism, from his early twenties.

32. Henry Highland Garnet, *Walker's Appeal, with a Brief Sketch of his Life . . . And also Garnet's Address to the Slaves of the United States of America* (New York, 1848), 92; Henry Highland Garnet, *A Memorial Discourse; by Rev. Henry Highland Garnet, Delivered in the Hall of the House of Representatives, Washington City, D.C. on Sabbath, February 12, 1865*, with an introduction by James McCune Smith, M.D. (Philadelphia, 1865), 69–74.

33. *Narrative of the Life of Frederick Douglass, an American Slave*, ed. Benjamin Quarles (Cambridge, Mass.: Harvard University Press, 1960), 66–67, 95; Waldo E. Martin, *The Mind of Frederick Douglass* (Chapel Hill: University of North Carolina Press, 1984), 29.

34. Soskis, *"Heroic Exile:* The Transatlantic Development of Frederick Douglass," 23–25.

35. Blassingame, *Frederick Douglass Papers*, Series One, 1:35, 42.

36. Cunliffe, *Chattel Slavery and Wage Slavery*, 9–10, 27, 69–70. In 1847, Oastler helped win the Factory Act limiting the work of such children to a ten-hour day.

37. Gilbert Francklyn, *Observations, Occasioned by the Attempts Made in England to Effect the Abolition of the Slave Trade* . . . (Kingston, Jamaica, 1788; repr., London, 1789), 10–12, 27–42, 74–75.

38. Cunliffe, *Chattel Slavery and Wage Slavery*, 39 and passim.

39. Ibid., 51–67.

40. Blassingame, *Frederick Douglass Papers*, Series One, 1:341–52.

41. Ibid., 342–43. Critics of Douglass could have stressed that the 1834 Poor Law also allowed families to be torn apart. "When families went to a workhouse, husbands, wives, and children were segregated into separate wards. Moreover, the poor, including children, could be sent away from their own parishes to work." In 1848 the radical Chartist Joseph Barker even "declared that the British upper classes made brutes of workers just as surely as did American slaveholders" (Betty Fladeland, "'Our Cause Being One and the Same': Abolitionists and Chartism," in *Slavery and British Society, 1776–1846*, ed. James Walvin (Baton Rouge: Louisiana State University Press, 1982), 71, 95.

42. Ibid., 352, 407.

43. For some of the key works on the antislavery debates, see David Brion Davis, *The Problem of Slavery in the Age of Revolution, 1775–1823* (Ithaca, N.Y.: Cornell University Press, 1975; New York: Oxford University Press, 1999); Thomas Bender, ed., *The Antislavery Debate: Capitalism and Abolitionism as a Problem in Historical Interpretation* (Berkeley: University of California Press, 1992); Betty Fladeland, *Abolitionists and Working-Class Problems;* Seymour Drescher, "Cart Whip and Billy Roller: Antislavery and Reform Symbolism in Industrializing Britain," *Journal of Social History* 15, no. 1 (Autumn, 1981): 3–24; Drescher, "Paradigms Tossed: Capitalism and the Political Sources of Abolitionism," in *British Capitalism and Caribbean Slavery*, ed. Barbara L. Solow and Stanley L. Engerman (Cambridge, UK: Cambridge University Press, 1987), 191–208; Davis, "Capitalism, Abolitionism, and Hegemony," in Solow and Engerman, *British Capitalism and Caribbean Slavery*, 209–27. In the Bender volume I try to answer the

criticisms of Thomas Haskell, which are quite different from those of Drescher and Fladeland. The last mentioned essay deals more with their argument and should make clear that I have always held that British abolitionism performed both "hegemonic" and progressive functions, depending in large part on time periods. I have learned much from Drescher's and Fladeland's deep research on the connections between British abolitionism and domestic reform, which I underplayed in the *Western Culture* volume that evoked all this debate. I also now see that my use of the Marxist terms "hegemony" and "hegemonic" proved to be a red flag that led to much misunderstanding and misinterpretation of my main argument. But, as I indicate here, I still stand by my thesis regarding the dual functions and ultimately progressive legacy of antislavery in Britain.

44. See especially Fladeland, " 'Our Cause Being One and the Same,' " 69–99; Fladeland, *Abolitionists and Working-Class Problems,* passim; Drescher, "Cart Whip and Billy Roller," 3–24.

45. Fladeland, *Abolitionists and Working-Class Problems,* 49.

46. Fladeland, " 'Our Cause Being One and the Same,' " 69; Patricia Hollis, "Anti-Slavery and Working-Class Radicalism in the Years of Reform," in *Antislavery, Religion, and Reform: Essays in Memory of Roger Anstey,* ed. Christine Bolt and Seymour Drescher (Folkestone, UK: Wm Dawson & Sons, 1980), 295–96.

47. Fladeland, " 'Our Cause Being One and the Same,' " 84–87.

48. *William Lloyd Garrison, 1805–1879, The Story of His Life, Told by His Children,* vol. 2, *1835–1840* (New York: The Century Co., 1885), 398, 400–401.

49. Walter M. Merrill, *Against Wind and Tide: A Biography of Wm. Lloyd Garrison* (Cambridge, Mass.: Harvard University Press, 1963), 172.

50. Henry Mayer, *All on Fire: William Lloyd Garrison and the Abolition of Slavery* (New York: St. Martin's Press, 1998), 293–95.

51. *William Lloyd Garrison, 1805–1879,* 2:399–400; Fladeland, " 'Our Cause Being One and the Same,' " 90. Thompson clearly had a good bit of influence on Garrison's and then Douglass's support of Chartism.

52. *William Lloyd Garrison, 1805–1879,* vol. 3, *1841–1860* (New York: The Century Co., 1889), 173; *The Letters of William Lloyd Garrison,* ed. Walter M. Merrill, *No Union With Slave-Holders, 1841–1849* (Cambridge, Mass.: Belknap Press of Harvard University Press, 1973), 161.

53. Fladeland, *Abolitionists and Working-Class Problems,* 49–73; Blassingame, *Frederick Douglass Papers,* Series One, 1:95–96n8; Fladeland, " 'Our Cause Being One and the Same,' " 89.

54. Fladeland, " 'Our Cause Being One and the Same,' " 80, 84, 89, 94; Fladeland, *Abolitionists and Working-Class Problems,* 63–73; Riva Berleant, "Joseph Sturge (1793–1859)," http://brycchancarey.com/abolition/sturge.htm.

55. Blassingame, *Frederick Douglass Papers,* Series One, 1:96n8, 249, 269–70, 295, 483n8; ibid., 3:614.

56. Ibid., 1:394–95.

57. While a number of historians have written that Douglass "called himself a Chartist," his actual statement, printed in his newspaper *North Star,* was part of an attack on the Chartists who had resorted to and defended violence in a great demonstration on April 11, 1848. After praising the British state for its many examples of peaceful reform, Douglass wrote as follows:

> With such advocates in Parliament, how absurd, monstrous and wicked it is for Chartists or any other class of reformers in that country, to dream of bloodshed as a means of furthering their cause! To do so is to deserve defeat. We are, if we understand Chartism, a Chartist; and we are even in favor of more radical forms than they have yet proposed; and still, for the time being, we rejoice they have failed in their 10th of April demonstration. A victory

gained by such means, would be far worse in the sequel than all the pain and mortification they must have experienced in their present signal failure. Away with all mobs and violence as a means of reform! We have experienced too much of this species of tyranny already.

"Chartists of England," *North Star,* July 14, 1848.

58. Seymour Drescher, *The Mighty Experiment: Free Labor versus Slavery in British Emancipation* (New York: Oxford University Press, 2002), 200–201.

59. Blassingame, *Frederick Douglass Papers*, Series One, 2:1847–54, 430, 435–36.

60. David S. Reynolds, *Mightier than the Sword: Uncle Tom's Cabin and the Battle for America* (New York: W. W. Norton, 2011), 117–28.

61. Ibid., 117–32. As Reynolds observes, Stowe increased the appeal of her book by stressing the importance of black honor, the strength of racial prejudice even in New England, and the fact that it was the slave system that was evil and that corrupted even Northerners like Simon Legree who went to live in the South. She was able to advance antislavery principles while dissociating herself from abolitionist rhetoric.

62. Amanda Foreman, *A World on Fire: Britain's Crucial Role in the American Civil War* (New York: Random House, 2010), 26–27.

EPILOGUE

1. [J. S. Mill], "The Slave Power," *Westminster Review*, n.s., 21 (1862): 490; David Brion Davis, *Slavery and Human Progress* (New York: Oxford University Press, 1984), 244–50.

2. *The Times,* Jan. 15, 1863, in *Abraham Lincoln: A Press Portrait*, ed. Herbert Mitgang, 2nd ed. (New York: Fordham University Press, 2000), 332–33 .

3. *The Times*, Oct. 7, 1862, quoted in Amanda Foreman, *A World on Fire: Britain's Crucial Role in the American Civil War* (New York: Random House, 2010), 319. This diatribe was in response to Lincoln's preliminary Emancipation Proclamation.

4. James M. McPherson, "What Drove the Terrible War?" *New York Review of Books,* July 19, 2011, www.nybooks.com/articles/archives/2011/jul14/what-drove—terrible-war/? [n.p.] I do not agree with McPherson's critique of Foreman's stress on the importance of some "progressives" who attacked the Lincoln administration's approach to slavery.

5. Foreman, *World on Fire*, xxiii.

6. Ibid., 317–19, 861; David Brion Davis, *Slavery and Human Progress*, 248.

7. James M. McPherson, *Battle Cry of Freedom: The Civil War Era* (New York: Oxford University Press, 1988), 383–86; McPherson, "What Drove the Terrible War?".

8. Foreman, *World on Fire*, 215, 743.

9. Ibid., 19, 180–82, 295, 741.

10. McPherson, *Battle Cry of Freedom*, 554; Foreman, *World on Fire,* 295.

11. Foreman, *World on Fire*, 320–26. Napoleon III remained interested in intervention even after Britain postponed any thought of action.

12. Ibid., 319–20, 326–30, 395–97.

13. Brian Jenkins, *Britain and the War for the Union,* vol. 2 (Montreal: McGill–Queens University Press, 1980), 214 and passim. Given the evidence recently presented by James Oakes that the Republican leaders in Lincoln's administration were dedicated from the start of the Civil War to undermine and abolish slavery, it is surprising to learn from Foreman that no effort seems to have been made to inform the British regarding the effects of the First Confiscation Act, which freed thousands of slaves. See James Oakes, *Freedom National: The Destruction of Slavery in the United States, 1861–1865* (New York: W. W. Norton, 2013). On the contrary, according to Foreman, "[Secretary of State] Seward's interdiction against calling the conflict a war for abolition was so strict that [America's minister Charles Francis] Adams was placed in the invidious

position of having to turn away Northern supporters who wanted to help." When a deputation from the British and Foreign Anti-Slavery Society visited the American legation in April 1862, "expressing interest and sympathy with our cause," Adams "could only say a few platitudes about voluntary emancipation after the war." Visitors were not satisfied and wanted to hear him promise abolition (Foreman, *World on Fire*, 221). The only explanation I can think of would be the desire to help convince the Border States that the Union was not trying to "interfere" with slavery in the states where it existed—the so-called "federal consensus," which was undermined by the Second Confiscation Act in the summer of 1862.

14. Walter Johnson, *River of Dark Dreams: Slavery and Empire in the Cotton Kingdom* (Cambridge, Mass.: Belknap Press of Harvard University Press, 2013), 5–17.

15. Ibid., 5–17, 330–94.

16. Ibid., 321, 393.

17. Ibid., 307–22. In addition to overinvestment, by the 1850s the Mississippi system was losing trade to canals and railroads, cotton was increasingly being transported eastward instead of southward, and according to the Southern press, the acquisition of Cuba would increase New Orleans's trade tenfold and convert the Gulf of Mexico into the New World's Mediterranean.

18. Ibid., 15, 304, 366–94.

19. From *Wikipedia*, the free encyclopedia.

20. Johnson, *River of Dark Dreams*, 15, 366–94.

21. Ibid., 14–15, 366–94.

22. *Encyclopaedia Britannica*, 11th ed., vol. 19 (1911), 344. While Britain and other Western European nations would have set an example of extensive imperialism, Britain would almost certainly have tried to block any major attempt to restore the African slave trade. Recognizing this, and desiring British recognition, the Confederates specifically prohibited any opening of the slave trade in their Constitution.

23. Seymour Drescher brilliantly examines the "reversion" to slavery in Soviet and Nazi Europe in the 1930s and 1940s in his masterful *Abolition: A History of Slavery and Antislavery* (New York: Cambridge University Press, 2009), 415–55. No other book offers such valuable material for a comparison of traditional chattel slavery with modern forms of coerced servitude.

24. Oakes, *Freedom National*. In part 3 I have copied many parts of my review of Oakes's book: "How They Stopped Slavery: A New Perspective," *New York Review of Books*, 60, no. 10 (June 6, 2013): 59–61.

25. Eric Foner, *The Fiery Trial: Abraham Lincoln and American Slavery* (New York: W. W. Norton, 2010), 108–9.

26. See especially David M. Oshinsky, *Worse Than Slavery: Parchman Farm and the Ordeal of Jim Crow Justice* (New York: The Free Press, 1996).

27. David Brion Davis, *Inhuman Bondage: The Rise and Fall of Slavery in the New World* (New York: Oxford University Press, 2006), 328.

28. Since writing *The Problem of Slavery in the Age of Revolution*, which does contain some claims regarding the economic decline of British West Indian slavery, I have been convinced on this point by the writings of Seymour Drescher, Robert W. Fogel, and Stanley L. Engerman, among others.

29. Drescher, *Abolition*, 415–55.

30. I am much indebted to Professor John Stauffer for sending me an impressive list of such examples.

31. I am indebted to Harold Brackman for this suggestion.

Index

Page numbers beginning with 345 refer to notes.

Aaron (biblical char.), 87
AASS, *see* American Anti-Slavery Society
Aberdeen, Lord, 286, 296
Abimelech, King, 102
abolitionists, abolitionism, xiii, xiv, xvi, 46
  animal stereotypes of blacks opposed
    by, 34
  and belief in divine intervention, 197
  Britain toured by, 294–304
  and compensation for slaves, 269–70
  free blacks as aid to, 54
  free blacks educated by, 194
  Fugitive Slave Law opposed by, 251–2
  fugitive slaves helped by, 247–50
  on insurrections, 4
  Liberia accepted by, 121–5, 361
  Liberia disdained by, 84
  paternalism of, 306
  and racial equality in West Indies, 73
  slave trade opposed by, 65, 67–8, 144,
    145
  and stigma of Haitian Revolution, 50–1
  as threat ot West Indian society, 74
  vagrancy acts protested by, 270–1
  views on cruelty and, 348
  see also Great Britain, and emancipation
Aborigines Protection Society, 303
Abraham, 109
Acadians, 93, 95
Accompong Maroons, 56
ACS, *see* American Colonization Society
Adam (biblical char.), 102
Adams, Charles Francis, 322, 323, 326, 329,
    402–3
Adams, John Quincy, 200, 277, 299

Address, to free blacks of New York City
    (AASS), 197–200, 205
Address to Free Colored Americans, An (Sarah
    Grimké), 200–1, 202–9, 211, 212, 215, 217
Address to the Inhabitants of the City and
    County of Philadelphia, 173, 174
"Address to the Slaves" (Garnet), 248–50
affranchis, 71–2, 73–4
Africa, Africans, 207, 382
  alleged inferiority of, 7
  penises of, 350
  see also Liberia; Sierra Leone
African Americans, *see* blacks
African Civilization Society, 122, 129
African Free Society, 169
African Lodge of Prince Hall Masonry, 210
African Masonic Lodge, 169
African Slave Trade, The (Buxton), 279
African Times, 135
African Union Society, 169
Agency Committee, 264–5, 270, 303
Akpan, M. P., 367
Albany African Church Association, 298
Albert, Prince Consort of England, 319
Alexandria, Va., 210
Ali, Dusé Mohamed, 135
Alicante, Spain, 96
Allen, Richard, 130, 171
  colonization movement attacked by, 173,
    179, 210
  kidnapping of, 171
Allen, William, 170
Alsatians, 127
Amalekites, 98
amalgamation, 145, 157

American Anti-Slavery Society (AASS), 7,
185, 186, 192, 193, 223, 226, 272, 274, 275,
279, 302
  Address, to free blacks of New York City by,
  197–200, 205
American Bible Society, 147
American Colonization Society (ACS), 83,
84, 106, 111, 114, 134, 156, 161, 278, 298, 299,
302, 368, 369, 376, 379, 399
  Annual Report (1824) of, 150
  Bacon's support for, 160
  blacks portrayed as Pilgrims by, 99
  British support for, xiv
  on comparisons with New World
    colonization, 108–10
  in conflict with Africans, 111–12
  falling revenue of, 133
  formation of, 167, 171
  free black hostility to, 120, 122–3, 164–6, 171–6,
    177, 181–2, 184, 185, 196, 210–11, 361, 373
  Garrison's support for, 186–7
  initial expedition of, 87–8
  Lincoln's praise for, 363
  modern hostility to, 84
  religious mission of, 97
  Sarah Grimké's attack on, 202
  on voluntary emigration to Liberia,
    122
  white abolitionists' change of mind toward,
    196, 197
*American Dilemma, An; The Negro Problem and
  Modern Democracy* (Myrdal), xii
American Revolution, 52, 80, 177, 295, 300,
  322
  blacks in, xv, 56–7, 64, 72–3
  clerical support for, 89
  as led by ruling class, 47
  and restrictions on slave trade, 48
  slave group consciousness in, 64
  as slave revolt, 390–1
  slaves freed in, 53, 168, 236, 244
*American Slavery as It Is: Testimony of a Thousand
  Witnesses* (Weld), 7–8
American Society for Free Persons of Color
  in Philadelphia, 179
Americo-Liberians, 106–21
  Africanisms of, 114
  African labor exploited by, 117–18, 119
  Congos assimilated by, 117
  Dei's disapproval of, 113–14
  physical labor seen as degrading by, 117
  population of, 119
  in skirmishes with Africans, 110, 111–12,
    114–15, 118
  superior attitude of, 113, 115–16
  worries of moral regression of, 106
  see also Liberia
Am I Not a Man and a Brother?, 51
Amis des noirs, 67–8, 249, 332

Amorites, 365
anciens libres, 74–5
Andover Seminary, 154, 160–1
Andover Society of Inquiry, 162–3
Anglo-Saxons, 221
animal cruelty, 348
animal Id, 32
animalization, dehumanization, xiii, 5–13,
  15–35, 40, 44, 206, 305–6, 333, 347
  in Americas, 8
  Bacon on, 194, 198
  definition of, 22
  emancipation's consequences and, 6
  equality and, 346
  evidence for, 9–13
  increasing scope of, 26–7
  in Jim Crow, 12
  meaning of, 15–26
  nature vs. nurture and, 346
  Sarah Grimké on, 203–4
  scientific, 7, 33–4
  at slave auctions, 11–12
  Walker on, xiii, 209, 212, 214
  Weld on, 7–8
  as white pathology of projection, 42
  see also domestication
animals, 22–6
  as automatons, 25–6
  domestication of, 23, 37
  sacrifice of, 24
Anthony, Aaron, 227
Anthony, Lucretia, 27
anthropodenial, 23
Antichrist, Der (Nietzsche), 15
Anti-Corn Law League, 303, 313
Antietam, Battle of, 320, 323, 324, 329
Antigua, 274–6, 280, 283, 285
Anti-Slavery Convention of American
  Women, 200–9, 386–7
  Address to Free Colored Americans of, 200–1,
    202–9, 211, 212, 215, 217
Anti-Slavery Reading Room, 243
apes, 30
Aponte, José Antonio, 78
Appeal to the Coloured Citizens of the World
  (Walker), 79, 162, 179, 184–5, 188, 209–16,
  218, 248, 297, 374, 388
"Appeal to the Women of the *Nominally* Free
  States, An," 200–1
Appiah, Kwame Anthony, 17, 289, 290
apprenticeship, 187, 206, 263, 268, 269–70, 271,
  273–4, 275, 281
  abolition of, 258, 260, 261, 276, 297, 303,
    316
Arabs, 30, 31, 95
Argentina, 333, 364, 371
  animalization in, 8
"Arguments Against Making Slaves of Men"
  (Hepburn), 167

Aristotle
    on animalization, 9
    "natural slave" idea of, xiii, 27, 30, 32, 34,
        35–6, 37, 38, 305, 333, 351
    on nature, 25
Arminianism, 152
Army, U.S., segregation in, xi
Aryans, 28
Ashmun, Jehudi, 111
assimilation, 54, 56, 93, 126, 127
    in Liberia, 106, 117
Assyrians, 85
Atlanta, Battle for, xvii
Atlantic Islands, 29
Augustine, Saint, 152–3
Auld, Hugh, 228, 229–30, 291
Auld, Sophia, 228
Auld, Thomas, 40, 227–8, 229–30, 291
Australia, 43, 99, 119, 371, 392
Austro-Hungarian Empire, 128, 130
Ayers, Eli, 111
Aztecs, 17

Baba, Ahmad, 30
Babylon, 106
Babylonian exile, 90
"back to Africa" movements, 43, 367
    see also Garvey, Marcus
Bacon, Leonard, 5–6, 7, 144–66, 352
    on caste system, 156, 220
    colonization report of, *see* "Report on
        Colonization"
Bailey, Frederick, *see* Douglass, Frederick
Bailey, Sarah, 227
Baldwin, James, 40–1
Baltimore, Md., 178, 188, 210, 245, 246, 302
Baltimore Society for the Protection of Free
    People of Color, 246
Banks, Joseph, 99
Baptists, 115, 265, 266
Baptist War, 256, 264–5
Barbadian Assembly and Council, 55
Barbadian insurrection, 4, 56, 77
Barbados, 272, 275
    free black population of, 62
    proportion of whites in, 58
    racial distinction in, 60
barbarians, 27
Barbary, 95
Barber, Mollie, 11
Barbot, Jean, 349
Barker, Joseph, 400
Barnett, Claude, 370
Basques, 127
Bassa Cove, 110, 116
Bay, Mia, 10–12
Bay of Fundy, 95
Beecher, Lyman, 152
Behn, Aphra, 51

Belgium, 140
Benezet, Anthony, 7, 172
Benjamin, Judah P., 375
Berbice, proportion of whites in, 58
Bercovitch, Sacvan, 362
bestiality, 26, 29
Bethel Church, 173, 180
BFASS, *see* British and Foreign Anti-Slavery
    Society
Bible, 23, 24–5, 36
    see also specific books
Bible Society, 160
Bill (slave), 229
Bioko, 117
Birmingham, U.K., 315, 316
Birney, Catherine H., 201, 386
Birney, James Gillespie, 5, 249, 279
Bishop, Abraham, 71
Bitter Canaan (Johnson), 370
Blackett, R. J. M., 297, 302–3
black Id, 21
Black Power movement, 140
blacks
    affection for Britain of, 197
    alleged future extinction of, 21–2
    as allegedly inferior, xiv, 3, 7, 31, 51–2, 145,
        155–6, 205–7, 213–14, 217, 218, 219–21, 328
    in American Revolution, xv, 56–7, 64, 72–3
    Civil War casualties of, 206
    in Congress, 332
    education of, 150, 192, 194–5, 198, 208, 211,
        221
    Haitian Revolution supported by, xiv
    Haiti migration to, xiv–xv, 43, 82, 96, 132,
        142, 174, 176–9, 180, 183
    incarceration rate of, 141
    income of, 141
    institutions developed by, 60
    intellectual attainment of, 207
    Jews and, 136–40, 374–6
    kidnapping into slavery of, 245
    leasing out of, 42
    racist stereotyping of, 27, 31, 38–9, 206,
        248–9, 282, 354–5
    as representative of dark reality, 42
    response to colonization of, 53–4, 162–6,
        210–11, 218, 381
    self-hatred of, 40–2
    as servants, 32
    temperance movement and, 199–200
    terms used for, 355
    unemployment of, 199
    voting rights of, 63, 156
    see also affranchis; Americo-Liberians; free
        blacks
"Black Spartacus," 51
Black Star Line and Negro Factories
    Corporation, 140
Blassingame, John, 352–3

Blight, David, 185, 191–2, 232, 233, 234
Blumenbach, Johann Friedrich, 34
Blyden, Edward Wilmot, 84, 97, 116, 123, 131, 133, 134, 135, 136, 137–8, 141, 373, 375
Bolívar, Simón, 360
Book and Slavery Irreconcilable, The (Bourne), 187
Border States, 329–30, 331
Boston, Mass., 178, 242, 245, 248
Boston Prison Discipline Society, 158–9
Boston Recorder, 266
Botany Bay, 73, 99, 159
Bourne, George, 151, 187
Bowyah, King, 116
Boyer, Jean-Pierre, 81, 82, 178
Brackman, Harold, 348
Brazil, 32, 255, 279, 283, 290, 325, 333, 335
  animalization in, 8
  emancipation in, xiii, 328
  free blacks in, 62
  in global agricultural depression, 120
  manumission in, 53
  maroon communities in, 236
  slaveholders in, 238
  slaves demanded by, 47–8
breeders, 8
Bretons, 127
British and Foreign Anti-Slavery Society (BFASS), 122, 303, 316, 318, 324, 403
British Dominica, 280
British Peace Society, 303
British West Indies, 283
  white refugees from French colonies in, 55
Brougham, Henry, 80
Brown, John, 218, 223, 224, 248, 253–4, 255
Brown, William Wells, 121
Brown v. Board of Education, xii
Buckle, Henry Thomas, 219
Buddhists, 25
Buffon, Georges-Louis de, 34
Buffum, James N., 292
Bureau of Investigation, 140
Burgess, Ebenezer, 111
Burke, Edmund, 26, 49
Burned-Over District, 299
Burns, Anthony, 248
Burns, Robert, 11
Bushnell, Horace, 155
Butler, Benjamin F., 255
Buxton, Priscilla, 268
Buxton, Thomas Fowell, 262, 263, 266–7, 270, 277, 280, 302, 361, 397
Byron, George Gordon, Lord, 19

Cairnes, John Elliott, 320
Caldwell, Elias, 166
Calhoun, John C., 252, 272, 274, 278, 282, 286, 296, 307, 393, 397
"Call for Rebellion" (Garnet), 248–50

Calvinism, 147, 150–1, 153–4, 157
Cambodia, 346
Campbell, Stanley W., 393
Canaan (Ham's son), 30, 350
Canaan (promised land), 88, 89, 90, 98, 99, 101–2
Canaanites, 27, 98, 102, 350, 365
Canada, 96, 333, 382
  African American immigration to, 96, 184, 232, 233, 235, 247
  black colony in, 299
Canary Islanders, 26, 365
cannibalism, 26
Canning, George, 264
Cape Colony, 76
Cape Mesurado, 111
Cape of Good Hope, 116, 171
Cape Palmas, 140, 367
Cape Verde, 365
Caribbean, 28, 32
  three-tiered society in, 58
Carlyle, Thomas, 288, 307
Caroline (slave), 229
Cary, Lott, 120
Cassey, James, 165
caste, 156, 220
Caucasians, 34
Central America, 132
Chad, 346
Channing, Henry, 142
Channing, William Ellery, 278
Charleston, S.C., 3, 133, 210
  racial distinction in, 59
  slave petition in, 64
  Vesey's planned insurrection in, 56, 78–9, 149, 209, 271
Chartist movement, xvi, 303, 304, 306, 312–14, 317–18
  Douglass's support for, 310, 334–5, 400, 401–2
Cheever, George Barrell, 87
Cherokees, 365
Chesapeake colonies, 32
Chicago's World's Fair, 45–6
Chicago Tribune, 352
Child, Lydia Maria, 200, 202, 233, 239, 240, 244
children, 23–4
Chile, 333
chimpanzees, 23, 29
China, 28
Chinese, 137
Chirino, José, 56
Christians, 28
Christian Spectator, 150
Christophe, Henri, 75, 76, 81, 82
Cincinnati, Ohio, 184, 245, 275
Cinque, 248
Circuit Courts, 251
City on a Hill, 45, 105, 106

"Civilization: Its Dependence on Physical Circumstances" (McCune Smith), 219
Civil Rights Act (1875), 131
civil rights movement, xii, 233
Civil War, U.S., xiii, 141, 166, 214–15, 244, 248, 259, 289, 319, 333, 388
  British views on, xvi, xvii, 290, 320–5, 402–3
  causes of, 233, 250
  fugitive slaves in, 254–5
  reburial program of Northern troops after, 206
Claiborne, William, 77
Clarke, Edward, 131
Clarkson, John, 368
Clarkson, Thomas, 48, 68, 146, 170, 181, 263, 270, 278–9, 299, 300, 302, 353, 358, 396, 399
Clay, Henry, 146, 172, 223, 250, 277, 278, 279, 280, 282, 363
Club Massiac, 66–7
Coates, Benjamin, 123
Cobbett, William, 312
Cobden, John C., 295–6
Cocke, John Hartwell, 114
cocoa, 119
Code noir, 65
coffee, 47, 50, 65, 119, 286
Coffin, William C., 232
Coker, Daniel, 88, 120, 362
Coleridge, Samuel Taylor, 23
colonization movement, xiv–xv, 4, 13, 83–90, 105–66
  abolitionist support for, 5–6
  Bacon's support for, 160, 194
  black opposition to, 53–4, 162–6, 210–11, 218, 381
  bombast used by, 108
  as civilizing mission, 107
  Exodus story and, 85–7, 88–9, 90
  of Garvey, *see* Garvey, Marcus
  Haiti's influence on, 83
  historians' dismissal of, 5
  modern hostility to, 84–5
  as necessitated by "Irremediable Degradation" of slaves, xiv
  pros and cons of, 140–3
  questionable assumptions of, 145–6
  as reversal of slave trade, 4–5, 144
  Russwurm's support for, 183–4
  slave insurrections and, 48–9
  white prejudice allegedly alleviated by, 107–8
  see also American Colonization Society; Liberia; Sierra Leone
Colored American, 392
Colored National Convention, 116
Colored Troops, U.S., 206
Colton, Charles Caleb, 19
Columbian Orator, 228, 232

Columbian Sentinel, 71
Columbus, Christopher, 36–7
Committee on Civil Rights, xii
Complete Suffrage Movement, 316
Compromise of 1850, 250, 393
Confiscation Acts, 329–30
Congos, 117
Congregationalists, 146, 147, 165–6
Congress, U.S.
  African Americans in, 332
  "gag rule" on slavery discussion in, 200, 234, 299
  slave petition to, 64
Connecticut, 147, 149, 156, 247
  gradual emancipation in, 246, 271, 346
Connecticut Society for the Promotion of Freedom, 378
Constantinople, 28
Constituent Assembly, 66, 68–9, 71
Constitution, U.S., 48, 75, 112, 142, 231, 252, 329
  emancipation and, 260
  see also specific amendments
Constitutional Convention, 245
Cook, James, 99
Coolidge, Calvin, 105
coolies, 260, 286, 346
Coppinger, William, 123, 131
cordon of freedom, 297, 302–3, 326, 331
Cornish, Samuel E., 162, 163, 164, 180, 182–3, 247, 383–4
Corn Laws (1846), 283, 303, 313, 315
cotton, xvi, 50, 65, 121, 261, 322–3, 326
Cotton, John, 101–3
counter-nationalism, 128
Covey, Edward, 40, 228–9, 305
Cowles, Samuel H., 162–6
Cox, A. L., 198
Craft, Ellen, 121
Craft, William, 121
Crashaw, William, 102
Cresson, Elliott, 298–300, 302
Crete, 365
Cromwell, Oliver, 100
Cropper, James, 263, 299
Crummell, Alexander, 84, 122, 123, 124, 130, 133, 181, 373
Crummell, Boston, 181
Cuba, 129, 255, 279, 283, 287, 290, 292, 325, 326–7, 328, 335, 403
  alleged slave insurrection plot in, 286
  emancipation in, xiii, 328
  free blacks in, 53, 62
  in global agricultural depression, 120
  runaway slaves to, 235
  slave insurrection in, 78
  slaves demanded by, 47–8
Cuffe, Paul, xv, 63, 84, 134, 165, 170–2, 173–4, 368
Cunliffe, Marcus, 295–6, 306, 307–8

Curaçao, 56
"curse of Ham," 12, 30, 350
Custis, George Washington Parke, 108
Cyprus, 365
Czechs, 127

Dalmatian coast, 28
Darfur, 346
Darrow, Clarence, 335
Darwin, Charles, 7, 8, 347
David, King, 101
Davis, Henrietta Vinton, 138
Davis, Jefferson, 323
Davis, Thomas F., 378–9
death camps, 346
DeBow's Review, 326
Debs, Eugene, 335
debt slaves, 27
Declaration of Independence, 142, 177, 330
Declaration of Rights (UNIA), 138
Declaration of the Rights of Man, 66
de Hirsch, Maurice, 364
dehumanization, *see* animalization,
    dehumanization
Dei, 112–13
Delaney, Martin R., 84, 120, 122, 123–4, 130–1,
    133, 136, 361, 371, 373
Delaware, 64, 322, 332
    free black population of, 62
DeLeon, Daniel, 335
Demerara-Essequibo, 58
Democratic Party, U.S., 214–15
    racism of, 224
Denmark, 283
Desaussure, William, 79
Descartes, René, 25–6, 27
de Sers, Mademoiselle, 97
Dessaline, Jean-Jacques, 48, 50, 75, 76–7, 80,
    135, 360
"Destiny of the People of Color, The"
    (McCune Smith), 218–21
Deuteronomy, 98, 393
de Waal, Frans, 23
Dickens, Charles, 307, 319
Dictionary of Synonyms, 22
Dinah (biblical char.), 102
Disraeli, Benjamin, 285
domestication, 23
    as model for slavery, 37–9
Dominica, 354
Douglas, Stephen A., 250, 330
Douglass, Anna, 291
Douglass, Frederick, xvi, 105, 130, 135, 136, 180,
    243, 290, 302, 334
    on animalization, xiii
    background of, 40
    British and Irish tour of, 291–2, 294–5,
        305–6, 308–11, 326
    on British emancipation, 258–60, 294, 311
    Cambria speech of, 291–4

Chartism supported by, 310, 334–5, 400,
    401–2
on economics of emancipation, 289
on emigration issue, 121–2, 132, 176
free blacks praised by, xiv, 193, 194, 206, 215
as fugitive, 226–32, 238, 244
fugitive slaves aided by, 230, 246
Haitian Revolution praised by, 45–7, 51, 52,
    82, 105, 352–3
"Heads of the Colored People" published
    by, 221–2
and internalization, 39–40, 333
Lincoln's praise for, 39–40
on need for free black elevation, 121, 206
in North Elba project, 223
as slave, 228–30, 239, 305
Sturge's relationship with, 316–17
temperance movement supported by, 199,
    316
on uniqueness of chattel slavery, 304, 313,
    334–5
violence accepted by, 223, 250, 254
Drake, Francis, 349–50
Drake, Kimberly, 391
Draper, Nicholas, 396
Dreams from My Father (Obama), 41–2
Dred Scott Decision, 121, 250, 318
Drescher, Seymour, xv, 262, 283, 285, 288, 289,
    290, 312, 349, 394, 401, 403
Dubnow, Simon, 127
Du Bois, W. E. B., 43, 135, 217, 225
    on Africa as spiritual frontier, 105–6, 113,
        367
Dutch Guiana, 50

Economist, 288
Edict of Expulsion, 93
Edict of Nantes, 95
Edinburgh Review, 307
education, 150, 192, 194–5, 198, 208, 211, 221
Edwards, Bryan, 4, 5, 272, 345, 396
Edwards, Jonathan, 151, 153–4, 155, 168
Egypt, xv, 28, 52, 89–90, 106, 138, 143, 162, 206,
    207, 365, 372, 374
elections, U.S., of 1864, xvii
Elkins, Stanley, 39, 205–6, 352, 355, 388
Ellison, William, 59–60
emancipation, 166, 320–37
    and alleged inferiority of blacks, 145
    British pressure for, 122
    French Convention's declaration of, 74
    gradual, 194
    in Haiti, 75
    immediate, xiv, 5, 161, 187–9, 193, 195–6,
        263–4, 274, 334
    in Northern U.S., xiii, 7, 217, 271
    by United Nations, 315
    see also Great Britain, and emancipation;
        Haitian Revolution; Thirteenth
        Amendment

Emancipation in the West Indies. A Six Months'
Tour in Antigua, Barbadoes, and Jamaica
(Thome and Kimball), 274–6, 277, 280
Emancipation Proclamation, xvi, 142, 255,
290, 320–1, 322, 324, 325, 329, 330, 332, 377
Emancipator, 247
Emanuel I, King of Spain, 364
Emerson, Ralph Waldo, 254, 257–8, 273, 394
Encyclopaedia Britannica, 328
Engels, Friedrich, 307
Engerman, Stanley L., 396
England
  Huguenots' escape to, 95
  medieval Jews in, 91–2
  see also Great Britain
Enlightenment, 33–4, 228, 257, 262, 334
environmentalism, 221, 346
Episcopal Theological Seminary, 123
Escoffery, Edward, 78
Estates General, 65
Ethiopia, Ethiopians, 34, 95
ethnocentrism, 32
evangelicals, 151–2, 154, 197, 211, 334
Everett, Edward, 277
evolution, 35, 37
Exodus, xv, 9, 27–8, 43, 85–7, 88–9, 90, 96, 97,
  143, 362
Expulsion, Edict of, 93

Falashas, 95
Faust, Drew Gilpin, 206
Federalist Party, U.S., 80
Felton, Rebecca Latimer, 21
Ferdinand II, King of Aragon, 91, 93
Fernando Po (Bioko), 117, 118, 370–1
Fiery Trial, The: Abraham Lincoln and American
Slavery (Foner), 330
Fifteenth Amendment, xvii, 325, 328, 332
Finkelman, Paul, 393
Finley, Robert, 171–2
Finney, Charles Grandison, 299
Firestone, 371
First Colored Presbyterian Church of New
  York, 163
First Confiscation Act (1861), 329
First Great Awakening, 168
First Temple, 90
First Zionist Congress, 364
Fitzhugh, George, 307
Fladeland, Betty, 312, 401
Flanders, 95–6
Flemings, 127
Florida, runaway slaves to, 235
Florida Territory, 200
Fogel, Robert William, 273–4
Foner, Eric, 142, 330
Foreman, Amanda, 322, 402
Forten, James, 79, 162–3, 165, 171, 172–6, 179,
  185, 186, 189, 190, 224–5
Fort Monroe, 255

Fourteenth Amendment, xvii, 325, 328, 332
Fox, Edward, 285, 286
Fox, Henry, 277
France, xvi, 65–74, 140, 158, 283
  British struggle for Caribbean with, 53, 57,
    72, 73
  colonies allowed autonomy on slavery by,
    69–70
  emancipation act and, 7
  foreign trade by, 65
  in Haitian Revolution, 44, 47, 74, 75–6, 80,
    359–60
  Haiti's bankruptcy and, 6, 178
  Jews expelled from, 364
  Liberian encroachment of, 116, 120
  Spanish struggle for Caribbean with, 72, 73
  U.S. Civil War viewed by, xvi, xvii, 320, 324
Franklin, Benjamin, 99, 100, 365
Franklin, John Hope, 229, 235
Franklin, Joseph Pitt Washington, 56
Frederick Douglass's Paper, 218, 221
Fredrickson, George M., 33, 107, 158–9, 368
free blacks, xiii, 193–225
  ambiguous status of, 57–8
  apprenticeship of, *see* apprenticeship
  barred from Northern schools and jobs, 7
  as danger to slave system, 52–61, 193
  Douglass's praise for, xiv, 193, 194, 206, 215
  employment of, 98
  First of August as holiday for, 258
  in Haitian Revolution, 54–6, 61–65
  as hostile to ACS, 120, 122–3, 171–6, 177,
    181–2, 184, 185, 196, 210–11, 361, 373
  land ownership by, 222–4
  of New York City, *Address* to, 197–200, 205
  portrayed as pilgrims, 98–9
  proportion in southern U.S., 357
  rights in French colonies won by, 65–74
  rights of, 61–5
  slaves' relationship with, 54–5, 60–1
  in Underground Railroad, *see*
    Underground Railroad
  see also Americo-Liberians; *gens de couleur*
    libres
Freedman's Bureau, 206
Freedom's Journal, 162, 179–83, 184, 190, 210, 297,
  298, 384
Freehling, William W., 5
free market, 283
Free Online Thesaurus, 22
free produce movement, 121
free soil, xvi, 6, 9, 231, 250, 255
free trade, 284–5
Frégier, Antoine-Honoré, 158
French and Indian War, 236
French Convention, emancipation declared
  by, 73
French Legislative Assembly, 71
French National Assembly, 66–7, 69–70, 71,
  72, 358

French Revolution, 3, 26, 64, 69, 128, 261, 262, 311
  slave group consciousness in, 64
  slaves freed in, 53
  and slaves' vindication of humanity, 48
Fry, Elizabeth Gurney, 277, 278
Fugitive Slave Law (1793), 64
Fugitive Slave Law (1850), 121, 194, 222, 233, 245, 248, 249–52, 253, 318, 393

"gag rule," 200, 234, 299
Gains, John, 371–2
Gallatin, Albert, 170
Gara, Larry, 233
Garibaldi, Giuseppe, 297
Garnet, Henry Highland, 9, 10, 38, 84, 129, 130, 248–50, 304–5, 308, 317, 371
  on emigration issue, 121–2
  Fugitive Slave Law opposed by, 121
  on Thirteenth Amendment, 142–3
Garrigus, John, 358
Garrison, William Lloyd, xii, xvi, 85–92, 160, 172, 174–6, 183, 223, 231–2, 292–3, 294, 295, 297, 300, 302, 308, 388, 399
  BFASS's opposition to, 318
  Chartism movement supported by, 313–14, 317
  colonization accepted by, 5, 186–7
  colonization repudiated by, 185–6, 189–91, 298, 383
  disunion rhetoric of, 251
  Fugitive Slave Law denounced by, 253
  immediatism of, 187–9
  pacifism of, 248, 254
Garvey, Marcus, xv, 43, 84, 132, 134–6, 138–40, 141, 166, 367
  ACS praised by, 134
  educated blacks castigated by, 135
  on Jews, 138–40, 376
  Liberia as viewed by, 134, 136, 373, 374
  Lincoln praised by, 377
  racial oppression welcomed by, 131
  racial purity favored by, 373
Geggus, David, 70, 74, 359, 360, 361
Genesis, 24–5, 350
Genius of Universal Emancipation, The (Lundy), 186, 263
genocide, 16–17, 21
gens de couleur libres, 55, 65, 66–8, 71, 73, 74
Georgia, 293
  Acadians supplied by, 95
  enlistment of black troops in American Revolution opposed by, 56–7
  slave trade banned in, 354
Germans, 137
Germany, 128, 297, 336
  Jews expelled from, 364
  U.S. military riots in, xi–xii
Gettysburg, Battle of, 331

Getumbe, 114
Gilbert, Humphrey, 100
Girard, Phillipe, 359–60
Gladstone, William E., 324
Glasgow Emancipation Society, 313–14
Gliddon, George R., 372
Gloucester, John, 172, 173, 179, 180
Goebbels, Joseph, 16
Gola, 114, 118
gold, 119, 392
Golden Rule, 18, 28
Goode, Mr., 205
Good Hope, Cape of, 116, 171
Göring, Hermann, 21, 94
Goterah, 115
Grain Coast, 111
Granada, 92, 93
Granville, Jonathan, 178
Granville Town, 110
Great Awakenings
  First, 168
  Second, 168, 211
Great Britain, 65, 140
  abolitionists' tours of, 294–304
  African colonization by, 116
  ancient barbarism of, 82
  criminals' deportation from, 43
  Douglass's tour of, 291–2, 294–5, 305–6, 308–11, 326
  French struggle for Caribbean with, 53, 57, 72, 73
  in Haitian Revolution, 44, 47, 49–50, 74, 76, 353–4
  human uniqueness assumed in, 26
  Liberian encroachment of, 116, 120
  Muslim stereotypes of blacks and, 31
  in Napoleonic Wars, 80
  parliamentary debate over slave registration in, 77
  racism, relative absence of, xiv
  Sierra Leone established by, 81
  slave trade abolished by, 49, 145, 256, 293, 311, 370–1, 403
  threat of insurrection in, 261–2
  U.S. Civil War as viewed by, xvi, xvii, 290, 320–5, 402–3
  see also England
Great Britain, and emancipation, xiii, 256, 257–71, 284, 297, 324, 334, 400–1
  Douglass's speeches on, 258–60, 294, 311
  economic impact of, 259–60, 284–90, 296, 397
  parliamentary debate over, 47, 256, 259, 284
  U.S. reaction to, 271–6
Great Chain of Being, 34
Great Depression, 10
Great Dismal Swamp, 236
Great Northern Migration, 132
Great Potato Famine, 306
Great Religious Revival, 299

Greece, ancient, 13, 27, 51, 148, 162
Greece, modern, struggle for independence
  of, 80
Greeks, 137
Greeley, Horace, 389
Green, Duff, 272
Green, John P., 136
Greenville settlement, 125
Grégoire, Abbé, 68
Grenada, 57, 74, 273
  proportion of whites in, 58
Grey, Lord, 267, 395
Grigg, Nanny, 77
Grimké, Angelina, 200–2, 308, 386, 387
Grimké, Sarah, 200, 201, 202–9, 211, 212, 215,
  217, 218, 386, 387
Guadeloupe, 57, 74, 75
Guiana, 265, 287, 354
gulags, 346
Gurley, Ralph Randolph, 106, 166, 369, 376
Gurney, Joseph John, 277–84, 286, 290, 397

Ha-'Am, Ahad, 373
Hahn, Steven, 236–7, 391
Haiti, xiii, 13, 96, 129, 135, 305
  African American immigration to, xiv–xv,
    43, 82, 96, 132, 142, 174, 176–9, 180, 183
  bankruptcy of, 6, 178
  British blockade of, 76
  as challenge to slaveholding regimes, 76–7,
    354
  color division in, 74–6, 81–2
  economic problems of, 80–1
  1801 Constitution of, 75
  as helpful to opponents of abolition, 81–2
  independence declared in, 76, 81, 354
  Napoleon's desire to reinstate slavery in,
    75, 76
  U.S. quarantine of, 81
  see also Saint-Domingue
Haitian Immigration Society, 178
Haitian Revolution, xiii, xiv, 3–4, 7, 44, 64,
    74–82, 193, 261, 271, 272, 396
  abolitionist movement and stigma of, 50–1
  abolitionists blamed for, 249
  British policy affected by, 49–50
  Douglass's praise of, 45–7, 51, 52, 82, 105, 352–3
  freedmen in, 54–6, 61, 65
  influence of, 51–2, 76–82, 83, 178
  McCune Smith's praise for, 217
  violence in, 4, 5, 6, 46, 55, 80, 198, 272, 282,
    321, 353
  Walker's praise of, 210
  as watershed, 45–52
Hall, Prince, 63
Hals, Frans, 30
Ham (biblical char.), 12, 30, 350
Hamilton, Alexander, 71
Harmon, Ernest N., xii
Harper, Robert Goodloe, 108, 166

Harpers Ferry raid, 218, 223, 248, 253–4
Harris, Sion, 115
Harrison, Jesse Burton, 91
Harrison, Robert Monroe, 286
Haskell, Thomas, 401
Hastings, Max, 347
Havana, 28
"Heads of the Colored People" (McCune
  Smith), 221–2
Hegel, Georg Wilhelm Friedrich, 333
Hegelians, 128
Helmsley, Leona, 348
Hemings, Sally, 219, 346
Henry III, King of England, 92
Henry VIII, King of England, 100
Hepburn, John, 167
Herzl, Theodor, 137, 364
Heyrick, Elizabeth, 187, 263, 264
Himmler, Heinrich, 16, 17
Hindus, 25
Hinks, Peter, 211, 212–13, 215–16
Hittites, 365
Hivites, 365
Hobsbawm, E. J., 128, 373
Holland, 95
Hollis, Patricia, 312
Holly, James Theodore, 84, 122, 132
Holocaust, 16, 17, 18, 21
Holy Roman Empire, 29
Homer, 36
Homestead Act (1862), 222
Hopkins, Samuel, 154, 168–9
Horniblow, Margaret, 239
Hosea, 362
House of Commons, British, 49, 264, 266,
  268, 269
House of Delegates, Virginia, 204
House of Lords, British, 269
House of Representatives, U.S., 63, 331
Howard, Josephine, 11
Howick, Lord, 262, 268
Huguenots, 91, 93, 95, 97
human origin, common, 34
human sacrifice, 26
Hume, David, 33, 263, 349
Hungarians, 130
Hungary, 297
Hutus, 16–17

Iberia, 29, 31, 37
Ibn Khaldūn, 30
Illinois, 245, 332
Immediate, Not Gradual Abolition (Heyrick), 187,
  263, 264
"immediatist movement," xiv, 5, 161, 187–9,
  193, 195–6, 263–4, 274, 334
*Incidents in the Life of a Slave Girl, Written by
  Herself* (Jacobs), 239, 240
India, 28, 127, 156, 220, 286, 321
Indian Ocean colonies, 76

Indians, 5, 141
indigo, 65
Indo-European races, 221
Industrial Revolution, xvi, 267, 294, 297
Industrial Workers of the World (IWW), 335
internalization, 13, 27, 35–42, 218, 305, 333
International Institute of African Languages
    and Cultures, 370
interracial marriage, 21
Iraq, 30
Ireland, 98, 100, 128, 138
    Potato Famine in, 306
Irish, 26, 127, 137
Isabella of Castile, 91, 93
Islam, 30–1, 115, 350
Israel, 52
    Operation Moses of, 95
Israelites, xv, 27, 85, 88–9, 97, 101, 129, 374
Italians, 137
Italy, 37, 95–6, 128, 297

Jacob (biblical char.), 102, 104, 366
Jacobins, 74
Jacobs, Harriet, 238–44, 391–2
Jacobs, Henry, 391
Jacobs, John S., 240–3
Jacobs, Joseph, 240–3
Jacobs, Louisa Matilda, 240, 241, 242, 243
Jacoby, Karl, 37, 351
Jamaica, 47, 56, 57, 73, 129, 140, 275, 281, 282–3,
    284, 287, 289, 335
    emancipation of, 260
    free black population of, 62
    free blacks in, 357
    Haitian Revolution celebrated in, 77
    Maroon War in, 74, 76
    slave insurrections in, 78, 256, 263, 264–6,
        271
    slave rights won in, 63–4
    slaves demanded by, 47
    three-tiered society in, 58–9
Jamaican Assembly, 61
Jamestown, 99, 102, 107, 181
Janjaweed, 346
Japanese Americans, 141
Jebusites, 365
Jefferson, Thomas
    aristocracy disdained by, 349
    colonization movement supported by, xv,
        5, 83, 90–1
    as concerned about slavery, 92, 149
    emancipation worries of, 214–15, 216–17, 219,
        220, 222, 330
    Haiti quarantined by, 81
    Hemings affair of, 219, 346
    on low achievements of black slaves, 51, 214
    race war feared by, 21
    and slavery in western territories, 331
    worries about slave revolt in Haiti, 71
Jeremiad, 89

Jericho, 98
Jerusalem, fall of, 90
Jesus, 257, 387
Jewish Colonization Association, 364
Jewish messianism, 90
Jewish nationalism, 127
Jews, Judaism, 16, 17, 18, 21, 28, 29, 130
    black relationship with, 136–40, 374–6
    deportation from Spain of, 43, 91, 92–4,
        95–6, 97, 364
    Nazi persecution of, 94–5
    rights of, 68
    seen as useful in medieval Europe, 91
    in Soviet Union, 95
Jim Crow, xi, 131, 137, 335
    animalization in, 12
Jocelyn, Simeon, 198
Joe Harris, King, 110
Johnson, Andrew, 206
Johnson, Charles Spurgeon, 117–18, 135, 369,
    370
Johnson, Hiliary R. W., 118
Johnson, James Weldon, 370
Johnson, Walter, 325–6
Jones, Absalom, 64, 86, 171, 172, 173
Jordan, Winthrop D., 20, 29, 348
Joshua, 98
Jubilee, 257, 261, 290
Jurieu, Pierre, 97
juvenilization, 38

Kansas, 326
Kansas-Nebraska Act (1854), 250
Kant, Immanuel, 33
Keller, Ralph A., 393
Kentucky, 245, 278, 322, 332
Kenyatta, Jomo, 140
Key to Uncle Tom Cabin, A (Stowe), 244
Kimball, J. Horace, 274–6, 277, 280
King, C. D. B., 106, 367, 374
King, Martin Luther, Jr., 140
Kings, Book of, 362
Kingston, 140, 276
Kizzel, John, 109, 368
Knibb, William, 265
Knox, Andrew, 391
Knox, Elijah, 391
Kossuth, Louis, 128, 297
Kristallnacht, 94
Kru, 105, 110, 115
Ku Klux Klan, 131, 141
Kupperman, Karen, 368

Lady of the Lake (Scott), 231
Lane Theological Seminary, 275
Lanson, William, 159
Las Casas, Bartolomé de, 36
Latimer, George, 246
Latin America, 10, 39
    free blacks in, 53

manumission in, 62
struggle for independnce in, 52, 53, 80
three-tiered society in, 58
Laurens family, 56
Lea, Henry Charles, 96
League of Nations, 336, 370
League of Nations International Commission
    of Inquiry into the Existence of Slavery
    and Forced Labor in the Republic of
    Liberia, 117
Leavitt, Joshua, 198, 279
Le Cap, 72
Lecesne, Louis, 78
Lecky, W. E. H., 290
Leclerc, Charles, 75–6
Lee, Luther, 252–3
Lee, Robert E., 254, 323, 324
Leidesdorff, William, 225, 390
Lester, Charles Edwards, 306
"Letter to the Women of Great Britain," 200
Levi, Master, 11
Leviticus, 27–8, 349
Liberator, 185, 186, 188–9, 232, 260, 300, 313, 319,
    383, 386
Liberia, xv, 81, 94, 105–25, 128, 134, 140, 141,
    142, 161, 177, 299, 302, 370
    abolitionists' disdain for, 84
    black abolitionist acceptance of, 121–5, 361
    British and French encroachment on, 116,
        120
    as civilizing mission, 107, 123
    constitutional republic founded in, 119–20
    disease in, 119
    emigration from, 96, 132
    exports from, 119
    Forten's negative comments on, 186
    Garvey's view of, 134, 136, 373, 374
    immigration into, 118–19, 133
    limits to continuing U.S. presence in, 369
    New World colonies vs., 106–7, 108–10,
        118–19, 181
    per capital income in, 371
    as religious mission, 97, 121, 122
    Russwurm's move to, 183–4
    as spiritual frontier, 105–6
    see also Americo-Liberians
Liberia Herald, 110, 125
Liberian Exodus Joint Steamship Company,
    133
Liberian Frontier Force, 118
Liberian Hotel, 159
*Liberty Line, The: The Legend of the Underground
    Railroad* (Gara), 233
Liberty Party, 223, 249
Libreville, 117
Lima, 32
limpieza de sangre, 93
Lincoln, Abraham, xvi, 157, 255, 290, 319, 321,
    328, 331–2, 377, 402
    admission of slave states disputed by, 234
    assassination of, 332
    colonization movement supported by, xv, 5,
        83, 141, 142, 146, 166, 363
    on Douglass, 39–40
    in election of 1864, xvii
    as moderate, 223–4
Linnaeus, Carl, 34, 351
Livingstone, David, 365
Locke, Alain L., 370
London, 332
London, Jack, 335
Long, Edward, 263
Louisiana, 77, 225, 329
    free blacks in, 357
    refugees in, 59
    slave revolt in, 56
Louisiana Purchase, 48, 61, 382
Louverture, Toussaint, xiv, 3, 4, 49, 51, 56, 135,
        149, 161, 334, 354
    capture of, 75, 80
    death of, 80
    gens de couleur mistrusted by, 73
    mulatto resistance crushed by, 74–5
    on side of Spanish, 73
Lovett, William, 317–18
Loyalists, 93
Luke, Saint, 257
Lundy, Benjamin, 185, 186, 187, 211–12, 263
Lyell, Charles, 307
lynchings, 15, 16, 18, 21, 141

Mack, Julian W., 139–40
Madagascar Project, 94
Madeira, 365
Madison, James, 5, 170
Magna Carta, 142
Magyars, 127
Maine, 64, 198, 219
malaria, 75, 132
Malays, 34
Malcolm X, 140, 376
Malinowski, Bronislaw, 370
Man and the Natural World (Thomas), 25
Mandinka, 115, 118
Manley, Norman, 140
Mansā Mūsā, 29
manual labor schools, 221
manumission, 54–5, 61, 149, 245–6
    of *anciens libres*, 74
    banning of, 65
    in Brazil, 53
    effect on slavery of, 62–3
    in Latin America, 62
    in Rome, 152
    Saint-Domingue laws restricting, 53
    U.S. laws restricting, 49
    Virginia law on, 168
Maracaibo, Venezuela, slave revolt in, 77
maroons, 56, 76, 236
Maroon War, 74, 76

Martin, Waldo E., Jr., 352
Marx, Karl, 297
Mary, 29
Maryland, 28, 64, 161, 163, 230, 245, 322, 323, 326, 332
    free black population in, 62
    runaway slaves from, 236
Mason, James, 393
Massachusetts, 147, 219
    slave petition in, 63, 168
    slavery outlawed in, 244, 332–3, 346
Massachusetts Anti-Slavery Society, 232
Massachusetts General Colored Association, 210
maternal associations, 208
Maurice, Saint, 29
Mauritius, 287
May, Samuel J., 232, 314
Mazzini, Giuseppe, 128, 297
McClellan, George B., xvii
McDaniel, W. Caleb, 297
McDuffie, George, 274
McFeely, William S., 228, 232
McGiffert, Michael, 89
McGuire, George Alexander, 138, 139
Mecca, 29
Memling, Hans, 30
Merriman, John M., 158
Mesurado, Cape, 111
Methodists, Methodism, 218, 266, 280, 395
Mexican-American War, 223, 250, 287
Mexico, 292
    runaway slaves to, 235
Mexico City, 32
Michigan, 332
Mickiewicz, Adam, 128
Middle East, 336
Mill, John Stuart, 219, 320
Mills, Samuel J., 111, 160–1, 171
Minkins, Shadrach, 248
minstrels, 43
Mirabeau, comte de, 67
Missionary Society, 160
Mississippi, 326
Mississippi Valley, 327, 329
Missouri, 322
Missouri Crisis, 144–5, 147, 149, 181
modernization, 126–7
Mohammed, Elijah, 140
molasses, 280
Mongolians, 34
Monroe, James, 100–1, 112
Monrovia, 105, 107, 114, 116, 133
Montaigne, Michel de, 19
Montesquieu, 349
Moody, T. W., 100
Moore, Samuel McDowell, 204, 387
Moors, 26, 91, 92, 95, 363
moral reform societies, 208
Moral Suasion Chartists, 314–15

Moravians, 280
More, Thomas, 100
Morgan, Edmund S., 103
Moriscos, 43, 92, 95, 96, 363
Mormons, 89
Morning Advertiser, 322
Morrison, Toni, 40, 41
Morton, Samuel George, 372
Morton, Thomas, 103
Moses, 87, 88, 90, 137, 138, 142
Moses, Wilson Jeremiah, 372–3
Mott, Lucretia, 200
Muhammad, Elijah, 376
mulattoes, 59, 66, 112–13, 130
    in Haitian Revolution, 74–6
Murray, Anna, 230
Muslims, 30–1, 115, 350
My Bondage and My Freedom (Douglass), 218
Myrdal, Gunnar, xii

Nantes, Edict of, 95
Napoleon I, Emperor of the French, xiv, 334
    end of New World ambitions of, 48
    Haitian Revolution and, 75–6
    slavery and slave trade reinstituted by, 262
Napoleonic Wars, 52, 80, 311
Napoleon III, Emperor of France, 324
Narrative of the Life of Frederick Douglass, an American Slave (Douglass), 236, 291
Nash, Gary, 390–1
Nashville American, 252
Nathan (biblical char.), 101
National Association for the Advancement of Colored People (NAACP), 137, 335
National Complete Suffrage Union, 303
National Convention of Colored Citizens, 248, 249, 250
National Era, 318
nationalism, 41, 84, 126–43, 216
    counter-, 128
    Liberia and, 120–5
National Negro Convention, 136
National Urban League, 137, 370
Native Americans, 34
    animalization of, 26
    end of U.S. wars with, 118
    persecution of, 98
    Puritan's brutality to, 103–4
    as slaves, 36–7, 236
    Virginia Company's concern for, 103
Nativity, 29
"natural slave," xiii, 27, 30, 32, 34, 35–6, 37, 38, 305, 333, 351
Navy, U.S., 117
Nazis, xv, 16, 17, 18, 21
Negro Convention Movement, 211
Negro Id, 43
neo-Darwinism, 35
Neolithic revolution, 37
neoteny, 37, 38

Netherlands, 92, 103, 334
 African colonization of, 116
 slave trade ended by, 287–8
Nevis, proportion of whites in, 58
New Bedford, Mass., 231
"New Divinity" theologians, 154
New England, 32, 63, 104, 107, 162, 169
New-England Anti-Slavery Society, 185
New France, 32
New Hampshire, 63
 slavery outlawed in, 346
New Haven, Conn., 146, 151, 154–5, 157–9,
 165–6, 298
New Haven Negroes, 156
New Jersey, gradual emancipation in, 245,
 271, 346
Newman, Richard S., 179, 184, 189
New Mexico, 250
New Orleans, La., 3, 326, 335, 403
New Orleans Bee, 271
New Poor Law (1834), 311
Newport, Matilda, 111
Newport, rebellion at, 312
New York, N.Y., 3, 32, 110, 163, 178, 205, 210,
 221, 230, 242, 245
New York African Free-School No. 2, 217
New York State, 332
 Burned-Over District, 299
 Emancipation Act of 1827 in, 217
 gradual emancipation in, 245, 346
New York Tribune, 244
New York Vigilance Committee, 231, 246–7, 392
Nicaragua, xvii, 326–8
Niebuhr, Reinhold, 18–19, 20
Nietzsche, Friedrich, 15
Niles' Register, 271
Nkrumah, Kwame, 140
Noah, 30, 102
Norcom, James, 238–43
Norcom, Mary, 239–40
North Carolina
 freedmen disenfranchised in, 55–6
 fugitive slaves in, 236
North Elba, 223–4
Northern states, U.S., slaves freed in, xiii, 7,
 217, 245, 271, 346
North Star, 243, 401
Northwest Ordinance, 245, 331
Notes on the State of Virginia (Jefferson), 214–15,
 216–17, 219, 220, 222
nouveaux libres, 74
Nova Scotia, 93, 236
Nussbaum, Martha, 23

Oakes, James, 328, 330, 402
Oastler, Richard, 306–7, 312
Obama, Barack, 20–1, 41–2, 43
O'Brien, Bronterre, 312
"Observations Concerning the Increase of
 Mankind" (Franklin), 99

Occasional Discourses on the Negro [later *Nigger*]
 Question (Carlyle), 288
O'Connell, Daniel, 269
Ogé, Vincent, 68–9, 358
Ohio, 245
 Black laws, 218
Olmsted, Frederick Law, 15
"On the Condition and Prospects of Haiti"
 (Russwurm), 178–9
Operation Moses, 95
Opportunity (National Urban League), 370
Orient Review, 135
original sin, 152–4, 159–60, 168
Oroonoko (char.), 51
Ottoman Turks, 28, 128
Oxford Thesaurus, 22

Pale of Settlement, 364
Palestine, 138, 139, 365
Palestinians, 127
Palmas, Cape, 140, 367
Palmerston, Viscount, 319, 323–4
Panama, Congress of, 360
Pan American Airways, 371
Park, Robert E., 370
Parliament, British, 234, 264
 emancipation debate in, 47, 256, 267–8, 272
Passion of Christ, 29
Patterson, Orlando, 11, 38–9, 152, 153, 354–5
Paul, Nathaniel, 292, 298, 299, 300–2
Paul, Saint, 152, 393
Payne, Daniel, 233
peace societies, 208
Pechméja, Jean de, 50
Peck, Solomon, 163
*Peculiar Institution, The: Slavery in the
 Ante-Bellum South*, xii
Peel, Robert, 285
Pennington, James W. C., 116–17, 121, 130, 231
Pennsylvania, 110, 245
 gradual emancipation in, 244, 346
Pennsylvania Abolition Society, 179
People's Charter, 318
Pequots, 103
Perizzites, 365
Persians, 30
Peru, 346
Peter, King, 111
Pétion, Alexandre, 56, 76, 82, 360
petits blancs, 72
Pharaoh (biblical char.), 52, 87, 90, 91, 97, 262
Phelps, Anson G., 120
Philadelphia, Pa., 3, 79, 110, 113, 169, 171, 173,
 178, 210, 242, 245, 332
 black convention in, 197
 fugitive slaves in, 230
 riot in, 194
 slave petition in, 64
Philadelphia Presbytery, 163
Philadelphia Resolution and Address, 176

Philadelphia Vigilance Committee, 233, 242
Philip, King, 104
Philip III, King of Spain, 91, 92, 96
Phillips, Wendell, 232
Philmore (abolitionist), 50
Phoenix High School for Colored Youth, 247
Phoenix Society, 198, 385
phrenology, 217, 219
Physical Force Chartists, 314
Pilgrims, 103, 133
Pinney, John B., 123, 124
Pitt, William, 49, 70
Plato, 23, 25, 32, 142, 351
"Plea for Africa, A" (Bacon), 151
Plymley, Joseph, 353, 358
Plymley, Katherine, 353, 358
Plymouth, 99, 107, 133, 181
Pointe Coupée, slave revolt in, 77
Poland, 94, 128, 297
Poles, 130
Poliakov, Leon, 96
Polk, James K., 223
Poor Laws, 311, 312, 396, 400
Portugal, Portuguese, 29, 31, 97, 283, 350, 364
Post, Amy, 243, 392
Post, Isaac, 243, 392
Presbyterians, 147, 154, 196
Preston, Dickson J., 229
Prichard, James C., 123
pride, sin of, 20
Prosser, Gabriel, 78
Puerto Rico, 328
Puritans, 43, 86, 89, 98, 101–3, 106–7, 368
Purvis, Robert, 185

Quaker African School, 172
Quaker and Agency Committee, 264–5, 270, 303
Quakers, 106, 110, 201, 243, 244, 262, 263, 279, 315
Quarles, Benjamin, 183, 235

race war, fear of, 21
racial order, 33–4
racism, 141, 157–9
    abolitionism and increase of, 145
    as absent from British slavery defenders,
        262–3
    in Enlightenment, 33–4, 349
    equality and, 346
    slavery and, 28–31
    see also animalization, dehumanization
Radical Abolitionists, 218
Raimond, Julien, 65, 69
Randle, Gloria T., 391
Rankin, John, 198
rape, 15, 21, 44, 249
Ray, Joe, 11
Raynal, Abbé, 51
Reconquista, 93
Reconstruction, 132, 133, 141, 332, 335
    Radical, 388

Redeemers, 84
Redkey, Edwin S., 132, 373
Redpath, James, 132
Reform Act (1832), 262, 266–7, 311
Reformation, 85, 107
Reid, Arthur L., 376
religion
    slavery and, 201–2, 207–9
    see also specific religions
Rembrandt, 30
Remond, Charles Lenox, 250, 292, 317
Renaissance, 25, 30
"Report on Colonization" (Bacon), 146–62,
    194, 377–8
Republican Party, U.S., 214–15, 328–30
    admission of slave states disputed by, 234
    as moderate, 223–4
reservations (Indian), 5
Retribution: The Battle for Japan, 1944–45
    (Hastings), 347
Revelation, Book of, 89
Reynolds, David, 319, 402
Rhineland, 95
Rhode Island, 156, 168, 219, 332
    gradual emancipation in, 346
Rigaud, André, 74
Rights of All, 179, 180, 184, 384
Rio de Janeiro, Brazil, 347
Roberts, Joseph Jenkins, 113, 114, 120, 121
Robespierre, Maximilien de, 69
Robinson, John, 103
Rome, 51, 82, 148, 162, 333
    manumission in, 152
Rotter, Gernot, 30
Royal Society, 34
rubber, 119
Rubens, Peter Paul, 30
Rugemer, Edward Bartlett, 272–3
Ruggles, David, 130, 231, 247
Runaway Slaves: Rebels on the Plantation
    (Franklin and Schweninger), 235
Russell, John, 323
Russia, 130, 139, 297, 324, 349, 373
Russian Empire, 128
Russwurm, John Brown, 120, 178–82, 183–4,
    190, 384
Rutledge, John, 56
Rutledge, John, Jr., 64
Rwanda, 16–17

St. Christopher, 280
Saint-Domingue, 3–4, 47, 69, 178
    aborted rebellion in, 68, 70–1, 72–3, 345, 360
    free black population of, 62, 65
    manumission restricted in, 53
    white secession promoted in, 72
    see Haiti
St. Kitts, 60
Saint Lucia, 74
Saint Vincent, 57, 74, 354

Samaria, 85
Sambo image, 38–9, 206, 248–9, 354–5
Samson, 150, 155
Sao Boso, 369
São Tomé, 365
Savannah, Ga., 277–8
Savoyards, 127
Sawyer, Samuel Tredwell, 240, 241, 242, 243
Scandinavia, 297
Schomburg, Arthur A., 370
Schweninger, Loren, 229, 235
scientific racism, xvii, 7, 21, 32, 33–5, 262
Scott, Walter, 231
Scramble for Africa, 289
Second Confiscation Act (1862), 329–30
Second Great Awakening, 168, 211
Séjourné, Madame, 4
Senate, U.S., 279
Seneca Falls Women's Rights Convention, 200, 243
Senior, Nassau W., 287
sensuality, 20
"Sentiments of the People of Color" (Garrison), 189–90
Sepoy Mutiny, 321
Sepúlveda, Juan Ginés, 36
serfs, 349
Sermon on the Mount, 105
Seward, William H., 322, 332
Sharp, Granville, 168
Sheba, Queen of, 29
Sherbro Island, 87–8, 111, 368
Sherman, William T., xvii
Shiites, 127
Sicily, 37, 365
Sieburt, Wilbur, 233
Sierra Leone, 56, 87–8, 109, 110, 111, 118, 134, 135, 169, 171–2, 236, 368
    Cuffe's colony in, 170–1
    founding of, 81, 83, 168
    as model for emigration projects, 169–70
Sikhs, 127
Sims, Thomas, 248, 251–2
Sinai, 365
Sinai covenant, 90
Sinclair, Upton, 335
Skipwith, Peyton, 114
slave auctions, 11–12
slave-catchers, 222
slaveholders, 237–8
slavery, slaves
    and admission of Missouri, 144–5
    as allegedly incapable of exercising power, 51–2
    animalization of, *see* animalization, dehumanization
    British oppression vs., 304
    Christianizing of, 26, 347
    Christians as, 167, 168, 350
    colonization of, *see* colonization movement

compared to other forms of oppression, 346
    contagion of liberty among, 48
    domestication as model for, 37–9
    etymology of word, 28, 348
    expansion westward of, 223
    freedmen's relationship with, 54–5, 60–1
    internalization and, 13, 27, 35–42, 218, 305, 333
    justification for, 12
    juvenilization in, 38
    legacy of, 39–42, 43
    legal challenges to, in U.S. to, 63
    legal petitions of, 63–4, 168
    manumission's effect on, 62–3
    physical cruelty of, 203
    in Plato's cosmology, 351
    poor whites and, 42
    racism and, 28–31
    renting out of, 229
    "road to extinction" argument and, xv, xvii, 325
    Sambo image and, 38–9, 206
    servility of, 212–13
    sex between masters and, 9–10
    U.S. Constitution and, 245
    women as, 36
    in World War II, 336
    worldwide outlawing of, 315, 336
slaves, fugitive, xvi, 205, 213, 226–55, 301
    as cause of Civil War, 233
    cities as assembly places of, 245–6
    in Civil War, 254–5
    Douglass's aid to, 230
    economic value of, 237
    female, 238–44
    number of, 233, 235–6
    rehumanization achieved by, 230–1
    on Underground Railroad, 238
    see also Fugitive Slave Law; maroons
slaves, insurrections of, 51
    abolitionist movement on, 4
    American Revolution as, 390–1
    associated with recently imported Africans, 48
    freedmen in, 56
    as less frequent after 1790, 77
    in Tigris-Euphrates delta, 30
    see also specific insurrections
slave trade, 4–5, 25, 110, 144, 269, 279, 319, 333
    alleged benefits of, 26
    American Revolution and restrictions on, 48
    British abolition of, 49, 145, 256, 293, 311, 370–1, 403
    British and French opposition to, 65, 67–8
    Dutch abolition of, 287–8
    Haitian Revolution attributed to, 48
    to Iberia and Atlantic Islands, 29, 350
    interstate, abolition of, 234
    Napoleon's desire to reinstate, 75

slave trade *(continued)*
  petitions against, 48
  possible reestablishment of, 287
  South Carolina's reopening of, 48
  U.S. abolition of, 380
Slave Trade Act (1819), 112
Slavs, 26, 28, 29, 348
Slim, William, 347
Smith, David Livingstone, 18
Smith, Gerrit, 5, 218, 222–3, 224, 389
Smith, Goldwin, 325
Smith, Henry, 18
Smith, James McCune, xiv, 108, 177, 216–25,
  297, 298, 308, 334, 389
Société des colons américains, 66
Society for the Mitigation and Gradual
  Abolition of Slavery, 263–4
Society of Inquiry, 155–6
Society of Inquiry Respecting Missions, 146,
  155–6
Society of West Indian Planters and
  Merchants, 264
Socrates, 142
solidarity, 128–9
Somerset decision, 311
"Sonnet to Chillon" (Byron), 19
Sonthonax, Léger-Félicité, 72
Souls of Black Folks (Du Bois), 225
South Africa, 371
South Carolina, 56, 245, 327, 382
  Acadians supplied by, 95
  black troops opposed in Revolution by,
    56–7
  slave trade reopened by, 48
Southern U.S.
  proportion of whites in, 58
  racial distinction in, 59, 60
  white refugees from French colonies in, 55
Soviet Union, xv, 95
Spain, Spaniards, 31, 95, 283, 326
  French struggle for Caribbean with, 72, 73
  in Haitian Revolution, 44, 47, 74
  Jews deported from, 43, 91, 92–4, 95–6, 97,
    364
  Moors deported from, 91, 92, 363
Spanish American War, 328
Spanish Louisiana, 47
Spectator, 322
Spence, Thomas, 79
Stampp, Kenneth M., xii
Standing Committee of West India Planters
  and Merchants, 268–9
Stanfield, John, 369, 370
Stanley, Edward, 258, 262, 268, 269, 284
State Department, U.S., 286, 367
Stauffer, John, 217, 221–2, 223, 253–4, 389
Stein, Judith, 367
Stephen, George, 262, 269
Stephen, James (the younger), 262
Stephen, James (the elder), 262, 263, 311, 395

Stewart, Maria, 211
Still, William, 233
Stockton, Robert Field, 111
Stoics, 153
Stowe, Harriet Beecher, xiv, 124–5, 169, 193,
  194, 236, 244, 250, 288, 319
Stuart, Charles, 260–1, 298–9
Sturge, Joseph, 270, 303, 306, 315–19
Sudan, 346
sugar, 47, 50, 280, 283, 284, 285, 286, 287, 335,
  354
Sugar Duties Act (1846), 284–5
Supreme Court, U.S., 94
Sweet, James H., 31
Swift, David, 182, 392
Switzerland, 95

Talmud, 98
T'ang Dynasty, 28
Tappan, Arthur, 5, 186, 198, 247
Tappan, Lewis, 5, 198, 247
taxes, 63, 64
Taylor, Nathaniel, 152, 154, 161
Teague, Hilary, 125
temperance movement, 194, 199–200, 208,
  211, 316
Tennessee, 161
  freedmen disenfranchised in, 55–6
Teutonic Knights, 29
Texas, 18, 287
  admission of, 234
Thatcher, George, 64
Thirteenth Amendment, xvii, 9, 142–3, 255,
  271, 290, 304, 325, 328, 330, 331–2
Thomas, Evan, 347
Thomas, Keith, 22–3, 25, 26
Thome, James A., 274–6, 277, 280
Thompson, Charles, 370
Thompson, George, 260, 261, 278, 308
Thompson, James, 335
Thoreau, Henry David, 254
Thornton, William, 169
Thoughts on African Colonization (Garrison),
  174–6, 189–90, 298
Tigris-Euphrates delta, 30
Tillich, Paul, 388
Timbucto, 223–4
Times (London), 71, 76, 259, 287, 288, 307, 321
tobacco, 63
Tom, King, 110
Tory Party, U.K., 267
To Secure These Rights, xii
transcendent whiteness, 20
Transvaal, 117
Trelawny Town Maroons, 56, 110
Trinidad, 50, 274, 286, 287, 354
  slaves demanded by, 47
tropical disease, 4
Trotsky, Leon, 139
Truman, Harry S., xii

Truth, Sojourner, 247
Tubman, Harriet, 234, 254
Tubman, William V. S., 371
Turkey, 95–6
Turnbull, David, 286
Turner, Henry McNeal, 132–4
Turner, Nat, 185, 204–5, 209, 248, 249, 271, 387
Tuscany, 333
Tuskegee Institute, 135, 137
Tutsis, 16–17
Tyler, John, 107, 316
Tyson, Edward, 19

Uganda, 364
Ulster, 100
Uncle Tom's Cabin (Stowe), 124–5, 193, 236, 250, 288, 318–19
Underground Railroad, 232–8, 246, 247, 253, 285–6
  blacks as organizers of, 234–5
Underground Railroad, The (Sieburt), 233
Underground Railroad and Freedom Center, 232
Unitarians, 147
United Nations, 315, 336
United States
  British pressure for emancipation in, 122
  free black population growth in, 61–2
  Haitian Revolution celebrated in, 79
  Haiti quarantined by, 81
  Muslim stereotypes of blacks and, 31
  population growth in, 61
  slave population growth in, 62
  West Indies as focus of, 283
United States Telegraph, 272
Universal Negro Improvement Association (UNIA), 88, 134–5, 138, 367
Upper Guinea, 111
Upper Mesopotamia, 85
Upshur, Abel, 285–6
urban frontier, 158
urbanization, 236
Utah, 250
"Utopia" (More), 100

Vai, 115
Van Buren, Martin, 277
Vandine, Charlotte, 172
Vastey, Pompée Valentin, 82
Venezuela, 56
Vermont, 65, 149, 168, 190
  slavery outlawed in, 244, 332–3, 346
Vesey, Denmark, 56, 78–9, 149, 209, 210, 248, 271, 355
Vicksburg, Battle of, 331
Victoria, Queen of Britain, 319
vigilance committees, 231, 233, 242, 246–7, 392
Vincent, Henry, 317–18
Virginia, 3, 28, 104, 148, 161, 162, 245, 248, 326
  Americo-Liberians from, 113

debate on emancipation and deportation in, 183–4, 204
free blacks in, 357
growth of black population in, 61–2
manumission banned in, 65
runaway slaves from, 236
slave conspiracies and revolts in, 4, 77–8, 185, 204–5, 209, 249, 271, 387
Virginia Argus, 78
Virginia Company, 103
Virgin Islands, 280
Vital, David, 373
Volney, Comte de, 123
Voltaire, 33, 349
voting rights, 63, 67, 156, 309, 316, 318

wage slavery, xvi, 296–7, 306–7, 311, 312, 334–5
Walker, David, 79, 162, 179, 183, 184–5, 188, 209–16, 218, 221, 248, 297, 305, 308, 333, 374, 388
  on animalization, xiii, 209, 212, 214
  colonization movement opposed by, 210
  death of, 210
  Haiti as influence on, 355
Walker, William, 326, 327–8
Walzer, Michael, 86, 89
Ward, J. R., 395
Ward, Samuel Ringgold, 121, 292, 303
War Department, U.S., 329
Wardlaw, Ralph, 256–7, 258
Ward Societies, 385
Warner, Robert A., 156
War of 1812, 177, 295, 322
  blacks in, xv, 171
Washington, Booker T., 135, 136
Washington, Bushrod, 166
Washington, D.C., 200, 210, 250
  abolition of slavery in, 234
Washington, George, 70, 71
Washington, Madison, 248
Water-Cure Hospital, 247
Watkins, William, 187, 188–9
Watson, J. L., 367
Weber, Benjamin David, 275
Webster, Daniel, 250, 277
Wedderburn, Robert, 79
Wedgwood, Josiah, 51, 358
Weekly Anglo-African, 179
Weizsäcker, Ernst von, 94
Weld, Theodore Dwight, 5, 7, 144, 260, 275, 299, 378, 387, 399
West Africans, 29–30
West India, 267
West India Bank, 285
West India Question, The: Immediate Emancipation Safe and Practical (Stuart), 260
West Indies, 62, 64, 67, 145, 193, 260, 264, 274, 279, 282–90, 300, 307, 315, 324, 353, 382
  black refugees from, 59
West Virginia, 329, 332

Wheatley, Phillis, 40
Whig Party, British, 267, 285
White, Charles, 34, 350
White Over Black (Jordan), 20
White Slaves of England, The (Cobden), 295–6
Whitfield, James M., 120
Whitman, Walt, 348
Wilberforce, William, 146, 147, 154, 181, 256,
    262, 264, 267, 278–9, 299–300, 302, 311, 395
Wilberforce Colony, 298
Wilkeson, Samuel, 115
Williams, Eric, 370
Williams, Peter, 247
Williamson, Adam, 73, 74
Willis, Cornelia Grinell, 243–4
Willis, Mary Stace, 243
Willis family, 242
Wilmington, N.C., 209, 210
Winch, Julie, 185
Windward Islands, 49
Winthrop, John, 45, 101, 105
Wisconsin Supreme Court, 250
women, 35
    as abolitionists, 200–9, 211
    as slaves, 36
Woodson, Grandville B., 125
Woodson, Lewis, 120
Woolman, John, 7

Worcester, Samuel, 161
Works Progress Administration (WPA),
    10–12, 304
World Antislavery Conventions, 297, 315
*World on Fire, A: Britain's Crucial Role in
    the American Civil War* (Foreman), 322
World War I, 139
World War II, 336
Wounded Knee, 118
Wright, Elizur, 161, 198
Wright, Henry Clarke, 317
Wright, Theodore S., 183, 189, 196, 225

xenophobia, 32
Xenophon, 38

Yancy, Allen, 370
Yellin, Jean Fagan, 239, 242, 391
yellow fever, 57, 75, 132
Yorktown, Battle of, 177
Young, Edward, 19
Young Ladies Domestic Seminary,
    243

Zanj, 30, 31
zebras, 37
Zeppie, Dwallah, 118
Zionism, 137, 138, 139, 362, 373

DAVID BRION DAVIS is Sterling Professor of History Emeritus at Yale University, and founder and Director Emeritus of Yale's Gilder Lehrman Center for the Study of Slavery, Resistance, and Abolition. He has written and edited sixteen books, the most recent of which was *Inhuman Bondage: The Rise and Fall of Slavery in the New World.* He is also a frequent contributor to *The New York Review of Books.* He lives outside New Haven, Connecticut.

A NOTE ON THE TYPE

This book was set in a type called Baskerville. The face itself is a facsimile reproduction of types cast from the molds made for John Baskerville (1706–1775) from his designs. Baskerville's original face was one of the forerunners of the type style known to printers as "modern face"—a "modern" of the period A.D. 1800.

Composed by North Market Street Graphics,
Lancaster, Pennsylvania

Printed and bound by Berryville Graphics,
Berryville, Virginia

Designed by Cassandra J. Pappas